*To Joan . . . for everything*
*To my mother and father*

# The Legal Environment of Business

**SECOND EDITION**

CHARLES R. MCGUIRE
Illinois State University

MERRILL PUBLISHING COMPANY
A Bell & Howell Information Company
Columbus  Toronto  London  Melbourne

Cover Photo: Journalism Services, Tim McCabe

Published by Merrill Publishing Company
A Bell & Howell Information Company
Columbus, Ohio 43216

This book was set in Electra and Franklin Gothic Condensed.

Administrative Editor: John Stout
Developmental Editor: Dwayne Martin
Production Coordinator: Carol Driver
Art Coordinator: Lorraine Woost
Cover Designer: Cathy Watterson

Photo Credits: © National Geographic Society, p. 4; © Supreme Court Historical Society (copies
by Ankers Photographers, Inc.), pp. 19, 96, 129

Library of Congress Catalog Card Number: 88-63749
International Standard Book Number: 0-675-21067-4
Printed in the United States of America
1  2  3  4  5  6  7  8  9—92  91  90  89

# The Legal
# Environment
# of Business

# PREFACE

*Every citizen should know what the law is, how it came into existence, what relation its form bears to its substance, and how it gives to society its fiber and strength and pose of fame.*

PRESIDENT WOODROW WILSON

While legal knowledge will not guarantee business success, a *lack* of legal knowledge will almost certainly guarantee failure, or at least a very frustrating and dangerous career. This text will not make students into lawyers—only years of concentrated study can do that. It is possible, however, to teach a great deal about the law and the legal system in the space of a single semester. That is the purpose of this textbook.

This textbook is aimed at a one-semester course in the legal environment of business. This second edition, like the first, is directed at the "legal environment" requirement of the American Assembly of Collegiate Schools of Business (AACSB). The text is organized around the definition of the law that flows from the AACSB requirement. That basic organizational scheme has remained unchanged from the first edition.

## THE AACSB STANDARDS FOR THE "LEGAL ENVIRONMENT"

In recent years, the legal environment of business has become a required subject of instruction in virtually every college of business in America. The AACSB requires every accredited business college to teach "a background of the economic and legal environment as it pertains to profit and/or non-profit organizations along with ethical considerations and social and political influences as they affect such organizations."

The following features reflect a concern for the AACSB standards:

## A DEFINITION OF THE LEGAL ENVIRONMENT OF BUSINESS[1]

Although the AACSB has left the definition of the term *the legal environment of business* up to member schools, it is clear that the term means something more than traditional business law. The term *legal environment* includes *both* traditional business law topics—such as contracts, agency, property, and business associations—and regulatory topics—such as labor law, securities regulation, and antitrust, to name a few. The legal environment also includes a major focus on the legal *process* and how the law works, rather than on lists of legal rules.

This text is based on a theoretical framework and definition of the legal environment of business. In a nutshell, that definition says that the legal environment of business consists of *all of the laws and legal controls on any of the relationships of the business firm.* That framework will be discussed in more detail in Chapter 1 (see p. 12).

## THE "ETHICAL CONSIDERATIONS" REQUIREMENT

Chapter 2 deals at length with ethics and their relationship to the law. Scattered throughout the text are "Pro and Con" sections that often raise ethical issues as well. And throughout the text, questions are raised about *why* the law is as it is, and whether the law results in substantial justice—both of which are ethical considerations. Chapter 2 also includes 16 common ethical problems that confront businesspeople in our society. These problems permit students to wrestle with these ethical issues *before* they meet them in real life.

## THE "SOCIAL AND POLITICAL INFLUENCES" REQUIREMENT

This text treats the law as part of the fabric of society, the result of social and political forces and the cause of social and political change. The law cannot be studied in a vacuum, and this text introduces each major topic with a discussion of the social and po-

---

1 The author's view of the meaning of the AACSB requirements was explained in McGuire, Logic and the Law Curriculum: A Proposed Conceptual Framework for "The Legal Environment of Business," 23 *American Business Law Journal* 479, (Winter, 1986). Parts of that definition are included in Chapter 1 of this text (see p. 12).

litical history that influenced the creation of the law. The text views the law as an ever-changing institution, responsive to the society and political environment of which it is a part.

## THE "NONPROFIT ORGANIZATIONS" REQUIREMENT

Coverage of nonprofit organizations means more than a brief discussion of charitable trusts. In fact, many of the most important actors in the business world are nonprofit organizations. Health care facilities, labor unions, political parties, political interest groups, educational institutions, and international organizations all influence and are a part of the business environment and the legal system. Major components of this text deal with such organizations and their legal and business relationships.

## DISTINGUISHING FEATURES NEW TO THE SECOND EDITION

In light of the changing legal scene, and particularly in light of our maturing profession, a number of changes were suggested by adopters, reviewers, colleagues, and friends. Those insights brought about a few major changes and a host of minor ones throughout the text.

### Reorganization of the Text

This text is "convertible" in the sense that it may fit any course outline. Instructors may take the chapters in any order they find appropriate. Some instructors may find securities law more important than employment law, for example, and may cover that chapter earlier in the semester without any loss of organization. Each chapter is free-standing and contains cross-references to other chapters to make reorganization easier. Some sample course outlines are found in the instructor's manual accompanying this text.

The text has been shortened and tightened considerably to make it more readable and understandable. Two chapters, dealing with taxation and economic regulation of business, have been deleted. The antitrust material has been compressed into two chapters rather than three, and much of the detailed regulatory material has been simplified and compressed. More charts and diagrams have been added to aid the student.

### Treatment of the Common Law

Perhaps the most important change in the second edition has been the addition of more business law material. With the change from a strict "business law" approach to a "legal environment" approach for the first (and in some instances, the *only*) course in law in many colleges and universities, many students have missed some of the important doctrines of business law. Those doctrines are essential to an understanding of the law and how the law applies to business.

To that end, the business law material has been expanded from two to five chapters in the second edition. Separate chapters on contracts, torts, property, agency, and business associations have been added (see Part 2, "The Common Law," Chapters 8–12). Portions of other chapters deal with common law–related areas as well, such as products liability and bankruptcy.

### International Law

The legal and business worlds are shrinking. It is now necessary to think about both business and the law from a worldwide perspective, and to take into account the legal systems of other nations and of the international system when making legal decisions. To reflect that concern, an entirely new chapter (Chapter 7) dealing with international law has been added.

### Computers and the Law

Chapter 10 contains an extensive new discussion of the law relating to computers, including the problems of copyrights and the protection of software. This emerging area remains on the frontiers of the law and is certain to affect most, if not all, business students of the 1990s.

### Products Liability

Products liability and safety are the subjects of an entire chapter (Chapter 14). That chapter includes a discussion of common law products liability under negligence, warranty, and strict liability theories, plus a consideration of government regulatory efforts at controlling product safety.

### Consumer Protection and Debtor-Creditor Relations

The discussion of consumer protection has been expanded to three chapters, including ones on deceptive advertising (Chapter 13), products liability (Chapter 14), and an entirely new chapter on debtor-creditor relations (Chapter 15). More material on products liability, bankruptcy, and collection practices is included, because those areas are likely to affect businesspeople and consumers alike.

### Employment at Will

The emerging doctrine of at-will employment has become far more important since the first edition was written. New court decisions and state statutes made on almost a daily basis limit the authority of employers to terminate employees, and those limits have severe implications for future business managers. Additional emphasis is placed on that doctrine and its implications in Chapter 11.

### Securities Law

Perhaps the most explosive changes in the relationship of law and business since the first edition appeared have been in the area of securities law and insider trading. Chapter 22,

"Securities Law," has been completely rewritten to place more emphasis on insider trading and other recent antifraud problems.

### Discrimination in Employment and Affirmative Action

Chapter 18, "Discrimination Law," contains new cases and discussions of emerging areas, including some of the most recent cases involving affirmative action and sexual harassment. The chapter continues the successful approach of the first edition by discussing several of the problems of discrimination, including housing, public accommodations, and credit discrimination, as well as the all-important problems of employment discrimination.

### Pro and Con

The second edition continues one of the best-received features of the earlier edition, that of the "Pro and Con" section. Two important changes have been made in these sections, however. First, the sections have been shortened and written by the author. Second, each "Pro and Con" now includes discussion questions to stimulate thought and classroom participation.

### Profiles

"Profiles" include important and interesting facts about the legal system that otherwise would not find a place in a business textbook. Short biographies of important jurists ("The Great Dissenter" [Oliver Wendell Holmes]—see p. 19), important historical background ("The Court Packing Plan and the Constitutional Revolution of 1937"—see p. 102), or important practical tips ("How to Choose a Lawyer"—see p. 9) are scattered throughout the text.

### Review Questions

Each chapter includes at least 10 review questions designed to promote thinking about the text. A few of the questions are designed to test important concepts and knowledge of terminology, and the balance deal with actual and hypothetical case problems drawn from the material in the chapter.

### Glossary and Appendices

The Glossary provides definitions of over 700 legal terms and phrases, including all terms in boldface in the text. The Appendices include the U.S. Constitution and excerpts of several important statutes, such as the Uniform Commercial Code, the federal antitrust laws, and the federal labor laws.

### Supplementary Materials

Students may also obtain a study guide to accompany this text. That study guide, prepared entirely by the author, follows the highly successful lead of the first edition by including detailed outlines of the text, lists of important terms, additional review questions, and exercises to test the student's knowledge of the text material. A comprehensive instructor's manual and test bank are also available to adopters. Like the study guide, these materials were prepared by the author.

### Case Selection

As in the first edition, the cases in this text were carefully chosen based on three criteria: *importance*, *clarity*, and *currency*, roughly in that order. In those rare and happy instances when the most important case was also clear and relatively current, the choice was easy. In all other circumstances, the author balanced the three criteria to find the best selection.

The text continues to include many of the most important cases in American legal history. Landmark cases are part of the legal culture and heritage of America, and students should be exposed to classic legal literature in the same way that they are exposed to classics in other disciplines. To exclude a discussion of *Marbury v. Madison* or *Palsgraf v. Long Island Railroad*, for example, from a course in law is like excluding Shakespeare from a course in English literature.

### ACKNOWLEDGMENTS

As in the first edition, the author's debts are immense. It would be legitimate to thank everyone who played any part in my intellectual development, including my parents, every teacher I ever had, together with a huge array of lawyers, judges, scholars, and authors who at one time or another made me *think*. I can only hope that this book also makes some students *think*. If so, it will have done its job.

Special thanks once again go to my colleagues at Illinois State University—Edmund Ficek, Dennis Kruse, and Carson Varner—who all helped with questions or advice. I also owe substantial thanks to Dean Andrew Nappi of the College of Business for his support. Finally, to all of my friends, fellow authors, and colleagues in the American Business Law Association and the Midwest Regional Business Law Association goes a deeply felt sense of comradery. To them I owe my belief that what we are doing is vital to the future of business in the United States.

Thanks must also go to Greg C. Anderson, Northern Illinois University; Renee D. Culverhouse, Auburn University at Montgomery; Steven B. Dow, Michigan State University; David Hoch, University of Southwestern Louisiana; Mary C. Keifer, Ohio University; D. Jeffrey Lenn, George Washington University; Nancy Reeves Mansfield, Georgia State University; Michael O. McDonald, University of Louisville; Sharlene A. McEvoy, Fairfield University; Marvin Narz, University of Montevallo; Robert T. Rhodes, Texas Christian University; Arthur F. Southwick, The University of Michigan; and Leo J. Stevenson, Western Michigan University, all of whom reviewed portions of the manuscript. Their insightful and helpful comments were crucial to the final product.

Finally, once again my most important debt is to my family. My mother and father provided their constant moral support, for which I will always be grateful. My wife, Joan, lovingly gave her help, advice, and support, as always; and the understanding of my sons, Patrick, David, Michael, and Chad, is greatly appreciated. As every author knows, it is the author's family who gives the most to any book. By the time my family reads this, we will have gotten in some of those golf matches, ball games, and fishing trips that were put off so Dad could finish THE BOOK.

While my debts for this book are enormous, the responsibility is simple. I alone am responsible for any errors, omissions, or faulty prose. Perhaps that is why writing is such a lonely chore, and why so few textbooks are written by a single author.

Charles R. McGuire
Illinois State University
Normal, Illinois

# CONTENTS

## PART 2

# The Common Law Foundations

## PART 3
# The Firm and Its Customers

# PART 4
# The Firm and Its Employees

# PART 5
# The Firm and the Public

Cases: *Prah v. Maretti; Calvert Cliffs Coordinating Committee v. AEC; Metropolitan Edison Co. v. People Against Nuclear Energy; Chevron, U.S.A., Inc. v. Natural Resources Defense Council*

Cases: *U.S. v. Falstaff Brewing Corp.; FTC v. Indiana Federation of Dentists; Matsushita Electric Industrial Co., Ltd. v. Zenith Radio Corp.*

## PART 6
# The Firm and Its Competitors

Cases: *U.S. v. Container Corporation of America; Jefferson Parish Hospital District No. 2 v. Hyde; Business Electronics Corp. v. Sharp Electronics Corp.*

## PART 7
# The Firm and Its Investors

Cases: *Dirks v. SEC; Basic Incorporated v. Levinson*

# C A S E S *

---

*The principal cases are in boldface type. Cases cited or discussed are in roman type.

# An Introductory Note to Students: On Studying the Law and Briefing Cases

Over the centuries, several hints and techniques have evolved to help lawyers and law students conquer the vast mountain of cases, statutes, and law review articles that they must read. Although students of the legal environment of business are not confronted with a mountain quite that high, some of those hints may be of help to those students as well.

## HINT 1: LEARN THE LANGUAGE OF THE LAW

The law, like any discipline, has its own language. This book is full of new terms, like *tort, trespass, plea, tender, mandamus, certiorari,* and a hundred others. Those terms must be learned, just as you would learn a foreign language. Understand them if possible, but memorize them if you must. At the back of this book is a *Glossary* that contains all of the special terms used in this text. Consult it often. You may also wish to consult a good legal dictionary from time to time.

There are also a number of terms that occur in everyday speech but also have a *special meaning* in the law. You may *think* that you know the meaning of terms like *complaint, contract, damages, negligence,* or *fraud,* but those terms and many others like them have very precise meanings in the law. Be sure to check the meaning of those special words.

## HINT 2: READ CAREFULLY, AND THEN REREAD AND REREAD AND . . .

You cannot read the law, or any textbook for that matter, in the same way that you read a novel or the newspaper. You will be far more successful in this course if you read *actively* rather than simply racing through the text to see how quickly you can finish.

Before you begin, it is helpful to quickly page through the chapter, noting the headings and boldfaced key concepts. Take a few minutes to think about where the chapter is going, ask yourself why each topic is included, and make a mental list of questions that

1

you would like to have answered by this chapter. At that point the real work of studying begins. Read *carefully*, taking notes in the margins or in a separate notebook. Underline key phrases and sections of the text. Then go back and review what you have learned, integrating the material. If necessary, memorize lists and definitions.

Be especially careful when you read the *cases* in the text. When judges write those opinions, they make every word count. Begin with the assumption that every word has a precise meaning and a special reason for being in the case. Make sure you understand the legal meaning of the terms used and why the case is presented in the chapter. It is impossible to skim through *Palsgraf v. Long Island Railroad* (p. 235), or any other decision, one time and come away with the full sense of the case. As one student put it, reading cases is almost like studying poetry. It cannot be done quickly, nor can it be done only once, if it is to be done well.

## HINT 3: PUT AWAY YOUR PREJUDICES

Political prejudices and labels, social and economic biases, and cracker-barrel philosophies all seem to interfere with the objective study of law. If we grew up hearing that "all lawyers are crooks" or "the law is just word play," and we are not willing to set those prejudices aside, we may have a very difficult time learning what the law is all about.

Almost every page in this text deals with political, social, and economic controversy. In these pages we will discuss almost every conceivable social, economic, and political dispute relating to business. After all, the business of law is *settling* controversies and disputes.

It will be difficult for students who have strong opinions on these subjects and who are not willing to pursue the study of law objectively to read *beyond* the controversy at hand and study the legal process as it deals with the issue. Lawyers are often accused of hypocrisy in being able to argue either side of a case. Yet this ability comes from seeing all sides of a case, reserving judgment until all of the evidence is in and all of the arguments have been made.

## HINT 4: ASK QUESTIONS ABOUT THE CASES

When studying the cases found in the text, it is vital that you understand the facts and procedural background of the case. First, be sure to note the **court** (U.S. Supreme Court, state supreme court, etc.) and **date** of the case. In most of the cases in this book, the facts are presented in edited form at the beginning. But even so, you should still ask yourself a standard series of questions about *every* case:

**1   Who are the parties?**
Who is the **plaintiff** (the person bringing the lawsuit)? Who is the **defendant** (the person who is sued)? Which of the parties is the **appellant** (person appealing the case)? Who is the **appellee** (person against whom the appeal is taken)? Almost every case in this text was written by the **appellate courts,** that is, courts that hear appeals of cases from the lower courts.

**2   What are the relevant facts?**
What happened in the case? What behavior is the plaintiff complaining of? What facts are *unimportant?*

**3    What is the plaintiff asking for?**

What relief is the plaintiff requesting? Is this a case for money damages, for an injunction, or for other relief (see p. 23)?

**4    What are the procedural facts?**

Who won in the lower court? On what basis (jury verdict, motion to dismiss, etc.—see Chapter 3) did that party win? Who appealed? To what court was the appeal taken?

**5    What were the arguments of the appellant?**

What is the basis of the appeal? What arguments did the appellant make to try to convince the appellate court to overrule the lower court's decision?

**6    What is the dispute about?**

What legal issues are involved? What is the practical effect of the case? What will happen to the defendant if the plaintiff is successful? What will the plaintiff gain?

**7    Who won on appeal?**

Was the decision of the lower court **affirmed** or **reversed**? Affirming a decision means the appellate court upheld the decision of the lower court, whereas reversing the decision means that the appellate court reached a conclusion different from the lower court's.

**8    What was the reasoning of the court in deciding the case?**

How did the court reach its conclusion? Did it rely on **precedent** (prior cases—see p. 24), public policy arguments, simple logic, or some other basis?

**9    What rules of law are illustrated by the case?**

This is perhaps the most important question for your purposes. Can you state, in your own words, a general rule that was established by the case? What are the implications of the case for the future?

## BRIEFING CASES

Over the centuries, lawyers and law students have devised a system of notetaking about legal decisions that may be of help to the legal environment student. To a large extent, a brief is merely a formal presentation of the questions in the preceding Hint 4. The briefing process focuses the student's mind and permits the student to make order out of chaos. Every brief has four major sections:

1    **Facts:** All of the relevant facts, i.e., all of the facts that *make a difference to the outcome of the case*, should be included. Usually the **procedural facts** are included as well, including what happened in the lower courts, who is appealing, and the reason why the appeal was taken.

2    **Issue:** In many ways the issue, or question that the case attempts to answer, is the most important part of the case brief. The purpose is to recognize the problems in the case from the facts. The facts should lead the reader to the issue.

3    **Judgment:** Normally, the judgment is a one-word answer to the issue. Some students prefer to use "Yes" or "No," whereas others prefer to use "Affirmed" or "Reversed." If that is the case, the student should be careful to frame the issue so that the answer makes sense.

4    **Reasons:** *Why* did the court decide the case as it did? This will probably be the

longest section of the brief. The reasons should be stated *in the student's own words*, although quotes from the opinion may be used sparingly. Figure I.1 shows a sample student brief of *Flagiello v. The Pennsylvania Hospital*, p. 25, the first case in the book.

## CASE CITATIONS AND FINDING THE LAW

In this course or later in your career you may need to look up legal cases or statutes. Many corporate offices maintain sets of statutes, looseleaf legal services, and even complete law libraries for the use of their employees. Although no one expects nonlawyers to do extensive legal research, you may find it helpful to be able to decipher citations and look up relevant statutes or cases.

Every case in this text has a **citation** to at least one set of books in which the case may be found. Those citations show the volume number, the set of books, and the page number where the case may be found (see Figure I.2). The citation also shows the court that decided the case and the year in which the case was decided.

Statutes (see p. 20) are cited in a slightly different manner from cases. The citation usually contains the **title,** a number of a section of the statutes, the name of the statutes, and a **section number.** Sometimes there are subsections to the statute as well. Although citations of state statutes usually follow a form similar to that for federal statutes, state systems vary widely.

*The Supreme Court:* Seated (left to right) are Justices Thurgood Marshall, William J. Brennan, Jr., Chief Justice William H. Rehnquist, Justices Byron R. White, and Harry A. Blackmun. Standing (left to right) are Justices Antonine Scalia, John Paul Stevens, Sandra Day O'Connor, and Anthony Kennedy.

Michelle D. Green

Legal Environment of Business

## Flagiello v. The Pennsylvania Hospital
### 417 Pa. 486, 208 A. 2d 193 (1965)

**Facts:** Mary Flagiello, while a paying patient of the Pennsylvania Hospital, was caused to fall and break her ankle through the negligence of two hospital employees. The Flagiellos brought suit against the hospital and the two employees for this loss. The hospital claimed that it was not responsible on the basis of the doctrine of charitable immunity. This doctrine says that charitable institutions are immune from suit due to negligence. The trial court dismissed the complaint, and the Flagiellos appealed to the Pennsylvania Supreme Court.

**Issue:** Should the doctrine of charitable immunity be overruled?

**Judgment:** yes.

**Reasons:** Historically, hospitals have been immune from suit under the doctrine of charitable immunity. Justice Musmanno, however, feels that this doctrine has now lost its justification. The court said that since Mary Flagiello was paying for her stay at the hospital, she was not receiving charity and that the hospital was, in fact, operating as a business in the legal sense of the term, and thus, subject to the obligations of a business.

The court stated that stare decisis does not bind the court if injustice would result. The court also said that legislation was not required to change prior judge-made law.

The decision ended the use of the charitable immunity doctrine, at least as it applied to charitable hospitals.

---

FIGURE I.1   Sample Student Brief

A. U.S. Supreme Court Cites

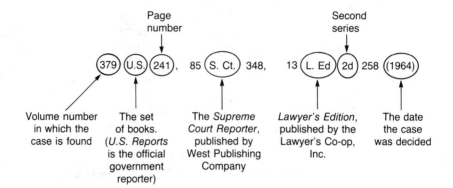

B. State Court Cites

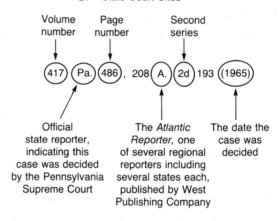

C. Federal Statutes

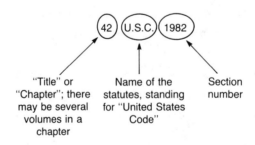

FIGURE I.2   Legal Citations

*Source.* The citation in part A is from *Heart of Atlanta Motel v. U.S.*, p. 108.
*Source.* The citation in part B is from *Flagiello v. The Pennsylvania Hospital*, p. 25.
*Source.* The statute in part C is part of the Federal Civil Rights Act of 1866.

# PART 1

# The Legal Process

An understanding of the legal environment of business requires an understanding of the American legal process. That process includes the philosophical, historical, and social input into the law; the relationship of ethics and the law; the nature of the American constitutional system; the procedures of and restraints on legislatures, courts, and administrative agencies; and the relationship of our legal system to others in the international environment. Those matters will be the subject of the first seven chapters.

The law is, first and foremost, a method of social control. Law is meant to restrain behavior into socially acceptable channels. In that sense, the law is the clearest expression of the ethics of society. When society, in the form of its elected representatives, its judges, its juries, and its appointed officers, decides that certain conduct is "wrong," that conduct will be declared "illegal." The relationship between law and the ethical norms of society is intimate and vital. As ethics change, so does the law.

The common question running through the first seven chapters is whether the structures of the law—the Constitution, the lawmaking authorities, the courts and their procedures, and the administrative agencies—are constructed properly to respond to the ethical and moral demands of society.

The law can be out of touch with the society it governs, and its prohibitions may have little to do with the needs, values, and ethics of the people. But the law may also be *too* responsive to the ever-changing currents and fads of society. Our question then is how best to structure the law to be both responsive to the needs of society and to control and regulate behavior in a way that benefits society.

# CHAPTER 1

# Introduction to the Legal Environment of Business

*The life of the law has not been logic; it has been experience.*

OLIVER WENDELL HOLMES
*The Common Law* (1881)

This may be the single most important book that you study during your years in college. Your career and your financial future may depend on how well this book does its job. That job is to teach you as much as possible about the law, the legal process, and the legal environment of business.

In many ways the law has received a bad reputation. Outlandish jury awards, conniving lawyers, and befuddled or unethical judges are part of American folklore. Many people recoil in horror from legal matters, envisioning brilliant but amoral lawyers hanging vulturelike over the shoulders of honest businesspeople. Others see the law as the source of unnecessary and costly "overregulation." To many students the law seems to be a vast and complex mystery, suitable for study only by those who intend to become lawyers.

Much of the folklore about the law is untrue, or at best is full of half-truths. Most jury awards are fair and correct, most lawyers and judges are highly ethical, and most of the time the law *protects* rather than takes advantage of the public. Regulations exist because elected representatives thought they were necessary, and may be undone if representatives see them as burdensome or unnecessary. And most importantly, nonlawyers not only *can* but *should* study the law.

The law is a tool of civilization. And as with any tool, we must learn to use it before it becomes helpful. It is particularly important that future businesspeople learn how the law works. People in business come in contact with legal matters on almost a daily basis. The purpose of this book is to teach you enough law so that it can be used as a tool rather than feared as an enemy.

## WHY STUDY LAW?

### Because Most Business Decisions Are *Legal* Decisions

Most business decisions involve legal considerations. Even the simplest business transaction, such as the sale of an item in a retail store, involves an incredible number of legal implications. Both the purchase of the item from the manufacturer and the sale to the consumer are legal contracts. Ownership of the item involves key elements of the

PROFILE

# How to Choose a Lawyer

One of the most important decisions any businessperson can make is the choice of legal counsel. It is not enough to simply flip through the telephone book, watch the advertisements on television, or hire someone who ran for political office. Even if someone has an interesting commercial or is politically active, he or she may not be the lawyer for you.

Use all sources available to you to seek out the right lawyer. Local and state bar associations often maintain lists of lawyers competent in certain areas, and accountants and banks are also a good source of information. Probably the best advertisements for any lawyer, like any product, are satisfied clients. Seek out friends or business acquaintances who have had similar problems and ask them whether they would use that attorney again. Be sure to ask whether the attorney answered all questions, made satisfactory fee arrangements, and was available to discuss the matter at reasonable times. Inquire about results, but remember that your friend's case may have been unwinnable.

Feel free to comparison shop. Visit lawyers in their offices, and describe the situation to each. Most lawyers will charge only a nominal fee (or nothing at all) for initial office consultations. Be sure to ask their fee for the matter, and whether they will put that fee in writing. Make a list of questions, based on what you know of the law.

If your legal problem involves a specialty area, such as securities law, antitrust, or patent law, ask your general practitioner for a referral. General practitioners understand that clients sometimes need specialized advice and will not (or should not) feel offended. Make sure he or she understands that you are willing to pay for work done in finding the right specialist and helping to watch over the case.

Above all, understand that when you hire a lawyer, you are hiring the lawyer's time and expertise, and that in part you are paying for many years of training. Be willing to compensate the lawyer fairly, because as the old saying goes, "Free legal advice is worth what you pay for it."

law of property. Pricing and advertising of the item may be subject to antitrust and other federal regulation. If credit is involved, the retailer may be required to inform the purchaser of his or her legal rights. If the item is defective, the retailer may be liable for money damages, both for the item and for any damage that it does.

It is not enough to see the marketing, management, financial, or accounting implications of a business decision. Those strategic matters are vital, of course, but underlying it all is the law. The law sets limits on business decisions and may make some business decisions inevitable. And some legal decisions arise so fast, or are so small, that it is impossible or impractical to call in legal counsel.

### Because Businesspeople Must Know the Law Well Enough to Know *When* to Call in Legal Counsel

Unfortunately, most lawyers are called in too late. Lawyers serve two functions: (1) to solve legal difficulties *after* they arise; and (2) to *prevent* legal difficulties. A businessperson must know enough law to see that legal problems may develop out of a particular course of action and that legal advice is necessary.

For example, assume that after graduation you are placed in charge of personnel in a small company. If your company is considering hiring some new employees, those decisions may well be covered by some federal affirmative action requirements, particularly if your company does work for the government (see Chapter 18). If you did not know what affirmative action was, or were unaware that such requirements *might* apply to your company, you might make some illegal hiring decisions that could cost your company the government contracts—and might also cost you your job.

Certainly, a lawyer might help *after* the damage was done, but a lawyer knowledgeable in such matters might have avoided the damage altogether. Most corporate attorneys practice **preventative law,** in the sense that they try to stop legal damage before it occurs. Although you may not be expected to know the intricate details of the law, you are expected to know that there are *legal implications* from what you do and to recognize *when* to seek legal advice.

### Because Businesspeople Must Know the Law Well Enough to Be Good Clients

A business client must know enough law to assist the lawyer. Clients must tell their lawyers *everything* about a case or a transaction, and that means that clients must know enough law to know what facts are important (see Figure 1.1).

For example, if a lawyer is hired to defend a suit brought by a customer who was injured by a defective product, it may be very important that the client has a sign posted stating "All Sales As Is." Although lawyers are trained in asking the right questions, some questions may simply never occur to them. Clients must know enough law to tell the lawyer *all* of the important facts.

### Because the Study of Law Makes You a Better Citizen

Politics and the law are two sides of the same coin. Citizens who understand the legal process will be able to think more clearly about public and political affairs and to vote or

1    Do not, under any circumstances, depend on "free" advice given by lawyers or nonlawyers. Lawyers must often research the law, even on everyday topics, and casual advice can be dangerous.

2    Tell your lawyer *everything*, no matter how insignificant or irrelevant it seems to you.

3    Keep your appointments, or telephone well ahead of time to cancel. A lawyer's time is valuable.

4    Discuss fees at the first meeting. You have a right to know how fees will be charged and to receive a written fee agreement.

5    Be willing to pay a reasonable fee, but be willing to question fee items you do not understand.

6    *Never* talk to anyone on the other side of a case without your lawyer's permission and presence, if possible.

7    Ask questions. Be sure your lawyer keeps you informed and that you understand why certain things happen, but don't call so often that you interfere with the lawyer's work.

8    Be willing to do groundwork. The lawyer cannot do a good job without your cooperation.

9    Keep copies of all documents. Keep a diary from the first instant you think you may be involved in litigation. Write down anything that happens involving the case, and include as much detail as possible. Take pictures of physical objects (such as auto damage) and date the photos.

10   If you are dissatisfied with the progress of your case or with your lawyer, discuss the matter with your lawyer. Some cases are simply unwinnable, and others that look simple become complex over time. You have a right to discharge the lawyer, but you will have to pay reasonable fees on the basis that you have agreed upon.

FIGURE 1.1    Ten Rules for Being a Good Client

take other political action more intelligently. Businesspeople, as leaders in their communities, are expected to take part in public affairs. It is far better to do so from a position of knowledge.

Participation in public affairs may also help your own business. For example, assume that your business may become the subject of regulation by a federal agency. If you understand the legal and administrative system (see Chapter 6), you will know that you may approach federal administrative agencies in writing and make your position clear to that agency. Your written comments may convince the agency to change its position.

### Because the Study of Law Clarifies the Relationship Between Business and Society

The study of law helps to build a clearer understanding of the place of business in American society. The background of the common law and the development of the law of contracts and property provide a basic understanding of the place of property and business rights in our heritage. An understanding of the commerce clause (see p. 101) makes clear the right of the government to regulate business. A study of the antitrust laws illustrates the place of economic analysis in public policy and legal analysis.

The law is the place where conflicts between public policy, the need for regulation, and private rights of businesspeople and others are resolved. An understanding of the law will provide a perspective on the relationship between business, government, and other parts of our society.

Above all, the law is the study of the real world. It is important for all business students to understand the theories of economics and finance, the details of accounting, and the methods of effective marketing and management. But each of those topics is an isolated *part* of the business world. The law deals with *all* of them as they affect business in the real world.

It is important to dispel one bit of homespun "wisdom" very early. The law does *not* consist of long lists of black-and-white rules. The law is full of greys. If anything is always true about the law, it is that *nothing* is always true about the law. There are no absolutes, no rules without exceptions; no perfect justice exists. The law is a vital thing, alive with change and controversy and exceptions. If this text teaches no more than that, it will have succeeded.

## THE NATURE OF THE LEGAL ENVIRONMENT OF BUSINESS

The place of an individual firm in the business world is complex. Every business has relationships with a great number of persons and institutions, and the sum total of those relationships may be defined as the *environment of business*. Businesses have relationships with eight major groups of persons or legal entities: competitors, suppliers, creditors, customers, employees, investors, the anonymous "public," and the various units of government (see Figure 1.2).

The *law* may be viewed as a method of controlling these relationships. Every law controls or regulates some relationship because the lawmaking authority found this control necessary or advisable. For example, the law of labor relations governs the relation-

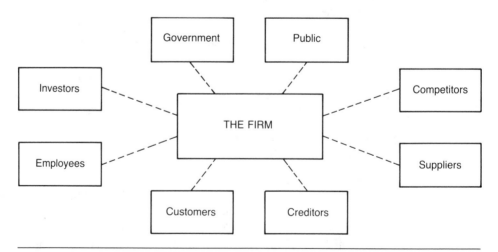

FIGURE 1.2    The Environment of Business

ship between a firm and its employees, the law of securities regulation governs the relationship between a firm and its investors, and antitrust law governs the relationship between a firm and its competitors and suppliers.

Each of the eight relationships of the business firm has legal implications. In each case, the law steps in at times to limit and control the relationships involved. Those legal limits and controls on the relationships between business and those with whom it deals may be termed the *legal environment of business.*

The relationship of business to government has the greatest impact on the other relationships because it includes the various regulations, statutes, and court decisions that regulate the other seven relationships. Those laws not only regulate relationships but in a few cases have *established* relationships where none existed, as in the case of the environmental laws designed to regulate the relationship between business and "the public."

Before we consider each of these relationships in detail, it is important that we discuss the framework of the law, including its philosophical and constitutional bases, the relationship between law and ethics, the organization and procedures of the courts and administrative agencies, and the relationship of the American legal system to international law. In large measure this is a description of the relationship of the firm to government. Those matters are discussed in Part 1, "The Legal Process." Part 2, "The Common Law," deals with the basic law relating to business, including the common law of contracts, torts, and property (including some emerging law relating to computers), and the law of agency and business associations.

Beginning with Part 3, we examine government regulation of the various relationships of the business firm. Part 3, "The Firm and Its Customers," deals with the relationship of the firm to consumers. Part 4, "The Firm and Its Employees," deals with the relationship of the firm to its employees. Part 5, "The Firm and the Public," deals with the two clearest cases of regulation of the firm's relationship to the public, in the form of discrimination laws and environmental protection laws. Part 6, "The Firm and Its Competitors," examines the relationship of the firm to its competitors, suppliers, and customers in the form of the federal antitrust laws. Part 7, "The Firm and Its Investors," considers the relationship of the firm to its investors in the federal securities laws.

## THE DEFINITION AND FUNCTIONS OF LAW

The term *law* is defined as "a rule of conduct or action prescribed or formally recognized as binding or enforced by a controlling authority."[1] It is important to note the necessity of *government* to that definition. A law, by definition, is enforced by some governmental body, whether local, state, or federal. The world is full of *unenforced* rules as well, such as moral and ethical sentiments, customs, and beliefs. But if those rules do not have the force of government behind them, they are not "law." As Oliver Wendell Holmes put it, "Law is a statement of the circumstances in which the public force will be brought to bear through courts."

---

1 *Webster's New Collegiate Dictionary*, G. & C. Merriam Co., Springfield, Mass., 1975, p. 646.

## The Law as a System of Social Control

The law is concerned with controlling behavior. In fact, *social control* is clearly the principal purpose of the law, and other purposes are only secondary. In some cases a legislature or a court may find that certain kinds of behavior cannot be tolerated. Such behavior is then prohibited and punishments or consequences are prescribed, as in the case of many criminal acts. In other cases a legislature or court may find that certain results should flow from certain acts. For example, if a person negligently harms another, courts and legislatures generally require the negligent person to pay for the loss. In either case, the power of the state stands behind the rules as established by the legislature or the court.

A game without rules is not a game at all, but mere disorder. The law establishes rules of behavior and makes sure that we follow them. Probably the clearest example of the law performing this function of social control is in the criminal law, where the heavy artillery of the legal system is found in the form of judges, prosecutors, prisons, and even the electric chair. Civil courts also provide rules of behavior, but in more subtle ways. Without those rules it is clear that our civilization could not exist as we know it.

## The Law as a Method of Dispute Settlement

A second function of the law is *settlement of disputes*. Few people can go through life without becoming involved in some major disputes with other people. Auto accidents, business contracts, property lines, and even marriages may result in conflicts that must be resolved. Most disputes involve fairly small scale clashes between individuals, but others may involve giant corporations or even classes of people. Without some mechanism provided to resolve those disputes, many of them would result in violence or other antisocial behavior. A major function of the courts is to settle those conflicts peacefully, without bloodshed or major social dislocation.

## The Law as a Means of Social Engineering

The law is also used to make policy choices. Every government must decide economic and social issues, usually through its legislature. Often the law is used to bring about planned social change through elected representatives. Progressive taxation, distribution of social security and welfare, environmental protection, antitrust laws, consumer protection, and discrimination statutes are all examples of the policy choices that must be made through the law.

More controversially, the courts are also agents of social change. The courts must decide specific cases, and those cases later act as **precedent** for later decisions. Those decisions are, in every sense of the word, public policy. In the American system, courts also have the right and duty to decide whether acts of the legislature are constitutional under the doctrine of **judicial review**.[2] Those decisions often require changes in society, such as instituting school desegregation, forbidding laws that prohibit abortion, or requiring police officers to advise arrested persons of their rights.

---

2 See Chapter 4, p. 94.

### The Law as a Means of Preserving Society

Finally, the law keeps society running smoothly. There is a strong element of tradition and consistency in the law, and that element makes sure that the machinery of society keeps running more or less as it did in the past. This *maintenance* function is largely implicit in the law. For example, a law against theft is also a law *to protect* the institution of private property. The law lends stability and predictability to our social and economic system by generally protecting the status quo.

## THEORIES OF LAW AND GOVERNMENT

The study of philosophy is usually not very appealing to today's down-to-earth business student. Philosophy seems to be, in the words of Voltaire, "when he who hears doesn't know what he who speaks means, and when he who speaks doesn't know what he himself means."

But the study of philosophy is especially central to the study of law, particularly in the United States. Unlike other systems of government, American institutions are based on a specific philosophy of government and law, the **natural rights theory**; and an understanding of that theory and its competitors is essential to a complete understanding of our entire political, legal, and regulatory system.

Throughout the history of human thought, philosophers have debated the nature and purpose of government and law. Even the earliest Greek philosophers, including Plato and Aristotle, dealt with issues such as why government must exist, the ideal structure of government, what sort of laws are good or proper, and the overriding problem of defining the term *justice*.

The questions raised by the early Greeks remain a vital part of the law even today. It is fairly common for a contemporary legal opinion to quote Plato or Locke or Jefferson. It is even more common that the ideas of these thinkers are implicit in statutes or judicial decisions. At the very least, philosophy is another major input into the law.

The questions raised by legal philosophy are perhaps as important as the answers it gives. Traditional legal and political theorists were concerned with the issues of why government exists and what the source of the authority of government is. Contemporary analysis of law centers around what function law should play in society and how best to describe the legal process. Implicit in the questions are the issues of what changes should be made in the law, whether the law is fair or just, and the relationship of government to the public.

### The Beginnings: The Divine Right of Kings

Perhaps the oldest and simplest theory of the origins and nature of government was the doctrine of the **divine right of kings.** This theory justified monarchies from the earliest times through the sixteenth century on the basis that the authority of the monarch came directly from God. A deity somehow "appointed" the king and authorized him and his descendants to rule. Usually the theory also either expressly or implicitly stated that the actions of the monarch are also directly authorized by God, with God actually acting through the king. Therefore, of course, rebellion is impossible and a sin, and only God may punish a wicked king, for "the king can do no wrong." Parts of the divine right theory influence the law even today, as, for example, in the doctrine that governments are generally immune from suit. It was not until the middle of the twentieth century that that doctrine began to fade, and it is still with us in many respects (see p. 225).

Beginning in the seventeenth century, the divine right theory lost its hold. The theory was weakened already by the revival of Greek thought in the Renaissance and the challenge to established authority in the Protestant Reformation. In the late 1600's newer and bolder theories of government began to replace the divine right theory, basing their thought on the primacy of man.

## The Theory of Power: Hobbes to Marx

One direction of the new thought was shaped by Thomas Hobbes (1588–1679). Hobbes believed that the sole basis of government and law was sheer, naked power. His theory began with the assumption that to determine the true source of government, we must view humanity in a "state of nature." In that original society, life must have consisted of a "war of each against all," which meant that life must have necessarily been "poor, nasty, brutish and short."

In a "war of each against all," the winner is obvious. The strongest must win the struggle, and with it win the right to rule. According to Hobbes, the original source of power of government is then *force*. Hobbes's views were tempered by the belief that enlightened human beings would give up their individual freedoms willingly in order to gain the protection of the stronger and avoid the consequences of the war of each against all.

A special brand of **Hobbesian philosophy** finds some prominence today. The theory of *economic determinism* states simply that wealth is power and that the desire for wealth motivates all people. As a result, economic determinism argues that the wealthy rule the governments of the world, and governments rule largely for the benefit of the wealthy.

To a large extent, economic determinism is an unorganized philosophy, full of cynical folk wisdom. There is an old Spanish proverb that says, "Laws, like the spider's web, catch the fly and let the hawk go free." Many cynics believe today that the rich are largely untouched by law and government and that government is largely run by the wealthy for their own benefit. In the words of Anatole France, "The law, in all its majestic equality, forbids all men to sleep under bridges, to beg in the streets, and to steal bread—the rich as well as the poor."

One attempt to build economic determinism into a coherent philosophy of government was made by Karl Marx. Marx believed that capitalists ruled government for their own ends and that the denial of economic justice would result in worldwide political revolution. Once economic justice was achieved, Marx said, there would be no need for government at all, and the state would "wither away."

## The Theory of Agreement: Natural Rights

Another theory of government came close on the heels of Hobbes's work. The *natural rights theory*, also known as the *compact theory* or *social contract theory*, was not new; it may be found in the thought of the early Greek and Roman philosophers. But aside from St. Thomas Aquinas (1225–1274), the theory lay dormant throughout the Middle

Ages. In the seventeenth century, the theory was reawakened in the thought of John Locke (1632–1704) and his followers.

The natural rights theory would agree that we should look to the state of nature for clues as to the source of government and would also agree that the original state of nature was disorganized and brutal. But here the natural rights theory parts company with Hobbes and states that humanity is *essentially good*. In order to avoid the conflict of the state of nature, people therefore agreed among themselves to give up their individual freedoms, or a part of them, and appoint some of their number as rulers for the common good and protection. Therefore, although the public gave up the right to rule itself, the ruler governed only by the consent of the governed. But the governed gave up only those rights that were necessary for government to exist, and the people retained other rights that could not be transferred, also known as *inalienable rights*. The agreement between ruler and governed was a **contract,** or *compact*, and a breach of the agreement gave the injured party a remedy, much as a breach of a private contract gives the innocent party a remedy under law.

The theories of Locke, Rousseau, and Montesquieu were quickly adopted by men like Paine, Adams, and Jefferson. Those American philosophers based both their right to revolt against the British king and their concept of how a government ought to be organized directly upon the natural rights theory of government. The American Declaration of Independence, with its statements of "unalienable rights" and the right of free people to alter or abolish governments that destroy those rights, is one of the clearest statements of natural rights philosophy.

Jefferson and his contemporaries were true to their philosophy. Not only did they base the revolution on natural rights principles, but for the first time they made the implicit social contract not only express but written. In a large sense, the American Constitution was merely an expression of the lawyer's adage, "get it in writing."

The philosophical issues raised by Hobbes and the natural rights theorists are still debated today, although on a much more sophisticated basis. Modern theorists continue to argue these issues within the contemporary environment. But the field has recently been invaded by the social scientists, who have their own theories and methods of analysis.

### Modern Schools of Legal Analysis

Almost every branch of modern social science has advanced its own theory purporting to explain the law. Separate theories of law have developed in the disciplines of history, sociology, and economics, each purporting to give a fairly complete picture of what the law is all about.

**The Historical School**    The historical view of law holds that the law and legal institutions are the result of historical forces of all kinds that drive the law to its present situation. The study of law cannot be divorced from the study of history and all of the social, political, economic, and even psychological forces that have brought our system of government to its present circumstances.

**The Sociological School**    Often blending with the historical school, sociology views the law as both an expression and a tool of social forces. The primary difference between the historical and sociological schools lies in the somewhat more value-oriented approach of the latter. Sociology implies that the law *ought* to respond to contemporary social forces more closely, whereas history merely describes the extent to which it does.

**The Economics School**   A latecomer to the field of legal analysis, economics teaches that most, if not all, of law may be analyzed according to traditional economic theory. Actors in the legal system are assumed to be rational people, interested in maximizing their welfare. As a result, such actors assess the costs and gains of legal actions in a manner very similar to the way in which consumers buy goods in the marketplace. For example, a person who is considering filing a lawsuit will weigh the costs of filing, including attorneys' fees, time spent in litigation, and even embarrassment at losing, against the possible gains of winning.

Such an analysis allows, at least theoretically, some measurement of legal actions and permits a more precise analysis of legal rules and institutions. Perhaps the most controversial argument of the economics school is that the law should *promote* economic efficiency, perhaps to the exclusion of other human values. The economics school has had a major influence on antitrust law in the late twentieth century (see Chapter 19).

### Legal Realism (Positivism)

Standing apart from the traditional philosophies of law and government and the analyses of social science, a final, practical-minded approach to the law is found in the analysis

---

## "The Path of the Law"
OLIVER WENDELL HOLMES
10 *Harvard Law Review* 809 (1897)

If you want to know the law and nothing else, you must look at it as a bad man, who cares only for the material consequences which such knowledge enables him to predict, not as a good one, who finds his reasons for conduct, whether inside the law or outside of it, in the vaguer sanctions of conscience. . . . Take the fundamental question: What constitutes the law? You will find some text writers telling you that it is something different from what is decided by the courts of Massachusetts or England, that it is a system of reason, that it is a deduction from principles of ethics or admitted axioms or what not, which may or may not coincide with the decisions. But, if we take the view of our friend the bad man, we shall find that he does not care two straws for the axioms or deductions but that he does want to know what the Massachusetts or English courts are likely to do in fact. I am much of his mind. The prophecies of what the courts will do in fact, and nothing more pretentious, are what I mean by the law.

of **legal realism**, or *positivism*. This school says that all we can be concerned about when we begin to analyze the law is a description of the law itself, aimed at a *prediction* of what the courts are likely to do.

The gist of the positivist school is *prediction* of the result of any particular case. Lawyers who are faced with a new case must predict the possibilities of success and advise their clients. Businesspeople who are thinking about a possible course of action must predict the legal results. Judges must predict the possibilities of being overruled on appeal. And those predictions are not always easy.

To a positivist, "the law" is not simply a list of statutes or cases. Those statutes and cases are merely *clues* to what a judge may do in a particular case. And some statutes and cases are not law to a positivist. For example, laws that are never enforced are not law, because they do not aid in the prediction of what a judge will do. According to that view, an unenforced law is no law at all; and quaint laws forbidding such things as "walking a hippopotamus down a wooden sidewalk after noon on Sundays," as one municipal ordinance does, are curiosities, but not laws.

---

PROFILE

## The Great Dissenter

Oliver Wendell Holmes (1841–1935), son of a Boston physician, poet, and writer of the same name, graduated from Harvard in 1861. He served as a lieutenant colonel in the Civil War and was wounded three times. One time under fire he shouted at a tall civilian, "Get down, you fool." Holmes later learned that the tall civilian was Abraham Lincoln.

Following the Civil War he entered Harvard Law School. In 1882 he was appointed to the Massachusetts Supreme Court and served as Chief Justice from 1899 to 1902. In 1902, President Theodore Roosevelt appointed him to the U.S. Supreme Court, where he served until 1932, when he retired at the age of 91.

Holmes was both a judge and a philosopher of law. His book *The Common Law* (1881) remains a classic of American legal thought. Holmes believed that the law was a growing and living organism, to be molded to the needs of a changing society. Law, to Holmes, was a product of society. His essay "The Path of the Law" remains a classic defense of legal realism.

In many ways far ahead of his times, Holmes found himself in dissent in so many cases in the Supreme Court that he became known as "The Great Dissenter." Many of those decisions were later adopted by the majority and became the law, although often long after his death. He is considered one of the most influential and distinguished judges ever to have served on the Supreme Court.

## CLASSIFICATIONS OF LAW

### "Law" by Its Origins

"The law" is found in written form in constitutions, treaties, statutes, case law, and administrative regulations. In the American legal system there is no such thing as an "unwritten law." The classification of law by its origins is really a consideration of the various places where one might look to determine what a court will probably do. It is, in the view of the positivist school, a prediction of the probable outcome of a case. Sometimes that prediction is very easy to make; at other times that prediction is extremely difficult and complex.

<u>Constitutions</u>    A constitution is a charter of government that expresses both the powers of government and the limits on the exercise of that power. *The Constitution* commonly refers to the federal constitution of 1789 and the twenty-six amendments enacted since that date (see Appendix A). But each state also has its own constitution, which is law in that state. The federal Constitution establishes a pecking order among the various laws. The so-called *supremacy clause* of the Constitution (article VI, section 2) provides that "[t]his Constitution . . . shall be the Supreme Law of the Land."

**Treaties**    Treaties between the United States and foreign governments have the binding force of law and bind the citizens of the United States to live by such agreements as well (see Chapter 7).

<u>Statutes</u>    Legislation duly enacted by either the federal Congress, state legislatures, or even local legislative bodies such as city councils or county boards is clearly law. These enactments are usually set out in list or book form as statutes (see Figure 1.3). Legislation passed by the federal Congress or state legislature is known as **statutes,** whereas legislation passed by local governments, such as cities or counties, is known as **ordinances.** Both are often compiled in books known as **codes.**

<u>Administrative Regulations</u>    The newest form of law involves administrative regulations and rules that are created by administrative agencies. Such agencies are created by the legislature through statutes, and the authority to make regulations is delegated to the agency by the legislature. An example of an administrative rule is shown in Figure 1.4 on p. 22.

In the strictest sense, such regulations are considered *rules*, not *law*. But because such rules contain sanctions and are enforceable by the courts, they belong in any list of the origins of law. Administrative agencies and the rules they make are discussed at greater length in Chapter 6.

<u>Case Law</u>    Judicial decisions written in opinion form and referred to by subsequent courts are "law" just as much as constitutions, treaties, or statutes. These decisions either interpret statutes, treaties, or constitutional provisions, or they state what the law is if there is no statute or constitutional provision. This latter type of decision has created the **common law,** or law by judicial decision. Case law and the doctrine of *precedent*, or **stare decisis,** will be discussed at length later in this chapter.

§ 1203. Hostage taking

(a) Except as provided in subsection (b) of this section, whoever, whether inside or outside the United States, seizes or detains and threatens to kill, to injure, or to continue to detain another person in order to compel a third person or a governmental organization to do or abstain from doing any act as an explicit or implicit condition for the release of the person detained, or attempts to do so, shall be punished by imprisonment for any term of years or for life.

(b)(1) It is not an offense under this section if the conduct required for the offense occurred outside the United States unless—

(A) the offender or the person seized or detained is a national of the United States;

(B) the offender is found in the United States; or

(C) the governmental organization sought to be compelled is the Government of the United States.

(2) It is not an offense under this section if the conduct required for the offense occurred inside the United States, each alleged offender and each person seized or detained are nationals of the United States, and each alleged offender is found in the United States, unless the governmental organization sought to be compelled is the Government of the United States.

(C) As used in this section, the term "national of the United States" has the meaning given such term in section 101(a)(22) of the Immigration and Nationality Act (8 U.S.C. 1101(a)(22)).

(Added Pub. L. 98–473, title II, § 2002(a), Oct. 12, 1984, 98 Stat. 2186.)

FIGURE 1.3    An Example of a Statute
*Source.* 29 U.S. Code § 1203

## Procedural and Substantive Law

**Procedural law** tells us the rules of the game. Court rules and procedures, including questions of which court should hear a case (rules of *jurisdiction* and *venue*), filing requirements, time limits, and discovery rules make up procedural law. **Substantive law** includes those parts of the law that create, define, and regulate the rights of parties in legal proceedings, such as the definition of a contract. Chapter 3 considers procedural law in detail, whereas the rest of this book deals with various areas of substantive law.

## Private and Public Law

Substantive law can be divided into two principal areas: **private law,** which deals with the relations between individuals, including corporations and the government as a private party; and **public law,** which deals with the relations between the individual and the government. Private law includes such areas as contracts, agency, torts, corporations, business organizations, and real property. Public law includes constitutional law, administrative law, and criminal law. Issues concerning the government's regulation of business generally involve the areas of public law, but the regulations may well affect areas of private law, as, for example, a zoning regulation (public law—relation of property owner to government) restricts the use and sale of private property (private law—relation of owner to buyer/lessee).

§ 1606.8 Harassment.

(a) The Commission has consistently held that harassment on the basis of national origin is a violation of Title VII. An employer has an affirmative duty to maintain a working environment free of harassment on the basis of national origin.

(b) Ethnic slurs and other verbal or physical conduct relating to an individual's national origin constitute harassment when this conduct: (1) Has the purpose or effect of creating an intimidating, hostile or offensive working environment; (2) has the purpose or effect of unreasonably interfering with an individual's work performance; or (3) otherwise adversely affects an individual's employment opportunities.

(c) An employer is responsible for its acts and those of its agents and supervisory employees with respect to harassment on the basis of national origin regardless of whether the specific acts complained of were authorized or even forbidden by the employer and regardless of whether the employer knew or should have known of their occurrence. The Commission will examine the circumstances of the particular employment relationship and the job functions performed by the individual in determining whether an individual acts in either a supervisory or agency capacity.

(d) With respect to conduct between fellow employees, an employer is responsible for acts of harassment in the workplace on the basis of national origin, where the employer, its agents or supervisory employees, knows or should have known of the conduct, unless the employer can show that it took immediate and appropriate corrective action.

(e) An employer may also be responsible for the acts of non-employees with respect to harassment of employees in the workplace on the basis of national origin, where the employer, its agents or supervisory employees, knows or should have known of the conduct and fails to take immediate and appropriate corrective action. In reviewing these cases, the Commission will consider the extent of the employer's control and any other legal responsibility which the employer may have with respect to the conduct of such non-employees.

**FIGURE 1.4    An Example of an Administrative Rule**
*Source. 29 C.F.R. § 1606.8, Rules of the Equal Employment Opportunity Commission*

## Civil and Criminal Cases

**Civil cases** are brought to redress some private wrong, such as a breach of contract. A unit of government, such as a city, county, state, or even the federal government, may bring a civil case as well, as in the case of a suit to obtain money due to the government. **Criminal cases** are brought by a unit of government against an individual who has injured the public at large. For example, a state may bring a criminal action against a person who strikes another. While real injury may have been suffered by the victim, the criminal law is concerned with the injury to *society* caused by that conduct.

The same conduct may be the subject of both a civil and a criminal case. For example, if a business engages in anticompetitive actions, the conduct may be a criminal violation of the federal antitrust laws. But the same conduct may be the subject of a civil action brought by persons injured by that conduct.

The burden of proof and rules of evidence in criminal cases are very different from those used in civil cases. The burden of proof in criminal cases is "beyond a reasonable doubt," whereas the usual burden of proof in civil cases is "by a preponderance of the evidence." Crimes are often divided into **felonies** (serious offenses) and **misdemeanors** (less serious offenses).

## Legal Remedies

The purpose of any lawsuit, whether civil or criminal, is to remedy some wrong. The injured party, which may be an individual or the state or federal government, asks the court to grant some remedy or sanction against the party that allegedly committed some wrong. In *criminal* cases, that remedy is some form of punishment for the wrongdoer. In *civil* cases the remedy takes the form of either **damages** or **equitable remedies.**

**Damages**    The most common remedy in civil cases is *damages*, or the payment of a sum of money from the wrongdoer to the injured party. Damages are of three basic forms. **Nominal damages,** or damages in name only (usually $1 and court costs), are awarded if the wrongdoer violated a right of the other party but caused no injury. For example, if someone walked across your lawn, you would be entitled to nominal damages for the technical trespass to land.

Compensatory damages are meant to compensate the injured party for his or her loss. The judge or jury must determine the value of the loss to the injured party and give judgment in that amount. For example, if someone owes you $100 on a debt and you sue, the court may award you $100 in damages, plus court costs (but probably not attorney's fees). Some damages are more difficult to determine. For example, if you suffer a broken leg in an accident, your damages include enough money to place you back in the same position you would have been in had the injury not occurred, including your medical bills, lost wages, and an amount to compensate you for pain and suffering. Compensatory damage claims are by far the most common type of lawsuit. **Punitive damages** are damages in excess of the plaintiff's actual loss, granted to punish the wrongdoer for an intentional or malicious act. For example, if a person defrauds you in the amount of $1,000, the court may award you $1,000 in compensatory damages, plus an additional amount to *punish* the wrongdoer. Punitive damages are sometimes called *exemplary damages*, because they make an example of the wrongdoer and deter others from similar acts.

**Equitable Relief**    The second form of civil remedy is **equitable relief.** Equitable relief takes the form of a court order, requiring a person to do, or not to do, a particular act. A general form of equitable relief is an **injunction,** which forbids a person from doing a certain act. An injunction might order your neighbor not to set foot on your property, for example. The more rare **mandatory injunction** requires a person to affirmatively perform an act. Another common form of equitable relief is **specific performance,** which is a court order requiring a person to comply with the exact terms of a contract. Such court orders are enforced through **contempt of court proceedings,** in which the person who violates such an order may be jailed or fined for failure to comply with a court order.

Both civil and criminal remedies may be available in cases involving government regulation. For example, the antitrust laws provide criminal penalties against individuals or corporations that violate those statutes, injunctive relief to stop future violations and/ or order changes in corporate structure, and civil damages in favor of injured persons. In fact, those damages may take the form of **treble damages,** a unique form of punitive damages, which give the injured party three times the actual loss. Usually, regulatory statutes provide for some type of injunctive relief, but often that relief is known by some other name, such as **cease and desist orders.** More rarely the regulatory statutes permit fines and civil damages. Imprisonment may not be ordered by an administrative agency.

## THE DOCTRINE OF *STARE DECISIS*

American courts follow the doctrine of *stare decisis*, which literally means "look to the decided cases." That doctrine, also known as the rule of **precedent,** means that lower courts are generally required to follow the decisions of higher courts in similar cases.

For example, a trial court in State A is bound to follow the decisions of the state supreme court in that state and is also bound to follow the decisions of the United States Supreme Court when the decisions of that court apply to State A. The only way the decision can be changed is for the appellate court that made the prior decision to change its mind, or for an even higher appellate court to make a contrary decision. The trial court is not bound if the new case is different in its essential facts (distinguishable) from the precedent, nor is the trial court bound by **dicta,** or gratuitous statements in a decision that are unnecessary to the final result of the case.

Judges are bound to follow precedent only by tradition and to some extent by codes of judicial ethics. Judges can, and often do, depart from precedent in proper cases: Judges may depart from precedent if the precedent is old, if the reasoning of the court that provided the precedent was poor, or if justice would not be served. Sometimes trial judges do so for the conscious purpose of forcing an appeal of a case that is covered by a precedent the court finds singularly bad.

*Stare decisis* is vital to two extremely important functions of the court. First, *stare decisis* is the method by which much of our law was *created*, through the development of the **common law.** Second, *stare decisis* is essential to the *interpretation* function of the courts.

### *Stare Decisis* and the Common Law

The term **common law** is used to refer to the *judge-made* law that developed in England. More specifically, the term refers to the body of principles and rules derived from the customs and usages of "immemorial antiquity" or from the judgments of courts recognizing and enforcing those customs and usages. In other words, the ancient unwritten law of England forms the background of "the common law."

Historically there were no statutes to guide the courts in many areas of the law, including such important areas as contracts, torts, agency, and property. From the beginning of English history, judges were confronted with disputes that had to be settled but found that no statutes had been made that resolved the problem before them. In fact, during the first few centuries of the development of the common law, there were no legislatures to make statutes. Those judges then decided the case based on notions of fairness, justice, custom, religious views, or other bases.

Over the centuries judges began to recognize the value of consistency in the law and began to develop the idea of precedent, or *stare decisis*. Judges made an effort to decide similar cases by similar rules. After judges became literate, some decisions were written down to give judges the benefit of another's reasoning. In this way, the vast amounts of "law" found in the common law were created.

The common law is just as binding as any statute, because in the final analysis it is what judges do that determines the nature of the law. The following decision illustrates both the concept of *stare decisis* and the nature of the common law.

## *Flagiello v. The Pennsylvania Hospital*

417 Pa. 486, 208 A.2d 193 (1965)

Mary Flagiello was a paying patient in the Pennsylvania Hospital, a charitable institution. Through the negligence of two employees of the hospital she was caused to fall and fracture her ankle. That injury in turn caused a longer hospital stay and more hospital expenses. Mrs. Flagiello and her husband (the plaintiffs) brought suit for their loss against the hospital and the two employees who allegedly caused the injury. The hospital (the defendant) claimed that it was not responsible for the injuries on the basis of an ancient common-law doctrine called *charitable immunity*. That doctrine provides that charitable (eleemosynary) institutions are immune from suit for their own negligence or the negligence of their employees. The trial court dismissed the complaint filed by the Flagiellos, and the Flagiellos appealed the decision to the Pennsylvania Supreme Court.

**Musmanno, Justice**    The hospital has not denied that its negligence caused Mrs. Flagiello's injuries. It merely announces that it is an eleemosynary institution, and, therefore, owed no duty of care to its patient. It declares in effect that it can do wrong and still not be liable in damages to the person it has wronged. It thus urges a momentous exception to the generic proposition that in law there is no wrong without a remedy. From the earliest days of organized society it became apparent that society could never become a success unless the collectivity of mankind guaranteed to every member of society a remedy for a palpable wrong inflicted on him by another member of that society. In 1844 Justice Storrs of the Supreme Court of Connecticut crystallized into epigrammatic language that wise concept, as follows: "An injury is a wrong; and for the redress of every wrong there is a remedy: a wrong is a violation of one's right, and for the vindication of every right there is a remedy."

On what basis then, may a hospital, which expects and receives compensation for its services, demand of the law that it be excused from responding in damages for injuries tortiously inflicted by its employees on paying patients? There is not a person or establishment in all civilization that is not required to meet his or its financial obligations, there is not a person or establishment that is not called upon by the law to render an accounting for harm visited by him or it on innocent victims. By what line of reasoning, then, can any institution, operating commercially, expect the law to insulate it from its debts?

The hospital in this case . . . replies to that question with various answers, some of which are: it is an ancient rule that charitable hospitals have never been required to recompense patients who have been injured through the negligence of their employees; the rule of *stare decisis* forbids that charitable hospitals be held liable . . . ; if the rule of charitable immunity is to be discarded, this must be done by the State Legislature; and that since hospitals serve the public, there is involved here a matter of public policy which is not within the jurisdiction of the courts.

Whatever Mrs. Flagiello received in the Pennsylvania Hospital was not bestowed on her gratuitously. She paid $24.50 a day [a rather substantial fee for hospital services in 1965.—Ed.] for the services she was to receive. And she paid this amount not only for the period she was to remain in the hospital to be cured of the ailment with which she entered the hospital, but she had to continue to pay that rate for the period she was compelled to remain in the hospital as a result of injuries caused by the hospital itself.

To say that a person who pays for what he receives is still the object of charity is a self-contradiction in terms. In the early days of public accommodation for the ill and the maimed, charity was exercised in its pure and pristine sense. Many good men and women, liberal in purse and generous in soul, set up houses to heal the poor and homeless victims of disease and injury. They made no charge for this care. . . . The wealthy and the so-called middle class were treated in their homes where usually there could be found better facilities than could be had in the hospitals. Charity in the biblical sense prevailed.

Whatever the law may have been regarding charitable institutions in the past it does not meet the conditions of today. . . . Hospitals today are growing into mighty edifices in brick, stone, glass and marble; many of them maintain large staffs; they use the best equipment that science can devise; they utilize the most modern methods in devoting themselves to the noblest purpose of man, that of helping one's stricken brother. But they do all this on a business basis, submitting invoices for services rendered—and properly so.

And if a hospital functions as a business institution, by charging and receiving money for what it offers, it must be a business establishment also in meeting obligations it incurs in running that establishment. One of those inescapable obligations is that it must exercise a proper degree of care for its patients, and, to the extent that it fails in that care, it should be liable in damages as any other commercial firm would be liable. . . .

If there was any justification for the charitable immunity doctrine when it was first announced, it has lost that justification today.

The appellee [Hospital] . . . insist[s] that if the charity immunity doctrine is to undergo mutation the only surgeon capable of performing the operation is the Legislature. We have seen however that the controverted rule is not the creation of the Legislature. This Court fashioned it, and, what it put together, it can dismantle.

Failing to hold back both the overwhelming reasons of rudimentary justice for abolishing the doctrine, and the rising tide of out-of-state repudiation of

the doctrine, the defendant Hospital . . . fall[s] back for defense to the bastion of *Stare Decisis*. It is inevitable and proper that they should do so. Without *stare decisis*, there would be no stability in our system of jurisprudence.

*Stare decisis* channels the law. It erects lighthouses and flies the signals of safety. The ships of jurisprudence must follow that well-defined channel which, over the years, has been proved to be secure and trustworthy. But it would not comport with wisdom to insist that, should the shoals rise in a heretofore safe course and rocks emerge to encumber the passage, the ship should nonetheless pursue the original course, merely because it presented no hazard in the past. The principle of *stare decisis* does not demand that we follow precedents which shipwreck justice.

*Stare decisis* is not an iron mold into which every utterance by a Court—regardless of circumstances, parties, economic barometer and sociological climate—must be poured, and, where, like wet concrete, it must acquire an unyielding rigidity which nothing later can change.

The history of law through the ages records numerous inequities pronounced by courts because the society of the day sanctioned them. Reason revolts, humanity shudders, and justice recoils before much of what was done in the past under the name of law. Yet, we are urged to retain a forbidden incongruity in the law simply because it is old. That kind of reasoning would have retained prosecution for witchcraft, imprisonment for debt and hanging for minor offenses which today are hardly regarded as misdemeanors.

There is nothing in the records of the courts, the biographies of great jurists or the writings of eminent legal authorities which offers the slightest encouragement to the notion that time petrifies into unchanging jurisprudence a palpable fallacy. As years can give no sturdiness to a decayed tree, so the passing decades can add no convincing flavor to the withered apple of sophistry clinging to the limb of demonstrated wrong. There are, of course, principles and precepts sanctified by age and no one would think of changing them, but their inviolability derives not from longevity but from their universal appeal to the reason, the conscience and the experience of mankind. No one, for instance, would think of challenging what was written in Magna Charta, the Habeas Corpus Act or the Bill of Rights of the Constitution of the United States. . . .

While age adds venerableness to moral principles and some physical objects, it occasionally becomes necessary, and it is not sacrilegious to do so, to scrape away the moss of the years to study closely the thing which is being accepted as authoritative, inviolable, and untouchable. The Supreme Court of Michigan said sagaciously in the case of *Williams v. City of Detroit* . . . that "it is the peculiar genius of the common law that no legal rule is mandated by the doctrine of *stare decisis* when that rule was conceived in error or when the times and circumstances have so changed as to render it an instrument of injustice."

The charitable immunity rule proves itself an instrument of injustice and nothing presented by the defendant . . . shows it to be otherwise. . . .

A rule that has become insolvent has no place in the active market of current enterprise. When a rule offends against reason, when it is at odds with every precept of natural justice, and when it cannot be defended on its own merits, but has to depend alone on a discredited genealogy, courts not only possess the inherent power to repudiate, but, indeed it is required by the very nature of judicial function, to abolish such a rule.

Of course, the precedents here recalled do not justify a light and casual treatment of the doctrine of *stare decisis*, but they proclaim unequivocally that where justice demands, reason dictates, equality enjoins and fair play decrees a change in judge-made law courts will not lack in determination to establish that change.

The judgments of the Court below are reversed. . . .

## Case Discussion Questions

1    Turn back to page 2 in the introduction and answer each of the questions about this case.
2    Does the fact that Mrs. Flagiello was a paying patient have anything to do with the result? Would the decision have been the same if she had been a charity patient?
3    What is the social and economic effect of this decision? Under the prior rule, who carried the risk of loss of injury suffered at the hands of a charity? After this case, who carries that risk?
4    Does the new rule of liability announced by the court apply to all charities, or just charitable hospitals?

### *Stare Decisis* and Interpretation

**Interpretation of Statutes**    Even when there is a statute, administrative regulation, or constitutional provision directly on point, the courts must often step in to interpret the meaning of the words in the statute. This need for interpretation is often difficult for laypersons to grasp. Words—even commonly used ones—often have several meanings, and the precise meaning given to a word or phrase may make a great deal of difference in a crucial case. Various phrases in the U.S. Constitution, such as "freedom of speech," "due process," "Commerce . . . among the several States," and "equal protection of the laws," are particularly subject to interpretation because of their breadth and vagueness. Many of the cases in this text involve an issue of construction (interpretation) of some statute or constitutional provision.

While the courts have a great deal of latitude in interpreting the words of statutes, constitutional provisions, and administrative regulations, there are many "rules of construction," often devised by the courts themselves, to aid the courts in interpreting legislative acts. It is often said that the goal of all statutory construction is to find *"the intent of the legislature,"* or, in the case of the federal Constitution, *"the intent of the framers,"* and give effect to that intent. Sometimes that intent is easy to determine, particularly if the legislature discloses its intent in the statute, or if the legislative record contains statements of the legislature's intent. But often such help is not available, and the courts must rely on other "rules of construction" to determine the true intent of the legislature (see Figure 1.5).

1    The words of a statute should be given their plain and natural meaning unless injustice or absurdity would result.

2    A statute should be interpreted, if possible, to have a legal and constitutional effect.

3    Criminal statutes are construed strictly against the government.

4    Tax statutes are construed in the manner that imposes the least burden on the taxpayer.

5    Statutes that change the common law are strictly construed.

6    Technical words are given their technical meaning.

7    *May* is permissive, whereas *shall* or *will* means "must."

8    Statutes should be interpreted as a whole, and all of the parts of the statute should be viewed to determine the intent of a part of the statute.

FIGURE 1.5    Some Basic Rules for the Interpretation of Statutes

When a court interprets a constitutional provision, statute, or administrative regulation, generally that interpretation has the same status in the law as the provision interpreted and, thus, becomes a part of the law. Therefore, if the Supreme Court interprets a provision of the U.S. Constitution, the Court's interpretation in effect becomes a part of the Constitution until either the Constitution is amended or the Court changes its mind. If Congress were to pass a statute declaring the Court's interpretation unlawful, that statute would be of no effect, because the Court's decision had the status of the Constitution itself.

**Interpretation and Case Law**    Sometimes even cases need interpretation. It is at this point that the distinction between the common law and interpretative functions of judicial decisions becomes fuzzy. In the *Flagiello* decision (pp. 25–27), the court's decision may be read in one of two ways. Either the doctrine of charitable immunity is completely dead, or the doctrine no longer applies to paying patients in charitable hospitals. Sometimes, as in the following case, the courts are required to clarify and interpret their own decisions.

## *Nolan v. Tifereth Israel Synagogue of Mt. Carmel*

425 Pa. 106, 227 A.2d 675 (1967) Sup. Ct. of Pennsylvania

Gertrude Nolan fell on the sidewalk in front of the defendant-synagogue's building, resulting in personal injuries. Mrs. Nolan and her husband brought this action against the synagogue, charging negligence. The synagogue raised the defense of charitable immunity, but the Nolans argued that the *Flagiello* case had overturned that doctrine in Pennsylvania. The lower court held that the synagogue was a nonprofit religious organization and was exempt from suit under the doctrine of charitable immunity. The case was dismissed, and the Nolans appealed to the state supreme court.

**O'Brien, Justice**    The opinion of the court below concludes that our decision in *Flagiello* abrogated the doctrine of charitable immunity only insofar as it related to an action . . . brought by a paying patient in a hospital. . . . Appellants, on the other hand, contend that *Flagiello* intended to, and did, put an end to the doctrine of charitable immunity in Pennsylvania. . . .

To hold that *Flagiello* is limited to the extent found by the court below and contended for by the appellee would produce an anomalous situation bordering on the bizarre. We would then be required to say that a paying patient in a hospital could recover for injuries sustained by him as the result of the hospital's negligence, while a nonpaying patient could make no such recovery. We would further be required to say that of all of the charitable institutions in the Commonwealth formerly beneficiaries of the doctrine of charitable immunity, only hospitals had lost the protection and all other charitable institutions retained it. Or, we might be required to say that payment of a fee for service is the criterion upon which a determination of who may recover against a charitable institution in tort is based, if indeed the decision in *Flagiello* is dependent on the circumstance of the plaintiff's having been a paying patient. Were such a conclusion reached, we might be required to hold that in cases such as the one at bar involving a religious institution, that a dues-paying member of the congregation could recover while another person not so situated could not, if indeed the organization were set up on the basis of fixed membership dues, as many religious organizations are.

We cannot conclude that our decision in *Flagiello* did nothing more than remove the protection of the doctrine from hospitals involved in tort litigation with paying patients, and therefore, lest the fact that such a situation was involved in *Flagiello* remain as a source of confusion, we here hold unequivocally that the doctrine of immunity of charitable institutions from liability in tort no longer exists in the Commonwealth of Pennsylvania.

The judgment of the court below is reversed, and the cause remanded for further proceedings. . . .

## Case Discussion Questions

1    How do the charities in *Flagiello* and *Nolan* differ? What relationship between the parties exists in the two cases? What remedies were the plaintiffs requesting?
2    Does this decision *change* the *Flagiello* decision or merely *explain* it?
3    Following *Nolan*, would you advise the local Boy Scout troop to get insurance? Why or why not?

---

Thus, although a decision may constitute binding precedent, it may also require interpretation. And, the lower courts are not bound by a decision if a new case is different in its essential facts (e.g., is **distinguishable**) from the precedent. In *Nolan*, the trial court thought that the *Flagiello* decision did not apply to charitable immunity in contexts other than paying patients in hospitals, and thus *distinguished* the case. But the trial court, as it turned out, was wrong.

Trial courts are not bound by dicta, or gratuitous statements in a decision that are not necessary for the final result. For example, many of the statements in the second full paragraph of the *Nolan* decision might be characterized as dicta, and no trial court is bound by such statements.

### Stare Decisis and the Organization of the Courts

The organization of the trial and appellate courts presents some tricky problems in applying the doctrine of *stare decisis*. Assume, for example, that Congress passes a statute prohibiting any person from killing any "deer, bear, wolf, or other large mammal in

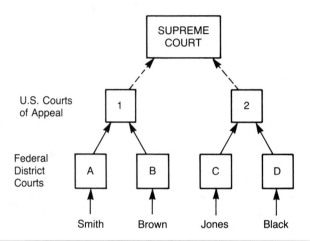

FIGURE 1.6    The Federal Court System (Simplified)*

*A more complete diagram of the Federal court system is found on p. 66.

federally protected territories." Assume also that Smith killed a whale in federally protected waters and was charged with a violation of that statute in Federal District Court A
(see Figure 1.6).

Federal District Court A would decide the question of whether a whale was the
kind of "large mammal" intended by Congress, using a variety of rules of construction
and ultimately looking to the intent of Congress. Assuming that that court convicted
Smith, Smith could appeal only to the U.S. Court of Appeals for Circuit 1. That court
might agree with the lower court and **affirm** the conviction, or disagree with the lower
court and **reverse** the decision. If anything further remained to be done in the trial
court, the appellate court would **remand** the case back to the trial court for further proceedings (see Chapter 3, p. 89, for a discussion of appellate procedure). The decision
would become precedent for all courts within the area served by Court 1. Thus,
if Brown were arrested for killing another whale and the case were tried in either Court
A or Court B, the judge in either court would be bound by the decision in *U.S. v.
Smith*.

On the other hand, if Jones were arrested for killing a whale and tried in either
Court C or D, the judges in those courts would *not* be bound by the *Smith* decision,
because they are not in Court 1's circuit.[3] The judges in those courts may view the
*Smith* case as helpful, or even persuasive, but they are free to disagree and rule differently. Similarly, if Jones were convicted and he appealed to Court 2, that court could
also disagree with Court 1. As a result, there would be a **split in the circuits** created by
the *Jones* case, a split that could be resolved only by the Supreme Court. In the meantime, the law would be different in two parts of the country.

---

3 While this is true in the federal courts and many state court systems, the precedent value of intermediate
  appellate court decisions in the state courts varies widely, either by statute or court decision. Thus, *Smith*
  may be binding or of little value as precedent.

Finally, to expand the point, if Black were arrested and tried in any of the district courts for shooting a *walrus*, neither the *Smith* nor the *Jones* decision would be binding. The judge might find both cases helpful or persuasive, but because the essential facts (i.e., the character of the mammal) are different, the cases would be distinguishable and the judge would be bound to follow neither decision.

## SUMMARY AND CONCLUSIONS

The study of the legal environment of business requires an understanding of the nature of law and the legal process, including the sources of American institutions and the powers of government. American legal and political theory is based on a specific theory of government and law, the theory of natural rights, in which the authority of government is derived from the consent of the governed.

"Law" is best viewed as predictions of what the courts will do. Clues to what the courts may do may be found in the expressions of written law, the Constitution, statutes, administrative rules, treaties, and judicial decisions. In all cases, the courts interpret those expressions, and the result, in the form of actual decisions, is the law.

The concept of *stare decisis*, or *precedent*, is central to the Anglo-American legal system. That doctrine requires lower courts to follow the decisions of higher courts in identical cases. The principle of *stare decisis* operates to create law in the form of the common law and also acts to aid in the interpretative function of the courts.

## PRO AND CON

# Should judges use their powers for "social engineering" purposes?

It is said that judges should find the law, not make it. But judges, particularly appellate court judges, sometimes use their authority to create new legal doctrines. The question is whether judges *should* be active in "creating" the law.

**Pro**   In actuality, judges cannot avoid creating law. The whole process of the common law means that entire areas of the law are left open for judges' policymaking. And make it they must, because even *not* deciding cases often means that policy is made through silence.

When a court interprets a statute, administrative regulation, or constitutional provision, its interpretation is "law" just as certainly as the statute, regulation, or constitutional provision is "law." And if those provisions are broad and ambiguous, such as "due process of law" as found in the fifth and fourteenth amendments of the U.S. Constitution, *whatever* interpretation is placed on the words by the courts is likely to make policy. Whether the interpretation is "liberal" or "conservative," it constitutes policymaking.

Judges tend also to be the last bastion of protection for the weak, the disadvantaged, and the minorities within our society. Our legislative process is based on the concept of majority rule, as it should be. But this means we are subject to the "tyranny of the majority." The rights of minorities, particularly unpopular minorities, are protected only by the law. And the only way in which the law may be used to protect minorities is for judges to interpret it, mold it, and even create it so that minority rights are not overridden. For example, it is highly unlikely that schools would have been desegregated in 1954 had it not been for the Supreme Court's decision in *Brown v. Board of Education of Topeka* (see pp. 448–449).

Finally, judges are in a unique position in fashioning law: they have legal expertise, which elected legislators may lack; they have independence from pressure groups and public opinion; and they have the leisure to pursue the law through the methods of scholarship and wisdom.

**Con**    In the United States only a legislature can make a law. In fact, the very term *legislature* means "lawmaking body." Legislatures are elected bodies, chosen by the citizens to make laws. They are constructed in such a manner that the citizens can have access to the legislature and bring pressure to bear when necessary to make sure that the public will is embodied in our laws. Judges, on the other hand, serve the public in other ways. Many judges are not elected and often serve for lengthy terms or even life. They do not represent the public—they represent "the law" instead. In that sense, creation of policy by the courts is singularly undemocratic.

The power of interpretation is *not* the power to make laws. Interpretation means *finding* the meaning of law, not *creating* the meaning. Courts therefore should be concerned with ascertaining and giving effect to the meaning of statutes, regulations, and constitutional provisions by looking to the *intent of the legislature* or, in the case of the Constitution, the *intent of the framers*. For example, it is highly unlikely that the framers of the Constitution intended that police officers be required to advise persons charged with crime of their rights. That is a *legislative*, not a *judicial*, function.

Creation of the common law clearly does involve lawmaking, but only by default. If a legislature does not like a common law result, it may change that result by statute. Some common law doctrines are so ancient and so entwined within our society and economy that any change in them—at least any essential change—should be done by elected representatives, and not by the judges. If a contemporary court were to change the basic elements of a contract today, the change would be highly unsettling to our society and economy. Such a change, if it is to be made, should be made by elected representatives, even though those elements were formed in the first instance by courts.

### Roundtable Discussion

1    Are judges responsive to the public will? Should judges try to follow public opinion? Why or why not? Why do you think judges serve very lengthy terms—even for life? Should judges be elected?

2    Should we be afraid of the "tyranny of the majority"? What protections exist for unpopular minorities? Who enforces those protections? What if a legislature, representing the majority, overrides those protections?

3    Should judges make policy? What do you mean by "policy"? Can judges *avoid* making policy?

---

## REVIEW QUESTIONS

1    What is the "legal environment of business"? Can you think of any other relationships of the business firm besides the eight relationships in Figure 1.2?

2    Explain the four principal functions of the law.

3    How are ethics and the law related? Would you lie if your employer required you to do so? Which is more important—honesty or loyalty? Would you still lie if the lie was illegal?

4    Explain the difference between *damages* and *equitable relief*. What kinds of damages are available?

5    What is the "common law"?

6    Explain how *stare decisis* works. *Why* do judges follow precedent?

7    Were the laws of Nazi Germany under Adolf Hitler valid? Under which of the philosophies of law would those laws be invalid? Why? Does it make a difference whether we are discussing a traffic law or Hitler's laws concerning the Jewish population?

8    By what right did the Nuremburg Court convict, sentence, and execute Nazi war criminals for committing acts that were perfectly legal under the laws of Germany? What conception of law does this illustrate?

9    An ordinance in a midwestern city makes

it illegal for "any person who is disfigured, grotesque, or otherwise obnoxious to public view" to be on the streets after dark. The law has never been enforced and carries no penalty. Is it still a law?

10    Falstaff had a bad day. He was standing on the sidewalk when he was struck by a car that was owned by Glendower House, a local charitable home for the aged. The car was being driven by Gadshill, one of the residents of the home, who was running an errand for the home. Falstaff survived the accident and was taken to Westmoreland Hospital, a local not-for-profit hospital. Falstaff was indigent and could not pay his bill, but the hospital had a policy of taking all patients regardless of financial condition. While Falstaff was a patient at the hospital, two nurse's aides dropped him, breaking his clavicle. Falstaff filed two lawsuits, one against the Glendower House and one against Westmoreland Hospital, charging negligence. How would each case be decided in Pennsylvania after the *Flagiello* case was decided? Of what importance is the *Nolan* case?

C H A P T E R    2

# Ethics and the Law

*I have gained this by philosophy: that I do without being commanded what others do only from fear of the law.*

ARISTOTLE
*Diogenes Laertius* (circa 350 B.C.)

*Laws are sand, customs are rock. Laws can be evaded and punishment escaped, but an openly transgressed custom brings sure punishment.*

MARK TWAIN
*The Gorky Incident* (1906)

**Ethics** are the standards by which each of us judges the conduct of ourselves and others as either "right" or "wrong." *Webster's* defines ethics as "1: the discipline dealing with what is good and bad and with moral duty and obligation 2a: a set of moral principles or values b: a theory or system of moral values. . . ."[1] Each of us has such standards, although they may vary with the way we were raised, our religious beliefs, and a host of other influences on our lives.

The law and ethics are parallel systems of social control. Our relationships with others, including the eight relationships of the business firm, are regulated both by the law and by our ethical and moral beliefs about how we should act (see Figure 2.1). Moral and ethical beliefs are *unenforced* except through social pressure. Sometimes it is necessary for the *enforced* requirements of the law to step in and force us to act in a certain way.

Business ethics have been a source of concern to businesspeople, lawyers, judges, academics, and the public for a very long time. Many people believe that unrestrained personal ambition, unbridled by concern for morality, ethics, or the public interest, is extremely dangerous. We are all praised for ambition and taught that we should strive to succeed, but there must be some checks on that ambition. The first and best check is, of course, self-discipline. But self-discipline may fail for any number of reasons. As a result, the law must step in to provide limits on ambition and enforce the morality, ethics, and interests of the larger society. Often, but not always, the law embodies underlying moral and ethical principles. In a broad sense, the law is the enforced expression of the ethics of society as determined by legislators, judges, and juries.

It is clear that the ethics of society are a major *input to the law*. In a democracy, what the majority believes to be right and wrong will tend to become the law, eith-

---

1 *Webster's New Collegiate Dictionary*, G. & C. Merriam Co., Springfield, Mass., 1975, p. 392.

U.C.C
Uniform Commerce Code
— Set of rules for commerce
for banking, money, doing business

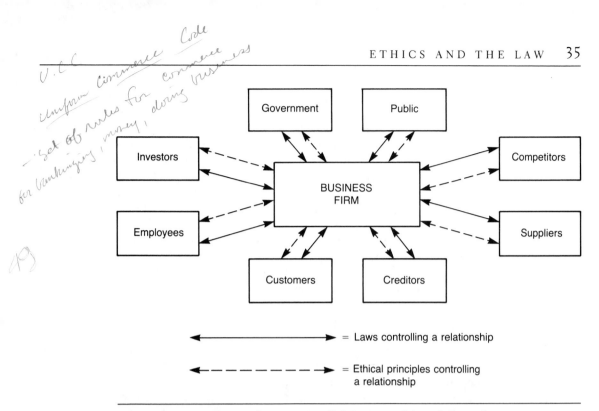

= Laws controlling a relationship

= Ethical principles controlling
a relationship

FIGURE 2.1   Ethics and Law as Parallel Systems of Social Control

er through the actions of legislatures or through court decisions and the principle of *stare decisis*. It is also clear that the law is an *input to ethics*. If certain conduct is made illegal (e.g., traffic laws), violating those laws tends to become somehow unethical or immoral. Ethics and the law therefore overlap, with some conduct being only illegal, some conduct being only unethical, and some conduct being both illegal and unethical (see Figure 2.2).

### The Place of Ethics in the Classroom

There is a great deal of disagreement about the place of ethics in the classroom. Some argue that such instruction belongs in the home and the church and has no place in a

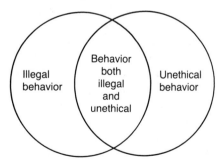

FIGURE 2.2   The Relationship Between Law and Ethics

university class. Others insist that it is not proper for a college instructor to "preach" to students. And indeed there are two common traps for ethical instruction at any level of public education. First, instructors and textbooks may end up preaching about ethics from the personal value system of the teacher or the author. Second, instructors and textbooks may merely proclaim that "it's all a matter of opinion" and simply admonish students to "let your conscience be your guide." Neither approach is satisfactory.

Ethics are highly personal matters, and it is quite inappropriate, particularly in an academic setting, to try to convince someone that a particular ethical system is "correct." But that does not mean that instruction in ethics is impossible or wrong. It means instead that instruction in ethics should encourage students to *think about* their personal ethical systems and work on them logically and consistently, so that when real ethical dilemmas arise, the student will have the intellectual tools with which to face them. This chapter merely aims at developing those intellectual tools.

## WHERE DO ETHICS COME FROM?

Each of us establishes his or her own notions of right and wrong. Clearly, our ethical systems are created over our lifetime and continue to evolve as we grow and mature. Those systems are influenced first by our parents and then later by others around us, including brothers and sisters, friends, counselors, and teachers. Beliefs about what is right and wrong are influenced by our religious beliefs, the books we read, and even the movies and television programs we see. Those individual ethical principles are sometimes called **personal ethics.**

Common personal ethical principles include honesty, truthfulness, tolerance, charity, and loyalty (see Figure 2.3). The precise mix of those values will vary with each person's upbringing, religion, education, and experience. Personal ethics tend to change over time. Whereas murder and thievery have probably always been considered wrong and have been outlawed at almost every time in history, notions of honesty, fair play, and loyalty have changed a great deal over the centuries. Ethical beliefs and laws that made good sense to our Puritan and Victorian ancestors seem curious anachronisms today.

### Cultural Sources of Ethics

Our ethical beliefs are likely to be quite similar to those of others who grew up in the same culture. Our ethical systems may be compared to snowflakes—each person's system is like every other person's in the larger aspects, but on close examination each person's ethics are slightly different, depending on the influences on that person's life. Most of our basic personal beliefs are derived from our *culture*, however.

The sources of the ethical principles of our culture are complex. Western civilization has a long and rich ethical tradition, including a variety of philosophies and religions that have intermingled and acted on one another to produce the stewpot of ethical notions in our world today. Without our even realizing it, each of those philosophies and religions has influenced our personal ethical beliefs.

Those cultural ethical beliefs are sometimes called **societal ethics.** Societal ethics include principles from all ideologies, such as communism, socialism, and democracy, and all religions, such as Christianity, Islam, and Buddhism. For example, the Judeo-

| Examples of Personal Ethics | Sources of Societal Ethics |
|---|---|
| Honesty | Religions |
| Truthfulness | Christianity |
| Sincerity | Judaism |
| Fairness | Islam |
| Impartiality | Buddhism |
| Loyalty | Other Eastern faiths |
| Reliability | Political ideologies |
| Dependability | Democracy |
| Trustworthiness | Marxism |
| Fairness | Socialism |
| Evenhandedness | The "work ethic" |
| Lack of oppression | Philosophies |
| Obedience to law | Ancient Greek philosophy |
| Community responsibility | Humanism |
| Tolerance | Mysticism |
| Charity | Modern philosophies |

FIGURE 2.3    Ethics and the Sources of Ethics

Christian heritage generally asks that people "love one another," and therefore we would expect people who follow Judeo-Christian beliefs to accept that principle. Societal ethics also include other principles that are accepted by groups of people but are not express principles of organized systems of belief. For example, many Americans consciously or subconsciously subscribe to the **work ethic,** which places a high value on hard work, sacrifice, and enterprise.

Societal ethics are important in understanding the background and development of the law. American law grew out of American culture and particularly out of the great societal ethics of democracy, the Jewish and Christian religions, and the work ethic. As a result, American law is very different from the law of other countries that do not share those values.

Students who may deal in international business must be sensitive to the ethical differences in cultures around the world. The cultural heritage of nations with Islamic, Hindu, or Buddhist backgrounds is fundamentally different from that of Western cultures; as a result, the ethical rules of the game will also be fundamentally different. It is vital to have some understanding not only of the basis of Western ethical culture but also of the ethical background of those with whom we deal in the international arena.

Ethical beliefs in Western cultures can be traced to three main sources: (1) Greek philosophy; (2) the Judeo-Christian religious heritage; and (3) the philosophical traditions of rationalism, humanism, and utilitarianism. Each plays a role in the development of personal ethics and in the creation of the law.

### Greek Philosophy

Western ethical thought began with the Greeks, especially Aristotle, who coined the term *ethics*. Aristotle argued that all people seek *happiness*, a point from which many other philosophers begin. Aristotle said that people could reach happiness only by practicing the *virtues* of courage, temperance, liberality, justice, good temper, prudence (good sense), and wisdom. The ultimate good life to Aristotle consisted of a contemplative use of the mind, and people can only be free to use their minds in that way if they practice the virtues. Therefore, only through the virtues can we arrive at the state of happiness.

The influence of the Greeks cannot be overstated. Greek philosophy had a major impact on later Christian thought, particularly with its revival in Western cultures during the Renaissance. That revival in turn resulted in the philosophical upheavals of the seventeenth and eighteenth centuries, including the creation of natural rights theories (see p. 16).

### Judeo-Christian Religious Influences

Perhaps the best-known and most widely accepted statement of ethical conduct is found in the Ten Commandments (Exodus 20:2–17). The Hebrew ethics of the Old Testament, sometimes called simply *The Law*, state the ethical duties of human beings in substantial detail, especially in the so-called *Covenant Code* (Exodus 21–23). Many of the Biblical stories, particularly those in the Old Testament, are "case histories" of moral and ethical problems resolved by reference to the law of God.

For many, the search for ethics stops here. Western culture is a joint creation of Greek thought and the Judeo-Christian heritage. Greek culture found its way into the thought of many of the early Christian thinkers and rose again during the Renaissance. Western ethical thought is in large measure the combination of those two streams of thought.

### Rationalism and Humanism

During the sixteenth century, philosophers began disputing the religious dogmas that had ruled Europe for a thousand years. Interest shifted from the supernatural to the natural, and philosophers tried to extend the teachings of science and mathematics into the area of philosophy. Human reason, rather than divine inspiration, became the source of moral authority. **Rationalism** believes that ethical values can be logically deduced through human reasoning.

The rationalist philosophies led to a number of other schools of thought, including **humanism,** which stressed the importance of human experience and developed philosophies independent of theology and religion. Many humanists taught that all people have dignity and worth and should command the respect of their fellow humans. That philosophy was embraced by such humanists of the American Revolution as Thomas Jefferson, Benjamin Franklin, and Thomas Paine. Rationalism and humanism also form the basis of **utilitarianism,** a philosophy particularly important to the law, and of the two predominant philosophies of the twentieth century—the ideas of *community* and *individualism*.

### Utilitarianism

*Utilitarianism* has had a major impact on political and economic thought in the last century. Utilitarianism originated in the thought of the English philosophers Jeremy

Bentham, James Mill, and his son, John Stuart Mill, and it found its fullest expression in John Stuart Mill's book *On Liberty*. Utilitarianism is an immensely practical philosophy with strong economic overtones.

Utilitarianism begins with Aristotle's premise that happiness is the greatest good. Therefore, Mill continues, a "good society" is one in which the greatest possible number of persons enjoy the greatest possible amount of happiness. Individual actions may be classed as "good" or "bad" by the amount to which they contribute to or detract from total human happiness.

The principles of utilitarianism are similar to the notion of marginal utility economics. If an action by an individual contributes more toward the total amount of happiness in the world, then that action should be undertaken. If it reduces total happiness, it should not be undertaken.

### Individualism and Community

Two societal ethics, both derived from rationalism and humanism, have dominated the world of the twentieth century. Since the eighteenth century, Western culture has been directed by the **individualist ethic.** In the middle of the nineteenth century a competitor arose in the form of the **community ethic.** Almost all political and legal debate can be characterized as a struggle between those poles.

Individualism in its purest form holds that the individual is supreme and society is merely a means of achieving and maximizing individual welfare. The American Bill of Rights is clearly an example of individualism in its purest form (see Chapter 5). Although individualism is almost second nature to contemporary America, the idea was a radical heresy in the eighteenth century, when the state, in the person of the king, was all-important. Individualism in its most extreme form may be found in **social Darwinism,** which believes that strong individuals *should* win as part of the "survival of the fittest," and in **laissez-faire** economics, which in its ultimate form holds that governments should never interfere in economic matters. Individualism may ultimately result in political **anarchy,** or the absence of all government.

The community ethic, on the other hand, holds that the welfare of society is supreme over the welfare of the individual. In its most extreme form, the community ethic believes that individuals may be used or even destroyed as a means to perfection of society. The ultimate form of the community ethic may be found in the writings of Karl Marx and forms the basis of communism, socialism, and other collectivist ideologies.

We may be tempted to reject all aspects of the community ethic and embrace individualism outright. But both the ethic of individualism and the community ethic have resulted in major economic, political, and personal miseries, when carried to their extremes. Whereas the community ethic rejects the importance of the individual, individualism may reject all notions of community. Whereas the community ethic in its extreme form results in the evils of communism and totalitarianism, individualism in its extreme form may result in sweat shops, consumer fraud, discrimination, environmental pillage, and monopoly.

There is a middle ground, one taken by most societies. Much of the history of the twentieth century—and much of the history of American law—may be viewed as an attempt to combine the best elements of individualism with the best elements of the community ethic. Our problem is not one of facing a stark choice between the

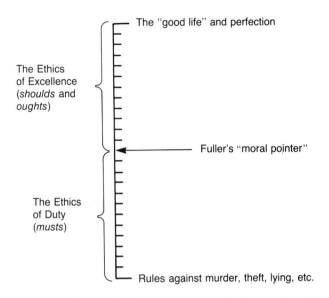

The "good life" and perfection

The Ethics
of Excellence
(*shoulds* and
*oughts*)

Fuller's "moral pointer"

The Ethics
of Duty
(*musts*)

Rules against murder, theft, lying, etc.

FIGURE 2.4    The Ethical Scale

individual and the community but one of finding the proper mix of the two ethics.

For example, many of the antidiscrimination statutes represent a choice between individualist and community notions. Individualism holds that each businessperson has the right to sell to whomever he or she chooses. Notions of community find that sellers should be prohibited from discrimination against buyers on the basis of race or other irrelevancies. The result is a compromise in which the worst elements of individualism are prohibited for the good of the larger community, while as much individual choice as possible is preserved.

## THE THEORY OF THE TWO ETHICS

One of the most valuable tools in analyzing ethics is the **theory of the two ethics.** Many philosophers have argued that each of us has within us *two* sets of ethical principles, and a great deal of our ethical difficulty is caused by our failure to recognize the existence of and difference between these two systems. Although the names of the two systems vary, we may call them the **ethics of duty** and the **ethics of excellence**[2] (see Figure 2.4).

### The Ethics of Duty and the Ethics of Excellence

The *ethics of duty* include those fundamental rules necessary for an organized society. Those ethics include most of the "thou shalt nots" of our culture, including our moral

---

2 Perhaps the clearest expression of the theory is Lon Fuller's book, *The Morality of Law* (New Haven, Conn.: Yale University Press, 1964), pp. 13–33. Fuller uses the term *morality of duty* for the ethics of duty, and the term *morality of aspiration* for the ethics of excellence. Fuller's work builds on philosophical notions dating back to Aristotle, and many other philosophers have established similar theories.

prohibitions of murder, violence, theft, lying, and cheating. Although we are often bound by the law not to violate these standards, we are also bound by moral and ethical standards to comply. These duties are essential to civilized society and are remarkably uniform from culture to culture. Almost every society forbids murder, for example, because a society that freely permits murder would soon drown in its own blood.

The *ethics of excellence*, on the other hand, contain our ideals of perfection and the good life. These are the "shoulds" and "oughts" of our society, including both our personal aspirations and our standards of perfect conduct. They contain our views of what constitutes a "good life." For perhaps too many, a good life means only personal wealth; for others it means physical pleasure, personal beauty, wisdom, virtue, or holiness. The ethics of excellence also contain our ideals of perfection in ethical matters, such as *total* honesty, *perfect* justice, and *complete* loyalty.

Adam Smith, a philosopher turned economist, used an analogy that may prove helpful in telling the difference between the two types of ethics. The ethics of duty may be compared to the basic rules of grammar, whereas the ethics of excellence may be compared to "the rules which critics lay down for the attainment of what is sublime and elegant" in writing. If we fail to follow the rules of grammar, our writing is automatically "bad"; but merely following the rules of grammar does not make our writing "good." We may be blamed for failing to follow the rules of grammar, but not for failing to write elegantly and with style. In Smith's words, the rules of perfection in ethics and in writing are both "loose, vague, and indeterminate, and present us rather with a general idea of the perfection we ought to aim at, than afford us any certain and infallible directions of acquiring it."

Smith's analogy points out a rather surefire test for determining the difference between an ethic of duty and an ethic of excellence. We tend to *blame* people for failing to live up to an ethic of duty, but we do not blame them for not living up to the ethics of excellence. On the other hand, we tend to *praise* people for reaching (or almost reaching, or even trying to reach) the ethics of excellence, but we do not praise people for living up to the ethics of duty. We do not praise people for *not* murdering, for example.

There is a gray area in between the two sets of ethics. For example, it is probably a universal ethic of duty to refrain from telling deliberate lies for selfish purposes. On the other hand, exhibiting total honesty or frankness is a laudable but perhaps unreachable goal. Between these extremes are "white" lies, silence when one should speak, and speaking the literal truth while implying something else by tone of voice, gesture, or expression.

## The Law and the Ethical Scale

At least in the United States, the law is chiefly concerned with enforcing the ethics of duty and only rarely is concerned with the ethics of excellence. That is not necessarily the case in other nations, where the law may be intimately involved in enforcing the ethics of excellence. In theocratic (church-based) states, for example, the law imposes religious duties, whereas in the Soviet Union the whole purpose of the system, at least in theory, is to create a "perfect" society and ultimately to create Soviet Man, an idealized perfect person. In both cases Professor Fuller might say that the "iron hand of imposed obligation may stifle experiment, inspiration, and spontaneity."

# The Moral Scale
LON L. FULLER

As we consider the whole range of moral issues, we may conveniently imagine a kind of scale or yardstick which begins at the bottom with the most obvious demands of social living and extends upward to the highest reaches of human aspiration. Somewhere along this scale there is an invisible pointer that marks the dividing line where the pressure of duty leaves off and the challenge of excellence begins. The whole field of moral argument is dominated by a great undeclared war over the location of this pointer. There are those who struggle to push it upward; others work to pull it down. Those whom we regard as being unpleasantly—or at least, inconveniently—moralistic are forever trying to inch the pointer upward so as to expand the area of duty. Instead of inviting us to join them in realizing a pattern of life they consider worthy of human nature, they try to bludgeon us into a belief we are duty bound to embrace this pattern. All of us have probably been subjected to some variation of this technique at one time or another. Too long an exposure to it may leave in the victim a lifelong distaste for the whole notion of moral duty. . . .

This line of division [or pointer] serves as an essential bulwark between the two moralities. If the morality of duty reaches upward beyond its proper sphere the iron hand of imposed obligation may stifle experiment, inspiration, and spontaneity. If the morality of aspiration invades the province of duty, men may begin to weigh and qualify their obligations by standards of their own and we may end with the poet tossing his wife into the river in the belief—perhaps quite justified—that he will be able to write better poetry in her absence. (From *The Morality of Law* (New Haven, Conn.: Yale University Press, 1964), pp. 9–10, 27–28. Reprinted by permission.)

## Ethical Problem 1: Ethics of Duty and Ethics of Excellence

Following graduation, you have become manager of a local office of a major corporation as well as being active in civic affairs. The local city council is considering passing an ordinance banning smoking in any public place, including any workplace in which nonsmokers may be present. In your office there are thirty employees, ten of whom smoke cigarettes. The city council has asked you for your personal and professional opinion about the ban on smoking. One of the city council members directly asks you at a public session of the council, "Is this a good law?"

Discussion Questions

1   Does this law enforce an ethic of duty or an ethic of excellence?
2   If this law is passed, has the moral pointer been moved? Which way?

**3**   Which of the functions of law described in Chapter 1 (see p. 13) does this law illustrate? How do you answer the question?

## THE NATURE OF ETHICAL DILEMMAS

The most difficult ethical questions involve **ethical dilemmas.** An ethical dilemma involves conflicting moral duties, each of which pushes an individual in a different direction. For example, the duty of honesty may conflict with the duty of loyalty, or the duty to obey the law may conflict with the duty to family.

### Ethical Problem 2: Ethical Dilemmas

A's child is dying of a rare blood disease. B, a chemist, has discovered a substance that may cure that disease. The cure costs $100 to manufacture, but B realizes that she may charge a great deal more for the treatment. A, a poor person, tries to raise the money but succeeds in raising only $300 of the $1,000 asked by B. A gives the $300 to B as a "down payment" and is unsuccessful in raising the balance. Finally, in desperation, A begs B to let him have the cure on credit, but B refuses.

- *Variation 1.* A burglarizes B's offices and steals the cure.
- *Variation 2.* A robs C's store, obtains the money, and buys the cure from B.

Discussion Questions

**1**   What ethical notions conflict in these examples? How would you resolve those conflicts?

**2**   Is A ethically "wrong" in Variation 1? Variation 2? In which case is A *more* wrong? Is B ethically wrong as well? How?

**3**   Should the law punish A in Variation 1? In Variation 2? What response should the law make in either case?

In Ethical Problem 2, the ethical duty not to steal conflicts with the ethical duty to save one's child's life. Although the conduct was clearly *illegal*, a judgment regarding its moral wrongness will depend on whether one finds the duty to obey the law or the duty to save a child's life more important.

Hidden in the example is another ethical dilemma. B's talent and work led to the cure in the first place, and by most ethical standards, B ought to be able to profit from that talent and work. Similarly, if B permits A to buy the cure for less than the price asked, she would set a precedent for future reductions. But B's conduct obviously conflicts with widely held moral beliefs about the importance of human life and the nature of charity. B, like A, may be both "right" and "wrong" depending on which ethical values are considered more important.

In determining the moral "rightness" of actions in ethical dilemmas, two factors appear to be extremely important in our culture: (1) the *motivation* or *state of mind* of the person involved; and (2) the *relationship of the parties*. Those two factors are often recognized by the law in determining legal guilt and responsibility as well.

## Motivation and State of Mind

Voluntariness is the basic mental state required by both the law and morality as a basis for guilt. We do not hold a person morally guilty for involuntary acts. We do not blame people for acts performed while unconscious or insane, or while under compulsion.

We also maintain a rough sort of hierarchy of voluntariness, depending on the amount of choice we have in the matter. Assume for example that X shoots Y. If X is unconscious at the time and the shooting results from an involuntary twitch of a finger, we would excuse X and call it an unfortunate accident. If X is insane, we would also tend to excuse the conduct, but chances are there would be more guilt attached, or at least we would be more suspicious. If X was intoxicated at the time, we would find him morally guilty, but perhaps less so than a person who had a clear mind at the time. The more choice a person has, the more moral responsibility that person will have.

## Ethical Problem 3: Voluntariness and Ethical Guilt

After graduation you are made sales manager for a computer firm. You have been negotiating to sell 150 computers to the ABC Company for quite some time. One night at a cocktail party you meet the purchasing agent for ABC, who has obviously had quite a lot to drink. During the course of the conversation the purchasing agent orally agrees to the purchase of the computers at a price *over* what you had been asking for the units. You hurriedly scribble the details down on a scrap of paper, and both of you sign the agreement. The next day the purchasing agent calls you, apologizes, and asks that the negotiations go on as if nothing had ever happened.

Discussion Questions

1   Is it unethical for you to insist on payment at the price agreed to at the party? What if your boss promises you a raise if you can make the deal go through at that price?

2   Should the purchasing agent be fired by ABC? Were his or her actions *voluntary*?

3   Should a court excuse the purchasing agent and ABC from *legal* liability on the agreement because the agent was intoxicated? Why?

**The Law and State of Mind**   The law generally follows our ethical notions of responsibility, particularly in the law of crimes and the law of torts. Civil law often makes a distinction between negligent and intentional acts (see p. 225). And almost every criminal statute has a mental element that must be proven before the defendant may be convicted of the offense. The prosecutor may be required to show that the defendant acted intentionally, knowingly, or with some specific intent, such as "with intent to defraud."

If a statute only requires proof of an intent to commit the act the statute prohibits, the crime in question is said to be a **general intent** one; but if it requires proof of some other intent, such as assault "with intent to kill" or writing bad checks "with intent to defraud," the crime is known as a **specific intent** crime.

State of mind may also be used as an aggravating or mitigating circumstance. Assault, which only requires proof of "intent to assault," is less aggravated than "assault with intent to kill," for example. Thus, it seems, the more voluntary an act is, the more both our ethical standards and our legal standards impose moral and legal guilt.

**Motivation and the Law**    **Motive** may be defined as the purpose for which an act is performed. Motive has a great deal to do with the amount of moral guilt attached to an act, but it has less to do with legal responsibility. In Ethical Problem 2, A's conduct was perhaps morally excusable because his motive was to save another's life. The same conduct undertaken to obtain some personal benefit, such as to sell the cure on the black market, would have been more morally guilty. The law does not often excuse behavior on the basis of "good motives." Motivation might be taken into account by the judge imposing a sentence as a matter of "aggravation and mitigation."

---

### Ethical Problem 4: Motivation and Ethical Guilt

After graduation, you become a real estate broker. Times have been hard, and you have only a few hundred dollars in the bank. One afternoon, you sell a house for $150,000. The buyer hands you a check for $5,000 to bind the deal, made out to you personally. The house belongs to one of your clients, and the money rightfully belongs to that client as well. You stand to make a commission of $9,000 on the sale, but the sale will not close until thirty days later. The ethical rules of your profession state that clients' money should immediately be placed in a separate bank account until closing. Should you do this, or should you instead use the money to (a) pay your secretary's salary, which is two weeks late; (b) pay for a badly needed operation for your mother; (c) pay your past-due rent and buy groceries for your family; or (d) throw a party to celebrate the sale?

Discussion Questions

1    Is placing such money in a personal account theft? Should the law punish you if you are caught? Does the answer depend on what you used the money for?

2    Are you *ethically* wrong to use the money? In all four instances? Are there degrees of ethical guilt here?

3    Can you think of any reasons for using the money that are *not* ethically wrong?

---

### Personal Relationships

Our relationships with the persons with whom we are dealing are important to our ethical conclusions. The complex web of human relationships establishes a similarly complex set of ethical standards with finely graded differences. The moral pointer seems to move up and down for each person with whom we deal.

**Intimate Ethics and Marketplace Ethics**    There appear to be two separate sets of widely recognized ethical standards. We use one set of standards to apply to family, friends, and neighbors—**intimate ethics.** Generally, we hold ourselves and others to a higher set of standards when dealing with such persons—more honesty, loyalty, and so on.

On the other hand, we maintain a different set of ethical standards when we deal with people in a business relationship—**marketplace ethics.** We deal with such persons on an "arm's length" basis and expect the same from them. This generally means a lower degree of trust, honesty, and the like. Everyone expects businesspeople to act shrewdly in business matters—unless the transaction involves a friend, relative, or neighbor of the businessperson.

### Ethical Problem 5: Personal Relationships and Ethics

You are employed in a part-time position in an appliance store. You are paid a percentage of each sale you make, and no salary. The store owner has several repossessed televisions for sale. No sign identifies the televisions as used, and the implication is that the sets are new. The owner has not told you anything about the sets, but you have overheard a full-time salesperson describing the sets to a customer as new. Jobs are tight, and you need this job to help finish school and to help support your sick mother. You have several customers interested in the sets: (1) several acquaintances from college, (2) your roommate, (3) your second cousin, (4) your brother, and (5) several strangers.

Discussion Questions

1    Do you tell *anyone* that the sets are used?

2    Do you make distinctions between the acquaintances and the strangers? Between your roommate, your second cousin, or your brother? Why or why not?

3    Is the appliance store owner guilty of unethical conduct? Is the other salesperson? What ethical notions are in conflict?

There are also finely graded differences within both intimate ethics and marketplace ethics. Within intimate ethics, we tend to treat close relatives with higher standards than distant relatives. If some of our relatives have breached their own intimate ethics in their treatment of us, we feel more free to treat them in a similar fashion. Some business relationships are of such closeness and such long duration that they become subject to an intimate ethics all their own. And relatives or friends may announce to each other that "this is business," which warns the parties that intimate ethics are suspended and marketplace ethics will be used for a particular transaction, at least temporarily.

**Personal Relationships and the Law**    The law recognizes the differences between marketplace ethics and intimate ethics in a variety of ways. As you will learn in Chapter 11, the law makes a distinction between **fiduciary relationships** and **arm's length transactions**. A fiduciary relationship is one of trust and confidence, such as between an attorney and client or between an employer and an employee. An arm's length transaction is the common business relationship. If a fiduciary relationship is found, the courts impose much higher duties on the fiduciary than in the ordinary arm's length transaction (see p. 286).

One way to look at the fiduciary duties is as an extension of intimate ethics to places where we would not expect to find them. The relationship between employer and employee or between corporate officer or director and the corporation is, after all, business, and we would ordinarily expect marketplace ethics to be used in any business relationship. But the law insists that a form of intimate ethics be used in many such relationships.

## Ethical Problem 6: Loyalty and Employment Relationships

You are employed by the XYZ Company as an assistant to the vice-president. You learn that the company is planning to buy land owned by Smith for construction of a new factory and that the company is willing to pay up to $50,000 per acre for this particular land, because it serves the company's needs very well. Smith is unaware of this figure, however, and the company has offered her only $5,000 per acre. Smith is a close personal friend. Should you tell Smith? Should you tell Smith on condition that she splits the profits with you?

Discussion Questions

1  Does your employer have a right to trust you? Should your employer, or any employer, deal with its employees on the basis of trust or at arm's length?

2  Do you violate any ethical duties to your employer by telling Smith? Do you violate any ethical duties to Smith by *not* telling her? What ethical notions are in conflict?

3  How should the law react if you tell Smith? What kind of action will your employer probably take? Is it justified?

One of the reasons for the distinction between intimate and marketplace ethics is *power* and the possibility that power will be abused. We expect intimate ethics in certain relationships because the parties are vulnerable to each other, and high ethical standards are a way of guaranteeing that such vulnerability will not be exploited. Friends and family members are vulnerable to each other because of the emotional commitment the parties have to each other. A "false friend" might exploit that emotional commitment and gain an unfair advantage. Our society tries to guard against such abuse by imposing very high ethical standards on such relationships. Similarly, employees (technically *agents*—see p. 274) have the power to bind employers to contracts or make the employer liable for torts. As a result, the law tries to insulate the employer from abuses of power by imposing higher legal duties.

Marketplace ethics have traditionally assumed some rough equality of power between the parties, which permits the parties to protect themselves against potential abuses. At the least, persons in a business relationship are forewarned that a different set of ethical standards applies. But if we are involved in an intimate relationship, we expect intimate ethics to apply. The law may not agree, however, as discussed in the following case.

## Eaton v. Sontag
387 A.2d 33 (Supreme Court of Maine, 1978)

Mr. and Mrs. Sontag and Mr. and Mrs. Eaton had been good friends for over fifteen years. The Eatons were in the process of developing a campground in Maine and were looking for a purchaser. During numerous social visits the Eatons "sounded out" the Sontags about purchasing the campground, and finally the Sontags agreed. The Sontags agreed to pay $80,000 for the property—$26,000 down, and the balance over three years.

The first summer the camp grossed $400, and the Sontags wrote the Eatons complaining that they had been overcharged by at least $25,000 and claimed that the Eatons had misrepresented the earning potential of the camp. Finally, the Sontags stopped making payments, and the Eatons brought an action seeking payment of the overdue installments. The Sontags counterclaimed, asking rescission of the contract and a refund of all of the money owed. The Eatons replied that the doctrine of *caveat emptor* ("let the buyer beware," see p. 328) applied to the case. The jury found for the Eatons, and the Sontags appealed.

**Dufresne, Active Retired Justice**    The charge of fraud which the defendants set out to prove against the plaintiffs . . . was that the Eatons misrepresented to them that the campsite was a gold mine; they had taken in fifteen hundred dollars in five weeks of their first season of operation; there was city water on the premises; the Sontags could live on the premises year round; also they failed to disclose that the value . . . of the campground did not reflect the true value of the property. . . .

The defendants argue on appeal that the past association of the parties as social friends for the period of fifteen years raised their relationship in connection with any business transaction between them to one of a confidential nature, and, under such circumstances, the rule of *caveat emptor* did not apply, but rather, there existed a duty on the part of the plaintiff vendors to disclose to the defendant vendees the plaintiff's financial embarrassment . . . instead of representing the operation as a gold mine opportunity. We disagree.

We agree . . . that the "fiduciary or confidential relation" concept when used in connection with improper influence affecting the validity of some transaction was one of broad application and that it embraced not only technical fiduciary relations such as may exist between parent and child, guardian and ward, attorney and client, etc., but may also encompass relationships wherein confidence is actually reposed in another by reason of their social ties. . . .

[We have held that] "[t]he salient elements of a confidential relation are the actual placing of trust and confidence in fact by one party in another *and a great disparity of position and influence* between the parties" . . . [court's emphasis]

[M]ere kinship itself . . . does not establish a confidential relation; *often relatives are hostile to each other or deal at arm's length and act independently and so are held not to have been [in] a confidential relation.* [court's emphasis]

[E]ven where specific facts tend to show intimate dealings, as between family members or friends, the existence of a confidential relationship remains a question of fact and need not be imposed by law. If the parties to a transaction are of mature years and in full possession of their faculties, their continuing life-long relation as [relatives] and friends will not give rise to a confidential relation as a matter of law unless there is evidence of superior intellect or will on the part of the one or the other, or of trust reposed or confidence abused.

The evidence here fails to disclose any particular dependence of one party upon the other's judgment for business transactions during their acquaintanceship of fifteen years. That one had developed a reliance on the other in a business way does not appear in this case. . . . That the parties believed in their mutual honesty, sincerity, and truthfulness on account of their social intercourse is not sufficient to constitute a confidential relationship as the term implies in the law. . . .

The assertion that the campsite operation is a gold mine was, and should have been understood to be . . . "seller's talk," i.e., "that picturesque and laudatory style affected by nearly every trader in setting forth the attractive qualities of the goods he offers for sale," and this even among friends. But such is not actionable. . . . The law recognizes the fact that sellers may naturally overstate the value and quality of the articles or property which they have to sell. Everybody knows this, and a buyer has no right to rely upon such statements. . . .

Furthermore, it is not fraud for one party to say nothing respecting any particular aspect of the subject property for sale where no confidential or fiduciary relation exists and where no false statement or acts to mislead the other are made, as was the case here. . . .

Every man has the right to ask any price he sees fit for the wares or lands he has to sell and the matter of fixing the price, even for friends who might be interested in their purchase may be predicated upon divers bases one of which may be what he thinks he can get for it from a prospective purchaser. To seek a price commensurate with one's investment in the property would not only be non-fraudulent in itself, but mere good business acumen.

Appeal denied.

### Case Discussion Questions

1   Was there a fiduciary relationship here? Is a life-long friendship enough to create a fiduciary relationship?

2   Did the Eatons defraud the Sontags? Did they tell them any lies? Did they fail to tell them anything that they should have told them? Was their conduct unethical?

3   Should the courts require relatives and close personal friends to announce "this is business" before beginning arm's length business dealings?

---

Marketplace ethics present other problems. Some persons are naively unaware of the two sets of standards, and others are aware of those standards but are unable to protect themselves because of great differences in power. In such cases the law has stepped in, either to restrict the power of one side or to "balance the power equation." Consumer protection laws, labor legislation, and securities regulation are examples of situations where the government has softened the rigors of marketplace ethics with some of the aspects of intimate ethics, thereby raising the "moral pointer."

## SOME COMMON ETHICAL PRINCIPLES

We tend to express our ethical values in terms of a few notions such as *honesty, loyalty,* and *fairness.* These terms are all generalizations, each referring to a *set* of ethical principles that may be related but that also often conflict. Many persons tend to generalize all ethics as *honesty,* for example, but it is clear that ethics mean far more than mere truthfulness and include loyalty, fairness, and diligence.

In the case of each ethical notion there is a range of duties, stretching from the most basic notions of the ethics of duty to the farthest reaches of the ethics of excellence. Honesty, for example, may mean only not telling outright lies or, instead, mean being totally frank. Our problem in each case is to locate our personal moral pointer somewhere on that scale, with regard for state of mind, motivation, and the relationships involved.

### Honesty

The term *honesty* may mean a great many things, including trustworthiness, truthfulness, fairness, reliability, sincerity, impartiality, or total candor, each of which might be a separate ethical standard.

At the ethics-of-duty level, we have a basic duty not to tell outright lies, similar to our legal duty not to indulge in fraudulent practices or perjure ourselves. Somewhere in the far reaches of the ethics of excellence, we may set standards of total frankness and candor and may, in fact, require "truth in all circumstances." But such total honesty is dangerous and may not be a virtue, as in the case of telling a lie to a murderer to protect his victim. Those who always tell the truth probably have few friends. Deciding the proper location of the moral pointer is not an easy task.

### Ethical Problem 7: Honesty

You have been called to testify in a lawsuit brought by a consumer for injuries caused by a defective product made by your employer. You are placed under oath, and the lawyer for the consumer asks you, "Did any tests made by your company disclose that this product could cause injury to consumers?" Very technically, no such tests exist, since the tests were run by an independent testing company. The tests disclosed that the product is extremely dangerous and should be taken off the market.

Discussion Questions

1   Do you volunteer the information about the independent tests?

2   Are you lying if you simply answer "no" under oath?

3   Is there a conflict of ethics here? What ethical notions may conflict? How do you resolve those conflicts?

The law does not require total frankness and candor in every situation, as shown by the *Eaton* case, but the law does require us to avoid fraud, or actual misrepresentation of facts. In fiduciary relationships, the law requires full disclosure, something similar to total candor. Federal regulation of deceptive advertising also requires more than merely refraining from fraud (see Chapter 14).

### Loyalty

*Loyalty* implies the existence of some relationship and requires one party to the relationship to give allegiance and fidelity to the other. This term, like *honesty*, has a variety of related meanings such as reliability, dependability, and trustworthiness.

At the ethics-of-duty level, loyalty merely requires what the agreement between the parties requires. In its ethics-of-excellence aspects, loyalty would require perfect fidelity, perhaps merging into a kind of fanatical allegiance and "other-centeredness." It has been argued that modern cynicism and self-centeredness have chipped away at the notion of loyalty.

Loyalty is essential to the legal doctrines underlying the law of business associations and corporations. Agents must show loyalty to their principals and cannot serve two masters (see p. 287). Partners must be loyal to each other and to the partnership (see p. 301). And corporate officers and directors must be loyal to their corporations or the stockholders (see p. 311).

Abstract loyalty presents some rather large problems, however. First, it is necessary to decide, loyalty to whom? A corporate manager may feel duties of loyalty to the firm itself, to its stockholders, to its customers, to the other members of management, to the board of directors, or to its employees. Loyalty also may conflict with other ethical notions. A firm may insist that its employees lie to customers, for example, in which case the employees' duty of loyalty directly conflicts with the duty of honesty. In fact, the duty of loyalty seems to create many of the most serious conflicts of ethics.

## Ethical Problem 8: Loyalty, Honesty, and Obedience to Law

After graduation, you begin working in a chemical business. During one lunchtime you decide to take a stroll along the river running next to the plant, and you notice a pipe with a slimy substance discharging into the river from the plant. You ask your supervisor about it, and she admits that it is waste from the plant. She also tells you that the expense of disposing of such materials properly is very high. That afternoon an Environmental Protection Agency inspector stops by and directly asks you if you know of any pollution from the plant.

Discussion Questions

1   What do you say, and why?

2   What ethical notions are in conflict? How would you resolve the conflict?

3   Would your answer change if your father owned the plant? If the waste being dumped could harm hundreds of people?

## Fairness and Lack of Oppression

One of the most ambiguous ethical notions is fairness or justice. Again the term *fairness* may have many meanings, including honesty, lack of bias or prejudice, equity, and reasonableness. One meaning of the term *fairness* has particular significance for business— that of lack of oppression or, as sometimes stated, "not taking advantage of others." In marketplace ethics one is always looking for an advantage to press; in intimate ethics one is restrained from pressing those advantages. Our problem again is just how far intimate ethics intrude upon the marketplace.

Oppression is related to power. In fact, the whole notion of oppression assumes that one party to a transaction has power over another and uses that power "too much." Thus, an employer who takes advantage of an employee's lack of bargaining power by offering low wages may be said to be guilty of oppression or unfairness. Similarly, a firm that takes advantage of a monopoly position to raise prices or a seller who takes advantage of a consumer's lack of bargaining skills or lack of knowledge may be said to be oppressing others.

## Ethical Problem 9: Fairness

Your first job is as sales manager of an appliance store. You learn rather quickly that while the store stays within the letter of the law, the store specializes in selling shoddy merchandise at high prices to people who cannot afford the goods. In fact, most of the goods are later repossessed and resold, and the purchasers are sued for the outstanding balance.

Discussion Questions

1   Do you keep the job? Why or why not? Are there any other strategies you might use rather than resigning?

2   Is this procedure "unfair"? How do you determine what is unfair?

In a broad sense, many of the government regulations studied in this text are an attempt to limit unfair advantage. Perhaps the clearest example is the national labor laws, which try to act as a "balancer" in the power equation between labor and management (see Chapter 16). Consumer protection statutes, securities regulations, antitrust laws, and even civil rights statutes are in a sense efforts to even out differences in power between business and other groups that society views as being oppressed.

### Obedience to Law

A strongly held ethical notion is that we should obey the law. "Respect for the law" is so deeply imbedded in our political traditions that it has become an ethic of duty. Our society cannot function without law, and the law cannot function without willing obedience on the part of the great majority of society.

The ethics of duty require us to obey the letter of the law, at the least. It should be clear by now that even obeying the letter of the law may not be an easy task, given the huge number of laws and regulations and the occasional difficulty of determining just what the letter of the law actually requires.

It is also clear that when the law makes illegal an act that is immoral as well, our ethics of duty make such lawbreakers doubly guilty—both for performing an immoral or unethical act and for breaking the law. But if the law merely prohibits an act that is "morally neutral," such as crossing the street against a red light or violating a building code, our ethical system still imposes moral guilt for simply violating the law itself. In such cases the party is not as morally guilty as in the first case. The criminal law sometimes makes a distinction between such laws, by distinguishing between **malum in se** (evil of itself) and **malum prohibitum** (evil only because it is prohibited) offenses.

The ethical duty of obedience to law breaks down when we are faced with a bad law. Not all laws are "good," and some, like "Jim Crow" segregation statutes, may conflict with basic ethical ideas. The notion that we should obey all laws conflicts directly with some basic ethical beliefs in such cases.

### THE SOCIAL AND COMMUNITY RESPONSIBILITIES OF BUSINESS

In the late twentieth century it has been argued with increasing frequency that businesses have social and community responsibilities, along with their private responsibilities to stockholders. Social and business thinkers argue that individual businesses and the communities of which they are a part are interdependent.

### Economic and Public Views of the Corporation

There is a deep debate between those who see the business corporation as merely an *economic* unit and those who see the corporation as a *public* or *social* body as well. Cer-

# Letter from Birmingham Jail
REV. MARTIN LUTHER KING, JR.

My Dear Fellow Clergymen: . . . .

You express a great deal of anxiety over our willingness to break laws. This is certainly a legitimate concern. Since we so diligently urge people to obey the Supreme Court's decision of 1954 outlawing segregation in the public schools, at first glance it may seem rather paradoxical for us consciously to break laws. One may well ask: "How can you advocate breaking some laws and obeying others?" The answer lies in the fact that there are two types of laws: just and unjust. I would be the first to advocate obeying just laws. One has not only a legal but a moral responsibility to obey just laws. Conversely, one has a moral responsibility to disobey unjust laws. I would agree with St. Augustine that "an unjust law is no law at all."

Now, what is the difference between the two? How does one determine whether a law is just or unjust? A just law is a man-made code that squares with the moral law or the law of God. An unjust law is a code that is out of harmony with the moral law. To put it in the terms of St. Thomas Aquinas: An unjust law is a human law that is not rooted in eternal law and natural law.

Any law that uplifts human personality is just. Any law that degrades human personality is unjust. All segregation statutes are unjust because segregation distorts the soul and damages the personality. It gives the segregator a false sense of superiority and the segregated a false sense of inferiority. . . . Hence segregation is not only politically, economically, and sociologically unsound, it is morally wrong and sinful. . . . Thus it is that I can urge men to obey the 1954 decision of the Supreme Court, for it is morally right; and I can urge them to disobey segregation ordinances, for they are morally wrong. . . .

I hope you are able to see the distinction I am trying to point out. In no sense do I advocate evading or defying the law, as would the rabid segregationist. That would lead to anarchy. One who breaks an unjust law must do so openly, lovingly, and with a willingness to accept the penalty. I submit that an individual who breaks a law that conscience tells him is unjust, and who willingly accepts the penalty of imprisonment in order to arouse the conscience of the community over its injustice, is in reality expressing the highest respect for law. . . .

We should never forget that everything Adolf Hitler did in Germany was "legal" and everything the Hungarian freedom fighters did in Hungary was "illegal." It was "illegal" to aid and comfort a Jew in Hitler's Germany. Even so, I am sure that, had I lived in Germany at the time, I would have aided and comforted my Jewish brothers. If today I lived in a Communist country where certain principles dear to the Christian faith are suppressed, I would openly advocate disobeying that country's anti-religious laws. (Abridged version of "Letter from Birmingham Jail" in *Why We Can't Wait*, by Martin Luther King, Jr.

Discussion Questions

1   How can we decide whether a particular law is unjust?

2   What happens to a society in which everyone is morally free to decide which laws to ignore?

3   Should the law punish those who violate laws out of a sense of conscience less severly than other lawbreakers? More serverly? Why?

tainly corporations have economic responsibilities to shareholders to maintain and increase profits. This traditional view of the corporation says quite simply that "the business of business is business" and recognizes only one group—the stockholders—to whom the corporation has loyalty. In fact, this view argues that it is a violation of management's duties to shareholders to undertake social responsibilities at the expense of corporate profits.

Others argue that corporations have a *public character* beyond such narrow economic purposes. Those people argue that corporations have several constituencies made up of groups that they affect directly, including shareholders, consumers, local communities, labor, and even "the public" regarding environmental and antidiscrimination matters. The public view of the corporation argues that corporate actions are not legitimate unless the corporation takes into account each of its constituencies. One function of management is to mediate between those constituencies.

One answer to the tension between the economic and public views of the corporation has been proposed by the American Law Institute in the following model statute.

## Principles of Corporate Governance and Structure: Restatement and Recommendations
AMERICAN LAW INSTITUTE
Tent. Draft. #2, 1984

A business corporation should have as its objective the conduct of business activities with a view to enhancing corporate profit and shareholder gain, except that, whether or not corporate profit and shareholder gain are thereby enhanced, the corporation, in the conduct of its business
(a) is obliged, to the same extent as a natural person, to act within the boundaries set by law,
(b) may take into account ethical considerations that are reasonably regarded as appropriate to the responsible conduct of business, and
(c) may devote a reasonable amount of resources to public welfare, humanitarian, educational, and philanthropic purposes.

### Some Proposed Corporate Social Responsibilities

The ALI draft seems to recognize the economic view of the corporation, with a nod to some social responsibilities of the firm. Some argue that the ALI draft does not go far enough and that corporations have other broader responsibilities. Some of those proposed responsibilities include (1) charitable giving; (2) affirmative action and minority group representation; (3) environmental action; (4) local community support; and (5) the use of "outside" directors.

## PRO AND CON

# Does business have social responsibilities?

**Pro**   Just as no man is an island, no business can isolate itself from the larger problems of the society. From a long-run point of view, the problems of poverty, crime, discrimination, homelessness, and the environment will affect every business just as they affect every individual. Business can only prosper in a prosperous society, and business must do its part to eradicate social ills. Business and society are both long-run phenomena.

Social responsibility extends *beyond* the law to include matters that are for the greater social good, perhaps even at the expense of corporate profits. Examples include giving gifts to charity; hiring handicapped or minority workers; placing "public" members on the board of directors; promoting community action by, for example, providing shelter for the homeless; and generally going further than the law requires in producing safe products, healthy work surroundings, or a clean environment.

But even from a selfish standpoint, it is good business to be socially responsible. Quality products, responsible use of the environment, and good workplace relations will, in the long run, create goodwill and product loyalty. Consumers are quite intelligent, and most are sensitive to shoddy products, environmental piracy, and exploitive employers, as are the news media.

Finally, business has no choice. If it does not act in a socially responsible manner, it will be *forced* to do so. Public interest groups and government will require socially responsible behavior if business fails to do so voluntarily. Political reality demands that business recognize its responsibilities. It is better to act responsible *voluntarily*, where there is some choice, than to endure further government regulation.

**Con**   The business of business is profits. Any corporate manager is the employee of the owners of the business—the stockholders. The stockholders in turn require the manager to make as much money as possible within the confines of rules established by law and by ethics. Some nonprofit businesses, of course, have other goals, such as the goals of a charitable hospital. But the business of most corporations is to maximize profits, not to spend their shareholders' money on social causes.

Any manager who decides, on his own, to embark on a program of social responsibility is in effect spending his employer's money, by reducing the amount available for dividends or profit-making activities. In some cases, such activities may increase prices as well, which means the manager is spending the consumers' money. The manager is in effect levying a *tax* on stockholders and consumers, a tax that those people did not vote for. Taxation of that sort should be left to the political process and the government.

This is not to say that socially responsible activities should not be accomplished by *someone*. Of course many of the activities that fly under the banner of "social responsibility" should be undertaken by society at large. But they are activities best done by government, not private business. We have established elaborate political mechanisms to deal with public policy questions, and those mechanisms involve public input, accountability, and the democratic process. Matters of social responsibility should be left to those institutions.

### Roundtable Discussion

1   The *Con* argument contends that managers must act in accordance with law and ethics. Is social re-

sponsibility one of the ethical notions of our society, or is it becoming one?

**2**   Should business act *beyond* the law? Should a business make its products *safer* than the law re-quires? Should it reduce pollution *below* government standards?

**3**   Do shareholders have a right to demand social responsibility from their managers? Is shareholder si-lence a sign that they don't want such behavior?

**Charitable Giving**   The level of corporate giving to charity is always in question. On one hand, corporations may support large numbers of groups existing for the public pur-pose through gifts to charity, such as the United Way fund, hospitals, universities, pub-lic broadcasting, and many others. Many argue that corporations should give back to society, because corporations are direct beneficiaries of that society. On the other hand, such gifts are direct reductions of shareholders' dividends.

**Affirmative Action and Minority Group Representation**   Although the law requires affirmative action in certain instances (see Chapter 18), the level of participation of mi-nority group members in corporate America presents a serious social problem. Efforts by corporations to strengthen that involvement help disadvantaged individuals, widen the stake of deprived groups in the business world, and build goodwill for the future. On the other hand, affirmative action programs are often expensive and inefficient, at least in the short run, because of the common requirement of additional training for members of disadvantaged groups.

**Environmental Action**   Again, the law makes certain requirements regarding environ-mental protection. But companies may go *beyond* the requirements of the law, either by reducing pollution more than the law requires or by moving faster than the law re-quires. Doing so would obviously clean our environment more quickly, but it also would cost money and place those companies at a competitive disadvantage, at least in the short run.

**Local Community Loyalty**   Many local communities are totally dependent on a par-ticular firm. If those firms move their operations, the local community may be irretriev-ably injured. The company's gain may mean losses of jobs and economic support for the entire community and may result in dying or stagnant cities and regions. Many ar-gue that corporations owe some loyalty to the local communities that support them. On the other hand, a failure to take advantage of cheaper labor or more advantageous busi-ness climates may harm the shareholders' return.

**Outside Directors**   Some corporations have experimented with "community" or "out-side" directors to represent the interests of consumer, environmental, labor, or affirma-tive action groups. Representatives of those groups may sit on corporate boards of direc-tors, providing broader perspectives than those elected by shareholders. That broader perspective may promote greater social responsibility, but it may also result in less con-centration on corporate profits.

### Ethical Problem 10: Community Responsibility

You are a member of the board of directors of a local corporation. The company is located in a small town of 3,000 people and has 100 employees. The corporation made $3 million in profits last year, which is to be distributed to shareholders. Before distribution of the profits, the following resolutions must be voted on by the board of directors: (1) a request for a $100,000 gift to the local United Fund; (2) a suggestion that the company install an affirmative action program (not required by law) next year, which will cost $250,000 to implement; (3) a suggestion that the company install new pollution scrubbers, not required by law, at an expense of $500,000; (4) a suggestion that the company move its facilities to another city, which would double the profits but leave 100 people unemployed and hurt the local community; and (5) a suggestion that the president of the union local, a local civil rights leader, and the president of a local college be given seats on the board of directors.

Discussion Question

- How do you vote on each matter, and why?

## THE ETHICS OF THE LEGAL PROFESSION

Lawyers are fiduciaries of their clients. That says a great deal about the nature of the ethical duties of lawyers. Like many other professionals, lawyers have adopted codes of ethics to explain the ethical duties of attorneys. Most of those codes are administered by the states but are based on the ABA (American Bar Association) *Model Rules of Professional Conduct* (see Figure 2.5).

Codes of ethics are enforceable by the state bar associations and ultimately by the state supreme courts. Lawyers may be disbarred, suspended, or reprimanded for violating those rules. The codes are far different from the codes of ethics of other business associations, which are often voluntary statements that are not binding or not enforceable.

## ETHICS AS AN ALTERNATIVE TO REGULATION

To many, American society in general and business in particular are "overregulated." Those people often argue that business can regulate itself through individual notions of ethics and through **codes of ethics** similar to those that regulate the conduct of lawyers, doctors, and other professionals. And, in fact, many industries and professions have adopted codes of ethics that detail the ethical duties of members of the profession or trade (see Figure 2.6). Such codes of ethics might take the place of enforced government regulation through law.

### Ethical Problem 11: Use of an Ethical Code

In the 1970's, Johnson & Johnson Company ran a very successful advertising campaign for their famous baby oil, promoting it as a tanning product ("Baby, Baby! Turn on the Tan with Johnson's"). In fact, baby oil speeded up the tanning process, and sales of baby

### Preamble

A lawyer is a representative of clients, an officer of the legal system and a public citizen having special responsibility for the quality of justice.

As a representative of clients, a lawyer performs various functions. As advisor, a lawyer provides a client with an informed understanding of the client's legal rights and obligations and explains their practical implications. As advocate, a lawyer zealously asserts the client's position under the rules of the adversary system. As negotiator, a lawyer seeks a result advantageous to the client but consistent with requirements of honest dealing with others. As intermediary between clients, a lawyer seeks to reconcile their divergent interests as an advisor and, to a limited extent, as spokesman for each client. A lawyer acts as evaluator by examining a client's legal affairs and reporting about them to the client or to others. . . .

**Rule 1.1 Competence.** A lawyer should provide competent representation to a client. Competent representation requires the legal knowledge, skill, thoroughness and preparation reasonably necessary for the representation. . . .

**Rule 1.6 Confidentiality of Information.** (a) A lawyer shall not reveal information relating to representation of a client unless the client consents after consultation, except for disclosures that are impliedly authorized in order to carry out the representation, and except as stated in paragraph (b).

(b) A lawyer may reveal such information to the extent the lawyer reasonably believes necessary: (1) to prevent the client from committing a criminal act that the lawyer reasonably believes is likely to result in imminent death or substantial bodily harm; or (2) to establish a claim or defense on behalf of the lawyer in a controversy between the lawyer and the client, to establish a defense to a criminal charge or civil claim against the lawyer based upon conduct in which the client was involved, or to respond to allegations in any proceeding concerning the lawyer's representation of the client.

**Rule 1.7 Conflict of Interest: General Rule.** (a) A lawyer shall not represent a client if the representation of that client will be directly adverse to another client, unless:

(1) the lawyer reasonably believes the representation will not adversely affect the relationship with the other client; and (2) each client consents after consultation.

**Rule 2.1 Advisor.** In representing a client, a lawyer shall exercise independent judgment and render candid advice. In rendering advice, a lawyer may refer not only to law, but to other considerations, such as moral, economic, social and political factors, that may be relevant to the client's situation. . . .

**Rule 4.1 Truthfulness in Statements to Others.** In the course of representing a client a lawyer shall not knowingly: (a) make a false statement of material fact or law to a third person; or (b) fail to disclose a material fact to a third person when disclosure is necessary to avoid assisting a criminal or fraudulent act by a client, unless disclosure is prohibited by Rule 1.6. . . .

**FIGURE 2.5**   Excerpts from the ABA *Model Rules of Professional Conduct* (Adopted 1983)

Source. Excerpted from the ABA *Model Rules of Professional Conduct*, copyright by the American Bar Association. All rights reserved. Reprinted with permission.

**Our Credo**
**Johnson & Johnson Co.**

We believe our first responsibility is to the doctors, nurses and patients, to mothers and all others who use our products and services.

- In meeting their needs everything we do must be of high quality.
- We must constantly strive to reduce our costs in order to maintain reasonable prices.
- Customers' orders must be serviced promptly and accurately.
- Our suppliers and distributors must be serviced promptly and accurately.

We are responsible to our employees, the men and women who work with us throughout the world.

- Everyone must be considered as an individual.
- We must respect their dignity and recognize their merit.
- They must have a sense of security in their jobs.
- Compensation must be fair and adequate, and working conditions clean, orderly and safe.
- Employees must feel free to make suggestions and complaints.
- There must be equal opportunity for employment, development and advancement for those qualified.
- We must provide competent management, and their actions must be just and ethical.

We are responsible to the communities in which we live and work and to the world community as well.

- We must be good citizens—support good works and charities and bear our fair share of taxes.
- We must encourage civic improvements and better health and education.
- We must maintain in good order the property we are privileged to use, protecting the environment and natural resources.

Our final responsibility is to our stockholders.

- Business must make a sound profit.
- We must experiment with new ideas.
- Research must be carried on, innovative programs developed and mistakes paid for.
- New equipment must be purchased, new facilities provided and new products launched.
- Reserves must be created to provide for adverse times.

When we operate according to these principles, the stockholders should realize a fair return.

FIGURE 2.6    A Corporate Ethics Code

oil had doubled as a result. At the time, there was little medical knowledge of the harmful effects of the sun. Some medical evidence was later presented to the company that tanning may cause skin cancer. You are manager of the baby oil division, and you are about to make a presentation to the executive committee regarding future advertising.

Discussion Questions

1   What recommendations do you make?

2   Does the Johnson & Johnson credo specifically speak to this issue? Does the *spirit* of the credo affect this issue?

3   In fact, Johnson & Johnson withdrew its advertising campaign. Is such a move against the company's best interests?

---

The argument that ethical codes can take the place of law has several problems: (1) most codes of ethics, unlike those of attorneys, doctors, and other professionals, are voluntary in nature and are unenforceable; (2) such codes of ethics may in fact be anticompetitive in nature or otherwise hurtful to the public welfare; (3) such codes will undoubtedly subordinate the will of some of the members of the industry to other members of the industry, but they will rarely subordinate the interests of the entire industry to the interests of the public.

## Enforceability of Ethical Codes

The argument that lawyers, doctors, and other professionals govern themselves admirably through codes of ethics and that other trades and industries might therefore adopt the same policy and avert government regulation has some problems. Law, medicine, and those other professions are *licensed* trades; in order to practice those professions one must obtain permission from the state, in the form of a license, to do so, and that license may be withdrawn. Thus, the codes of ethics are not voluntary in any sense, and in fact are an *adjunct of* government regulation, not a *replacement for* regulation. And many argue that even those professions do not do a good job of policing themselves.

## Actual Harm from Ethical Codes

Although codes of ethics generally have a positive effect on an industry, their use may in fact involve harm to the public. Those codes may be little more than efforts to restrain trade between members of the profession or trade. Ethical codes for real estate brokers, attorneys, and other professionals have been found to be ways to fix prices and eliminate competition, by requiring competing members of the profession not to undercut certain "suggested" prices.

## Differing Ethical Interests

Ethical codes can only regulate activities *within* a profession or trade and can have little impact on relations of the industry to other industries or to the society as a whole. It is one thing, for example, to regulate the activities of lawyers or stockbrokers or accountants who adversely affect individuals within their own industries. It is a totally different problem to adopt and enforce ethical duties that subordinate the entire business of law, investment advice, or accountancy to the interests of the larger society or economy.

These considerations do not mean, of course, that codes of ethics are useless nor that they should not be adopted. Trade associations and professional organizations have done a great deal of good through their adoption of codes of ethics by way of defining and refining the ethical duties of members of their respective trades and professions. It just means that codes of ethics are limited in their ability to replace government regulation.

## SUMMARY AND CONCLUSIONS

There is a close relationship between ethics and the law. Ethics, or standards and rules of conduct of human relations, are the learned duties of people towards other people. Many of those ethical duties have, over time, become embodied in and sanctioned by the law.

One way to look at ethics is as two distinct systems, the ethics of duty and the ethics of excellence. The ethics of duty provide basic rules essential for the survival of society and civilization, whereas the ethics of excellence provide our goals, aspirations, and standards of perfection. At least in democratic societies, the law is generally concerned with the ethics of duty. There seems to be strong agreement about the ethics of duty, but opinions regarding the ethics of excellence vary widely.

Common ethical duties include honesty, loyalty, fairness, obedience to law, and community responsibility. Each of those duties has a variety of meanings, and those meanings may conflict. Those duties may conflict as well, and the resolution of those conflicts must be a matter of personal decision, although reflection on ethical matters and reference to the law may help.

Ethics is an input to the law, but law is also an input to ethics. The two systems, legal and ethical, are often parallel. As ethics change, the law also must change through the courts and legislatures. And as the law changes, ethics also change because of our social values of obedience and respect for the law.

Ethical codes are sometimes viewed as an alternative to government regulation, but they are of limited usefulness. Such codes are often unenforceable, may create actual harm, and can have a limited effect on professional activities that are in the interest of the group enacting the code.

## REVIEW QUESTIONS

1  What are ethics? What influences determine an individual's ethical system?

2  Make up your own list of ethics of duty, and make it as complete as possible. Compare that list with that of a friend. Now make up a list of your ethics of excellence and compare that to the same friend's. Are the two lists different? Why?

3  Can you think of an instance where the law enforces an ethic of excellence? Why is it more difficult for democratic societies to embed

ethics of excellence in the law than it is for totalitarian societies? Shouldn't we be trying to make our society the best it can possibly be? What's wrong with using the law to enforce the ethics of excellence?

4  Do state of mind, motivation, and relationships play a part in our ethical judgments? Why or why not?

5  Is there a real distinction between marketplace ethics and intimate ethics? Is business just a game with different rules? Should it have dif-

ferent rules? Shouldn't we just apply the same high standards of intimate ethics to all our dealings?

6    As an ambitious business graduate, you are rapidly climbing the corporate ladder. Your immediate superior, who is also ambitious, asks you to negotiate a contract and directly instructs you to lie to the other party to the contract. You have three choices: (a) violate your superior's instructions and tell the truth, and hope the contract goes through anyway; (b) inform your superior's boss of the instruction to lie and ask for guidance; and (c) go ahead and lie. What do you do, and why?

7    The company for which you work is under investigation for violations of the antitrust laws, laws with which you vehemently disagree on grounds of principle. The Department of Justice has directly subpoenaed all records in your possession. In those records you know there is evidence of price fixing, which will probably result in indictment and conviction of your company. There is a strong possibility that if the company is convicted, the adverse publicity will put the company out of business and put you out of a job. Failure to turn over the evidence or destruction of the evidence is a federal offense as well, but probably no one would ever know. What do you do, and why?

8    You are in desperate need of cash to finance your final semester in college. You also own an old car. Recently a mechanic told you that although the car still sounds good and runs quite well, it actually is in need of a major mo-

tor overhaul that will cost $700, and that the car could "quit" at any time. The retail value of the car, if it is in good condition, is $1,800. You decide to sell the car, and you have three offers—from your roommate, your brother, and a total stranger. How much do you tell each of them about the engine defect? If there is a difference, explain why.

9    Your employer is involved in a large contract dispute with another company that results in a lawsuit against your firm. From your classes in business law, you know that if your company can prove that the other firm or its representatives agreed to take certain products back that were sold to your firm, your firm will win the case. You are friendly with the sales manager of the other firm, and you met with him for lunch and played tennis on several occasions. He never agreed to take those products back, however. You also know it is your word against his, and that if your testimony wins the case, you can expect a sizable raise. What do you do, and why?

10    You are assigned as foreign sales manager for your firm in another nation. After several unsuccessful attempts to sell your products, you learn that it is the custom in that country to pay bribes to purchasing agents. Such bribes are illegal in both that nation and in the United States, but in that nation the enforcement authorities receive 10% of the bribe and look the other way. Your competitors have been bribing purchasing agents for years. Do you pay a bribe? Why or why not?

CHAPTER 3

# The American
# Court System

*Lawsuit. n., A machine which you go into as a pig
and come out as a sausage.*

AMBROSE BIERCE
*The Devil's Dictionary* (1906)

*Lawyers are better to work with or play with or fight
with or drink with, than most other varieties of
mankind.*

HARRISON TWEED

An important part of the legal environment of business is the machinery of the courts.
The purpose of this chapter is to describe the nuts and bolts of the American court systems, both federal and state, including their organization and some of the rules of the
game that apply in those courts.

## THE ADVERSARY SYSTEM

Before we begin, it is important to understand that the Anglo-American system of law is
based on the **adversary system,** a process with historical roots in trial by combat. The
adversary system assumes that the truth will emerge from a clash of able and opposing
forces. The issues are framed by the lawyers for either side; and issues not raised, objections not made, and points not challenged are all generally waived. The function of the
judge is to rule on contested points, and judges usually do not play an active role in the
case.

Rules of pleading and evidence all assume that each lawyer will use only those procedures that will help his or her client's case. It is then up to the **trier of fact** (a jury or
a judge without a jury) to decide the truth after hearing all sides presented capably and
forcefully. The trial judge in a jury trial acts as **trier of the law** to rule on contested legal
points.

The major competitor to the adversary system is the **inquisitorial system,** which is
used in much of the rest of the world. In such a system the primary goal of all participants is to ascertain the truth. Judges tend to take a very active role in such a system.
The primary difference is the assumption in the inquisitorial system that the truth can
be found by a thorough (and, one hopes, even-handed) search for it, whereas the adver-

sary system is based on the assumption that truth will be found through the clash of conflicting interests.

## The Role of the Lawyer and the Legal Profession

A character in one of Shakespeare's plays once advised, "Let's kill all the lawyers" [*Henry VI*, Act IV, scene ii], and the quote is often used to show that Shakespeare held lawyers in contempt. But the speaker in Shakespeare's play was a criminal and a revolutionary who feared that lawyers would undermine his cause. Lawyers are, in many ways, the protectors of our civilization and our democracy.

Lawyers are professionals. Almost all lawyers today have spent three or more years in graduate study and have been awarded the degree of *Juris Doctor*. Although not all lawyers practice law (many are corporate executives or are involved in law enforcement or teach), those who practice must pass a difficult state bar examination.

Lawyers are subject to a strict code of ethics imposed by their state bars. A lawyer must conform to that code strictly or be subject to *disbarment* (expulsion) or suspension from the practice of law. That code requires absolute honesty, total lack of conflicts of interest, and full disclosure to clients. (See p. 58 for a sample of the *ABA Model Rules of Professional Conduct*.)

Lawyers have two principal functions toward their clients. First, they are *counselors*, giving legal advice (and sometimes personal and practical advice). Second, lawyers are *advocates*, arguing cases for the clients in court, before administrative agencies, or elsewhere. It is absolutely crucial that a lawyer operate from a base of complete knowledge, and clients *must* tell their lawyers everything in order to obtain effective representation. Lawyers cannot divulge any matters disclosed to them by their clients because of the attorney's code of ethics and because of the *attorney-client privilege*.

Apart from their duties to their individual clients, lawyers also hold a public trust. They are *officers of the court* and owe certain duties to the courts, the legal profession, and our democracy, as well as to their clients. Lawyers tend to be active in civic and political affairs, and many legislators and political officers have a legal background.

## The Need for an Actual Dispute: Cases and Controversies

Courts will not decide problems that are not real disputes. Section 2 of article III of the Constitution provides that "[t]he judicial Power shall extend to all Cases . . . [or] Controversies. . . ." The **case or controversy requirement** has resulted in several doctrines that effectively prohibit the federal courts from acting unless an *actual dispute* is pending. Most state courts follow the federal lead and require an actual dispute as well.

Neither cases that are **moot**, or already resolved in some fashion, nor ones that are not **ripe** for decision will be considered by the courts. The case or controversy requirement also prohibits the federal courts from giving **advisory opinions**. That means that the federal courts cannot rule on the constitutionality of an action before the action is taken. Only one state, Massachusetts, permits its courts to use advisory opinions, although several foreign nations, including Canada, permit the practice.

### The Need for Injury: Standing to Sue

Only injured parties can sue. The concept of *legal* injury is not as simple as it first appears, however. If your best friend is killed in an auto accident, you cannot sue even though you have suffered a real loss. But her family, from whom she may have been estranged, does have a right to sue for the legal injury they suffered. The family has standing to sue, that is, the right to bring the lawsuit, but you do not. In every case the party bringing the action must have suffered some kind of *legally recognized injury* in order to have standing to sue.

## COURT ORGANIZATION: FIFTY-TWO COURT SYSTEMS

One of the most unique and complicating factors in the American court system is that there are fifty-two such systems. The federal courts are organized by Congress to handle federally related matters and cases that demand federal supervision, and each state has established its own court system to hear cases within its borders. The fifty-second court system is the special set of courts established by Congress to hear cases in the District of Columbia. Sometimes the American court system is called a *dual* system, referring to the state and federal systems; but that term is misleading, because each state maintains its own separate court system. The existence of so many court systems gives rise to many of the problems we will consider.

### Sources of Judicial Organization

The U.S. Constitution provides almost no guidance for the establishment and organization of the federal courts. Article III only provides for the establishment of "one supreme Court, and . . . such inferior Courts as the Congress may . . . ordain and establish." The lower federal courts, including the U.S. district courts and U.S. courts of appeals, have all been created by acts of Congress.

Some state constitutions are quite detailed in the types of courts established, whereas others, like the federal Constitution, are vague and leave much to the state legislature. A common feature is that the salary of judges may not be diminished while the judge is in office. Some states, like the federal government, select judges by appointment of the chief executive (governor) with the advice and consent of the legislature. Others provide for election of judges by popular vote, followed by retention elections, in which the public votes on whether the judge should continue in office after a specified period of time.

### The Typical Three-Tiered Court System

The federal courts and a large minority of state courts are organized on a three-tiered basis similar to that shown in Figure 3.1. At the lowest level are the **trial courts.** In the federal system the trial courts are known as **U.S. district courts;** and in the state systems they are known by a variety of names, including circuit courts, county courts, courts of general session, courts of common pleas, and superior courts, among others. In the federal system, the nation is divided into districts, at least one in each state, and each dis-

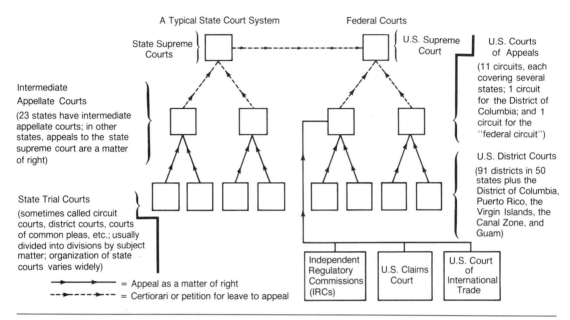

A Typical State Court System          Federal Courts

State Supreme Courts

U.S. Supreme Court

U.S. Courts of Appeals
(11 circuits, each covering several states; 1 circuit for the District of Columbia; and 1 circuit for the "federal circuit")

Intermediate Appellate Courts
(23 states have intermediate appellate courts; in other states, appeals to the state supreme court are a matter of right)

U.S. District Courts
(91 districts in 50 states plus the District of Columbia, Puerto Rico, the Virgin Islands, the Canal Zone, and Guam)

State Trial Courts
(sometimes called circuit courts, district courts, courts of common pleas, etc.; usually divided into divisions by subject matter; organization of state courts varies widely)

⟶ = Appeal as a matter of right
⤑ = Certiorari or petition for leave to appeal

Independent Regulatory Commissions (IRCs)

U.S. Claims Court

U.S. Court of International Trade

FIGURE 3.1   The American "Dual" Court System

trict contains a U.S. district court. Normally, state systems place a separate trial court in each county, although there are variations.

Everything above the trial court level is an **appellate court,** because almost all cases reach those courts through appeal from decisions of a trial court. The federal system and twenty-three states have intermediate appellate courts, where most appeals are heard the first time. In the federal system, the nation and its foreign territories are divided into twelve geographic regions, each of which has a U.S. court of appeals (see Figure 3.2). Because the District of Columbia receives a large volume of cases from federal administrative agencies, it has a separate circuit. The thirteenth U.S. court of appeals is the U.S. Court of Appeals for the Federal Circuit, which hears cases from the district courts involving patents, trademarks, unfair competition, various claims against the government, and appeals from the U.S. Claims Court, the U.S. Court of International Trade, and from certain administrative agencies.

Not all states have intermediate appellate courts. The bare majority of states maintain only a set of trial courts and a state supreme court, and appeals from the trial court proceed directly to the state supreme court. In such states, the state supreme court must hear all appeals directed to it, because the concept of due process under the Constitution means that a litigant has the right to at least one review of his or her case by a higher court.

### The U.S. Supreme Court

The highest court in the American system is the **U.S. Supreme Court.** That court hears cases from the U.S. courts of appeal and from the state supreme courts. The U.S. Supreme Court consists of nine justices, appointed for life by the President with the advice

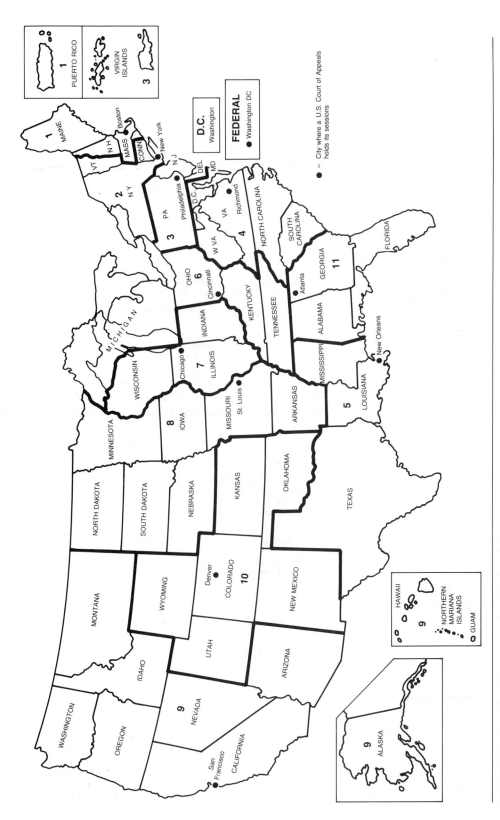

FIGURE 3.2    The Thirteen Federal Judicial Circuits

and consent of the U.S. Senate. The size of the Supreme Court, and to some extent the type of cases it may hear, is determined by the U.S. Congress. In fact, one of the very earliest congressional acts, the **Judiciary Act of 1789,** established the Supreme Court's size (although it has changed several times), created the federal district courts, and established the general outlines of federal jurisdiction.

Most of the cases that the Supreme Court hears come to it through **certiorari.** In such cases, the Court has the discretion to *deny certiorari, which means that the case is not heard,* or to *grant certiorari,* which means that the Court will hear the case. A vote of four of the nine justices is necessary to grant certiorari. In the vast majority of cases certiorari is denied, which means that the decision of the lower court will stand. The Court *must* hear cases that are categorized as **appeals.** The most common cases include those in which a state supreme court has upheld a state statute or struck down a federal statute on constitutional grounds, or where a federal court has struck down a state statute on constitutional grounds. In a few isolated instances, known as **original jurisdiction,** the Supreme Court will act as a trial court. Those cases are established by the Constitution itself, and include cases affecting ambassadors and those in which a state is a party.

## JURISDICTION AND VENUE

The term **jurisdiction** means the right of a court to hear a case. It may refer to either **subject matter jurisdiction,** meaning the class of cases a court may hear, or **personal jurisdiction,** which refers to the right of a court to subject a particular person to its judgment.

### Subject Matter Jurisdiction

The subject matter jurisdiction of a court is usually set by statute. Subject matter jurisdiction may be either **general,** meaning the court may hear *any* case, or **limited,** in the sense that the court may hear only certain kinds of cases. For example, the U.S. Court of Claims may only hear claims against the U.S. government. Most courts, including federal courts, are limited in the types of cases they may hear.

Many state courts are referred to as *courts of general jurisdiction,* but that phrase is somewhat misleading, because most state courts are divided into specialized areas, such as small claims, criminal, civil, probate, and equity courts, none of which have unlimited authority to hear *all* types of cases.

Sometimes two or more courts will have overlapping jurisdiction to hear the same case, in which case it is said that the courts have **concurrent jurisdiction.** For example, in some cases both the federal courts and state courts may have authority to hear the same case.

### Personal Jurisdiction

*Personal jurisdiction,* or the right to subject an individual to the judgment of the court, generally depends on the physical availability of the parties within the area served by the court. Originally, in English history, this meant that the sheriff arrested the defendant and physically brought him or her to court. If the defendant was outside of the area where the sheriff had authority, the defendant could not be brought before the court, and therefore no action was possible. Today, personal jurisdiction is most often obtained

---

## Uniform Interstate and International Procedure Act
COMMISSIONERS ON UNIFORM STATE LAWS (1962)

Section 1.03 *Personal Jurisdiction Based upon Conduct*
(a) A court may exercise personal jurisdiction over a person, who acts directly or by an agent, as to a cause of action or claim for relief arising from the person's
(1) transacting any business in this state;
(2) contracting to supply services or things in this state;
(3) causing tortious injury by an act or omission in this state;
(4) causing tortious injury in this state by an act or omission outside this state if he regularly does or solicits business, or engages in any other persistent course of conduct, or derives substantial revenue from goods used or consumed or services rendered, in this state;
(5) having an interest in, using, or possession of real property in this state;
(6) contracting to insure any person, property, or risk located within this state at the time of contracting. . . .

---

by having the sheriff serve a paper on the defendant, ordering him or her to appear in court or respond in writing to a claim (see p. 75).

A major factor in personal jurisdiction is the question of **due process** under the fourteenth amendment (see p. 133). That amendment requires *fairness* in court proceedings, and subjecting a defendant to jurisdiction in a state where he or she has few contacts could be highly unfair and might be a violation of due process.

**Long-arm statutes** create a legal fiction, namely that by doing certain acts within a state, a person consents to the jurisdiction of the courts of that state. Thus, by transacting business within a state by driving on its highways or by owning property within the state, a person may become subject to the laws and courts of that state, regardless of the person's citizenship or residence.

Each state's long-arm statute varies slightly. If personal jurisdiction is sought under long-arm statutes, and the defendant is physically present outside of the state where the suit is filed, the defendant must still be notified by *service of process*, usually served by the sheriff or other officer in the state where the defendant is present.

It is possible for a state to exercise jurisdiction on the basis of a long-arm statute in a case where the defendant has very minimal contact with the state. That may result in due process objections, as the following case indicates.

---

## World-Wide Volkswagen Corp. v. Woodson
444 U.S. 286, 100 S. Ct. 559, 62 1. Ed. 2d 490 (1980)

Harry and Kay Robinson purchased an Audi automobile from Seaway Volkswagen in Massena, New York in 1976. Seaway had purchased the automobile from World-Wide Volkswagen, a distributor in the New York–New Jersey area. The car had been manufactured by Audi NSU Auto Union Aktiengesellschaft and imported by Volkswagen of America. Both Seaway and World-Wide were incorporated in New York and had their only place of business in that state.

In 1977, the Robinson family moved to Arizona. As they passed through Oklahoma, the car was struck from behind, causing a fire that severely burned Kay Robinson and two of her children. The Robinsons brought a *products liability* action [see Chapter 13] against Audi, Volkswagen of America, World-Wide and Seaway in Oklahoma state courts. World-Wide and Seaway objected to the exercise of jurisdiction by the Oklahoma courts on the grounds that they had no connection with the state of Oklahoma with the single exception of the car in question in this case. They filed a separate case for a *writ of prohibition* against the trial judge in the Oklahoma courts (Woodson) asking that he be barred from exercising jurisdiction.

The Supreme Court of Oklahoma denied the writ on the grounds that personal jurisdiction over both World-Wide and Seaway was authorized by the state's "long-arm" statute. World-Wide and Seaway appealed to the U.S. Supreme Court.

**Mr. Justice White Delivered the Opinion of the Court**    Oklahoma's long-arm statute contained a provision identical to Section 1.03 (a)(4) of the *Uniform Interstate and International Procedure Act*. The Supreme Court of Oklahoma held that the products sold are so mobile "that petitioners can foresee its possible use in Oklahoma" and that "given the retail value of the automobile, . . . the petitioners derive substantial income from automobiles which from time to time are used in the State of Oklahoma."

The Due Process Clause of the Fourteenth Amendment limits the power of a state court to render a valid personal judgment against a nonresident defendant. . . . Due process requires that the defendant be given adequate notice of the suit . . . and be subject to the personal jurisdiction of the court. . . . In the present case, it is not contended that notice was inadequate; the only question is whether these particular petitioners were subject to the jurisdiction of the Oklahoma courts.

As has long been settled, . . . a state court may exercise personal jurisdiction over a nonresident defendant only so long as there exist "minimum contacts" between the defendant and the forum State. . . . The concept of minimum contacts, in turn, can be seen to perform two related, but distinguishable functions. It protects the defendant against the burdens of litigating in a distant or inconvenient forum. And it acts to ensure that the States through their courts do not reach out beyond the limits imposed on them by their status as coequal sovereigns in a federal system.

The protection against inconvenient litigation is typically described in terms of "reasonableness" or "fairness." We have said that the defendant's contacts with the forum State must be such that maintenance of the suit "does not offend 'traditional notions of fair play and substantial justice'." . . . The relationship between the defendant and the forum must be such that it is "reasonable . . . to require the corporation to defend the particular suit which is brought there." Implicit in this emphasis on reasonableness is the understanding that the burden on the defendant, while always a primary concern, will in an appropriate case be considered in light of other relevant factors, including the forum State's interest in adjudicating the dispute . . . ; the plaintiff's interest in obtaining convenient and effective relief, . . . at least when that interest is not adequately protected by the plaintiff's power to choose the forum; . . . the interstate judicial system's interest in obtaining the most efficient resolution of controversies; and the shared interest of the several States in furthering fundamental substantive social policies. . . .

Applying these principles to the case at hand, we find in the record before us a total absence of those affiliating circumstances that are a necessary predicate to any exercise of state court jurisdiction. Petitioners carry on no activity whatsoever in Oklahoma. They close no sales and perform no services there. They avail themselves of none of the privileges and benefits of Oklahoma law. They solicit no business there either through salespersons or through advertising reasonably calculated to reach the State. Nor does the record show that they regularly sell cars at wholesale or retail to Oklahoma customers or residents or that they indirectly, through others, serve or seek to serve the Oklahoma market. . . .

It is argued, however, that because an automobile is mobile by its very design and purpose it was "foreseeable" that the Robinsons' Audi would cause injury in Oklahoma. Yet "foreseeability" alone has never been a sufficient benchmark for personal jurisdiction under the Due Process Clause. . . .

If foreseeability were the criterion a local California tire retailer could be forced to defend in Pennsylvania when a blowout occurs there . . . ; a Wisconsin seller of a defective automobile jack could be hauled before a distant court for damage caused in New Jersey; or a Florida soft drink concessionaire could be summoned to Alaska to account for injuries happening there. Every seller of chattels would in effect appoint the chattel his agent for service of process. . . .

When a corporation "purposefully avails itself of the privilege of conducting activities within the forum State," it has clear notice that it is subject to suit there, and can act to alleviate the risk of burdensome litigation by procuring insurance, passing the expected costs on to customers, or, if the risks are too great, severing its connection with the State. . . .

Because we find that petitioners have no "contacts, ties, or relations" with the State of Oklahoma, the judgment of the Supreme Court of Oklahoma is reversed.

## Case Discussion Questions

1  In what courts could the Robinsons have brought this case? Why did they choose Oklahoma?
2  What criteria does the court use to determine whether the court used is reasonable?
3  Where must the Robinsons bring this case now? Is that fair to the Robinsons?

## Federal Jurisdiction

There are two major grants of federal jurisdiction—**federal question jurisdiction** and **diversity jurisdiction**—and a series of more specific grants sometimes known as **special federal question jurisdiction.** Unless a case fits within one of the grants of federal jurisdiction, the federal courts may not hear the case. As a result, the federal courts are considered *courts of limited jurisdiction.* Federal court jurisdiction is established by an act of Congress, and thus may be changed at any time by another act of Congress.

**Federal Question Jurisdiction**    Under 28 U.S. Code 1331 the federal courts have the authority to hear cases arising under the federal Constitution or under federal law. The principal question in such cases is whether the plaintiff's claim is one "arising under" federal law. A right or immunity created by federal law must be a basic element of the plaintiff's complaint. Federal jurisdiction is not conferred if the federal issue arises as a defense to the claim, or if the federal law is not the basis of the plaintiff's claim but is merely incidental to the complaint.

**Diversity Jurisdiction**    Under 28 U.S. Code 1332, the federal courts have authority to hear cases in which no plaintiff and no defendant are residents of the same state and the amount in question exceeds $10,000. The purpose of diversity jurisdiction is to protect out-of-state parties from potential unfairness in the courts of another state. Diversity jurisdiction extends to citizens of foreign nations as well.

# Mas v. Perry
489 F.2d 1396 (5th Cir. 1974)

Jean Paul Mas, a citizen of France, and Judy Mas were married at her home in Jackson, Mississippi. At the time both were graduate students at Louisiana State University in

Baton Rouge, Louisiana. They returned to Baton Rouge and rented an apartment from Oliver H. Perry. Unknown to Mr. and Mrs. Mas, Perry had installed two-way mirrors in their bedroom and bathroom, and watched them during the first three months of their marriage.

Jean Paul and Judy Mas stayed in Baton Rouge for approximately two years, and then moved to Park Ridge, Illinois. It was their intention to return to Baton Rouge for more course work, and then they were undecided where they would reside. They discovered that they had been watched and brought this action for deprivation of privacy in federal court in Louisiana under federal diversity of citizenship. Perry moved to dismiss the case at the close of the plaintiffs' case on the ground that Judy Mas was a citizen of Louisiana at the time the events took place. It was clear that Jean Paul Mas was a citizen of France, however. The trial court denied the motion, and the jury returned a verdict of $5,000 for Jean Paul Mas and $15,000 for Judy Mas. Perry appealed.

**Ainsworth, J.**   This case presents questions pertaining to federal diversity jurisdiction under 28 U.S.C. 1332, which . . . provides for original jurisdiction in federal district courts of all civil actions that are between . . . citizens of different States or citizens of a State and citizens of foreign states and in which the amount in controversy is more than $10,000. . . .

It has long been the general rule that complete diversity of parties is required in order that diversity jurisdiction obtain, that is, no party on one side may be a citizen of the same State as any party on the other side. . . . To be a citizen of a State within the meaning of section 1332 a natural person must be both a citizen of the United States and a domiciliary of that State.

For diversity purposes, citizenship means domicile; mere residence in the State is not sufficient. A person's domicile is the place of "his true, fixed, and permanent home and principal establishment, and to which he has the intention of returning whenever he is absent therefrom . . ." A change in domicile may be effected only by a combination of two elements: (a) taking up residence in a different domicile with (b) the intention to remain there.

It is clear that at the time of her marriage Mrs. Mas was a domiciliary of the State of Mississippi. . . . Mrs. Mas' Mississippi domicile was disturbed neither by her year in Louisiana prior to her marriage nor as a result of the time she and her husband spent at LSU after their marriage, since for both periods she was a graduate assistant at LSU. Though she testified that after marriage she had no intention of returning to her parents' home in Mississippi, Mrs. Mas did not effect a change of domicile since she and Mr. Mas were in Louisiana only as students and lacked the requisite intention to remain there. Until she acquires a new domicile she remains a domiciliary, and thus a citizen, of Mississippi. . . .

Thus the power of the federal district court to entertain the claims of appellees in this case stands on two separate legs of diversity jurisdiction: a claim by an alien against a State citizen; and an action between citizens of different States. . . .

Affirmed.

## Case Discussion Questions

1´   Why do you suppose Mr. and Mrs. Mas filed this case in federal court, rather than in the local state courts?

2   Is there any question about federal jurisdiction over *Mr.* Mas? Why or why not? What is the question about jurisdiction over *Mrs.* Mas?

3   What is the difference between "residence" and "domicile"?

In diversity cases such as the *Mas* decision the plaintiff must allege damages in an amount in excess of the jurisdictional amount of $10,000. There must be a probability that the value of the matter in controversy exceeds that amount. It does not matter, as in the *Mas* decision, that the plaintiff ultimately receives less than $10,000, and the federal courts have jurisdiction to award lesser judgments if the evidence does not warrant an amount over $10,000. Courts are reluctant to dismiss actions for lack of the jurisdictional amount unless there is a "legal certainty" that the plaintiff will not recover that amount.

**Special Federal Question Jurisdiction**    Many federal statutes, such as the federal antitrust, labor, securities, or bankruptcy laws, create a right to sue under those laws. Although general federal question jurisdiction would provide the right to use the federal courts in those cases in any event, those statutes expressly confer federal jurisdiction independent of the general statute. Sometimes those statutes provide rather unique procedures as well, such as statutes providing that some cases[1] are to be heard by three-judge panels of the district court with a direct appeal to the U.S. Supreme Court.

**Removal to the Federal Courts**    Quite often both the state and federal courts have jurisdiction over the same case. In the *Mas* case, for example, Mr. and Mrs. Mas might have brought their action in the Louisiana state courts. In such a case, the state and federal courts have concurrent jurisdiction. A defendant sued in a state court other than his own state's may petition the federal court for **removal.** If the case could have been filed in the federal court in the first place, removal will be granted.

**State Law in the Federal Courts**    A central question in diversity cases is what law—state or federal—should be applied by the federal courts. As a result of *Erie R.R. v. Tompkins,*[2] federal courts hearing diversity cases are to apply the law of the state in which they are sitting.

For example, if A, a citizen of Montana, sues B, a citizen of Idaho, over a contract executed in Montana, and suit is brought in federal district court in Idaho, the court will apply Idaho law to the case. There is no federal law of contracts to apply to the case. Federal *procedure* would still be used, unless federal procedures would change the outcome of the case, in which case state procedures would be used by the federal courts.

**Conflicts of Laws**    Over the years, a number of common law rules have developed to deal with situations in which the laws of two states conflict. For example, in the case of torts (see Chapter 9) such as auto accidents, the court hearing the case is to apply the law of the state where the tort occurred. In contracts actions, the general rule is that the courts are to apply the law of the state where the contract was made, even if suit is brought in some other state.

Conflicts of law rules are important for diversity actions in federal courts. In the preceding example regarding the Montana plaintiff suing in Idaho federal district court over a contract made in Montana, the federal district court would apply Idaho law. But Idaho law includes the conflicts of law principle that the law of the state where the contract was made should be applied. As a result, the federal court would end by applying Montana contracts law to the case.

---

1 Such cases include injunctions against state regulatory statutes, suits to review some Interstate Commerce Commission orders, some government civil antitrust cases, suits under some civil rights statutes, and suits challenging the constitutionality of federal statutes.

2 304 U.S. 64, 58 S. Ct. 817, 82 L. Ed. 1188 (1938).

**Venue**    **Venue** is the choice between two courts, each of which has proper jurisdiction over the subject matter and persons involved in a case. Venue is usually set by statute and identifies a convenient court for the parties to litigate a dispute. In the federal system, venue provisions specify the district or districts in which suit may be brought. Thus, although the federal courts may have jurisdiction, there may only be one federal district in which suit may be properly brought. Often that district is where the defendant resides (because it is the defendant who is being forced to defend), where a corporation is incorporated or does business, or where the transaction giving rise to the litigation took place. In state court systems, venue statutes typically establish the proper county where an action may be brought under similar principles.

## SPECIAL REMEDIES

Unusual cases, particularly those that challenge government actions and regulations, often demand special remedies other than a traditional lawsuit for money damages or for equitable relief. Three such remedies are of special importance to the study of the relationship of government to business: **class action suits, declaratory judgment actions, and mandamus.**

### Class Actions

Under both the *Federal Rules of Civil Procedure* and state codes of procedure, *class actions may be brought by representatives of a class of people*. Under the Federal Rules, such actions may be brought if (1) the class is so numerous that it would be "impracticable" for each member of the class to appear in person; (2) there is a common question of law or fact; (3) the claims of the representatives are "typical" of the claims of members of the class; and (4) the representatives will "fairly and adequately" protect the interests of the class.

Class actions may be brought by any group. Cases have been brought on behalf of injured purchasers of a certain product; members of a race, religion, or native American tribe; and certain classes of voters, to name a few.

The representatives of the class must attempt to notify all members of the class and permit those members to join the lawsuit if they so request. The damages recoverable are the loss to the entire class, and an effort must be made to distribute the damages to all members of the class. Class actions may not be filed without court permission, and courts may dismiss the action if the class is not defined properly.

### Declaratory Judgments

Another unusual remedy seems to contradict both the case or controversy and standing requirements. *Declaratory judgment* actions involve neither damages nor injunctive relief but ask the court to declare the rights of the parties under the law. For example, a theater owner who wishes to show a film that might be obscene under a local ordinance may find himself in a difficult situation. If he shows the film, he will be prosecuted and will risk a finding of guilt. On the other hand, the film may not be obscene, and he would have given up the profits from the film unnecessarily. The owner who wishes to test the film against a threatened prosecution might file a declaratory judgment action.

A judge would "declare the rights" of the parties and determine the film's obscenity before it was exhibited.

This is close to the sort of hypothetical question not permitted by the case or controversy requirement, and in some cases, a declaratory judgment might be refused if there is no actual controversy. The procedure is also useful in private actions, such as insurance and patent cases. Jury trials are often available.

## Mandamus

A *mandamus* action, resulting in a *writ of mandamus*, orders a public official to perform an act required by law. Such actions may be brought to force regulatory agencies to perform their required duties, but they are not available to force performance of discretionary acts.

## THE COURSE OF A LAWSUIT

The basic rules governing trial court procedures are identical for all kinds of cases, from the simplest collection case to the most complex antitrust action. In the federal courts, trial procedure is governed by the *Federal Rules of Civil Procedure*, a modern code of procedure first adopted by the Supreme Court in 1937. The Federal Rules introduced many innovations into civil procedure which have been widely adopted by the states. Several states have adopted the Federal Rules almost in full. Figure 3.3 shows a flow chart of civil litigation from beginning to end.

### The Pleadings and Service of Process

The **pleadings** in a lawsuit include the initial papers filed by all of the parties in a case, including **complaints, answers, counterclaims, cross-claims,** and **third-party complaints.** Sometimes, **motions to dismiss** are included in the term as well.

**The Complaint**    After an alleged civil wrong has been committed, the wronged party may initiate court action by filing a document called a *complaint* (sometimes called a *petition*) with the clerk of the proper court. The complaint tells the story of the wrong and the resulting injury to the **plaintiff,** or complaining party. Under the federal rules, a complaint must include "(1) a short and plain statement of the grounds upon which the court's jurisdiction depends . . . , (2) a short and plain statement of the claim showing the pleader is entitled to relief, and (3) a demand for judgment for the relief to which he deems himself entitled." State rules often demand more complex pleadings.

Complaints may be as short as a half page in simple cases or a hundred pages or more in complex cases. The purpose is to notify the court and the opposing parties of the substance of the claim. The plaintiff will be required to pay a filing fee when the complaint is filed in an amount that often varies with the size of the claim.

**Service of Process**    After the complaint is filed, the **defendant,** or person sued, must be given notice of the suit in order to defend the case. The clerk of the court prepares a document, called a **summons,** that tells the defendant that suit has been filed and gives the defendant instructions on what to do. Usually the defendant must file an answer to

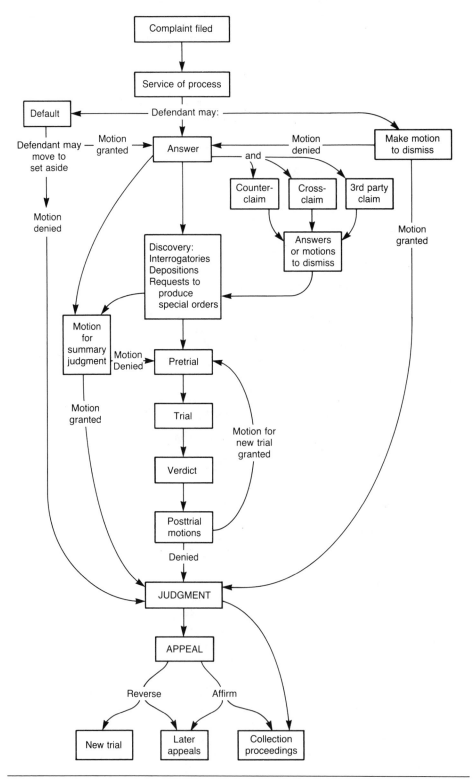

FIGURE 3.3    A Flowchart of Civil Litigation

the complaint or some other response within a certain time (twenty days in the federal courts), although in some instances the defendant will be required to appear in court. Service of process may be made on the defendant in one of four ways:

1    *Personal service* means physical delivery of the documents to the defendant. The U. S. marshal, the sheriff, or in some instances a private process server will hand the documents to the defendant. Personal service is preferred to other forms of contact, since the defendant clearly has actual notice of the suit.

2    *Substituted service* means physical delivery of the documents to some agent of the defendant, such as an attorney, employee, or a member of the defendant's family. Court rules are usually quite specific about which persons may receive service.

3    *Service by certified mail* is usually possible only in smaller cases under some states' rules. A return receipt signed by the defendant is usually required.

4    *Service by publication* is available in limited circumstances. If the defendant has left the state or is in hiding, or in cases involving real estate located in the jurisdiction of the court, many states permit the plaintiff to publish a notice in the "legals" of a newspaper. The notice must usually be published several times, be worded well enough to notify the defendant of the nature of the claim, and appear in a newspaper of general circulation. Often the plaintiff must obtain court approval before publication.

### Defendant's Responses to Complaints

Once the defendant has been served, there are several responses that can be made. The principal responses are **defaults, motions to dismiss,** and **answers.** In addition, the defendant may also file lawsuits in the form of **counterclaims, cross-claims,** and **third-party complaints.**

**Default**    It is vital that a defendant do what the summons requires. Failure to comply with the instructions on a summons will probably result in a **default judgment** against the defendant, which means that the plaintiff has won the case without a trial. Default judgments may be set aside by the court, but only after a showing that the defendant intended to respond and any failure to respond was not the result of bad faith.

**Motions to Dismiss**    A *motion to dismiss* is the defendant's statement to the court that the plaintiff's complaint is legally defective and should be dismissed. The dismissal may be *without prejudice,* which means the plaintiff may amend his complaint or file another lawsuit, or *with prejudice,* which means that the case is over and the plaintiff must appeal the dismissal in order to proceed.
    One of the most common grounds for a motion to dismiss is *failure to state a cause of action.* A **cause of action** is a legally recognized claim, one upon which the courts have granted relief in the past. For example, the courts have never recognized a claim of injury resulting solely from an insult. Therefore, if the plaintiff were to file a complaint stating such a claim, the defendant could move to dismiss based on failure to state a cause of action. Numerous other defects can also be raised by motions to dismiss, including lack of jurisdiction, release or waiver of the claim, bankruptcy, the statute of limitations, and many others.

Often the court will dismiss the complaint but give the plaintiff the opportunity to amend the complaint. In some cases, this may happen several times until the plaintiff finally "gets it right." The plaintiff may elect to "stand on the complaint" and appeal if a recognized cause of action cannot be stated.

Similar to motions to dismiss are *motions to strike* and *motions for a more definite statement*. A motion to strike asks that certain sentences, paragraphs, or words be stricken from the complaint. A motion for a more definite statement asks that material in the complaint be clarified. Such motions may not be used as a "fishing expedition" for evidence, however.

**Answers**    Every complaint that is not dismissed with prejudice must ultimately be answered. The *answer* is a relatively simple document that either admits, denies, or states that a party is without information to answer each allegation of the complaint. Failure to admit an allegation in bad faith may result in an order to pay the expenses of proving the allegation at trial. Sometimes answers contain **affirmative defenses,** which state that the defendant agrees with the allegations of the complaint but has something substantial to add to the story. For example, if the plaintiff sues to collect a debt, the defendant may agree that the debt was made but raise as an affirmative defense the fact that the plaintiff gave the defendant a release. Affirmative defenses, counterclaims, cross-claims, and third-party complaints all must be answered by the opposing party as well.

**Counterclaims and Set-Offs**    The defendant also has the option of suing the plaintiff in the same case. In an auto accident case, A may sue B, and B, believing that he was in the right, may file a **counterclaim** against the plaintiff. A **set-off** is a credit claimed by the defendant arising from an independent transaction. Thus, A, a carpenter, may sue B, a building supply dealer, for failing to provide materials according to a contract. B may claim a set-off from A for amounts due on another contract.

The federal rules provide for two types of counterclaims: (1) *compulsory counterclaims* are those arising from the same occurrence or transaction as the original complaint; and (2) *permissive counterclaims*, roughly equivalent to set-offs, are *any* claims the defendant may have against the plaintiff. Compulsory counterclaims must be filed or will be barred, whereas defendants *may* file permissive counterclaims, and failure to file them will not bar them in the future in a separate action.

Filing a counterclaim changes the names of the parties somewhat. The defendant becomes the *defendant-counterplaintiff* and the plaintiff becomes the *plaintiff-counter-defendant.*

**Cross-Claims**    Suits between parties on the same side of a lawsuit are called *cross-claims*. Thus, if a plaintiff has sued two or more codefendants, one of the codefendants may sue another codefendant by filing a cross-claim. For example, if A was injured by flying glass resulting from a collision between cars driven by B and C, she or he may sue both in the same case. If B feels the collision was C's fault, he or she may file a cross-claim against C. The parties become the *cross-plaintiff* and *cross-defendant.*

**Third-Party Complaints**    A defending party also has the right to bring in new parties to the lawsuit. Under the Federal Rules, such a *third-party complaint* may be filed by any defending party against any person "who is or may be liable to him for all or part of the plaintiff's claim against him." The party filing such a complaint is the *third-party plaintiff*, and the person against whom it is filed is the *third-party defendant*.

## Discovery

Perhaps the most important innovation of the Federal Rules was the liberalization of the **discovery** process. At least in the federal courts, the day of the surprise witness and the "bluff" are over. Today, as a result of discovery procedures available in most courts, a lawyer should know the details of his opponent's case as well as his own when the trial begins.

After the *Federal Rules of Civil Procedure* were adopted in 1937, many states also adopted liberalized discovery rules. Some states do not go quite as far as the Federal Rules, but for the most part there has been a national revolution in court procedures centered around the discovery rules.

**Depositions**    **Depositions** are meetings between the lawyers, a court reporter, and either a party or a witness in the case. The *deponent* (the party or witness) is placed under oath, and the lawyers may ask questions "reasonably calculated to lead to the discovery of admissible evidence." The questions and answers are transcribed by the court reporter, and a typed transcript of the proceedings is prepared. That transcript may be used to contradict or impeach the testimony of the deponent in the trial or may be introduced if the deponent is dead or unavailable for trial. Witnesses may be compelled to attend a deposition by **subpoena,** or court order.

**Interrogatories**    **Interrogatories** are lists of written questions sent to a party. The questions must be answered under oath within a specific time limit. The interrogatories may also be used to impeach or contradict a party at trial, and failure to answer may result in severe sanctions.

**Requests to Produce**    With **requests to produce,** a party may request any other party to produce and make available for copying "any designated documents"; to inspect, copy, or test any tangible thing; or permit entry onto land for the purpose of inspection, measurement, or testing. The opposing party may be under a continuing duty to send new evidence, documents, or other material to the person requesting it until the trial is over. The only exceptions are the "work product" of an attorney and privileged material.

**Special Orders**    Other discovery techniques provide for *physical or mental examinations* of parties and **requests for admission.** The latter is simply a list of written questions submitted to a party, demanding that the party admit or deny them. If they are admitted, they need not be proven at trial. If denied in bad faith, the court may assess the costs of proving them at trial against the party denying them. Parties may be required to submit *witness lists* to the opposing party long before trial, and failure to include a name may result in the exclusion of that witness.

**Scope and Purpose of Discovery**    Discovery has several purposes. Discovery shortens trial time considerably and saves tax money, because lawyers need not thrash about for evidence during the trial. Discovery also lessens the possibility of injustice by assuring thorough investigation of the facts before trial. Also, discovery encourages settlement by making the parties aware of the strengths and weaknesses of the case.

The federal courts and most state courts view discovery very liberally, holding that almost everything is discoverable. The *Federal Rules of Civil Procedure* provide that "Parties may obtain discovery regarding any matter, not privileged, which is relevant to the subject matter involved in the pending action." It does not even matter that the matters sought to be discovered will be inadmissible at the trial if the information sought appears "reasonably calculated to lead to the discovery of admissible evidence."

## Pretrial Motions

After the pleadings are settled, two motions are available to the parties to attempt to dispose of the case: (1) a motion for **judgment on the pleadings** and (2) a motion for **summary judgment**.

**Motion for Judgment on the Pleadings**    A motion for *judgment on the pleadings* asks the court to simply look at the pleadings filed to determine whether there is a remaining issue. If not, the court may grant judgment to either party. For example, if a defendant were to admit all of the allegations of a complaint, the plaintiff might file a motion and obtain judgment without the time and expense of trial. The motion is rarely filed and even more rarely granted.

**Motion for Summary Judgment**    In many controversies there is no dispute about the facts between the parties. Their dispute centers rather on the legal effect of those facts. In such cases, either party may move for *summary judgment*, and the moving party must show that there is *no material question of fact* in the case. He or she does so by filing affidavits, depositions, answers to interrogatories and other materials along with the motion. The opposing party may agree that there is no material question of fact, or may file counteraffidavits and materials showing that a dispute actually exists. If the court finds any material question of fact, it must deny the motion. If no such question of fact exists, the court may proceed to decide the case on the remaining legal dispute.

A common example would involve a suit on a contract. The parties may agree that the contract was signed and that certain work was performed under the agreement, but they may disagree as to the legal effect of a contract. Either or both parties might file a motion for summary judgment, and the judge would simply decide the legal issue.

Summary judgment eliminates unnecessary trials. Even if such a case were to go to jury trial, the trial judge would still have the right to decide the legal issues in the case. Therefore, no party is deprived of his or her right to trial by jury by the summary judgment procedure.

## Pretrial Conferences

In federal cases and under most state procedures, the attorneys and the judge will meet a few weeks prior to trial at a **pretrial conference**. At that conference, the court will attempt to simplify the issues and complete all of the "detail work" on motions and discovery. One of the other matters commonly raised by the courts is the possibility of settling the case.

## The Trial

Trials may be heard either by a jury or by a judge sitting without a jury. The usual order of trial is shown in Figure 3.4. Equity cases, such as actions for an injunction, are heard by a judge alone. Although the seventh amendment guarantees trial by jury in civil cases "at common law," the Supreme Court has held that equity cases are not common law cases. As a result, the right to trial by jury in civil cases exists only if the case is of the kind tried by the ancient English common law courts in 1789, when the Constitution was ratified.

The jury is often called the *trier of the facts* or the *fact finder*, and the judge (or "the court") is often called the *trier of the law*. In a jury trial, the jury decides what the facts are, but it is the judge's responsibility to determine the law applicable to the case and tell the jury what that law is. It is also the judge's function to run an orderly trial and rule on questions of procedure and admissibility. An appeal may come only on errors of law committed by the judge, and not on the basis that the jury made an error in the facts. In nonjury, or **bench trials,** the judge is both fact finder and trier of the law.

**Jury Selection**   Traditionally, juries were made up of twelve persons. Recently, courts have experimented with juries of less than twelve, usually six, with some success. The Supreme Court has ruled that a six-person jury is permissible even in criminal trials, and federal courts now use six-person juries in all cases. Jurors should be selected at random from the community. Most jury selection is based upon voter registration lists, although stories occasionally appear about a judge who orders the sheriff into the streets to "draft" jurors when the available panel runs out.

At the beginning of the trial, the judge and attorneys must select the jury. Prospective jurors are questioned by the court and the attorneys[3] to discover any hidden biases or personal relationships with the parties. If the juror discloses any reason why he or she could not act as juror, the juror may be **challenged for cause.** The attorneys are also permitted a varying number of **peremptory challenges** in which no cause need be shown. Challenges result in dismissal of prospective jurors. The initial questioning of the jurors is often called **voir dire examination.**

**Opening Statements**   Opening statements are brief statements by the attorneys to give the jurors a bird's eye view of the evidence in the case. Under some state procedures, the plaintiff must describe all of the elements of the case in the opening statements or be subject to dismissal, although this practice is losing ground.

**Presentation of Evidence**   After the opening statements, the parties present their proof. All evidence, with the exception of **stipulations** (agreed evidence), must be brought in through witnesses. The party having the burden of proof (almost always the plaintiff) has the right to present evidence first and also has the right to close by presenting rebuttal

---

3 Practice varies widely. In many federal courts, attorneys rarely examine jurors. In some state courts, all examination is conducted by attorneys.

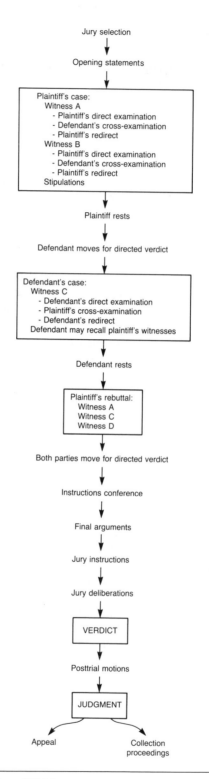

FIGURE 3.4    The Order of Trial

evidence. Throughout all trial procedure, the general rule is that the party who opens has the right to close.

The plaintiff's case may consist of one or more witnesses. The plaintiff will conduct a **direct examination** of each witness, then the defendant has the right to **cross-examine** the witness, and then the plaintiff may conduct a **redirect examination** of that witness. If the plaintiff's redirect brings up new matters not covered in the defendant's cross-examination, the defendant may have a right to a recross-examination, until no new matters have been brought up in the last examination by the opposition. After all of the plaintiff's witnesses have been examined in this manner, the plaintiff will **rest**. The defense then presents its proof in the same way, but in the defendant's case the defendant's attorney presents the direct examination and the plaintiff may cross-examine, and so on. All exhibits must be brought into court through witnesses as well.

**Subpoenas and Subpoenas *Duces Tecum***    A *subpoena* is an order from a court to a witness to appear and testify. It is often issued to the witnesses in a trial, but it is also available in the federal system and in most states to force a witness to appear at a deposition. Failure of the witness to appear is a violation of a court order and constitutes contempt of court, punishable by fine or imprisonment.

A **subpoena *duces tecum*** is also available at trial and sometimes in the discovery process. That order requires a witness who possesses evidence to appear and testify, bringing that evidence to court. Failure to comply is again a contempt of court.

It is important to distinguish a *subpoena* from a *summons*. A summons is a notification to a defendant that suit has been filed and that he or she must either file an answer or appear in person. A subpoena is a court order to a witness to appear in court. Failure to comply with the directions on the summons may result in a default judgment but does not result in contempt of court or any punishment for failure to appear.

**Motion to Dismiss at the Close of Plaintiff's Case**    After the plaintiff's case, the defendant usually makes a *motion to dismiss*, arguing that the plaintiff has not proven the required elements of its case. Thus, if the plaintiff failed to prove the existence of a contract in a contract action, the court might dismiss the action before the defendant is forced to put on its defense. It is important that the defendant make that motion even if it seems clear that the plaintiff has indeed proven its case, because the right to appeal on those grounds may be waived if the motion is not made. Similarly, the grounds for appeal on the basis of a lack of evidence would be that the trial judge made an *error of law* in failing to grant the motion. No appeal is possible on the grounds that the jury was simply wrong; the appeal instead is based on the judge's error in permitting the case to proceed on the basis of insufficient evidence. At this point, however, the judge must give the benefit of the doubt to the plaintiff, and if there is any evidence on which a jury might base a verdict for the plaintiff, the trial judge must permit the case to go forward and must deny the motion.

**The Burden of Proof**    As a general rule, the party making an allegation has the burden of proving it. The plaintiff has the burden of proving the allegations of the complaint, and the defendant has no duty to disprove those allegations. Conversely, the defendant has the burden of proving affirmative defenses, and the plaintiff need not disprove them.

# The Rules of Evidence

Over the centuries, rules of evidence have been devised to determine whether particular types of evidence should be permitted to be used in court. If evidence is allowed, it is *admissible*; if it is not allowed, it is considered *inadmissible*.

**Relevant evidence** is evidence that helps the parties arrive at the truth regarding one of the issues in the case. Thus, if the issue is whether A killed B, it would be relevant to prove that A was the beneficiary of B's life insurance policy, but it would not be relevant to show that A had a bad driving record (unless B were killed with an automobile).

**Prejudicial evidence** may in fact be relevant but is *inflammatory*; that is, it could influence the fact finder beyond its relevance. For example, a set of full-color photographs of the injuries caused by an accident prior to their treatment would be relevant, as tending to show the extent of the injuries, but might be so prejudicial that a judge would exclude them regardless of their relevance.

**Hearsay** statements are statements by a witness in court as to a statement made out of court by a person who is unavailable, introduced to show the truth of the out-of-court statement. For example, in a prosecution of A for the murder of B, if C testifies that D told her (C) that he had witnessed the murder, C's testimony of what D said would be hearsay and inadmissible. The reason for its inadmissibility is that D is not available to be cross-examined by A's lawyer. There are numerous exceptions to the hearsay rule, however.

**Opinion evidence** is, as a general rule, inadmissible. Witnesses may only testify to *facts* within their knowledge, and not to their *opinions*. Some opinion testimony is permissible if the opinion is based on fact and is within the common experience of laypersons, such as an estimate of the speed of a vehicle by a person who drives a car.

**Experts** may give opinions on other matters. Expert witnesses must be qualified by establishing their credentials. Once qualified, the expert may be asked a hypothetical question within his or her field of expertise. Experts may not give opinions on the **ultimate issue** of guilt, innocence, or liability, however.

**Privileges** have been developed over the centuries to protect certain kinds of relationships. For example, the *marital privilege* says that one spouse may not be required to testify against the other because such a requirement would undermine the marital relationship and mitigate against honesty between spouses. Other privileges include the *attorney-client privilege*; the *physician-patient privilege*; and the *priest-penitent privilege*. All are based on the need for confidentiality and trust in those relationships.

The rules of evidence vary widely between states, and much of the law of evidence is of judicial creation. Some states and the federal courts have adopted statutory rules of evidence—*The Federal Rules of Evidence*—which provide some guidance for the courts.

The usual civil burden of proof is *by a preponderance of the evidence*. This burden requires proof by the plaintiff that leads the jury to find that the existence of a fact is more probable that not. This does *not* mean a larger number of witnesses or longer testimony or more exhibits. It means simply that the jury believes that a fact is more probably true than not true, and such a belief is often based on the *credibility* (believability) of witnesses.

In a few civil cases, such as charges of fraud, undue influence, and certain types of will contests, the burden is said to be by *clear, strong, and convincing evidence*. The exact phrasing of this burden varies among the states, such as "clear and convincing" or "clear, unequivocal, satisfactory, and convincing." It is generally agreed that these burdens simply mean that a certain fact is highly probable in light of the evidence.

**Final Argument**    After all the evidence has been received, the attorneys will be permitted a **final argument,** in which the attorneys may summarize the evidence and try to convince the jury to rule in their favor. A century ago, in the "golden age of jury speeches," lawyers like Daniel Webster, William Jennings Bryan, and later Clarence Darrow often presented ringing and emotional speeches to the jury. Although emotional arguments still have a substantial impact, the trend in modern courtrooms is toward closely reasoned and logical statements of the proof. Attorneys are permitted wide latitude in their arguments to the jury.

**Jury Instructions**    After final arguments, the jury will be instructed on the law that is to be applied to the case. The judge will usually read prepared instructions, which have been discussed and argued by the attorneys during an earlier break in the trial. Many states and the federal courts have prepared books of final instructions that are used in most cases. One of the most common grounds for appeal is that the judge presented an erroneous instruction. Many courts permit the jury to take the instructions into the jury room when they deliberate.

**Verdict**    A civil jury verdict is usually in two parts: (1) the finding of **liability,** that is, whether the complaint has been proven; and (2) the amount of *damages*, if any. Sometimes, the court will submit **special verdicts** to the jury in the form of specific questions for the jury to answer. The judge will then decide the case based on the answers to these questions.

**Motion for Directed Verdict**    Before the verdict is rendered, either party may move for a **directed verdict.** The court will direct a verdict in favor of the moving party unless there is *substantial evidence* favoring the other side. Substantial evidence means that there is some credible (believable) evidence on which a jury could rely to base a verdict for the nonmoving party. If the verdict is directed, judgment will be entered for the moving party, and the jury will not deliberate.

**Posttrial Motions**    After the verdict is rendered, two other motions are possible: (1) a *motion for judgment notwithstanding the verdict*, also known as a **motion for judgment n.o.v.,** may be made on the grounds that the jury's verdict was based on insufficient evidence; and (2) a *motion for new trial* may be made if there has been a substantial legal error in the trial. A common basis for appeal is the trial court's refusal to enter a directed verdict, grant a motion for judgment n.o.v., or order a new trial. Usually judgment n.o.v. and new-trial motions are made in a single *posttrial motion.*

**Judgment**    After all posttrial motions have been argued and denied, the court will enter **judgment** on the verdict. The court's judgment permits the winning party to try to collect the judgment through a variety of collection procedures. In addition, the judgment constitutes a final order that may be appealed. Only on very rare occasions will courts permit **interlocutory appeals,** or appeals prior to a final judgment.

## Alternative Dispute Resolution

Although the court system resolves many of the disputes in our society, there has been a recent move to try to find other ways of resolving conflicts. Court delays, expense, and the size of some cases have encouraged development of other ways of resolving disputes.

**Small claims courts** are designed to handle matters in which the amount in controversy is very low, such as under $1,000. A judge hears the case, often without lawyers, and takes a far more active role in the case than usual by questioning witnesses and researching legal points.

**Arbitration** requires an agreement between the parties that they will submit the dispute to a neutral third party. The decision of that party is binding. Formal arbitration agreements are often found in commercial and labor contracts. The agreement to arbitrate may be made either before or after a dispute arises. Some courts require **court-annexed arbitration** in small cases or divorce cases, but often dissatisfied parties may demand a trial before the court.

**Private judging** involves hiring a private judge, often one retired from the bench, to resolve the dispute by legal standards. It is essentially a formal type of arbitration.

**Mediation** is a process in which a neutral third party assists the parties to reach a negotiated settlement. The mediator does not have the power to render a binding solution but simply seeks to bring about agreement through persuasion. **Court-annexed mediation** is also required in some courts for small cases and domestic disputes, particularly those involving child custody. Many communities, and even some private firms, have established **ombudspersons,** who are third parties who receive and investigate complaints and perhaps act as mediators.

**Minitrials** are confidential processes, either before or during legal proceedings, in which lawyers present an abbreviated version of the case before a panel of managers of disputing firms who have authority to settle and a neutral advisor. After the presentation, the managers decide whether to settle the case. If no settlement is made, the parties may resort to formal court proceedings.

## CRIMINAL PROCEDURE

The criminal courts operate almost identically to the civil courts, and a flowchart of criminal procedure is found in Figure 3.5. The jury selection process, the order of presentation of proof, the order of examining witnesses, the basic rules of evidence, final argument, and the instructions to the jury are all substantially alike. There are some major differences between civil and criminal cases, however.

### Initiation of Charges

Charges may be filed in criminal cases in two ways: (1) **indictment,** which is a charge made by a grand jury; and (2) **information,** which is a complaint filed by the prosecutors. Although citizens may begin the process by making a complaint to the prosecutor, the discretion of whether to file a charge lies solely in the hands of the prosecutor or grand jury. A common distinction is between *felonies,* which are offenses punishable by imprisonment in a penitentiary, and *misdemeanors,* which are offenses punished by imprisonment in some facility other than a penitentiary (such as a county jail) or by fine only. State classifications vary widely.

Prosecutors, also known as *district attorneys* or *state's attorneys* or, in the federal system, *United States attorneys*, have the freedom to charge or not to charge. **Prosecutorial discretion** means the prosecutor is free to file or not to file a charge as he or she sees fit and to dismiss or **plea bargain** the case after it is filed.

### Discovery

Discovery in criminal cases is more limited than in civil cases. The defendant is generally not required to supply much information to the prosecution because of the fifth amendment's *privilege against self-incrimination*. Both the prosecution and the defense may be required to furnish witness lists, and the prosecution is often required to furnish police reports and records, chemical tests, and other documentary evidence. Depositions and interrogatories are used only in exceptional circumstances, such as to take the testimony of a dying witness.

### Pretrial Motions

The defendant often moves to dismiss the charges on the grounds that the indictment or information is *defective*. Defects include failure to identify the defendant properly or to state all of the elements of the offense. Another common pretrial motion is the **motion to suppress** evidence. If evidence is seized illegally, as through an illegal search and seizure, the defendant may move to exclude that evidence. If granted, the evidence could not be introduced at trial under the *exclusionary rule*, discussed in Chapter 4. In such motions, the burden of proof is on the prosecution to show that the evidence was seized legally.

### The Trial and Burden of Proof

The basic rules for proceeding in a criminal case are identical to those in a civil case. The prosecution must present its proof first, and the defendant is under no obligation to disprove any of the prosecution's evidence.

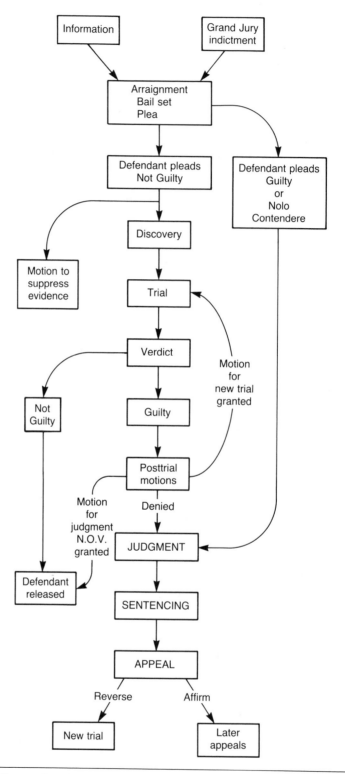

FIGURE 3.5   A Flowchart of Criminal Litigation

The burden of proof in criminal cases of *beyond a reasonable doubt* is different from civil cases in both the amount of proof that the prosecution must present and the nature of the belief that must exist in the minds of the jurors. In civil cases, a mistake in favor of the plaintiff is no worse than a mistake in favor of the defendant. But in a criminal case the possibility of a mistake in favor of the state is far worse than a mistake in favor of the defendant, because the defendant's liberty or even life may be in jeopardy.

One classic definition of *reasonable doubt*, as used in numerous cases, provides some help in defining this troublesome phrase: "It is that state of the case, which, after the entire comparison and consideration of all the evidence, leaves the minds of jurors in that condition that they cannot say they feel an abiding conviction, to a moral certainty, of the truth of the charge."

Other definitions emphasize that jurors should not overstress mere possibilities or imaginary doubts. An imaginative mind could always find a doubt in any case. But the prosecution must only prove its case beyond a *reasonable* doubt. A great many courts resolve the difficulty of defining reasonable doubt by refusing to define the term for jurors in the court's instructions.

Often the term *beyond a reasonable doubt* is confused with its relative, the **presumption** of innocence. That means that an accused person is presumed (or assumed) to be innocent unless and until the jury renders a verdict against the defendant. That presumption follows the defendant throughout the trial, and the defendant never has the burden of proving that innocence.

## Sentencing

In almost all instances, the sentence imposed on the defendant after a finding of guilt is up to the judge. In a few isolated and rare instances, the jury may recommend a particular sentence, especially in cases involving the death sentence. Statutes provide the available sentences for each offense, including imprisonment, fines, and probation; and as long as the judge imposes a sentence authorized by the statute, the sentence itself usually cannot be appealed.

## Plea Bargaining

Just as most civil cases are settled before coming to court, most criminal cases end in agreed dispositions through the *plea-bargaining* process. Generally, the defendant agrees to plead guilty either to the principal charge or to a lesser charge in return for a recommendation by the prosecutor of a specific sentence lighter than the maximum sentence available. Proponents of plea bargaining argue that the process is necessary because of the case load of the courts and prosecutors.

## APPELLATE PROCEDURE

All appellate courts, from the intermediate state appellate courts to the U.S. Supreme Court, operate in much the same way. After the trial court enters a final judgment, any party may file a **notice of appeal.** That document alerts the court and the opposing parties that an appeal is pending. The notice of appeal must be filed within thirty days of the entry of final judgment in the federal courts. The party appealing is now known as the **appellant,** and the opposing party is called the **appellee.**

The appellant must order the **record on appeal,** including all court documents and the transcript of proceedings. Shortly after the record is filed, the **appellant's brief** is due. The brief is a written argument, detailing the claims of error in the trial court and arguments of law, including citations of cases and statutes dealing with those claims. The **appellee's brief** is due somewhat later. The appellant has the right to file an **appellant's reply brief** dealing with matters raised by the appellee's brief. Later briefs are possible at the discretion of the court. Briefs are sometimes also filed by *amicus curiae,* or friends of the court, who are nonparties interested in the litigation. For example, if the constitutionality of a federal law is in issue in a private lawsuit, the U.S. Attorney General usually appears as *amicus curiae* to aid the court.

At a later date, the appellate court may order *oral argument.* The attorneys for the parties will appear before the appellate judges who will decide the case to present their arguments orally. Appellate judges sit in **panels** of three or more judges; and if all of the judges of the court hear a case, they are said to sit *en banc.* After the oral argument, the court will usually take the case *under advisement* while it makes its decision. The court will vote on the case, and one of the judges in the majority will write a decision and an opinion, which is later published.

The order of the court may affirm (agree with) the decision of the lower court, in which case the decision of the lower court will stand. Or, the court may reverse the decision of the lower court, which means that the appellate court will enter a judgment different from that entered by the lower court. Or, if matters remain to be done by the lower court, such as holding a new trial, the appellate court may reverse and remand the decision back to the lower court for further proceedings. Appellate courts never hear trials and almost never take evidence. Following the appellate court's judgment, the parties are free to appeal to an even higher court.

## RES JUDICATA

Once a case has been heard and finally decided by a court, it can never be heard again, under the concept of *res judicata* (literally, "the thing has been decided"). The concept is ancient and is based on the idea that there should be an end to a case. If A sues B for an auto accident, and if a final judgment is rendered, A may never again sue B on those facts. Likewise, if B did not file a compulsory counterclaim in that action, he or she may not sue A either.

A closely related concept that applies only to criminal cases is **double jeopardy,** found in the fifth amendment to the U.S. Constitution. Double jeopardy means that a person cannot be tried twice for the same offense or for different offenses arising from the same facts. If, for example, a defendant was found not guilty of robbery, the prosecutor could not file **lesser-included offenses** such as assault, battery, and theft against the defendant based on the same incident.

Appellate courts can and often do order new trials after an appeal, and sometimes trial courts order new trials as well. A criminal defendant may not be retried after an acquittal, however, even if the prosecution attempts to appeal. State appeals in criminal cases are usually restricted to interlocutory matters, such as an appeal of a ruling on evidence, because to do otherwise would constitute double jeopardy.

## SUMMARY AND CONCLUSIONS

American courts are organized in a dual system involving both federal and state courts. Both systems include trial, intermediate appellate, and supreme courts. Questions of authority to hear cases are settled by the concepts of jurisdiction and venue. Jurisdiction includes both subject matter jurisdiction and personal jurisdiction. Federal subject matter jurisdiction provides for diversity, federal question, and special federal question jurisdiction.

Three extraordinary actions are available in certain instances. Class actions, declaratory judgments, and mandamus suits are extremely valuable in contesting government actions. These cases are governed by the same basic trial procedures as other cases.

Trial procedure is dictated in the first instance by the due process clause of the Constitution, which requires fair procedures. Pretrial procedure in civil cases involves the pleadings, discovery, and motions phases of litigation. The trial procedure is generally dictated by the rule that "whoever opens has the right to close." Criminal procedure follows much the same procedure as civil cases, with the exceptions of the method by which charges are brought, the discovery phase, and the burden of proof.

Appellate procedure is generally confined to reviewing the lower court's conduct of the trial to determine whether there was a legal error. Appellate procedure is quite similar in all appellate courts, requiring submission of the record and briefs and oral argument, although minor differences may occur. An appellate court may affirm, reverse, or reverse and remand the decision of the trial court. The opinion of the appellate court then becomes precedent for all trial courts within the appellate court's jurisdiction.

## REVIEW QUESTIONS

1   Describe and diagram the American dual court system. Why are there two sets of courts in the United States? Are there good and valid reasons for having two sets of courts?

2   Explain the difference between federal question and diversity jurisdiction. Do you think sufficient state bias really exists to give cause for federal diversity jurisdiction?

3   What law do the federal courts apply in diversity cases? Under the *Erie* doctrine, what if a federal court finds that a state law is unjust, immoral, or just plain wrong? Must it still apply the law? Should it refuse on ethical grounds to apply such a law?

4   Are advisory opinions advisable? What's wrong with a legislature getting an advance opinion from the state supreme court on whether a piece of pending legislation will be constitutional? Wouldn't such a procedure save a lot of trouble later? Should that court be bound by its advisory opinion when a real controversy comes before it later on?

5   Why may an appellate court only review errors of law and not errors of fact? Do you suppose it might have something to do with the fact that the appellate court did not see the witnesses testify but only read the transcript? If trials are videotaped, should this rule be changed?

6   Cunningham purchased a Ford automobile for $11,221.40 and had nothing but problems. After driving the car for 12,000 miles, he sued Ford under a warranty theory for the entire purchase price. An expert testified that because of the mileage, the car was now worth $1,800 less. Is there federal jurisdiction? [*Cunningham v. Ford Motor Co.*, 413 F. Supp. 1101 (1976).]

7   Brown, a resident of New York, made a contract with White, a resident of California. The contract was made in Illinois. If White defaults on the contract, in which courts may Brown sue White? What courts have jurisdiction? What courts have venue? What state's law would be applied in each case?

8   Curtis filed suit under Title VIII of the federal Civil Rights Act to enjoin discrimination by Loether in rental of housing and for damages caused by Loether's discrimination. Loether demanded a jury trial. Title VIII makes no mention of jury trials, and discrimination actions were unknown at common law. Should Loether get a jury trial? [*Curtis v. Loether*, 415 U.S. 189, 94 S. Ct. 1005, 39 L. Ed. 2d 260 (1974).]

9   Page, a citizen of Great Britain and a student at the University of Wisconsin, married a citizen of the United States. Mrs. Page, a resident of Illinois, was working on her master's degree in business administration at the University of Wisconsin at the time, although she continued to maintain her residence at her parents' home in Illinois and voted in that state. The couple had made no plans regarding their residence after their graduation. On a trip back to visit Mrs. Page's parents in Illinois, they were involved in a traffic accident in Illinois with Bane, a resident of Illinois, and both were injured severely. May they bring an action in federal court? If so, what law will that court apply?

10   Grey and Erpingham had entered into an employment contract, and Grey alleged that Erpingham owed her money on the deal, which Erpingham denied. Grey filed suit, and the summons was delivered to Ely, a deputy sheriff, for service of process. Ely, who was very overworked, threw the summons away and falsely claimed that he had delivered the summons to Erpingham. When Erpingham failed to appear, Grey moved for a default judgment, which was granted. Some time later Erpingham learned of the judgment and moved to set it aside. Does he have a remedy?

CHAPTER 4

# The American Constitution

*We are under a Constitution, but the Constitution is what the judges say it is.*

CHIEF JUSTICE CHARLES EVANS HUGHES (1907)

The source of all government authority in the United States is the people. Under the theory of natural rights, the people join together in a compact, or agreement, for mutual aid and protection. The American Constitution is that agreement, in written form. The agreement was made by representatives of the people who met in the Constitutional Convention in 1787. The representatives formed a federal government out of the states, granted that government very specific powers to rule, and placed certain limits on the privilege of ruling. That document, which is reproduced in full in Appendix A, forms the foundation of all American law.

## BACKGROUND OF THE CONSTITUTION

Even before the defeat of the British at Yorktown, the young American nation had begun the business of running its own affairs. The Second Continental Congress had proposed the Articles of Confederation as early as 1777; but those articles—the first attempt at a written constitution—did not become effective until March 1781. The articles were little more than a treaty or alliance between independent and sovereign nations and soon proved highly unworkable.

In the summer of 1787, delegates met in Philadelphia for the purpose of amending the Articles of Confederation. That meeting has come to be known as the **Constitutional Convention.** The delegates, chosen by the legislatures of the states, were a remarkable group of men. The fifty-five delegates included Washington, Franklin, Hamilton, and Madison, as well as lesser-known but equally brilliant men such as Roger Sherman, James Wilson, and John Dickinson. The delegates were young, with an average age of forty-two, and twenty-nine of the delegates were lawyers.

We know little of the internal workings or debates of the Convention. The members immediately pledged themselves to secrecy in order to prevent undue disturbance to "the public repose." We know that the delegates immediately breached their instructions, which were to amend the Articles of Confederation. Instead, they scrapped that document altogether and began anew.

On September 17, 1787, the finished document was signed. The delegates left the convention well aware of the political revolution they had begun. Upon leaving the

93

hall, Benjamin Franklin was stopped by a woman who asked him what sort of government the delegates had given the country. Franklin replied, "A republic, madam, if you can keep it." An outline of the major provisions of the Constitution is provided in Figure 4.1.

The Constitution provided that it would become effective upon ratification by nine states. The ratification process revived all of the old sectional arguments and added a philosophical dispute about the power of a central government in relation to the states and the people. The fight for ratification was led by the delegates themselves, especially Hamilton, Madison, and John Jay, who wrote a series of essays arguing for ratification, later collected as the **Federalist Papers.** Many of the arguments regarding the "intent of the Framers" in contemporary debates on constitutional issues are based upon those essays, particularly since little is known of the actual debates within the Constitutional Convention.

By July 26, 1788, eleven states had ratified the Constitution, two more than the Constitution required. In 1789 the first Congress met, and the new nation had begun. Within two years, ten amendments would be made to the original document as a result of substantial pressure from the states and from the public. Those amendments are known as the **Bill of Rights.**

## THE DOCTRINE OF JUDICIAL REVIEW

One of the most unique features of the new American government was that it provided *limits* on the power of the federal government. Those limits first took the form of **specific grants** of power to the three branches of government. Those specific grants implicitly permitted the federal government to act only if the power to act was specifically granted within the Constitution. Later the Bill of Rights would add some very explicit limits on the power of government to act.

It is one thing to make a law and quite another to enforce it. Although the Constitution clearly limits the authority of government to act, nowhere does the document state what happens if government goes beyond those limits. Some, such as Andrew Jack-

| Article I | Created Congress and granted it specific powers |
|---|---|
| Article II | Created the Presidency and granted that office specific powers |
| Article III | Created the Supreme Court and gave Congress the power to create lower courts |
| Article IV | Specified federal-state relations |
| Article V | Described the amendment process |
| Article VI | Miscellaneous<br>1 Took on pre-Constitution debts<br>2 Stated the supremacy clause<br>3 Required oaths of office |
| Article VII | Specified the ratification process |
| 26 Amendments | |

FIGURE 4.1    An Outline of the Constitution

son, believed that each branch of government should oversee itself and seemed to believe that no single branch, such as the judiciary, had the right to tell another branch what to do. In Jackson's view, each branch of government was *coequal*.

## Judicial Review of Acts of Congress

For fourteen years after the ratification of the Constitution in 1789, there was no fixed plan to deal with occasions when Congress went too far. The Constitution itself was silent on the matter, but in 1803 Chief Justice John Marshall "found" the right of *judicial review* in the Constitution in *Marbury v. Madison*, a case that has been called the most important decision in American jurisprudence. *Marbury* only affected the right of the Supreme Court to review acts of Congress, but it implicitly affected the right of the Court to review acts of the executive branch and the states as well.

## Marbury v. Madison
5 U.S (1 Cranch) 137, 2 L. Ed. 60 (1803)

Under a provision of the Federal Judiciary Act of 1789, suit could be brought directly in the Supreme Court of the United States to force a public officer to do his duty. Marbury brought suit against Madison directly before the Supreme Court to order Madison to deliver a commission as a judge that had been signed by President John Adams. The issue was whether the law that gave the Supreme Court the power to hear such cases conformed to article III of the Constitution, which set the limits of jurisdiction of the Supreme Court. Marshall decided that it did not, and then the question became whether the Supreme Court had the authority to rule that law—or *any* law—unconstitutional and void.

**[T]he Following Opinion of the Court was Delivered by the Chief Justice [Marshall]**    The question, whether an act, repugnant to the constitution, can become the law of the land, is a question deeply interesting to the United States; but, happily, not of intricacy proportioned to its interest. It seems only necessary to recognize certain principles, supposed to have been long and well established, to decide it. . . .

Certainly, all those who have framed written constitutions contemplate them as forming the fundamental and paramount law of the nation, and consequently, the theory of every such government must be, that an act of the legislature repugnant to the constitution, is void. . . .

It is emphatically, the province and duty of the judicial department to say what the law is. Those who apply the rule to particular cases, must of necessity expound and interpret that rule. If two laws conflict with each other, the courts must decide on the oper-

ation of each. So, if a law be in opposition to the constitution, if both the law and the constitution apply to a particular case, so that the court must either decide that case, conformable to the law disregarding the constitution; or conformable to the constitution, disregarding the law; the court must determine which of these conflicting rules governs the case: this is of the very essence of judicial duty.

. . . [T]he peculiar expressions of the constitution of the United States furnish additional arguments in favor of [the proposition]. The judicial power of the United States is extended to a case's arising under the constitution. Could it be the intention of those who gave this power, to say that in using it, the constitution should not be looked into? That a case arising under the constitution should be decided without examining the instrument under which it arises? This is too extravagant to be maintained. . . .

There are many other parts of the constitution which serve to illustrate this subject. It is declared, that "no tax or duty shall be laid on articles exported from any state." Suppose, a duty on the export of cotton, or tobacco or of flour; and a suit instituted to recover it. Ought judgment to be rendered in such a case? Ought the judges to close their eyes on the constitution, and only see the law?

From these, and many other selections which might be made, it is apparent that the framers of the constitution contemplated that instrument as a rule for the government of courts, as well as of the legislature. Why otherwise does it direct the judges to take an oath to support it? . . . How immoral to impose it on them, if they were to be used as the instruments, and the knowing instruments for violating what they swear to support!

. . . . If such be the real state of things, this is worse than solemn mockery. To prescribe, or to take this oath becomes equally a crime.

It is also not entirely unworthy of observation, that in declaring what shall be the supreme law of the land, the constitution itself is first mentioned; and not the laws of the United States, generally but those only which shall be made in pursuance of the constitution have that rank.

Thus, the particular phraseology of the constitution of the United States confirms and strengthens the principle, supposed to be essential to all written constitutions, that a law repugnant to the constitution is void; and that courts, as well as other departments, are bound by that instrument.

## Case Discussion Questions

1    Does the Constitution say anything about judicial review? If not, where did Marshall find that doctrine?

2    Could we get along without judicial review? Could, as Andrew Jackson argued, each branch of government be the judge of the constitutionality of its own actions?

3    What function does judicial review play in our constitutional system?

---

The *Marbury* decision has been called a "legal and logical *tour de force*, because by giving up a little power, the Court assumed a great deal of power. *Marbury v. Madison* gave the Court the right to oversee and void any act of Congress that it considered unconstitutional. The decision has also been called a usurpation of power by the Court, because the branches of government are coequal and the right of judicial review is not found expressly in the Constitution.

---

PROFILE

# John Marshall

John Marshall (1755–1835) was born on the Virginia frontier and had little formal education, but he came to be known as the greatest Chief Justice ever to sit on the Supreme Court. After distinguished service in the Revolutionary War, he studied law on his own and became a lawyer in 1781. He served as a diplomat in the famous "XYZ Affair," a U.S. Congressman, and Secretary of State under John Adams. In 1801, Adams appointed Marshall to the Supreme Court to take the place of an ailing Oliver Ellsworth. Adams hoped that Marshall would place limits on the new Demo-

*continued*

crat-Republican President, Thomas Jefferson. By coincidence, Jefferson was Marshall's cousin, but they were bitter enemies.

The election of 1800 was a bitter contest between the Federalist party, and their incumbent President John Adams, and the upstart Democrat-Republicans and their candidate, Thomas Jefferson. The Federalists lost the election badly, losing the Presidency and control of both houses of Congress. Adams and the lame-duck Federalist Congress resolved to retain as much power as possible by appointing as many Federalists as possible to government positions, especially the judiciary.

The lame-duck Congress also created a large number of new federal judgeships, including forty-two justices of the peace for the District of Columbia. Adams nominated Federalists, including William Marbury, for these posts. Adams stayed up much of the night before Jefferson's inauguration signing the appointments. As a result, those appointed were called the *Midnight Judges*. Arguably, the commissions had to be "delivered" to the persons nominated to complete the appointment process. The commissions were not delivered; and James Madison, the new Secretary of State under Thomas Jefferson, refused to deliver Marbury's commission. Marbury then sued Madison directly in the Supreme Court under a provision of the Federal Judiciary Act of 1789 that permitted such suits. It fell to John Marshall to write the opinion, and the result was *Marbury v. Madison*, possibly the most important legal decision in American history.

Marshall served on the Court for thirty-four years and rendered some of the most important decisions ever made by the Court. *Marbury v. Madison*, with its creation of judicial review, *McCulloch v. Maryland* and its broad interpretation of government power, *Gibbons v. Ogden* and its expansive definition of commerce, and many lesser-known decisions established the starting point of American constitutional law.

Marshall, a Federalist, believed in a strong central government and a strong Supreme Court. When Marshall was appointed, the Supreme Court was respected so little that it was difficult to convince men to serve. When he died, the Court was strong and vital, and the structure and principles of American government were well established. Marshall's opinions became the basis of much of American constitutional law for the next 200 years.

## Judicial Review of State Court Decisions

*Marbury* did not end the problems of judicial review. Although the decision gave the Court the right to review acts of Congress, it did not speak to the issue of judicial review of *state* court actions. The problem was whether the United States Supreme Court had the authority to review and void decisions of state courts. State courts jealously guarded their own supremacy, and the issue was a major problem in the developing federalism of the new nation.

The issue was not resolved until 1816 in the rather bizarre case of *Martin v. Hunt-*

*er's Lessee.*[1] In that case, Justice Joseph Story held that the U.S. Supreme Court had the right to review decisions of the state supreme courts, although this generated much controversy and some threats of armed rebellion. In a broad sense, the issue of judicial review of state court decisions involved questions of the power of the federal government over the states, an issue that was finally resolved in the Civil War.

## The "Styles" of Judicial Review

Although almost everyone would agree that the courts should have the right of judicial review, a substantial disagreement remains over how that right should be exercised. As part of the answer we must consider the philosophical and legal thought of the judge—whether he or she is *liberal* or *conservative*, if those terms have any real meaning. But a far more important issue, going beyond individual politics, is the judge's view of his or her function and that of the Constitution. Three categories of judicial thought have been identified: (1) **neutralists,** (2) **restraintists,** and (3) **activists.** Although no judge consistently fits a single type, the categories are useful in interpreting judicial opinions and in making legal forecasts.

**The Neutralist Approach**    The neutralist school, sometimes called the *absolutist school*, finds certain fixed principles of justice in the Constitution. These principles are absolute and unchanging and should be applied to all cases. Judges are treated as mere conduits through which justice and the law speak, never as policymakers or quasi-legislators. Judges of this sort, perhaps best exemplified by Justice Hugo Black (1886–1971), generally rely on the plain meaning of the Constitution. Black, for example, looked at the first amendment guarantee of free speech as such an absolute. The amendment says Congress may make *no law* regarding free speech, and Black believed that "no law" meant exactly what it said. There could be no exceptions, no compromise, no balancing of interests. And this was true regardless of how beneficial the judge might think a particular law might be. Personal politics must be put aside in favor of consistency and the plain language of the Constitution.

**The Restraintist Approach**    Advocates of judicial restraint find themselves embarrassed by the existence of judicial review, and although they are unwilling to give up the power to review acts of the other two branches, they generally counsel restraint in exercising that power. They generally see the Court as the least powerful branch of government—in Hamilton's terms, "the least dangerous branch"—in that it cannot enforce its decisions on its own, but rather must depend on the goodwill of the executive branch. Therefore, restraintists generally avoid confrontation with the other, more powerful branches of government except on rare and crucial occasions. Generally, restraintists ask that the Court *avoid* constitutional questions whenever possible. Law is viewed not as a set of immutable principles but as the history of the resolution of past problems, and the best result is usually found by balancing the interests of the parties to the controversy. Restraintists, like Oliver Wendell Holmes (see *Profile*, p. 19), Benjamin Cardozo (1870–1938), and Louis Brandeis (1856–1941), to name a few, feel that law should be

---

1  14 U.S. (1 Wheat.) 304, 4 L. Ed. 97 (1816).

TABLE 4.1   The Current Supreme Court

| Judge | Judicial Style* | Appointed | Date of Birth | Appt. By |
|-------|-----------------|-----------|---------------|----------|
| William Rehnquist | R | 1972 | 1924 | Nixon |
| William Brennan | A | 1956 | 1906 | Eisenhower |
| Byron White | R | 1962 | 1917 | Kennedy |
| Thurgood Marshall | A | 1967 | 1908 | Johnson |
| Harry Blackmun | A(?) | 1970 | 1908 | Nixon |
| John P. Stevens | R | 1975 | 1920 | Ford |
| Sandra Day O'Connor | R | 1981 | 1930 | Reagan |
| Antonine Scalia | R | 1986 | 1936 | Reagan |
| Anthony Kennedy | R(?) | 1988 | 1936 | Reagan |

*R = Restraintist
 A = Activist

"prudently found," not "made" by the Court. Many of the judges recently appointed to the Court are considered to be judicial restraintists, including all of the judges appointed by Presidents Nixon, Ford, and Reagan.[2] After appointment, Justice Blackmun has taken a more activist position on many issues, and some argue that Justice O'Connor is moving in that direction on some issues, particularly those involving church-state relations (see Table 4.1).

**The Activist Approach**   The third approach, called the *activist* or the *preferred freedoms* approach, finds the balancing test advocated by the restraintists to be very distasteful, because it usually results in favoring the interests of the stronger members of our society. Judicial activists see it as part of the Court's role to be an advocate and protector of the interests of the weak and disadvantaged groups in our nation. They also make a distinction between economic interests and civil rights and liberties. In the former case, the activists will accept the balancing tests of the restraintists, and therefore the two groups often find themselves allied in those cases. In cases involving civil rights and liberties, the activists find such rights to be fundamental guarantees, or preferred freedoms, and therefore will not permit a balancing of interests to take place. In such cases judicial activists are often allied with judicial neutralists. Important activists include Earl Warren (Chief Justice from 1953–1969), William O. Douglas (1939–1975), William Brennan (appointed 1956), and Thurgood Marshall (appointed 1967).

## THE POWERS OF GOVERNMENT

The federal government received specific **enumerated powers** that are expressly set forth in the Constitution. The rest of the authority to govern is expressly "reserved to the

---

**2** President Carter made no appointments to the Supreme Court.

States," both under the theory implicit in the Constitutional idea and expressly under the tenth amendment.[3]

## The Powers of Congress

Congress received the clearest statement of its powers in article I, section 8 of the Constitution. That section contains a long list of specific enumerated powers given to Congress, such as the power to lay and collect taxes, regulate commerce, coin money, and many others.

Congress also has **implied powers.** The implied powers of Congress are based upon the necessary and proper clause, article I, section 8, clause 18, of the Constitution, which grants Congress the right to "make all laws necessary and proper for carrying into Execution the foregoing [enumerated] Powers."

The necessary and proper clause was first interpreted by the Supreme Court in a decision that rivals *Marbury v. Madison* in importance. In *McCulloch v. Maryland*,[4] Justice John Marshall interpreted the necessary and proper clause as granting the federal government the right to use any legitimate *means* of bringing about the *goals* established by the specific grants of power. *McCulloch v. Maryland* clearly expanded federal power and gave the federal government a great deal of flexibility. Under the necessary and proper clause, Congress has exercised many powers not specifically granted by the Constitution, such as the power to take property under eminent domain for public purposes, create corporations, exclude and deport aliens, and even enact the Federal Criminal Code.

## The Powers of the Executive

Compared to the legislative grants of authority, the powers of the President seem quite limited. The President may make certain official appointments (such as members of the Supreme Court), grant reprieves and pardons, make treaties subject to the advice and consent of the Senate, and temporarily fill Congressional vacancies. But, the lack of formal grants of power notwithstanding, the President has become extremely powerful over the years, especially through the administrative process (see Chapter 6). Congress has delegated a great deal of authority to the President or to administrative agencies within the executive branch.

## The Powers of the Courts

The powers of the courts are defined in general terms in article III, but the Constitution is quite vague regarding that power. Congress is given the power to set the size and the organization of the lower federal courts. One of the first actions taken by the first Congress was to pass the federal Judiciary Act of 1789. That act provided for the formation of lower federal trial courts and the division of the nation into judicial districts. The act also specified what types of cases the federal courts might hear. The Judiciary Act also specified that the Supreme Court should consist of six justices.

Although much of the Judiciary Act has changed over the years, the act has always

---

3 The tenth amendment provides that "[t]he powers not delegated to the United States by the Constitution, nor prohibited by it to the States, are reserved to the States respectively, or to the people."

4 17 U.S. 316, 4 L. Ed. 579 (1819).

existed in one form or another. Two important changes involved enlarging the Supreme Court to nine justices and the creating of "second-tier" appellate courts, called U.S. courts of appeals. Both of those changes took place in 1896. It is important to remember that Congress may, at any time, change the organization or makeup of the federal courts, remove or enlarge federal court jurisdiction, or alter the size of the Supreme Court.

## PREEMPTION AND THE PROBLEM OF FEDERALISM

One of the more controversial issues throughout American history is the relationship between the states and the federal government. Under the Articles of Confederation, the states were virtually sovereign nations, and the fear of a strong centralized government was a major issue in the debate over ratification of the Constitution. In the debates, Alexander Hamilton favored a centralized government, whereas Thomas Jefferson and his followers favored dispersing power among several "levels" or "layers" of government. In a way, the Constitution of 1789 was a compromise between these conflicting philosophies, a compromise resulting in massive conflicts that ultimately led to the Civil War. A part of that compromise was **federalism,** or the existence of semi-independent states along with a relatively strong central government.

Initially, the reasons for federalism and the existence of multiple levels of government lay in the fear of tyranny. The more points of access to the government, the more the public could hope to influence and limit the excesses of government. Modern arguments favoring more state and local controls that exclude the national government have been based on ideas of efficiency. It is argued that local and state control over various programs involves less waste and a greater degree of responsiveness to local concerns.

Two constitutional provisions are relevant to the continuing debate over the relative roles of the state and federal governments. The tenth amendment assures that powers not delegated to the federal government are "reserved to the States respectively, or to the people." And the **supremacy clause** (article VI, clause 2) provides that the "Constitution and the Laws of the United States which shall be made in Pursuance thereof . . . shall be the supreme Law of the Land."

The most common issue of federal-state relations continues to be the authority of the states to govern areas concurrently with the federal government. If a state law and a federal law purport to govern the same problem and the two laws conflict, the state law is **preempted** by the federal law. That means that under the supremacy clause, the state law must give way to the federal law. Although the issue may be stated in simple terms, the problem is often complex. The courts may be asked to determine whether laws really do conflict in such situations, which involves a comprehensive analysis of both laws. And even if the laws do not directly conflict, the problem may be one in which Congress has the exclusive authority to act, in which case the state law is also preempted. In some situations, too, it may have been Congress's intention that no one, including itself, should act in the field.

## THE COMMERCE CLAUSE: A CASE STUDY
## IN CONGRESSIONAL POWER

Perhaps the most important change brought about by the Constitutional Convention was the adoption of article I, section 8, clause 3, the **commerce clause.** This deceptively

*Commerce Clause*

simple clause gave Congress the authority to "regulate Commerce with foreign Nations, and among the several States, and with the Indian Tribes." These simple words have been called "the fount and origin of vast power" and "the direct source of the most important powers which the Federal Government exercises in time of peace." From civil rights to consumer protection, the commerce clause is the source of authority for most of our present regulatory environment.

Yet this was not always so. For the first hundred years of its existence, the clause was a sleeping giant, giving little power and rarely, if ever, used. Beginning with the creation of the Interstate Commerce Commission in 1887, the clause was used by Congress as the basis for the creation of regulatory agencies. But even then, it was not until 1937 that Congress obtained any real power to regulate the day-to-day affairs of business.

The first decision to consider the scope of the commerce clause was the famous *Gibbons v. Ogden* decision.[5] The case was partly a preemption problem, dealing with the issue of whether a New York monopoly granted to Robert Fulton to operate his famous steamboat on Lake Erie conflicted with the commerce clause. Chief Justice John Marshall's definition of the term *commerce* lives on in decisions today. "Commerce," said Marshall, "undoubtedly is traffic, but it is something more; it is intercourse. It describes the commercial intercourse between nations, and parts of nations, in all its branches." The Court ruled that New York had attempted to regulate commerce in this sense, and therefore had attempted to control something exclusively within federal power.

Commerce clause questions are commonly centered on one of two issues: (1) whether a state regulation has interfered with exclusively federal matters and (2) whether an action by Congress has gone beyond the scope of the authority granted to it by the commerce clause.

---

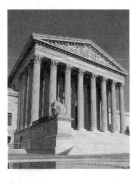

PROFILE

## The Court-Packing Plan and the Constitutional Revolution of 1937

In 1929 the nation was plunged into the Great Depression. Three years later, Franklin Roosevelt was elected President on his promise to end the economic chaos of that time. He and the Democratic majority in Congress set about enacting various statutes designed to bring economic recovery. Most of those statutes were aimed at regulating manufacturing operations in some manner, but under the authority of the commerce clause. Time after time, the Su-

---

5  22 U.S. (9 Wheat.) 1, 6 L. Ed. 23 (1824).

preme Court held those statutes unconstitutional with reasoning similar to that used in *Hammer v. Dagenhart.*

In 1937, after Roosevelt's reelection, two key portions of the New Deal were up for review before the Supreme Court, including the National Labor Relations Act and the Social Security Act, along with a major case concerning the right of states to regulate labor. Frustrated by the prior decisions that had nullified his program for recovery and secure in his second term of office, Roosevelt moved against the Court. On March 9, 1937, Roosevelt proposed an amendment to the Judiciary Act—later termed the **court-packing plan.**

The court-packing plan relied on the ability of the U.S. Congress to set the size of the Supreme Court. Roosevelt asked Congress to establish a variable size for the Court by permitting the President to appoint a new justice every time a current justice reached the age of seventy. Roosevelt justified the program by pointing to the "nine old men" on the court and asking the nation to save itself from "judicial hardening of the arteries." At the time the plan was proposed, six justices were over the age of seventy. Thus, the size of the Supreme Court would have been increased to fifteen members, and Roosevelt could have appointed six new members, more than enough to give him a majority on the Court. Roosevelt's plan was introduced in Congress but encountered heavy resistance, even among members of his own party, and it was withdrawn.

While the plan was being considered, the Court announced three decisions indicating a shift in judicial policy toward federal regulation of business under the commerce clause and state regulation of business under the police powers. In *NLRB v. Jones & Laughlin Steel Co.* (p. 107), the Court vastly expanded the reach of the commerce clause. In *Helvering v. Davis*[6] the Court refused to hold the Social Security Act unconstitutional in the face of a claim that it violated federal taxing powers. And in *West Coast Hotel v. Parrish* (p. 113) the Court all but did away with the doctrine of economic substantive due process, the doctrine that had been used to hold many state regulations of labor unconstitutional.

Although scholars disagree over whether the Supreme Court "knuckled under" to the pressure of the court-packing plan, it is clear that 1937 signaled a major legal change, sometimes called the **constitutional revolution of 1937.** Only one judge, Justice Owen Roberts (1875–1945), changed his vote, but that vote was crucial and was, according to a commentator of the time, "the switch in time that saved nine."

## State Regulation of Commerce: The Police Power

From 1824 until the 1890s, the vast majority of cases dealt with the issue of whether a state law in some way conflicted with federal power over commerce. In one sense this is a preemption question, a conflict between a state power and a federal power.

The authority of states to regulate in any field is generally derived from the so-called

---

6 301 U.S. 619, 57 S. Ct. 904, 81 L. Ed. 1307 (1937).

**police power** of the states. The police power is the power of a state to enact laws for the purposes of *health, welfare, safety,* and *morals.* It is one of the reserved powers of the states, under the tenth amendment, although it is not mentioned specifically there or anywhere else in the Constitution. On many occasions, the courts have held the police power to be an "inherent power of government."

The police power gives the states ample power to regulate many intrastate[7] aspects of business, but those state regulations may well conflict with federal authority under the commerce clause. Generally, a state law regulating commerce may be defective in one of two ways: (1) the state law may *discriminate against interstate commerce* and (2) the state law may *unduly burden interstate commerce.*

**Discrimination against interstate commerce** means some form of favoritism of local business over out-of-state business. Such discrimination may take the form of boycotts, embargoes, taxes, or other regulations that affect out-of-state business adversely. Such state regulations were a moving force in the push for a Constitutional Convention in 1787. Generally speaking, the courts frown on state laws that treat commerce from outside the state differently from internal commerce.

An **undue burden on interstate commerce** is an even-handed yet burdensome regulation that affects interstate commerce. *Every* state law that affects interstate commerce presents a burden on that commerce. The question is whether that burden is *undue* or *unreasonable.* Since the state law affects both intrastate and interstate commerce equally, the courts are reluctant to hold such laws unconstitutional. The following case discusses the attitude of the courts towards both state discrimination towards and burdens on interstate commerce.

---

## Maine v. Taylor
477 U.S. 131, 106 S. Ct. 2440, 91 L. Ed. 2d 110 (1986)

The State of Maine enacted a statute that prohibited importing any live bait fish into the state. Taylor, the owner of a bait business, imported 158,000 live golden shiners, a common minnow used as live bait in sport fishing, from outside the state. He was indicted by a federal grand jury under a federal law that made it a crime to import fish or wildlife "taken, possessed, transported or sold in violation of any law . . . of any State." Taylor moved to dismiss on the grounds that Maine's statute violated the commerce clause. The motion was denied, and Taylor was convicted. He appealed to the U.S. court of appeals, which reversed. The State of Maine then appealed to the U.S. Supreme Court under a special statute allowing such appeals.

**Justice Blackmun Delivered the Opinion of the Court**    Once again, a little fish has caused a commotion. . . .

The Commerce Clause of the Constitution grants Congress the power "[t]o regulate Commerce with foreign Nations, and among the several States, and with the Indian Tribes." Although the Clause thus speaks in terms of powers bestowed upon Con-

---

7 The term *intrastate* means within one state; the term *interstate* means between states. Often the courts use the term *commerce* to refer only to *interstate* commerce.

gress, the Court long has recognized that it also limits the power of the States to erect barriers against interstate trade. Maine's statute restricts interstate trade in the most direct manner possible, blocking all inward shipments of live baitfish at the State's border. Still . . . this fact alone does not render the law unconstitutional. The limitation imposed by the Commerce Clause on state regulation is by no means absolute, and the States retain authority under their general police powers to regulate matters of legitimate local concern, even though interstate commerce may be affected.

In determining whether a State has overstepped its role in regulating interstate commerce, this Court has distinguished between state statutes that burden interstate transactions only incidentally, and those that affirmatively discriminate against such transactions. While statutes in the first group violate the Commerce Clause only if the burdens they impose on interstate trade are clearly excessive in relation to the putative local benefits, statutes in the second group are subject to more demanding scrutiny. . . . [O]nce a state law is shown to discriminate against interstate commerce either on its face or in practical effect, the burden falls on the State to demonstrate both that the statute serves a legitimate local purpose, and that this purpose could not be served as well by available nondiscriminatory means.

The prosecution experts testified that live baitfish imported into the State posed two significant threats to Maine's unique and fragile fisheries. First, Maine's population of wild fish—including its own indigenous golden shiners—would be placed at risk by three types of parasites prevalent in out-of-state baitfish, but not common to wild fish in Maine. [Two of those types of parasites were found in Taylor's confiscated shipment.—Ed.] Second, non-native species inadvertently included in shipments of live baitfish could disturb Maine's aquatic ecology to an unpredictable extent by competing with native fish for food or habitat, by preying on native species, or by disrupting the environment in more subtle ways. The prosecution experts further testified that there was no satisfactory way to inspect shipments of live baitfish for parasites or commingled species. . . .

The Commerce Clause significantly limits the ability of States and localities to regulate or otherwise burden the flow of commerce, but it does not elevate free trade above all other values. As long as a state does not needlessly obstruct interstate trade or attempt to place itself in a position of economic isolation, it retains broad regulatory authority to protect the health and safety of its citizens and the integrity of its natural resources. The evidence in this case amply supports the District Court's findings that Maine's ban on the importation of live baitfish serves legitimate local purposes that could not adequately be served by available nondiscriminatory alternatives. This is not a case of arbitrary discrimination against interstate commerce; the record suggests that Maine has legitimate reasons, apart from their origin, to treat out-of-state baitfish differently. The judgment of the Court of Appeals setting aside appellee's conviction is therefore reversed.

**Justice Stevens, Dissenting**    There is something fishy about this case. Maine is the only State in the Union that blatantly discriminates against out-of-state baitfish. . . . Although golden shiners are already present and thriving in Maine (and, perhaps not coincidentally, the subject of a flourishing domestic industry), Maine excludes golden shiners grown and harvested (and, perhaps not coincidentally, sold) in other States. This kind of stark discrimination against out-of-state articles of commerce requires rigorous justification by the discriminating State. . . .

Significantly, the Court of Appeals, which is more familiar with Maine's natural resources . . . than we are, was concerned with the uniqueness of Maine's ban. That court felt, as I do, that Maine's unquestionable natural splendor notwithstanding, the State has not carried its substantial burden of proving why it cannot meet its environmental concerns in the same manner as other States. . . .

## Case Discussion Questions

1   What is the police power purpose of this state law?

2   Does the state law place an undue burden on interstate commerce? Does it discriminate against interstate commerce?

3   Does the state of Maine have an economic interest in keeping out-of-state baitfish out of the state? Is this simple economic protectionism?

### Federal Regulation under the Commerce Clause

While the states may regulate commerce under their police powers, the federal government may also regulate interstate commerce. The commerce clause seems to indicate that federal authority over commerce is **plenary;** that is, total and absolute. And today the commerce clause is interpreted to give Congress authority to regulate anything (1) **in commerce** or (2) that **affects commerce.**

In our society of rapid communication and transportation and economic interdependence, this means that there is little that Congress may not regulate. As the *Heart of Atlanta Motel* decision (p. 108) indicates, if Congress finds a connection with interstate commerce, it may impose regulations for any purpose, including nonbusiness or noncommercial reasons. And the relationship to interstate commerce may be quite remote and indirect as well.

But this was not always the case. At the beginning of the twentieth century, congressional power was restricted to matters that were "in" interstate commerce, and then only for commercial or business purposes. The story of the changes in the Court's interpretation of the commerce clause during the twentieth century illustrates the capability of the Supreme Court to change its mind, the impact of political events on the Court, and the impact of the Court's decisions on our nation.

**Restricted Powers—the Early Cases**   During the late 1800's Congress began to pass statutes designed to help the social welfare of the nation. Congress was concerned with abuses of the common man, such as child labor, sweatshops, protection of female workers, and what it saw as abuses of corporate power. Congress met these problems through the creation of regulatory agencies like the Interstate Commerce Commission, the passage of the antitrust statutes, and the passage of statutes that outlawed the interstate shipment of goods made with child labor. All of these statutes were passed based on the authority of the commerce clause.

It was not long before those statutes were challenged in the Supreme Court. In cases such as *Hammer v. Dagenhart,*[8] the Court took an extremely restricted view of these regulations. That case, for example, involved an attempt by Congress to control child labor by outlawing the shipment, in interstate commerce, of goods mined by people under the age of sixteen. The Court held that the federal regulation of commerce went too far, because its effect was to regulate something "purely local," namely manufacturing and mining. Justice Oliver Wendell Holmes dissented on the grounds that Congress has the power to regulate commerce, and that federal power is not lessened because it has an "indirect effect" on local manufacturing.

As a result of the *Hammer* decision and others like it, federal regulation of "purely local" matters, such as manufacturing, was impossible. Federal power over interstate commerce was restricted to the interstate transportation of goods, and no regulation could be imposed that had an impact on local matters, especially if the federal government regulated for some noncommercial purpose.

**Enlarged Federal Power over Commerce**   In 1937, as a direct result of the threat to the Court posed by President Roosevelt's court-packing plan (see p. 102), the Supreme

---

8 247 U.S. 251, 38 S. Ct. 529, 62 L. Ed. 1101 (1918).

Court shifted its position in dramatic fashion in the following landmark case that still determines the outlines of federal power today.

## National Labor Relations Board v. Jones & Laughlin Steel Co.
301 U.S. 1, 57 S. Ct. 615, 81 L. Ed. 893 (1937)

The National Labor Relations Act (see Chapter 16) outlawed a variety of "unfair labor practices" and gave authority to the National Labor Relations Board to determine whether an action by an employer was an unfair labor practice. The NLRB found that the respondent, Jones & Laughlin Steel, had engaged in such practices and had therefore violated the act. Those practices included discrimination against members of a union with regard to hiring and tenure, coercion and intimidation of employees in order to interfere with unionization efforts, and discharge of employees active in the union. The NLRB ordered Jones & Laughlin to cease and desist from such practices and to reinstate several employees with back pay. Jones & Laughlin refused to comply, and the NLRB petitioned the U.S. court of appeals to enforce its order. That court refused, holding that the order of the NLRB was beyond the constitutional grant of authority under the commerce clause. The NLRB appealed to the Supreme Court, which granted certiorari.

**Mr. Chief Justice Hughes Delivered the Opinion of the Court**   . . . [T]he respondent argues (1) that the Act is in reality a regulation of labor relations and not of interstate commerce; [and] (2) that the Act can have no application to the respondent's relations with its production employees because they are not subject to regulation by the federal government. . . .

[The Court described in detail the operations of Jones & Laughlin Steel, which operated mines in Michigan and Minnesota, operated coal mines in West Virginia, operated its own tugboats and towboats on interstate and intrastate waterways, manufactured steel in Pennsylvania, and owned and operated steel fabricating plants in New York.]

Summarizing these operations, the Labor Board concluded that the works in Pittsburgh and Aliquippa (Pennsylvania) "might be likened to the heart of a self-contained, highly integrated body. They draw in the raw materials from Michigan, Minnesota, West Virginia, Pennsylvania in part through arteries and by means controlled by the respondent: they transform the materials and then pump them out to all parts of the nation through the vast mechanism which the respondent has elaborated."

. . . Respondent says that whatever may be said of employees engaged in interstate commerce, the industrial relations and activities in the manufacturing department of respondent's enterprise are not subject to federal regulation. The argument rests upon the proposition that manufacturing in itself is not commerce. . . .

The Government . . . argued that these activities constitute a "stream" or "flow" of commerce, of which the Aliquippa manufacturing plant is the focal point, and that industrial strife at that point would cripple the entire movement. . . .

The fundamental principle is that the power to regulate commerce is the power to enact all appropriate legislation for its protection and advancement . . . to adopt measures to promote its growth and insure its safety . . . to foster, protect, control and restrain. . . . That power is plenary and may be exerted to protect interstate commerce, no matter what the source of the dangers which threaten it. . . . Although activities may be intrastate in character when separately considered, if they have such a close and substantial relation to interstate commerce that their control is essential or appropriate to protect that commerce from burdens and obstructions, Congress cannot be denied the power to exercise that control. . . . Undoubtedly the scope of this power must be considered in the light of our dual system of government and may not be extended so as to embrace effects upon interstate commerce so indirect and remote that to embrace them, in view of our complex society, would effectually obliterate the distinction between what is national and what is local and create a completely centralized government. . . . The question is necessarily one of degree.

The close and intimate effect which brings the subject within the reach of federal power may be due to activities in relation to productive industry although the industry when separately viewed is local. . . .

In view of respondent's far-flung activities, it is idle to say that the effect would be indirect or remote. It is obvious that it would be immediate and might be catastrophic. We are asked to shut our eyes to the plainest facts of national life and to deal with the question of direct and indirect effects in an intellectual vacuum. . . . When industries organize themselves on a national scale, making their relation to in-terstate commerce the dominant factor in their activities, how can it be maintained that their industrial labor relations constitute a forbidden field into which Congress may not enter when it is necessary to protect interstate commerce from the paralyzing consequences of industrial war?

Reversed.

## Case Discussion Questions

1    Under the earlier doctrine of *Hammer v. Dagenhart*, would the federal government be able to regulate labor in this way? Why or why not?

2    What kinds of activities may the federal government regulate after this case?

3    Has the Court gone too far? Is this what the framers intended by the commerce clause? How do you know?

**Contemporary Dimensions of the Commerce Power**    Following the *Jones & Laughlin Steel* decision, other decisions refined the federal power until it was clear that Congress could indeed regulate manufacturing and other local business so long as they "affected Commerce" in some way. In the years that followed, Congress came to rely extensively on the commerce clause as the source of much of its authority to enact a variety of regulatory measures. In 1964 the full scope of the commerce power became evident in the following decision:

# Heart of Atlanta Motel v. U.S.
379 U.S. 241, 85 S. Ct. 348, 13 L. Ed. 2d 258 (1964)

In 1964, Congress passed Title II of the Civil Rights Act. That statute provided that "places of public accommodation," including hotels, motels, restaurants, motion picture theatres, and sport arenas, could not discriminate against nor segregate patrons on the basis of race, color, religion, or national origin, if those establishments "affect commerce." The act specifically defined *affecting commerce* as serving or offering to serve interstate travelers, or obtaining food, gasoline, or other products that had moved "in commerce," or presenting films, performances, or athletic teams that had moved "in commerce."

The Heart of Atlanta Motel was a large metropolitan motel in downtown Atlanta, Georgia. The motel solicited patrons through national advertising and was located near interstate highways. Approximately 75% of its patrons came from out of state. Prior to the passage of the act, the motel had followed a practice of refusing to rent rooms to black travelers, and it stated that it intended to do so in the future. The motel filed an action for a declaratory judgment and for an injunction to restrain the enforcement of the act. A three-judge panel sustained the validity of the act and issued an injunction against the motel, restraining it from violating the act. The motel appealed.

**Mr. Justice Clark Delivered the Opinion of the Court** The appellant contends that Congress in passing this Act exceeded its power to regulate commerce under Article I, section 8, clause 3 of the Constitution of the United States. . . .

The appellees counter that the unavailability to Negroes of adequate accommodations interferes significantly with interstate travel, and that Congress, under the Commerce Clause, has power to remove such obstructions and restraints.

. . . [T]he record of [the] passage [of the Act] . . . . is replete with evidence of the burdens that discrimination by race or color places upon interstate commerce. . . . This testimony included the fact that our people have become increasingly mobile with millions of all races traveling from State to State; that Negroes in particular have been the subject of discrimination in transient accommodations, having to travel great distances to secure the same; that often they have been unable to obtain accommodations and have had to call upon friends to put them up overnight. . . . These exclusionary practices were found to be nationwide, the Under Secretary of Commerce testifying that there is "no question that this discrimination in the North still exists to a large degree" and in the West and Midwest as well. . . . This testimony indicated a qualitative as well as quantitative effect on interstate travel by Negroes.

The former was the obvious impairment of the Negro traveler's pleasure and convenience that resulted when he continually was uncertain of finding lodging. As for the latter, there was evidence that this uncertainty stemming from racial discrimination had the effect of discouraging travel on the part of a substantial portion of the Negro community. . . .

The power of Congress to deal with these obstructions depends on the meaning of the Commerce Clause. Its meaning was first enunciated 140 years ago by the great Chief Justice John Marshall in *Gibbons v. Ogden*. . . . In short, the determinative test of the exercise of power by the Congress under the Commerce Clause is simply whether the activity sought to be regulated is "commerce which concerns more than one state" and has a real and substantial relation to the national interest. . . .

The same interest in protecting interstate commerce which led Congress to deal with segregation in interstate carriers and the white slave traffic has prompted it to extend the exercise of its power to gambling . . . to criminal enterprises . . . to deceptive practices in the sale of products . . . to fraudulent security transactions . . . to misbranding of drugs . . . to wages and hours . . . to members of labor unions . . . to crop control . . . to discrimination against shippers . . . to the protection of small business from injurious price cutting . . . to resale price maintenance . . . to professional football . . . and to racial discrimination by owners and managers of terminal restaurants. . . .

That Congress was legislating against moral wrongs in many of these areas rendered its enactments no less valid. In framing Title II of this Act Congress was also dealing with what it considered a moral problem. But that fact does not detract from the overwhelming evidence of the disruptive effect that racial discrimination has had on commercial intercourse. It was this burden which empowered Congress to enact appropriate legislation, and given this basis for the exercise of its power, Congress was not restricted by the fact that the particular obstruction to interstate commerce with which it was dealing was also deemed a moral and social wrong.

It is said that the operation of the motel here is of a purely local character. But, assuming this to be true, "if it is interstate commerce that feels the pinch, it does not matter how local the operation that applies the squeeze." . . . Thus the power of Congress to promote interstate commerce also includes the power to regulate the local incidents thereof, including local activities in both the States of origin and destination, which might have a substantial and harmful effect upon that commerce. One need only examine the evidence which we have discussed above to see that Congress may—as it has—prohibit racial discrimination by motels serving travelers, however "local" their operations may appear.

We, therefore, conclude that the action of the Congress in the adoption of the Act as applied here to a motel which concededly serves interstate travelers is within the power granted it by the Commerce Clause of the Constitution, as interpreted by this Court for 140 years. It may be argued that Congress could have pursued other methods to eliminate the obstructions it found in interstate commerce caused by racial discrimination. But this is a matter of policy that rests entirely with the Congress and not with the courts. How obstructions in commerce may be removed—what means are to be employed—is within the sound and exclusive discretion of the Congress. It is subject only to one caveat—that the means chosen by it must be reasonably adapted to the end permitted by the Constitution. We cannot say that its choice here was not so adapted. The Constitution requires no more.

Affirmed.

## Case Discussion Questions

1    For what purposes may Congress regulate interstate commerce?
2    Why isn't this motel "purely local"? How does it affect interstate commerce?
3    How substantial must the effect on interstate commerce be before the federal government may regulate?

It seems clear that the federal power over commerce allows congressional regulation of much of American life. The issue of whether regulation is better handled by the states or by the federal government is a matter of policy for Congress, rather than a constitutional issue for the Supreme Court. The clause is really "the direct source of the most important powers which the Federal Government exercises in time of peace."

## PRO AND CON

# Should the Constitution be interpreted to reflect the changing needs of society?

One of the deepest arguments in constitutional law is whether the Constitution should be interpreted to reflect the changing needs of society, or "strictly" to conform to the intent of the framers of the document. The question is just how "flexible" the Constitution should be.

This debate surfaced again in 1987 during Senate confirmation hearings on the nomination of Judge Robert Bork to the U.S. Supreme Court. The Senate rejected the nomination, in part because Judge Bork adopted a very strict construction of the Constitution.

**Pro**    The Constitution must be interpreted to meet the changing demands of society. The Constitution was intentionally written in broad and sweeping terms, such as "due process," "commerce among the several states," and "equal protection" to give future lawmakers and judges flexibility to adapt the document to changes in society, the economy, and technology. While the founding fathers could not anticipate changes such as computers, air travel, television, and the international economy, they did anticipate *change* and provided for it through the broad language of the Constitution.

To speak of the "intent of the framers" is, except in the broadest sense, to speak nonsense. We know little of the debates of the Convention, and it is rarely possible to learn the "intent" of any large body. In all likelihood, there were thirty-nine separate intentions, one for each of the people signing the document. Even Jefferson, Marshall, Hamilton, and Madison disagreed among themselves over the meaning of the document. It was part of the genius of these men that they gave us a document that could endure change.

The real purpose of "strict construction" is to resist change. It is to tie the Constitution to the status quo, no matter what changes fate has in store for us. The Constitution will become irrelevant if it stands still and society continues to change.

A constitution created for a rural, preindustrial

frontier state cannot work for an urban, industrial world leader. The Constitution, born in a different era, must have the durability and flexibility to grow and encompass new situations and meet new needs. It guides by general principle, not by specific beliefs of individual eighteenth-century men.

**Con**   The only guide we have to the true meaning of the words of the Constitution is the intent of the framers, the men who wrote the document. The founding fathers even put a process for change in the document, in the form of the amendment process. Nowhere does the document provide for any other method of change, and especially none through the judicial process.

The power to interpret the Constitution is the power to determine meaning, not change the content. If a constitutional provision is plain, the court must determine meaning solely from the words themselves. If the words are unclear, it is the Court's duty to determine the meaning of the framers and the history of the Constitution.

When activists say the Constitution is a living document, they are really saying the Constitution has nothing to say to us and the judges are free to "make law." The Constitution must guide judicial decisions. Without that guide, we are giving judges an authority that we reserve for legislators.

While history may provide us with scant records of the Constitutional Convention, we must look to them, to the *Federalist Papers*, and to the meaning of words in the eighteenth century for guidance. If we do not, there is no fixed point of reference for the Constitution. If that is the case, unelected judges will be free to impose their own moral judgments and political beliefs on the rest of us.

## Roundtable Discussion

1   What sources would you look to to determine the intent of the framers of the Constitution? Are those sources reliable?

2   Amending the Constitution is *very* difficult. Does it mean anything that the Constitution has only been amended 26 times in 200 years?

3   How should judges use the power of judicial review? Does it make any sense to rely on the intent of the framers? If judges do not rely on the intent of the framers, what should they look to?

## PROTECTION OF ECONOMIC FREEDOM

The remaining question is whether the Constitution imposes limits on economic regulation, either by the federal government or by the states. There are only three provisions that even remotely touch on the area of economic regulation: (1) the **contracts clause** of article I, section 10; and the (2) **due process** and (3) **equal protection** clauses, both of which are found in the fourteenth amendment.

### The Contracts Clause

Article I, section 10 of the Constitution provides that "No State shall . . . pass any . . . Law impairing the Obligation of Contracts." Early interpretations of the clause seemed to promise that the clause would be interpreted broadly to prevent state regulation of business and commercial affairs. During the nineteenth century, the clause was used to invalidate many state business regulations.

But the states also have broad police powers, as indicated previously, to regulate for the purposes of health, welfare, safety, and morals. At the end of the nineteenth century the states began to use that right to regulate a wide variety of business-related activities. The Supreme Court held fairly early that the right of the state to regulate was superior to the contracts clause. It became clear that regulations which were "in the public interest" would be permitted, even though they may affect contractual obligations in some way.

The contracts clause had two other significant problems. First, the clause only prohibited *state* laws that impaired contractual relations and, therefore, had no impact on federal laws. Second, the clause related only to *contracts*, a word that was given a restrictive definition quite early. As a result, business activities that did not involve legal contracts were unaffected.

Recently the Supreme Court held that the contracts clause may be used to invalidate a state law regulating contracts if (1) the state law substantially impairs contractual relationships or (2) the state has no "significant and legitimate public purpose" behind the regulation. A significant and legitimate public purpose is defined as remedying a broad and general social or economic purpose.[9] As a result of the difficulties inherent in the clause, most challenges of government regulations were diverted to other areas, such as substantive due process or economic equal protection.

## Substantive Economic Due Process

The due process clause was added to the Constitution with the fourteenth amendment in 1868 and specified that no state shall "deprive any person of life, liberty or property, without due process of law." The first Supreme Court decision to deal with the application of the due process clause to business regulation came in 1873.[10] That involved a Louisiana statute aimed at cleaning up the Mississippi River and controlling cholera, which was caused by pollution coming from the slaughterhouses. The state had effectively created a monopoly in one large slaughterhouse and had made any other meat-processing facilities illegal. The law deprived the owners of their livelihood in the hopes of controlling pollution at that one location. The Supreme Court ruled that the law did not violate the due process rights of the other owners, however.

But in the next twenty years the membership of the Court changed, and in 1897 the Supreme Court ruled that state regulation of contracts could violate the doctrine of **substantive economic due process.** One of the principal cases establishing the doctrine of economic due process was *Lochner v. New York.*[11] That case involved a New York statute that prohibited employers from allowing employees to work more than sixty hours per week. Clearly there were police power purposes for the law, but the Court held that the real purpose was to limit the contract between employer and employee and that such limits were a deprivation of "life, liberty or property without due process of law." Again, Justice Holmes disagreed in one of his most famous dissents.

The *Lochner* analysis reached its apex in a 1923 decision, *Adkins v. Children's Hospital,*[12] which struck down a federal minimum wage law as "a naked, arbitrary exercise of the legislative power." The combination of the restricted view of the federal power over commerce and the limitations on state police powers established by the doctrine of economic due process made it virtually impossible to regulate labor or economic matters at either level.

But again the membership of the Court was to change, and the pressures for public

---

9 *Energy Reserves Group, Inc. v. Kansas Power and Light Company,* 459 U.S. 400, 103 S. Ct. 697, 74 L. Ed. 2d 569 (1983).

10 *Butcher's Benevolent Association v. Crescent City Livestock Landing & Slaughterhouse Co.* (The Slaughterhouse Cases), 83 U.S. 36, 21 L. Ed. 394 (1873).

11 198 U.S. 5, 25 S. Ct. 539, 49 L. Ed. 937 (1905).

12 261 U.S. 525, 43 S. Ct. 394 (1923).

regulation of wages and hours took their toll on the Court. Finally, in 1937, following the announcement of the court-packing plan (see p. 102), the doctrine of economic due process was to fall in the following decision.

# West Coast Hotel v. Parrish
300 U.S. 379, 57 S. Ct. 578, 81 L. Ed. 703 (1937)

A 1913 Washington state statute established a minimum wage for women and minors. The plaintiff was not paid the minimum wage and brought suit to recover the difference between that wage and her actual salary. The trial court ruled against her on the basis of *Lochner* and *Adkins v. Children's Hospital*, and she appealed to the state supreme court. That court ruled in her favor, and the defendant appealed to the U.S. Supreme Court.

**Mr. Chief Justice Hughes Delivered the Opinion of the Court**    The principle which must control our decision is not in doubt. The constitutional provision invoked is the due process clause of the Fourteenth Amendment. . . . In each case the violation alleged by those attacking minimum wage regulation for women is deprivation of freedom of contract. What is this freedom? The Constitution does not speak of freedom of contract. It speaks of liberty and prohibits the deprivation of liberty without due process of law. In prohibiting that deprivation, the Constitution does not recognize an absolute and uncontrollable liberty. Liberty in each of its phases has its history and connotation. But the liberty safeguarded is liberty in a social organization which requires the protection of law against the evils which menace the health, safety, morals, and welfare of the people. Liberty under the Constitution is thus necessarily subject to the restraints of due process, and regulation which is reasonable in relation to its subject and is adopted in the interests of the community is due process. . . .

The power under the Constitution to restrict freedom of contract has had many illustrations. That it may be exercised in the public interest with respect to contracts between employer and employee is undeniable. [The Court discussed a variety of other minimum wage–maximum hours statutes that had been sustained and other regulations of the contract between employer and employee.]

In dealing with the relation of employer and employed, the Legislature has necessarily a wide field of discretion in order that there may be suitable protection of health and safety, and that peace and good order may be promoted through regulations designed to insure wholesome conditions of work and freedom from oppression. . . .

We think that the views thus expressed are sound and that the decision in the *Adkins* Case was a departure from the true application of the principles governing the regulation by the state of the relation of employer and employed. . . .

There is an additional and compelling consideration which recent economic experience has brought into a strong light. The exploitation of a class of workers who are in an unequal position with respect to bargaining power and thus relatively defenseless against the denial of a living wage is not only detrimental to their health and well being but casts a direct burden for their support upon the community. What these workers lose in wages the taxpayers are called upon to pay. . . .

Our conclusion is that the case of *Adkins v. Children's Hospital* . . . should be, and it is, overruled. The judgment of the Supreme Court of the State of Washington is affirmed.

## Case Discussion Questions

1    What is the hotel's argument? How has the state deprived the hotel of "due process" by this law?

2    Does this law have a valid police power purpose? What is it?

3    Why did the Court overrule the *Adkins* case?

### Economic Equal Protection

The fourteenth amendment also contains the famous *equal protection clause*, which guarantees the "equal protection of the laws" to all persons. Generally speaking, the equal protection clause prohibits a state from making unlawful classifications. It has been used to prohibit classifications based on race, sex, religion, and a variety of other criteria (see Chapters 5 and 18).

Every statute classifies in some way. A tax statute classifies between those who pay the tax and those who do not. Even a statute against murder classifies us into "murderers" and "nonmurderers" and discriminates against the murderers. Obviously, the equal protection clause cannot be read to prohibit *all* classification. The tough question is, What kind of classifications are prohibited by that amendment?

As a general rule, classification schemes in statutes are permitted if the legislature that made the law had a **rational basis** for making the classification. That is, if the legislature had a good reason for classifying as it did, the statute will stand. There are some important exceptions, such as classifications that deal with *fundamental liberties* (liberties protected by the Bill of Rights) and certain *suspect classes* (such as race or sex) in which a much stricter test, known as **strict scrutiny,** is used.

The application of equal protection principles to economic regulation came late and did not last long. Equal protection was first applied to economic matters in 1957 in the case of *Morey v. Doud*.[13] That case involved an Illinois statute that prohibited currency exchanges from selling money orders unless the money orders were issued by the American Express Company. Other money order issuers challenged the law on the grounds that it discriminated in favor of American Express, and the Supreme Court agreed, striking down the law.

The doctrine of economic equal protection under the *Morey* decision did not stand for long. The decision seemed to indicate that a state could not discriminate against businesses under almost any circumstances. But, clearly, there are circumstances where the legislature has a *rational basis* for favoring one business over another. In 1976 the Supreme Court considered a case that, on its face, was a flagrant violation of equal protection principles under the rule of *Morey v. Doud*.

---

## City of New Orleans v. Dukes
427 U.S. 297, 96 S. Ct. 2513, 49 L. Ed. 2d 51 (1976)

During the early 1970s there had been a tremendous rise in the number of pushcart food vendors in the French Quarter of New Orleans. In an effort to preserve the atmosphere of the French Quarter, the city passed an ordinance prohibiting all pushcarts except those that had been in operation more than eight years. Dukes had operated such a pushcart for two years, and to prevent elimination of his business, he filed suit to challenge the constitutionality of the ordinance. He relied expressly on *Morey v. Doud* in his case. The Court of Appeals had held the law unconstitutional under that case, and the city appealed.

---

13 354 U.S. 457, 77 S. Ct. 1344, 1 L. Ed. 2d 1485 (1957).

***Per Curiam***[14]    When local economic regulation is challenged solely as violating the Equal Protection Clause, this Court consistently defers to legislative determinations as to the desirability of particular statutory discriminations. . . . Unless a classification trammels fundamental personal rights or suspect classifications such as race, religion, or alienage, our decisions presume the constitutionality of the statutory discriminations and require only that the classification challenged be rationally related to a legitimate state interest. States are accorded wide latitude in the regulation of their local economies under their police powers, and rational distinctions may be made with substantially less than mathematical exactitude. Legislatures may implement their program step by step . . . in such economic areas, adopting regulations that only partially ameliorate a perceived evil and deferring complete elimination of the evil to future regulations. . . . In short, the judiciary may not sit as a superlegislature to judge the wisdom or desirability of legislative policy determinations made in areas that neither affect fundamental rights nor proceed along suspect lines. . . . In the local economic sphere, it is only the invidious discrimination, the wholly arbitrary act, which cannot stand consistently with the Fourteenth Amendment. . . .

The Court of Appeals held in this case, however, that the "grandfather provision" failed even the rationality test. We disagree. The city's classification rationally furthers the purpose which the . . . city had identified as its objective . . . that is, as a means "to preserve the appearance and custom valued by the Quarter's residents and attractive to tourists." . . . The legitimacy of that objective is obvious. The City Council plainly could further that objective by making the reasoned judgment that street peddlers and hawkers tend to interfere with the charm and beauty of a historic area and disturb tourists and disrupt their enjoyment of that charm and beauty, and that such

vendors in the Vieux Carre, the heart of the city's tourist industry, might thus have a deleterious effect on the economy of the city. They therefore determined that to ensure the economic vitality of that area, such businesses should be substantially curtailed in the Vieux Carre, if not totally banned.

Nevertheless, relying on *Morey v. Doud* . . . as its "chief guide," the Court of Appeals held that even though the exemption of the . . . vendors was rationally related to legitimate city interests on the basis of facts extant when the ordinance was amended, the "grandfather clause" still could not stand because "the hypothesis that a present eight year veteran of the pushcart hot dog market in the Vieux Carre will continue to operate in a manner more consistent with the traditions of the Quarter than would any other operator is without foundation." . . . Actually, the reliance on the statute's potential irrationality in *Morey v. Doud* . . . was a needlessly intrusive judicial infringement on the State's legislative powers, and we have concluded that the equal protection analysis employed in that opinion should no longer be followed. *Morey* was the only case in the last half century to invalidate a wholly economic regulation solely on equal protection grounds, and we are now satisfied that the decision was erroneous. *Morey* is . . . essentially indistinguishable from this case, but the decision so far departs from proper equal protection analysis in cases of exclusively economic regulation that it should be, and it is, overruled.

## Case Discussion Questions

1   Was there a valid police power purpose for the ordinance?
2   Did the city have a reasonable basis for classifying pushcart operators as it did? What reason existed for the classification?
3   Why did the Court overrule *Morey v. Doud?*

---

Although the *Dukes* case expressly overruled *Morey v. Doud*, the whole concept of economic equal protection is not dead. But decisions after *Dukes* make it clear that the courts will uphold a statute against such a claim if there is evidence that the classification scheme is debatable and has a *rational basis*. The simple fact that legislation is "wrong" is not enough.

---

14 Literally, "by the court." A unanimous opinion by the whole court without any judge's name on it.

## A NOTE ON POLITICS

Lawyers, like all professionals, tend to suffer from professional myopia. While legal restrictions found in the Constitution and the concept of judicial review furnish some extremely important checks on possible government overreaching, they are clearly not the only checks on government by any means. The formal checks supplied by our Constitution would be meaningless unless they were widely accepted by our society and our political system.

Many of the same provisions found in our Constitution, including our Bill of Rights, are found in the "charters" of many other countries, including some dictatorships and even some Communist nations. The difference appears to be that the American people and their politically elected representatives, for the most part, really believe what the Constitution says.

Law and politics are intimately intertwined. The final result of the political process is the creation of laws in the form of statutes passed by elected representatives. And that political process is itself in turn "controlled" by the legal process, both in the form of Constitutional limitations and the process of judicial review. Law and politics are in fact two sides of the same coin.

But our political system is based to a large extent on the concept of majority rule. The electoral process and the method of passing laws in our legislatures are both based on democratic principles, which is to say that whoever or whatever gets the most votes wins. Although that concept is essential to democratic government, it raises the specter of "the tyranny of the majority," in which the will of the many may run roughshod over the interests of the few.

To some degree the tyranny of the majority is controlled by American sensitivity to the rights of minorities and an innate sympathy for the underdog. But the founding fathers, and particularly the common people of the late eighteenth century, did not trust those informal restrictions. Instead, two years after the ratification of the Constitution, ten amendments were added to the document to act as bulwarks against the authority of the state and the authority of the majority. Those amendments, known as the Bill of Rights, are the subject of the next chapter.

## SUMMARY AND CONCLUSIONS

Although government has the power to act within the guidelines supplied by the Constitution, there are limits on the exercise of government power. Those limits are supplied, in the first instance, by the grant of power itself, since government can only act within the grant of power, whether express or implied.

One of the most important limits on government power is the principle of judicial review. Under that doctrine, which was "found" by John Marshall in the famous *Marbury* decision, the Supreme Court has the authority to review and hold unconstitutional the acts of other branches of government or the states.

What began as an attempt to provide a uniform system of regulation over commerce has become the source of much of the federal authority to regulate commerce. On one hand, the commerce clause acts to restrict state authority to discriminate against or unduly burden interstate commerce. On the other hand, the clause has provided the authority for the federal government's authority to regulate such different areas as civil rights, labor, and antitrust.

The concept of economic freedom must be examined within the context of the Constitution itself. Generally the courts have taken a "restraintist," or balancing-of-interests, approach to economic freedom and government regulation of business. This is opposed to the usual "activist" position as taken in the area of civil liberties, an area to be examined in the next chapter.

## REVIEW QUESTIONS

1  What is *judicial review?* Where did it come from? Should judges have the right of judicial review? Could each branch of government be the sole judge of the constitutionality of its own actions?

2  What are the granted powers? How do they differ from the implied powers? Why is the concept of granted powers so important to the American system?

3  Explain the difference between *interstate* and *intrastate* commerce. What authority does the federal government have over each? What authority do the states have over each? Where does that authority come from?

4  Was Roosevelt's court-packing plan legal? Ethical? Why or why not? Do you think the framers of the Constitution intended this result?

5  Under the preemption doctrine and the federal power over commerce, taken together, can you think of anything which Congress could not regulate today?

6  An Arizona statute made it illegal to operate a train consisting of more than fourteen passenger cars or seventy freight cars in the state for safety reasons. The practical effect of the statute was that trains entering Arizona had to drop off cars at the border, to be picked up by other trains not over the limit. Is the statute constitutional? [*Southern Pacific Co. v. Arizona*, 325 U.S. 761, 65 S. Ct. 1515, 89 L. Ed. 1915 (1945).]

7  All states require some kind of mud flaps on trucks, but Illinois decided that "contour" mud flaps would provide more safety benefits. Those mud flaps were legal in all other states except Arkansas, which required "straight" mud flaps. The result was that any truck traveling through both Arkansas and Illinois would have to change mud flaps during the trip. Is the Illinois statute constitutional? [*Bibb v. Navajo Freight Lines, Inc.*, 359 U.S. 520, 79 S. Ct. 962, 3 L. Ed. 2d 1003 (1959)].

8  The City of Madison, Wisconsin, passed an ordinance that required all milk sold within the city to be processed within five miles of the center of Madison so that local inspectors could inspect the milk. The effect was that no milk processed in other states could ever be sold in Madison. Is the ordinance constitutional? [*Dean Milk Co. v. Madison*, 340 U.S. 349, 71 S. Ct. 295, 95 L. Ed. 329 (1951)].

9  The Federal Consumer Protection Act makes extortionate debt collection practices a federal crime. Perez loaned money to a local butcher and threatened the butcher and his family when the money was not paid back. Perez was prosecuted under the federal law, and he claimed that the transaction was entirely "local" and therefore beyond federal jurisdiction. What result would you expect and why? [*Perez v. U.S.*, 402 U.S. 146, 91 S. Ct. 1357, 28 L. Ed. 2d 686 (1971)].

10  Ollie's Barbeque, a local restaurant in Birmingham, Alabama, refused to serve blacks. There was evidence that few, if any, interstate travelers ate at Ollie's, that Ollie's did not advertise at all, and that in fact all of Ollie's supplies were purchased from local distributors. Some of those distributors received their supplies from out of state, however. (a) Is Ollie's outside the scope of the Civil Rights Act of 1964? (b) Is the application of that act to Ollie's unconstitutional? Why or why not? [*Katzenbach v. McClung*, 379 U.S. 294, 85 S. Ct. 377, 13 L. Ed. 2d 290 (1964)].

# CHAPTER 5

# The Bill of Rights

*The right to be let alone is the underlying principle of the Constitution's Bill of Rights.*

ERWIN N. GRISWOLD, DEAN, HARVARD LAW
SCHOOL, ADDRESS, 1960

The American **Bill of Rights,** consisting of the first ten amendments to the Constitution, is one of the most remarkable legal and political documents in the world. First, it is a statement of things the government may not do. The very idea that a government was in any way restricted in its actions was a revolutionary concept in a time when most nations were ruled by absolute monarchs. Second, the Bill of Rights is written in language that is both meaningful and vague. The amendments impose strict limits on government action, but in language flexible enough to adapt to changing social, economic, and political circumstances.

Third, it might be argued that the relatively few words of the first ten amendments contain *all* of the essential conditions for political liberty and democracy. The first amendment has been called the "heart of political democracy," and it is difficult to envision any other necessary conditions for democratic government aside from those guaranteed by the Bill of Rights. And, finally, Americans and American courts have taken the Bill of Rights seriously. Following the American lead, many other nations have adopted bills of rights, some copied almost verbatim from ours. But in many such nations those bills of rights lie forgotten and unused.

All this makes it even more curious that the original Constitution contained no bill of rights. Federalists had opposed a bill of rights during the Constitutional Convention on the grounds that by specifying certain rights, other unspecified rights might go unprotected. Alexander Hamilton also argued that a Bill of Rights might provide an argument that government had powers other than those expressly granted by the Constitution. Hamilton saw no need to prohibit actions that the government had no power to carry out in the first place, and he contended that prohibiting those things expressly provided an argument to those who claimed that the government had powers beyond those specifically granted.

But the nation was unwilling to accept a Constitution without a bill of rights. A grassroots cry arose across the nation demanding a list of protected freedoms. Some states refused to ratify the Constitution unless the framers promised to add a bill of rights, and other states made "conditional ratifications" providing that ratification would be revoked unless a bill of rights was added. It seemed that the bitter memories of British excesses were too fresh in the minds of the American people.

In the end the supporters of a bill of rights had their way. Prominent men throughout the nation made promises that if the Constitution was ratified, they would immediately move to add a bill of rights by amendment. The body of the Constitution was ratified in 1789, and on December 15, 1791, the Bill of Rights was formally amended to the Constitution.

## THE NATURE OF THE BILL OF RIGHTS

At the outset we are faced with a problem of definition. Most simple definitions of the Bill of Rights include only the first ten amendments. But if we mean by the term *Bill of Rights* all those parts of the Constitution that protect individual liberty from governmental interference, we must include much more. One observer[1] has counted sixty-three separate, express guarantees of individual freedom in the Constitution. These include several in the body of the Constitution, such as the contracts and supremacy clauses; all of the specific guarantees in the first ten amendments; and all of the guarantees in later amendments. Many reasonable people argue that the term *Bill of Rights* should include at least the thirteenth, fourteenth, and fifteenth amendments, with their prohibitions of slavery, protection of voting rights, and the equal protection and due process clauses. We use the latter definition in this chapter (see Figure 5.1).

It is impossible to do justice to the Bill of Rights in the space of a single chapter of a textbook. Each amendment, and in fact each phrase in each amendment, has been subjected to close judicial interpretation and development. Rather than presenting a superficial survey of all of the amendments, this chapter considers a few of the major provisions in some depth.

The choice of provisions to discuss is somewhat arbitrary. This chapter discusses the first amendment in some detail, principally because it is so important to our political-legal system and because it has substantial relevance to business through its **commercial speech** doctrine. We will also consider the criminal procedure amendments—the fourth, fifth, and sixth amendments—primarily because every educated person should have some knowledge of those provisions and because they also have a relevance to business when a firm is subjected to administrative or criminal investigation. The chapter also considers two fourteenth amendment provisions, the due process and equal protection clauses, because of their overriding significance to many areas discussed later in the text. Finally, we consider the right of privacy and the possibility that other rights exist beyond those expressly granted by the Constitution.

The basic notion behind the Bill of Rights is that the people are the source of government and not the other way around. The rights specified in the Bill of Rights are not *granted* by government, because they are not government's to grant. All rights are *retained* by the people, except those that are expressly granted to government under the enumerated and implied powers. The Bill of Rights, therefore, is merely a formal statement that government has no power to regulate in certain areas or in certain ways. But that does not mean that other rights, ones not expressed in the Constitution, are not also retained by the people.

---

1 Irving Brant, *The Bill of Rights* (Indianapolis: Bobbs-Merrill, 1965), pp. 3–15.

### Amendment I (1791)

Congress shall make no law respecting an establishment of religion, or prohibiting the free exercise thereof; or abridging the freedom of speech, or of the press; or the right of the people peaceably to assemble, and to petition the Government for a redress of grievances.

### Amendment II (1791)

A well regulated Militia, being necessary to the security of a free State, the right of the people to keep and bear Arms, shall not be infringed.

### Amendment III (1791)

No soldier shall, in time of peace be quartered in any house, without the consent of the Owner, nor in time of war, but in a manner to be prescribed by law.

### Amendment IV (1791)

The right of the people to be secure in their persons, houses, papers, and effects, against unreasonable searches and seizures, shall not be violated, and no Warrants shall issue, but upon probable cause, supported by Oath or affirmation, and particularly describing the place to be searched, and the persons or things to be seized.

### Amendment V (1791)

No person shall be held to answer for a capital, or otherwise infamous crime, unless on a presentment or indictment of a Grand Jury, except in cases arising in the land or naval forces, or in the Militia, when in actual service in time of War or public danger; nor shall any person be subject for the same offence to be twice put in jeopardy of life or limb; nor shall be compelled in any criminal case to be a witness against himself, nor be deprived of life, liberty or property, without due process of law; nor shall private property be taken for public use, without just compensation.

### Amendment VI (1791)

In all criminal prosecutions, the accused shall enjoy the right to a speedy and public trial, by an impartial jury of the State and district wherein the crime shall have been committed, which district shall have been previously ascertained by law, and to be informed of the nature and cause of the accusation; to be confronted with the witnesses against him; to have compulsory process for obtaining witnesses in his favor, and to have the Assistance of Counsel for his defense.

### Amendment VII (1791)

In Suits at common law, where the value in controversy shall exceed twenty dollars, the right of trial by jury shall be preserved, and no fact tried by jury, shall be otherwise reexamined in any Court of the United States, than according to the rules of the common law.

### Amendment VIII (1791)

Excessive bail shall not be required, nor excessive fines imposed, nor cruel and unusual punishments inflicted.

### Amendment IX (1791)

The enumeration in the Constitution, of certain rights, shall not be construed to deny or disparage others retained by the people.

### Amendment X (1791)

The powers not delegated to the United States by the Constitution, nor prohibited by it to the States, are reserved to the States respectively, or to the people.

. . .

FIGURE 5.1   The Bill of Rights

**Amendment XIV** (1868)

Section 1. All persons born or naturalized in the United States, and subject to the jurisdiction thereof, are citizens of the United States and of the State wherein they reside. No State shall make or enforce any law which shall abridge the privileges or immunities of citizens of the United States; nor shall any State deprive any person of life, liberty or property, without due process of law; nor deny to any person within its jurisdiction the equal protection of the laws.

FIGURE 5.1   Continued

### *Stare Decisis* and Interpretation Revisited

Like any other statute or constitutional provision, the provisions of the Bill of Rights may be and must be interpreted by the courts. Those interpretations then, of course, become binding precedent for future court decisions.

Two issues are especially important in interpretations of the Bill of Rights. The first is that there is a special need for interpretation in matters relating to the Bill of Rights, because the language used is so broad and vague. This does not mean that the amendments are without meaning, however. It is part of the special genius of the American Constitution that it provides both a direction and fixed rules for government and flexibility for future adaptions through judicial construction.

The second issue deals with the status of judicial decisions interpreting the Constitution. Those interpretations have the status of the document itself, and in effect become a part of the Constitution. Those constructions may be changed by later court decisions or by decisions of higher courts, but until that time they are constitutional law. Thus, the decisions of the U.S. Supreme Court, especially, have the same status as the Constitution itself and cannot be changed except by a later decision of the Supreme Court or by Constitutional amendment. A congressional act, for example, that purports to change the effect of a Supreme Court decision interpreting the Constitution would be of no effect.

Finally, before we begin consideration of some selected parts of the Bill of Rights, a word of warning to students seems appropriate: *Read the amendment first!* The precise language of the Constitution is extremely important to the interpretations by the Court, and a full understanding of the cases is impossible without a knowledge of what the document says. And, even if you are familiar with the Constitution, or think you are, there are likely to be some surprises.

### THE FIRST AMENDMENT

It has been argued that the first amendment is the heart of American political freedom. That amendment deals with freedom of speech, freedom of the press, freedom of religion, freedom of assembly, and the right to petition the government. The first amendment is sometimes said to protect *freedom of conscience* because it guarantees the rights of all persons to believe as they wish, to express those beliefs openly, and to attempt to use those beliefs to influence the government.

The first amendment is based on Thomas Jefferson's **marketplace theory** of public thought. That theory assumes that each person is intelligent and discerning and that all ideas should be permitted into the "marketplace of ideas." Since people are intelligent, they will "buy" the good and true ideas and reject the bad and false ones. But government cannot and should not intervene and tell us which ideas to accept or reject. Later theorists would point to totalitarian dictatorships, where thought control and book burning are the first orders of business.

### Freedom of Speech

The first amendment is written in absolute terms: "Congress shall make *no* law . . . abridging freedom of speech. . . . " The amendment on its face indicates that the federal government simply cannot pass a law dealing with speech under any circumstances.

But in at least four areas the courts have used a balancing-of-interests approach that permits Congress to limit the right of free speech when other social interests predominate. Those areas are (1) advocacy of crime or revolution; (2) commercial speech; (3) obscenity; and (4) **defamation, libel,** and **slander** (see p. 229). In all four instances the result has been restrictions on the right of individuals to speak. Our discussion will be restricted to the problems of advocacy of crime or revolution and commercial speech. The latter is quite relevant to many areas of business, and the former goes to the very heart of the first amendment.

*(handwritten margin note: (1) can't be VIOLENT)*

Underlying all of the discussion of limits on free speech is the *slippery slide* problem. That is, once one limit is placed on free speech, the next limit is that much easier to defend, until the clear language of the first amendment is swallowed up by exceptions. For example, once we permit an exception for defamation or obscenity, it becomes easier to impose other exceptions such as limits on commercial speech or even on political speech.

**Advocacy of Crime or Revolution**   Some of the most serious issues facing American democracy have arisen in the context of the "advocacy of crime or revolution" exception to the first amendment. It is clear that freedom of "political speech" is absolutely essential to democracy. Opposition political parties, spokespersons for minority positions, and the media must be free to criticize the government openly. Limits on the right to speak out are seen as the first step towards tyranny. But on the other hand, some people believe that criticism may sometimes go too far and damage the public good.

Although the courts are extremely sensitive to the need to protect political speech, limits on political speech have been imposed by the court if the speech presents a *clear and present danger* of crime or revolution. Later cases have required that lawless action must be imminent before speech may be limited.[2] For example, the government may not prohibit speech that merely advocates revolution unless actual violence is imminent. Other decisions have involved issues of what is "speech"—including cases of so-called *symbolic speech* of language on T-shirts, marches, and gestures—and of whether speech can be more severely limited in certain places at certain times. For example, it is permissible to restrict picketing and marches on army bases, in courtrooms, or near jail facilities.

2 *Brandenburg v. Ohio,* 395 U.S. 444, 89 S. Ct. 1827, 23 L. Ed. 2d 430 (1969).

**Commercial Speech: The First Amendment and Advertising**  A second major exception to the absolute terms of the first amendment's protection of freedom of speech is *commercial speech*. State and federal legislatures and administrative agencies often attempt to regulate the nature and content of advertising. Those regulations have been challenged on the basis of the first amendment. Like advocacy of crime or revolution, regulation of advertising has been subjected to a balancing test, weighing the right to advertise against the government's interest in regulating.

The general rule for many years seemed to be that commercial speech, principally advertising, had little to do with the purposes of the first amendment and therefore could be regulated without fear of challenge. As a result, many government agencies undertook to limit or prohibit various types of advertising. Examples of such restrictions include Federal Trade Commission regulations prohibiting "false and misleading" advertising; limits on advertising by certain trades or professions, such as attorneys and public utilities; and prohibition or limitation of certain forms of advertising, such as forbidding the use of outdoor signs.

Finally, in 1976, the Supreme Court provided some protection for advertising as a form of protected speech. The following decision expanded the protections of the first amendment to include typical commercial advertisements.

---

## *Virginia State Board of Pharmacy v. Virginia Citizens' Consumer Council*
425 U.S. 748, 96 S. Ct. 1817, 48 L. Ed. 2d 346 (1976)

*broadened the right of pharmacist to adv. the price of perscription drug*

A Virginia statute made it a crime for pharmacists to advertise prices on prescription drugs, on the basis that such advertising was unprofessional. The Virginia Citizens' Consumer Council brought suit to declare the statute unconstitutional under the first amendment. Their goal was to create price competition between pharmacists and thereby to lower prices for prescription drugs. The district court struck down the statute, and the state board appealed.

**Mr. Justice Blackmun Delivered the Opinion of the Court**  Our pharmacist does not wish to editorialize on any subject, cultural, philosophical, or political. He does not wish to report any particularly newsworthy fact, or to make generalized observation even about commercial matters. The "idea" he wishes to communicate is simply this: "I will sell you the X prescription drug at 'Y' price." Our question, then, is whether this communication is wholly outside the protection of the First Amendment.

We begin with several propositions that already are settled or beyond serious dispute. It is clear, for example, that speech does not lose its First Amendment protection because money is spent to project it, as in a paid advertisement. . . . Speech likewise is protected even though it is carried in a form that is "sold" for profit . . . and even though it may involve a solicitation to purchase or otherwise pay or contribute money. . . .

Our question is whether speech which does "no more than propose a commercial transaction," . . . is so removed from any "exposition of ideas," . . . and from "truth, science, morality, and arts in general, in its diffusion of liberal sentiments on the administration of Government" that it lacks all protection. Our answer is that it is not.

Focusing first on the individual parties to the transaction that is proposed in the commercial advertisement, we may assume that the advertiser's purpose is a purely economic one. That hardly disqualifies him for protection under the First Amendment. . . .

As to the particular consumer's interest in the free flow of commercial information, that interest may be as keen, if not keener by far, than his interest in the day's most urgent political debate. . . . Those whom the suppression of prescription drug price information hits the hardest are the poor, the sick, and particularly the aged. . . .

Generalizing, society also may have a strong interest in the free flow of commercial information. . . . Advertising, however tasteless and excessive it sometimes may seem, is nonetheless dissemination of information as to who is producing and selling what product, for what reason, and at what price. . . .

Arrayed against these substantial individual and societal interests are a number of justifications for the advertising ban. These have to do principally with maintaining a high degree of professionalism on the part of licensed pharmacists. . . . Price advertising, it is argued, will place in jeopardy the pharmacist's expertise and, with it, the customer's health. . . .

There is, of course, an alternative to this highly paternalistic approach. That alternative is to assume that this information is not in itself harmful, that people will perceive their own best interests if only they are well enough informed, and that the best means to that end is to open the channels of communication rather than to close them. . . . It is precisely this kind of choice, between the dangers of suppressing information, and the dangers of its misuse if it is freely available, that the First Amendment makes for us.

In concluding that commercial speech, like other varieties, is protected, we of course do not hold that it can never be regulated in any way. Some forms of commercial speech regulation are surely permissible. . . .

[The Court listed four permissible regulations of commercial speech: (1) the time, place, and manner of advertising; (2) misleading, deceptive, and false advertising; (3) advertising of transactions that are themselves illegal; and (4) broadcast media regulations.—Ed.]

What is at issue is whether a State may completely suppress the dissemination of concededly truthful information about entirely lawful activity, fearful of that information's effect upon its disseminators and its recipients. Reserving other questions, we conclude that the answer to this one is in the negative.

The judgment of the District Court is affirmed.

## Case Discussion Questions

1  Was there a valid police power purpose behind the state law?

2  Why had advertising gone unprotected by the first amendment prior to this time? How does advertising differ from other forms of speech?

3  Is this the kind of speech that the authors of the first amendment had in mind in 1791? Does that make a difference?

---

In 1980 the Supreme Court explained the doctrine of commercial speech even further and proposed a four-step analysis in all such cases. The case involved a state utility regulation that banned all advertising promoting the use of electricity by a public utility on the theory that a controlled monopoly need not spend its customers' money on advertising. The Court overturned the regulation on the grounds that the commission had not shown that a less extensive regulation would do as well. In the decision the Court said that the analysis of commercial speech should involve a specific type of analysis.

In commercial speech cases, then, a four-part analysis has developed. At the outset, we must determine whether the expression is protected by the First Amendment. For commercial speech to come with that provision, it at least must concern lawful activity and not be misleading. Next, we ask whether the asserted governmental interest is substantial. If both inquiries yield positive answers, we must determine whether the regulation directly advances

## PRO AND CON

# Should the first amendment prohibit *all* regulation of advertising?

**Pro**    The issue of advertising regulation usually arises in the context of some product that is considered unhealthy, dangerous, or contrary to community standards. For example, there has been some discussion of banning advertising of cigarettes, liquor, or "soft-porn" materials.

Clearly, it is permissible to ban certain products completely, such as dangerous drugs, explosives, or firearms. If a product cannot be sold, it is also clear that advertising may be forbidden. The problem arises when goods are not *forbidden*, but merely regulated.

There is no "bright line" between products. If we ban advertising of cigarettes, this provides an easy precedent for those who would ban advertising of other legal products that might be harmful, such as liquor, "soft porn," or even automobiles. The only clear division is between those products that are *legal* and those that are *illegal*. If the product is legal, advertising the product must be legal.

Whenever the government seeks to limit speech, it runs the risk of beginning a slide down the "slippery slope" to further regulation of all speech. Today's advertising regulation becomes another blow at the wedge in *all* speech. Will it end by saying that "we regulated advertising, so why can't we ban all *political* advertising?" If so, the whole purpose of the first amendment has been subverted. It is better not to draw lines between legal products at all, even if we have to accept some advertising that we consider bad.

**Con**    There is a major difference between "commercial" speech and the kind of speech that the first amendment was created to protect. The purpose of the first amendment is to protect *political* speech and criticism of the government. Without that protection, free democratic government cannot exist. But the same cannot be said for advertising of commercial products. That advertising serves no political purpose at all and consequently ought to be subject to regulation by government at all levels.

In fact, such regulation already takes place. Even *Virginia Pharmacists* permits regulation in several areas. The courts also permit "special rules" for advertising aimed at children. And no one suggests that we cannot regulate fraudulent, false, or misleading advertising under the guise of the first amendment.

In a large sense, protection of commercial speech is essentially the revival of "economic due process" under the guise of the first amendment. Both doctrines argue that there is something sacred about the free-market economy, when in fact the Constitution says nothing at all about economic freedom. Even Chief Justice William Rehnquist has argued in dissent in the "commercial speech" cases that recognition of commercial speech opens a Pandora's box that ought to remain closed.

Rehnquist's consistent point has been that commercial speech is different from political speech and should have no first amendment protection. The clear point of the first amendment is to protect *political* speech, not speech of every kind.

### Roundtable Discussion

1    Does it make any sense to appeal to the "intent of the framers" in this dispute?
2    Can you draft a constitutional amendment that would address the concerns of both sides?
3    Should we permit advertising of cigarettes? Liquor? Firearms? "Soft porn"? Should we permit advertising of those products *to children*? How would you control such advertising without violating the first amendment?

---

the governmental interest asserted, and whether it is not more extensive than is necessary to serve that interest.[3]

In 1986 the Supreme Court held that restrictions on advertising of *legal* activity (gambling, where gambling is legal) were not unconstitutional under the four-step analysis of *Central Hudson*. The Court held that since the legislature could have outlawed

---

3 *Central Hudson Gas & Electric Corp. v. Public Service Commission of New York*, 447 U.S. 557, 100 S. Ct. 2343, 65 L. Ed. 2d 341 (1980).

the activity entirely, it could also limit the activity by prohibiting advertising.[4] That decision has been criticized on the grounds that a state *could* outlaw a huge array of activities under its police power, and the decision therefore seems to undercut all protection of commercial speech.

### Freedom of the Press and the Problem of Prior Restraint

Closely tied to the right to speak is the right to publish. In a day of mass media, the right to speak out on issues would be of little value without the right to publish those views to the public. The framers viewed freedom of the press as an essential part of political freedom and the Jeffersonian marketplace concept of freedom of speech.

Like freedom of speech, the Constitutional guarantee of freedom of the press is phrased in absolute terms: "Congress shall make *no law* . . . abridging the freedom . . . of the press." But, as with freedom of speech, the Court has carved out various exceptions and limitations on that freedom through various balancing tests. First, the court has generally permitted regulation of the same four areas as in freedom of speech, namely, (1) advocacy of crime or revolution, (2) commercial speech, (3) obscenity, and (4) defamation.

**Prior restraint** is really another name for advance censorship, a problem that has troubled the courts for years. On one hand, if certain material is somehow bad for the public, as is arguably the case in obscenity, it would seem that public authorities should not be limited to penalties after the harmful material is published, but the government should be able to protect the public in advance. But granting that right to public authorities opens a whole Pandora's box of issues: Who is to make the decision? How is that decision to be made? What standards are to be applied?

The Court has imposed substantial limits on advance government censorship. Those limits (1) provided that the state must have the burden of proving the published material violates established guidelines, (2) afforded the publisher of the material the opportunity to have a judicial determination of the case at some point, and (3) required that the censor's decision be speedy. The courts have viewed any prior restraint very strictly and have found that prior restraint against publishing even classified material carries "a heavy presumption against its constitutionality."[5]

### Freedom of Religion

The third part of freedom of conscience is freedom of belief, generally referred to as freedom of religion. The first amendment makes *two* specific guarantees regarding freedom of religion: (1) that Congress may not make a law "respecting an establishment of religion" and (2) that Congress may not make a law "prohibiting the free exercise" of religion. The first guarantee generally prohibits state *support* of religious activities, and the second generally prohibits government *interference* with religious activities.

---

4 *Posadas de Puerto Rico Associates v. Tourism Company of Puerto Rico*, 478 U.S. 328, 106 S. Ct. 2968, 92 L. Ed. 2d. 266 (1986).
5 *New York Times v. U.S.* (the *Pentagon Papers* case), 403 U.S. 713, 91 S. Ct. 2140, 29 L. Ed. 2d 822 (1971).

**The Establishment Clause**    The first guarantee against the "establishment of religion" was aimed at preventing state religions and state discrimination against those who fail to adhere to the "official" religion. The problems inherent in that clause have provided many of the major constitutional controversies in our history, including the debate over school prayer and whether evolution and creationism can, must, or should be taught in the public schools.

In a business context, the debate has centered on laws that require businesses to close on Sundays, the day of rest for the majority of Americans—but by no means *all* Americans. The Court has held that Sunday closing laws are constitutional, because such laws have nonreligious purposes as well as religious ones.[6]

The courts have also ruled that other religious activities are a part of the American tradition and are therefore permissible. Examples include having "In God We Trust" on our coins, opening the congressional day with prayer, and allowing municipal maintenance of a manger scene during the Christmas season.

**The Free Exercise Clause**    The second part of freedom of religion is aimed at preventing government interference with belief. But that clause, like other parts of the first amendment, has been subjected to a balancing test. In a classic case involving door-to-door solicitations by Jehovah's Witnesses in a heavily Catholic neighborhood, the state arrested the solicitors for unlawful solicitation. Although the Court held the application of the law to the defendants violated their first amendment rights, it stated in the course of the decision that

> No one would contest the proposition that a State may not by statute wholly deny the right to preach or to disseminate religious views. . . . It is equally clear that a State may by general and nondiscriminatory legislation regulate the times, the places, and the manner of soliciting upon its streets, and of holding meetings thereon; and may in other respects safeguard the peace, good order and comfort of the community, without unconstitutionally invading the liberties protected. . . .[7]

As a result, states have constitutionally forbidden bigamous marriages, snake handling, and other practices that invade the "peace, good order, and comfort of the community."

In a business context, some of the most important cases deal with laws that have an adverse effect on individuals because of their religious beliefs. For example, unemployment compensation laws usually deny benefits to those who are fired because of misconduct. But that "misconduct" may be required by their religious faiths, and denial of benefits may result in a denial of the free exercise of their religious beliefs.

For example, the Court has ruled that benefits cannot be denied to individuals who refuse to work on their religious sabbath,[8] or to an individual who refuses to work on military equipment because of religiously based pacifist beliefs.[9] On the other hand, the

---

6 *McGowan v. Maryland*, 366 U.S. 420, 81 S. Ct. 1101, 6 L. Ed. 2d 393 (1961).

7 *Cantwell v. Connecticut*, 310 U.S. 296, 60 S. Ct. 900, 84 L. Ed. 1213 (1940).

8 *Sherbert v. Verner*, 374 U.S. 398, 83 S. Ct. 1790, 10 L. Ed. 2d 965 (1963); *Hobbie v. Unemployment Appeals Comm'n.*, 480 U.S. ———, 107 S. Ct. 1046, 94 L. Ed. 2d 190 (1987).

9 *Thomas v. Review Board*, 450 U.S. 707, 101 S. Ct. 1425, 67 L. Ed. 2d 624 (1981).

Court has held that benefits may be denied to persons who illegally used the drug *peyote* in connection with ceremonies of native American religions.[10]

## THE CRIMINAL PROCEDURE AMENDMENTS

The fourth, fifth, and sixth amendments have a great deal to say about the procedures that must be used in criminal arrests and trials in the United States. The founding fathers were quite sensitive about their individual rights in criminal proceedings, because many of the British excesses prior to the Revolution had involved abuses of criminal procedure. Blanket or "sweep" searches of entire cities, arrest without cause, and long-term secret confinement had been principal weapons of the British forces both before and during the American Revolution. It is little wonder that the public insisted upon protections in the Constitution against such government conduct.

On the other hand, a great deal of criticism has been levelled at the courts and the Constitution itself based upon so-called legal technicalities, which supposedly permit guilty persons to go free because of official misconduct. Those technicalities arose in large measure because of the Supreme Court's interpretation of those amendments during the 1950s and 1960s. Those broad interpretations have been limited somewhat by later interpretations by the Court.

### Business and the Criminal Law

Many business-related statutes and regulations are actually criminal statutes, such as the antitrust laws, portions of the Internal Revenue Code, and parts of the securities laws, to name a few. Investigations into possible violations of those laws involve the same searches, seizures, interrogations, arrests, and indictments as the investigation of any burglary. Similarly, the protections of the Bill of Rights, including protections against unreasonable searches and self-incrimination, apply with full force to searches of business records, OSHA inspections of business premises, and interrogation by IRS officials.

Businesspeople are also often victims of crime or may find themselves as witnesses in criminal proceedings, from shoplifting to securities frauds. Perhaps the only way to survive the frustrations of such proceedings and the delays inherent in the criminal law is to understand the reasons for the process.

### The Exclusionary Rule

Perhaps the largest issue overriding all of the criminal procedure amendments is how those amendments can be enforced. Clearly, persons injured by official misconduct may have the right to file civil lawsuits against public officials and government agencies that abuse their rights, but such lawsuits are often difficult to prove (especially if the plaintiff is a convicted felon) and provide little deterrent against official misconduct. Similarly, some official misconduct, such as some searches and seizures, are themselves violations of the criminal law (e.g., "burglary" and "theft"); and the police officers involved could be charged criminally. But realistically, that option often is not available

*attempt by gov't to deter illegal police conduct*

---

10 *Smith v. Employment Division,* —— U.S. ——, 108 S. Ct. 1444, —— L. Ed. 2d —— (1988).

PROFILE

# The Warren Court

In 1953, President Eisenhower appointed Earl Warren (1891–1974), a former prosecutor and Republican governor of California, as Chief Justice of the Supreme Court. Warren quickly brought together a coalition of activist Justices that was to last until his retirement in 1969. Those Justices included, at different times, Hugo Black, William J. Brennan, Tom C. Clark, William O. Douglas, Abe Fortas, Arthur Goldberg, Thurgood Marshall, and Potter Stewart.

This group of Justices, known collectively as the *Warren Court*, was responsible for some of the most far-reaching decisions of the Supreme Court. Their decisions ended school desegregation, required "one-man, one-vote" for state legislatures, outlawed state-required school prayer, "found" the right of privacy in the *Griswold* decision, and instituted many criminal procedure reforms, as in the *Miranda* and *Gideon* decisions discussed in this chapter.

A great deal of resistance developed to the decisions of the court, including calls for impeachment of Warren and other Justices by the Ku Klux Klan and other groups. Later decisions of the Court under Chief Justices Warren Burger and William Rehnquist limited the effect of some of the decisions, but their general effect was not undone and remains with us.

because of the close relationship that must exist between prosecutors and the police. Consequently, although the Constitution forbids certain types of police misconduct, there was simply no effective way to enforce those rights.

In 1914 the Supreme Court announced the **exclusionary rule** as an attempt to deter some illegal police conduct.[11] From 1914 to 1961, that rule applied only to the federal government. The exclusionary rule provides simply that evidence obtained in violation of any of the provisions of the Constitution cannot be introduced in a court proceeding. If evidence is seized or found in violation of the fourth amendment's prohibition of unreasonable searches and seizures, the fifth amendment's protection against self-incrimination, or the sixth amendment's protection of the right to counsel, such evidence cannot be introduced in a later trial.

In 1961 the exclusionary rule was applied to state court proceedings as well in the famous case of *Mapp v. Ohio.* As Mr. Justice Clark noted:

> There are those who say, as did justice (then judge) Cardozo, that under our constitutional exclusionary doctrine, "[t]he criminal is to go free because the constable has blundered."

---

11 *Weeks v. U.S.*, 232 U.S. 383, 34 S. Ct. 341, 58 L. Ed. 652 (1914).

No search warrant is needed
1    In a search incident to a lawful arrest.
2    To inventory contents of property lawfully in the hands of the police.
3    If items are in plain view, and the officer is in a place where he or she has a right to be.
4    If the suspect has consented to the search.
5    In a search for an individual if the police are in "hot pursuit."
6    In a search of a motor vehicle if the police have probable cause to search.
7    If the police have probable cause and the search is otherwise reasonable.
8    If an officer has a reasonable suspicion that an individual is armed and dangerous and the officer needs to stop and frisk the suspect for weapons.

FIGURE 5.2    Exceptions to the Warrant Requirement

. . . In some cases this will undoubtedly be the result. But . . . "there is another consideration—the imperative of judicial integrity." . . . The criminal goes free, if he must, but it is the law that sets him free. Nothing can destroy a government more quickly than its failure to observe its own laws, or worse, its disregard of the charter of its own existence.[12]

Over time the exclusionary rule developed a number of technical procedural rules dealing with the nature of search warrants, the scope of interrogation, and the times when a lawyer must be present. In the early 1980's the Supreme Court began to chip away at the rule with what it termed *common sense exceptions*. For example, the Court has said that if a search is conducted pursuant to a defective search warrant, the evidence seized may still be introduced if the officer was not responsible for the defect and acted in good faith.[13] Similarly, evidence found illegally may still be introduced if it would have been inevitably discovered through legal means.[14]

## The Fourth Amendment: Unreasonable Searches and Seizures

The fourth amendment prohibits all "*unreasonable* searches and seizures" and requires the existence of **probable cause** before a warrant may be issued. Search warrants are obtained by police officers or other officials on the basis of an affidavit showing that the officer has probable cause to believe that contraband, evidence of a crime, or even an individual is to be found on certain property. The warrant is issued by a judge who must make an independent judgment based on the evidence presented in the affidavit.

The fourth amendment does not require a search warrant in every case, however, and the courts have permitted warrantless searches in several situations (see Figure 5.2). But aside from those exceptions, a warrant is generally required in order to provide an independent judicial analysis of the facts of the case before a search is permitted.

From a business standpoint, perhaps the most important application of the search and seizure doctrines occurs in administrative inspections. A great number of adminis-

12 *Mapp v. Ohio*, 367 U.S. 643, 81 S. Ct. 1684, 6 L. Ed. 2d 1081 (1961).
13 *Massachusetts v. Sheppard*, 468 U.S. 981, 104 S. Ct. 3424, 82 L. Ed. 2d 737 (1984).
14 *Nix v. Williams*, 467 U.S. 431, 104 S. Ct. 2501, 81 L. Ed. 2d 3771 (1984).

trative agencies are required by law to conduct various types of inspections. Health department officials must inspect restaurants, building inspectors must inspect construction projects, environmental protection officers must inspect facilities that may pollute, and OSHA inspectors must inspect workplaces. The following case considers the limits on administrative inspections as searches under the fourth amendment.

# New York v. Burger

—— U.S. ——, 107 S. Ct. 2636, 96 L. Ed. 2d 601 (1987)

A New York state statute provided that businesses that dismantle automobiles must register with the state and permit an inspection of their premises, without a warrant, by any police officer. New York City police detectives appeared at Burger's junkyard and demanded to inspect the premises. During the inspection, the detectives found several automobiles and parts that were listed as stolen. Burger was charged with possession of stolen property. He moved to suppress the evidence on the grounds that the statute permitting a warrantless search was unconstitutional under the fourth amendment. The trial court denied the motion, and the Appellate Division affirmed; but the New York Court of Appeals (the highest court in the state, equivalent to the supreme court in other states) reversed. The state appealed to the U.S. Supreme Court.

**Justice Blackmun Delivered the Opinion of the Court** The Court long has recognized that the 4th Amendment's prohibition on unreasonable searches and seizures is applicable to commercial premises, as well as to private homes. An owner or operator of a business thus has an expectation of privacy in commercial property, which society is prepared to consider to be reasonable. This expectation exists not only with respect to traditional police searches conducted for the gathering of criminal evidence but also with respect to administrative inspections designed to enforce regulatory statutes. An expectation of privacy in commercial premises, however, is different from, and indeed less than, a similar expectation in an individual's home. This expectation is particularly attenuated in commercial property employed in "closely regulated" industries. . . .

Because the owner or operator of commercial premises in a "closely regulated" industry has a reduced expectation of privacy, the warrant and probable-cause requirements, which fulfill the traditional 4th Amendment standard of reasonableness for a government search, have lessened application in this context. Rather, we conclude that . . . where the privacy interests of the owner are weakened and the government interests in regulating particular businesses are concomitantly heightened, a warrantless inspection of commercial premises may well be reasonable within the meaning of the 4th Amendment.

This warrantless inspection, however, even in the context of a pervasively regulated business, will be deemed to be reasonable only so long as three criteria are met. First, there must be a "substantial" government interest. . . . [The Court gave as examples the need to regulate mining for health and safety reasons and the need to regulate firearms to prevent crime.—Ed.]

Second, the warrantless inspections must be necessary to further the regulatory scheme. For example, we [have] recognized that forcing mine inspectors to obtain a warrant before every inspection might alert mine owners or operators to the impending inspection. . . .

Finally, the statute's inspection program . . . must provide a constitutionally adequate substitute for a warrant. In other words, the regulatory statute must perform the two basic functions of a warrant: it must advise the owner . . . that the search is being made pursuant to the law and has a properly defined scope, and it must limit the discretion of the inspecting officers. [That is,] it must be carefully limited in time, place and scope. . . .

The New York regulatory scheme satisfies the three criteria. . . . First, that State has a substantial interest in regulating the vehicle-dismantling and automobile-junkyard industry because motor vehicle theft has increased in the State and because the problem of theft is associated with this industry. . . . Second, regulation of the vehicle-dismantling industry reasonably serves the State's substantial interest in eradicating automobile theft. It is well established that the theft problem can be addressed effectively by controlling the receiver of, or market in, stolen property. . . . Third, [the statute] provides a "constitutionally adequate substitute for a warrant." The statute informs the operator . . . that inspections will be made on a regular basis. . . . [The statute] also sets forth the scope of the inspection and, accordingly, places the operator on notice as to how to comply with the statute. . . . Finally, the "time, place and scope" of the inspection is limited, to place appropriate restraints upon the discretion of the inspecting officers. The officers are allowed to conduct an inspection only "during regular and usual business hours." And the permissible scope of these searches is narrowly defined: the inspectors may examine the records, as well as "any vehicles or parts of vehicles which are subject to the record keeping requirements of this [statute]. . . ."

[Reversed.]

**Justice Brennan, with Whom Justice Marshall . . . and Justice O'Connor Join . . . Dissenting . . .**    Burger's vehicle-dismantling business is not closely regulated (unless most New York City businesses are), and an administrative warrant therefore was required to search it. . . . Neither the general junk industry nor the vehicle-dismantling industry, are or ever have been pervasively regulated. . . .

The implications of the Court's opinion, if realized, will virtually eliminate 4th Amendment protection of commercial entities in the context of administrative searches. No state may require, as a condition of doing business, a blanket submission to warrantless searches for any purpose. I respectfully dissent.

## Case Discussion Questions

1    What is a "closely regulated" business? Why is there an exception from the warrant requirement in the case of those businesses?
2    What requirements does the court impose before a warrant is not necessary?
3    Did Burger ever agree to the inspection of his premises? Explain.

### The Fifth Amendment: The Privilege Against Self-Incrimination

Certainly, the truth is a major consideration in any civil or criminal proceeding. But that truth should only be obtained while the integrity of the individual is protected. If truth were the only consideration, we could shoot the defendant full of truth serum and simply ask him. American law has gone to a great deal of trouble to preserve the dignity of the individual, and a major part of that effort is the right not to convict one's self through compelled testimony.

Like the fourth amendment, the fifth amendment is enforced through the exclusionary rule and results in some guilty persons being freed. And, like the fourth amendment, the right attaches to more than mere police investigations; it has also been applied to administrative investigations.

The most important fifth amendment case is clearly <u>Miranda v. Arizona</u>.[15] That case established the rule that suspects must be warned of their rights prior to any interrogation while the suspect is in custody. Suspects must be informed that they have a right to remain silent; that anything they say can and will be used against them in court; that they have a right to an attorney present during questioning; and that if they cannot

*may be required to testify in a civil case not criminal*

---

15    384 U.S. 436, 86 S. Ct. 1602, 16 L. Ed. 2d 694 (1966).

afford an attorney, one will be appointed without charge. Warnings must be given before questioning; and if during questioning the suspect indicates that he or she wishes to consult with an attorney, questioning must stop. It is important to note that *Miranda* only bars the use of evidence obtained through a confession or statement taken in violation of the rules under the exclusionary rule; it does *not* automatically result in a dismissal of the charges if there is other evidence.

The basis of the *Miranda* decision is that the fifth amendment prohibits *involuntary* confessions. Clearly, that includes confessions obtained through physical threats, violence, and even torture. *Miranda* is aimed at more subtle *psychological* compulsion to speak, which the Court found always exists during police interrogation.

The warnings only need be given during **custodial interrogation,** that is, when the suspect is in the custody of the police. As a result, *threshold confessions*, where the suspect walks into the police station and admits guilt before questioning and before he or she is taken into custody, are admissible.

The *Miranda* decision has itself been the subject of substantial interpretation, including further definition of custodial interrogation. Later decisions, particularly those in the 1980's, have tended to limit the *Miranda* holding. A 1984 decision, for example, held that *Miranda* warnings need not be given after routine traffic stops, because traffic violators are not in custody.[16]

### The Sixth Amendment: The Right to Counsel

The sixth amendment provides that "In all criminal prosecutions, the accused shall enjoy the right . . . to have the Assistance of Counsel for his defense." Whereas persons accused of crimes in federal court have always enjoyed that right, persons accused in state courts did not receive full protection under the sixth amendment until 1963, when the Court decided *Gideon v. Wainwright* (see p. 135).

The right to counsel involves far more than the right to a lawyer at trial. The Supreme Court has noted that the right to counsel is rather illusory if **critical stages** of the case have already passed. Defendants, both guilty and innocent, may emerge from a secret pretrial interrogation after having made damaging admissions from which no attorney can save them. The year after *Gideon* was decided, the Supreme Court held that the right to counsel attached during interrogations,[17] and the *Miranda* decision can be viewed as simply requiring that the defendant be informed of that right.

Much of the later law on the right to counsel has dealt with the question of whether particular stages of the proceedings are critical and therefore require the presence of an attorney. For example, the Court has held that a defendant has a right to the presence of an attorney during "line-ups,"[18] but that rule was later limited to line-ups prior to indictment by a grand jury.

### DUE PROCESS

One of the murkiest areas of constitutional law deals with the meaning of the phrase "due process" as it is used in both the fifth and fourteenth amendments. The term *due*

---

16 *Berkemer v. McCarty*, 468 U.S. 420, 104 S. Ct. 3138, 82 L. Ed. 2d 317 (1984).
17 *Escobedo v. Illinois*, 378 U.S. 478, 84 S. Ct. 1748, 12 L. Ed. 2d 977 (1964).
18 *U.S. v. Wade*, 388 U.S. 218, 87 S. Ct. 1926, 18 L. Ed. 2d 1149 (1967).

*process* is itself general and vague. That vagueness is compounded by the fact that the term appears *twice* in almost identical phrasing, once in the fifth amendment and again in the fourteenth. It is probably no overstatement to say that the vast majority of constitutional law cases involve an interpretation of the due process clauses.

Under both the fifth and fourteenth amendments, it is traditional to divide due process theory into two broad categories: (1) **substantive due process, involving questions of** whether laws are themselves fair; and (2) **procedural due process,** involving issues of the fairness of court and administrative procedures. *(how you get there)*

## Substantive Due Process and the Selective Incorporation Doctrine

*14th amend applies many of the rights listed under the federal Constitution to the states*

In 1833, Chief Justice John Marshall ruled that the Bill of Rights did not apply to *state laws*, but only to *federal* actions.[19] Marshall felt it was obvious from the intent and the wording of the first ten amendments that they were directed against the federal government alone, and that citizens were amply protected against state actions by state constitutions. That interpretation, at least technically, remains the law.

In 1868, the fourteenth amendment was adopted as the second of the Civil War amendments directed toward slavery. It was thought necessary to include a second due process clause to apply to state actions in the aftermath of slavery and the Civil War. The initial cases to interpret the meaning of due process as applied to the states took the position that the term meant "fundamental fairness," and as long as state laws did not "shock the conscience of the court" the states had met their duty under the fourteenth amendment due process clause. Many of those early decisions dealt with state social welfare laws that were held unconstitutional under the doctrine of substantive economic due process (see p. 112).

In those early cases, Justice John Harlan stood alone in dissent, arguing that the term *due process* was a shorthand way of applying *all* of the standards of the Bill of Rights to the states, and arguing that the fourteenth amendment totally "incorporated" the first ten amendments and made them applicable to the states.

The Supreme Court has never fully accepted Justice Harlan's view, but has instead adopted a process of **selective incorporation.** Under that doctrine, only those portions of the Bill of Rights that are *implicit in the concept of ordered liberty* are made applicable to the states by the fourteenth amendment due process clause.[20]

For example, if a state violates an individual's right of free speech, the Court has held that the concept of free speech is "implicit in the concept of ordered liberty" and is therefore included in the concept of due process. Most of the provisions of the Bill of Rights have been applied to the states through the process of selective incorporation, but the Court has never applied the provisions of the second or third amendments nor portions of the seventh amendment to the states.

The process of selective incorporation and the standards to be used have never been fully defined. The following decision, which is also a landmark case in the area of right to counsel, provides some background on that process.

---

**19** *Barron v. The Mayor and City Council of Baltimore*, 32 U.S. (7 Pet.) 243, 8 L. Ed. 672 (1833).

**20** This test was first announced in an opinion by Justice Cardozo in *Palko v. Connecticut*, 302 U.S. 319, 58 S. Ct. 149, 82 L. Ed. 288 (1937).

# Gideon v. Wainwright
372 U.S. 335, 83 S. Ct. 792, 9 L. Ed. 2d 799 (1963)

Clarence Earl Gideon was charged with breaking and entering with intent to commit theft, a felony, in the Florida state courts. Gideon asked that a lawyer be appointed to represent him, because he did not have enough money to hire one. The trial judge refused, because under Florida law only defendants in capital cases were entitled to a lawyer without charge. Gideon then conducted his own defense, in the words of the Court "about as well as could be expected from a layman." Gideon was convicted and sentenced to serve five years in prison. While in prison, Gideon filed a petition with the Florida Supreme Court, claiming that his sixth amendment right to counsel had been violated. That petition was denied, and Gideon, without the aid of counsel, appealed that decision to the U.S. Supreme Court. The Supreme Court appointed counsel for Gideon in that Court, and granted certiorari.

There was a major precedent exactly on that point: In *Betts v. Brady*,[21] a 1942 case with virtually identical facts, the Supreme Court had held that defendants in state courts did not have the right to counsel except in *capital cases* (death sentence). That case had held that "refusal to appoint counsel for an indigent defendant charged with a felony did not necessarily violate the Due Process Clause of the 14th Amendment." On the other hand, an even earlier case[22] had held that state defendants charged with capital cases *have* the right to counsel under the sixth and fourteenth amendments.

**Mr. Justice Black Delivered the Opinion of the Court**    Since the facts and circumstances of the two cases are so nearly indistinguishable, we think the *Betts v. Brady* holding if left standing would require us to reject Gideon's claim that the Constitution guarantees him the assistance of counsel. Upon full reconsideration we conclude that *Betts v. Brady* should be overruled.

We think the Court in *Betts* had ample precedent for acknowledging that those guarantees of the Bill of Rights which are fundamental safeguards of liberty immune from federal abridgment are equally protected against state invasion by the Due Process Clause of the Fourteenth Amendment. This same principle was recognized, explained, and applied in *Powell v. Alabama* . . . where the Court held that . . . the Fourteenth Amendment "embraced" those "fundamental principles of liberty and justice which lie at the base of all our civil and political institutions," even though they had been "specifically dealt with in another part of the Federal Constitution." . . . In many cases . . . this Court has looked to the fundamental nature of the original Bill of Rights guarantees to decide whether the Fourteenth Amendment makes them obligatory on the States.

Explicitly recognized to be of this "fundamental nature" and therefore made immune from state invasion by the Fourteenth, or some part of it, are the First Amendment's freedoms of speech, press, religion, assembly, association, and petition for redress of grievances. For the same reason, though not always in precisely the same terminology, the Court has made obligatory on the States the Fifth Amendment's command that private property shall not be taken for public use without just compensation, the Fourth Amendment's prohibition of unreasonable searches and seizures, and the Eighth's ban on cruel and unusual punishment. . . .

We accept *Betts v. Brady*'s assumption, based as it was on our prior cases, that a provision of the Bill of Rights which is "fundamental and essential to a fair trial" is made obligatory upon the States by the Fourteenth Amendment. We think the Court in *Betts* was wrong, however, in concluding that the Sixth

21 316 U.S. 455, 62 S. Ct. 1252, 86 L. Ed. 1595 (1942).
22 *Powell v. Alabama*, 287 U.S. 45, 53 S. Ct. 55, 77 L. Ed. 158 (1932).

Amendment's guarantee of counsel is not one of these fundamental rights.

Not only these precedents but also reason and reflection require us to recognize that in our adversary system of criminal justice, any person haled into court, who is too poor to hire a lawyer, cannot be assured a fair trial unless counsel is provided for him. This seems to us to be an obvious truth. Governments, both state and federal, quite properly spend vast sums of money to establish machinery to try defendants accused of crime. Lawyers to prosecute are everywhere deemed essential to protect the public's interest in an orderly society. Similarly, there are few defendants charged with crime, few indeed, who fail to hire the best lawyers they can get to prepare and present their defenses. That government hires lawyers to prosecute and defendants who have the money hire lawyers to defend are the strongest indications of the widespread belief that lawyers in criminal courts are necessities, not luxuries. The right of one charged

with crime to counsel may not be deemed fundamental and essential to fair trials in some countries, but it is in ours.

The judgment is reversed and the cause is remanded to the Supreme Court of Florida for further action not inconsistent with this opinion.

Reversed.

[The case was retried in Florida, and this time Gideon was given a lawyer. At that trial, Gideon was found not guilty of all charges by a jury.—Ed.]

## Case Discussion Questions

1    Read the sixth amendment. Is *Betts v. Brady* or *Gideon* more within the spirit of that amendment?
2    What is the selective incorporation doctrine? How does it apply to this case?
3    Had the circumstances changed since the Court decided *Betts v. Brady?* Or had the personnel on the Court changed?

### Procedural Due Process

A second meaning of due process, both under the fifth and fourteenth amendments, is *fair procedures.* Whenever a unit of government tries to take away "life, liberty, or property," the persons involved are entitled to procedures such as a hearing, notice of charges, and a right to present their side of the story. Generally speaking, the more important the interest involved, the more formal the procedures that must be used. Thus, a case involving the death penalty would require extremely formal procedures, but a suspension from high school would involve very informal procedures.

Each procedural due process case is different. The court must first determine that the "protected interest" in the case is in fact "life, liberty, or property" and therefore protected by the due process clause. Once that determination is made, the court must then determine "what process is due," that is, how formal the procedures must be to protect the specific interest involved. Those procedures are then tailored to fit the situation (see *Mathews v. Eldridge,* p. 154).

Due process procedures have been required in cases of suspension or revocation of a driver's license; suspension from school for disciplinary reasons; denial of time off for good behavior in prisons; termination of electrical service by a municipal power company; suspension of welfare payments; dismissal of teachers, police officers, fire fighters, and university professors; and immigration proceedings, among others. But, in each case, the degree of formality of the procedures varied with the importance of the interest being threatened by government action, the risk of an erroneous deprivation of the interest without procedural guarantees, and the value of added procedures.

Due process requires both administrative and courtroom procedures to be basically fair. Although many of the components of a fair trial are specifically set out in the Constitution—such as the right to trial by jury, the right to counsel, and the right to be free from cruel and unusual punishments—other aspects of a fair trial not found in the Constitution have been supplied by interpretation of due process. For example, the courts have held that "mob domination" of trial proceedings, excessive limits on cross-examination by a defendant, the denial of a public trial, and insufficient time to prepare for trial are all denials of due process.

## EQUAL PROTECTION

The concept of equal protection under the fourteenth amendment has already been discussed in Chapter 4 in the context of economic liberties. But the equal protection clause applies to far more than economic freedoms and, in fact, may apply to any statute that imposes an impermissible classification scheme.

Every statute inevitably classifies—who is to be taxed, who is to be charged with a crime, who must submit to regulation, and the like. Such classification cannot be avoided, but neither may such statutes make **invidious discriminations,** that is, classifications based on impermissible categories.

The fourteenth amendment was enacted in part to prohibit such invidious discrimination, but it did not explain what sorts of classifications were impermissible. Over the years, the court has established two tests to determine whether a classification scheme is impermissible. In most instances, the courts use the **reasonable basis test,** but in two very important areas the courts impose the more exacting **strict scrutiny test.**

### The Reasonable Basis and Strict Scrutiny Tests

In most cases the general question in equal protection cases is whether the legislature had a **reasonable basis** for its classification scheme. For example, in *City of New Orleans v. Dukes* (p. 114), the Court found that the city council had a reasonable basis for treating some pushcart vendors differently from others and, therefore, held that the classification scheme was permissible.

But, if a classification scheme involves **fundamental liberties** protected by the Bill of Rights, or a **suspect classification,** the courts will use a much higher standard—the so-called strict scrutiny test. Under that test, the classification will be held to violate the equal protection clause unless the legislature can demonstrate there is no other way to accomplish a valid state objective.

The question of whether a particular group belongs in a suspect class depends on three factors: (1) whether membership "carries an obvious badge, such as race or sex do"; (2) whether treatment of members of the group has been historically severe and pervasive; and (3) whether members of the class have been subjected to the "absolute deprivation" of benefits available to nonmembers of the group.

In the twentieth century, the equal protection clause has been used to invalidate laws that required racial discrimination in the schools and elsewhere, racial restrictions on voting rights, underrepresentation of urban majorities in legislatures (one-man, one-vote), and many others. Perhaps the greatest area of activity in the development of the equal protection clause has been in racial discrimination. That topic will be discussed at length in Chapter 18.

## The Problem of State Action

By its express terms, the fourteenth amendment only limits action on the part of *states*. The amendment has nothing to say about *private* discrimination, as in the case of a landlord who refuses to rent to a person because of race, for example. Clearly, Congress and the states may enact statutes to prohibit various types of private discrimination (see Chapter 18); but if no such statute exists, the fourteenth amendment does not prohibit private discrimination.

In *Shelley v. Kraemer* (see p. 446), a 1948 Supreme Court decision, the Court held that judicial enforcement of such private discrimination constituted state action and therefore violated the equal protection clause. In that case, a state court was asked to enforce a discriminatory provision in a real estate deed that prohibited blacks from purchasing property. The Supreme Court held that the court order enforcing that private discrimination was state action and therefore in violation of the equal protection clause.

## THE RIGHT OF PRIVACY AND THE PROBLEM OF "OTHER RIGHTS"

The Bill of Rights contains other specific guarantees aside from those discussed so far. Our discussion has not included any mention of the second, third, seventh, eighth, ninth, or tenth amendments, and it should be clear that a great deal of law surrounds those amendments as well. Our selection of amendments to discuss has reflected a rather arbitrary opinion of which amendments are "more important" and consideration of which provisions are likely to be most important to the ordinary citizen and businessperson.

Even though the Constitution seems to contain a rather complete list of necessary civil liberties, it remains at least possible that there are *other* rights, not specified in the Constitution. That conclusion is bolstered by the somewhat vague and mystical reference in the ninth amendment to "other rights." Although the Bill of Rights does a good job of setting out essential civil liberties, it is possible that the founding fathers missed something. This does not mean that the authors of the Bill of Rights were in any way sloppy or lacked intelligence. It may mean only that the times have changed since 1791, and new rights are necessary to protect us from overzealous government. The possibility of new rights remained only a theory until 1965, when the following case was decided.

## Griswold v. Connecticut
381 U.S. 479, 85 S. Ct. 1678, 14 L. Ed. 2d 510 (1965)

Connecticut law made the use of birth control devices illegal and also prohibited anyone from giving information on the use of such devices. The executive director and medical director of a planned parenthood association were found guilty of dispensing such information and fined $100 each. They appealed the convictions to the Supreme Court.

**Mr. Justice Douglas Delivered the Opinion of the Court**    We are met with a wide range of questions that implicate the Due Process Clause of the Fourteenth Amendment. . . . We do not sit as a super legislature to determine the wisdom, need, and propriety of laws that touch economic problems,

THE BILL OF RIGHTS

business affairs, or social conditions. The law, however, operates directly on an intimate relation of husband and wife and their physician's role in one aspect of that relation.

[Previous] cases suggest that specific guarantees in the Bill of Rights have penumbras, formed by emanations from those guarantees that help give them life and substance. . . . Various guarantees create zones of privacy. The right of association contained in the penumbra of the First Amendment is one. . . . The Third Amendment in its prohibition against the quartering of soldiers "in any house" in time of peace without the consent of the owner is another facet of that privacy. The Fourth Amendment explicitly affirms the "right of the people to be secure in their persons, houses, papers and effects, against unreasonable searches and seizures." The Fifth Amendment in its Self-Incrimination Clause enables the citizen to create a zone of privacy which the government may not force him to surrender to his detriment. The Ninth Amendment provides: "The enumeration in the Constitution, of certain rights, shall not be construed to deny or disparage others retained by the people."

The Fourth and Fifth Amendments were described . . . as protection against all governmental invasions "of the sanctity of a man's home and the privacies of life." We recently referred in *Mapp v. Ohio* . . . to the Fourth Amendment as creating a "right to privacy, no less important than any other right carefully and particularly reserved to the people." . . .

We have had many controversies over these penumbral rights of "privacy and repose." . . . These cases bear witness that the right of privacy which presses for recognition here is a legitimate one.

The present case, then, concerns a relationship lying within the zone of privacy created by several fundamental constitutional guarantees. And it concerns a law which, in forbidding the *use* of contraceptives rather than regulating their manufacture or sale, seeks to achieve its goals by having a maximum destructive impact upon that relationship. Such a law cannot stand. . . . Would we allow the police to search the sacred precincts of marital bedrooms for telltale signs of the use of contraceptives? The very idea is repulsive to the notions of privacy surrounding the marital relationship.

We deal with a right of privacy older than the Bill of Rights—older than our political parties, older than our school system. Marriage is a coming together for better or for worse, hopefully enduring, and intimate to the degree of being sacred. It is an association that promotes a way of life, not causes; a harmony in living, not political faiths; a bilateral loyalty, not commercial or social projects. Yet it is an association for as noble a purpose as any involved in our prior decisions.

Reversed.

## Case Discussion Questions

1   What does the ninth amendment mean? Do you think the framers intended a right of privacy in the Constitution?
2   Which view of the Constitution—activist, neutralist, or restraintist—does this decision illustrate?
3   What is privacy? What kinds of activities would you expect to be protected by this decision?

---

The concept of the "right of privacy" has been applied to hold unconstitutional a variety of state statutes punishing consensual sexual conduct and was the basis of the Supreme Court's decision in *Roe v. Wade*,[23] the controversial case which held state statutes prohibiting abortion unconstitutional. As Mr. Justice Blackmun argued in that case,

> The Constitution does not explicitly mention any right of privacy. In a line of decisions, however . . . the Court has recognized that a right of personal privacy or a guarantee of certain areas or zones of privacy, does exist under the Constitution. . . . They also make it clear that the right has some extension to activities relating to marriage . . . procreation . . . contraception . . . family relationships . . . and child rearing and education. . . .

---

23  410 U.S. 113, 93 S. Ct. 705, 35 L. Ed. 2d 147 (1973).

> This right of privacy . . . is broad enough to encompass a woman's decision whether or not to terminate her pregnancy.

It is clear that new rights may be discovered and applied to the state and federal governments at any time. Following *Griswold,* no other new rights have been found so far, but the importance of *Griswold* is that it lays the foundations for the discovery of other rights. That doctrine, perhaps more than any other, makes clear the idea of an ever-changing Bill of Rights, adjusting to social and economic changes through judicial interpretation.

## SUMMARY AND CONCLUSIONS

The Bill of Rights, broadly defined to include at least the fourteenth amendment, provides the clearest limitations on the powers of government. Many believe that the first amendment contains the essential political rights necessary to any free state. It seems clear that the freedoms of speech and press are necessary to political democracy, because without them opposition to the government would be impossible. Although the first amendment is phrased in absolute terms, the courts have permitted some exceptions

---

### Drug Testing and the Right of Privacy

One of the most important applications of the right of privacy deals with the problem of drug testing by employers. Clearly, the right of privacy as developed in *Griswold* applies only to *governmental* intrusions on privacy, and not to private ones. Some federal courts have ruled that drug testing of federal employees or employees subject to federal regulation (e.g., railroad workers) is barred by the right of privacy.

Just as clearly, employees are generally subject to the *employment-at-will* doctrine (see p. 291), which says that employees may be fired for any reason, or for no reason, and that employers may therefore place any condition of employment (such as taking a drug test) on continued employment.

Some states have broad constitutional provisions protecting privacy against *private* action. Recently, a San Francisco jury awarded $475,000 to an employee discharged because she refused to take a drug test, based on such a provision in the California constitution. Other states have adopted or are considering statutes limiting drug testing to workers in hazardous and safety-related jobs.

Certainly, a mandatory drug test invades the kind of "zone of privacy" envisioned by the Supreme Court in *Griswold*. But just as certainly there are major issues of job safety and even public safety in some jobs. The issue of job privacy also raises other troublesome issues, such as lie detector tests, monitoring of employees' telephone calls, confidentiality of employee records, and even genetic screening for tendencies toward certain diseases. The courts and legislatures will undoubtedly be considering those issues in the years to come to strike some balance.

and allowed governments to regulate advocacy of crime or revolution, obscenity, commercial speech, and defamation.

When considered together with freedom of religion, the first amendment seems to protect a general "freedom of conscience." Freedom of religion involves two aspects: (1) freedom from governmental interference with religious beliefs (the free exercise clause) and (2) freedom from governmental support of particular religious bodies or beliefs (the establishment clause).

The fourth, fifth, and sixth amendments, taken together, provide protections against governmental abuse of the criminal process. Those amendments contain, among others, protection against unreasonable searches and seizures, protection against abuses of the privilege against self-incrimination, and guarantees of the right to counsel. However, many of those protections are not limited to criminal prosecutions but include administrative searches and interrogations by taxing and administrative officers.

The due process clause of the fourteenth amendment operates on two levels: first, it requires that procedures in trials and administrative hearings be "fair"; and, second, it has applied many of the protections of the first ten amendments to the states under the selective incorporation doctrine. The equal protection clause of the fourteenth amendment prohibits any state-backed invidious discrimination.

The Bill of Rights may be expanded and stretched. New rights may be "discovered" under the broad phrasing of the ninth and fourteenth amendments, and the existing rights under the express amendments may be changed through judicial interpretation of their meaning. In the words of John Marshall, the Constitution was "intended to endure for ages to come, and consequently, to be adapted to the various crises of human affairs." It is the peculiar genius of the American Constitution that it at once erects barriers to government overreaching and makes those barriers flexible enough to account for social, economic, and political necessity.

## REVIEW QUESTIONS

1  What is the Bill of Rights? What amendments does it include?

2  Some of the framers of the Constitution felt that the Bill of Rights was unnecessary and even dangerous. Do you think they were correct? Have historical events proven them correct?

3  Many commentators have argued that the first amendment is far more important than any other amendment, especially when it deals with matters of conscience, such as politics and religion. Do you agree?

4  In the 1960's, several courts held that marches by civil rights demonstrators through white areas of cities were protected by the first amendment, as long as the marchers themselves remained peaceful. Should cities be able to ban such marches if people watching the marchers might become violent? Before you answer, consider that the answer must be the same for those civil rights marchers as for a parade of American Nazis and for a Ku Klux Klan march. Should the answer be the same for all three marches?

5  Do you think the exclusionary rule ties the hands of the police? Do you have a better alternative to assure that the police will follow constitutional procedures? Is it a fair criticism of the exclusionary rule to say that it protects the guilty and only very rarely the innocent?

6  What is the right of privacy? Where did it come from? Do you think the framers of the Constitution intended us to have a general right

of privacy? In an age of computer information gathering, should we have a right of privacy?

7) A group of university students gathered at a jail in Florida to protest continuing local policies of racial segregation within the jail. The sheriff ordered the protestors to leave the premises, and when they refused, had them arrested for trespass. The protestors were in an area of the jail restricted from the public. Has the sheriff violated the protesters' right of free speech? [*Adderly v. Florida*, 385 U.S. 39, 87 S. Ct. 242, 17 L. Ed. 2d 149 (1967).] Would it make a difference if they were in a public area? [See *Edwards v. South Carolina*, 372 U.S. 229, 83 S. Ct. 680, 9 L. Ed. 2d 697 (1963).]

8) You are the manager of a large department store in a downtown area. One morning you arrive at work to find that a small religious sect has set up a loudspeaker in front of your store and is using it to harangue passersby. They also insist on passing out literature to people entering and leaving your store. Can you take any action? Can the police require them to leave? Can they be arrested?

9) A local ordinance provides that it is illegal to erect any billboard within the city limits that advertises cigarettes, liquor, travel to states where gambling is legal, firearms, or automobiles. Is the ordinance constitutional?

10) Routine warrantless inspections were made by officials of the Occupational Safety and Health Act to assess compliance with federal health standards. Barlow's, Inc., an electrical contractor, contended that such inspections violate the fourth amendment. Are such inspections searches? Has Barlow's consented to the search by voluntarily conducting a business subject to such searches? [*Marshall v. Barlow's, Inc.*, 436 U.S. 307, 98 S. Ct. 1816, 56 L. Ed. 2d 305 (1978).] (See p. 161.)

11) A New York statute made it a crime for any person to sell or distribute contraceptives to any person under the age of 16 and also made it illegal to display or advertise contraceptives. Does this statute violate the first amendment, the right of privacy, or both? [*Carey v. Population Services International*, 431 U.S. 678, 97 S. Ct. 2010, 52 L. Ed. 2d 675 (1977).]

# C H A P T E R    6

# Administrative Agencies

*> unique to our systems*
*seem to do all three*
*functions ( legislative,*
*executive, judicial )*

*[Administrative agencies] have become a veritable fourth branch of the Government.*

JUSTICE JACKSON, DISSENTING
*FTC v. Ruberoid Co.*, 343 U.S. 470 (1952)

In many ways, the study of contemporary American government is the study of administrative agencies. Almost all domestic, and some foreign, policy is carried out through a huge variety of commissions, boards, bureaus, and agencies. Although administrative agencies have few fans and many critics, the growth of agencies has been viewed as a necessary response to the growing complexity of governing a modern nation.

Without agencies, Congress would be required to enact every administrative rule into law through its formal processes. This task would be physically impossible, and the rules would be of questionable value. Congress would have to assign every radio and television channel, set rail and truck routes and rates, specifically describe every type of unfair labor and trade practice, set discount rates for financial institutions, draft specific regulations for each nuclear power plant, and perform a host of functions far beyond its abilities and expertise. And enforcement of these laws would take place through the courts, vastly increasing their caseloads.

Since 1887, Congress has used administrative agencies to handle much of the "detail work" of government. Agencies permit the use of expertise to make rules, eliminate the need for Congress to regulate in a detailed and day-to-day manner, and eliminate some of the caseload from the federal courts.

*rulemaking*
*promulgating*

Agencies did not, in Justice Frankfurter's terms, "come like a thief in the night," but rather have been developing for centuries. Their origins go back to the powers of the medieval English sheriffs. A sophisticated agency was created in England as early as 1385. Delegations of power to cabinet officers were made by the first American Congress in 1789. It is vital to note, however, that the Constitution makes no mention of administrative agencies.

## ORGANIZATION OF AGENCIES

Administrative agencies are classified as either **line agencies** or as **independent regulatory commissions** (IRCs). Until 1887, all agencies were line agencies, that is, subordinate parts of cabinet offices. Line agencies are under the direct control of the President and are usually headed by a single administrator, who serves at the pleasure of the President. For example, the Internal Revenue Service is a subunit of the Treasury Department, and the Commissioner of Internal Revenue is appointed and may be removed by the President. Line agencies may be created by executive order of the President, although authority to make rules, investigate, and adjudicate claims is often delegated to such bodies by Congress.

Independent regulatory commissions (IRCs), on the other hand, were created by Congress to limit the political control of the President. The Interstate Commerce Commission was created as the first federal IRC in 1887. That body regulates railroads, and Congress was fearful that President Benjamin Harrison, who had been a railroad lawyer, would not permit strict control of the railroads. Typically, IRCs are headed by a board, rather than by a single head. The members of the board are appointed by the President, but for staggered terms longer than that of the President. Often the membership is required to be *bipartisan*, that is, made up of a certain number of members of each political party. Board members cannot be unilaterally removed by the President (see Figure 6.1).

## TRENDS IN ADMINISTRATIVE AGENCIES

Beginning in 1930, several new agencies were created to meet the challenges of the Great Depression, including the National Labor Relations Board (NLRB) and the Securities and Exchange Commission (SEC). Three trends that began in that era have had a profound effect on the development of administrative agencies: (1) standardization of administrative procedure; (2) concern with administrative efficiency; and (3) a move from purely "economic" regulation towards "social" regulation. In the 1970's a new trend toward *deregulation* emerged, resulting in the limitation of administrative power in some areas. And in the late 1980's, a trend toward *re-regulation* seems to be developing.

### Standardization of Administrative Procedure

Before 1947, every agency had its own rules of procedure, different from those of every other agency. During the late 1930's, a move toward uniform procedures began, which ended in 1947 with congressional approval of the **Administrative Procedure Act** (APA). Much of the discussion of administrative procedures in this chapter will be based upon that act, because it applies to "each authority of the Government of the United States" except Congress, the courts, and the governments of territories, possessions, and the District of Columbia. Many states have adopted similar statutes prescribing uniform procedures for state agencies.

### Concern with Efficiency and Power

With the rise in power of agencies came criticism of agencies on two bases: first, that agencies were not accountable to the public; and, second, that agencies were often mismanaged and inefficient. In part, the introduction of the APA was a response to those criticisms. A second response has been the appointment of several presidential commissions to study the management of agencies.

A. An IRC: The Federal Trade Commission

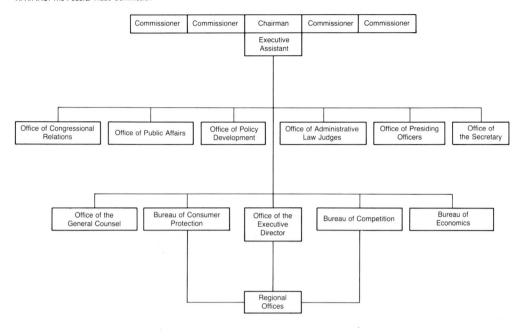

B. A Line Agency: The Environmental Protection Agency

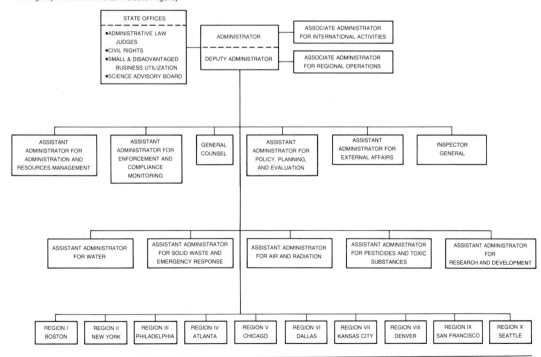

FIGURE 6.1 Comparison of IRCs and Line Agencies
*Source. U.S. Government Manual,* 1987.

## Economic and Social Regulation

Until the 1930's, almost all regulation dealt with *economic* areas. **Economic regulation** is detailed regulation of prices, routes, and output of various industries. Economic regulation is usually applied to public utilities, transportation, and communication. In those industries, an administrative agency makes the basic business decisions of price, output, routes, and even entry into the industry—decisions that other industries make on the basis of supply and demand.

**Reasons for Economic Regulation**    There are both economic and political reasons for economic regulation. The three principal reasons are (1) that such firms may be "natural monopolies," (2) that the industries may be subject to "ruinous competition," and (3) that some of the regulated firms *requested* to be regulated.

A *natural monopoly* is a business in which only one firm can efficiently supply the product, and the existence of more than one firm would mean that prices would in fact go up. Such industries are usually marked by very large capital investments, such as power plants, transmission lines, or pipelines, and duplication of those facilities would mean increased costs and prices. But since such firms are monopolies, they may charge monopoly prices or cut back output unless they are regulated.

Other industries are said to be subject to *ruinous competition*. That means that entry costs are so low that virtually anyone may enter the field, reducing profits for all. For example, during the Great Depression of the 1930's, many unemployed workers bought a truck and entered the trucking field, compressing profits for the older firms. Those older firms lobbied the government for regulation of the field, especially with *licensing and certification* procedures, through which government can keep new entrants out of the field.

Finally, many regulated industries have actually *sought* regulation to protect themselves from competition or to regulate competitors. For example, it is clear that the railroads actively sought regulation by the Interstate Commerce Commission at various times to stop cutthroat competition among themselves. The railroads also lobbied for regulation of the trucking industry to protect themselves from competition.

**Methods of Economic Regulation**    Economic regulation generally involves two principal activities by administrative agencies. Such agencies generally are involved in **licensing and certification,** which means a choice of who gets the business. For example, broadcast licenses of radio and television stations are issued after a determination that a particular licensee would best serve the public "interest, convenience and necessity." Currently, many state and local governments are involved in issuing **franchises,** or licenses to operate, to cable television stations.

A far more complex activity involves **rate making,** or the establishment of prices, price structures, routes, and rates. Agencies generally establish prices on a *cost plus reasonable profit* basis. The agency determines the costs of the firm to be regulated and then permits a fair profit over that cost. It is often difficult to establish costs, because many of the costs of the regulated firm (executive salaries, advertising, etc.) are within its control. It is also difficult to establish a "fair" profit, because there are few comparisons between monopoly public utilities and private industries.

**Social Regulation**    During the 1930's, in partial response to the social problems caused by the Depression, another type of regulation developed, generally called **social welfare regulation.** It generally includes such areas as occupational safety and health, consumer product safety, equal opportunity, and environmental protection. Sometimes those laws are divided into two broad categories: **protective legislation,** which shelters the public from some danger; and **entitlement legislation,** which provides aid for the needy, disabled, or disadvantaged. Many laws, like social security, have both protective and entitlement aspects.

## Deregulation

In the 1970's, the pressure for regulatory reform became enormous. Attacks on "red tape" and "excessive paperwork" joined with philosophical and economic objections to regulation to produce political pressure for regulatory reform. Both Presidents Carter and Reagan were elected, at least in part, on their pledges to reform the federal bureaucracy. In the period after 1976 many government regulations were repealed or amended.

Originally, the term **deregulation** was applied to the removal of *economic* regulation of specific industries, such as transportation, communications, and energy transmission. Economic regulation of those industries had been criticized for many years. In some instances, the original justification had vanished, as in the case of federal regulations to protect the fledgling commercial airlines of the 1930's. In other cases, such as trucking, economists challenged the theory of *ruinous competition* as merely an effort to avoid the rigors of the marketplace.

Soon the term *deregulation* acquired a much different and broader meaning. The creation of dozens of new administrative agencies resulted in a large number of regulations aimed at specific social problems, such as those issued by the Occupational Safety and Health Administration (OSHA) and the Consumer Product Safety Commission (CPSC), among others. Critics argued that the sheer number of regulations made the economy less productive. But while agreement has existed regarding the need to deregulate some areas of economic regulation, no such agreement has arisen regarding social regulation.

## Cost–Benefit Analysis

The largest single change in the administrative process arising from the demand for deregulation has been the adoption of **cost–benefit analysis.** That theory requires that the costs of a new regulation, including the government's cost of administering the program and industries' cost of compliance, must be weighed against the benefits of the regulation. The process was begun by President Ford in 1974 and continued by President Carter. Cost–benefit analysis was expanded by President Reagan by requiring the Office of Management and Budget (OMB) to review all regulations and conduct cost–benefit analyses when preparing the budget of the executive branch.

## PRO AND CON

# Should "cost–benefit analysis" be used to assess administrative agencies?

**Pro**    Administrative agencies must make political choices. Those choices involve whether to make a rule and what kind of rule to pass. Those choices are often unguided and have no real criteria provided by the delegation of power in the enabling act. Cost–benefit analysis injects certainty into the process of making choices by administrative agencies by reducing the decision to simple levels of dollars and cents.

Administrative decisions about rules involve trade-offs. The issue of nuclear power involves a question about the health of people living near a nuclear power plant, but it also involves the health of people who must mine the coal that must be used if nuclear power is not used. Cost–benefit analysis can eliminate the guesswork from such choices.

Administrative choices often involve the intensity of preferences. A particular rule may involve a matter of life or death, or, like many consumer safety rules, may pass unnoticed. Administrators must make choices based on those differing intensities, and cost–benefit analysis may help them by weighing intensity.

It is no response to say that these choices involve "untraded goods." Actuarial tables exist to determine the value of human life, for example. We ask jurors and legislators to determine the monetary value of such goods as clean air, safety, and injury every day. Administrative agencies may do the same.

Cost–benefit analysis is a tool for making difficult choices. The essential question is, if administrators do not use cost–benefit analysis, what sort of criteria *will* they use?

**Con**    Cost–benefit analysis is a sham. First, the regulated businesses are often the only source of data about costs; therefore, those industries, with their vested interests, can affect the process a great deal. And administratively, cost–benefit analysis is itself costly. The weighing process itself is relatively expensive in money and in time.

The question of the evaluation of "benefits" is very difficult. For example, the Consumer Product Safety Commission estimated a substantial decrease in infant mortality because cribs no longer may have the kind of bars that strangle children. But it is very difficult to say how many lives would be saved, or what the value of any single life saved will be. Other untraded goods, such as clean air, the existence of wilderness, an extra margin of safety in our products or workplaces, freedom from racial or sexual discrimination, or even the presence in the world of the bald eagle, the snail darter, or the grizzly bear, simply cannot be measured in dollars and cents.

Perhaps most importantly, cost–benefit analysis is already built into the process. The judgments of what sort of rules to enact is a political judgment, made initially by elected representatives, who then delegate the responsibility to others. Cost–benefit analysis is a way for the executive to "short-circuit" the political process by eliminating regulations that have been adopted by the will of the elected representatives.

### Roundtable Discussion

1    In which kinds of decisions should cost–benefit analysis be used? Are there decisions where it should *not* be used?
2    Could cost–benefit analysis be adapted to social legislation?
3    If administrative decisions are *political*, shouldn't they be made by the legislature?

### Re-regulation

In the late 1980's it became clear that deregulation had gone too far in some areas. After 1986, Congress began to reconsider some of the regulations that had been discarded under deregulation and began reimposing some of those rules. **Re-regulation** became particularly important in the product- and workplace-safety areas and in environmental protection. It is difficult to tell whether re-regulation will be a long-term trend.

## THE DELEGATION OF POWER

Agencies are created by the legislature. Congress or a state legislature first passes a law creating an agency and then passes an **enabling act,** which *delegates* power to the agency to make *rules.* Later enabling acts may delegate additional power to the agency (see Figure 6.2).

Only the legislature can make a law. Strictly speaking, administrative rules are not laws but *rules* with the force of law. The difference seems to be a semantic fiction, but it is crucial to preserving the constitutionality of agencies under the doctrine of the separation of powers.

### Policy and Standards

A major question involves how broad the **delegation** of power may be. Must the legislature spell out in detail what sort of rules the agency may make, or may it delegate total authority to the agency? The problem involves the separation of powers concept, because if the grant is too broad, the legislature will have delegated the authority to "make law" to an agency. On the other hand, if the grant is too specific, Congress will have defeated its own purposes in establishing an agency.

In 1935 the Supreme Court ruled that congressional delegations of power may be

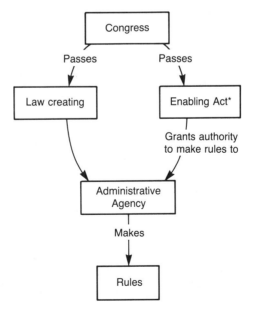

*Enabling legislation (the power to make rules) may be found in the law creating the agency or in a separate law.

FIGURE 6.2    The Delegation of Power to Administrative Agencies

too broad and violate the concept of separation of powers.[1] The Court held those delegations unconstitutional because Congress had not included a *standard* against which agency action could be measured, and "Congress has declared no policy, has established no standard, has laid down no rule. There is no requirement, no definition of circumstances and conditions." In the words of Justice Cardozo, "[T]he delegated power of legislation which has found expression [in these cases] is not canalized within banks that keep it from overflowing. It is unconfined and vagrant."

No U.S. Supreme Court case after 1935 has held a delegation of power unconstitutional. In 1944 the Court seemed to say that enabling acts need no longer set standards for administrative rule making, but need only establish a congressional *policy* against which the administrative agency's rules might be judged.[2] The difference between *policy* and *standards* is one of degree, and the failure of the courts to "demand that Congress do its job" has been severely criticized.

### Administrative Agencies and the Separation of Powers

The separation of powers problem is inevitable because of the split personality of most agencies—part executive, part legislative, and part judicial. In 1983 the Court held that the legislature did not have the right to exercise control over administrative actions through the **legislative veto**. A legislative veto involves a delegation of authority to an agency but with the provision that administrative action may be overridden by a vote of one or both houses of Congress. The legislative veto, which was first used in the 1930's, has appeared in over 200 major pieces of legislation.

## *Immigration and Naturalization Service v. Chadha*
462 U.S. 919, 103 S. Ct. 2764, 77 L. Ed. 2d 317 (1983)

Chadha, holder of a British passport, overstayed his nonimmigrant student visa in the United States. The Immigration and Naturalization Service filed an action to deport him, and Chadha filed an application to suspend the deportation with the Attorney General under provisions of the Immigration and Naturalization Act. Under section 244 of that act the Attorney General had the authority to suspend deportation if an alien is of good moral character and if the deportation would result in extreme hardship. According to the act, if either house of Congress passed a resolution stating that it did not favor the suspension of deportation, the Attorney General was required to deport the alien. The House of Representatives voted to override the Attorney General's suspension in Chadha's case on the grounds that no extreme hardship had been shown. Chadha appealed, first to the Board of Immigration Appeals and then to the U.S. court of appeals, which held the legislative veto unconstitutional. The government petitioned for certiorari to the U.S. Supreme Court.

---

1 *Schecter Poultry Corp. v. U.S.*, 295 U.S. 495, 55 S. Ct. 837, 79 L. Ed. 1570 (1935); and *Panama Refining Co. v. Ryan*, 293 U.S. 388, 55 S. Ct. 241, 79 L. Ed. 446 (1935).
2 *Yakus v. U.S.*, 321 U.S. 414, 64 S. Ct. 660, 88 L. Ed. 834 (1944).

**Mr. Chief Justice Burger Delivered the Opinion of the Court**  [T]he fact that a given law or procedure is efficient, convenient, and useful in facilitating functions of government standing alone, will not save it if it is contrary to the Constitution. Convenience and efficiency are not the primary objectives—or the hallmarks—of democratic government, and our inquiry is sharpened rather than blunted by the fact that Congressional veto provisions are appearing with increasing frequency in statutes which delegate authority to executive and independent agencies. . . .

The Constitution sought to divide the delegated powers of the new federal government into three defined categories: legislative, executive and judicial, to assure as nearly as possible that each Branch of government would confine itself to its assigned responsibility. The hydraulic pressure inherent within each of the separate Branches to exceed the outer limits of its power, even to accomplish desirable objectives, must be resisted. . . .

Examination of the action taken here by one House . . . reveals that it was essentially legislative in purpose and effect. In purporting to exercise power defined in Art. 1, §8, cl. 4 to "establish an uniform Rule of Naturalization," the House took action that had the purpose and effect of altering the legal rights, duties and relations of persons, including the Attorney General, Executive Branch officials and Chadha all outside the legislative branch. . . . The one-House veto operated in this case to overrule the Attorney General and mandate Chadha's deportation; absent the House action, Chadha would remain in the United States. Congress has *acted* and its action has altered Chadha's status. . . .

Since it is clear that the action by the House . . . was not within any of the express constitutional exceptions authorizing one House to act alone, and equally clear that it was an exercise of legislative power, that action was subject to the standards prescribed in Article 1. The bicameral requirement, the Presentment Clauses, the President's veto, and Congress' power to override a veto were intended to erect enduring checks on each Branch and to protect the people from the improvident exercise of power by mandating certain prescribed steps. To preserve those checks, and maintain the separation of powers, the carefully defined limits on the power of each Branch must not be eroded. To accomplish what has been attempted by one House of Congress in this case requires action in conformity with the express procedures of the Constitution's prescription for legislative action, passage by a majority of both Houses and presentment to the President.

The choices we discern as having been made in the Constitutional Convention impose burdens on governmental processes that often seem clumsy, inefficient, even unworkable, but those hard choices were consciously made by men who had lived under a form of government that permitted arbitrary governmental acts to go unchecked. There is no support in the Constitution or decisions of this Court for the proposition that the cumbersomeness and delays often encountered in complying with explicit Constitutional standards may be avoided, either by the Congress or by the President. With all the obvious flaws of delay, untidiness, and potential for abuse, we have not yet found a better way to preserve freedom than by making the exercise of power subject to the carefully crafted restraints spelled out in the Constitution.

We hold that the Congressional veto provision in §244(c)(2) . . . is unconstitutional. . . . Accordingly the judgment of the Court of Appeals is affirmed.

**Justice White, Dissenting**  The prominence of the legislative veto mechanism in our contemporary political system and its importance to Congress can hardly be overstated. It has become a central means by which Congress secures the accountability of executive and independent agencies. Without the legislative veto, Congress is faced with a Hobson's choice: either to refrain from delegating the necessary authority, leaving itself with a hopeless task of writing laws with the requisite specificity to cover endless special circumstances across the entire policy landscape, or in the alternative, to abdicate its lawmaking function to the executive branch and independent agencies. To choose the former leaves major national problems unresolved; to opt for the latter risks unaccountable policymaking by those not elected to fill that role. Accordingly, over the past five decades the legislative veto has been placed in nearly 200 statutes. . . .

Theoretically, agencies and officials were asked only to "fill up the details," and the rule was that "Congress cannot delegate any part of its legislative power except under a limitation of prescribed conduct." . . . Chief Justice Taft elaborated the standard . . . "If Congress shall lay down by legislative act an intelligible principle to which the person or body authorized to fix such rates is directed to conform, such legislative action is not a forbidden delegation of legislative power." In practice, however, restrictions on the scope of the power that could be delegated diminished and all but disappeared. . . .

If Congress may delegate lawmaking power to independent and executive agencies, it is most difficult to understand Article I as forbidding Congress from also reserving a check on legislative power for itself. Absent the [legislative] veto the agencies receiving delegations of legislative or quasi-legislative power may issue regulations having the force of law without

bicameral approval and without the President's signature. It is thus not apparent why the reservation of a veto over the exercise of that legislative power must be subject to a more exacting test. . . .

## Case Discussion Questions

1    What was the purpose of the legislative veto?
2    Is the legislative veto unfair or unwise? What is Justice White's argument?
3    Which portions of the Constitution does the legislative veto violate?

---

Following the *Chadha* decision, the Supreme Court ruled that portions of the *Gramm-Rudman Act* were unconstitutional on similar grounds. That law delegated power to the Comptroller of Currency (an administrative agency) to make automatic cuts in the federal budget. The Court cited *Chadha* and held that the delegation violated the separation of powers.[3]

## ADMINISTRATIVE RULE MAKING

Once a delegation of authority is made to an agency, the agency may make rules within its grant of authority. At the federal level, these rules become a part of the *Code of Federal Regulations*, a collection of all existing agency rules. The rules have "the force of law." Rules are also made by agencies at the state level with similar effect. The APA provides for two rule-making procedures: (1) **formal rule making** and **informal** or **notice and comment rule making.**

### Formal Rule Making

*Formal rule making* involves a trial-type hearing preceding the adoption of a rule. If a statute requires that rules be made "on the record," formal rule-making procedures must be used. Those procedures include a formal hearing, similar to a courtroom trial, including presentation of evidence, the right of cross-examination, and the right of appeal or review. Formal rule making is extremely time-consuming and costly. Only a few federal statutes (by one count, only fifteen laws) require formal procedures. Perhaps the most important statute requiring formal procedures is the federal Food, Drug and Cosmetic Act of 1938.

### Notice and Comment: Informal Rule Making

*Informal rule making*, sometimes called *notice and comment rule making*, has been called "one of the greatest inventions of modern government"[4] because of its compromise of governmental efficiency and citizen access to public affairs. Almost all federal rule making takes place under notice and comment procedures.

---

3 *Bowsher v. Synar*, 478 U.S. 714, 106 S. Ct. 3181, 92 L. Ed. 2d 583 (1986).
4 Kenneth Culp Davis, *Administrative Law*, 6th Ed. (St. Paul, Minn.: West Publ. Co., 1975), p. 448.

The APA requires that *notice* of any proposed rule making must be published in the *Federal Register,* a daily publication of the federal government, unless all of the people subject to the rule are somehow personally served or have actual notice of the rule-making proceedings. The notice must detail the time, place, and nature of the proceedings, the legal authority under which the rule is proposed, and the terms or substance of the proposed rule. Interested parties must then be given an opportunity to *comment,* either personally or in writing. Virtually all comments are made in writing (see Figure 6.3).

The purpose of notice and comment rule making is to assure public access to the rule-making process. Agencies need not permit oral comment, but they must permit an opportunity for written comments by members of the public. A small number of statutes, such as the Magnuson-Moss Warranty Act (see p. 330), provide that the agency *must* permit oral comment.

Certain types of rules are excluded from the requirements of notice and comment, including rules governing management and personnel matters, and matters that are considered adjudicatory (discussed later in this chapter). Interpretative rules (that is, rules which interpret statutes or other rules) must be published in the *Federal Register* but are not subject to notice and comment requirements.

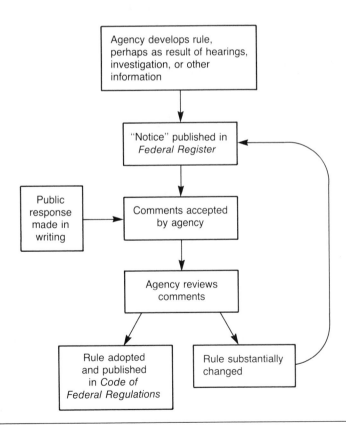

FIGURE 6.3    Notice and Comment Procedures

## ADMINISTRATIVE ADJUDICATION

Many agencies have the duty to judge various claims in a manner similar to the way in which courts adjudicate claims. For example, the National Labor Relations Board adjudicates claims between employees and employers. Other agencies adjudicate claims of citizens against the agencies themselves, such as claims for benefits under the Social Security Act. Examples of adjudicatory hearings before administrative agencies are almost endless, including license applications, appeals of tax and zoning decisions, disciplinary hearings in prisons, and even decisions regarding the expulsion or suspension of children from school. All of those examples and many more require the administrator to act as a judge. The question then is what kinds of procedures the administrator, acting as a judge, must use.

### Due Process and the Adjudicatory Function

As noted in Chapter 4, the fifth and fourteenth amendments provide that no person may be deprived of "life, liberty, or property, without due process of law." Many administrative procedures involve potential deprivations of liberty and property. For example, an increase of a real estate tax assessment clearly deprives the owner of property by making the tax bill higher; similarly, if the Federal Trade Commission or the Securities and Exchange Commission imposes an administrative order on a firm, the firm may have been deprived of property or even some forms of liberty. For decades due process rights had to be granted if a person was to be deprived of a *right*, but not if the person was to be deprived of a *privilege*. For example, a driver's license was considered a privilege. Under the old interpretations, the state could suspend or revoke that license without first giving that person a hearing, an opportunity to present the other side of the case, or notice of the proceedings.

In the 1960's this old right-privilege doctrine came under substantial criticism and was finally laid to rest in *Goldberg v. Kelly*,[5] the famous "welfare rights" case. That case held that due process procedures must be followed when a state agency attempts to terminate welfare payments, and that a hearing is required *prior* to that termination. According to a long line of cases following *Goldberg*, fair procedures must be used whenever a *protected interest* is involved, and such interests have been found in a large variety of situations, from school expulsions and suspensions to parole revocations to termination of welfare and social security benefits. The following case discusses the nature of the hearing and other procedures that must be afforded if a protected interest is threatened.

---

# Mathews v. Eldridge
424 U.S. 319, 96 S. Ct. 893, 47 L. Ed. 2d 18 (1976)

Eldridge, who received disability benefits under the Social Security Act, was informed by the Social Security Administration that the agency had found that his disability had

---

5  397 U.S. 254, 90 S. Ct. 1011, 25 L. Ed. 2d 287 (1970).

ended and that his benefits would not be continued. The letter to Eldridge also advised him that he could request additional time to submit other relevant information. Eldridge responded by letter, disagreeing with the administration's finding, but submitting no new information. The agency made a final determination and terminated Eldridge's benefits but allowed him a hearing *after* the benefits were terminated. Instead of taking advantage of that posttermination hearing, Eldridge filed suit, claiming that the agency's procedures did not afford him due process. The court of appeals held for Eldridge, finding that the agency's procedures violated the fifth amendment due process clause. The administrator of the Social Security Administration appealed the judgment to the Supreme Court.

**Mr. Justice Powell delivered the opinion of the Court** The issue in this case is whether the Due Process Clause of the Fifth Amendment requires that prior to the termination of Social Security disability benefit payments the recipient be afforded an opportunity for an evidentiary hearing. . . .

Procedural due process imposes constraints on governmental decisions which deprive individuals of "liberty" or "property" within the meaning of the Due Process Clause of the Fifth or Fourteenth Amendments. The Secretary [of HEW, the defendant in the case] does not contend that procedural due process is inapplicable to terminations of social security disability benefits. He recognizes, as has been implicit in our prior decisions, that the interest of an individual in continued receipt of these benefits is a statutorily created "property" interest protected by the Fifth Amendment. . . . Rather, the Secretary contends that the existing administrative procedures . . . provide all the process that is constitutionally due before a recipient can be deprived of that interest.

This Court consistently has held that some form of hearing is required before an individual is finally deprived of a property interest. . . . The "right to be heard before being condemned to suffer grievous loss of any kind, even though it may not involve the stigma and hardships of criminal conviction, is a principle basic to our society." . . . The fundamental requirement of due process is the opportunity to be heard "at a meaningful time and in a meaningful manner." Eldridge argues that the review procedures available to a claimant before the initial determination of ineligibility becomes final would be adequate if disability benefits were not terminated until after the evidentiary hearing state of the administrative process. The dispute centers upon what process is due prior to the initial termination of benefits, pending review.

In recent years this Court increasingly has had occasion to consider the extent to which due process requires an evidentiary hearing prior to the deprivation of some type of property interest even if such a hearing is provided thereafter. . . .

These decisions underscore the truism that "[d]ue process, unlike some legal rules, is not a technical conception with a fixed content unrelated to time, place, and circumstances. . . . [D]ue process is flexible and calls for such procedural protections as the particular situation demands." . . . Accordingly, resolution of the issue whether the administrative procedures provided here are constitutionally sufficient requires analysis of the governmental and private interests that are affected. . . . More precisely, our prior decisions indicate that identification of the specific dictates of due process generally requires consideration of three distinct factors: first, the private interest that will be affected by the official action; second, the risk of an erroneous deprivation of such interest through the procedures used, and the probable value, if any, of additional or substitute procedural safeguards; and finally the government's interest including the function involved and the fiscal and administrative burdens that the additional or substitute procedural requirement would entail. . . .

Since a recipient whose benefits are terminated is awarded full retroactive relief if he ultimately prevails, his sole interest is in the uninterrupted receipt of this source of income pending final administrative decision on his claim. . . .

The Secretary concedes that the delay between a request for a hearing before an Administrative Law Judge and a decision on the claim is currently between 10 and 11 months. Since a terminated recipient must first obtain a reconsideration decision as a prerequisite to invoking his right to an evidentiary hearing, the delay between the actual cut-off of benefits and final decision after a hearing exceeds one year.

In view of the torpidity of this administrative review process, and the typically modest resources of the family unit of the physically disabled worker, the hardship imposed upon the erroneously terminated disability recipient may be significant. Still, the disabled worker's need is likely to be less than that of a welfare recipient. In addition to the possibility of access to private resources, other forms of government assistance will become available where the termination of disability benefits places a worker or his family below the subsistence level. . . .

By contrast, the decision whether to discontinue disability benefits will turn, in most cases, upon "routine standard, and unbiased medical reports by physician specialists." . . . To be sure, credibility and veracity may be a factor in the ultimate disability assessment in some cases. But procedural due process rules are shaped by the risk of error inherent in the truth-finding process as applied to the generality of cases, not the rare exceptions. . . .

In striking the appropriate due process balance the final factor to be assessed is the public interest. This includes the administrative burden and other societal costs that would be associated with requiring, as a matter of constitutional right, an evidentiary hearing upon demand in all cases prior to the termination of disability benefits. The most visible burden would be the incremental cost resulting from the increased number of hearings and the expense of providing benefits to ineligible recipients pending decision. No one can predict the extent of the increase, but the fact that full benefits would continue until after such hearings would assure the exhaustion in most cases of this attractive option. . . .

We conclude that an evidentiary hearing is not required prior to the termination of disability benefits and that the present administrative procedures fully comport with due process.

The judgment of the Court of Appeals is reversed.

**Mr. Justice Brennan, with Whom Mr. Justice Marshall Joins, Dissenting**   I would add that the Court's consideration that a discontinuance of disability benefits may cause the recipient to suffer only a limited deprivation is no argument. It is speculative. Moreover, the very legislative determination to provide disability benefits, without any prerequisite determination of need in fact, presumes a need by the recipient which is not this Court's to denigrate. Indeed, in the present case, it is indicated that because disability benefits were terminated there was a foreclosure upon the Eldridge home and the family's furniture was repossessed, forcing Eldridge, his wife and children to sleep in one bed. . . . Finally, it is also no argument that a worker, who has been placed in the untenable position of having been denied disability benefits, may still seek other forms of public assistance.

## Case Discussion Questions

1   What is the three-part test described in this case?
2   What is the protected interest in this case? What kind of hearing is required?
3   How would the three-part test in this case be applied to (a) the firing of a police officer; (b) revocation of a driver's license; (c) revocation of "time off for good behavior" as a disciplinary matter in a prison; (d) revocation of a license to transact business as a restaurant?

---

The *Mathews* "balancing test" has been applied in a variety of situations in cases that followed. The precise nature of the due process procedures required in each case depends on the balancing of the three factors mentioned in *Mathews*: (1) the nature of the interest involved, (2) the possibility of erroneous deprivation and whether additional procedures will relieve that possibility, and (3) the nature of the state interest in not providing such additional procedures.

As a general rule, the more important the interest being protected, the more formal the procedures used by the agency. If the interest is minor, such as a ten-day disciplinary suspension from school, due process only requires an informal conference with the decision maker and the right to present one's side of the case. On the other hand, in cases where the interest is more important, such as a revocation of parole or of time off

There appear to be ten potential "ingredients" of due process. Which of the ten ingredients will be required depends on the outcome of the *Mathews* balancing test.* Those potential ingredients of due process include the following:

1   *Notice.* A timely and adequate statement, either oral or written, of the nature of the charges and the time and place of any hearing

2   *Right to confront witnesses.* The right to be present when witnesses contrary to one's position are giving evidence

3   *Oral arguments.* The right to state one's position to the decision maker

4   *Evidence.* The right to present evidence orally, as is done in courtrooms

5   *Cross-examination.* The right to use cross-examination techniques in questioning adverse witnesses

6   *Discovery.* The right to obtain disclosure of evidence by the agency or the adverse party prior to the hearing, if any

7   *Attorney.* The right to have an attorney present and, in some instances, to have an attorney appointed without charge

8   *Record.* The right to have the proceedings recorded in some way and to have the decision on the record as well

9   *Decision.* The right to have a statement of the decision maker's reasons for the result and an indication of the evidence relied upon

10   *Decision maker.* The right to an impartial decision maker, rather than one with an obvious bias

FIGURE 6.4    The Ingredients of Due Process

* See Paul Verkuil, "A Study of Informal Adjudicative Procedures," 43, *University of Chicago Law Review*, 739, 760 (1976).

for good behavior from a prison term, a very formal hearing is required, affording all of the ingredients of due process (see Figure 6.4) in a proceeding much like a courtroom trial.

### Adjudication Procedure under the APA

The APA provides detailed rules for the conduct of adjudicatory hearings. These rules apply to "every case of adjudication" by agencies, with a few exceptions. Those exceptions include employee selection and tenure, military and foreign affairs matters, and the certification of worker representatives (unions) under the National Labor Relations Act. The act provides for many of the ingredients of due process, such as notice, oral presentation of arguments and evidence, representation by an attorney, discovery, and an impartial decision maker.

**Administrative Law Judges**    There appears to be a strong potential for conflicts of interest in many agency cases, because the "prosecutor" and "judge" are both employees of the same agency. Courts have held that *potential* bias is not the same as *actual* bias, and that the courts will not presume bias exists unless it is shown that the decision maker is actually prejudiced.

In federal agencies the problem of bias has been partially resolved through the appointment of **administrative law judges (ALJs)**. ALJs are hired by an agency to act as hearing officers in adjudicatory hearings, but they cannot be fired by the agency. The tenure and compensation of ALJs are governed by the Civil Service Act, thereby guaranteeing some independence.

**The Adjudicatory Process**    The usual pattern of decision making in the federal system involves the assignment of a case to an ALJ. The ALJ may conduct a prehearing conference, which serves many of the same purposes as pretrial conferences in the courts. A hearing is held later, at which the ALJ administers oaths, issues subpoenas, rules on evidence, and regulates the course of the hearing in a manner similar to a courtroom trial. The parties may submit written briefs to the ALJ, who takes the case under advisement for further study.

Finally, the ALJ issues a proposed report, or initial findings of law and fact, which is forwarded to the agency. Usually, the ALJ does not make the final decision; that task is reserved for the agency itself, but the record and the proposed report by the ALJ form the basis for that decision, and in the majority of cases the agency will follow the proposed report of the ALJ. Following the decision of the agency, an appeal may be filed in the courts (see Figure 6.5.)

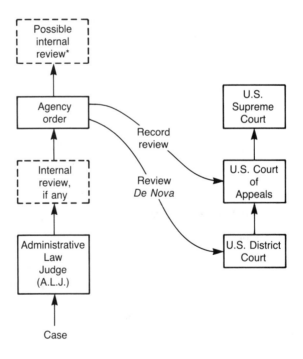

*If granted, an appeal to the courts would start from here.

FIGURE 6.5    The Adjudicatory Process

## Judicial Review of Administrative Actions

One of the oldest controversies in administrative law involves the issue of whether the courts should be permitted to overrule agency rulings. On one side of the controversy are those who point to the possibility of agency abuse and arbitrary conduct and who would require that agency actions be subject to review by the courts. On the other side are those who say that the whole point of agencies is to give the responsibility for making a decision to experts in the area and that the courts are simply not competent to rule.

Some administrative determinations are excluded from judicial review by statute. The APA provides that acts of Congress may state that there shall be no judicial review of the actions of an agency. Such **preclusion of review** by statute is fairly rare and is viewed strictly by the courts, but it is constitutional under Congress's authority to set the jurisdiction of the federal courts under article III of the Constitution.

Most administrative decisions proceed through some kind of *administrative review* within the agency itself, from a regional or local board to a national board, or from a lower-level administrative officer to a higher-level officer or board. But once the final authority of the agency has spoken, an aggrieved party usually has the right to appeal to the courts.

In the federal arena this usually means an appeal directly from the agency to the U.S. courts of appeals (see Figure 6.5). In some instances, Congress has designated a specific U.S. court of appeals to hear cases from a particular agency, in many cases the U.S. Court of Appeals for the Federal Circuit. In other cases, any U.S. court of appeals with proper venue may hear the case. The courts of appeals hear such cases in much the same manner as appeals from the lower federal courts, based on the record of proceedings before the administrative agency. This is known as a **record review.**

In a few instances, parties have a right to present the evidence again before the courts, under the concept of **review de novo.** Such appeals are heard by trial courts rather than appellate courts, and the parties effectively retry the case. The decisions of the trial courts may in turn be appealed to the appellate courts in the usual fashion. Review *de novo* procedures are almost nonexistent in the federal system and rare in state systems.

**Judicial Review under the APA**    The APA specifies six circumstances in which agency adjudicatory decisions may be reviewed by the courts (see Figure 6.6). In addition, the courts have found two other circumstances in which they have authority to review administrative decisions: (1) questions of law and (2) interpretation of constitutional, statutory, and administrative terms.

Many of the rules imposed by the APA are based on the idea of **judicial deference** to agencies. That is, courts generally defer to the expertise of agencies and to the powers given to agencies by the legislature. For example, the *substantial evidence rule* (see Figure 6.6, section 706 E) is based on the reluctance of the courts to second-guess agency findings of fact, particularly those based on the agency's expertise. The courts will overrule the agency if there is not substantial evidence on the record to support the agency's finding. The term *substantial evidence* means only that there must be *some* evidence on the record that the agency could have believed. Similarly, if the agency had the power

*(handwritten margin notes: once you have gotten to a federal Court of appeal Court will not second guess facts presented in case.)*

**Section 706. Scope of Review** To the extent necessary to decision and when presented, the reviewing court shall decide all relevant questions of law, interpret constitutional and statutory provisions, and determine the meaning or applicability of the terms of an agency action. The reviewing court shall (1) compel agency action unlawfully withheld or unreasonably delayed; and (2) hold unlawful and set aside agency action, findings and conclusions found to be: *(handwritten: unfounded)*

A)  Arbitrary, capricious, an abuse of discretion, or otherwise not in accordance with law.

B)  Contrary to constitutional right, power, privilege, or immunity.

C)  In excess of statutory jurisdiction, authority, or limitations, or short of statutory right.

D)  Without observance of procedure required by law.

E)  Unsupported by substantial evidence in a case. . . .

F)  Unwarranted by the facts to the extent that the facts are subject to trial de novo by the reviewing court.

FIGURE 6.6    Standards for Judicial Review Under the Administrative Procedures Act

to do an act, the courts will not second-guess the agency merely because it finds the decision unwise.

Although agencies may be especially competent in their areas of expertise, the courts are by definition expert in determining legal issues. The courts jealously guard their right to determine what the law is and interpret the various constitutional and statutory provisions, including the rules of the agency itself.

**The Doctrine of Exhaustion of Remedies**    **Exhaustion of remedies** is a traditional doctrine of administrative law which requires a party who is challenging an agency ruling to use all of the administrative remedies and procedures available to challenge the decision before taking the case to the courts. The basis for the doctrine is a combination of judicial economy and respect for the decisions of other branches of government.

The exhaustion doctrine has been applied in a fairly flexible manner. Generally speaking, the doctrine is not applied in cases challenging the adequacy of the very administrative procedures that the doctrine would require to be exhausted, or where the administrative procedures or remedies are not available as a matter of right, or where the application of the doctrine produces extremely harsh results. Civil rights actions are not subject to the doctrine, although the Court has never explained the exception except to say that the constitutional challenge in such cases is "sufficiently substantial" to justify not imposing the rule.

## ADMINISTRATIVE INVESTIGATION

In order to fulfill their various rule-making, adjudicatory, and administrative duties, agencies often are required to investigate factual matters. Such investigation is generally considered to be an *executive* function. For rule-making purposes, for example, agencies must collect data in order to make informed judgments when enacting a new rule, or in deciding whether a rule is necessary. Likewise, in making decisions on licensing, deciding claims of adverse parties, or determining issues in enforcement actions, agencies need to obtain facts. Agencies often act as "police officers" to determine whether violations of law have occurred; therefore, agencies need investigative powers in order to ferret out such violations.

Usually the power to investigate, together with many of the investigative tools, is given to an agency by the enabling act, although some of the powers are implied from the authority to enforce the law. One of the principal investigatory powers is the authority to issue subpoenas requiring an individual to appear before an agency or officer.

Unlike subpoenas issued by a judge, administrative subpoenas are not **self-executing;** that is, failure to appear before the agency in response to a subpoena does not automatically subject the violator to contempt proceedings. In order to enforce the subpoena, the document itself must be issued by a judge, or a judge must issue an order requiring the individual to appear. At that point, if the person still refuses to appear, the court may order him to show cause why he should not be held in contempt.

Subpoenas are not the only investigation techniques available to agencies. In some instances agency personnel are authorized to conduct searches, much like those by police officers. Under such circumstances the issue arises whether the administrative officers must comply with fourth amendment standards regarding searches and seizures, and whether they must obtain search warrants. The following landmark case dealt with searches to determine compliance with Occupational Safety and Health Administration (OSHA) standards.

---

## Marshall v. Barlow's, Inc.
436 U.S. 307, 98 S. Ct. 1816 56 L. Ed. 2d 305 (1978)

The Occupational Safety and Health Act empowered agents of the Secretary of Labor to search work areas of any employment facility to find safety hazards and violations of OSHA regulations. No search warrant was required for such inspections under the act. The respondent refused to permit a search without a warrant, and the Secretary applied for a court order compelling Barlow's to admit the officers. Barlow's requested an injunction against warrantless searches. The district court ruled that a warrant was required and that the sections of OSHA which permitted searches without a warrant were unconstitutional. The Secretary appealed.

**Mr. Justice White Delivered the Opinion of the Court** The Secretary urges that warrantless inspections to enforce OSHA are reasonable within the meaning of the Fourth Amendment. . . . This Court has already held that warrantless searches are generally unreasonable, and that this rule applies to commercial premises as well as homes. [W]e have held: "[E]xcept in certain carefully defined classes of cases, a search of private property without proper consent is unreasonable unless it has been authorized by a valid search warrant." . . . [W]e also ruled: ". . . The businessman, like the occupant of a residence, has a constitutional right to go about his business free from unreasonable official entries upon his private commercial property. The businessman, too, has that right placed in jeopardy if the decision to enter and inspect for violation of regulatory laws can be made and enforced by the inspector in the field without official authority evidenced by a warrant." . . . It therefore appears that unless some recognized exception to the warrant requirement applies, . . . a warrant [is required] to conduct the inspection sought in this case.

The Secretary urges that an exception from the

search warrant requirement has been recognized for "pervasively regulated businesses," . . . and for "closely regulated" industries "long subject to close supervision and inspection." . . . These cases are indeed exceptions, but they represent responses to relatively unique circumstances.

The Secretary submits that warrantless inspections are essential to the proper enforcement of OSHA because they afford the opportunity to inspect without prior notice and hence preserve the advantages of surprise. . . . To the suggestion that warrants may be issued *ex parte* and executed without delay and without prior notice, thereby preserving the element of surprise, the Secretary expresses concern for the administrative strain that would be experienced by the inspection system, and by the courts. . . .

We are unconvinced, however, that requiring warrants to inspect will impose serious burdens on the inspection system or the courts, will prevent inspections necessary to enforce the statute, or will make them less effective. . . .

Whether the Secretary proceeds to secure a warrant . . . his entitlement will not depend on his demonstrating probable cause to believe that conditions in violation of OSHA exist on the premises. Probable cause in the criminal sense is not required. For purposes of an administrative search such as this, probable cause justifying the issuance of a warrant may be based . . . on a showing that "reasonable legislative or administrative standards for conducting an . . . inspection are satisfied. . . ."

We hold that Barlow was entitled to a declaratory judgment that the Act is unconstitutional insofar as it purports to authorize inspections without warrant. . . .

**Mr. Justice Stevens, with Whom Mr. Justice Blackmun and Mr. Justice Rehnquist Join, Dissenting** Because of the acknowledged importance and reasonableness of routine inspections in the enforcement of federal regulatory statutes such as OSHA, the Court recognizes that requiring full compliance with the Warrant Clause would invalidate all such inspection programs. Yet, rather than simply analyzing such programs under the "reasonableness" clause of the Fourth Amendment, the Court holds the OSHA program invalid under the Warrant Clause and then avoids a blanket prohibition on all routine, regulatory inspections by relying on the notion that the "probable cause" requirement . . . may be relaxed whenever the Court believes that the governmental need to conduct a category of "searches" outweighs the intrusion on interests protected by the Fourth Amendment. . . .

Fidelity to the original understanding of the Fourth Amendment therefore leads to the conclusion that the Warrant Clause has no application to routine, regulatory inspections of commercial premises. . . .

## Case Discussion Questions

1  Does this decision protect business from OSHA inspections? What does OSHA need to know before it undertakes an inspection?
2  How does this case relate to *New York v. Burger* (p. 131)?
3  What purpose does the search warrant serve?

## REMEDIES AGAINST IMPROPER ADMINISTRATIVE ACTS

If a person is injured as a result of improper actions of an administrative agency, several forms of relief are available. **Injunctions** may be available to order an agency to stop acting, and **declaratory judgments** are sometimes used to declare the rights of the parties in relation to the agency.

Under some circumstances, **civil lawsuits**, claiming money damages, may be filed against the agency itself, against the unit of government of which the agency is a part, or against the individual officer. The primary problem with lawsuits of this kind is the doctrine of **sovereign immunity**, which says that the government cannot be sued without its permission. The doctrine is derived from ancient common law and is based on the theory that the king can do no wrong. The doctrine caused some very unfair results, and substantial sentiment arose to do away with the doctrine.

Finally, in 1946, Congress passed the **Federal Tort Claims Act,** which provided in part that "The United States shall be liable . . . relating to tort claims, in the same manner and to the same extent as a private individual under like circumstances."

The act contained several exceptions from liability, however, and two of those exceptions are directly applicable to suits against administrative officers. The first exception provides that certain intentional torts, such as libel, slander, misrepresentation, deceit, and others, cannot form the basis of a suit against the government. Many of the acts of administrative agencies are "intentional acts" and would therefore fall within this exception. A 1974 amendment reduced the impact of this exception substantially by withdrawing the exemption for suits based on assault, battery, false imprisonment, false arrest, abuse of process, and malicious prosecution by federal investigative or law enforcement officers.

The second exception deals with claims based on the "exercise or performance or the failure to exercise or perform a discretionary function or duty on the part of a federal agency or an employee of the Government." This exception seems to say that if Congress has given an agency the discretion to do an act, the agency may not be sued for performing or not performing the act. The discretionary duty exception extends to the acts of subordinates carrying out orders based on such discretionary authority.

Although suits against the government or an agency may not be available, actions may be available against the individual officers who committed the wrong. Generally speaking, such suits may be based on common law principles of liability, various civil rights statutes, or the Constitution itself. Officers may also be cloaked in some form of immunity. Judges have "absolute immunity" from suit while acting in their judicial capacity even if their actions are malicious or undertaken in bad faith. Legislators are immune from suit for their votes and for various activities undertaken in their capacity as legislators, such as speeches before the legislature. Administrators are generally immune from suit if they are acting within their sphere of duties and the acts are performed in good faith and in a reasonable manner.

States have a double protection from civil lawsuits. The common law doctrine of sovereign immunity applies to state governments as well as to the federal government, and states are also protected by the eleventh amendment.[6] During the 1960's and 1970's many states enacted statutes similar to the Federal Tort Claims Act, with varying degrees of liability.

## PUBLIC ACCESSIBILITY TO THE
## ADMINISTRATIVE PROCESS

During the 1960's and 1970's, a trend developed toward more citizen access to the administrative process and accountability of agencies to the public they serve. Aspects of that trend include the Freedom of Information Act, the Privacy Act, "government in the sunshine" laws, "sunset" legislation, and the Ethics in Government Act.

---

6 The eleventh amendment provides: "The Judicial Power of the United States shall not be construed to extend to any suit in law or equity, commenced or prosecuted against one of the United States by Citizens of another State, or by Citizens or Subjects of any Foreign State."

### Federal Freedom of Information Act

One concern regarding administrative agencies is the amount and type of records that are kept secret from the public. In 1966 the APA was amended by adding the **Freedom of Information Act.** Prior to this amendment, government was only required to release records to "persons properly and directly concerned" with the records, and records could be kept secret if it was in the public interest to do so. The Freedom of Information Act changed that long-standing policy by requiring any agency to make available records requested by any person. Agencies now have the burden of proving that the records fit within any of the exceptions to the act, such as trade secrets, personnel and medical files, and matters dealing with national security and foreign policy. Requests for records may be directed to the agency, and the agency must respond within ten days. Federal court actions are available to force an agency to produce the records.

### Federal Privacy Act

Another concern during the 1970's was the sheer amount of information that the government had collected or might collect in the future about individuals. That concern resulted in 1974 in the **Federal Privacy Act,** again an amendment to the APA. The act gives citizens control over the information collected about them by requiring agencies to report the existence of all systems of records maintained on individuals. The act further requires that the information be accurate, complete, and up-to-date, and provides procedures whereby individuals can inspect records and correct inaccuracies. Agencies cannot share information with other agencies, and they must keep an accurate record of all of their disclosures of information. There are exemptions for law enforcement and CIA files, classified documents concerning national defense and foreign policy, and government employment matters. Persons dissatisfied with agency action may appeal to higher authorities within the affected agency and may file federal court actions.

### Sunshine Statutes

**Sunshine statutes,** also termed *open meeting laws,* have been adopted by the federal government and all fifty states. Such laws require that government meetings be held in public, but the degree of openness and the types of meetings subject to such laws vary considerably.

At the federal level, a 1976 amendment to the APA provides for public meetings of advisory committees, study panels, and ad hoc committees within the executive branch, and to congressional committees in the legislative branch. The principle was also applied to Congress through resolutions passed by both houses of Congress. The act applies only to multiheaded federal agencies, generally meaning independent regulatory commissions, and not to single-headed bodies. In addition, federal bodies may go into *executive session*, or closed session, simply by majority vote.

### Sunset Legislation

A 1970's innovation in administrative law is so-called **sunset legislation,** which provides for automatic expiration of certain regulatory statutes and agency enabling acts. The purpose of such laws is to require legislative review of the agency from time to time, and an affirmative vote of the legislature is necessary if the agency is to continue in existence. Without automatic expiration, some agencies might continue to operate indefinitely, even though their purpose is fulfilled or they have ceased to be useful.

### Ethics in Government Act

The **Ethics in Government Act,** passed in 1978, was aimed at "influence peddling" by former government officials. After government employees left their jobs, they often took positions with lobbyists or law firms dealing with the government to take advantage of their knowledge and contacts. The Ethics Act prohibits officials from aiding private parties with which they were involved while in office for a period of two years, and in some cases forever. The law also prevents all contact between the former official and his agency for one year after leaving office. Criminal penalties and administrative sanctions are available as remedies.

### Equal Access to Justice Act

The **Equal Access to Justice Act** of 1982 attempts to deal with the problem of the costs of suing the government. Many people do not contest government actions because it is so expensive to do so. The Equal Access to Justice Act permits courts to award attorneys' fees if the government has not acted in a manner that was "substantially justified."

Attorneys' fees may only be awarded to people with a net worth of under $1 million, businesses worth less than $5 million with fewer than 500 employees, and charitable and religious tax-exempt organizations with fewer than 500 employees. The claimant must also have won in court to be eligible, and the court must have found that the government's original position was not "substantially justified."

### SUMMARY AND CONCLUSIONS

Much of American government policy is made by administrative agencies in their rule-making, adjudicatory, and investigative functions. Such agencies are initially created through a legislative act or executive order and are given power through an enabling act, which delegates the authority to make rules to the agency. Issues of separation of powers are inherent in the nature of such delegations, and many of those issues are as yet unresolved.

The federal Administrative Procedure Act governs the procedures used by agencies at the federal level. That act provides procedures for making rules and adjudicating claims, and it contains the federal Freedom of Information Act, Privacy Act, and Open Meeting Act. In its adjudicatory capacity, an agency is also subject to constitutional restrictions under the due process clauses.

Judicial review of agency decisions is available, but generally the courts defer to the judgment of the agency. The courts will review questions of law and will also review agency decisions if they constitute an abuse of discretion or are not based on substantial evidence, or if the actions are otherwise invalid under the Administrative Procedure Act. Courts will generally refuse to review actions if the party asking the review has failed to exhaust the available administrative remedies.

During the 1960's and 1970's concern with agency accountability and power produced several restrictions on agency authority, including the Freedom of Information

Act, Privacy Act, and "government in the sunshine" acts. Similar concerns gave rise to the push towards deregulation of various industries during the same period.

## REVIEW QUESTIONS

1  Is there a real distinction between the "rules" of an administrative agency and the "laws" made by a legislature? Isn't the whole theory of delegation of authority a legal fiction?

2  Can you defend the statement that notice and comment rule making is "one of the most creative and important jurisprudential developments of the century"?

3  Should judges defer to the judgment of agencies in their rule-making functions? Always? Under what circumstances should such deference *not* be paid?

4  Which of the ten ingredients of administrative due process are most important? Which should *always* be accorded?

5  Should all administrative agency meetings be open to the public?

6  The FTC issued a complaint against several major advertisers, claiming that their advertisements were false and deceptive. The hearing was scheduled for several months later. The firms brought a separate declaratory judgment action in federal court in the hopes of getting the matter resolved sooner. Will the court grant a declaratory judgment?

7  James was a recipient of public assistance. A caseworker for the local department that provided the aid insisted on inspecting James's home to see if there was any change in her circumstances. James insisted that the agency obtain a search warrant. (1) Must the agency obtain a warrant? (2) May the agency terminate James's public aid if she fails to permit entry without a warrant? [*Wyman v. James*, 400 U.S. 309, 91 S. Ct. 381, 27 L. Ed. 2d 408 (1971).]

8  What due process procedures should be required in each of the following cases? (1) Revocation of a driver's license because of conviction of driving while intoxicated; (2) firing of a police officer of twenty years for accepting small bribes; (3) finding a firm guilty of antitrust violations and imposition of a $1 million fine; (4) taking away the license of a stockbroker for insider trading violations; (5) requiring a firm to clean up a major oil spill.

9  The Internal Revenue Service issued a summons to Euge to give handwriting samples to IRS agents so that those agents could check his signature against those on bank accounts that the agents believed Euge held under an assumed name. Euge refused, and the agency requested the court to order Euge to give the samples. Must he do so? [*U.S. v. Euge*, 444 U.S. 707, 100 S. Ct. 874, 63 L. Ed. 2d 141 (1980).]

10  Rivers wishes to become a real estate broker, and in the state in which Rivers lives, she must be licensed by the State Board of Real Estate. That Board turned Rivers down because of "moral turpitude," because she had been convicted of shoplifting twenty years ago. There is an appeal to the Secretary of State, but the Secretary of State need not hear such cases if he doesn't want to; and in the last twenty years the Secretary of State has never overruled the State Board. May Rivers file suit in court without first applying for an appeal?

CHAPTER 7

# International Law

Business students at the end of the twentieth century cannot avoid dealing with international law and business. A grocery chain in Tennessee that wants to purchase Danish hams is introduced to the world of letters of credit and import restrictions. A California manufacturer of athletic shoes discovers that a Hong Kong firm is flooding the market with cheap imitations that infringe its patents. An Iowa company wants to export its grain to Czechoslovakia. A New York television manufacturer is faced with unfair competition by Japanese competitors subsidized by their government. A Texas oil company finds that its property in the Mideast has been expropriated by its host country. Even if these firms never considered themselves "international," they face problems of international law and business.

The international legal system is very different from and far more complex than the domestic legal system. First and foremost, there is no central legal authority in the international system. As a result, international law is enforced by a hodge-podge of international courts, national courts, arbitration organizations, and political bodies. Legal definitions of contracts may differ widely between nations, and language differences may create differences in interpretation. Nations with an English background use a common law system, while much of the rest of the world refuses to recognize the doctrine of *stare decisis*. Communist nations have developed legal doctrines far different from those in much of the rest of the world. Developing countries have vastly different interests from those of the industrialized nations. As a result of these and many other factors, the international legal system is far less predictable than the familiar American legal system.

This chapter provides an overview of international law. First, we will briefly look at some definitions and the problem of whether there is such a thing as "international law," since there is not a common government or monopoly of force in the international arena. We will then review the basic institutions of international law and the techniques by which disputes may be settled in the international arena. The chapter will conclude with some of the more important doctrines of international law, especially regarding some of the problems surrounding international trade.

## SOME TERMS AND CLASSIFICATIONS

**Nations, States, and Countries**    In international affairs, the term **state** refers to politically sovereign bodies who make up the world, such as the United States, Sweden, the USSR, and many others. The term **country** also means some sovereign political body. Those terms are sometimes used interchangeably with the term **nation.** On the other hand, *nation* may also be used properly to mean some homogeneous group of people who look at themselves as a group, regardless of political independence or geographic borders. For example, Eskimos, Uzbeks, Germans, and Moslems might all owe more allegiance to some ethnic or language group than to some artificial political state.

**Sovereignty**    The term **sovereignty** is vital in international affairs and international law. That term means the supreme political power and authority over a geographic area. For example, the government of France has sovereignty over the geographical area within its jurisdiction. On the other hand, the Soviet region of Byelorussia is not a "sovereign" nation, nor are the American states.

It is sometimes said that the only thing standing in the way of true international law is sovereignty. That is because each nation jealously guards its sovereignty. The courts of the United States cannot compel action against a citizen of Argentina living in Argentina, because Argentina is a sovereign nation. There is no true international law because there is no central authority with a monopoly of force to enforce international law. For example, if you break a traffic law, you may be required to appear in court. If you fail to appear, or fail to pay the fine, the police or sheriff will physically arrest you. If you do not cooperate, the authorities may use all necessary force to make you comply. The ultimate power of law is the monopoly of force.

But in the international arena, no such monopoly of force exists. Each nation has its own monopoly of force as part of its sovereignty and may protect its citizens from the force threatened by other nations. One of the reasons why "international law" cannot outlaw war is that nations are unlikely to give up their sovereignty and monopoly of force to any international group, legal or otherwise. It therefore seems to make little sense to speak of "international law."

In another sense, there *is* a real "international law." It is not as absolute as a state legal system, such as that of the state of Utah or the nation of France. It is instead a combination of vague and uncertain notions, enforced haltingly and inconsistently by world tribunals, regional organizations, and national and state court systems. Sanctions imposed by those courts may not be enforceable in the same way or to the same extent that decrees of state courts are enforced, but often other ways exist to enforce those sanctions.

**Treaties**    A **treaty** is an agreement between sovereign states. Treaties may be either **bilateral,** meaning between *two* states, or **multilateral,** meaning between several states. Treaties are sometimes called **conventions,** particularly when they involve several countries. The United Nations and other international bodies have proposed **draft conventions** on many occasions to the world community for their consideration. A draft convention is a kind of model treaty which the nations may accept or not.

Treaties with the United States must be *ratified* by the U.S. Senate before they become effective, even though they are negotiated by the executive branch. Once ratified, treaties have the force of law and are second only to the U.S. Constitution in the rank order of law as imposed by the supremacy clause (see p. 101).

**Tariffs, Duties, and Embargoes**    A **tariff** is a tax on imports. A *protective tariff* protects local business from foreign competition, whereas a *retaliatory tariff* is enacted in response to another country's tariff. A **duty** may either be a tariff on imports or a tax on *exporting* goods. An **embargo** is a complete bar to transportation of certain goods into or out of a country.

## A BRIEF OVERVIEW OF INTERNATIONAL LAW

International law is the body of rules that nations are expected to observe in their relations with one another. Most rules have developed from *customs*, some as much as 2,500 years old, followed by civilized nations. For example, even the ancient Greeks followed the custom of not mistreating ambassadors of other nations. Other doctrines have been recognized in treaties or in the judicial decisions of individual nations. In the late 1600's, Hugo Grotius, a Dutch statesman, argued that all nations should follow certain international rules of conduct, and he developed many of the rules that are followed even today. For his efforts, Grotius is often called the father of international law.

International law is often divided into three major categories. First, the **Law of Peace** establishes the rights and duties of nations at peace with one another. Every state has a right to existence, legal equality, jurisdiction over its territory, ownership of property, and diplomatic relations with other nations. Most of the principles and problems of international business are parts of the Law of Peace and are established by custom or treaty. Peace is considered the normal relationship between states.

Second, the **Law of War** provides restrictions on nations at war with one another. For example, surrendering enemy soldiers cannot be killed and must be treated as prisoners of war. Even in World War II most nations followed that rule most of the time, although the same cannot be said for recent conflicts, such as Vietnam. The Law of War is often violated and is impossible to enforce except through world opinion or the threat of retaliation.

Third, the **Law of Neutrality** requires that neutral nations must be respected. For example, warring nations may not move troops across neutral territory. During World War II, Switzerland remained neutral for the entire war, even though its territory lay in the heart of the war zone. Of course, Switzerland occupies a unique place in the international arena because of its unbending neutrality and its usefulness as a center for international diplomacy and commerce.

### An International Business Transaction

Probably the most common international business transaction is a simple sale of goods by a citizen of one country to a citizen of another. In such a transaction the seller may worry about not being paid after the goods are shipped, while the buyer will not want to pay unless the goods have arrived, or at least have been shipped. The buyer will also be concerned about whether the goods meet the requirements of the contract and will want to pay only after having inspected the goods. Payment terms may cause problems because of currency fluctuations and the difficulty of converting currencies. And finally, international disruptions such as wars, revolutions, and terrorist attacks may make international transactions far riskier than domestic ones.

Because of the distances and risks involved, most international transactions are arranged as **documentary sales.** In the contract of purchase the parties will agree to payment through a **letter of credit.** A letter of credit is a promise by the buyer's bank, known as the **issuing bank,** to the seller that the issuing bank will pay the contract amount to the seller if the seller produces documentary evidence in the form of a **bill of lading** (a negotiable receipt from the shipper) that the seller has shipped the goods (see Figure 7.1.)

Step A

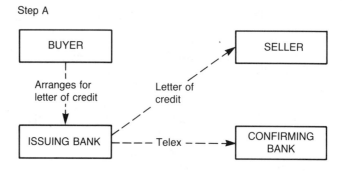

Step B

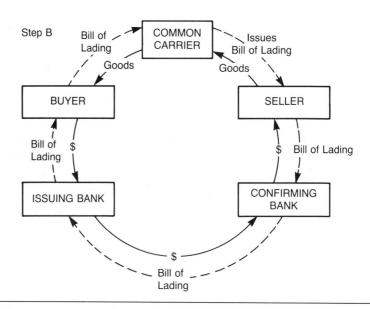

FIGURE 7.1   An International Business Transaction

The buyer's bank will ordinarily telex its correspondent bank, known as the **confirming bank,** located near the seller, advising that it has opened a letter of credit in favor of the buyer and stating all of the details of the letter of credit contract (see Figure 7.1, step A). The seller will then ship the goods by some common carrier, such as a shipping company, who gives the seller a bill of lading. If the seller meets all of the terms of the contract and provides the confirming bank with the bill of lading, the confirming bank will then pay the seller.

The confirming bank then sends the bill of lading to the issuing bank and is paid. The issuing bank then releases the bill of lading to the buyer after it has been paid, and the buyer may obtain the goods from the carrier with the bill of lading, often after a right of inspection granted by the contract (see Figure 7.1, step B).

Although this system appears relatively simple, there are a number of complications. The nations involved may have established trade quotas or embargoes. Language difficulties may result in differences in interpretation of the documents. The law of contracts may not be the same in the seller's and buyer's countries, even though a draft treaty, known as the **Convention on International Sales of Goods,** has been proposed and accepted by many nations. If such complications develop, it may be necessary to file suit in one country or another, or before some international court.

## INSTITUTIONS OF INTERNATIONAL LAW

A variety of institutions may decide disputes in the international arena. Some of those institutions are not "courts" in the traditional sense, but instead are major actors in the international system that decide disputes between governments and private parties. Those institutions include the **United Nations,** the **International Court of Justice,** the **European Economic Community** (the **Common Market**), the **Council for Mutual Economic Aid** (COMECON), the **World Bank,** and the **International Monetary Fund** (IMF). Finally, much of the work of international law is done by national court systems.

### The United Nations

The *United Nations* itself, while not a court in the traditional sense, does try to resolve disputes involving its member states. The United Nations was created following World War II in 1945 out of the wreckage of the League of Nations. The *General Assembly* consists of representatives of all member nations. The *Security Council* is charged with keeping world peace, and the *Economic and Social Council* has several duties, including enhancing human rights and helping people to achieve a better way of life. The *Trusteeship Council* watches over territories that are not yet self-governing, and the *International Court of Justice* administers international law. The *Secretariat* helps all of the other organs do their job more efficiently. There are also several specialized agencies, as shown in Table 7.1.

Disputes between nations may be resolved through votes of the General Assembly or within the various specialized agencies. Nations may refuse to be bound by those decisions, but the members may impose economic sanctions or even create armed peace-keeping forces, such as those in Korea, Lebanon, and other parts of the world.

### The International Court of Justice

The *International Court of Justice*, or the *World Court*, is the principal judicial organ of the United Nations. It was created in 1945 and was preceded by the Permanent Court of International Justice, which was created by the League of Nations in 1920 and dissolved in 1946. The World Court consists of fifteen members elected by the members of the UN or other countries who have elected to join in the court. Members serve for nine years, and one-third of the members are elected every three years.

Private individuals and corporations cannot institute proceedings before the World Court. Actions may be brought by (1) states that are members of the UN, (2) states that

TABLE 7.1    Specialized Agencies of the United Nations

| Name | Function |
| --- | --- |
| Food and Agricultural Organization (FAO) | Helps improve farm production, forests, and fisheries |
| Intergovernmental Maritime Consultative Organization (IMCO) | Encourages cooperation in shipping practices |
| Int'l Civil Aviation Organization | Works for greater air safety and standard flying regulations |
| Int'l Development Association | Lends money for development |
| Int'l Finance Corporation | Lends money for smaller developments |
| Int'l Labor Organization | Helps improve working conditions |
| Int'l Monetary Fund (IMF) | Helps adjust differences between money systems to encourage trade |
| Int'l Telecommunications Union | Helps solve problems of radio, telephone, and satellite communications |
| United Nations Educational, Scientific and Cultural Organization (UNESCO) | Encourages education, science, and culture |
| Universal Postal Union | Works for cooperation in the delivery of mail |
| Int'l Bank for Reconstruction and Development (World Bank) | Lends money for projects like dams, power plants, and railroads |
| World Health Organization | Deals with worldwide health problems |
| World Intellectual Property Organization | Protects artistic and literary works and trademarks |
| World Meteorological Organization | Encourages cooperation in weather forecasting |

have elected to join the court, and (3) states that have accepted the jurisdiction of the court without becoming formal members. States in category 2 have agreed to support the court financially, and states in category 3 have subjected themselves to the jurisdiction of the court and undertake to comply with its decisions. A state may bring an action in its own name on behalf of its citizens, but it is usually quite difficult to convince a government to do so.

**Advisory Opinions**    The World Court has the authority to make *advisory opinions* on any legal question submitted by the United Nations or its specialized agencies. Private parties may not request advisory opinions. Although advisory opinions are generally not binding, the **Convention on the Privileges and Immunities of the United Nations** provides that advisory opinions given in disputes between the United Nations on one hand and a member of the UN on the other "shall be accepted as decisive by the parties."

**Compulsory Jurisdiction in Disputed Cases**    The jurisdiction of the World Court includes (1) all cases referred to it by the parties, (2) all matters provided for in the UN

Charter, and (3) all matters provided for in other treaties or conventions. States may also *agree* to submit other cases to the court, including matters involving

1   The interpretation of a treaty;

2   Any question of international law;

3   The existence of fact which, if established, would constitute a breach of any international obligation;

4   The nature and extent of reparations to be made for breach of any international obligations.

If two states agree to accept the jurisdiction of the court over those four matters, or any of them, **compulsory jurisdiction** exists. Many states have accepted the jurisdiction of the court over the four grounds of compulsory jurisdiction. Thus, if two nations (both of which have agreed to be bound by the four grounds of compulsory jurisdiction) have a dispute, the court has jurisdiction and may decide the case. The United States has *conditionally* accepted the jurisdiction, stating that it reserves the right to bring only certain cases before the court.

The International Court of Justice has established its own rules for deciding cases. It does not accept the notion of *stare decisis*, although it does strive for consistency of its decisions. The selection in the box below establishes the material to which the court will look when it makes a decision.

Enforcement of decisions of the International Court of Justice depends on the goodwill of the parties. The UN Charter provides that if a party fails to perform the obligations of a judgment, the other party "may have recourse to the Security Council, which may, if it deems necessary, make recommendations or decide upon measures to be taken to give effect to the judgment."

On the whole, there has been remarkable compliance with the judgments of the court, although some nations have ignored judgments against them. No case has been taken to the Security Council to decide on measures to be taken to enforce a judgment.

---

# Article 38 of the Statute of the Court of the International Court of Justice

1   The Court, whose function is to decide in accordance with international law such disputes as are submitted to it, shall apply:

   (a) international conventions, whether general or particular, establishing rules expressly recognized by the contesting states;

   (b) international custom, as evidence of a general practice accepted as law;

   (c) the general principles of law recognized by civilized nations;

   (d) . . . judicial decisions and the teachings of the most highly qualified publicists of the various nations, as subsidiary means for the determination of rules of law.

It is not yet clear whether the Security Council may order a state to comply with a judgment, or whether the Security Council may direct or authorize the use of force to enforce a judgment.

## The World Bank and the IMF

Two other agencies of the UN are especially important to business. The *International Bank for Reconstruction and Development*, sometimes called the *World Bank*, exists to make loans to countries for development of major projects, such as dams, roads, and irrigation systems. It lends money to governments and private organizations in member countries. The bank not only gets loan funds from member countries but also borrows in the world money market. It also encourages private investment in member nations.

The *International Monetary Fund* (IMF) is a specialized agency of the UN that seeks to achieve high economic growth and high employment among member nations. The IMF serves as a consultant on world money problems and seeks to stabilize exchange rates and maintain orderly exchange arrangements.

## The European Economic Community (EEC)

The *European Economic Community* (EEC) was created by the **Treaty of Rome** of 1957. The members include Belgium, Denmark, France, West Germany, Greece, Ireland, Italy, Luxembourg, the Netherlands, Portugal, Spain, and the United Kingdom.

The EEC began as a **common market** of states, in which there are no internal tariffs between members and a common external tariff. There are several other common markets or free-trade associations in the world, including the Latin American Integration Association (LAIA), the Central American Common Market (CACM), the Andean Community (ANCOM), and the Caribbean Common Market (CARICOM). Others are emerging in Africa and Southeast Asia.

The EEC is a limited political federation for some economic and social purposes. The community itself has the power to act *within* the territories of the member states. The "Grand Design" of the founders of the EEC was that Western Europe would evolve into a new, federated state by movement from a free-trade area to a common defense force to political unification. Those expectations have in part resulted in virtually binding laws created by the union itself. Member states are required by the terms of the Treaty of Rome to enforce the EEC's law, even if that law conflicts with the law of the state.

The EEC functions through the **Assembly,** also known as the **European Parliament,** which is elected directly by the people of Western Europe and functions as a legislative body. The **Council** consists of one of the ministers of each of the member states, who meet to discuss specific issues of interest, and the **Commission,** which is a permanent administrative body made up of fourteen members appointed for four-year terms by agreement of the parties. The **Court of Justice** consists of eleven members appointed for six-year terms. The Court of Justice serves not only the EEC but also the European Coal and Steel Community and the European Atomic Energy Community. Parties in cases before the court may include individuals and firms, as well as member states or institutions.

## COMECON

The *Council for Mutual Economic Aid* (COMECON) is an East European organization similar to the EEC. Its members include Bulgaria, Cuba, Czechoslovakia, East Germany, Hungary, Poland, Rumania, and the USSR. Its purposes are similar to those of the EEC, but it has not been as successful because of the dominance of the Soviet Union and the reluctance of smaller states to play the roles expected of them.

## INTERNATIONAL DISPUTE RESOLUTION

International disputes may be resolved (1) through the national courts of the states involved, (2) through some international court, (3) through international arbitration, (4) through negotiation and diplomacy, or (5) through the use of force, including war.

### National Court Systems and International Law

Most disputes between individuals in the international arena are resolved through the national court systems of one of the states in which one of the individuals is a citizen. For example, if a citizen of the United States is involved in a dispute with a citizen of France, the dispute may be resolved in the courts of the United States or in the courts of France, assuming that either court has jurisdiction over both the parties and the subject matter of the dispute. The issue of jurisdiction in such cases is often important, and will be discussed further (see p. 177).

In the United States, the federal courts have jurisdiction over diversity cases in which a citizen of a foreign state is a party and if more than $10,000 is in issue (see p. 71). That assumes that the federal courts may exercise *personal jurisdiction* over the foreign party. A summons may be served in foreign countries through a variety of procedures, and a judgment may be entered against foreign nationals. On the other hand, enforcing that judgment may be difficult.

**The Court of International Trade**    The *United States Court of International Trade* was created by Congress to review civil actions arising out of import transactions and certain federal statutes affecting international trade. The nine members of the court are appointed by the President, and not more than five members may belong to the same political party. The court has jurisdiction over the entire United States and may hold hearings abroad as well.

The Court of International Trade has exclusive jurisdiction to decide any civil action *against* the United States, its agencies, or its officers arising from any law involving imports, tariffs, duties, or embargoes, and any civil action brought *by* the United States concerning an import transaction. The court also hears all antidumping (see p. 184) and countervailing duty (see p. 185) cases. The court functions much like a U.S. district court, and decisions of the Court of International Trade may be appealed to the Court of Appeals for the Federal Circuit, and, ultimately, to the U.S. Supreme Court.

### International Courts

As noted previously, a variety of international courts exist, including both the International Court of Justice and a variety of regional or special-purpose courts. Those courts and their jurisdiction are always established by treaties. Their real power depends on the continued acknowledgment of jurisdiction by the parties involved.

### International Arbitration

The process of arbitration requires that the parties to a dispute agree to submit the problem to a neutral third party whose decision is binding on the parties. International arbitration of disputes has existed for over a century. The first instance of international arbitration involved claims by the United States that Great Britain had not acted as a "neutral" during the Civil War. The parties agreed to submit both government and private claims to a "Mixed Commission" consisting of representatives of the United States, Great Britain, Brazil, Italy, and Switzerland.

As a result of that successful arbitration, an agreement known as the *Convention for the Pacific Settlement of International Disputes* was established in 1899, and it is still in force. That convention established a panel of arbitrators and a method of deciding the machinery for arbitration. Each party to a case selects two arbitrators, only one of whom may be a national of that party. The four arbitrators then select an *umpire*. If the four arbitrators cannot agree, a third nation appoints the umpire. The third nation is determined according to an extremely complex procedure.

Arbitration is generally more popular than judicial action in international courts. Only a few treaties require the submission of disputes *before* the dispute arises, and even then nations often include reservations of matters in the "vital interests" of the nations.

In 1965 the **International Center for Settlement of Investment Disputes** was created by the World Bank and submitted to the world community for consideration. The center is available to arbitrate any dispute arising out of an investment between a state and a national of another state. The parties must agree in writing to the jurisdiction of the center and cannot withdraw.

The effectiveness of the awards of international arbitration commissions depends on the willingness of the parties to abide by the decisions. There has been remarkable compliance with those awards, but in some cases disputes over the awards have delayed final compliance for years.

### Negotiation and Diplomacy

Because of the lack of effective enforcement mechanisms in international matters, negotiation and diplomacy become vital methods of settling disputes. A common feature of many international agreements is the creation of mechanisms that make conciliation easier and more effective. Many observers argue that the principal benefit of the UN itself is the establishment of a permanent place and procedures whereby the parties to disputes can conveniently settle their differences through compromise.

### The Use of Force

The ultimate dispute resolution technique in the international arena is, of course, armed force. Although there is an international Law of War, that law consists exclusively of customs which may be (and have been) broken by warring nations who believe it necessary to do so.

The Charter of the United Nations imposed an important philosophical limitation on the use of force by United Nations members. That charter provides that "All Members shall refrain in their international relations from the threat or use of force against the territorial integrity or political independence of any state, or in any other matter inconsistent with the Purposes of the United Nations."

The charter also provides that the Security Council has primary responsibilities for maintaining international peace and security. The right of individual or collective self-defense in the event of an armed attack is expressly preserved by the charter.

## SOME DOCTRINES OF INTERNATIONAL LAW

There are numerous customs of international law that have been observed by civilized nations, but a few of those are particularly important to an understanding of the international legal system. Those doctrines are (1) **jurisdiction,** (2) the doctrine of **sovereign immunity,** (3) the **"act of state" doctrine,** and (4) the **rights of aliens before foreign courts.**

### International Jurisdiction

The meaning of the term *jurisdiction* in international relations is identical to its meaning within a state. Jurisdiction means the right of a state, under international law, to subject certain persons, events, or places to its rules of law. Jurisdiction in international law may be based on the *territorial principle*, the *nationality principle*, or the *protective principle*.

Most jurisdictional rules in international law rely on the **territorial principle.** If conduct takes place *within the territory* of a state, that state has the jurisdiction to deal with it. This is true even if the *effect* of the conduct is outside the territory of that state. For example, if a British merchant sends a defamatory letter to a Spanish citizen, Great Britain has jurisdiction to deal with the problem.

On the other hand, events entirely outside of a nation that have an effect within the nation do not confer jurisdiction on that country. For example, if a French citizen publishes a defamatory letter *in France* about an American citizen, the American courts would have no jurisdiction, although the French courts would. If the defamatory letter had been sent to America, the American courts could deal with it. The issue in such cases is whether there are sufficient contacts with a nation to justify taking jurisdiction.

## *Koster v. Automark Ind., Inc.*
640 F.2d 77
U.S. Court of Appeals, 7th Circuit (1981)

Automark, a corporation doing business in Illinois, agreed to purchase "up to 600,000 valve cap gauges" from Hendrik Koster, a citizen of the Netherlands. The agreement was executed in Milan, Italy, following a series of letters between Koster and Automark, and the gauges were to be manufactured in Switzerland. Automark never ordered any gauges, and Koster never shipped any gauges; and under American law it is doubtful that this promise would be considered a contract.

Koster filed suit in Amsterdam, the Netherlands, and Automark never appeared to defend. The Amsterdam court rendered a default judgment against Automark for $66,000, the price of the gauges. Koster then brought suit in the U.S. district court in Illinois, where Automark's business was located. The trial court granted enforcement of the judgment, and Automark appealed.

**Harlington Wood, Jr., Circuit Judge** The business contacts described above are insufficient to reach the minimum level needed to satisfy due process requirements prerequisite to enforcement of the Dutch default judgment. . . . Whether it be Wisconsin or the Netherlands, the standard of minimum contacts is the same. . . .

Automark's *only* contacts with the Netherlands were eight letters, and possibly a telegram and a transatlantic telephone call all preliminary to the meeting in Italy. [S]uch contacts cannot be held to satisfy jurisdictional requirements, otherwise use of the . . . telephone and mail service to communicate . . . would give jurisdiction to any state into which communications were directed. Such a result would make virtually every business subject to suit in any state with which it happened to communicate in some manner. That clearly would not satisfy the demands of due process. . . .

The Netherlands lacks an adequate relationship to defendant's presence and conduct to justify trial of the case in that country. The interests of international business are better served by protecting potential international purchasers from being unreasonably called to defend suits commenced in foreign courts which lack jurisdiction according to our recognized standards of due process. . . .

[Reversed.]

## Case Discussion Questions

1    What contacts existed between the Netherlands and the parties to this agreement?
2    Did the fact that this contract would have been unenforceable in the United States play any role in this case?
3    Where might this case have been brought? Do other nations recognize our doctrine of procedural due process?

---

If conduct takes place partly within a nation and partly outside of it, as in the case of a series of transactions, any nation in which essential portions of the transactions took place has jurisdiction. For example, a series of contracts that depend on each other but were made in several different countries may be the subject of judgments in any nation involved. If conduct takes place inside of a nation but involves events outside of the nation, the nation may deal with the entire conduct. For example, a person who acquires stolen goods in Mexico and then brings those goods into the United States may be found guilty of possession of stolen goods in the United States.

Nations may also impose jurisdiction under the **nationality principle,** by enacting laws that deal with their own citizens. Thus, the United States may enact laws that bind its own citizens, no matter where they are located. An American citizen traveling abroad who tries to bribe an official of a foreign nation may be found guilty of violating the Foreign Corrupt Practices Act, for example (see p. 186).

Finally, under the so-called **protective principle,** a state also has jurisdiction over conduct that occurs outside of its territory but which threatens its security as a state or the operation of its governmental functions. For example, American law may make it a crime to misrepresent facts on a visa application that is used to enter the United States, even though the visa is issued in a foreign nation.

## The Doctrine of Sovereign Immunity

The doctrine of *sovereign immunity* says that governments are immune from suits brought in the courts of other nations. For example, the courts of the United States have little or no jurisdiction to render a judgment against the government of Mexico. Generally speaking, sovereign immunity protects not only the state itself but also the head of state, the government, the foreign minister, other public ministers or agents of the state, and any corporations created as agencies of the state. For example, the Soviet Union has refused to make any reparations for damages caused in other nations by the Chernobyl nuclear accident on the basis of sovereign immunity.

Because of the growth of government-sponsored commercial activity, problems of sovereign immunity have become more important in recent years. Communist nations, which maintain state foreign-trade monopolies, have demanded absolute immunity from suit, even when suits are based on wholly commercial activities. Other nations have rejected the application of sovereign immunity in such cases.

In 1976 the U.S. Congress adopted the **Foreign Sovereign Immunities Act.** That statute provides that a foreign state is normally immune from the jurisdiction of the federal and state courts, *unless* (1) the foreign state waives its immunity or (2) the claim is based upon commercial activities of a foreign government carried on in the United States or causing a direct effect in the United States. The act also provides that any action against a foreign nation in state courts may be removed to the federal courts.

## The Act of State Doctrine

Closely related to the concept of sovereign immunity is the *act of state doctrine.* That rule says that the courts of one nation will not sit in judgment of the acts *of the government* of another. Any remedy for government actions must come through diplomatic processes or international courts, if at all. Most nations accept a modification of that theory that distinguishes between *public acts* of governments and *private acts* of governments. A private act is one that is performed as though by an individual, rather than in the sphere of governmental functions.

For example, an auto accident between a U.S. embassy car in Austria and a car driven by an Austrian citizen would be a *private* act, and the U.S. government might be sued in Austrian courts. The rule requires that the courts look to *the act itself,* and not to the purpose of the act. Thus, in the auto accident example, even if the car was being used for government purposes at the time of the accident, the U.S. government would be liable.[1]

Commercial acts undertaken by governments are generally considered to be private acts and subject to the jurisdiction of local courts. For example, if a government purchases land in another nation, the transaction is private and is subject to the jurisdiction of the local courts.

Communist states do not accept the distinction between public and private acts. *All* commercial trade with communist states constitutes acts of state because of the govern-

---

1 See *Collision with Foreign Government Owned Motor Car,* 40 Int'l Law Rep. 73 (Supreme Court of Austria, 1970).

ment monopoly over foreign trade under the communist system. Those nations argue that the distinction between private and public acts is a device invented by capitalist states to destroy the state monopoly in foreign trade. Many nations do not recognize the Soviet argument and hold Soviet foreign-trade missions liable for commercial actions.

# Banco Nacional de Cuba v. Sabbatino
376 U.S. 398, 84 S. Ct. 923 (1964)

Farr, Whitlock & Co., an American commodity broker, had contracted to purchase Cuban sugar from Compania Azucarera Vertientes de Cuba (C.A.V.), a Cuban corporation owned principally by American stockholders. After the sugar was loaded on a ship, the ship was seized by the Cuban government to serve as an example for other countries to follow "in their struggle to free themselves from the brutal claws of Imperialism."

In order to obtain the sugar, Farr, Whitlock & Co. entered into a contract with the Cuban government for purchase of the same sugar. C.A.V. then brought this action in U.S. district court to stop payment to the Banco de Nacional de Cuba, an instrumentality of the Cuban government, claiming that the sugar was still its property. The Cuban government argued that the seizure was an act of state and therefore immune from judicial action in the United States. The district court held that the taking was invalid under international law and that the act of state doctrine did not apply. The court of appeals affirmed, and the Banco Nacional de Cuba appealed.

**Mr. Justice Harlan Delivered the Opinion of the Court**    The classic American statement of the act of state doctrine, which appears to have taken root in England as early as 1674, . . . is found in *Underhill v. Hernandez*, [which said]:

Every sovereign State is bound to respect the independence of every other sovereign State, and the courts of one country will not sit in judgment on the acts of the government of another done within its own territory. Redress of grievances by reason of such acts must be obtained through the means open to be availed of by sovereign powers as between themselves.

. . . [R]ather than laying down and reaffirming an inflexible and all-encompassing rule in this case, we decide only that the Judicial Branch will not examine the validity of a taking of property within its own territory by a foreign sovereign government . . . in the absence of a treaty or other unambiguous agreement regarding controlling legal principles, even if the complaint alleges that the taking violates customary international law.

There are few if any issues in international law today on which opinion seems to be so divided as the limitations on a state's power to expropriate the property of aliens. There is, of course, authority . . . for the view that a taking is improper under international law if it is not for a public purpose, is discriminatory, or is without provision for prompt, adequate, and effective compensation. However, Communist countries, although they have in fact provided a degree of compensation after diplomatic efforts, commonly recognize no obligation on the part of the taking country. . . . It is difficult to imagine the courts of this country embarking on adjudication in an area which touches more sensitively the practical and ideological goals of the various members of the community of nations. . . .

If the Executive Branch has undertaken negotiations with an expropriating country, but has refrained from claims of violation of the law of nations, a determination to that effect by a court might be regarded as a serious insult, while a finding of compliance with international law would greatly strengthen the bargaining hand of the other state with consequent detriment to American interests. . . .

However offensive to the public policy of this country and its constituent States an expropriation of this kind may be, we conclude that both the national interest and progress toward the goal of establishing the rule of law among nations are best served by maintaining intact the act of state doctrine. . . .

[Judgment reversed.]

Case Discussion Questions

1   Restate the act of state doctrine in your own words.

2   What is the purpose of the act of state doctrine? What diplomatic trouble could the United States cause if the courts could rule differently in this or similar cases?

3   What options remain open to C.A.V. and its American stockholders?

## Nationality and Treatment of Aliens

A nation is under no duty to admit nationals of another state into its territory and may deport them at any time. If aliens are admitted, they may be subjected to restrictions on the length of their stay, the places they may travel, and the activities they may engage in. Aliens are also subject to the laws of the nations in which they are present, and special legal rules may be established for them. For example, aliens may be excluded from engaging in various commercial activity, from owning real property, and from exercising civil and political rights, such as voting or holding public office. As a general rule, the alien's legal rights are no better or worse than those of local nationals. Thus, an American citizen in Hungary has the same legal rights and duties as Hungarian citizens, although the Hungarian government may impose additional restrictions on aliens.

## *Lehndorff Geneva, Inc. v. Warren*
74 Wis. 2d 369, 246 N.W.2d 815
(Supreme Court of Wisconsin, 1976)

Lehndorff Geneva, Inc. (Lehndorff) was a Texas corporation qualified to do business in Wisconsin. All of the stock of Lehndorff was owned by nonresident aliens who were citizens of West Germany. Lehndorff owned and wished to exercise options on certain land in Wisconsin.

A Wisconsin state statute provided that it was unlawful for any *nonresident* alien or any corporation more than 20% of the stock of which was owned by nonresident aliens to own more than 640 acres of real estate in Wisconsin. All land over that amount was to be forfeited to the state. Lehndorff brought this action for a declaratory judgment that (1) the statute was unconstitutional under the equal protection clause of the U.S. Constitution and (2) the forfeiture of land violated international law. The trial court held that the statute was constitutional and legal under international law. Lehndorff appealed to the Supreme Court of Wisconsin.

**Day, Justice**   Aliens within the jurisdiction of the state are unquestionably entitled to the equal protection of the laws. In considering the applicability of these decisions [in cases cited] . . . two points emerge. The first is that these cases deal only with resident aliens; second, the question of whether nonresident aliens constitute a suspect class has not been decided. . . .

*Graham v. Richardson* [403 U.S. 365, (1971)] was the first in a line of recent cases to hold that "classifications based on alienage, like those based on nationality or race, are inherently suspect and subject to close judicial scrutiny." . . . This court is now called on to decide whether nonresident aliens have the same rights as resident aliens with respect to the purchase of real property. . . .

[T]he inequity of singling out aliens [turns] on characteristics of resident aliens. Like citizens, they pay taxes, serve in the military and contribute to economic growth. It is the class of resident aliens and not aliens worldwide who are similarly situated to citizens. . . .

None of these considerations appears in the instant case, in which foreign nationals who reside outside our borders have voluntarily associated with each other simply to have an investment vehicle here. The duties and burdens shared by the resident alien in common with the citizen entitles him to most of the benefits enjoyed by citizens. But burden sharing, except the payment of taxes in connection with the ownership or development of the land, is lacking in the case of the nonresident aliens in the case before us. . . .

Alien land laws pre-date our Declaration of Independence; they became part of the fabric of state law as the colonies received the common law from England. The right of a sovereign state to restrict land ownership by aliens is deeply imbedded in our law. Land law became primarily a problem of local state law. In general, a state [may] increase or decrease the disabilities of aliens in whatever manner it might choose.

The state argues that absentee ownership of land can be potentially detrimental to the welfare of the community in which it is located and persons who are neither citizens nor residents are least likely to consider the welfare of the community in which the land is located. . . .

We conclude that [the statute] does not violate the equal protection clause of the United States Constitution, [nor] principles of international law.

[Judgment affirmed.]

## Case Discussion Questions

1    Restate in your own words the equal protection argument of the plaintiffs in this case.
2    Why does the court make a distinction between *resident* aliens and *nonresident* aliens?
3    As a policy matter, should the courts restrict ownership of land by aliens? What about ownership of corporate stock?

---

Under some circumstances, aliens may ask the state of which they are nationals to press claims on their behalf against a foreign state. A French citizen may press the French government to intercede with the United States government if he or she believes that the U.S. government has injured him or her, for example. If the act of the foreign state was wrong under international law, the citizen may obtain some redress on a *state-to-state* basis.

Legal actions by one state against another on behalf of its citizens may take place if (1) the injury was caused directly by the other state, such as confiscation of property of an alien by the state, or (2) the injury was caused by a failure of the state to provide redress for an injury inflicted by some private person. Under those circumstances, the state that has wronged an alien must make **reparations,** not to the individual harmed, but to the *state* of which the individual is a national. That state, of course, may pay the reparations to the individual who was harmed.

In general, there is no duty on a state to press a claim for injuries to a national caused by a foreign state at the international level. Under the law of the United States, no citizen has a legally enforceable right to force the government to press the claim. If a claim is pressed, it is under the exclusive control of the government, which may settle or waive the claim in its discretion. Generally speaking, the individual who is harmed must exhaust all remedies before the courts of the nation which was responsible for the injury before he or she can request his or her government to press the claim.

## REGULATION OF INTERNATIONAL TRADE AND INVESTMENT

As a practical matter, a nation may buy what it wants from anyone, or discriminate against foreign buyers or sellers in any way. It can exclude foreign buyers or sellers and may prohibit foreign investment. It can sell its goods abroad under any terms that it pleases; and it may maintain tariffs, embargoes, quotas, or any other device that it desires.

There seems to be a natural inclination on the part of many nations towards **protectionism**. If large numbers of foreign products are made available, many domestic industries may suffer and jobs may be lost. The result may be political pressure for high import duties or even embargoes on certain products that compete with domestic industries.

On the other hand, protectionism often results in retaliation. Foreign governments whose products are the subject of high duties or embargoes may respond with equally high duties or embargoes on products coming from nations imposing such restrictions. The results are more industries hurt, more jobs lost, and loss of the benefits of international trade.

### Protection of Trade

The fast-changing environment of the world economy demands that some kind of order be imposed on international trade. Much of that order is imposed through treaties. Those agreements establish trade rules between the nations involved and often establish systems of legal redress for governments and private parties. The most important treaty related to foreign trade is the **General Agreement on Tariffs and Trade** (GATT).

**General Agreement on Tariffs and Trade**    The *General Agreement on Tariffs and Trade* (GATT) is a series of treaty rules developed immediately following World War II as an early effort of the United Nations. GATT essentially requires a **most favored nation clause** in every trade agreement established by a member country. A most favored nation clause requires that *every* nation be treated identically to the *most favored nation* in customs duties, tariffs, and export duties, and in the procedures by which those duties and tariffs are carried out. Similarly, imported products are to be treated identically to domestic products for purposes of regulation and taxation.

GATT includes several exceptions from most favored nation treatment. Perhaps the most important is for regional economic organizations, such as the EEC, which are not required to provide most favored nation status to others as compared to members of the organization. Another exception provides that developing states are not required to follow most favored nation practices in all instances.

### Protection of Foreign Investment

The protection of foreign investment revolves around the problem of **expropriation of property** by foreign governments. Expropriation means a seizure of foreign-owned property. Expropriation is generally considered legal if the seizing government pays fair compensation for the property seized. For example, the fifth amendment to the U.S. Constitution permits seizures for public purposes if "just compensation" is paid. If fair compensation is not paid, the seizure becomes a **confiscation** which may be the subject of legal action in national or international courts. Expropriation and/or confiscation is often followed by **nationalization,** in which the seized property becomes the property of the seizing government. For example, following the Cuban Revolution, large amounts of property owned by American companies and individuals were nationalized, that is, taken from the American owners to become the property of the Cuban state.

The general rule of international law is that changes in government do not affect the property rights of foreign nationals. If property is taken from foreign nationals, those owners may pursue claims through local courts; and if no remedy is obtained, the owners may ask their nations to seek reparations through international means.

In 1963 and 1964 the U.S. Congress passed a series of statutes known as the **Hickenlooper Amendments,** which withhold all U.S. government assistance to any nation that has nationalized or expropriated property that is owned by American citizens or companies with at least 50% American ownership. These statutes became part of the **Foreign Assistance Act of 1964,** the principal law that establishes foreign aid. The same doctrine applies to contracts that are nullified and discriminatory taxes that have the effect of expropriating American property.

Some efforts have been made to create an international machinery for the settlement of investment disputes. The Organization for Economic Cooperation and Development has established a *Draft Convention on the Protection of Foreign Property.* That convention prohibits any nation that accepts the convention from depriving a foreign national of property, unless (1) the measures are taken in the public interest and with due process of law, (2) the measures are not discriminatory, and (3) there is some provision for payment of just compensation. Similarly, the World Bank submitted a convention to its members establishing the International Center for Settlement of Investment Disputes, which has authority to decide all legal disputes regarding investments between member states.

## American Laws Regulating Foreign Investments

The U.S. government may control foreign investments made by U.S. citizens. Congress has passed a variety of laws dealing with investments in foreign nations, in order to protect either U.S. trade or the integrity of domestic American law.

**Export Control**    The **Export Administration Act of 1979** authorizes the President to prohibit the export of certain goods or technology to certain countries. As a general rule, most exports are covered by a **general license** and may be freely traded. The Department of Commerce has created a *Control List,* however, and exporters of certain commodities must obtain a **validated license** before trading may take place. Trading of other goods, such as arms and ammunition, narcotic drugs, and nuclear equipment and supplies, is restricted by other agencies, such as the Department of Defense. The **Trading with the Enemy Act of 1917** also prohibits exports to certain specified countries.

**Antidumping Laws: The Trade Agreements Act of 1979**    **Dumping** means selling goods in a foreign country at less than the comparable price in the exporting nation. For example, foreign firms may sell televisions in the United States for less than the same sets sell for in the firms' domestic market. If the exporting nation protects its domestic industries from competition through import controls or otherwise, the exporting nation may unfairly maintain its position in the domestic market and expand its position in the foreign market. For example, computer chips made in the Far East have been dumped in the United States, probably to force American manufacturers from the market.

In 1979 Congress passed the **Trade Agreements Act,** a statute that requires an additional import duty on foreign goods when dumping is proven. Proof of dumping requires (1) that the Secretary of the Treasury must determine that a class of merchandise is being or is likely to be sold in the United States at *less than fair value* (LTFV), that is, that the goods are to be sold in the United States at a price less than they are being sold for in the foreign market; and (2) that the International Trade Commission must determine that a domestic industry is being materially injured or threatened or the establishment of domestic industry is being retarded.

**Countervailing Duties: The Problem of Export Subsidies**    Some nations actively support exporters by providing government subsidies to firms that sell goods abroad. Such subsidies enable those sellers to compete more effectively with foreign sellers in the foreign markets. For example, if South Korea provided a subsidy to South Korean car manufacturer/exporters, those manufacturers could sell their automobiles at a lower price in the United States, perhaps undercutting American auto manufacturers.

The Trade Agreements Act of 1979 provides that if the government determines that such a subsidy has been given, and that an American industry is materially injured, is threatened with material injury, or the establishment of an industry in the United States is materially retarded, a **countervailing duty,** in the form of an import duty, will be imposed. That duty will be in the amount of the subsidy.

**Antitrust Laws and the Webb-Pomerene Act**    The United States maintains some of the most developed of all of the world's **antitrust laws** (see Chapters 20 and 21). The principal goal of those laws is to maintain and develop economic competition between domestic firms and to encourage competitive markets and practices. Those laws prohibit several anticompetitive practices, such as price fixing, monopolization, and certain mergers.

Many foreign nations actively *encourage* many of the practices prohibited by the American antitrust laws. For example, some nations actively subsidize large companies and even maintain a state financial interest in those firms. The result is that foreign firms may have a competitive advantage over American firms in international markets and the domestic American market. The **Webb-Pomerene Act of 1918** exempts certain conduct on the part of American export traders from the antitrust laws. To be eligible, the traders must not restrain trade in the United States.

A major issue in antitrust law has become whether American courts have jurisdiction to deal with foreign companies that have entered into conduct that would violate American antitrust law if performed within the United States, and that has an anticompetitive effect within the United States.[2] For example, if a group of Swiss watchmakers agreed to set prices on goods shipped to the United States, the price-fixing agreement

---

2 See *Matsushita Electric Industrial Co., Ltd. v. Zenith Radio Corp.*, p. 548.

would be illegal if made in the United States. And the effect of such an agreement would be to raise prices for Swiss watches in the United States. The sole issue is whether the courts of the United States have jurisdiction over the case.

If conduct abroad has a direct effect on domestic trade, the U.S. courts may hear the case (see p. 177). This means that American firms and foreign firms operating within the United States or abroad may be held liable under American antitrust laws. If a foreign nation also has an interest in regulating the same conduct, American courts apply a **jurisdictional rule of reason,** which means that the American courts balance the interests of the United States with the interests of the foreign nation to determine whether to exercise jurisdiction.

**Overseas Private Investment Corporation**   The **Overseas Private Investment Corporation** (OPIC) was created in 1979 as an agency of the U.S. government created to encourage private investment in foreign nations. The **Investment Insurance Program** provides investment guarantees and insurance against expropriation of property, war, revolution, and inconvertibility of currency.

To be eligible for such insurance, the investor must be a U.S. citizen or a company in which at least 50% of the owners are U.S. citizens. The investment must be in a developing country that has entered into an investment guaranty program with the United States. The project must be approved by the host country and OPIC. OPIC favors projects in nations with low per capita incomes and requires that the project serve the host nation's economic and social needs.

**The Foreign Corrupt Practices Act**   The **Foreign Corrupt Practices Act of 1977** was directed at the problem of bribery of foreign officials by U.S. firms. The central provision of the law makes it a federal crime for any American business to give or pay anything of value to "any foreign official for the purpose of influencing any act or decision of such foreign official." Small "facilitating" or "grease" payments are permitted to assure that goods will be treated identically to other goods (e.g., to assure that goods will not be delayed in customs). Penalties include up to a $1 million fine for firms and a fine of up to $10,000 and/or five years imprisonment for individuals. The law also requires *all* firms to maintain detailed financial records and accounts to assure that bribes are not included in some general accounting category, such as "payments for services."

In many parts of the world, bribery is a way of life, and some civil servants expect to supplement their income through bribery. The Foreign Corrupt Practices Act may in fact hinder some American companies in competing with foreign firms, and it is sometimes viewed as an attempt to impose American morality on the rest of the world.

## SUMMARY AND CONCLUSIONS

The international legal arena is unlike any domestic legal system. There is no monopoly of force standing behind international law to enforce its doctrines and demand compliance. Instead, international law depends on world opinion, custom, and a developing recognition of the need for legal order in the international system.

International law is often divided into three major categories. The Law of Peace establishes the rights and duties of nations at peace with one another. Most of the principles and problems of private citizens dealing in international business are parts of the

Law of Peace and are established by custom or treaty. The Law of War provides restrictions on nations at war with one another. The Law of Neutrality requires that neutral nations must be respected.

A variety of institutions may decide international disputes. Some of those institutions are not courts in the traditional sense, but rather are major actors in the international system that decide disputes between governments and private parties. Those institutions include the International Court of Justice, the United Nations and some of its subdivisions, the European Economic Community (the Common Market), the Council for Mutual Economic Aid (COMECON), the World Bank, and the International Monetary Fund (IMF).

International disputes may be resolved (1) through the national courts of the states involved, (2) through some international court, (3) through international arbitration, (4) through negotiation and diplomacy, or (5) through the use of force, including war.

Most jurisdictional rules in international law rely on the territorial principle. If conduct occurs *within* the territory of a state, that state has the jurisdiction to deal with it. This is true even if the *effect* of the conduct is outside the territory of that state. It is also clear that nations may impose jurisdiction under the nationality principle by enacting laws that deal with their own citizens. Finally, under the so-called protective principle, a state also has jurisdiction over conduct that occurs outside of its territory but which threatens its security as a state or the operation of its governmental functions.

The doctrine of sovereign immunity says that governments are immune from suits brought in the courts of other nations. Closely related to the concept of sovereign immunity is the act of state doctrine. That rule says that the courts of one nation will not sit in judgment of another government's acts within its own territory. Most nations accept a modification of that theory that distinguishes between public acts of governments and private acts of governments.

A great deal of international law deals with the protection of international trade and investments. The United States has made numerous agreements with other nations establishing rules of trade, generally based on the "most favored nation" idea established by the General Agreement on Tariffs and Trade (GATT). The United States has also encouraged foreign investment through international agreements that protect such trade and through American statutes that encourage and protect foreign investment by American firms.

## REVIEW QUESTIONS

1 List and explain the methods by which international disputes involving private corporations are resolved.

2 Define and explain the position in the international legal arena of the following: (1) the International Court of Justice, (2) the UN, (3) GATT, (4) the EEC, (5) the World Bank and the IMF, and (6) international arbitration.

3 What is the problem of enforceability in international law? How is it resolved?

4 How does the United States seek to regulate and promote foreign investment?

5 Explain the "act of state" doctrine.

6 You own 52% of the stock in the Slippery Banana Company in the nation of Nogalez. After a revolution, the new Nogalez government

nationalizes your company and refuses to make any reparation. Do you have a remedy?

7   Your firm has entered into a trade agreement with the government of East Germany, which defaults on payments under the contract after having received all of the goods your company shipped. Do you have a remedy?

8   Your firm is interested in locating a new plant somewhere overseas and has to choose between several different countries. The firm is also fearful of political unrest and the possibility of nationalization in several of these countries. What advice would you give the firm?

9   All Swiss watch manufacturers make an agreement that they will ship watches to the United States and charge the identical (high) price for their goods. Do the American antitrust laws provide any remedies for this obvious antitrust violation?

10   A Japanese car manufacturer charges the equivalent of $15,000 for its automobiles in Japan but charges only $12,000 for the same car in the United States, a price at least $3,000 under the price for comparable American cars. What action can the U.S. government take, if any?

# PART 2

# The Common Law Foundations

The system of private law in which business operates is a major part of the legal environment of business. How contracts are made, what kind of private liability a businessperson may expect for wrongful acts, the nature of property rights, and other aspects of the common law are clearly a major component of the legal atmosphere in which business finds itself.

The term *common law* is usually applied to the body of law that developed in England. The term refers to that body of principles and rules of action derived from the customs and usages of "immemorial antiquity" or from the judgments of courts recognizing and enforcing those customs and usages. In other words, the ancient unwritten law of England is "the common law."

To a large extent, the common law developed from the common sense and logic of the ancient English kings and the judges they appointed to keep the peace during England's savage history. Those rules developed in a time before there were statutes, or even legislatures. At that time, *all* law was "judge-made" law.

Over the centuries, the kings and judges saw the value of consistency in the law and began to develop the idea of precedent, or *stare decisis*. Judges made an effort to decide similar cases by similar rules. After judges became literate, some decisions were written down to give each judge the benefit of another's reasoning. In this way, the vast amount of "law" found in the common law was created—law that in many instances remains valid and binding today.

Much of our current law can be traced back to the earliest decisions of the common law. State legislatures may pass statutes that change common law rules, and modern judges may overrule ancient decisions, but that sort of action is relatively rare. A large part of the contemporary law of property, contracts, torts, agency, and business associations can be traced directly back hundreds of years to the English courts of the Middle Ages. Many new areas of the law, created either by statute or by judicial decision, are merely reflections of that same common law past. In that sense, the common law is the foundation upon which all of our contemporary law is built.

Ethical judgments are implicit in much of the private common law. The law of contracts is built upon the assumption that each person should keep his or her promises, and the law of contracts is merely a way of insuring that those promises are kept. The law of torts is built upon the assumption that each person should be responsible for the harm that he or she causes, and tort law is a method of enforcing those values of responsibility. Underlying much of English history is the almost sacred heritage of private property, and the earliest common law decisions protected and regulated the ownership of property. The law of agency is built upon the assumption that a servant, employee, or agent should be faithful, obedient, and diligent in serving his or her employer. From these ancient ethical values the modern law of contracts, torts, property, and business associations was formed.

# CHAPTER 8

# The Law of Contracts

*An oral contract is not worth the paper it's written on.*

ATTRIBUTED TO SAMUEL GOLDWYN

The history of commerce is to a large extent the history of contract law. It is probably no overstatement that commerce—and even Western civilization—could not have developed unless promises were enforced through the judicial system. But it would be impossible to enforce every promise. Some promises are made unwisely, some are made in jest, and some are so minor that the law should not get involved. One of the principal functions of contract law is to decide which promises should be enforced.

Before we begin consideration of the law of contracts, it is important to dispel one common misconception: A contract is *not* a piece of paper. A contract is an intangible thing—a promise, or set of promises, that will be enforced by the courts. In some cases the law may require further evidence of the existence of a promise, such as a written document. But when we use the term *contract*, we mean only the promise, or the intangible and subjective "agreement" of the parties, and not a piece of paper.

## THE DEVELOPMENT OF THE LAW OF CONTRACTS

The law of contracts is old, perhaps as old as law itself. Elements of contract law appear in the Bible and in the Code of Hammurabi and were well developed in the law of ancient Rome. But the true development of the law of contracts took place within the common law of England. As ancient English judges heard disputes between individuals, they were often forced to decide whether a particular promise should be enforced. Over time, the decisions of those judges tended to become more consistent and ultimately were written down. Those decisions became the common law of contracts, the basis of all contemporary contract law.

For centuries, contract law was a branch of property law. English society depended heavily on property rights, and contract law was a necessary addition to show how property was transferred. With the development of international trade during the fifteenth and sixteenth centuries, English merchants found the heavy details of property-contract law to be too slow and cumbersome for their uses. Merchants developed an entire system of private courts to decide their disputes speedily and in accordance with the needs of business. This system of mercantile courts and the doctrines they used to decide disputes are known as the **Law Merchant.** Many of the doctrines of the Law Merchant became firmly embedded in the law of England.

**The Restatement of Contracts**    In 1932, the **American Law Institute (ALI),** a private association of lawyers, judges, and scholars, published the **Restatement of Contracts,** which attempted to "restate" the common law of contracts in simple and organized form. The *Restatement of Contracts* is not law, nor does the *Restatement* attempt to change the law, but merely to "restate the law as it is, not as new law." Nevertheless, the *Restatement* has been quite influential in simplifying and unifying the law of contracts throughout the United States.

**The Uniform Commercial Code**    The most significant event in modern contract law is the development of the **Uniform Commercial Code** (UCC). Virtually all contract law is developed in state courts, which means that the law in every state differs somewhat from the law of every other state. With the development of a national economy early in the twentieth century, it became obvious that differences in state contract law resulted in an inefficient legal-economic system.

In the 1940's, the American Law Institute and the **National Conference of Commissioners on Uniform State Laws,** another private group, began joint work on a proposed Uniform Commercial Code. The UCC was initially approved in 1952, with subsequent editions in later years. Forty-nine states, the District of Columbia, and the Virgin Islands have adopted the UCC entirely. The fiftieth state, Louisiana, has adopted some parts of the UCC.

The UCC does not displace all contract law. It contains eleven articles covering commercial transactions, but the UCC does not cover contracts involving real property, employment, and some sales of intangibles (see Figure 8.1). If the UCC does not apply, the common law controls the transaction.

### Definition and Classification of Contracts

Perhaps the most widely adopted definition of the term *contract* is that adopted by the *Restatement:* "A promise or set of promises for the breach of which the law gives a remedy, or the performance of which the law in some way recognizes as a duty." That definition, widely adopted by the courts, makes clear that a contract is not a physical thing, but rather a promise that the courts will enforce.

**Express and Implied Contracts**    An express contract is expressly stated in words by the parties, either orally or in writing. Such contracts must contain a strict set of elements—those of *mutual agreement, consideration, legality of object,* and *legal capacity of the parties.*

**Implied-in-fact contracts** are based on the same principle of mutual consent as express contracts and must contain the same elements. The sole difference is that the promises of the parties are never spoken or put down on paper but are implied from the conduct of the parties. For example, assume that X, a professional window washer, drives her clearly marked truck up to Y's business and, while Y is watching, proceeds to

| | |
|---|---|
| Article 1 | **General Provisions.** Construction of the Act, definitions, and principles of interpretation |
| Article 2 | **Sales.** Contracts for the sale of tangible personal property |
| Article 2A* | **Leases.** Contracts for the lease of tangible personal property |
| Article 3 | **Commercial Paper.** Promissory notes, drafts, checks and related documents |
| Article 4 | **Bank Deposits and Collections.** How checks and other items are cleared through banks and the liabilities of parties, including banks |
| Article 5 | **Letters of Credit.** Engagements by a bank to honor demands for payment against a customer |
| Article 6 | **Bulk Transfers.** Sales of a major part of the seller's materials, supplies, merchandise, or inventory not in the ordinary course of business |
| Article 7 | **Warehouse Receipts, Bills of Lading, and Other Documents of Title.** Documents used to transfer title to property that has been stored or shipped through a warehouse or shipping company |
| Article 8 | **Investment Securities.** Stocks, bonds, and other investment securities |
| Article 9 | **Secured Transactions.** The law of security interests in personal property, such as liens on property to secure payment of debts |
| Article 10 | **Effective Date and Repealer.** Includes provisions regarding transfer from common law to the Code |
| Article 11 | **Effective Date and Transition Provisions.** Includes provisions regarding transfer from old UCC to newer editions |

FIGURE 8.1 The Uniform Commercial Code

*Approved in substance by the ALI and the National Conference of Commissioners on Uniform State Laws, but not yet widely adopted.

wash the front window of Y's store. Although no promise was expressed, Y would probably be held liable on the contract, because the promise to pay would be implied.

**Quasi-Contracts** In some circumstances the courts will imply the existence of a contract in the absence of any real promise, under the doctrine of **quasi-contract.** In effect, the law is saying that to deny an obligation would be to enrich one person at the expense of another unjustly. For example, if a doctor renders medical aid to a child whose parents have neglected her, the law will imply a contract to pay for those services even in the absence of a promise, and even when no promise would ever have been made. The law will impose liability as a matter of social policy.

**Formal and Informal Contracts** A **formal contract** is one that has specific requirements beyond the general requirements of any contract. For example, a **negotiable instrument** requires certain "magic words" for its creation. Similarly, **checks** or **bank drafts** also require specific formalities before they are effective. All other contracts without such additional requirements are **informal contracts.** Even large and important written agreements, such as a merger agreement between two corporations or a construction agreement to build a skyscraper, would be informal contracts.

**Unilateral and Bilateral Contracts**   Contracts are also classified by the number and direction of promises made. In many contracts, the **promisor** (person making a promise) expects a return *promise* from the **promisee**. This is known as a **bilateral contract.** For example, if X says to Y, "I promise to give you $400 if you promise to give me your motorcycle," and Y accepts, *two* promises have been made: X has promised to give Y $400, and Y has promised to give X the motorcycle.

On the other hand, the promisor may expect an *act* from the promisee. This is known as a **unilateral contract.** For example, if X says to Y, "I promise to give you $400 *if you give me your motorcycle,*" Y may obligate X only by actually giving the motorcycle to X. Only one promise has been made (see Figure 8.2).

**Validity, Voidability, and Enforceability**   A **valid contract** is one that fulfills all of the requirements of a contract. A **void contract** is one that lacks one or more of those same essential requirements. It is in fact not a contract at all.

A **voidable contract** is a contract that fulfills all of the essential requirements of a contract, but that binds only one party and not the other. The party who is not bound has the option of enforcing the contract. For example, if a contract is made with a minor, the contract is generally voidable at the option of the minor (see p. 205).

An **unenforceable contract** also fulfills all of the elements of a contract, but the courts refuse to enforce it for some reason. For example, a contract with a person who subsequently files bankruptcy is a valid contract, but it may be unenforceable because of the bankruptcy.

**Executed and Executory Contracts**   Contracts may also be classified according to the state of their performance. An **executed contract** is one that has been completely performed by all parties. An **executory contract** is one that has not been performed by the

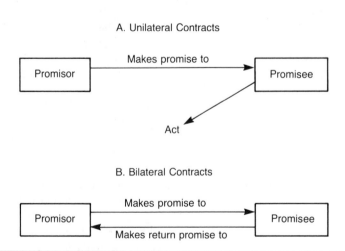

A. Unilateral Contracts

Promisor — Makes promise to → Promisee

Act

B. Bilateral Contracts

Promisor — Makes promise to → Promisee
Makes return promise to

FIGURE 8.2   Unilateral and Bilateral Contracts

parties. Contracts may also be *partially executed* and *partially executory*, if something remains to be done by one or more parties.

## THE ELEMENTS OF A CONTRACT

Every express contract contains four basic elements: (1) **mutual agreement,** (2) **consideration,** (3) **legality of object,** and (4) **capacity of the parties to contract.** In addition, some kinds of contracts must be evidenced by additional proof, usually a writing of some kind.

### Mutual Agreement

The parties to a contract must agree to its terms. It is often said that the parties must have a *meeting of the minds* regarding the contract. Usually this comes about through an **offer** made by the **offeror** (person making an offer) to the **offeree** (person to whom the offer is made), containing all of the essential terms of the agreement. The offer must be accepted in some way, and together the *offer* and *acceptance* form the **mutual agreement.**

The law has adopted the **objective theory of contracts.** That means that the law will look to outward clues to the intent of the parties, and the secret intentions of the parties will mean nothing. The courts will look to what the parties *said* or *did* rather than to what they *intended.* For example, an offer made as a joke will still bind the parties if a reasonable person would understand the offer to be a real invitation to make a contract.

**The Offer**  An *offer* is a proposal to make a contract, made by the offeror and communicated to the offeree. It is sometimes said that an offer creates a **power of acceptance** in the offeree, because the offeree can create a contract simply by accepting the offer.

*Definiteness of Terms*  The offer must be sufficiently definite to set out the essential terms of the contract, including the parties, the subject matter, the price, and the time of performance. The parties are ordinarily self-evident, and the time of performance will be considered to be a "reasonable time" if no specific time is established in the offer. But the subject matter and the price must be specifically established to create a valid offer.[1]

Certain communications may or may not be offers. The critical question is *whether the party manifested an intent to be presently bound to the promise made* if the offer is accepted. For example, "I would sell you my car for $400 if you were twenty-one years of age" is not an offer, because the words indicate no intention to be presently bound to the promise.

Advertisements use the term *offer,* but advertisements are not usually considered to be offers to make a contract in the legal sense. Ads are usually considered to be *invitations to make an offer,* because they usually omit two essential elements: the quantity of goods and the intended acceptor. If those two elements can be satisfied from the ad, it will be considered to be an offer.

 *Communication of the Offer*  An offer must be *received* before it can be accepted. If X writes a letter to Y, offering to sell a car for $1,000, and Y writes a letter to X, offering to buy

---

1 Under the UCC, even these terms may be left open. For example, if the price is not established in the contract, the court will imply a reasonable price at the time of delivery.

the same car for the same price, and the two letters cross in the mail, no contract has yet resulted. Neither party's communication was prompted by the expectation of a contract.

An offeree does not have the power to accept an offer until it has been communicated to him or her in the manner intended by the offeror. Even if a person knows of another's intention to make an offer, the offer cannot be accepted until it is actually made, and made in the manner intended by the offeror.

 **Termination of Offers**   An offer cannot remain outstanding forever. Offers may be terminated through (1) lapse of time, (2) revocation, (3) rejection and counteroffer, (4) death or destruction of a person or thing essential for performance, and (5) death or insanity of the offeror or offeree, and by (6) supervening illegality.

*Lapse of Time*   If an offer sets a specific time within which acceptance must be made, the offer will terminate at that time. If the offer simply says that the acceptance must be made within a certain time, such as "within ten days," that period begins to run from the date the offer is received. If X writes to Y on June 1, and Y receives the letter on June 3, Y has until June 13 to accept the offer. If there is a delay in the mails, the offer will begin to run at the time it would have been received if the offeree knew or should have known of the delay. If no time is stated in the offer, the offer will lapse after a *reasonable time*.

---

## Newman v. Schiff

778 F.2d 460
U.S. Court of Appeals (8th Cir., 1985)

Schiff, a self-styled "tax rebel," appeared on a nationwide live TV broadcast of CBS's program "Nightwatch" between 3 and 4 A.M. During the broadcast, Schiff argued American citizens are not required to file federal income tax returns and said, "If anybody calls this show—I have the Code—and cites any section of this Code that says an individual is required to file a tax return, I'll pay them $100,000."

Newman, a lawyer, heard an excerpt of the broadcast on the "CBS Morning News." When he arrived at work, he researched the issue and located several sections of the Internal Revenue Code that demonstrated that tax returns must be filed. Newman then called CBS, claiming the $100,000. CBS forwarded the demand to Schiff, and Schiff refused to pay. Newman brought suit in U.S. district court, claiming a breach of contract. The district court held that Newman's acceptance was too late and entered judgment for Schiff. Newman appealed.

**Bright, Senior Circuit Judge**   It is a basic legal principle that mutual assent is necessary for the formation of a contract. . . . Courts determine whether the parties expressed their assent to a contract by analyzing their agreement process in terms of offer and acceptance. An offer is the "manifestation of willingness to enter into a bargain, so made as to justify another person in understanding that his assent to that bargain is invited and will conclude it." *Restatement (Second) of Contracts* Sec. 24.

In the present case, Schiff's statement on "Nightwatch" . . . constituted a valid offer for a reward. In our view, if anyone had called the show and cited the code sections that Newman produced, a contract would have been formed and Schiff would have been obligated to pay the $100,000 reward, for his bluff would have been properly called.

Newman, however, never saw the live CBS "Nightwatch" program. . . . Newman saw the CBS Morning News rebroadcast of Schiff's "Nightwatch" appearance. . . . The rebroadcast constituted a newsreport and not a renewal of the original offer. An offeror is the master of his offer and it is clear that Schiff by his words, "If anybody calls this show . . ." limited his offer in time to remain open only until the conclusion of the live "Nightwatch" broadcast. . . .

Although Newman has not "won" his lawsuit in the traditional sense of recovering a reward that he sought, he has accomplished an important goal in the public interest of unmasking the blatant nonsense dispensed by Schiff. For that he deserves great commendation from the public.

Affirmed but without any costs against John Newman.

## Case Discussion Questions

1  What was the offer? To whom was the offer made? By its terms, how long did the offer last?
2  Had Newman been watching "Nightwatch," pulled the tax code off the shelf, and called in during the program, what would have been the result? What if the call had been placed three minutes after the program left the air?
3  Is the result fair? Should the common law be changed by statute to deal with cases such as this?

---

**Revocation**   The general rule is that an offeror may revoke an offer at any time prior to acceptance. This is true even if the offeror has promised to keep the offer open for a certain length of time. Before a revocation is effective, it must ordinarily be communicated to the offeree. An offer will also be revoked if the offeree learns indirectly that the offeror no longer intends to be bound by the offer. For example, if the offeree learns, prior to acceptance, that the offeror has sold the goods that had been offered to him, the offer is considered to be revoked.

Some kinds of offers are not revocable at the will of the offeror. Those offers include (1) offers supported by consideration (options), (2) offers made irrevocable by statute, and (3) offers to make unilateral contracts. An **option** is a contract offer in which the offeree has paid to keep the offer open for a specific length of time. The UCC also provides that **firm offers** for the sale of goods made by *merchants*, which state that they will not be revoked for a period of time, are in fact irrevocable for that time. Firm offers must be in writing and signed by the offeror. In almost all states, an offer to make a unilateral contract becomes irrevocable once performance has begun. And in some instances, the courts will refuse to permit an offeror to revoke an offer out of simple fairness on the basis of **estoppel** (see p. 203).

**Rejection and Counteroffer**   A **rejection** of the offer terminates the offer. The rejection is effective at the time it is received by the offeror. For example, A offers to sell her car to B for $400. B writes a letter to A rejecting the offer and mails it. After mailing the rejection, B changes his mind and personally accepts the offer before the rejection can reach A. A contract exists, because the rejection must reach A before it is effective.

A **counteroffer** is treated as a rejection by the courts. If A offers to sell her car to B for $400, and B says to A, "No, but I'll pay $300," the initial offer at $400 is dead and B cannot accept it, even if A rejects B's offer to pay $300. The counteroffer is treated just like an original offer and may be accepted to create a contract.

One of the most difficult questions of interpretation considers the difference between a counteroffer and an *inquiry into terms*. In the preceding example, if B were to reply to A's initial offer by saying, "I'm considering your offer. Would you take $300 now and my IOU for $100?" the initial offer would not be dead and could be accepted by B if A did not respond positively.

*Death or Destruction of a Person or Thing Necessary for Performance*    If a person is necessary to performance, the death of that person prior to acceptance will terminate the offer. For example, if A offers to pay B $500 to watch over C, A's elderly mother, and C dies before B accepts, the offer terminates. Similarly, the destruction of a thing necessary for performance prior to acceptance will terminate the offer. For example, if A has offered to buy a racehorse from B, and the racehorse dies prior to B's acceptance, the offer is at an end.

*Death or Insanity of the Offeror or Offeree*    The death or insanity of the offeror terminates the offers he or she has made, because the offeree cannot make a valid acceptance. The offeree need not know of the offeror's death or insanity for the offer to terminate. Similarly, the death or insanity of the offeree terminates the offer, because the offeree can no longer accept the offer, and only the intended offeree may accept.

*Subsequent Illegality*    If, while an offer is outstanding, the proposed contract becomes illegal, the offer is at an end. For example, if A offered to sell B a case of whiskey, and a law was later passed making the sale of whiskey illegal, A's offer would terminate.

**Acceptance**    The nature of the acceptance will vary with whether the offer is unilateral or bilateral. In order for a contract to result, an acceptance of a *bilateral* offer must be (1) clear and unmistakable (unequivocal) and (2) communicated to the offeror in a timely manner (although not necessarily received by the offeror). A *unilateral* offer is accepted by the performance of an act by the offeree, with knowledge of the offer and with the intention that performance of the act constitute acceptance. A mere promise to perform the act is not an acceptance.

It is sometimes said that the acceptance must be the *mirror image* of the offer. The acceptance may not insist on something to which the offeror is not entitled. If the offeree changes some essential term of the offer, or insists on something beyond the offer to which the offeree is not entitled, a counteroffer results. The Uniform Commercial Code permits the offeree to vary the terms of the offer in some cases dealing with the sale of goods.

As a general rule, silence cannot be an acceptance of a bilateral offer. For example, if A receives an offer to sell encyclopedias in the mail, and the offer states, "Your silence will mean that you want us to ship all fifty volumes. If you don't want them, let us know by return mail," no contract results from the offeree's silence.

*Communication and Time of Acceptance*    An acceptance generally must be *dispatched* (sent) to the offeror through some *authorized* mode of communication, or *received* if it is sent through some *unauthorized* mode of communication, before a contract results. This doctrine is sometimes called the **mailbox rule,** because an acceptance is effective *from the moment it is deposited into a mailbox*, if the mail is an authorized means of communication. An acceptance will be effective when it is received if the offer specifies that it must be received.

An authorized means of communication is any mode of communication expressly or impliedly authorized by the offeror ("Please send your acceptance by telegram"). The offeror impliedly authorizes the use of the same means of communication used to make the offer. Some states also provide that any means of communication that is *faster* than the authorized means is also authorized.

Since rejections are generally effective when received by the offeror, and acceptances are generally effective when sent, it is possible for the offeror to receive the rejection first, not knowing that the offeree has sent a later acceptance. The courts generally protect the offeror by stating that if the offeror has changed position in reliance on the rejection, the offeree cannot enforce the contract.

**Consideration**    The second essential element in any contract is **consideration.** Consideration is generally defined as the *inducement to a contract*. One classic definition says that consideration is "the cause, motive, price or impelling influence which induces a contracting party to enter into a contract." Consideration must be a **bargained-for exchange,** and consideration must constitute **legal detriment** to the promisee or **legal benefit** to the promisor.

*Bargained-For Exchange*    Consideration requires that the promises made be the result of a *bargain*. There need not be an exchange of equivalent things or services; in fact, the matters exchanged need not have any value at all. For example, if A were to say to B, "I promise to give you $10,000 as a gift," A's promise would be unenforceable, because it would be a promise to make a gift, made without consideration. If B were then to hand A a pencil, there would be an exchange, but not a *bargained-for* exchange. If A had said, "I will give you $10,000 *if you give me your pencil*," the exchange would be bargained for, and consideration would exist.

*Legal Detriment and Legal Benefit*    Consideration must be a legal detriment or a legal benefit—but not necessarily an *actual* detriment or benefit. Legal detriment is defined

---

## Restatement (Second), Contracts, Section 71

1 To constitute consideration, a performance or a return promise must be bargained for.

2 A performance or return promise is bargained for if it is sought by the promisor in exchange for his promise and is given by the promisee in exchange for that promise.

3 The performance may consist of (a) an act other than a promise, or (b) a forbearance, or (c) the creation, modification, or destruction of a legal relation.

4 The performance or return promise may be given to the promisor or to some other person. It may be given by the promisee or by some other person.

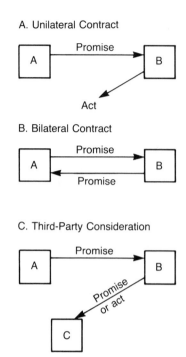

FIGURE 8.3    Consideration

as (1) doing, or promising to do, an act that one was not already legally obligated to perform; or (2) refraining from doing, or promising to refrain from doing, an act that one was not already legally obligated to refrain from doing. Similarly, legal benefit may be defined as receiving something that one has no prior legal right to receive.

For example, in the classic case of *Hamer v. Sidway*,[2] an uncle promised to pay his nephew $5,000 if the nephew would refrain from drinking, using tobacco, swearing, and playing cards or billiards for money until he was twenty-one. After age twenty-one, the nephew asked for the money, and the uncle's executor (the uncle had died in the meantime) refused payment on the grounds that the nephew had actually *benefitted* by refraining from such "immoral and unhealthy" activities. The court held that the nephew's acts in refraining from the activities constituted a legal detriment, because he had given up things *that he had no prior legal duty* to refrain from doing.

The law does not require that consideration move from the promisee to the promisor. The consideration may move from a third party to the promisor. For example, A may pay B $500 in exchange for B's promise to paint C's house. There is consideration for B's promise, but the consideration came from A, not C (see Figure 8.3).

*Adequacy of Consideration*    As a general rule, the courts will not inquire into the *adequacy of consideration*, but only into its *existence*. The courts are not concerned with

2  124 N.Y. 538, 27 N.E. 256 (Ct. of Appeals of New York, 1891).

whether the parties made a fair bargain or equal exchange of consideration, but only that consideration is actually present. For example, if A promises to sell his new car to B for $10, the courts will not look to see whether the price paid is fair or a good bargain. As many cases have pointed out, the courts are not in the business of making bargains for the parties to a contract.

If a party is seeking to show certain defenses, such as mistake, misrepresentation or fraud, duress or undue influence (see pp. 212–215), the inadequacy of the consideration may be important evidence of such defenses. Some courts will look at the adequacy of consideration if the difference in value is so grossly inadequate as to "shock the conscience of the court." This **peppercorn theory** is actually an expression of the rule that inadequacy of consideration is evidence of fraud. The following case illustrates this minority theory.

## O'Neill v. DeLaney
92 Ill. App. 3d 292, 415 N.E.2d 1260
Appellate Court of Illinois, 1980

James and Jeannette DeLaney and Nicholas O'Neill were good friends. The DeLaneys also owned a painting by Peter Paul Rubens, entitled *Hunting the Caledonian Boar*, that was worth at least $100,000 (and perhaps much more). On August 18, 1970, James DeLaney sold the painting to O'Neill for $10 "and other good and valuable consideration." A written contract was signed, although Jeannette DeLaney did not sign the agreement and, in fact, did not know of the contract. No other consideration except "love and affection" was given for the painting. The painting stayed in the DeLaney apartment except for brief periods when O'Neill hung it in his apartment.

In 1974 the DeLaneys filed for a divorce, and Mrs. DeLaney claimed an interest in the painting. O'Neill filed this action, claiming that he owned the painting and asking for a declaratory judgment. The suit was filed against both Mr. and Mrs. DeLaney. Mr. DeLaney admitted that he sold the painting, but Mrs. DeLaney denied that any such sale ever took place, or in the alternative, that the consideration was insufficient. O'Neill argued that since consideration existed, the court should not inquire into the adequacy of that consideration. The trial court held for Mrs. DeLaney, and O'Neill appealed.

**Lorenz, Justice** An offer, an acceptance, and consideration are the basic elements of a contract. Consideration to support a contract is any act or promise which is of benefit to one party or disadvantage to the other. Whether there is consideration for a contract is a question of law for the court. Generally, courts will not inquire into the sufficiency of the consideration which supports a contract. However, where the amount of the consideration is so grossly inadequate as to shock the conscience of the court, the contract will fail. The adequacy of consideration for a contract is to be determined as of the time of entering

the contract. Evidence of this gross inadequacy of consideration has been considered by some Illinois courts as tantamount to fraud. Professor Corbin in his treatise on contracts explained the underlying analysis employed by courts to strike down contracts for grossly inadequate consideration as follows:

The gross inadequacy of the consideration . . . may tend to support the conclusion that the parties did not actually agree upon an exchange, that the "peppercorn" [a term signifying a useless and valueless item used as consideration] was not in fact bargained for by the promisor. If it was not bargained for, it was not a consideration. . . . The rule that market equivalence of consideration is not required, and that the value of the consideration is to be left solely to the free bargaining process of the parties, leads in extreme cases to absurdities. . . .

In such extreme cases, Professor Corbin concluded that "the stated consideration is a mere pretense" and no contract exists. . . .

In the present case, the painting was purportedly sold to the plaintiff for "$10 and other good and valuable consideration." Plaintiff expressly testified that "other good and valuable consideration" meant the love and affection plaintiff and James Paul DeLaney had for one another. In Illinois, love and affection does not constitute legal consideration. Thus, the only remaining valid consideration for the transaction was the tender of $10. As we noted above, the adequacy of consideration must be determined as of the time of entering the contract. Plaintiff stated that at

the time he purchased the painting, it was worth $100,000 if not authenticated and several hundred thousand dollars if authenticated as an original Rubens. . . . A purchase price of ten dollars for such a valuable work of art is so grossly inadequate consideration as to shock the conscience of this court, as it did the trial court's. To find ten dollars valid consideration for this painting would be to reduce the requirement of consideration to a mere formality. This we will not do. . . .

Affirmed.

## Case Discussion Questions

1  What is consideration? What was the alleged consideration in this case?
2  What is the "peppercorn theory"? How was it applied in this case?
3  Why don't courts get involved in determining whether consideration is adequate or not? Why did the court do so here?

*Past Consideration*    As noted earlier, consideration is defined in part as doing or promising to do something that one has no prior legal duty to do. Promising or doing something that one is already under a legal obligation to do is known as **past consideration.** Past consideration is not sufficient consideration to support a contract.

Performance of an already existing contract duty is past consideration. For example, assume A has entered into a contract with B to build a house for $60,000. If A decides to quit, B's promise to pay A $10,000 more if he finishes the job is without consideration. But if A promises to do more than the original contract called for, such as add carpeting to the family room, B's promise to pay more has consideration and is binding.

*Adjustment of Debts*    If A owes B $100, B's promise to accept $75 in full payment is generally past consideration and unenforceable. A had a prior obligation to pay the full amount, and B's promise amounts to a gift of $25. If there is some dispute about the debt, such as the amount owed or whether the debtor is responsible for the debt, the creditor's agreement to accept a lesser amount is consideration, however. In that case, the creditor is giving up the right to receive the full amount, and the debtor is giving up the right to contest liability for the amount due. Similarly, if the debt is not yet due, a promise to pay a lesser amount prior to the due date is also made with consideration.

Current cases and statutes have cut deeply into the preexisting duty rule, and the trend in modern courts is to permit parties to enforce modifications of contracts made without additional consideration. In transactions in goods under the UCC, such modifications in existing contracts are binding without consideration. Several states have passed statutes recognizing payment of a smaller sum as consideration for the release of a debt.

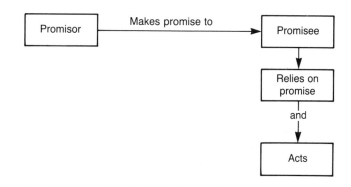

FIGURE 8.4    Promissory Estoppel

*"Moral" Consideration*    One of the knottiest issues of consideration deals with the problem of a promise made to pay an unenforceable debt. If A owed B an old debt of $500 that is barred by the statute of limitations, the debt is unenforceable. But if A makes a new promise to pay the debt, the general rule is that such promises are indeed enforceable. It is sometimes said that a new promise to pay an unenforceable debt is supported by **moral consideration.**

It is the *new* promise that is being enforced. For example, if A owes B $1,000 and A goes bankrupt, the entire obligation is discharged. If A later promises to pay B $500, B may only enforce the new promise and recover the $500.

*Promissory Estoppel: Enforcement Without Consideration*    Under certain circumstances the courts will enforce a promise when no consideration exists, under the doctrine of **promissory estoppel.** That doctrine holds that a promise will be enforced when equity and fairness require it, even without consideration. The four elements of promissory estoppel are that (1) the promisor must make a promise, (2) the promisor should reasonably have expected the promise to induce action or forbearance, (3) the promise must in fact have induced action or forbearance by the promisee or a third party, and (4) injustice can only be avoided by enforcement of the promise (see Figure 8.4). For example, if A pledged $10,000 to her church, and in reliance on the pledge, the church made a contract to have some construction work done, A may be *estopped* to deny the promise.

# *Loranger Construction Corp. v. E.F. Hauserman Co.*

356 Mass. 757, 384 N.E.2d 176
Supreme Judicial Court of Massachusetts, 1978

The plaintiff, a general contractor, was preparing its bid for certain construction at the Cape Cod Community College. The specifications called for removable metal partitions, and the plaintiff contacted the defendant, and the defendant prepared a "quotation" or "estimate" of $15,900 for supplying and installing the partitions. There was no consideration for the quotation, but the defendant knew that the plaintiff would use these figures in submitting its overall bid on the project.

The general contract was awarded to the plaintiff in June of 1968. In September the plaintiff sent the defendant an unsigned contract form including the $15,900 figure. The defendant rejected the subcontract, and the plaintiff had to go to another company. The plaintiff engaged another company, which charged $23,000 for the work.

The plaintiff sued on the basis of estoppel, claiming that the defendant had made a promise on which the plaintiff had relied to its detriment. The jury awarded the difference in price to the plaintiff. The defendant appealed, and the intermediate appellate court affirmed. The defendant appealed to the Supreme Court of Massachusetts.

**Braucher, Justice**   1   *The offer or promise.* The defendant argues that the "quotation" or "estimate" . . . was not an offer or promise, but merely an invitation to further negotiations. . . . Of course it was possible for the sales engineer [who made the quotation] to invite negotiations or offers. But it was also possible for him to make a commitment. We think the jury were warranted . . . in finding that the estimate . . . was an offer or promise.

2   *Reliance on the promise.* It seems clear enough . . . that the evidence made a case for the jury on the basis of the plaintiff's reliance on the defendant's promise. "An offer which the offeror should reasonably expect to induce action or forbearance of a substantial character on the part of the offeree before acceptance and which does induce such action or forbearance is binding . . . to the extent necessary to avoid injustice." Restatement (Second) of Contracts Sec. 89B(2). . . .

[Affirmed.]

### Case Discussion Questions

1   Was there consideration for the promises contained in the quotation made by the defendant? Were there any promises?
2   What are the elements of estoppel?
3   Had the plaintiff relied on the defendant's promises? How?

---

**Legality of Object**   A contract that (1) is itself illegal; (2) involves the commission of an illegal act; or (3) is against public policy is generally *void.* All of these types of contracts somehow involve "illegality."

If a contract is considered illegal, it is considered void and will not be enforced. The courts generally take a hands-off attitude and simply leave the parties where they are, refusing to aid either party. Sometimes the courts will restore the parties to their position prior to the contract (the *status quo ante*), particularly in cases of withdrawal by one party before the illegal act was committed. And, whenever possible, the courts will divide the contract into legal and illegal portions and enforce the legal portions of the agreements.

The result of this "hands off" policy is that some parties may profit from an illegal contract while others will suffer. For example, assume that A and B enter into a gambling contract in a state where gambling is illegal, and A loses her house to B. If A later thinks better of the matter and sues to recover the house, the courts may refuse to help A, just as they would refuse to help B obtain a deed if A refused to sign one. The courts will leave the parties where they found them.

Sometimes the parties are not equally at fault. If one of the parties to an illegal agreement is somehow less "at fault" than the other, the courts may aid that party. One party may be unaware of the illegality or less involved in the illegal venture. The parties are said to be not **in pari delicto,** that is, not of equal fault.

For example, a law may make it illegal to hire child labor. If A hires B, a child, and then refuses to pay B's salary, B could still sue for the wages. Even though the contract was illegal and even though B may have known of the illegality, the courts will still provide a remedy to B because B is a member of the class of persons that the statute was intended to protect.

**Capacity of Parties**    Although everyone is presumed to have full capacity to make a contract, three types of persons may show that they did not have full contractual capacity: (1) minors, (2) intoxicated persons, and (3) mentally incompetent persons.

*Contracts Involving Minors*    The **age of majority,** or time of adulthood for purposes of contracts, is established by statute in virtually every state. The two most common ages are eighteen and twenty-one, and there is a trend toward the lower age. If a minor makes a contract, the agreement is generally *voidable* at the option of the minor until, and for a reasonable time after, the minor reaches the age of majority. Contracts for *necessaries* cannot be voided by a minor, however.

The act of voiding the contract is called **disaffirmance.** Disaffirmance may be express (through written or spoken words) or implied (through some act or course of conduct). Disaffirmance may be made at any time up to the age of majority, or within a reasonable time after the minor reaches the age of majority (see Figure 8.5).

The courts differ on the duties of a minor upon disaffirmance of a contract. The majority view is that the minor need only return the consideration that the minor is capable of returning. That means that if the consideration received by the minor is lost, destroyed, damaged, or used up, the minor has the duty only to return what is left. The minority view is that the minor has a duty to return all of the consideration or pay the value of the consideration.

Upon disaffirmance, the other party to the contract has the duty to return the consideration received from the minor, or its value. A minor may **ratify,** or confirm that he or she is bound to the agreement, but that can only occur after the minor has reached the age of majority. Ratification may be done expressly, implicitly through a course of conduct, or by a failure to disaffirm within a reasonable time. Once ratified, the contract cannot be disaffirmed.

Most states hold that the minor may still disaffirm a contract, even if the minor misrepresented his or her age at the time of contracting. Some states have statutes that make it impossible for the minor to disaffirm such contracts, however, and others require the minor to return all of the consideration received under such circumstances. Finally, minors who misrepresent their age may be liable in tort for fraud, even if they are permitted to disaffirm the contract in which the fraud took place.

While a minor may generally avoid a contract, he or she cannot avoid a contract made for **necessaries** of life, such as food and shelter. The minor's parents may be liable for the necessaries as well, either under state statutes or under a theory of quasi-contract (see p. 193).

Any adult who agrees to be bound to ("cosigns") any contract made by a minor will continue to be bound, regardless of whether the contract is disaffirmed and regardless of whether it is for necessaries.

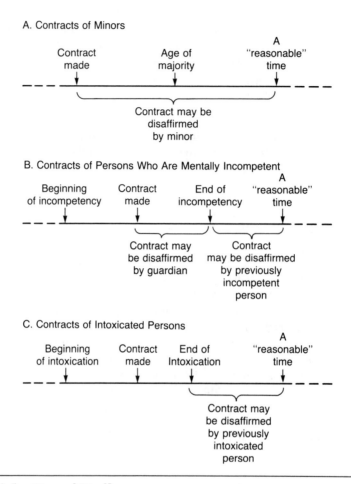

FIGURE 8.5    Time of Disaffirmance

*Mental Competency*    If a person is adjudged insane or incompetent by a court, the contracts that he or she may make after such a finding are *void*. In such circumstances, the courts will ordinarily appoint a **guardian** or other personal representative to act on behalf of the incompetent person, and that representative has the sole authority to make contracts on behalf of the incompetent person.

If a person has not been adjudged insane or incompetent but actually is incompetent, contracts made by that person are *voidable* at his or her option. Since the person is incompetent, he or she may disaffirm such contracts only upon regaining sanity or during any sane periods. Such contracts may also be disaffirmed by the guardian or personal representative, once such a representative is appointed by a court (see Figure 8.5).

*Intoxication*    Intoxicated persons may also disaffirm contracts made while they were intoxicated. The courts require that the person have been so intoxicated that he or she did not understand the transaction and its legal consequences. Under such circumstances, the contract may be disaffirmed (once the intoxicated person sobers up), and both parties will be required to return the consideration received (see Figure 8.5).

## THE STATUTE OF FRAUDS

Although it is almost always a good idea to "get it in writing"—if for no other reason than that people have imperfect memories—there has never been a general rule that a contract must be in writing. In fact, the general rule is that an oral contract is just as binding as a written one.

Oral contracts present several problems of proof, however. If an oral contract is the basis of a lawsuit, the party claiming a contract will swear that the contract exists and will testify to its terms. The opposing party may deny that the contract exists at all or may dispute the terms. It will then be up to a jury or a judge to decide who is telling the truth.

In 1677 the English Parliament began wrestling with the problem of fraud and perjury in oral agreements and ended by passing one of the most far-reaching statutes ever designed by human legislatures. The Statute of Frauds has been adopted with little change by almost every English-speaking jurisdiction in the world, and a large number of non-English-speaking nations as well. It is the law today in all fifty states (with minor variations), and its approach has also been adopted in the UCC.

The Statute of Frauds presents a kind of compromise between permitting all oral contracts to be enforced and requiring that all contracts be in writing. In essence, the Statute requires additional proof beyond oral testimony in cases involving certain types of contracts. That proof usually, but not always, amounts to a written agreement of some kind, although that "writing" may be very informal.

### Satisfying the Statute of Frauds: What Kind of Writing?

The original Statute of Frauds provided that none of the types of contracts could be enforced "unless the agreement . . . or some memorandum or note thereof, shall be in writing, and signed by the party to be charged therewith, . . . . " The note or memorandum may be informal, as long as it contains some basic elements, including (1) the names of the parties, (2) a reasonably certain description of the subject matter of the contract, (3) the terms and conditions of the promises made, and (4) the signature (or even initials) of the party to be charged. The "note or memorandum" requirement may be satisfied by integrating several writings, such as several business letters. In fact, only one of the writings must be "signed by the party to be charged," as long as the writings refer to each other, or if the signed writing is physically attached to other writings by the party to be charged.

### The "Part Performance" Doctrine

In two instances no writing at all is required, as long as there has been some **part performance of the contracts.** In contracts for the sale of an interest in land, an oral contract may still be enforced if it is accompanied by (1) the taking of possession by the buyer *and either* (2) part or full payment *or* (3) the making of improvements to the prop-

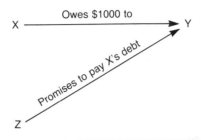

FIGURE 8.6    Contract to Pay the Debt of Another

erty. And, in contracts for the sale of goods over $500, the UCC[3] relaxes the note or memorandum requirement substantially. No note or memorandum is required if (1) payment has been made and accepted, or delivery has been made and accepted; (2) the goods are specially manufactured; or (3) the party admits the contract in court.

### Contracts Included Within the Statute of Frauds

The Statute of Frauds only applies to six types of contracts that are specifically described by the statute. These contracts are (or were, in 1677) considered to be the types of contracts most likely to be the subject of fraud, either because there is a particular incentive for fraud in the contract, or because the agreements are so important.

Contracts to Answer for the Debt of Another    A contract to pay a debt of another must be evidenced by a writing to be enforceable. For example, if X owes Y $1,000, and Z says to Y, "I promise to pay you if X doesn't," Z's promise is unenforceable unless Y obtains some written "note or memorandum" signed by Z (see Figure 8.6). In order for the Statute of Frauds to apply, the debt must be X's debt, and not in any sense Y's debt. The statute only applies to **collateral** obligations of the promisor, not **primary** ones, that is, debts for which the promisor has received some consideration.

Contracts by a Personal Representative to Pay the Debts of a Decedent    Closely related to the first type of contract are contracts by a personal representative to pay the debts of a decedent (deceased person) personally. When a person dies, the courts will usually appoint some person to act on the decedent's behalf to manage the decedent's affairs. That personal representative is known either as an **administrator** (if the decedent died without making a will) or an **executor** (if the decedent had made a will).

Only the decedent's estate is liable for the debts of the decedent. There is no obligation for the heirs, family, or personal representative of the decedent to pay the decedent's debts. If the estate is insufficient to pay the debts, the creditors of the decedent will share the estate, subject to some priorities among themselves, but they cannot collect additional sums from the family or personal representative.

Occasionally, however, the personal representative may promise to pay the decedent's debts personally, either for business reasons or to preserve the family honor. In

---

**3** UCC Sec. 2–201.

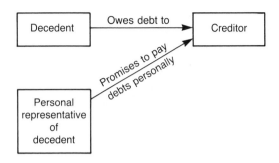

FIGURE 8.7    Contracts by a Personal Representative to Pay the Debts of a Decedent

such cases, the promise is unenforceable unless there is a "note or memorandum" signed by the personal representative (see Figure 8.7).

**Contracts for the Sale of an Interest in Land**    In seventeenth-century England, land was the entire basis of society. One's wealth, rank in society, and even military status were determined by whether one owned land and how much land one owned. It is not surprising, therefore, to find contracts for the sale of an interest in land protected by the Statute of Frauds.

The crucial question in this area is the definition of "an interest in land." This provision covers not just contracts to sell land, but any agreement selling an *interest* in land. Such interests include a promise to buy or sell the land itself, an option to purchase land, an agreement to sell an easement, and a mortgage or other security interest in the land. In most states a lease is considered to be personal, not real, property (see p. 246) and is not covered by the statute, but many states have passed statutes requiring long-term leases of a year or more to be in writing as well.

**Contracts in Consideration of Marriage**    Love was not an important consideration in many marriages in 1677. Many marriages were arranged as business deals, including the transfer of dowries between the bride's family and the groom. Such marriages were an important factor in the social system, and it is little wonder that they were protected by the Statute of Frauds. The rule did not cover mutual promises to marry but did include other consideration transferred as a result of the marriage. For example, if A promises to transfer property to B if he will marry C (A's daughter), a note or memorandum in writing signed by A is necessary.

Although such contracts are rare today, this provision does have a modern application. Many people sign **antenuptial agreements,** that is, ones prior to marriage. Such contracts provide that in the event of a divorce, the property owned by the parties will be divided in a particular way. Such contracts are generally considered to fall within the Statute of Frauds, and a note or memorandum is required.

**Contracts Not to Be Performed Within One Year**    Any contract that cannot be performed within one year must be evidenced by a note or memorandum. The provision has been interpreted to mean "impossible to perform by its terms." It must be clear from the contract itself that it cannot be performed within a year, as in an employment contract that lasts for two years. If it is *possible* that the contract could be performed within a year, no note or memorandum is necessary. For example, a contract to insure A's house against fire loss for three years is capable of performance within a year, because A's house could burn down tomorrow, and an oral contract would be enforceable.

**Contracts for the Sale of Goods over the Value of $500**    The original Statute of Frauds provided that a contract for the sale of goods "for the price of ten pounds" was within the Statute. The Uniform Commercial Code, responding to the inflation of three centuries, changed the value of the goods to $500.[4]

**Other Contracts That Must Be in Writing**    The six categories served the law well in 1677, but additions became necessary over the next 300 years. Those additions took three forms: (1) contracts for the sale of a security, (2) contracts for certain types of security interests, and (3) contracts for the sale of intangible personal property. All of those additions are found in the Uniform Commercial Code.

### THE PAROL EVIDENCE RULE

The **parol evidence rule** may be stated as follows: When a contract has been reduced to writing, and the parties intend that the writing be a complete statement of their agreement, they may not contradict the writing by evidence of prior agreements, either written or oral.

The parol evidence rule is based on the notion of **integration** of the agreement. That is, when parties enter into the negotiation of a contract, all of their offers, counteroffers, concessions, and tentative agreements are integrated into the final agreement, which is reduced to writing. All of the previous negotiations are "integrated" into the final written contract. It would defeat the intent of the parties to permit one of them to resurrect one of the prior tentative agreements, offers, or concessions. As a result, the parol evidence rule says that **extrinsic** (outside) evidence of those prior negotiations cannot be used to contradict or vary the terms of the written agreement. Generally speaking, the contract must be interpreted by looking at the meaning of the document itself, not at outside evidence (see Figure 8.8).

### Exceptions to the Parol Evidence Rule

Although prior and contemporaneous agreements may not be admitted to vary or contradict the terms of a written agreement, evidence of such agreements may be introduced for other purposes. Those purposes are (1) to explain ambiguities in the written document; (2) to show that one of the parties lacked capacity to contract; (3) to show the existence of a defense, such as fraud, mistake, duress, and undue influence; (4) to prove conditions to performance of the contract; and (5) to supply missing terms or correct typographical errors.

### ASSIGNMENTS AND DELEGATIONS

A party to a contract may make an **assignment** of rights or a **delegation** of duties under the contract. In an assignment, a party to a contract may assign rights under that con-

---

4 Sec. 2–201.

Like statutes, contracts often need interpretation by the courts. Over the centuries, the courts have devised a series of rules of interpretation of contracts. Those rules are not hard and fast and often conflict. Some of those rules are as follows:

**1**   The purpose of interpretation of a contract is to give effect to the *intent of the parties*.

**2**   Common words are given their everyday meaning. Some words have acquired substantial hidden *legal* meanings, however.

**3**   The interpretation of words in a contract may be influenced by prior dealings between the parties or the usage of terms in the trade.

**4**   Printed form contracts are construed strictly against the party that supplied the form if there is no opportunity for the other party to negotiate. Such agreements are called **contracts of adhesion.**

**5**   Handwritten terms are given effect over typewritten terms, and typewritten terms are given effect over printed terms, if there is a conflict.

**6**   Under the UCC, every contract imposes an obligation of good faith in its performance or enforcement.

**7**   The definition of the term *reasonable time* depends on the nature, purpose, and circumstances of the action. Under the UCC the term *seasonably* means within a reasonable time.

FIGURE 8.8   Interpretation of Contracts

tract to another. In Figure 8.9, A and B have entered into a contract in which A owes certain duties to B and has certain rights owing from B. A may *assign* the rights under the contract to C, and B then owes those rights to C. For example, B may owe money to A under the contract. A may assign the right to receive that money to C.

The **assignor** (the person transferring the rights) may make the assignment in any form, although the Statute of Frauds may apply and require a writing. The **assignee** (person to whom the rights have been transferred) has the right to sue for those rights, but the **obligor** (person owing the rights) may assert any defenses he or she may have against the assignee as well as against the assignor. For example, in Figure 8.9, if A was guilty of fraud in dealing with B, B may raise A's fraud as a defense in a suit by C.

A *delegation* involves the transfer of duties to a third party. In Figure 8.10, A may transfer the duties that he or she owes to C. Under those circumstances C must now do

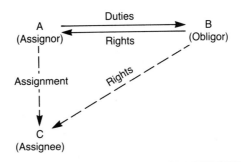

FIGURE 8.9   Assignment of Rights

what A had promised to do. The **delegator** transfers duties to the **delegatee,** but certain kinds of duties are nondelegable, especially those that involve some unique personal ability or personal service. For example, a rock group could not delegate its duties to perform at a concert to a 1940s-style crooner.

### Third-Party Beneficiary Contracts

Parties may make contracts in order to benefit a third party. Two types of third-party contracts may generally be enforced by the third party. A **donee beneficiary contract** involves a contract to make a gift to a third party. For example, A and B may make a contract in which A pays B $400, and B gives a car to C. C could enforce the contract and force B to give the car *if* it was the intent of the parties to make a gift to C (see Figure 8.11, part A). **Creditor beneficiary contracts** are also enforceable by the third party. Such a contract would exist if A and B make a contract in which A sells an item to B, and B is to pay the price to C, a creditor of A, in order to pay A's debt (see Figure 8.11, part B).

**Incidental beneficiary contracts,** in which the benefit derived by the third party is only incidental to the contract, cannot be enforced by the third party. For example, if city X makes a contract with paving company Y to pave the street in front of Z's home, Z certainly obtains a benefit, but that benefit is incidental, and Z could not sue Y or X to enforce the contract.

## CONTRACT DEFENSES

Genuine agreement between the parties may be affected by several contract defenses. Those defenses include matters that seriously disrupt the bargaining process, including **fraud, mistake, duress, undue influence,** and **unconscionability.** When those matters are present, courts may give relief from liability, even though the elements of a contract are present.

### Fraud

*Fraud* is generally defined as (1) a misrepresentation (2) of a material fact (3) made with knowledge of the falsity of the statement and with intent to cause another to act, (4) which in fact causes another to act to his or her detriment or injury.

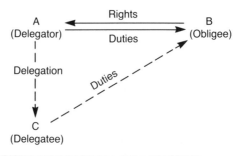

FIGURE 8.10    Delegation of Duties

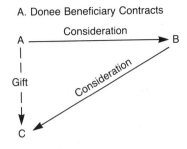

A. Donee Beneficiary Contracts

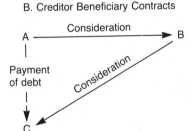

B. Creditor Beneficiary Contracts

FIGURE 8.11   Third-Party Beneficiary Contracts

A misrepresentation usually must be some affirmative act in the form of spoken or written words about some fact. Silence may be fraud if there is a duty to speak. For example, if there are **latent defects** (defects that are hidden and cannot be discovered by an ordinary inspection), there is a duty to call those defects to the attention of the other party. Similarly, if a party makes a statement that he or she believes to be true, and later finds out that the statement is false, he or she has a duty to correct those statements. Finally, persons in a fiduciary relationship (see p. 286) have an affirmative duty to tell their principals everything they know about a transaction.

The matter misrepresented must be *material*. That means that the fact must have been a substantial factor in creating the contract. The matter misrepresented must have been about a *fact* as well, which means that statements of opinion cannot be fraudulent. The person making the statement must *know* that it is false at the time the statement is made and must make the statement with the intent to convince another person to enter into the contract.

The person to whom the statement is made must *justifiably* rely upon the statement to his or her injury or detriment. In the usual case, this means that the party to whom the fraudulent statement is made believes the statement and enters into a contract as a result. That person must be *justified* in relying on the statement, which means that if the person to whom the statement is made either *knew* or *should have known* that the statement was false, no fraud can result.

An innocent misrepresentation, in contrast to fraud situations, involves a misstatement of facts that is not intentional. Usually, the party making the misrepresentation actually believes the facts to be as he or she represents them to be. Such cases are treated as mutual mistakes (see below), and contracts entered into as a result of innocent misrepresentations are voidable.

**Fraud in the Inducement and Fraud in the Execution**    There are two general types of fraud: (1) **fraud in the inducement,** which applies to misrepresentations made about the subject matter of the contract in order to convince the other party to enter the contract, and (2) **fraud in the execution,** which applies to misrepresentations made about the contract itself. The difference is crucial, because in general a finding of fraud in the inducement makes the contract *voidable* at the option of the defrauded party, whereas a finding of fraud in the execution makes the contract *void.*

For example, assume A and B enter into negotiations for the sale of A's car, and A tells B that the car only has 30,000 miles, when in fact it has 130,000 miles. A's representations are a fraud in the inducement, because they relate to the subject matter of the contract (the car) and were made to induce B to enter into the contract. On the other hand, if A were to switch contract documents when B was about to sign the agreement, so that B signed a contract giving the price as $10,000 instead of $3,000, A's representation that B was signing the proper document would be a fraud in the execution. In the first instance, the contract would be *voidable* at B's option, whereas in the second, the contract is *void* because no real agreement ever took place. Generally speaking, all parties have a duty to read the written contracts that they sign. But if a party misrepresents the character or essential terms of a proposed contract and induces a party to sign the contract without reading it, the contract is *void* because no real mutuality existed.

### Mistake

A contract requires a "meeting of the minds." If the parties are operating under a mistake about a material fact, such a meeting of the minds does not exist and no contract has been formed. The contract is void and never really existed. The courts make a clear distinction between *unilateral* and *mutual* mistakes of fact. A unilateral mistake of fact is one in which only one of the parties to the contract is mistaken. A mutual mistake of fact occurs when both parties to the contract are mistaken about a material fact.

A unilateral mistake of fact is usually not a defense to a contract. The courts take the position that the parties to a contract are responsible for their own mistakes and should have to live with them. Contracts entered into by mutual mistake are voidable at either party's option. If the mistake is serious enough and goes to the heart of the bargain, no contract is formed at all, and the contract is void.

### Duress

*Duress* simply means *compulsion.* A person who is the victim of a threat that deprives him or her of the freedom to decide voluntarily whether to enter into a contract has acted under duress, and the contract is voidable at that person's option. Generally speaking, the threat must be of an unlawful action, such as the threat of physical violence. The courts apply a subjective test in determining whether duress is present. The courts will consider such matters as the victim's physical attributes, age, training, state of health, and education in determining whether the threat actually influenced the victim to enter the agreement.

## Undue Influence

*Undue influence* involves one party taking advantage of another party through (1) a fiduciary relationship or (2) the mental infirmity of the other party. Like duress, undue influence involves an overpowering of the will of the victim, although there is no actual threat.

If a fiduciary relationship (see p. 286) is found, the dominant party to a contract between them must not "overpersuade" the dependent party. All of the facts must be disclosed, and the dependent party must be given every opportunity to resist the contract. Some courts even say that contracts between such parties are presumed to be tainted by undue influence and require the dominant party to show that the dependent party acted out of his or her own free will.

## Unconscionability

The doctrine of *unconscionability* was introduced with the Uniform Commercial Code and was originally applied only to contracts for the sale of goods (tangible personal property). That doctrine simply says that a court may refuse to enforce a contract, or a part of a contract, which the court finds to be unconscionable.

The Uniform Commercial Code does not define the term *unconscionable*, but the courts generally interpret that word to mean "unfair" or that the contract "shocks the conscience of the court." The doctrine of unconscionability has slowly evolved over time. Some courts have expanded the doctrine by common law means to other types of contracts, such as employment contracts or real estate agreements. Although the law of unconscionability is still evolving, the courts seem to place a great deal of emphasis on the relative bargaining power of the parties. Main considerations seem to be the relative intelligence and business sophistication of the parties. Even if no actual fraud, duress, or undue influence was present, the courts may still find the contract unfair and hold it unenforceable.

## PERFORMANCE OF CONTRACTS

A **discharge** means that a party's duty to perform under a contract is terminated. It is obvious that a party's duty to perform a promise is discharged by **full performance** of the promise. The act is finished, and there is no remaining duty to perform. The vast majority of contracts are discharged in this manner, simply because most people keep their promises.

A **tender** of performance is an unconditional offer and attempt to perform. If one party makes a proper tender, and that tender is refused, the tendering party's duty to perform is discharged. For example, assume that A agrees to sell a typewriter to B for $100. If A appeared at the proper time with the typewriter, and B refused to pay, A's duty to perform would be discharged. That means that A may sue B for **breach of contract** and might obtain either damages or some equitable remedy.

## Substantial Performance

The law generally does not require full, literal performance of a duty in order for discharge to take place. It is enough that **substantial performance** has taken place. For example, assume that A has agreed to build a house for B for $40,000. A full, detailed set of plans is provided to A, and A is to finish the house in accordance with those plans. A works diligently on the house and completes the house according to the plans, except that he is unable to obtain some of the wallpaper that was specified in the plans. A has substantially performed his duties under the agreement, and B has a duty to pay A the agreed price, less the value of the wallpaper.

## Breach of Contract

A failure to perform one's duties under a contract is a *breach of contract*. That failure to perform gives the other party to the contract a right to damages or other remedy and may terminate the nonbreaching party's duty to perform.

Not every breach is a discharge. Only a **material breach** is a discharge of the other party's duties. A material breach is defined as a failure to substantially perform duties under the contract. Sometimes courts ask whether the breach goes *to the essence of the contract*, that is, whether the breach defeats an essential purpose of the agreement.

Sometimes a party to a contract may have a serious question in his or her mind about whether the other party will ever perform the contract. For example, one party may state that he or she will not perform when performance is due. The doctrine of **anticipatory breach** applies to such cases, and the innocent party has the right to treat the contract as breached and his or her own duties as discharged. In some cases the innocent party may also have a right to damages.

**Breach of Time of Performance Provisions**    Many contracts contain a time limit within which performance must be completed. If no time provision is expressly stated in a contract, the courts will generally provide a time limit of a *reasonable time* for completion of the contract. What constitutes a "reasonable time" will vary with the type of contract, the expectations of the parties, and the customs and usages of the trade.

If the contract expressly states a completion date, the doctrine of material breach generally applies. If a party completes his or her performance after that date, the question will be whether the lateness of performance is substantial or not. Damages are available to compensate for any loss caused by delay. Some contracts clearly state that *time is of the essence*. In such a case, performance by the date specified is a necessary condition to performance by the other party, and any deviation from the date specified is a material breach and a discharge of the other party's performance.

## Termination by Agreement

The parties to a contract may *agree* to discharge their obligations under the contract. If both parties to an agreement later agree that the contract will be changed or terminated, there is no good reason not to enforce that later agreement. Termination by agreement may occur through **rescission, accord and satisfaction, release,** or **covenant not to sue.**

**Rescission**    A *rescission* is an agreement between the parties to abandon a contract. The rescission is also a contract, totally separate from the original contract. The consideration usually consists of each party giving up his or her rights under the contract in consideration of the other party's giving up rights as well.

**Accord and Satisfaction**    An *accord* is a contract in which one party agrees to render and the other party agrees to accept performance different from that called for in the original contract. The *satisfaction* occurs when the performance is rendered. Only the two together—accord *and* satisfaction—discharge the prior obligation. Simply making the accord is of no effect until the satisfaction occurs.

It is important that such agreements be based on legal consideration (see p. 202). For example, if A owes B $100 on December 1, an agreement to accept $50 on December 1 is not an accord, because B gave up the right to receive $50 and A gave up nothing. Usually an accord and satisfaction take place when the debt is disputed or when the due date has not yet arrived.

If an accord is made, but no satisfaction is rendered, the party to whom the debt is owed may sue on the original debt. By failing to comply with the accord, the debtor has in effect breached the new contract. The effect is to revive the original debt, but the creditor may elect to enforce the accord agreement instead.

**Release and Covenant Not to Sue**    A *release* is not necessarily a contract, but is instead a formal method of discharging obligations. Most states have adopted some form of release by statute, which, once executed, extinguishes a claim forever. Those forms often contain certain "magic words" which mean that the claim is forever discharged. Courts are very reluctant to reinstate claims once a release has been signed and will do so only after a clear showing of fraud, duress, or undue influence.

On the other hand, a *covenant not to sue* is a contract in which one party agrees not to sue the other in return for a payment of money. The agreement is a bar to lawsuits, because the party agreed not to sue. For example, A agrees not to sue B if B pays A $5,000 by January 1. A cannot sue B prior to January 1. If B fails to pay by January 1, no satisfaction is possible and A may sue B, either on the old obligation or on the new one.

If a release is given to one joint obligor, *all* of the joint obligors are released. For example, if A is owed money by B and C *jointly*, and A gives B a release, C is also discharged. That is *not* true if A gives B a covenant not to sue.

### Termination by Operation of Law

There are a variety of means by which an obligation may be discharged that have nothing to do with the performance or breach of the obligation or with any agreement by the parties. These miscellaneous methods of discharge are discharges **by operation of law,** because they involve basic policies imposed by statute or the courts.

**Statute of Limitations**    Every state maintains a **statute of limitations** which provides that a party cannot bring a lawsuit after a certain period of time. In fact, states usually maintain a whole series of statutes for different types of actions. The statutes of limitations for written contracts are generally longer than for oral agreements, but the UCC provides a period of four years for both oral and written contracts.

**Bankruptcy**    A **discharge in bankruptcy** is a bar to actions by a creditor to enforce a debt, including obligations under a contract. Only certain types of obligations are dischargeable under the federal bankruptcy law (see p. 383).

**Impossibility**    Generally speaking, if a contract becomes impossible to perform after it has been made, the parties are discharged. If performance has begun, the majority rule says that the party who has begun performance may recover in quasi-contract for the performance that was in fact rendered. Performance must be *objectively* impossible, rather than merely more difficult. That is, performance must be either legally or physically impossible.

If the subject matter of a contract is destroyed through no fault of the parties after a contract is made, the parties are discharged. For example, if the contract is for the sale of an automobile and the automobile is damaged beyond repair while legally parked on the street, the parties are discharged.

In a contract for personal services, the death or illness of the party who is to supply the personal services makes the contract objectively impossible. If A agrees to paint B's portrait and A dies, the contract has become objectively impossible and will be discharged.

**Frustration of Purpose**    **Frustration of purpose** occurs when the main purpose of the contract has been frustrated by some unforeseeable event. There are four elements to the doctrine of frustration of purpose: (1) the event that leads to the frustration was not reasonably foreseeable, (2) there is a total or nearly total destruction of the value of the contract to one party, (3) the event frustrating the contract occurred after the contract was formed but before performance was due, and (4) the main purpose of the contract was clear to the parties.

The doctrine of frustration was created by some English cases around the turn of the century. Those cases dealt with leases of rooms along the parade route for the coronation of a new king. The leases were for one day only and were very expensive. The new king became ill, and the coronation was postponed. English courts held that the purpose of the contracts had been frustrated, and they permitted rescission.

A second doctrine, that of **commercial impracticability**, is closely related to the doctrine of frustration. Commercial impracticability means that performance will be discharged if performance itself is "impracticable" because of some intervening event. Impracticability does not mean mere hardship or mere added cost, nor does it mean objective impossibility. Usually it means that the costs have escalated so sharply that the contract is outside of the ordinary risks run by business. Commercial impracticability is a new and emerging doctrine, drifting somewhere between the older doctrines of impossibility and frustration.

**Alteration**    If one of the parties to a contract makes a **material alteration** of the contract document, the *other* party to the contract is discharged. The innocent party may treat the contract as discharged, or he or she may enforce the contract as it existed prior to the alteration or even as altered.

## CONTRACT REMEDIES

Remedies for breach of contract fall into two large categories. Damages, in the form of money, are the most common type of remedy (see p. 23). If damages are insufficient or inadequate, the courts may allow some type of equitable remedy. The courts prefer to compensate any loss, including contract losses, with damages. In fact, it is necessary to show that an injured party has *no adequate remedy at law* (meaning damages) before equitable remedies become available.

### Damages

There are three main types of damages: (1) nominal damages, or damages in name only available for the vindication of any right; (2) compensatory damages, to compensate the injured party for loss, and (3) punitive damages, intended to punish the wrongdoer (see p. 23). Punitive damages are not available in contract actions. Fraud is both a contract defense and an intentional tort, and punitive damages are available when fraud is shown *as a tort*. The fraud must be intentional in order to merit punitive damages. Contract law is almost exclusively concerned with compensatory damages, but there are some specialized types of damages as well.

**Compensatory Damages in Contract Actions**    In the event of a breach of contract, the innocent party may bring an action for compensatory damages. The general rule of compensatory damages is that the injured party should be paid a sum of money sufficient to place him or her in the same position he or she would have been in had the contract been performed.

**Special (Consequential) Damages**    **Special** or **consequential** damages are those beyond the standard damages ordinarily allowable and only indirectly caused by the breach of contract. Such damages may be recovered only if they were reasonably contemplated by the parties at the time the contract was made and it can be reasonably inferred that the breaching party assumed the risk of liability for such losses.

The classic English case of *Hadley v. Baxendale* established the rule for consequential damages. In that case, a mill owner contracted with a wagon driver to deliver a broken drive shaft to London for repairs. The driver delayed an unreasonable length of time in making the delivery. The mill owner had no other shaft and lost profits as a result of the delay. The court limited the mill owner to standard damages because it was not reasonably foreseeable that the entire mill would be shut down.

**Liquidated Damages**    It is sometimes difficult to determine the extent of loss in a contract. A **liquidated damages** clause is a provision in a contract in which the parties agree to the amount of damages in advance. For example, it is common in construction contracts to provide that if the building is not finished in time, the contractor will be liable for damages of a certain amount for every day of delay.

On the other hand, the courts will not enforce a *penalty* or *forfeiture* provision in a contract. It is sometimes difficult to tell the difference between a liquidated damages clause and a penalty clause. If a provision is *called* a penalty or forfeiture, it will be unenforceable, regardless of the amount of the penalty. And if the clause is the product of a reasonable effort to forecast damages, it will be considered to be a liquidated damages provision. That means, of course, that at the time the contract was formed, it must have appeared that damages would be difficult to determine.

**Mitigation of Damages**    An injured party generally has the duty to **mitigate damages,** that is, to reduce the damages suffered because of a breach of contract. If the injured party fails to take action to reduce the loss, the courts will reduce the amount recovered by the amount that could have been saved by mitigation of damages. Mitigation of damages commonly is an issue in employment contracts, contracts for the sale of goods, construction contracts, and leases.

### Equitable Remedies

The law has a strong bias in favor of *legal* remedies, that is, damages. In fact, before equitable remedies become available, it must be shown that there is *no adequate remedy at law*. That means, quite simply, that money damages cannot "make the plaintiff whole." The law will provide equitable remedies only in exceptional circumstances. Such remedies include **specific performance, injunctions, rescission** and **restitution,** and **reformation.**

**Specific Performance**    The most common equitable remedy in contracts actions is *specific performance,* which is a court order to actually perform the contract. If a person later refuses to perform the contract, the court may find him or her in contempt of court and impose a fine or imprisonment.

Specific performance is available in contracts for the sale of goods only if the goods involved are unique. For example, a contract to sell a painting by Van Gogh would be specifically enforceable, because the payment of money would not place the injured purchaser back in the same position he or she would have been in had the contract been completed. Specific performance is also available in contracts for the sale of land. Land is considered to be unique under all circumstances, because no two pieces of land are in the same place.

It is not clear which parties to a contract may obtain specific performance. The *purchaser* of land or unique goods may obtain a decree of specific performance, because the purchaser has lost the right to the unique property and cannot be made whole through damages. State decisions vary regarding whether the *seller* may obtain specific performance.

**Injunctions**    *Injunctions,* or court orders requiring a person not to do something, have some limited uses in contract cases. Injunctions are sometimes used to require parties to employment contracts not to work for someone else, or to require parties who have agreed not to compete to comply with their contracts.

For example, assume that A has sold B her business and as part of that contract has agreed not to compete with B for a certain time. If A later violates that agreement and enters into competition with B, B may be able to obtain an injunction requiring A to cease such competition.

**Rescission and Restitution**   There are a variety of situations in which a party has the right to *rescind* (cancel) a contract. Any contract that is voidable at the option of one or both parties is subject to rescission, including cases of fraud, duress, undue influence, certain types of incompetency to enter into a contract, and others. Parties may also agree to rescind a contract. In such cases, each party must put the other party back in the same position he or she would have been in had the contract never been formed. That means that each party must give back what has been received under the contract.

If a party has a right to rescind, but the other party to the agreement refuses to cooperate, the party may sue for *restitution*. Restitution is an equitable remedy in which the court orders the parties to restore each other to their position prior to the formation of the contract. Sometimes restitution requires the payment of the equivalent value of money. Again, failure to comply with an order of restitution may be a contempt of court and is punishable by a fine or imprisonment.

**Reformation**   *Reformation*, sometimes known as the *blue pencil rule*, is an equitable remedy in which the court modifies the contract to conform to the true intentions of the parties. Traditionally, reformation was only available in cases of mutual mistake of fact, usually to supply a missing term of the contract or to change a term that is obviously wrong as a result of a typographical error. In recent years, reformation has become available in some courts for fraud or commercial impracticability, although those courts are in a small minority.

### Election of Remedies

It is usually up to the injured party who brings a lawsuit to **elect** between the various remedies available. It is not possible to obtain inconsistent remedies, such as damages for breach of contract and restitution, because restitution means the contract never existed. One cannot obtain damages for breach of a contract that does not exist. Consistent remedies include damages and specific performance, damages and reformation, and damages and an injunction.

### SUMMARY AND CONCLUSIONS

The law of contracts is of common law origin. Recent developments such as the *Restatement of Contracts* and the Uniform Commercial Code have introduced some stability and continuity into the law.

A contract is not a piece of paper. It is instead a promise, or set of promises, for the breach of which the law provides a remedy. A contract generally has four elements: mutual agreement, consideration, legality, and capacity of parties. Some types of contracts must be evidenced by a note or memorandum under the Statute of Frauds.

Contracts are subject to a series of defenses, including fraud, duress, undue influence, and mistake. Those defenses deal with whether the parties had a true "meeting of the minds."

In the event of a breach of contract or the existence of some defense, two general categories of remedies are available to the injured party: (1) money damages may be awarded and (2) equitable remedies such as specific performance, injunctions, restitution, or reformation may be awarded.

## REVIEW QUESTIONS

1   Why couldn't we require *all* promises to be in writing? Before you answer, consider all of the promises you have made in the last week.

2   Explain the differences between (a) *unilateral* and *bilateral* contracts; (b) *valid, void, voidable,* and *unenforceable* contracts; and (c) *executory* and *executed* contracts. Give examples of each.

3   What is the "mirror image" rule regarding offers and acceptances?

4   Explain the concept of consideration in your own words.

5   Explain and give examples of *fraud, duress, undue influence,* and *mistake.*

6   Hacienda Golf Course posted a sign which stated "$5,000 to anyone shooting a hole-in-one at this course." Gibson shot a hole-in-one but did not know of the offer until he returned to the clubhouse. Is he entitled to the money? [*Las Vegas Hacienda, Inc. v. Gibson*, 359 P.2d 85 (1961).]

7   Fledgby offers to sell Wilfer a parcel of land for $5,000 in writing, stating that the offer will remain open for thirty days. Under which of the following circumstances does a contract between Fledgby and Wilfer result?

   **a** Wilfer replies "I will pay $4,500." Fledgby declines, and Wilfer writes back, accepting the $5,000 offer.

   **b** Wilfer replies, "Won't you take $4,500?" Fledgby declines, and Wilfer writes back, accepting the $5,000 offer.

   **c** Ten days after Wilfer received the offer, Sampson offers Fledgby $6,000 for the property, which Fledgby accepts. Three days later Wilfer writes to Fledgby, accepting the $5,000 offer.

   **d** Two days after receiving Fledgby's offer, Wilfer writes back to reject it. The next day, before Fledgby receives the rejection, Wilfer sends a telegram to Fledgby to accept the offer.

8   Brownlow promised his nephew Oliver that if Oliver would go to college and get his degree, he would give Oliver $10,000. Oliver went to college. (a) Is there consideration for the promise? (b) Could Brownlow withdraw the promise the day before graduation?

9   Pidger, a noted violin expert, visited Dartle's violin shop. He found a violin that he knew to be a genuine Stradivarius, worth at least $100,000. Dartle had priced the violin at $100. Pidger purchased the instrument for $100 without disclosing the information or his true identity. Does Dartle have a remedy? Would it make a difference if Pidger learned that the violin was a Stradivarius *after* he purchased it?

10   Skiffins owned an apartment building and leased an apartment to Boffin for a term of one year at $350 per month. After three months, Boffin breached the agreement and moved out. If Skiffins sued Boffin, how much may he recover? Must Skiffins mitigate damages? How?

# CHAPTER 9

# The Law of Torts

*Even a dog knows the difference between being tripped over and being kicked.*

OLIVER WENDELL HOLMES

The term **tort** includes many of the most common and controversial types of lawsuits filed today. Examples of torts include *intentional* acts, such as assault, battery, false imprisonment, and dozens of others; *negligent* acts, including matters such as "slip and fall," and auto accident cases; and *strict liability* or *no-fault liability* cases, such as products liability[1] and others. In many ways, tort law is the cutting edge of civil law today.

One of the most common definitions of the term *tort* is that of a civil wrong, other than a breach of contract, for which the courts will provide a remedy. That definition, although perhaps the best we can do, is quite unsatisfactory. The definition makes the law of torts a "legal garbage can," into which we may toss every action that does not fit within the other classifications of the law. Thus, vastly different actions such as fraud, assault, automobile accidents, and products liability claims can all be called torts.

## THE PURPOSE OF THE LAW OF TORTS

The primary purpose of tort law is to *compensate* individuals for losses arising out of human activities. Western culture demands that those who injure others make good the loss that they cause. The law of torts adjusts these losses and provides compensation for injuries sustained by one person as the result of the wrongful conduct of another.

But on what basis should we adjust those losses? The early common law imposed no requirement of *fault* on the part of the person causing the loss and simply provided that if a person *caused* an injury, that person must compensate the injured party. Even today people who innocently trespass on another's land are liable.

In the nineteenth century the common law began requiring proof of some kind of fault before recovery would be permitted. This requirement, in turn, resulted in the requirement of a **mental element** in tort cases, such as intention or negligence. For the most part, that requirement is still with us.

In the mid-twentieth century legal scholars and lawmakers began rethinking the whole basis of tort law. The requirement of fault often left persons uncompensated for losses and permitted persons who had in fact caused an injury to escape liability. For example, a manufacturer who permitted a dangerous product to go on the market effectively *caused* the injuries that resulted, but he or she might escape liability because of

---

1 The law of products liability is considered in detail in Chapter 13.

the difficulty of proving fault. The result has been a retreat from fault and toward *strict liability*, or liability without fault.

The law of torts also provides a tool of social policy. Many tort disputes could easily result in bloodshed if the law did not step in. In doing so, the law must balance the scales between an individual's right to protection and another individual's right to freedom of action. Often there is a third element to be weighed, that of the public interest. When that element is thrown into the equation, it is impossible for the courts to avoid "social engineering" through the judicial process.

For example, there is a clear tension between the economic interests of manufacturers and sellers and the product-safety interests of consumers. The law of torts has stepped in, chiefly through judicial decision, to create the law of **products liability** and regulate the area. The judicial decisions in that area have arguably done more to create a safe-product environment than all of the government regulation of product safety. And inevitably, those decisions have affected our economic, social, and business structure. The notion of strict liability in tort, the law of products liability, and government regulation of product safety are discussed in detail in Chapter 13.

## The Impact of Liability Insurance

The concept of liability insurance has had a massive impact on the system of tort law. Liability policies can be purchased for almost every kind of activity, including automobile use, medical coverage, legal or accountants' malpractice, products liability, and homeowner's liability, among others. Such policies generally provide that the insurance company will pay compensation to a person injured as a result of the policyholder's activities covered by the policy, up to certain specified sums. Policies may also provide that the insurance company will provide counsel and court costs.

Some argue that the major change that has taken place in the tort system in the twentieth century—a shift from a "fault" to a "no-fault" system—can be attributed to the existence of liability insurance. It is also clear that the existence of liability insurance has caused the erosion of immunities against tort liability (see *Flagiello v. Pennsylvania Hospital*, p. 25). It is also argued that jury verdicts are higher because jurors will more readily assess damages against an insurance company. In most states, juries are not supposed to know that the defendant is insured, but juries probably guess that there is insurance in most cases. Some states have considered being honest with the jury and disclosing the fact of insurance. A problem exists, of course, in cases where the jury guesses that insurance exists when it really does not.

## The Elements of a Tort

There are four broad requirements in every tort: (1) a legally recognized *duty*, including a *mental element*; (2) a *breach* of that duty; (3) an injury, or *damages*; and (4) *proximate cause*, or a causal relation between the breach of duty and the injury. It is necessary to prove all four elements in every tort case. If a new set of facts can be brought within the four elements, a new tort may be judicially created.

**The Duty**    Legal *duties* arise in a large variety of ways. Some duties, such as the duty not to go over the speed limit or not to murder another person, are created by statute. Others, such as the duty not to commit negligent acts, may be created by the courts. All people are under a duty to conform their conduct to all of the duties imposed upon us and to refrain from doing things that the law, either statutory or common law, tells us not to do.

**The Mental Element**    A part of the duty element of any tort is the *mental element*, or the mental posture of the defendant at the time the tort is committed.

There are three large categories of torts: **intentional, negligent,** and **strict liability.** Intentional torts require that the person committing the tort—the **tortfeasor**—intended to bring about a result. Negligence requires that the tortfeasor fail to act in the way in which a reasonable and prudent person would have acted under like circumstances. And strict liability means liability without fault. In strict liability cases, the tortfeasor will be liable regardless of the mental posture he or she had at the time the act was committed. Some states create a fourth category of **reckless conduct,** or aggravated negligence, and permit the recovery of punitive damages in such cases.

Even children and insane persons are generally liable for their torts. If a specific mental element is required for proof of a tort, such as the intent to cause bodily harm, children and insane people who are mentally incapable of forming that intent may escape liability.

**The Breach of Duty**    Once the legal duty is established, including the required mental element for the specific tort, the plaintiff must also prove that the defendant in some way *breached*, or failed to live up to, the duty imposed upon him or her.

**Proximate Cause**    The breach of duty must *cause* the injury. That statement is deceptively simple, for causation is often the most difficult of the four elements to prove. Philosophically, all events in the world are interrelated. If a person commits a tort, that tort would not have taken place unless his mother had given birth to him, but it would be silly and senseless to make her liable because she "caused" the tort. The law only considers the **proximate,** or "nearest," **cause.** But the problems do not end by simply requiring the cause to be proximate. (Other problems of *foreseeability* and *direct causation* are discussed in the *Palsgraf* case, p. 235.) Although the problem of causation is discussed in the context of negligence, it is important to remember that causation is a required element in all torts.

**Injury (Damages)**    The breach of duty must cause some **injury** to the plaintiff before the courts will permit recovery. If the defendant has breached some right of the plaintiff, such as a technical trespass to the plaintiff's land, the plaintiff may recover **nominal damages,** usually $1 and court costs. Most tort cases involve **compensatory damages,** in which the object is to pay the plaintiff that sum of money that will place the injured party in the same position he or she would have been in had the injury not occurred. In cases of intentional (and in some states, reckless) torts, **punitive damages** may be awarded to punish the wrongdoer.

### Tort Immunities

Some groups have historically enjoyed immunity from liability for torts, including governmental bodies and charities. Although those immunities generally still exist, they have been under substantial attack in the twentieth century, and major exceptions have arisen.

For centuries it was an accepted rule of law that "the king can do no wrong" and that suit against the government—for any reason—was impossible. The doctrine was transferred intact to the United States; and for many years it was impossible to sue the federal government, the state governments, or municipal governments under the doctrine of **governmental immunity.**

However, the federal government has consented to be sued in a wide variety of actions. As early as 1887 federal law gave blanket permission to file suit in private contract actions against the government. In 1946 Congress passed the *Federal Tort Claims Act,* which permitted suits against the federal government in most cases. Most states have also placed limits on the absolute doctrine of governmental immunity and now permit some kind of recovery against state and local governments.

Since the middle of the nineteenth century, courts have generally held that charities, such as religious institutions, hospitals, and societies to aid the poor, were immune from suit under the doctrine of **charitable immunity.** In the middle of the twentieth century, courts began to rethink this rule, and virtually every state has overturned the rule of charitable immunity, either through judicial decision or through statute. (See *Flagiello v. Pennsylvania Hospital,* p. 25.)

## INTENTIONAL TORTS

*Intent,* for purposes of tort law, is an intent to bring about a result that will invade the legally protected interests of another. It is not a hostile intent, nor does the term mean any desire or motive to harm another. The tortfeasor may have only intended a practical joke or may have even intended to help the victim. As long as the defendant intended a particular result, he or she may be held liable.

Intent may also be broader than a desire to bring about a result. It includes those consequences that the actor believes are substantially certain to follow. A person who fires a gun into a crowd may hope that no one will be hit, but he or she knows that it is unavoidable that the bullet will hit someone. On the other hand, acting with mere knowledge that a risk may exist—short of a certainty—is not intent. Such conduct may be negligence or even recklessness, but it does not constitute the intent that the law requires.

It is clear that the law treats intentional acts more harshly than it treats negligent acts. Punitive damages are often available in such cases to deter future wrongdoing. Unlike negligent torts, the law will also "transfer" intent between victims. If A intends to strike B but misses and strikes C, the law will "transfer" the intent to C, and permit C to sue for an intentional tort.

There are dozens of intentional torts, and new ones may be created at any time as the law finds interests that need to be protected. This chapter discusses some of the most common intentional torts. Intentional torts dealing with unfair competition and deceptive marketing are discussed in Chapter 14, and those dealing with environmental protection are considered in Chapter 19.

### Assault and Battery

**Battery** is an intentional contact with a person that is harmful or offensive. **Assault** means an apprehension of a battery, also intentionally caused.

The contact required for a battery may be a touching of the person or anything attached or connected to the person, such as clothing, a chair, or a car. It is not essential that the person be aware of the contact at the time it occurs. A doctor who performs an operation without the consent of the patient or the patient's family commits a battery, for example.

---

## Manning v. Grimsley

643 F.2d 20 U.S. Court of Appeals, First Circuit (1981)

Manning and others were seated in the right-field bleachers in Boston at a baseball game between the Boston Red Sox and the Baltimore Orioles. A wire mesh fence separated the field from the bleachers. Ross Grimsley, a pitcher for the Orioles, was warming up in the "bull pen" immediately adjacent to the right-field bleachers, and the Boston fans in those bleachers continuously heckled him. Grimsley looked at those fans on several occasions.

At the end of the third inning, after Grimsley's catcher had left his position and was walking to the bench, Grimsley faced the bleachers and wound up as though to pitch in the direction of the bull-pen plate. The ball traveled at a speed of 80 miles per hour toward the bleachers, went through the fence, and hit the plaintiff.

Manning filed a battery suit against Grimsley and the Orioles in federal court under diversity jurisdiction (see p. 71). The district judge directed a verdict for the defendant, and the plaintiff appealed.

**Wyzanski, Senior District Judge**    We are of the view that from the evidence that Grimsley was an expert pitcher, that on several occasions immediately following heckling he looked directly at the hecklers, not just into the stands, and that the ball traveled at a right angle to the direction in which he had been pitching and in the direction of the hecklers, [and] the jury could reasonably have inferred that Grimsley intended (1) to throw the ball in the direction of the hecklers, (2) to cause them imminent apprehension of being hit, and (3) to respond to conduct presently affecting his ability to warm up and, if the opportunity came, to play in the game itself.

The foregoing evidence and inferences would have permitted a jury to conclude that the defendant Grimsley committed a battery against the plaintiff. This case falls within the scope of *Restatement*

*Torts 2d*, Section 13[2] which provides . . . that an actor is subject to liability to another for battery if intending to cause a third person to have an imminent apprehension of a harmful bodily contact, the actor causes the other to suffer a harmful contact. . . . Section 13 . . . is supported by a substantial body of American cases. . . . The whole rule and especially that aspect of the rule which permits recovery by a person who was not the target of the defendant embody a strong social policy including obedience to the criminal law by imposing an absolute civil liability to anyone who is physically injured as a result of an intentional harmful contact or a threat thereof directed either at him or a third person. . . . It, therefore, was error for the district court to have directed a verdict for defendant Grimsley. . . . [Reversed.]

---

2 The full text of section 13 provides: An actor is subject to liability to another for battery if (a) he acts intending to cause a harmful or offensive contact with the person of the other or a third person, or an imminent apprehension of such a contact, and (b) a harmful contact with the person of the other directly or indirectly results. [Court's footnote].

Case Discussion Questions

1    Did Grimsley *intend* to hit the plaintiff? Some other person? Or did he merely intend to hit the fence? Does it matter?

2    Didn't the plaintiff bring this conduct on himself through the heckling? Should that conduct excuse Grimsley's actions?

3    What does *intention* mean, according to the *Restatement?*

---

No actual contact is necessary for an assault. All that is required is an apprehension of an imminent battery. Assault is a purely mental tort, and the injury is the fear of a battery, together with any resulting physical injury. It is sometimes said that a mere verbal threat is not an assault and that there must be some physical action—such as shaking a fist—before the defendant is liable. The courts seem to be moving away from that position, however.

It is clear that a battery must be *imminent* for an assault to take place. The person who says, "I'm going to punch you in the nose tomorrow," has not committed an assault. The threat cannot be conditional, such as, "If you were not wearing glasses, I would hit you," because the defendant is in effect saying that he or she is *not* going to commit a battery.

For an assault to take place, the defendant must have the *apparent present ability* to carry out the threat. A defendant in a body cast lying in a hospital bed who shouts, "I'm going to hit you," does not have the apparent present ability to carry out the threat and is not liable for assault.

**Defenses to Battery: Self-Defense**    The privilege of self-defense permits a person who is attacked to use all *reasonable force* to prevent any threatened harmful or offensive bodily contact, or any confinement. Force may also be used to protect third persons. The defense extends not only to situations where real danger exists, but also to ones where it reasonably appears to exist.

The defendant must use only that degree of force necessary under the circumstances, and there is no right to use force after the assailant is disarmed or helpless, or the danger is past. If the assailant has withdrawn from the encounter and has clearly indicated the withdrawal, there is no privilege to renew the conflict. The state courts do not agree on whether a person must attempt to escape from the attack before using deadly force to resist the attack. The law in this area is far from clear, and the best rule appears to be that deadly force should only be used as a last resort.

Typically, force may be used to defend property under the same general rules as self-defense or defense of others. Only force reasonable to put an end to the invasion of property is a defense, and there is no privilege to use force calculated to cause death or serious bodily injury in defense of property unless there is also a threat to personal safety.

### False Imprisonment

The tort of **false imprisonment** and the closely related tort of **false arrest** protect the interest of the individual to move about freely. No real *imprisonment* is necessary as long as the plaintiff is not free to move about as he or she pleases. The plaintiff must be aware of the restriction of movement, and the defendant must have intended to restrict the movement of the plaintiff. Like assault, the injury is a mental one and includes compensation for physical discomfort, loss of time, and any resulting physical illness or injury. False imprisonment is commonly found when police officers or security guards have no legal authority to arrest an individual, as when they do not have probable cause to make an arrest.

### Infliction of Mental Distress (Outrageous Conduct)

*[handwritten margin note: Can't sue for emotional distress in and of itself. Must be an injury involved.]*

One of the most wide-ranging intentional torts, the **infliction of mental distress,** has only been recognized in the past few decades, and the law in this area is still developing. Liability may result if (1) the defendant's conduct is extreme and outrageous; (2) the acts are intentionally committed; and (3) they result in some mental injury to the plaintiff, such as fear, distress, or upset.

Recovery has been permitted in cases involving spreading of a rumor that the plaintiff's son had hanged himself, sending of a bloody rat to a person, use of outrageous collection practices, mishandling of dead bodies, and a proposal to a woman to "take it out in trade."

### Trespass

The term **trespass** has a long and complex history in the law. Initially the term meant any wrongful conduct, similar to the current use of the term *tort*. Today the term means an interference with property rights and includes both **trespass to land** and **trespass to personal property.**

Trespass to land technically involves no intent. A person is liable for trespass to land by any physical invasion of the rights of another in land, as by physically walking across land or by otherwise harming the plaintiff's interest in land.

Trespass must be a voluntary act, but it need not be an "intentional" or even a "negligent" act. For example, a person who cuts down a tree that falls on the land of another is liable. A related tort, **private nuisance,** involves invasions of one's right to own and enjoy land without any physical invasion, as by noxious odors, noise, or immoral conduct (see p. 471).

Trespass to personal property involves a similar invasion of property rights in personal property. Personal property is defined as moveable property (property that is not land or permanently affixed to land), such as a car or a TV (see p. 246). Unlike trespass to land, an intent to invade another's property interest is required. In most jurisdictions some actual injury to the property must also occur. The closely related tort of **conversion** is an interference with the plaintiff's right of dominion over personal property, as in the case of theft of the property or refusal to turn over property to which the plaintiff is entitled. In conversion actions the property is effectively "sold" to the defendant, who is forced to pay the value of the property.

### Defamation (Libel and Slander)

The tort of **defamation** is made up of two other torts known as **libel** and **slander**. Libel is a written communication, and slander is an oral communication. The law makes little distinction between libel and slander today and considers them to be the same tort.

Defamation consists of a false communication that tends to hold the plaintiff up to hatred, contempt, or ridicule, or tends to injure the reputation of the plaintiff. It is defamation *per se* to accuse anyone of committing a crime or of having a disease, a businessperson of being dishonest, or a woman of being unchaste (the rule has never been applied to a man). In those four instances the law assumes an injury, and the plaintiff may recover nominal damages plus any compensatory and punitive damages he or she may prove. Other accusations may also be defamatory, but proof of actual injury is necessary for recovery.

The truth is a defense to a defamation action, and the defendant has the burden of proving the truth of the statement. Retraction of the statement will be considered in mitigation of damages. Because of first amendment concerns, the Supreme Court has held that *public figures* cannot recover for defamation unless the statement was made with knowledge that it was false or with reckless disregard of the truth.

### Misuse of Legal Process

The legal process can be used wrongfully to harm another, as in the case of a person who convinces a prosecutor to bring false criminal charges against another. Even if the person is found not guilty in court, substantial harm may have been done to the individual's reputation and financial well-being. As a result of those possibilities, the law recognizes three torts dealing with the legal process.

**Malicious prosecution** deals with criminal cases and requires proof that (1) a criminal proceeding was instituted (or continued) against the plaintiff by the defendant; (2) the proceedings were terminated in favor of the accused; (3) no probable cause for the proceeding existed; and (4) the defendant was motivated by "malice," that is, some other purpose than that of bringing an offender to justice. If the defendant really believed that the plaintiff was guilty and had probable cause to believe that the plaintiff had committed the offense, no action exists.

**Wrongful civil proceedings** require a lack of probable cause to believe that grounds for a civil action exist, and malice is required. **Abuse of process** deals with the use of service of process or other court papers in a malicious manner. The plaintiff need not prove that the action was terminated in his or her favor or that court papers were obtained without probable cause. A common example is extortion of money through the threat of civil process.

### Invasion of Privacy

The tort of **invasion of privacy** dates back only to the beginning of the twentieth century, and it is still developing. The tort usually involves one of three major theories.

**Intrusion on physical solitude or seclusion** is perhaps the broadest theory. Cases involving illegal searches and home invasions clearly involve an invasion of privacy, but other cases have involved eavesdropping, wire tapping, window peeping, and even persistent telephone calls. Cases based on intrusion have recently been filed by employees against drug testing, use of lie detectors, and body searches.

**Public disclosure of private facts** includes situations in which the defendant makes public objectionable and offensive facts about a person that are considered private. An early sensational case involved a movie about a person who was a reformed prostitute, made without her permission. Other cases involve publishing that a person does not pay his or her debts, or publishing a picture of a person without his or her consent. Records that are otherwise available to the public may be made public. Publicity about *public figures* is generally protected by the first amendment, and the news media may report matters of news and public interest.

The final tort involved in invasion of privacy is **appropriation of the plaintiff's name or likeness.** Using the likeness of an actor or other public figure for advertising purposes without consent is the usual way in which the tort is committed. The name or likeness must be used for the defendant's advantage, as in advertising or in a corporate name.

### Intentional Business Torts

Several intentional torts specifically affect business relationships, including **interference with contracts, interference with a prospective advantage,** and **malicious discharge.** Other competitive torts are considered in Chapter 14.

The tort of *interference with contracts* means that one person may not intentionally interfere with the plaintiff's rights under an existing contract. The defendant must know of the existence of the contract, and the law seems to require some kind of "bad motive," although the exact nature of that motive varies from state to state. For example, if A has a contract to purchase goods from B, C's attempt to convince A to breach the contract to get the business would be a tortious interference with contract.

The tort of *interference with a prospective advantage* means some intentional deprivation of another's future business advantage, where the means employed, or the defendant's purposes, are improper, and the plaintiff must lose some business advantage that can be measured, such as future benefits. It is, of course, permissible to compete for business as long as the purpose of competition is simply to acquire a larger market share. In one case, attempts by a banker to put a barber out of business by setting up a competing shop and undercutting prices were held improper, because the banker's motives were based on intense personal hatred rather than economic motives.

The tort of interference with a prospective advantage has in turn resulted in a series of other torts falling under the general category of **unfair competition.** Those torts include **passing off** one's goods as the goods of another; **product simulation** and **misappropriation,** or copying the design or shape of another's product; and **false advertising.**

### Malicious Discharge

A rapidly developing tort involves *malicious discharge* of employees. The **at-will employment doctrine** holds that employees may be discharged at any time, for any reason or for no reason at all, just as employees may leave employment at any time for any reason. But recent decisions indicate that if the employer acts *maliciously*, that is, from some improper motive, the employee may be able to file suit. For example, discharging an employee because she filed a worker's compensation action has been held actionable (see p. 292). The outlines of this tort are just beginning to emerge.

### Defenses to Intentional Torts

Over the centuries of common law experience, several general defenses to intentional torts have evolved. A **privilege** relates to conduct that the courts find to be socially beneficial. Thus, although a technical tort has been committed, the courts will permit a balancing of interests and a finding that the tort should be excused. For example, a physician has the right to provide medical care in an emergency even though that care may involve a technical battery. If a person reasonably believes that he or she has a legal justification for a tort, such as self-defense, but is operating under a **mistake,** he or she may be excused from liability.

**Good Samaritan Laws**    Many states have adopted statutes to deal with the problem of people who are found liable after trying to help another person. In other cases, judicial decisions have also dealt with the same problem. Such persons have committed a technical battery and may be liable in the absence of some change in the law.

**Good Samaritan laws** provide a privilege, sometimes restricted to doctors or other health care professionals who stop to aid an injured person. Those statutes often provide that no recovery is possible unless the person helping is guilty of negligence. Some statutes go further and require gross negligence or recklessness before the helper may be found liable.

**Consent**    **Consent** to a tort by the plaintiff bars all recovery. For example, one who invites another to strike him cannot later sue for assault. On the other hand, consent will be ineffective if (1) the person lacked capacity to consent, based on infancy, intoxication, or mental incompetence; (2) the consent was coerced; (3) the consent was given while the person was mistaken about the nature and quality of the invasion intended; or (4) public policy prevents a valid consent, as in the case of laws against dueling, aiding another in a suicide attempt, or sexual conduct with a minor.

**Necessity**    A person who acts to prevent a threatened injury from some cause unconnected to the plaintiff may be able to rely on the defense of **necessity.** For example, a defendant who shoots the plaintiff's rabid dog will have a defense to a suit for destruction of property.

## NEGLIGENCE

*Negligence* is a child of our complex and dangerous world. The concept of negligence arose, probably not coincidentally, at the same time as the Industrial Revolution. As the world became more risky, the law began to require compensation from those who subjected others to unreasonable risks.

At the outset, it is necessary to distinguish between negligence and an *unavoidable accident*. Negligence is defined as the failure to act as a reasonable and prudent person would act under like circumstances. An unavoidable accident is an occurrence that is not intended and that could not be foreseen or prevented by the exercise of reasonable precautions. Unavoidable accidents do not result in liability, but injuring others through negligence does.

### The Duty of Due Care

Under the common law, every person has a duty to use that degree of care that a reasonable and prudent person would use in like circumstances. Sometimes the definition is shortened even further to require only that the defendant use *due care*, although the two definitions mean exactly the same thing.

# Lannon v. Taco Bell, Inc.

708 P.2d 1370 Colorado Court of Appeals, 1985

Lannon, a cab driver, approached the counter of a Taco Bell restaurant located in a bad neighborhood. He noticed a man with a gun behind the counter removing money from a floor safe and began to back away. In doing so, he bumped into a person who turned out to be a second robber. Lannon ran to the parking lot, and the man with the gun fired at Lannon through a window. The bullet struck Lannon in the hand. Lannon brought this action against Taco Bell, charging negligence. Lannon argued that Taco Bell had not taken reasonable precautions, including hiring an armed guard. The jury found for Lannon, and Taco Bell appealed.

**Pierce, J.**   Taco Bell contends that the issue of whether it breached a duty to this plaintiff by failing to employ an armed guard should not have been submitted to the jury. We disagree.

Before liability can be found in a negligence action, the existence of a duty of care must be determined. This is a question of law. . . . Whether the law should impose a duty requires consideration of the risk involved, the foreseeability and likelihood of injury as weighed against the social utility of the actor's conduct, the magnitude of the burden of guarding against the injury or harm, and the consequences of placing the burden upon the actor.

Business proprietors do have a duty to exercise reasonable care for the protection of persons on the premises, and that duty includes taking reasonable measures to prevent or deter reasonably foreseeable acts, and to alleviate known dangerous conditions. Where injury can be foreseen, there is a duty to act so as to avoid it. . . .

Whether the defendant owed a duty to the class in which the plaintiff found himself is a question of law for the court based on the foreseeable appreciable risk of harm. Whether the defendant has in fact breached that duty is a question for the jury. . . .

. . . [T]he trial court concluded that the evidence presented regarding the effectiveness of armed guards in other establishments in the area, the history

of frequent robberies at this particular establishment and throughout the general area, and the great risk of serious injury to those present during a robbery, established a duty on the part of Taco Bell to use reasonable means to alleviate a known dangerous condition. . . .

Hence, the factual issue here is whether Taco Bell breached its duty to Lannon because of its failure to take reasonable steps to prevent foreseeable armed robberies on its premises and that issue was an appropriate one for jury determination. It is for the jury to decide whether a reasonably prudent defendant, under the same or similar circumstances, would have taken available precautions. If Taco Bell should have, then the duty was breached. . . . The trial court was thus correct in refusing to enter a directed verdict in favor of Taco Bell. [Reversed on other grounds.]

## Case Discussion Questions

1   What is negligence? What acts of the defendant does the plaintiff allege to be negligence?

2   Did Taco Bell have a duty to Lannon? Where did that duty come from?

3   What duties do business establishments have with regard to their customers? How could Taco Bell have discharged its duties?

In the typical negligence action, the plaintiff will prove the conduct of the defendant to the jury. The jury will then compare the conduct of the defendant with the conduct of a hypothetical "reasonable person." If the jury finds that the defendant's conduct was not the same as that of the reasonable person, the defendant will be found guilty of negligence.

**The Reasonable Person**    The standard against which we all are measured is an external and objective one, that of "the reasonable person." The reasonable person is not described for the jury in negligence cases. The jury must determine what a reasonable person would do under the circumstances. The courts assume that the reasonable person is a person of "ordinary prudence," not to be identified with any specific person who might occasionally do unreasonable things, but rather with a hypothetical person who always does the reasonable and prudent thing.

The reasonable person is not necessarily a supercautious individual or "devoid of human frailties and constantly preoccupied with the idea that danger may be lurking in every direction about him at any time." The physical characteristics of the reasonable person are identical with those of the defendant. Thus, if the defendant is blind, he or she will be held to the standard of the reasonable *blind* person.

The standard for the mental abilities of the defendant is an objective one, however. In a famous statement, Justice Oliver Wendell Holmes said, "The law takes no account of the infinite varieties of temperament, intellect, and education which make the internal character of a given act so different in different men. It does not attempt to see men as God sees them, for more than one sufficient reason." In fact, the law will generally hold even insane persons and persons with mental defects accountable in negligence for their actions. The sole exception is children, who are held to the standard of children of "like age, intelligence, and experience." In tort law, the individual must, for the most part, conform to the standards of the community. Even children are held to the standard of reasonable care that would be exercised by a child of like years and intelligence. Insanity is generally no defense to negligence.

**Special Skills: Negligence as Malpractice**    If a person has special skill, knowledge, or intelligence, the law will require that the person use it. Cases have held accountants, lawyers, doctors, experienced ski instructors, construction superintendents, and coaches liable for failing to use a *higher* level of skill than that of the rest of humanity within their field of expertise. This is the definition of **malpractice.**

Those who undertake any work calling for a special skill are required not only to exercise reasonable care but also to possess a standard minimum of special knowledge and skill. A physician will be held to the standard not of the reasonable *person*, but of the reasonable *physician*. The same is true of dentists, pharmacists, psychiatrists, veterinarians, lawyers, architects, engineers, accountants, and many other professionals. Specialists will be held to an even higher standard—the reasonable brain surgeon as opposed to the reasonable general practitioner, for example.

**Recklessness**    For some limited purposes it is necessary to make finer divisions of negligence, although that practice is fading. Some states permit recovery of punitive damages for **reckless conduct,** and others have **automobile guest statutes** that require proof that the driver of an automobile be guilty of reckless conduct before the driver can be found liable to a passenger.

Recklessness is sometimes defined as *willful and wanton misconduct*, that is, a conscious disregard of a known risk. It is considered to be conduct somewhere between intentional acts and negligent acts. It is highly unreasonable conduct justifying punishment in the form of punitive damages in addition to compensatory damages for the actual loss.

### Injury (Damages)

Negligence cases are generally actions for compensatory damages. Although nominal damages are available, they are rarely awarded in negligence actions. Punitive damages are not available in negligence actions because the purpose of punitive damages is to deter future acts, and negligent acts, unlike intentional acts, cannot be deterred.

The purpose of compensatory damages is to place the injured plaintiff back in the same position he or she would have been in had the tort not occurred. Since many negligence actions involve personal injuries, compensatory damages include matters such as medical bills, lost work, and pain and suffering. Damage awards must also include such matters as *future* expenses, such as medical expenses and loss of earning capacity.

### Proximate Cause

One of the more difficult problems in all of tort law is the problem of causation. First, it is clear that the defendant must have *actually caused* the injury to the defendant. This requirement is sometimes called **proximate cause**. That is, the injury would not have occurred without the negligent act of the defendant. In the usual case this is resolved through the **but-for** test, that is, but for the negligence of the defendant, the injury would not have occurred.

Legal policies of causation seem to divide into two theories. First, proximate cause may mean *foreseeability* in the sense that the defendant will not be held liable unless it was foreseeable that the conduct would cause an injury. Second, proximate cause may mean *direct cause*, in the sense of consequences that are directly traceable to the actions of the defendant. The following classic case illustrates the two theories and their application to some rather complex facts in what has been called "a law professor's dream of an examination question."

## *Palsgraf v. Long Island Railroad*
248 N.Y. 339, 162 N.E. 99 (N.Y., 1928)

A passenger was running to board a train operated by the defendant, Long Island Railroad Co. One of the defendant's guards negligently tried to help the passenger board the moving train and, in doing so, dislodged a package carried by the passenger. The package fell near the tracks, and sparks from the wheels of the train set the package on fire. Inside the package were fireworks, which exploded with some force. The concussion from the explosion overturned a set of scales located some distance away from the loading platform. The scales fell on the plaintiff, Mrs. Palsgraf, and severely injured her. A jury found that the defendant's guard was negligent but that no harm to the plaintiff could possibly have been anticipated. In spite of these findings, the plaintiff won in the trial court. The railroad appealed.

**Cardozo, C.J.**     The conduct of the defendant's guard, if a wrong in its relation to the holder of the package, was not a wrong in its relation to the plaintiff, standing far away. Relatively to her it was not negligence at all. Nothing in the situation gave notice that the falling package had in it the potency of peril to persons thus removed. Negligence is not actionable unless it involves the invasion of a legally protected interest, the violation of a right. "Proof of negligence in the air, so to speak, will not do." . . . If no hazard was apparent to the eye of ordinary vigilance, an act innocent and harmless, at least to outward seeming, with reference to her, did not take to itself the quality of a tort because it happened to be a wrong, though apparently not one involving the risk of bodily insecurity, with reference to someone else. "In every instance, before negligence can be predicated of a given act, back of the act must be sought and found a duty to the individual complaining, the observance of which would have averted or avoided the injury." . . .

. . . What the plaintiff must show is a wrong to herself; i.e., a violation of her own right, and not merely a wrong to someone else, nor conduct "wrongful" because unsocial, but not a "wrong" to any one. . . .

The law of causation, remote or proximate, is thus foreign to the case before us. . . . If there is no tort to be redressed, there is no occasion to consider what damage might be recovered if there were a finding of a tort. . . .

The Judgment of the . . . Trial Term should be reversed. . . .

**Andrews, J. (Dissenting)**     . . . We deal in terms of proximate cause, not of negligence. . . . Due care is a duty imposed on each one of us to protect society from unnecessary danger, not to protect A, B, or C alone. . . .

The proposition is this: Every one owes to the world at large the duty of refraining from those acts that may unreasonably threaten the safety of others. . . . Unreasonable risk being taken, its consequences are not confined to those who might probably be hurt. . . .

. . . What is a cause in a legal sense, still more what is a proximate cause, depends in each case upon many considerations, as does the existence of negligence itself. Any philosophical doctrine of causation does not help us. A boy throws a stone into a pond. The ripples spread. The water level rises. The history of that pond is altered to all eternity. It will be altered by other causes also. Yet it will be forever the resultant of all causes combined. Each one will have an influence. . . . Each cause brings about future events. Without each the future would not be the same. Each is proximate in the sense it is essential. But that is not what we mean by the word. Nor on the other hand do we mean sole cause. There is no such thing. . . .

. . . What we do mean by the word "proximate" is that, because of convenience, of public policy, of a rough sense of justice, the law arbitrarily declines to trace a series of events beyond a certain point. This is not logic. It is practical politics. Take our rule as to fires. Sparks from my burning haystack set on fire my house and my neighbor's. I may recover from a negligent railroad. He may not. . . . We said the act of the railroad was not the proximate cause of our neighbor's fire. . . . The words we used were simply indicative of our notions of public policy. . . .

. . . A chauffeur negligently collides with another car which is filled with dynamite, although he could not know it. An explosion follows. A, walking on the sidewalk nearby is killed. B, sitting in a window of a building opposite, is cut by flying glass. C, likewise sitting in a window a block away, is similarly injured. And a further illustration: A nursemaid, ten blocks away, startled by the noise, involuntarily drops a baby from her arms to the walk. We are told that C may not recover while A may. As to B it is a question for [a] . . . jury. We will all agree that the baby might not. Because, we are again told, the chauffeur had no reason to believe his conduct involved any risk of injuring either C or the baby. As to them he was not negligent. . . .

. . . The true theory is, it seems to me, that the injury to C, if in truth he is to be denied recovery, and the injury to the baby, is that their several injuries were not the proximate result of the negligence.

And here not what the chauffeur had reason to believe would be the result of his conduct, but what the prudent would foresee, may have some bearing—*may* have some bearing, for the problem of proximate cause is not to be solved by any one consideration. It is all a question of expediency. There are no fixed rules to govern our judgment. There are simply matters of which we may take account. . . . There is in truth little to guide us other than common sense.

There are some hints that may help us. The proximate cause, involved as it may be with other causes, must be, at the least, something without which the event would not happen. The court must ask itself whether there was a natural and continuous sequence between cause and effect. Was the one a substantial factor in producing the other? Is the effect of cause on result not too attenuated? Is the cause likely, in the usual judgment of mankind, to produce the result? Or by the exercise of prudent foresight, could the result be foreseen? Is the result too remote from the cause, and here we consider remoteness in time and space. . . . We draw an uncertain and wavering line, but draw it we must as best we can. . . .

[In the present case] Mrs. Palsgraf was standing some distance away. How far cannot be told from the record—apparently 25 or 30 feet, perhaps less. Except for the explosion, she would not have been injured. . . . So the explosion was a substantial factor in producing the result. . . . The only intervening cause was that, instead of blowing her to the ground, the concussion smashed the weighing machine which in turn fell upon her. There was no remoteness in time, little in space. . . . [I]njury in some form was most probable.

Under these circumstances I cannot say as a matter of law that the plaintiff's injuries were not the proximate result of the negligence. . . . The judgment appealed from should be affirmed. . . .

## Case Discussion Questions

1   Was it foreseeable that *someone* would be harmed by the defendant's guard's negligence? Who? Was it foreseeable that the *plaintiff* would be injured? Should that make a difference?
2   What is the basis of Justice Cardozo's decision? How do we determine whether a duty is owed to someone?
3   What is the basis of Justice Andrews' dissenting opinion?

## Proof of Negligence

The burden of proof in negligence cases, as in virtually every civil case, is on the plaintiff. The plaintiff is required to prove the elements of negligence by a preponderance of the evidence. Although ordinary rules of evidence apply in negligence cases, two important considerations need further explanation: (1) the place of statutes in civil negligence actions and (2) the doctrine of *res ipsa loquitor*.

 **The Place of Statutes: Negligence Per Se and Evidence of Negligence**   Negligence is a common law matter, and the duties required of a reasonable person are ordinarily established by judicial decision. The standard of conduct required of a reasonable person may also be established by statute, and the effect of those statutes will vary from state to state.

Not every statute will impose civil liability. Generally speaking, the courts will impose civil liability for violation of a criminal statute only if the purpose of the statute is to protect persons from a particular risk. For example, the purpose of a statute that prohibits going through a stop sign is to protect others on the highway. The courts will probably find that a person who goes through a stop sign has violated the duty of care in a negligence action, as well as having violated a criminal statute in a criminal action.

Once the statute is determined to protect the class of persons in which the plaintiff is included against the risk of harm that has in fact occurred, the question becomes one of the legal *effect* of violation. Two rules are used by the courts: (1) such violation will be considered **negligence per se**; and (2) such violation will be considered **evidence of negligence**.

The majority of courts treat a violation of statute as a conclusive showing of negligence, or *negligence per se*. That is, the jury has no power to relax the standard set by the statute. For example, proof that the defendant violated a speed limit is negligence, and the defendant could not show that, given the circumstances at the time, it was perfectly reasonable to violate the speed limit.

A number of states hold that the violation of a statute is not *automatically* negligence, however. In these states, violation of statutes is treated merely as *evidence of negligence*, and permits the jury to find that, under the conditions existing at the time, it was reasonable to violate the statute. For example, on a clear day without much traffic, it might not be unreasonable to drive a few miles per hour over the speed limit, and in those states the jury might find the defendant innocent of negligence in spite of a technical violation of the speed limit.

 **Res Ipsa Loquitor**    In some cases it is extremely difficult to prove negligence on the part of the defendant, even though most reasonable people would conclude that negligence exists. For example, if an airplane crashes, it will be extremely difficult to prove to the jury precisely *how* the airline was negligent—through pilot error, equipment malfunction, or defect in the plane—but it is extremely unlikely that negligence did *not* exist. In some cases the law will permit the use of the doctrine of **res ipsa loquitor,** which literally means, "the thing speaks for itself." That doctrine provides that the burden of proof will shift to the defendant to prove that negligence did *not* exist if the plaintiff can prove (1) that the event is of a kind which ordinarily does not occur in the absence of someone's negligence; (2) the event is caused by an agency or instrumentality within the exclusive control of the defendant; and (3) the event must not have been due to the voluntary action of the plaintiff.

For example, in an airline crash, the plaintiff must show that airplane crashes do not ordinarily take place in the absence of someone's negligence; that the airplane was under the exclusive control of the airline; and that the plaintiff did not contribute to the crash. In that case, the plaintiff has not proven actual negligence, but the evidence is sufficient to shift the burden to the airline to prove that the crash occurred because of some cause other than its own negligence.

### Defenses to Negligence

Once negligence has been proven, the defendant may prove that a defense to that charge exists. The two most common defenses to negligence are **contributory negligence** and **assumption of risk.**

**Contributory Negligence**    *Contributory negligence* is negligent conduct on the part of the plaintiff that contributes to the plaintiff's injury. If the plaintiff is contributorily negligent, he or she cannot recover for any loss suffered. For example, if the defendant negligently operates an automobile and injures the plaintiff, but the plaintiff is also negligent, the plaintiff will not be able to recover. Recovery will be barred even if the plaintiff is only 1% negligent and the defendant is 99% negligent.

The strict contributory negligence rule may result in substantial injustice, and some exceptions have developed. One exception, known as the doctrine of **last clear chance,** says that even if the plaintiff is contributorily negligent, he or she may still recover if the defendant could have avoided the injury. Usually this rule is applied if the plaintiff is in a position of "helpless peril," such as being stranded in the middle of a road due to his or her own negligence. If the defendant had the "last clear chance" to avoid striking the helpless plaintiff, the plaintiff may still recover.

**Comparative Negligence** The doctrine of **comparative negligence** has developed recently in many states to replace contributory negligence in some cases. Although used chiefly in automobile accident cases, the rules of comparative negligence have been applied to other tort actions, such as maritime accidents and railroad accidents, and a few states have enlarged the doctrine to include all tort cases.

Comparative negligence involves an apportionment of damages based on the relative fault of the parties. If a person suffered $10,000 in injuries but was 20% at fault in the incident, the damages would be reduced by 20%, permitting the party to recover $8,000. The precise form of comparative negligence varies a great deal between states.

---

### PRO AND CON

## Is tort reform necessary?

**Pro** The common law tort system no longer works and is in need of reform. The result of the tort system has been huge jury verdicts that result in skyrocketing liability insurance premiums. Many professionals, especially doctors, have been forced to withdraw services in areas where liability suits are most common. Municipal governments have been forced to cut back on riskier services, such as swimming pools and even playground equipment. And some products have been taken off the market because of the possibility of large jury verdicts and high insurance premiums.

Several parts of the tort system are to blame. First, noneconomic loss, such as pain and suffering, is simply an invitation to the jury to award huge sums. Punitive damage claims likewise give juries carte blanche to award injured parties any figure they desire. Attorney's contingent fees, in which the lawyer takes a set percentage of any recovery, encourage lawyers to take high-risk cases in hopes of winning huge awards. Lawyers may even file frivolous "nuisance" suits in order to obtain a small, quick settlement. The move to comparative negligence and away from contributory negligence encourages plaintiffs to file suits in many more cases than before and results in some recovery in most cases.

State legislatures, and even the federal Congress, must make major changes in the tort system. One essential change is an absolute cap on noneconomic loss and punitive damages. For example, California has a $250,000 limit on noneconomic loss in medical malpractice cases. Some limit on contingency fees is also necessary, perhaps even outlawing them entirely. Disciplinary procedures should be used against lawyers who file frivolous cases. And we should reevaluate the move to comparative negligence, perhaps reinstituting contributory negligence. Finally, we must consider whether tort cases, or some of them, should be considered in some new way, perhaps through a state-operated system of arbitration, eliminating the jury entirely.

The tort system has outlived its usefulness. Sympathetic juries and highly capable plaintiffs' attorneys have created a litigious society where everyone sues at the slightest provocation. The result is much higher insurance costs to business and the loss of some highly productive and highly necessary businesses and professions. Reform is essential.

**Con** The tort system has done its job for centuries and continues to do that job effectively. The problem lies not in the tort system, but in a far riskier environment. The insurance industry, and those subject to liability suits, are simply trying to shift those risks to the injured parties, rather than accepting the notion that those responsible for injury should bear those risks.

In fact, jury awards have *not* increased dramatically. Median jury awards from 1960–1984 have remained at about $20,000, adjusted for inflation. Even in the medical malpractice area, the rise in median jury awards has been less than the increase in inflation between 1974 and 1984. Many have argued that the real "crisis" was caused by a decline in investment earnings by insurance companies and unwise insuring of very risky ventures in the early 1980s.[3]

Any absolute cap on noneconomic damages means depriving some injured plaintiffs of real compensation for their losses. Under the California cap, noted in *Pro*, a patient who suffers brain damage as a result of malpractice by an anesthesiologist may recover (1) the costs of medical care; (2) lost wages (if any), including future wages; and (3) $250,000 to cover all pain and suffering. Such a result is inhumane and totally unrealistic.

Similarly, caps on punitive damage awards mean that jurors can no longer take the wealth of the defendant into account in determining an appropriate punishment. A $250,000 punitive damage award has little or no deterrent effect on a huge corporation and may be viewed as a simple cost of doing business.

Limits on contingent fees mean simply that some plaintiffs will not be able to obtain legal representation. Often lawyers charge higher percentages for smaller or more difficult cases. If a limit is placed on the contingent fee, lawyers may not take those cases. Outlawing the contingent fee completely will mean that poor clients will not be able to afford legal representation at all. And imposing disciplinary sanctions against lawyers who file "frivolous" cases will mean that lawyers will not file cases based on new theories, and the law itself will remain stagnant. Undoing the progressive movement toward comparative fault means returning to the legal dark ages where the slightest negligence on the part of the plaintiff might bar recovery.

To undo the tort system means undoing centuries of legal history and denies the constitutional right to trial by jury to determine both liability and damages. Before such changes are made, we must be very sure that there is a real crisis and that the remedy is not worse than the problem.

## Roundtable Discussion

1   Should caps be placed on noneconomic loss in all cases? Should contingent fees be outlawed? Should they be limited? How?
2   Is there a real need to reform tort law? How would you reform it?
3   How should risks be allocated between the injured party and the person or firm causing the injury? Should insurance even be a consideration in allocating that risk?

---

**Assumption of Risk**   If the plaintiff voluntarily accepts a known risk, the doctrine of *assumption of risk* says that the party may not recover from an otherwise negligent defendant. For example, a plaintiff will be held to assume the risk of being hit by a foul ball while attending a baseball game, because it is common knowledge that foul balls are sometimes hit into the stands.

It is important that the plaintiff know of the risk prior to assuming it. If a person had never seen a baseball game, as in the case of a foreign visitor unfamiliar with the game, no assumption of risk would occur. Similarly, the plaintiff must *voluntarily* assume the risk. A three-year-old child accompanying her parents to the ballgame would not assume the risk of being hit by a foul ball, for example.

### Joint and Several Liability

There is often more than one person who is legally responsible to the injured party. For example, if A and B are both operating automobiles negligently and collide, and the collision injures C walking by on the sidewalk, C has a right to sue *either* or *both* A and B. Other examples might include a common duty, as in the case of the duty of a property owner and a city to maintain a sidewalk.

---

3 See "The Manufactured Crisis," 51 *Consumer Reports*, Aug. 1986, p. 544.

In such cases of shared responsibility, the general rule is that the parties are **jointly and severally liable;** that is, the parties are each equally liable to the plaintiff. The plaintiff may sue either or both and obtain a judgment against either or both. The plaintiff has only the right to one **satisfaction** (payment) of the judgment, however.

### Trespassers, Invitees, and Licensees

Often, people are injured while on the land or property of another. For example, a supermarket customer may slip on a mashed piece of fruit, or a visitor in a home may be injured because of a faulty sidewalk.

Generally speaking, a *trespasser* assumes the risk of any injury through negligence. There are some exceptions to that rule, as in cases involving known trespass by large numbers of people, or in cases in which the owner knows of the trespasser's presence. In such cases, the courts impose a duty to use reasonable care under the circumstances for the safety of the trespasser. If the trespasser is a child, the landowner may be liable for injuries caused by negligence if the possessor of the land knows that children are likely to trespass, under a theory known as **attractive nuisance.**

The courts often make a distinction between **licensees** and **invitees.** A licensee is *permitted* to enter on land, whereas an invitee is *encouraged* to enter on land. For example, a person who is permitted to stand on a person's front porch to get out of the rain without obtaining actual permission would be a licensee. A person coming to the same house on business and at the invitation of the owner will be an invitee. Curiously, social guests are often classified as licensees, although this rule seems to make little sense.

A landowner owes few duties to a licensee except to refrain from injuring the licensee intentionally. On the other hand a landowner owes an invitee the duty of reasonable care, both against dangers of which he or she has knowledge and those which with reasonable care he or she might discover.

## STRICT LIABILITY

The term **strict liability** means that there is no consideration given to the mental element of the person committing the tort. There is no requirement that the plaintiff prove that the defendant intentionally or negligently interfered with a protected interest. Strict liability has been applied in a few types of cases for centuries. Recently, the concept has been applied to *products liability* cases. That application is considered in detail in Chapter 13.

### Traditional Strict Liability Torts

Common law strict liability torts were recognized in three distinct areas: (1) liability for the acts of animals; (2) liability for fire; and (3) liability for abnormally dangerous things and activities.

**Liability for Animals**    It has been the law since biblical times that the owner of animals of a kind likely to roam and do damage is strictly liable for the injury that they do. Thus, if livestock damage another's crops, the owner will be liable regardless of any fault in permitting them to roam. This rule is not accepted in some western states, nor does it apply to domestic pets, such as cats and dogs. Many states and municipalities have imposed strict liability by statute on the owners of dogs running free, however.

Owners of *dangerous* animals are liable for *any* harm that they cause. This rule generally applies to animals not usually kept by people, such as monkeys, wolves, and poisonous snakes. Owners of domestic animals, such as dogs and cats, are not liable unless the possessor knew, or had reason to know, of an abnormally dangerous propensity of the animal. This is the source of the almost-correct statement that "every dog gets one bite," because until the dog bites someone, there is no reason to believe the animal has any abnormally dangerous characteristics. That propensity could be demonstrated in other ways, such as by training the dog to attack, however.

**Liability for Fire**    The early common law imposed strict liability for *any* fire damage to another's property, even if a fire spread from one person's house to another's. That rule was later modified so that fires that started accidentally would not impose liability. But if the fire started in the course of an *abnormally dangerous activity*, the courts have imposed a strict liability rule. Thus, a fire started by sparks from a railroad train will impose liability on the railroad. Courts have also found negligence in many cases where an intentionally set fire has gotten out of hand.

**Liability for Abnormally Dangerous Things and Activities**    In 1868 the English courts decided a famous decision known as *Rylands v. Fletcher*,[4] which established the rule of strict liability in tort for any *abnormally dangerous things and activities*. That case, which involved the flooding of mine shafts following the construction of a reservoir, held that the defendant was liable, regardless of the fact that the defendant had not been negligent. Building a reservoir in such an area was held to be an abnormal and inappropriate activity in an area in which there were large numbers of mine shafts.

The rule of *Rylands v. Fletcher* has been applied to a large number of other situations. Use and storage of explosives, pile driving, use of certain chemicals, emission of smoke and gas, and many other "nonnatural" activities have been held to subject persons to liability. Airlines are strictly liable both for sonic-boom damages and for the damage from the debris of airline crashes. It appears likely that the same rule will be applied to falling rockets and to nuclear emissions.

For strict liability to exist, there must be some kind of **ultrahazardous activity.** An ultrahazardous activity is one that (1) involves a risk of serious harm to the person, land, or property of another that cannot be eliminated by the exercise of utmost care and (2) is not a matter of common usage. If a person undertakes an ultrahazardous activity, it is said that he "acts at his peril." That means that an actor is liable for his or her conduct even without negligence or intent.

The same rules of proximate cause apply in such cases as are applied in negligence cases. This sometimes means that the defendant is liable only for *foreseeable* losses, or losses that are related to the type of harm threatened by the activity. Generally speaking, assumption of risk is a defense to strict liability, but contributory negligence is not.

The field of *products liability* developed directly from the liability imposed for ab-

---

4 H.L. 330 (1868)

normally dangerous activities. That area deals with the problem of injuries suffered as a result of dangerous or defective products. Products liability is perhaps the fastest growing area of tort law, marked by a major expansion of the concept of strict liability in the last few decades. Products liability is considered in detail in Chapter 13.

## SUMMARY AND CONCLUSIONS

The law of torts includes all private civil actions other than a breach of contract, including intentional, negligent, and strict liability actions. Every tort has four elements: (1) a legally recognized duty; (2) a breach of that duty; (3) an injury, or damages; and (4) a proximate causal connection between the breach of duty and the injury.

Intentional torts require proof of an intent on the part of the tortfeasor to bring about a result that will invade the legally protected interests of another. Every intentional tort has certain elements, including the mental element of intent. Intentional torts include assault, battery, false imprisonment, infliction of mental distress, defamation, several types of misuse of legal process, and several business torts.

Negligence is defined as the failure to use due care, or the care that a reasonable person would use under like circumstances. Some people, including many professionals, are held to a higher standard required by their professions. In some instances of strict liability, the courts do not require proof of a mental element and will hold the defendant liable without fault upon proof that the defendant committed the act alone. At common law, strict liability was restricted to incidents involving dangerous animals, fire, and ultrahazardous activities. The most activity in recent tort law has been in the field of products liability.

## REVIEW QUESTIONS

1 What is a tort? Why are torts sometimes called a "legal garbage can"?

2 Explain the difference between *intentional*, *negligent*, and *strict liability* torts. Why do we treat intentional torts more harshly than the other types? Why should *fault* make a difference? Is there a better way to apportion the risk of loss?

3 Justice Oliver Wendell Holmes once said, "'[D]etached reflection cannot be demanded in the presence of an uplifted knife." What did he mean in the context of the law of self-defense?

4 Who is the "reasonable person"? Why don't we define the reasonable person better for jurors? Is anyone *always* a "reasonable person"?

5 Explain the difference between contributory

negligence and comparative negligence. Which system is more fair?

6 Katko entered a vacant farmhouse owned by Briney to find and take old bottles and fruit jars that might be antiques. Briney had set up a shotgun wired to the door in an interior room. The gun was aimed at knee level. Katko opened the door and suffered permanent injuries to both legs. Katko sued Briney for battery. What result would you expect? [*Katko v. Briney*, 183 N.W.2d 657 (Iowa, 1971).]

7 Mrs. George's adult son had purchased goods from the Jordan Marsh Company and had failed to pay for them. Jordan Marsh employees then falsely alleged that Mrs. George had guaranteed the debt and (a) called her late at night, (b) repeatedly mailed bills to her marked "ac-

count referred to law and collection department," and (c) charged the bills to her personal account. Soon after, Mrs. George's health deteriorated, and she had two heart attacks. She sued Jordan Marsh, claiming intentional infliction of mental distress. What result would you expect? [*George v. Jordan Marsh Co.*, 268 N.E.2d 915 (1971).]

8   After a typical reunion at Yale University, Guilford, an alumnus, felt the need to relieve himself and walked toward a small clump of bushes. The bushes were actually the top of a tree growing below a cliff on the other side of the wall. No warning signs were present, although it is doubtful whether Guilford could have read them. Guilford stepped over the wall and fell through the tree to the ground below, injuring himself severely. He sued Yale, and Yale responded by arguing that he was either a trespasser or a licensee. Guilford claimed that he was an invitee, since one purpose of the reunion was to solicit funds. What result would you expect? [*Guilford v. Yale University*, 23 A.2d 917 (Conn., 1942).]

9   An employee of Fisher negligently parked a truck along a highway. A car driven by Gunther collided with the rear of the truck. Gunther was also negligent. Lynch ran to the scene to help the injured, and, with the aid of others, helped Gunther and his wife from the car, which was on fire. Lynch found a pistol in the car, which he handed to Gunther for safekeeping. Gunther was delirious, and shot Lynch in the foot. Lynch sued Gunther, the truck driver, and Fisher. Are any of them liable? [*Lynch v. Fisher*, 24 So.2d 513 (La., 1948).]

10   Whitcomb ran a construction company. While attempting to begin the foundation for a building, he decided to use dynamite to blast through the bedrock. Whitcomb used every conceivable precaution, hired experts to do the blasting, and even posted armed guards to keep people a safe distance away. (a) A group of college students made their way past the guards to watch the blasting and were injured by flying debris. (b) Windows were broken several miles away. (c) Riley, who had a nervous disorder, suffered a heart attack after hearing the explosion several miles away. In which case(s) is Whitcomb liable?

# CHAPTER 10

# The Law of Property, Patents and Copyrights, and Computers

The law of property is central to the history of the Anglo-American legal system. The earliest common law cases dealt with the rights of property. To a large extent, the laws of contracts, torts, and business associations all depend on and grew out of the law of property. This chapter considers the nature of property law and the law surrounding *intellectual property* (the law of patents, copyrights, and trademarks). Finally, the chapter discusses the law surrounding the development of computers.

## THE NATURE OF OWNERSHIP: A BUNDLE OF RIGHTS

Although property and ownership are central to Western legal and political thought, it is difficult to describe what it means to "own" something. Perhaps the easiest method of describing ownership is as a **bundle of rights.** The owner of property has a series of rights in property that will be protected by legal action. Among those rights are the rights to **possession, use, disposition,** and **title.**

The right to *possession* refers to the right to possess the property physically. Not all owners of property have that right, especially if they have leased the property to another. The right to *use* the property usually, but not always, accompanies the right of possession. The right to *dispose* of property means the right to transfer the property to another, to sell it, give it away, or even, within limits, to destroy it.

Perhaps the most troublesome aspect of ownership is the right to *title*. Ownership of some types of property is evidenced by some kind of paper certificate, as, for example, a deed to land or a certificate of title for a motor vehicle. But some property has no certificate or other evidence of title. For example, there is no paper "title" to this book. The term *title* means both the *right* of ownership and any *documents* that show ownership.

### The Law of Trusts: Division of Property Rights

One important application of the bundle of rights is in the law of **trusts.** In a trust, the owner of property (known as the **settlor**) transfers legal title to another party, known as the **trustee,** for the benefit of another, known as the **beneficiary.** The trustee holds legal title to the property, but many of the aspects of ownership (such as the right to use or receive profits) belong to the beneficiary.

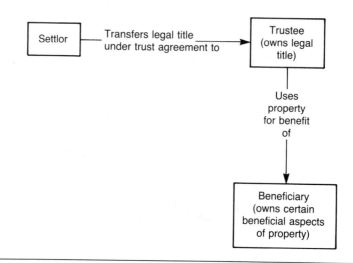

FIGURE 10.1    Trusts

For example, A may transfer a ranch to B, as trustee, for the benefit of A's children. B legally "owns" the property but may be required under the trust agreement with A to pay over the profits from the ranch to the children (see Figure 10.1).

## REAL AND PERSONAL PROPERTY

Property is divided into two classes: (1) **real property,** or land, anything permanently affixed to land, and interests in land, and (2) **personal property,** a residual category covering all other property.

It is sometimes difficult to tell whether certain property should be classified as real or personal property. A borderline class involves **fixtures,** or property that is attached to real estate. For example, a contract for the sale of a piece of real estate generally includes the sale of all fixtures on the property. But it is sometimes difficult to determine whether something is really "part of the land," such as curtain rods, window air conditioners, or growing crops.

The courts generally apply a three-part test to determine whether a piece of property is a fixture: (1) whether the property is "affixed" to the land, or to the improvements on the property; (2) whether the property aids in the use of the property or will injure the property if it is removed; and (3) the intent of the party who affixed the property to the land. If the court finds that the property is a fixture, it will "follow the land" in any sale or transfer. For example, a kitchen stove that may be removed by simply unscrewing a pipe is personal property, whereas an underground electrical system is part of the real estate. Growing crops are usually considered personal property, because the intent of the parties is that they be severed from the real estate.

## PERSONAL PROPERTY

Personal property may be either *tangible* or *intangible.* That is, it may have a physical existence or not. For example, tangible personal property includes a paper clip, this book, or a forty-ton crane. Some personal property may be intangible and have no physical existence, such as a patent, a copyright, or a share of corporate stock; but such property may be *represented* by a piece of paper, such as a stock certificate.

One type of intangible property right is sometimes called a **chose in action,** or a legal claim or right to sue another. Under some circumstances the owner of a chose in action may transfer that right to others in much the same way that other property rights may be transferred.

### Transfer of Personal Property

Personal property may be transferred to others in a variety of ways. Although state law may require filing or assignment of certificates of title in some cases (e.g., automobiles or boats), those requirements are the exception. Transfer of personal property may be made (1) by sale; (2) at death; (3) by gift; (4) through the doctrines relating to lost, mislaid, or abandoned property; (5) by accession; or (6) by confusion. Sales of property are valid if the underlying contracts are valid.

Property owned by a person at his or her death will be transferred to others. If the person died **testate** (with a will) the property will go to those persons designated in the will, subject to certain rights of the decedent's spouse or children. If the person died **intestate** (without a will) the property will be transferred to the people described in the state **law of descent and distribution,** a state statute providing the order of succession to property.

A valid **gift** will transfer ownership of the property from the **donor** (person making the gift) to the **donee** (person receiving the gift). A mere promise to make a gift is unenforceable for lack of consideration in the absence of estoppel, however (see p. 203). In order for a gift to be valid, both **donative intent** and **delivery** are necessary. Donative intent means the intent of the donor to make a gift, rather than an intent to make some other transaction. Delivery means that the property must be actually or constructively delivered to the donee. The donee must also *accept* the gift. There may be instances in which the donee may refuse the gift (e.g., for tax reasons, or a gift of a pet python).

**Lost property** is defined as property of which the owner has accidentally parted with possession. For example, if a watch band breaks and the watch falls off in the street without the knowledge of the owner, the property is lost. The finder of lost property is generally entitled to possession of the property to the exclusion of everyone except the true owner. The owner of the place where the property is found may have the right to the property if the finder is a trespasser or the property is found in a private place, such as inside a home.

Property is considered **mislaid** if the owner intentionally placed the property in a certain place and then forgot where he or she put it. The owner of the place where mislaid property is found is entitled to possession of the property to the exclusion of everyone except the true owner, on the assumption that the true owner will remember where the property was left and return to reclaim it. **Abandoned property** is property of which the owner has intentionally given up possession. The first person to take possession of abandoned property has the right to the property, even to the exclusion of the original owner, because there was an intent to give up ownership.

**Accession** means the right to own things that become a part of things already owned. For example, if A owns some lumber, and B takes that lumber by mistake and builds a table and chairs through his own labor, the wood (and the chair) still belongs to A. The increased value of the wood in its new form is an accession to value. Generally speaking, the courts award the final product to the owner of the raw material, unless the value has been substantially enhanced and the person taking the raw materials did not act willfully.

The doctrine of **confusion of goods** involves situations in which goods belonging to two or more people become inseparably mixed. The doctrine is particularly relevant to **fungible** goods, that is, goods that are identical in all respects and usually sold by weights or measures, such as by the pound or bushel. If the confused goods are of the same kind, value, and quality, and if the amounts contributed by each are known, each owner simply receives a proportional amount of the whole. If the goods cannot be proportionately divided, perhaps because of variations in the goods, the owners generally become **tenants in common** in the whole (see Table 10.2). If the confusion has come about as a result of an intentional act, the wrongdoer usually loses everything.

## Bailments

A **bailment** is defined as the rightful possession of goods by a person who is not the owner. The law of bailments covers a large number of situations, including finders, people with lawful possession of mislaid property, and borrowers of property. A person with the lawful possession of the property of another is a **bailee**, whereas the owner of the property is known as a **bailor**.

**Liabilities of Bailees**    Whether a bailee is liable to the bailor for property that is lost, damaged, or destroyed depends on the classification of bailments. There are three types of bailments: (1) bailments for the *sole benefit of the bailee* (e.g., you borrow your neighbor's lawnmower to mow your lawn); (2) bailments for the *sole benefit of the bailor* (e.g., you gratuitously hold a package that is delivered to your neighbor until she returns home); and (3) *mutual benefit* bailments (you pay a repairman to take your stereo and repair it).

In bailments for the sole benefit of the bailee, the bailee is held to a standard of *great care* and will be liable to the bailor if the property is lost, damaged, or destroyed as a result of even slight negligence. On the other hand, in bailments for the sole benefit of the bailor, the bailee is held to a standard of only *slight care* and is liable only for gross negligence. Finally, in the case of a mutual benefit bailment, the bailee is liable only for *ordinary care* and will be responsible only if the property is lost, damaged, or destroyed as a result of ordinary negligence.

Those liabilities only apply in the case of bailed property that is lost, damaged, or destroyed. If a bailee delivers goods to a person who has no legal right to the goods, the bailee is *strictly liable* to the bailor. That is, even if the bailee has not been negligent, he or she will be held liable.

**Limitation of Liability by Contract**    Many professional bailees, such as parking lots, coat checks, or repair persons, attempt to limit their liability for items left with them by some kind of printed contract. For example, many parking lots provide a receipt with a disclaimer of liability printed on the back or post a sign disclaiming liability. Such disclaimers of liability are not favored by the courts and are ineffective against intentional or reckless conduct by the bailee, because they are against public policy. The courts may give effect to disclaimers of liability if the provision limiting liability is clear and is communicated to the bailor before the contract is made.

## Carr v. Hoosier Photo Supplies, Inc.
441 N.E.2d 450 Supreme Court of Indiana, 1982

The Carr family took a "once in a lifetime" vacation in Europe, and Mr. Carr took eighteen rolls of film on the trip. He had purchased the film from another retailer, but on his return Carr took the film to the defendant Hoosier Photo Supplies for processing. He received a receipt for each roll of film, and the following notice was printed on the reverse side of the receipt:

> Although film price does not include processing by Kodak, the return of any film or print to us for processing or any other purpose will constitute an agreement by you that if any such film or print is damaged or lost by us or any subsidiary company, even though by negligence or other fault, it will be replaced with an equivalent amount of Kodak film and processing and, except for such replacement, the handling of such film or prints by us for any purpose is without other warranty or liability.

Carr did not read the notice. The boxes of film also contained a similar limitation of liability as to Kodak. Either Hoosier or Kodak, to whom the film was shipped for processing, lost four rolls of film, including 150 exposures of the Carr family's European relatives.

Carr brought suit, and the trial court held that the limitations of liability were ineffective and gave judgment for Carr in the amount of $1,013.60. Kodak and Hoosier appealed.

**Givan, Chief Justice**     That either Kodak or Hoosier breached the bailment contract, by negligently losing the four rolls of film, was established in the stipulated agreement of facts. Therefore the next issue raised is whether either or both . . . may limit their liability as reflected on the film packages and receipts. . . .

When a party can show that the contract, which is sought to be enforced, was in fact an unconscionable one, due to a prodigious amount of bargaining power on behalf of the stronger party, which is used to the stronger party's advantage and unknown to the lesser party, causing a great hardship and risk on the lesser party, the contract provision, or the contract as a whole, if the provision is not separable, should not be enforceable on the grounds that the provision is contrary to public policy. The party seeking to enforce such a contract has the burden of showing that the provision was explained to the other party and came to his knowledge and there was in fact a real and voluntary meeting of the minds and not merely an objective meeting [of the minds].

[T]he stipulated facts foreclose a finding of disparate bargaining power between the parties or lack of knowledge or understanding of the liability clause by Carr. The facts show Carr is an experienced attorney who practices in the field of business law. . . . Moreover, it was stipulated he was aware of the limitation of liability. . . .

Contrary to Carr's assertions, he was not in a

"take it or leave it position" in that he had no choice but to accept the limitation of liability. . . . Carr and other photographers like him do have some choice in the matter of film processing. They can, for one, undertake to develop their film themselves. They can also go to independent film laboratories not a part of the Kodak Company. . . .

The Court of Appeals' opinion in this case is hereby vacated. The cause is remanded to the trial court with instructions to enter a judgment . . . in the amount of $13.60.

[Reversed.]

### Case Discussion Questions

1   What kind of bailment is this? What degree of care did the defendants owe the plaintiff? Why did the Kodak Company include the limitation of liability on its film?
2   What were the real losses of the plaintiffs? How would the damages be computed for such losses?
3   Was there any true bargaining in this case? Is it important that the plaintiff was a lawyer? Do you think the same judgment would have resulted if the plaintiff had not been a lawyer?

**Rights of Bailees**    Whether a bailee has the right to use the property left in his or her possession will depend on the agreement between the parties. If there is no agreement, the courts will consider whether it is reasonable for the bailee to use the property. The bailee has a right to be paid for any services performed in connection with the bailed property. If there is no agreement, the bailee may recover reasonable compensation and reimbursement for expenses.

**Common Carriers and Innkeepers**    A **common carrier** is a bailee that holds itself out to the public as a transporter of goods or people. A common carrier is generally available to the public, whereas a **private carrier** or **contract carrier** is available only to people chosen by the carrier. Common carriers are generally divided into **common carriers of goods** and **common carriers of passengers.**

A common carrier of goods is strictly liable for goods in its possession, except in five instances: (1) acts of God, (2) acts of public enemies, (3) the negligence of the bailor (e.g., improper packaging), (4) the inherent nature of the goods (e.g., perishable goods), and (5) acts of a public authority (e.g., quarantine by public health officials). If a loss takes place as a result of any other cause than those five causes, the carrier is strictly liable for loss during *carriage* (actual transportation) of the goods.

On the other hand, common carriers of passengers are not strictly liable for injury to passengers. Such carriers are held to a high degree of care, but if the carrier shows that it met that duty, it is not liable. The baggage of passengers is treated under the liability of a common carrier of goods.

The common law imposed the same liability on **innkeepers** as it imposed on common carriers of goods, but most states have modified that liability by statute. Under these statutes if an innkeeper provides a safe or other place of safekeeping for valuables, it is strictly liable only for a limited dollar value of goods. That limitation and the availability of the safe must be posted in each room under most statutes.

## REAL PROPERTY

Most property law grew up in the context of land. Land is a unique commodity, and the complexities of the law of *real property* reflect the reverence paid to it by the early common law.

Land is three dimensional. It is often said, somewhat inaccurately, that "property boundaries extend downward to the center of the earth and upwards to infinity." That doctrine is not quite correct, although it was a more accurate statement before the invention of the airplane. Today the proper rule appears to be that property boundaries extend upwards as far as reasonably necessary for the use and enjoyment of the surface of the land.

An owner also owns the property down so far as necessary to the use and enjoyment of the land. If an adjoining landowner drills a well that intrudes on the plane of a neighbor's property line, extended to the center of the earth, the adjoining landowner is guilty of a trespass. An exception exists for the withdrawal of fluid substances. If a landowner drills an oil well under his property without ever breaking the plane of a neighbor's property, the landowner is free to withdraw oil even though the oil deposit lies under both properties.

### Estates in Land

Many of the complexities of the common law of property involve the theory of **estates in land,** or interests in real estate. Estates in land are in turn classified as either **freehold estates,** referring to ownership interests, or **leasehold estates,** referring to nonownership leased interests. Leasehold estates are discussed later in the chapter in the section on "Landlord and Tenant Law" (p. 255).

The person transferring an estate in land is known as the **grantor,** and the person to whom an estate is transferred is the **grantee.** In almost all cases, estates in land are transferred either by a **deed,** or formal document of conveyance, or a **will** by a deceased person. Each form of freehold estate grants a different type of ownership interest. The nature of the freehold estate granted is determined by the language used in the deed or will that conveys the property (see Table 10.1).

### Concurrent Interests

The term **concurrent ownership** refers to ownership of the same piece of property by two or more persons at the same time. Both real estate and personal property may be owned concurrently. Concurrent ownership of personal property, such as joint bank accounts, automobiles, or corporate stock, is often regulated by state statutes.

Concurrent interests in property are important to estate planning. Husbands and wives often wish to avoid delays in court probate and some inheritance taxes by creating a **joint tenancy** in property. A joint tenancy results in the *automatic* transfer of the property to surviving joint tenants at the death of one of them. This **right of survivorship** is not present in other forms of concurrent ownership (see Table 10.2 on p. 253).

### Other Property Interests

**Easements, Licenses, and Profits**   An **easement** is a right to use land, such as the right of a utility company to enter onto land to make repairs, or the right of a neighbor to use a driveway. A special type of easement, known as **profits a prendre** or simply *profits,* permits the holder to enter on the land and remove some part of that land, such as coal, gravel, or timber. A **license** is a permission by a landowner to enter on land. Such a

TABLE 10.1     Estates in Land

| Estate | Deed or Will Language | Interest Granted |
|---|---|---|
| Fee Simple | "To A and his/her heirs forever" | Total ownership |
| Fee Simple Determinable | "To A, so long as alcoholic beverages are not served on the premises" | Total ownership unless and until the condition is broken, at which time it reverts automatically to prior owner or some designated person; that person has a *possibility of reverter*. |
| Fee Simple Subject to a Condition Precedent | "To A, but if the property is used for the sale of alcoholic beverages, B shall have the right to reenter and repossess the property" | Same as fee simple determinable, but reversion to B is not automatic; B has to exercise *right of reentry*. |
| Life Estate | "To A for life, then to B" | A has right to possess and use property for life. B owns a *remainder*. |
| Life Estate *pur autrie vie* | "To A for the life of C, then to B" | Same as life estate, except *measuring life* is some other person. |
| Dower* | None: Conferred by law | A ⅓ life estate to a widow in all real property owned by her husband during marriage. |
| Curtesy* | None: Conferred by law | Same as dower, but refers to a husband's interests in his wife's property. |

*Have been replaced in many states with a *forced share* of all property owned at death.

license is not considered to be an interest in land, and the license may be revoked at any time. For example, a ticket to a ballgame or permission of a farmer to hunt on land are both licenses.

**Homestead Rights**     Most states have statutes that protect family stability by providing that all or a portion of the family *homestead* is exempt from the claims of creditors. Such statutes often set a dollar value of property that cannot be taken by creditors to satisfy debts. Creditors can often reach the balance of the property above the homestead acreage or value. For example, if a statute provided a homestead exemption of $5,000, and A owned property worth $20,000, a creditor owed $25,000 could force the sale of the property. The creditor would receive $15,000, and the debtor would keep $5,000.

## Transfer of Real Estate

Real estate, like personal property, may be transferred by sale, by gift, or on death. Our discussion will center around three areas: (1) transfers by **adverse possession,** (2) transfers caused by *death*, and (3) **deeds.**

**Adverse Possession**     Property may be transferred without a deed and without the intent of the original owner of the property through *adverse possession*. Adverse possession requires that a person hold property for a period of time set by statute, usually from fifteen

TABLE 10.2    Concurrent Interests

| Interest | How Created | Nature of Interest |
| --- | --- | --- |
| Tenancy in Common | Two or more persons own property together; no formalities required. | Upon death of a tenant in common, property goes to deceased tenant's heirs, who become tenants in common with other tenants. Interests are undivided and transferrable. Interests may be proportionate (of different size). |
| Joint Tenancy | (1) "Magic words" in deed or will: "To A and B in joint tenancy, with the right of survivorship, and not as tenants in common"; (2) "Four unities" of time, title, interest, and possession. Means joint tenants must take property at the same time, in the same document (title), have equal shares (interest), and have equal rights to possession. | Upon death of a joint tenant, property *automatically* goes to surviving joint tenant(s) equally. Interests are undivided and are transferrable. Transfer of one joint tenant's interest creates a tenancy in common with new party. |
| Tenancy by the Entirety | Same as joint tenancy between married persons, in states where permitted. "Magic words" may differ. | Same as joint tenancy, but one spouse cannot transfer his/her interest without other spouse's permission. |
| Community Property | Marriage, residence in state where community property laws exist | All property acquired during marriage is divided equally (or in some states, divided "equitably"). At death, ½ of community property goes to surviving spouse. |

to twenty years. The possession of the property must be *actual, visible, open, notorious, exclusive,* and *hostile,* although the definitions of these terms vary somewhat from state to state. At the end of the period of possession the adverse claimant will own the land. In order to protect his or her right to sell the land the adverse claimant may file a **suit to quiet the title.** The period of possession is sometimes shortened (e.g., to seven years in many states) if the adverse claimant has paid the real estate taxes for the period of possession. Several adverse claimants may "tack" their possessions together to form the entire period. For example, if A holds land for five years, B for ten years, and C for five years, C will take title if the statute of limitations is twenty years.

**Transfer by Death**    Real estate, like personal property, may be transferred at the death of the owner. If the owner had a valid *will,* the real estate will be transferred to the persons designated in the will. If no will exists, the property will be transferred under the state statute of *descent and distribution.* Dower, curtesy, and/or state *forced share* statutes may limit the ability of an owner to disinherit spouses and children.

A valid will must be in writing, with few exceptions. Most states provide strict requirements for the form of a will, including a requirement that the will be witnessed by two or more people, that it be signed, and that it contain certain formal words.

An estate will usually go through **probate** unless the estate is so small that it is exempt under some states' laws. A will may appoint an **executor** to handle the details of probate, or, if there is no will, the court will appoint an **administrator.** Probate includes (1) **marshalling of assets,** that is, collecting the assets of the decedent and reducing them to cash, if necessary; (2) **payment of the decedent's debts;** and (3) **distribution** of the remaining assets to the heirs of the decedent. If the estate is insufficient to pay the debts of the decedent, the estate will be divided proportionately between creditors who have filed claims against the estate. Heirs are not responsible for the decedent's debts beyond their share of the estate.

**Deeds**   The written documents that transfer real estate are known as *deeds*. The precise requirements of a deed are set by state statute and differ somewhat from state to state. At a minimum, such statutes require that the deed contain: (1) identification of the grantor and grantee; (2) words of conveyance; (3) a description of the land; (4) the grantor's signature; and (5) in some jurisdictions, the signature of two witnesses. Deeds also often contain (6) a statement of consideration; (7) covenants (promises) of title; and (8) a statement of existing mortgages, easements, and restrictions. The deed must also be delivered to the grantee.

*Types of Deeds*   Deeds are generally classified by the type of **covenants** (promises) that are made by the grantor. A **warranty deed** is the "best" type of deed that a grantee can obtain, because it contains the most promises by the grantor about the title being conveyed.

In a warranty deed the grantor automatically gives (1) the **covenant of seizin,** that the grantor has good title to the property and the power to convey it; (2) the **covenant against encumbrances,** that the land is not subject to any mortgages, liens, easements, leases, or other encumbrances except as specifically noted in the deed; (3) the **covenant of quiet enjoyment,** that no one with a better title will evict the grantee; and (4) the **covenant of further assurances,** that the grantor promises to do anything necessary to make the title good. A grantor may limit any covenant by listing exceptions in the deed.

A **quitclaim deed** merely conveys whatever interest the grantor may have in the property and makes no warranties about the title to the property. If the grantor has no interest, the deed conveys no interest; if the grantor has full ownership, that interest will be conveyed by the quitclaim deed.

A **special warranty deed** is a kind of compromise between a general warranty deed and a quitclaim deed. Such a deed contains all of the covenants that were found in the general warranty deed, except that the grantor warrants only that *the grantor* did not create a title defect. Defects created by prior owners are not covered.

*The Recording Process and Title Security*   Once a deed is executed and delivered, the deed must be *recorded* with the appropriate public office, normally the county recorder of deeds. The purpose of recording is to put others on notice that the transaction has taken place, and recording provides constructive notice of the transfer. An unrecorded deed is effective between the parties, but it is not effective as to others with no knowledge of the transaction.

The recording process provides a mechanism by which people who are thinking about acquiring land can assure themselves that there are no title defects. Since all real estate documents are public records, a **title search** can be run to verify that there are no outstanding claims on the title. Often people who are about to acquire land will obtain (or require that the grantors obtain) **title insurance** guaranteeing the property against such title defects, based on a title search conducted by an insurance company.

### Public Control of Real Estate

Property can be controlled in a variety of ways by federal, state, and local government units. There are laws against specific uses of property, such as laws against using property in a way that would create a public nuisance. There are also a variety of environmental protection laws that prohibit certain uses of property that create environmental hazards (see Chapter 19). All government units have the right of **eminent domain** as well. Many units of government impose **zoning ordinances,** and all states impose **real estate taxes.**

**Eminent Domain**    *Eminent domain* is the ability of government to take private property for public purposes. For example, a state government may take land in order to build a new highway. The state may condemn private property for any *public purpose*, although the government need not put the property to *public use*. For example, a city may condemn a private building as part of a downtown redevelopment program and then transfer the property to another private landowner for some new private use.

The principal limit on the right of eminent domain is found in the fifth amendment to the Constitution, which provides: " . . . nor shall private property be taken for public use, without just compensation." The government must pay for the property taken and must follow due process procedures in taking the property. The term *private property* means any legal right in property, including the right to transact business on the property.

**Zoning**    All states permit municipalities to enact *zoning ordinances* which restrict the use of property in certain areas. Such ordinances ordinarily establish classifications for certain areas and provide for injunctions or even criminal penalties for violation. A typical ordinance will divide uses of land into residential, commercial, and industrial uses, with subdivisions within each class.

**Real Estate Taxes**    State and local governments often impose taxes on the ownership of real property. Those taxes are usually expressed as a percentage of the assessed value of the property, and local authorities generally assess all of the real property in their jurisdictions on a regular basis. A large proportion of the income of local governments comes from property taxes, including funding for local schools, police and fire protection, and other government services.

## LANDLORD AND TENANT LAW

A lease is neither fish nor fowl. On one hand, a lease is a *contract* between landlord and tenant. On the other, a lease is a *conveyance* of an interest in real property. As a result, the law of landlord and tenant is a blend of real estate and contract law concepts.

Landlord and tenant law has common law roots, but many statutory changes have been made. In the 1970s the **Uniform Residential Landlord and Tenant Act** was created by the National Conference of Commissioners on Uniform State Laws. Thirteen states have adopted the act in whole or in part. In addition, most states have enacted statutes dealing with specific problems, particularly the law of eviction.

A **lessor** is the owner or landlord of the property, and a **lessee** is the tenant. A lease is usually a contract and falls within the Statute of Frauds. No special provision exists to cover leases, although the original intent of Parliament was that leases fall within the provision covering agreements "not to be performed" within one year (see p. 209). Generally, if a lease can be performed within a year, an oral lease is permissible. Leases of a longer term must be evidenced by some note or memorandum in writing.

## Leasehold Estates

Earlier we discussed freehold estates, or ownership interests. Now we turn to **leasehold estates,** or nonownership interests in land. Those estates are sometimes called **tenancies.** The four basic types of tenancies are (1) **tenancies for a fixed term,** (2) **periodic tenancies,** (3) **tenancies at will,** and (4) **tenancy at sufferance.** Each provides different rights for both lessors and lessees, particularly in relation to termination of the tenancy.

A lease for any definite term—a day, a week, a month, a year, or a century—is a *tenancy for a fixed term.* A tenancy for a fixed term terminates automatically at the end of the term specified in the lease, and in the absence of an agreement to the contrary the landlord need not give any notice of termination to the tenant.

A lease that gives the tenant possession for successive identical periods of time is known as a *periodic tenancy.* The period is usually for month to month, although it is possible to have periodic tenancies from day to day, week to week, year to year, or any other length of time. Periodic tenancies may be created by agreement of the parties, or under some state statutes, may result from a **holdover,** that is, the failure of the tenant to turn over possession after the expiration of a tenancy for a fixed term. Periodic tenancies continue until notice is properly given to terminate the tenancy.

At common law, the landlord must give six months' notice to terminate a tenancy from year to year. If the period is less than one year, the landlord must give one full period's notice before termination. For example, if A leased an apartment to B on a month-to-month basis, and either party wishes to terminate the lease on April 1, notice of termination must be given on or before March 1. Modern state statutes vary these rules somewhat.

Any lease that can be terminated at any time by either party is known as a *tenancy at will.* If a lease does not specify any duration, a tenancy at will results. At common law no notice was necessary to terminate a tenancy at will, but modern statutes often provide for some notice of termination.

Unlawful holding of property is known as *tenancy at sufferance.* Such a tenancy usually results from holding over at the expiration of a tenancy for a fixed term, although the landlord has the option to treat such a holdover tenant as either a trespasser or as a new tenant, possibly creating a periodic tenancy under many state statutes.

## Rights and Liabilities of Landlord and Tenant

As in all contract law, the rights and liabilities of parties to a lease are established by the agreement between the parties. There are a few statutes that specify certain rights and liabilities even if a lease exists. In the absence of a lease or if a lease is silent, the common law has developed certain doctrines to fix the rights and liabilities of the parties.

**The Covenants of Possession and Quiet Enjoyment**    The law implies a promise by the lessor in all leases that the lessee will have possession of the property. The lessor agrees, even if such a term is not written into the lease, that the lessee will be able to take possession of the property, and that there are no legal barriers to the tenant's possession. The lessor also impliedly agrees under this covenant that the tenant will not be evicted during the lease term, if the tenant is not in default on the lease.

**The Landlord's Duty to Repair: The Implied Warranty of Habitability**    At common law, the doctrine of *caveat emptor* ("let the buyer beware") applied to leases, and the landlord had no duty to repair the leased premises in the absence of a lease provision to the contrary. Even the common law recognized exceptions to *caveat emptor* and imposed a duty of making repairs on the landlord in cases of short-term leases of furnished dwellings, leases of buildings under construction, and cases where the landlord was guilty of fraud.

Beginning about 1970,[1] the courts began applying a new implied warranty to residential leases. That warranty, the **implied warranty of habitability**, provides in a deceptively simple manner that the landlord warrants that the property will be *habitable*, that is, livable, and that the landlord will keep the premises in repair.

Because the law is in a state of flux on the application of the warranty, it is difficult to make many statements about the rule. Several states have adopted statutes that impose the warranty, and many others have adopted the warranty through judicial decision. Exceptions are sometimes provided for leases of single-family homes, agricultural leases including residential structures, or long-term leases. Some decisions only apply to apartments or to dwellings covered by a municipal housing code.

The issue of what is *habitable* is also not consistent between states. Some states require strict compliance with local housing codes, and *any* violation (e.g., a cracked window or leaky faucet) is a violation. Others merely use the housing code as a guide and impose other standards (e.g., "fit for human habitation") through statute or judicial decision.

Probably the most controversial aspect of the implied warranty of habitability deals with the remedies available to tenants once the warranty is breached. A breach of the warranty results in a **constructive eviction,** which gives rise to a right of tenants to withhold rent and sue for damages, but tenants may also be required to move out of the premises. That remedy is often ineffective because tenants, rather than wanting to move from the premises, only want to force the landlord to make needed repairs.

Cases usually arise when the tenant refuses to pay rent after the landlord has failed to make some needed repair. The landlord then sues for back rent and for possession, and the tenant then raises the warranty of habitability as a defense. Almost all jurisdictions permit the use of the defense. Most states then reduce the rent (or eliminate it entirely) for the period during which the defects exist, and the tenant is permitted to

---

1 *Javins v. First National Realty Corporation*, 138 U.S. App.D.C. 369, 428 F.2d 1071 (1970).

remain in possession. Some states require the tenants to pay the rent to the court until repairs are made. The court then pays the landlord a portion of that fund based on the reduced value of the property once repairs are finished and returns the balance to the tenants.

**Landlord's Duty to Repair: Business Property**    The landlord's duty to repair in *business* leases is often treated differently than in residential leases. Tenants in business leases do not have the differences in bargaining power that are commonly associated with residential leases. The duty to repair in business rentals is usually imposed by the lease itself, but the common law provides a variety of remedies to the tenant, including the right to abandon the property and the right to remain in possession and obtain damages.

---

## American National Bank and Trust Co. of Chicago v. K-Mart Corporation

717 F.2d 394
U.S. Court of Appeals for the Seventh Circuit, 1983

K-Mart leased several buildings for its retail stores from the American National Bank, as trustee under several land trusts. The bank initially brought this suit based on a lease provision that called for additional rents if a supermarket was erected on the properties. K-Mart counterclaimed for breach of the landlord's obligation to repair and maintain the stores. The case was removed to federal court on the basis of diversity jurisdiction.

The lease contained a general covenant by the landlord to "repair and maintain" the premises. The evidence showed that K-Mart had expended $205,000 for "minor maintenance," including painting of the stores, parking lot maintenance, and lawn maintenance. K-Mart also claimed damages to one of the stores caused by the landlord's failure to repair the roof and parking lots, and asked damages of $725,000, representing 10% of the gross rents for the period of the lease. K-Mart tried to introduce the testimony of a real estate appraiser to testify to the state of disrepair and how the disrepair of the stores affected the leasehold value. The trial judge excluded that testimony. The jury found for K-Mart in the amount of $205,000. Both parties appealed.

**Nichols, Circuit Judge**    [The court found that the lease did not provide for additional rents for subleases unless new structures were built for the subleased supermarkets and dismissed the appeal by the Bank.—Ed.]

Under Illinois law, a tenant has various remedies available on breach of landlord's covenant to repair. The tenant may (1) abandon the premises if they become untenantable by reason of the breach, (2) remain in possession and recoup damages in an action for rent, (3) make the repairs and deduct the cost from the rent or sue landlord for the cost, or (4) sue

landlord for breach of the covenant and recover the damages usually measured by the difference between the rental value of the premises in repair and out of repair. . . .

This [latter] theory of damages is known as diminution of rental value and reflects the sum a tenant is entitled to recover to restore him to the position he would have been in had he received the benefit of his bargain, that is, the benefit of the premises in repair. Contrary to landlord's contention, this is not a "novel theory . . . " but is a proper, if not universal, measure of compensatory damages for breach of duty to repair, though of course the 10% figure may be excessive and would not bind the jury. . . .

Diminution of rental value is, by definition, the difference in value of the property in and out of repair. Obviously, this theory of damages requires proof of the reasonable rental value of the premises had the landlord fulfilled its obligation under the lease to keep the premises in repair, and proof of the reasonable rental value of the premises "as is," that is, the reasonable rental value of the premises in disrepair. The question of value is, of course, the proper subject for expert testimony.

We find that the district court erred in excluding this expert testimony. . . . We therefore vacate the jury award . . . and order a new trial on the issue of damages.

## Case Discussion Questions

1   How does this lease differ from the ordinary residential lease? Was there real bargaining between the parties in this case? Should residential and business leases be treated the same?

2   Describe the factors that might be considered in determining "diminution of rental value." What kind of evidence would be helpful in proving that loss?

3   What other remedies might the lessee have chosen? Why did it choose this one?

**Tenant's Duty Not to Commit Waste**    Tenants have a duty not to commit **waste** of the property. That is, the tenant is under a duty both to care for the property and not to injure the property in any way that would injure the landlord's interests. In fact, the common law imposed a duty on the tenant to make *tenantable repairs*, that is, repairs necessary to secure the property and assure that it would not be damaged. For example, if a window was loose or broken and rain could wash in and damage the structure, the tenant was under a duty to repair the window.

**Tort Liability of Landlord and Tenant**    The common law rule, arising from the doctrine of *caveat emptor*, is that the landlord is not liable for injury or property damage resulting from a dangerous condition on the leased premises. In such cases, the tenant was liable to third parties for injuries caused by defects in the premises caused after the beginning of the lease. Since *caveat emptor* has been severely restricted, it stands to reason that the rule of landlord immunity has also changed.

Today the landlord is often under a duty to repair, and if someone is injured as a result of the failure to repair, the landlord may be liable in negligence. Modern case law imposes liability on landlords for defective conditions in the premises in six situations: (1) dangerous conditions known to the lessor but not disclosed to the lessee, (2) dangerous conditions known (or which should be known) to the lessor that exist when possession of the property is transferred, (3) dangerous conditions on premises leased for admission to the public, (4) dangerous conditions on parts of land in the lessor's control (e.g., hallways or other common areas), (5) dangerous conditions in premises that the lessor has agreed to repair, and (6) dangerous conditions caused by the lessor's negligence in making repairs.

### Termination of the Landlord-Tenant Relationship

Most leases are terminated by fulfillment of all of the terms of the agreement. A lease may be automatically extended simply by **holding over,** or failing to move. Leases may also be terminated as a result of the *default* of either party. Defaults may result in remedies, such as *distress for rent, eviction,* and *damages.*

**Holdover Tenants**    If a tenant holds over after the termination of an estate for a fixed period, the common law provides that the landlord may either (1) treat the holdover tenant as a trespasser or (2) treat the tenant as a tenant for a further term.

In the first instance, the landlord may have the tenant evicted from the premises and sue for damages; in the second instance, the tenant is considered to have renewed the lease on identical conditions and for an identical rent. For example, a tenant for a year who holds over will be held to another term of a year. The common law provided that a holdover creates a tenancy from period to period, for a term identical to the original term. A holdover of a tenancy for a month creates a month-to-month tenancy; a holdover of a tenancy for a year creates a year-to-year tenancy; and so on.

Most states have adopted statutes that modify the common law somewhat. In many states the duration of the periodic tenancy will be identical to the rent installments called for by the original lease. For example, if a lease is for a year but rent is paid on a monthly basis, a holdover tenant will be treated as a month-to-month tenant (see Figure 10.2).

**Tenants' Defaults**    Certainly the most common form of tenant **default** is a failure to pay rent. But a lease usually imposes a variety of other obligations on the tenant, such as promises to keep the premises in good condition, not to keep pets, to permit entry by the landlord for inspection, and not to use the premises for unlawful purposes. Any violation of a lease provision is a default and may result in eviction or any other remedy provided by the lease, including payment of damages.

In the absence of a lease provision, the common law also imposes duties on tenants. Those duties include the duty not to commit waste, make structural changes in the leased premises, or remove fixtures, even if the fixtures were added by the tenant. **Trade fixtures** (fixtures used in a trade or business) may be removed by the lessor before the end of the lease term, as long as no damage to the property occurs.

**Remedies for Default**    If a default occurs, the landlord has a variety of remedies available. First, if a provision of the lease describes the remedies, the landlord and tenant will be bound by those terms. Second, all states have adopted statutes that establish the rights of eviction and damages for tenant defaults. Such statutes may override lease provisions for remedies.

**Self-help** means the landlord's use of practical, nonlegal means to obtain possession of the premises. For example, physically moving the tenant from the premises or padlocking the premises to keep the tenant out are effective, though dangerous, means of

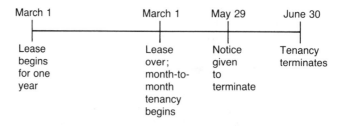

FIGURE 10.2    Holdover Resulting in Month-to-Month Tenancy

self-help. Many states expressly forbid self-help, and its use is generally frowned upon by the courts. At the least, such procedures are dangerous and may result in tort or even criminal actions against the landlord.

**Distress for rent** involves the landlord's right to seize and keep or sell personal property belonging to the tenant in payment of past-due rent. The common law permitted a landlord to seize and sell personal property, even in the absence of a lease provision. Distress for rent has been abolished by statute in many states, although landlords may retain a **lien** (secured claim) on the tenant's personal property that may be foreclosed through judicial proceedings.

*Actual and Constructive Eviction*  **Actual eviction** occurs when the landlord deprives the tenant of the use of the property. In such cases the tenant's duty to pay rent is suspended. For example, if the landlord forcibly takes the property away from the tenant, the tenant's duty to pay rent is terminated, or at least suspended if the property is only temporarily taken away.

A **constructive eviction** means the value of the leased premises to the tenant has been destroyed and requires a breach of some duty on the part of the landlord. For example, a landlord often has the duty to maintain the premises under city codes, by provisions of the lease itself, or under the implied warranty of habitability. If the landlord breaches that duty, the tenant may be considered to be constructively evicted. If a constructive eviction has taken place, the tenant's duty to pay rent has ceased, but the tenant often must vacate the premises.

Even though eviction procedures vary widely from state to state, a few generalizations are possible. State laws often provide accelerated or **summary procedures** to permit landlords to obtain possession after a default, including shortened time limits if the default involves a failure to pay rent. Statutes require the landlord to give the tenant some written **notice to quit,** or notice to leave the premises, following a default but before filing suit. That notice to quit may require the tenant to leave within a very short time, such as five days.

State statutes also usually provide for some **expedited trial date.** Following delivery of the notice to quit and the expiration of the time limit provided, the landlord may file an action, often known as **forcible entry and detainer,** sometimes before a special court established to hear such matters. A trial may be held within a very short time, often five days after a summons has been delivered to the tenant. No answer is required, but the defendant must be permitted to raise defenses at that trial. If the landlord is given possession of the property, a **writ of execution** is issued, and the tenant is ordered to leave the premises. If the tenant fails to leave, the sheriff may forcibly remove the tenant.

A variety of state and local statutes enacted for the benefit of tenants, such as housing codes, depend on "whistle blowing" by tenants for enforcement. Landlords may, under those circumstances, be tempted to find any excuse to evict the complaining tenant. Tenants faced with such a situation may use the defense of **retaliatory eviction.** Some states also prohibit landlords from raising rents or withholding services in retaliation for tenant whistle blowing.

*Damages*  The measure of damages for a tenant's default is the amount of money necessary to place the landlord in the position it would have been in had the injury not occurred. If the default involves waste or damage to the property, actual loss may be determined by the value of the premises before and after the default. If the default involves a failure to pay rent, the measure of damages is the rent owed. If the tenant holds over, many states provide a **double rent penalty,** requiring the tenant to pay twice the amount of rent due unless the landlord elects to treat the holdover as the beginning of a new tenancy.

*Abandonment and Surrender: The Landlord's Duty to Mitigate*    If a tenant moves out of leased premises before the end of the lease term, it is said that the tenant has *abandoned and surrendered* the premises. The tenant has signed a contract promising to pay rent for a period, however, and the tenant has a responsibility to pay rent to the end of the lease term.

On the other hand, the landlord is under a duty imposed by the common law of contracts to **mitigate damages.** For that reason, the landlord must seek to reduce its damages by releasing the property if possible. This means that the landlord must reasonably accept new tenants and apply their rent to the rent due from the abandoning tenant. The landlord need not rent those premises ahead of other vacant property, however.

In some states the original lease is treated as terminated and the tenant is liable only for the rent while the premises remain vacant. In others the original lease remains in effect, and the original tenant must pay any difference between the amounts received by the landlord and the amount due under the lease.

## INTELLECTUAL PROPERTY: PATENTS, COPYRIGHTS, AND TRADEMARKS

Article I, section 8, clause 8 of the Constitution provides that "The Congress shall have Power . . . To Promote the Progress of Science and useful Arts, by securing for limited Times to Authors and Inventors the exclusive Right to their respective Writings and Discoveries." The United States has maintained a patent and copyright system since 1790, and although the system has undergone many changes, the federal government has granted limited monopolies to inventors and authors ever since. The grant to an inventor is known as a **patent;** and the grant to an author, composer, lyricist, illustrator, or photographer is a **copyright.** A related type of exclusive right to use a brand name or advertising symbol is a **trademark.**

It may seem contradictory that the federal government at once prosecutes monopolization under the Sherman Act[2] and grants monopolies in the form of patents, copyrights, and trademarks. But in another sense, granting patent rights *protects* competition. Establishing a new product, process, or writing takes a great deal of work and often a large financial investment. Granting a limited monopoly encourages work and investment, which means that new products, processes, and writings will enter the marketplace.

Second, no inventor or writer would publicize his or her invention or writing until it was absolutely necessary without the protection of the patent or copyright system, thus

---

2 See Chapter 20.

slowing "the Progress of Science and the useful Arts." The patent system permits the early disclosure and use of such inventions and their availability to the public and removes the need for secrecy that would otherwise cloak inventions throughout their lives.

## The Patent System

The federal Patent Act grants "for the term of seventeen years . . . the right to exclude others from making, using, or selling the invention throughout the United States." Once a patent is properly applied for and granted, it becomes a form of intangible personal property and may be bought, sold, traded, given away, leased, or licensed for the use of others. Licensees of patents usually pay a **royalty,** or license fee, to the owner of the patent.

Under the Patent Act, "Whoever invents or discovers any new and useful process, machine, manufacture, or composition of matter, or any new and useful improvement thereof, may obtain a patent therefor." The courts have found four requirements for patentability: inventiveness, novelty, utility, and subject matter.

The standard of *inventiveness* means that the invention must not be an obvious discovery "to a person having ordinary skill" in the art or science involved. Merely making a well-known item out of a new material is not inventive, nor is putting together two well-known inventions. *Novelty* means that the invention was previously unknown, and *utility* means that it is useful.

The *subject matter* requirement means that only certain kinds of inventions are patentable. Mathematical formulas, fundamental laws of nature, and managerial techniques, while all highly useful, are not patentable. In *Diamond v. Chakrabarty*,[3] the Supreme Court held that a human-made bacterium developed to break down crude oil was patentable and overruled a Patent Office determination that living things are not patentable. The court held that the bacterium was a *manufactured* item, not a phenomenon or law of nature.

## The Copyright Process

A **copyright** grants an exclusive right to the holder to print, publish, copy, and sell books, periodicals, plays, music, artworks, photographs, motion pictures, and other materials. As specified in 1978, that protection lasts for the life of the creator plus fifty years, and materials may be copyrighted for a maximum period of fifteen years from the date of publication or 100 years from the date of creation.

In order to secure a copyright, the author or publisher must print a copyright notice on the material (see the back side of the title page in this book, for example), produce at least three copies of the piece, and register the publication with the Copyright Office. Registration is not necessary to establish the copyright, because a copyright exists from the moment of creation, but it is necessary to obtain a right to sue.

If registration has been accomplished properly, the act authorizes suits against persons who use the copyrighted materials without permission. Such actions are called *infringement actions*, and a person who uses such materials may be liable for damages

---

3 447 U.S. 303, 100 S. Ct. 2214, 65 L. Ed. 2d 159 (1980).

caused by unauthorized use. The courts may issue an injunction against such use in the future.

A major exception is the **fair use** doctrine, which permits the use of copyrighted material without permission for purposes of criticism, comment, news reporting, teaching, scholarship, or research. The following decision considers a major infringement issue, copying television programs using videotape recorders.

# *Sony Corp. v. Universal City Studios* (The Betamax Case)
464 U.S. 417, 104 S. Ct. 774, 78 L. Ed. 2d 574 (1984)

Sony Corporation manufactures home videotape recorders (VTRs) and markets them through retail establishments. Universal owns the copyrights on some of the television programs that are broadcast on the public airwaves. Universal brought an action in federal district court, claiming the VTR consumers had been recording some of respondent's copyrighted works and thereby had infringed its copyrights, and that Sony was liable for such copyright infringement because of their marketing of VTRs. The district court denied all relief to the petitioners, but the court of appeals reversed and held the manufacturer and some retailers of VTRs guilty of "contributory infringement." Sony appealed to the Supreme Court.

**Mr. Justice Stevens Delivered the Opinion of the Court** . . . Copyright protection "subsists . . . in original works of authorship fixed in any tangible medium of expression." . . . This protection has never accorded the copyright owner complete control over all possible uses of his work. Rather, the Copyright Act grants the copyright holder "exclusive" rights to use and to authorize the use of his work . . . including reproduction of the copyrighted work in copies. . . . All reproductions of the work, however, are not within the exclusive domain of the copyright owner; some are in the public domain. Any individual may reproduce a copyrighted work for a "fair use" . . .

The Copyright Act provides the owner of a copyright with a potent arsenal of remedies against an infringer of his work, including an injunction to restrain the infringer from violating his rights, the impoundment and destruction of all reproductions of his work made in violation of his rights, a recovery of his actual damages and any additional profits realized by the infringer or a recovery of statutory damages, and attorneys' fees.

The two respondents in this case do not seek relief against the Betamax users who have allegedly infringed their copyrights. Moreover, this is not a class action on behalf of all copyright owners who license their works for television broadcast, and respondents have no right to invoke whatever rights other copyright holders may have to bring infringement actions based on Betamax copying of their works. . . . It is . . . the taping of respondents' own copyrighted programs that provides them with standing to charge Sony with contributory infringement. To prevail, they have the burden of proving that users of the Betamax have infringed their copyrights and that Sony should be held responsible for that infringement.

The Copyright Act does not expressly render anyone liable for infringement committed by another. . . . The absence of such express language in the copyright statute does not preclude the imposition of liability for copyright infringements on certain parties who have not themselves engaged in the infringing activity. For vicarious liability is imposed in virtually all areas of the law. . . .

If vicarious liability is to be imposed on petitioners in this case, it must rest on the fact that they have sold equipment with constructive knowledge of the fact that their customers may use that equipment to make unauthorized copies of copyrighted material. . . .

The question is thus whether the Betamax is capable of commercially significant noninfringing uses. . . . [O]ne potential use of the Betamax plainly satisfies this standard, however it is understood: private, noncommercial time-shifting in the home. It does so both (A) because respondents have no right to prevent other copyright holders from authorizing it for their programs, and (B) because . . . even the unauthorized home time-shifting of respondents' programs is legitimate fair use. . . .

On the question of potential future harm from time-shifting, the District Court offered a more detailed analysis of the evidence. It rejected respondents' "fear that persons 'watching' the original telecast of a program will not be measured in the live audience and the ratings and revenues will decrease," by observing that current measurement technology allows the Betamax audience to be reflected. . . . It rejected respondents' prediction "that live television or movie audiences will decrease as more people watch Betamax tapes as an alternative," with the observation that "[t]here is no factual basis for [the underlying assumption.]" . . . It rejected respondents' "fear that time-shifting will reduce audiences for telecast reruns," and concluded instead that "given current market practices, this should aid plaintiffs rather than harm them." . . . And it declared that respondents' suggestion "that theater or film rental exhibition of a program will suffer because of time-shift recording of that program" . . . "lacks merit." . . .

It may well be that Congress will take a fresh look at this new technology, just as it so often has examined other innovations in the past. But it is not our job to apply laws that have not yet been written. Applying the copyright statute as it now reads, to the facts as they have been developed in this case, the judgment of the Court of Appeals must be reversed.

[Justice Blackmun, Justice Marshall, Justice Powell, and Justice Rehnquist dissented.]

## Case Discussion Questions

1   Who is really infringing the plaintiff's copyrights in this case? Why is the plaintiff concerned? Why didn't the plaintiff sue individual VTR users?
2   What is a "commercially significant noninfringing use?" Did the Court find one in this case?
3   What is the purpose of the copyright laws? Is this decision within the spirit of those laws? Should the copyright laws be amended to take VTRs into account?

## Trademark Protection

A **trademark** or **tradename** is any distinctive mark, symbol, word, phrase, or picture used to identify a particular corporation or product. The federal *Lanham Act* of 1947 permits individuals to register trademarks with the Patent Office. Such registration creates no rights but establishes federal recognition to use the trademark. Tradenames must be registered in each state. Scandalous, obscene, disparaging, or deceptive trademarks may not be registered.

After registration, the user may stop others from using the trademark. In such cases, the user may sue infringers for damages or for an injunction against future uses. Section 43(a) of the Lanham Act prohibits the use of "any false description or representation" in connection with any goods or services placed in commerce and permits persons likely to be damaged by the false description or representation to bring suit in federal court. Most federal courts permit competitors to sue for false representations concerning their products.

Trademarks may be licensed in much the same manner as patents, and such licensing often forms the basis of **franchise agreements.** In such agreements, the **franchiser** permits the **franchisee** to use the trademark of a nationally known firm on condition that the franchisee pays a **royalty** (payment for use) and perhaps that the franchisee purchase goods and services from the franchiser. A trademark may be lost by abandonment, that is, by failing to use it on products.

## COMPUTER LAW

Like the invention of the automobile, the airplane, and even the typewriter, the development of computers has posed new challenges for the law. "Computer law" is not a specific branch of the law but is merely an adaptation of existing law. The adaptations will continue as technology grows, resulting in even more changes in the legal environment.

Some of the most important computer-related problems include contracting for the purchase and lease of computer products, protection of software, computer crime, and privacy.

### Purchase and Lease of Computer Products

As discussed in Chapter 8, contracts for the sale of *goods* are controlled by the Uniform Commercial Code, whereas many other kinds of transactions, including contracts for *services*, are covered by the common law of contracts. Computer *hardware* (the physical components of a computer system) is *goods* within the meaning of the Uniform Commercial Code. On the other hand, transactions for computer services, including specially designed *software* systems (programs, assistance, service, and sometimes instruction manuals), are often controlled by the common law of contracts.

Courts generally prefer to apply the UCC for three reasons. First, the UCC is a more modern system and is integrated with other commercial transactions under the UCC. Second, the UCC basically abolishes the doctrine of *caveat emptor* ("let the buyer beware") and imposes a variety of **product warranties** (see p. 328), whereas the common law retains the doctrine of *caveat emptor* and requires that parties negotiate their own protection of product quality. Third, the UCC includes the doctrine of *unconscionability* (see p. 215), which may be important in sales to consumers.

The physical aspects of software (disks, tapes, manuals, etc.) are "goods" as well, but the importance of software lies not in those physical attributes but in the electronic impulses and information within the software. The question of whether software is "goods" becomes even more difficult when a program is custom made, or when a firm contracts to purchase a specially made "turnkey" system, with custom-designed hardware and software.

The courts are divided on whether the consumer purchased "goods" or "services" in such cases. If the court finds the consumer was purchasing goods, the UCC will apply; if the consumer was purchasing services, the common law of contracts will apply. The courts seem to prefer to apply the UCC if possible, except in the case of consultant services or a custom-designed program that involves little tangible property.

A related problem deals with creative sales-lease arrangements involving computers. The UCC applies to "transactions in goods," but some of the provisions of the UCC apply to "sales of goods." Many computer products are the subject of leases and licensing agreements. A true rental agreement is not a sale, and the lessee does not receive the protections of the UCC. But leasing arrangements may be found to be "sales" if the lease includes an option to purchase or otherwise indicates that the purchaser will receive title to the property.

### Warranties, Products Liability, and Computers

A malfunction in a computer may cause millions of dollars in damages. For example, a malfunction in a computer that controls robotic equipment in an automobile-manufacturing plant could cause damage to the robotic equipment and to dozens of new automobiles. Similarly, a malfunction in a computer that controls accounts receivable for a major credit card company could result in huge losses.

Generally speaking, the law of product **warranties** controls those situations. These warranties are explored more fully in Chapter 13. Many computer manufacturers and systems sellers give **express warranties** with their products, making certain promises about the condition of the product and its uses. Those express warranties are treated as part of the contract and may impose liability on the seller or manufacturer in the event of a breach. The injured purchaser may recover damages, including a reduction in the purchase price for defective goods. The injured purchaser may also recover additional amounts for injuries beyond the product itself, although an express warranty may limit liability.

The UCC imposes certain **implied warranties** on the sale of goods. The **implied warranty of merchantability** is given only by a seller who is a merchant with respect to the goods sold. The warranty has several requirements, including that the goods pass without objection in the trade, are of fair average quality, or are fit for the *ordinary purposes* for which such goods are intended. If the products are not "merchantable," the purchaser may sue for damages caused by defective equipment, including both the decrease in value of the product and any damage that it may do.

The **implied warranty of fitness for a particular purpose** is created when the purchaser communicates specific intended uses different from the ordinary purposes for the product. It is also necessary for the buyer to rely on the seller's expertise in selecting the product. For example, sending a supplier precise business requirements for a computer system, along with instructions to fill those requirements, will often result in the creation of the warranty. The buyer may recover the decreased value of the product and any other damage that the defective product may have caused.

## Liability for Defective Programs

If a computer program is defective, the computer programmer, or the company that employs a programmer, may be liable under both contract and tort theories.

Express warranties are not restricted to the UCC, and if a programmer makes representations about the program to the user, the programmer may be liable in contract. For example, if the programmer says, "This program will fulfill all of your needs," that statement may become a warranty that the program will perform as required. Express warranties may result from advertising, statements in brochures or manuals, or from oral statements by sales personnel. Programmers may restrict their liability by language in the contract by which they agree to design the program. Injured purchasers may sue for any loss directly traceable to the defective program. Third parties who are injured also have a right to sue.

The UCC may apply if a court decides that computer programs, embodied in disks or part of a larger "turnkey" system, are "goods," within the code. Many decisions have held that packaged programs intended for consumer sale are goods within the meaning of the UCC. In such circumstances, the implied warranties of merchantability and fitness for a particular purpose will apply to the program itself. Purchasers of defective programs may then sue for the reduced value of the program, together with any special damages. Injured third parties may also sue.

Injured parties may also have the right to sue in *tort* for damages resulting from deficient or defective programs. Clearly, the programmer is liable for any fraud or misrepresentation. For example, a false statement that others had successfully used the product made to induce purchase of the product could result in both compensatory and punitive damages. Programmers may also be guilty in *negligence* for a lack of due care in writing the program. It is not yet clear what standard of care is imposed on computer programmers, but the courts are tending toward treating programmers by a special standard of care for programmers alone, much like other professionals. Injured parties must prove that any damage was the result of a program error, rather than a data error or hardware defect, and must show what the programmer should have done to avoid the error.

Finally, *strict liability* may be imposed on programmers in certain situations. If a product is made in a defective manner and causes physical injury, the manufacturer may be held liable without proof of fault (see p. 242). If a computer program is part of a larger product that injures someone, strict liability may be used to create liability. The law in this area is still developing, but some cases have held programmers strictly liable. For example, one case involved an action against the designer of a computerized sawmill that caused the death of a worker because the mill continued to operate in the "off" position as a result of a programming error.[4]

## Protection of Software

Computer software may be duplicated quickly and easily, wiping out the potential profits to the firm that expended time and money to develop it. Software producers often seek shelter under the federal patent, copyright, and trademark laws, and under state trade secret laws.

**Patent Law**    It is difficult for computer programs to satisfy the requirements of federal patent law. Patents are available only for nonobvious, novel, and useful inventions. Mental processes and mathematical formulas are not patentable, and because many computer programs merely mimic mental processes and involve mathematical formulas, they are often not patentable.

On the other hand, computerized processes that do more than perform mathematical computations may be patentable. It appears that programs designed to produce some physical result or that transform a computer into some other machine are patentable. Computerized typesetting machines and language translators have been patented, for example.

**Copyright Protection**    Computer programs may be protected by federal copyright law. All published and visible copies of the work must contain a notice of copyright. That notice may be displayed in several ways, including any copies that are machine readable, such as on a terminal, on printouts, or on labels on containers holding copies of the program. Registration is necessary to obtain a right to sue. The Semiconductor Chip Protection Act of 1984 also gives copyright protection to the circuits built into silicon chips used in computers and other electronic equipment.

---

4 *Holdsclaw v. Warren and Brewster,* 45 Or. App. 153, 607 P.2d 1208 (1980).

In 1980 the Copyright Act was amended to include computer programs, but the same amendment permits persons who buy copyrighted software to make copies and adaptations for their own use and even to transfer copies under certain circumstances. The 1980 amendment made it clear that copyright law only protects against unauthorized *copying*, not against unauthorized *use* of the underlying ideas. And because the copyright law only protects the *expression* of an idea, and not the idea itself, others may take the same idea and express it differently—as in similar programs. The result is that copyright law provides only limited protection for computer programs, and "reverse engineering" remains a major problem.

## Apple Computer, Inc. v. Formula International, Inc.

725 F.2d 521
U.S. Court of Appeals, Ninth Circuit (1984)

Apple Computer, Inc., brought this action for an injunction against Formula International, Inc. Formula is a wholesaler and retailer of electronic parts and kits. In 1982, Formula began selling a computer kit under the trademark "Pineapple." The computer was designed to be compatible with software written for the Apple II computer. Two computer programs were embodied in the semiconductor devices called ROMs (Read Only Memory). Formula conceded that those programs were substantially similar to two programs for which Apple had registered copyrights.

Apple brought suit, claiming copyright, trademark, and patent infringement, as well as unfair competition. Formula counterclaimed for antitrust violations. The district court granted Apple's request for an injunction, and Formula appealed.

**Ferguson, Circuit Judge**    Formula asserts that the district court erred in granting the preliminary injunction by relying on the legal premise that the Copyright Act . . . extends protection to all computer programs regardless of the function which those programs perform. Formula contends that the computer programs involved in this lawsuit, because they control the internal operation of the computer, are only "ideas" or "processes," and therefore, unlike application programs, they are not protected by copyright. ("In no case does copyright protection for an original work of authorship extend to any *idea, procedure, process, system, method of operation, concept, principle,* or *discovery,* regardless of the form in which it is described, explained, illustrated, or embodied in such work.") Formula also points to the idea/expression dichotomy recognized in case law, and contends that a computer program is protected under the Copyright Act only if the program embodies expression *which is communicated to the user when the program is run on a computer.*

Formula's position, however, is contrary to the language of the Copyright Act, the legislative history of the Act, and the existing case law. . . .

In 1974, the National Commission on New Technological Uses of Copyright Works (CONTU) was established by Congress to consider to what extent computer programs should be protected by copyright law. The CONTU Final Report recommended that the copyright law be amended "to make it explicit that computer programs, to the extent that they embody an author's original creation, are proper subject matter of copyright." . . .

In 1980, Congress accepted the CONTU . . . [and] recommended statutory changes. . . . Among other changes . . . the Copyright Act was amended to add the following definition of "computer program":

A "computer program" is a set of statements or instructions to be used *directly* or *indirectly* in a computer in order to bring about a certain result.

. . . Formula's reliance on the idea/expression dichotomy to argue that computer programs are copyrightable only if they provide expression to the computer user is misplaced. The distinction between ideas and expression is intended to prohibit the monopolization of an idea when there are a limited number of ways to express that idea. . . . This rule is the logical extension of the fundamental principle that copyright cannot protect ideas. In the computer context this means that when specific instructions, even though they are previously copyrighted, are the only and essential means of accomplishing a given task, their later use by another will not amount to infringement. . . . When other language is available, programmers are free to read copyrighted programs and use the ideas embodied in them in preparing their own works. . . .

Apple does not seek to copyright the method which instructs the computer to perform its operating functions but only the instructions themselves. Apple introduced evidence that numerous methods exist for writing the programs involved here. . . . Thus, Apple seeks to copyright only its particular set of instructions, not the underlying computer process. . . . Affirmed.

## Case Discussion Questions

1  What *exactly* did Apple copyright? What interest is it trying to protect in this case?
2  What is the "idea/expression" problem? How does it apply to this case?
3  After this decision, can a computer manufacturer sell a computer that will run Apple programs? Explain.

**Trademark Law**   Many forms of innovative software have adopted well-known trademarks or tradenames (for example, Appleworks, WordStar, WordPerfect, Visi-Calc, dBase III, and Lotus 1-2-3). Those trademarks promote brand loyalty and provide substantial protection to the owners, because they accompany the programs themselves. Trademarks do not protect the underlying program from copying, but they protect the trademark and tie consumers to particular brands of software.

**Trade Secrets**   The common law provides protection for computer programs through the law of **trade secrets.** A trade secret is any formula, device, procedure or compilation used in business that the owner maintains as a secret. There is no registration process, and any owner injured by the theft of a trade secret may bring a common law action for damages or for an injunction. The owner must maintain secrecy, which results in a variety of security procedures and confidentiality agreements in the computer business. For example, employees of computer firms often must sign agreements promising not to disclose trade secrets, even after they leave the firm.

**Licensing Rights in Software**   All of the methods of copyright protection—patent, copyright, trademark, and trade secret—give the owner exclusive property rights. The owner must sell those rights in some way to obtain a financial return. This is most often accomplished through a **licensing agreement,** which limits the rights of the licensee in duplicating or using the program in return for the right to use the program for certain purposes. The precise type of license will vary somewhat, depending on whether the owner has patent, copyright, trademark, or trade-secret protection.

Often these licenses include a limit on the number of copies of the program that can be made (one back-up copy is common) and may require that the program be used only on a specific machine. Extended rights are sometimes available to large corporations or other groups. For example, the owner of a word processing program may agree that a university may make 100 copies of its program for use by faculty or students.

A second important form of license agreement is made between an independent computer programmer and a software marketing firm, permitting the firm to sell the programmer's product. Such licenses usually contain conditions that all rights remain in the programmer and that *royalties* will be paid to the programmer on sale of the program.

A difficult practical question involves computer programs that are mass marketed, because it is often not feasible to require every retail purchaser to sign a formal document agreeing to the limitations of the license. A possible solution involves **shrink-wrap licenses.** A shrink-wrap license is an agreement on the plastic coating of a software package that provides that a purchaser who breaks the plastic wrap to gain access to the software automatically agrees to the license limitations. Those limits usually include a promise that the purchaser will not copy the program (except for back-ups).

## Crimes Involving Computers

Many existing criminal statutes do not apply to crimes involving computers. For example, traditional theft statutes must be stretched, often beyond their meaning, to apply to the theft of computer time or of information by "hackers." As a result of these difficulties, many new state and federal criminal statutes have been adopted, and many others are under consideration.

The **Electronic Funds Transfer Act** governs all electronic transfers of funds, such as direct deposits of payroll and benefits checks, and automated teller machines. The act makes it a crime to use, sell, furnish, or transport in interstate commerce any counterfeit, fictitious, altered, forged, lost or stolen credit card, or similar device used in electronic funds transfers. Violation is punishable by up to ten years' imprisonment and/or a fine of up to $10,000.

The **Counterfeit Access Device and Computer Fraud and Abuse Act of 1984** makes it a crime to "knowingly access" a computer to obtain restricted government information or to obtain financial records from any financial institution or consumer reporting agency. The act also prohibits using, modifying, destroying, or preventing the use of a computer operated for the U.S. government.

Many states have adopted criminal statutes dealing with computer use as well. Many of these statutes forbid computer fraud, theft of computer time, accessing of a computer to obtain restricted or private information, or alteration or destruction of information held in a computer's memory in order to defraud any person.

## The Problem of Privacy and the Computer

Computers can collect and hold a great deal of information about individuals, far more than was feasible before their development. Almost at the same time that the computer was developed, the Supreme Court began recognizing a constitutional right of privacy (see p. 138). The Court has held that data collection does not invade individual privacy rights if there is a legitimate state interest in collecting the data and if there are adequate safeguards for protecting confidential information.[5] Private tort actions are also

---

5 *Whalen v. Roe*, 429 U.S. 589, 97 S. Ct. 869, 51 L. Ed. 2d 64 (1977).

possible for breach of privacy, based either on the constitutional right of privacy or on common law theories.

A variety of federal laws also protect individuals from some kinds of intrusive data collection. The federal **Fair Credit Reporting Act of 1970** provides detailed regulation of consumer credit reporting agencies (see p. 373). The **Right to Financial Privacy Act of 1978** forbids financial institutions from giving the government access to customers' financial records without the customers' consent, unless a valid subpoena, search warrant, or court order is obtained. And the **Counterfeit Access Device and Computer Fraud and Abuse Act of 1984** makes it a crime to access a computer to obtain information in a file of a consumer reporting agency or record of a financial institution without authorization.

## SUMMARY AND CONCLUSIONS

Property ownership is best described as a *bundle of rights* that the law will protect, including the rights of possession, use, disposition and title. The law of property includes both *personal* and *real* property. Personal property, that is, anything that is not land or affixed to the land, is often divided into tangible and intangible property. The law of *bailments* deals with the problem of property that is temporarily left in the possession of another.

Real property is the source of much of Anglo-American common law, with its estates in land, including both freehold, or ownership, estates and leasehold estates. Real estate may be transferred by deed or upon death. Leases of real property are both conveyances of an interest in real estate and a contract.

Federal patent and copyright law governs the protection of intellectual property. Inventors and authors may obtain a limited monopoly for their works. Neither law is adequate to protect computer programs fully, however. The development of computers has resulted in some important challenges to the common law of property. Much of the law relating to computers is statutory, because the common law of property does not mesh well with the new technology.

## REVIEW QUESTIONS

1  What is the difference between real property and personal property? Tangible and intangible personal property? How can an intangible, such as a copyright, be considered "property"?

2  Explain, with examples, how the various estates in land and joint tenancy would be helpful in estate planning.

3  Is a lease a conveyance of land or a contract? Explain. What is the implied warranty of habitability? How is that warranty protected? What remedies are available to a landlord for a tenant's default?

4  How may intellectual property be protected? What is the difference between a patent, a copyright, and a trademark?

5  Orlick parked his car in Hubble's Parking Garage. Someone broke into the car and stole a tape deck and several pieces of luggage stored in the trunk. What rights does Orlick have if (1) he took his keys with him and chose what space to park in? (2) he left the keys with Hubble, who chose where to park the car? (3) in both cases, a large sign behind the desk said "Not responsible for items left in cars"?

6   Mr. and Mrs. Brownlow purchased a home and had it titled in joint tenancy. Following an argument, Mr. Brownlow adjourned to the St. Giles Pub and, after several hours, sold his interest in the home to Monks, the bartender. (1) Is such a transfer possible? (2) What are the interests, if any, of Mr. and Mrs. Brownlow and Monks? (3) How could such a situation be avoided?

7   Wren leased an apartment for herself and her six children at the Field Lane Apartments. After moving in, Wren found that only one room had heat, the plumbing worked on alternate Tuesdays, and the cockroaches were larger than some of the rats. She refused to pay rent until the apartment was made livable, but also refused to move because she had nowhere else to go. Field Lane sued for possession, and Wren raised the defects as a defense. What result would you expect?

8   Assume that you have designed a new word processing program that far exceeds anything on the market. You know that it will be an instant success and probably make you very wealthy, if you can market it. What can you do to protect the program from (1) being directly copied and sold by other programmers and (2) having copies sold at retail but copied time after time, depriving you of numerous sales?

9   Farmingdale Furniture purchased a new computer system from the Lemon Computer Company to do its accounts receivable. The system was custom designed and installed by Lemon's experts, including specially written software. After installation, the computer automatically sent out bills to 10,000 customers, but over half of the bills were wrong. Many of the bills erroneously said "Paid in Full," and over 1,000 excellent customers were turned over to collection agencies. Several customers sued Farmingdale, charging slander of credit. Does Farmingdale have a remedy against Lemon? Do the customers?

10   In 1987 the IBM company introduced a new operating system for its computers. IBM obtained patents, copyrights, and trademark protection as far as the law allows. May other computer manufacturers adopt the same operating system or one like it? Why or why not?

# CHAPTER 11

# The Law of Agency

A store clerk selling a tube of toothpaste, a corporate officer purchasing a billion-dollar piece of real estate, a lawyer trying a case, and an accountant filling out a client's tax return are all *agents.* **Agency** relationships include a wide variety of employment and representative relationships and form the basis of many other areas of law, including the fields of labor relations and business associations.

The definition of *agency* is one of the broadest in the law. According to the *Restatement of Agency*, section 1, an agency is a relationship between two persons in which one "shall act on [the other's] behalf and subject to his control." The person who acts on another's behalf is known as an **agent.** The person on whose behalf an agent acts is known as a **principal.**

An agency is a **consensual** relationship. That is, the agency relationship exists *by consent* of the parties. On the other hand, no contract or other formal agreement is necessary in most agencies. Such contracts may exist, of course, but are generally not necessary to the formation of an agency.

Once an agency is formed, the principal has given the agent some *authority to act* on his or her behalf. As a result, the agent may have the authority to bind the principal to contracts with third persons, to make the principal liable for torts, or to do other matters. This power to bind the principal is in turn controlled through the concept of **fiduciary duties,** which imposes substantial duties on the agent.

## TYPES OF AGENCIES

The term *agency* includes two major types of legal relationships: (1) the **master-servant** relationship and (2) the **principal–independent contractor** relationship. In addition, agents are often classified as *general agents*, *special agents*, or *subagents.*

**Master-Servant Relationships**　　The most common form of agency relationship is a *master-servant relationship* (Figure 11.1), which includes most types of employment relationships. In the master-servant relationship, the **master** is a principal who controls or has the right to control the physical conduct of the **servant** in the performance of the agency. The term *servant* is not limited to people who perform menial tasks, but may include highly skilled workers and even executives and professionals if the master has the right to control their performance. Servants may or may not have the authority to bind their masters to contracts, depending on the nature and extent of the authority granted by the principal. Servants *will* bind masters to torts under the doctrine of *respondeat superior* (see p. 279) under many circumstances.

**Principal–Independent Contractor Relationships**　　The second major form that an agency may take is the *principal–independent contractor relationship* (Figure 11.2). In such a relationship the principal has no right of control over the physical actions of the

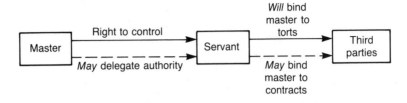

FIGURE 11.1    Master-Servant Relationship

independent contractor (agent) in the physical performance of his or her actions. Such persons contract for their performance and are often independent businesspeople. For example, if the XYZ Company hires A to be a receptionist, he will be a servant. On the other hand, if XYZ hires A, an independent sales agent, to sell its product along with several other product lines handled by A, A will be an independent contractor. Principals will be bound under many circumstances for the contracts made by agents on their behalf, but principals are generally not liable for the torts of independent contractors.

**Employer–Independent Contractor Relationships**    A final relationship is not an agency relationship at all. The **employer–independent contractor** relationship is a contractual relationship that involves no control, physical or otherwise, over the actions of the independent contractor, and which involves no authority to bind the principal to contracts (see Figure 11.3).

The chief difference between a principal–independent contractor relationship and an employer–independent contractor relationship lies in the ability of the independent contractor to bind the principal to contracts. In a principal–independent contractor relationship, the independent contractor has the authority to bind the principal to contracts with third persons. That authority does not exist in an employer–independent contractor relationship.

For example, if A hires B, a roofer, to install a new roof on her house, B will usually have no authority to bind A to contracts, and A will usually not have the power to control the physical performance of B's work. As a result, B is not considered to be A's agent, but an employer–independent contractor relationship will have been established.

**General and Special Agents**    A **general agent** is one authorized to conduct a series of transactions involving some continuity of service. A **special agent,** on the other hand, is an agent authorized to conduct a single transaction. Thus, if A hires B to sell any and all real estate that A owns or may own in the future, B is a general agent. But if A hires B to sell a specific parcel of land, B is a special agent.

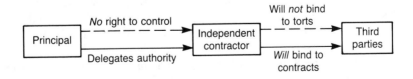

FIGURE 11.2    Principal–Independent Contractor Relationship

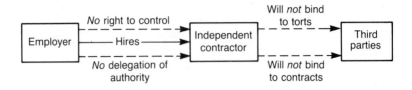

FIGURE 11.3    Employer–Independent Contractor Relationship

**Subagents**    A **subagent** is an agent appointed by an agent. A subagent is subject to the control of both the principal and the agent. Usually a subagent cannot be appointed without the express or implied authorization of the principal. For example, A may appoint B as her agent to sell her home. B, in turn, may appoint C to do the actual work. A will have the authority to control both B and C.

## CREATION OF AGENCIES

Agencies can be created in five basic ways: (1) by **agreement;** (2) by **ratification;** (3) by **estoppel;** (4) by **apparent authority;** and (5) by **operation of law.**

**Agency by Agreement: Express and Implied Agencies**    Most agencies are created by *agreement*, in the sense that both parties consent to the creation of the agency and to the grant of authority to act. That authorization may be given *expressly*, in words, or *impliedly*, by conduct of the parties. Ordinarily, an agency is created when the principal displays an intention that another shall act for him or her and the agent consents. No contract is necessary, and no consideration is necessary for the service by the agent.

Although agencies may be created both orally and in writing, the so-called **equal dignity rule** requires that an action creating an agency must be executed with the same formality as the law requires for the act itself. For example, if A is to sell real estate for B, B must authorize A to do so with a writing that satisfies the Statute of Frauds (see p. 207). A **power of attorney** is a written agency authorization, often established and required by statute, which authorizes a person to act as an **attorney-in-fact** for specific transactions. It is usually not necessary for an attorney-in-fact to be a lawyer.

**Implied authority** follows from the express authority granted by the principal. Implied authority includes (1) the authority to use all reasonable means to accomplish express authority, (2) the authority to perform according to general customs or usages in the trade, and (3) the authority to take necessary actions in an emergency.

For example, assume that A appoints B as his agent to travel to another city to sell A's products, and B travels to that city in A's automobile. Under those facts, B would have the authority to make arrangements for a tow truck after the car broke down, arrange for a rental car, if that was the custom in the trade, and take potential customers to lunch, if it was necessary to accomplish the authority granted.

**Agency by Ratification**    An *agency by ratification* takes place when an individual performs an act on behalf of another without the authority to do so, and the "principal" later agrees to be bound by the act. For example, if A sells a parcel of B's land to C without authority from B, B may later ratify the transaction and accept the contract. A principal may ratify a transaction either expressly, by words, or impliedly, such as by accepting the benefits of the transaction.

The ratification *relates back* to the date of the transaction. For example, if a transaction occurs on July 15 but is not ratified until August 1, the agency will be treated as having existed since July 15 once ratification takes place. The principal must have knowledge of all of the material facts at the time of the ratification, and the principal must ratify the entire transaction, and not just parts of it.

**Agency by Estoppel**    Even though no actual agency may exist, a principal may be bound to the actions of a purported "agent" by the doctrine of *agency by estoppel*. That doctrine says that out of fairness the principal cannot deny the existence of an agency if three elements are present: (1) the principal has, through intentional or negligent action, created the appearance that the agent has authority to act; (2) the third party has, in good faith, reasonably relied upon the appearance of authority; and (3) the third party changes its position to its detriment in reliance upon the appearance of authority.

For example, assume that A owns a valuable oil painting. B, an art dealer and confidence trickster, approaches C and offers to sell the painting, without authority from A. C calls A to inquire about the sale, and through negligence, or perhaps thinking the whole thing is a joke, A tells C that B has authority to sell. If C reasonably relies on A's representation, the law would say that A is "estopped to deny" that B had authority to sell the painting.

**Agency by Apparent Authority**    Closely related to the agency by estoppel is the doctrine of *agency by apparent authority*. That doctrine holds that if the "principal" places a person in a position where it reasonably appears to third persons that the "agent" has the authority to act, the principal will be bound by the agent's actions. The third party's belief that the purported agent is authorized to act must be *reasonable*, and the third party has the duty to investigate if there is a question in his or her mind.

For example, assume that P, a store owner, asks A to watch the store for a few minutes while P runs an errand. While P is gone, T, a sales representative for a supplier, stops by and sells A a large order of supplies. If T reasonably believed that A was authorized to make such an order, P will be bound since she placed A in a position where it reasonably appeared to T that A had authority to act.

Apparent authority differs from agency by estoppel in that in an agency by estoppel the third party relies upon the "principal's" representations that the "agent" has authority, whereas in apparent authority the third party relies on other facts. In both cases the law imposes an agency relationship to remedy an otherwise unjust situation.

**Agency by Operation of Law**    There are some situations in which the law imposes an agency where none exists. Such agencies automatically arise by *operation of law*, rather than through some act of the parties. For example, many states impose **nonresident motorist statutes,** which provide that any motorist using the highways of the state automatically authorizes the Secretary of State of that state to act as his or her agent in accepting service of process (see p. 69).

**Legal Capacity of Principals and Agents**   Since an agency is a consensual relationship, any person with legal capacity to give consent may be a principal. A corporation can only act through human beings and has the authority both to appoint agents and to act as a principal or as an agent. Infants may be both principals and agents, but a minor's appointment of an agent is considered *voidable* at the option of the minor. A mentally incompetent person generally cannot appoint agents. Both infants and mental incompetents may act as agents, but they may not be liable under the *fiduciary duties*. Although some degree of capacity is required, the capacity necessary to act as an agent is not as great as that needed to form a contract.

## TERMINATION OF AGENCIES

Agencies cannot last forever. Agencies may be terminated by (1) *lapse of time*, (2) *agreement*, (3) *accomplishment of purpose*, and (4) *operation of law*.

**Termination by Lapse of Time**   Generally speaking, an agency exists either for a stated term, such as a day, a week, or a year, or if no stated term exists, for a reasonable time. A reasonable time is generally considered to be the time reasonably necessary to carry out the agency. In employment contracts where no term is expressed, the duration depends on the intent of the parties. The burden of proving that an agreement was to last for a definite time is on the party asserting that time. If no definite term exists, the agreement is considered to be "at will," and either party may terminate the agreement at any time. Even a contract for "permanent employment" may be considered to be a contract terminable at the will of either party (see p. 291).

**Termination by Agreement**   Since an agency is created through the consent of both parties, the relationship can be severed by consent of the parties or by the action of either party. The agent may *renounce* the agency, or the principal may *revoke* the agent's authority.

A party may have the *power* to terminate an agency, but not the *right* to do so. If A has hired B to work for a year, B may renounce the agency at any time, and the law will not force B to continue to work. Similarly, A may revoke the agency at any time, and the law will not force A to continue to employ B. On the other hand, although either party has the power to terminate the agency, that termination may constitute a breach of contract, and the innocent party has the right to sue for damages.

*Agencies Coupled with an Interest*   Historically, the only agencies that could not be terminated were **agencies coupled with an interest.** That means that if, along with the creation of the agency, the agent also receives some kind of interest in the subject matter, the agency cannot be revoked by the principal. For example, if A borrows money from B and gives B the right to sell certain property if the loan is not paid, A has created an agency. If an agency only were involved, A could revoke the agency at any time. But B also has gained an interest in the property, because it secures the repayment of the debt. Under those circumstances, the courts would not permit A to revoke the agency and destroy B's security for the loan.

**Termination by Accomplishment of Purpose**    If the purpose of the agency is fulfilled, the agency is terminated. If P empowers A to sell P's house and the house is sold, the agency is over. Although this may seem obvious, it is important in terminating the implied powers of the agent. In the example, A may have implied powers to contract for certain services, such as termite inspections or title insurance, and the accomplishment of the purpose also terminates A's implied powers.

**Termination by Operation of Law**    Aside from an act of the parties or accomplishment of purpose, there are a variety of situations in which the law considers the agency to be terminated. Those situations are said to terminate the agency by operation of law, and include (1) death or (2) incompetence of a party, (3) bankruptcy of the principal, (4) destruction of the subject matter, (5) dissolution of a partnership or corporate principal, and (6) subsequent illegality of the agency.

**Necessity of Notice to Third Parties**    An act of the parties may terminate an agency, but it is sometimes necessary to notify third parties of the termination of the agency. For example, if A terminates B's authority to purchase goods on A's behalf, B may still retain *apparent authority* to purchase. In order to terminate that apparent authority, A must give actual notice to third parties that B cannot deal on A's behalf any longer. Actual notice need not be given if an agency has been terminated by operation of law.

## RESPONDEAT SUPERIOR

The modern doctrine of *respondeat superior*, or "let the superior respond," says that a *master* will be liable for the torts of his or her *servants* committed *within the scope of the servant's employment*. This doctrine, sometimes called **vicarious liability,** imposes responsibility upon the master regardless of the master's fault or lack of fault. Part of that rule is that if a principal *authorizes* an agent to commit an act, and a tort results, the principal should be liable to the person injured.

It is important to make a distinction between a principal's liability based on *respondeat superior* and liability based on *actual negligence*. If a principal is negligent in hiring an agent, in failing to supervise or train an agent, or in a number of other ways, the principal is liable in actual negligence. But the principal may also be liable *without* fault of any kind, based on the doctrine of *respondeat superior*.

For example, if a department store clerk tries to arrest an alleged shoplifter and commits a tort in the process, a court might find that the clerk was acting outside the scope of his or her employment, so that the store would not be liable under *respondeat superior*. But the same court might find the store guilty of actual negligence for failure to train or supervise the clerk.

Under *respondeat superior*, if a servant injures a third party, the third party has an action against *both* the master and the servant. The master and servant are *jointly and severally liable*. That is, the third person may sue either the master or the servant, or both. The third party is only entitled to one recovery, however.

If a servant commits a tort that subjects an employer to liability under respondeat superior, the employer generally has the right to **indemnification** from the servant. That means that the servant may have to pay the damages after all, but to the master rather than to the servant. Conversely, if an agent is required to commit a tort by an employer, the agent generally has the right to indemnity from the employer.

## Who Is a Servant?

Employers are only liable for the torts of their *servants*. As noted earlier, agents are often divided into the categories of servants and independent contractors. The distinction between servants and independent contractors is one of fact, and the courts will look to a variety of factors to determine whether a particular agent is a servant or an independent contractor.

Such factors include the extent of control the master may exercise over the details of the work; the kind of occupation, and whether the work is usually done under the direction of the employer or by a specialist without supervision; the skill required in the particular occupation; whether the employer or the workman supplies the tools and the place of work; the length of time for which the person is employed; the method of payment, whether by the time or by the job; whether or not the work is a part of the regular business of the employer; whether or not the parties believe they are creating the relation of master and servant; and whether the principal is or is not in business. In all cases, the determining factor is the master's right to **control** the servant's actions. The following case discusses the problem of control in the context of medical malpractice and the so-called "captain of the ship" doctrine.

---

## Rockwell v. Kaplan

404 Pa. 574, 173 A.2d 54 Pennsylvania Supreme Court, 1961

Rockwell had surgery to remove a small bursa from his right elbow. The surgery was performed by Dr. Kaplan, and Dr. Stone was the anesthesiologist. Stone was busy at the time and directed Dr. Jimenez, a resident physician, to administer the anesthetic. Jimenez did so in such a way as to cut off the blood supply to the left arm. Neither Jimenez nor Stone told Kaplan, and Kaplan did not learn of the mistake until it was too late to save the arm. The arm was amputated, and Rockwell sued Stone and Kaplan. The trial court rendered judgment against both, and Kaplan appealed. (The court sustained the judgment against Stone on the basis of both actual negligence and *respondeat superior* for Dr. Jimenez's actions in another opinion.) The following decision relates solely to the case against the surgeon.

**Bok, Justice**    As for Dr. Kaplan's responsibility for Dr. Stone's negligence, Dr. Stone testified that a surgeon could use the hospital's anesthesiologist or bring in his own. Dr. Kaplan testified that he was "the boss of the surgical end of it," and that "as long as Dr. Stone had anything to do with the anesthesia I was perfectly satisfied." He chose the hospital in which Dr. Stone worked and chose a general rather than a local anesthetic. Dr. Stone testified that Dr. Kaplan had the authority to ask or tell him what sort of anes-

thesia he wanted, although it was not the practice at the . . . [h]ospital to do so. Dr. Kaplan said that if it was best for his patient's safety he could discontinue the operation and tell the anesthesiologist to stop giving anesthetic, particularly in minor elective surgery. . . .

"A servant is the employee of the person who has the *right* of controlling the manner of his performance of the work, irrespective of whether he actually *exercises* that control or not." [citing cases] . . .

Dr. Kaplan and Dr. Stone did not disagree in their testimony . . . nor can there be doubt based on common sense that Dr. Stone acted on Dr. Kaplan's business: he had to or the surgeon could not operate. The undisputed evidence clearly shores up the instruction of the trial judge: "And in the eyes of the law, in this case, Dr. Stone was the agent for a step in the operative procedure, the anesthesia step. He was the agent of Dr. Kaplan."

It is clear . . . that doctors are subject to the law of agency and may at the same time be agent both of another physician and of a hospital, even though the employment is not joint.

[Judgment Affirmed.]

**Jones, J., Dissenting**    In the case at bar, Dr. Kaplan neither prescribed nor was he advised of the use of [this anesthetic]; he did not administer it, was not present when it was administered and, in fact, did not know of it until hours later. Moreover he exercised no direction, control, or authority over Drs. Stone and Jimenez. . . . Dr. Kaplan was simply using the

hospital facilities and its personnel, a service for which Rockwell would be billed directly.

The [anesthetic] was administered, outside of Dr. Kaplan's presence, in the induction room over which . . . he was not the "captain of the ship"; over the personnel in that room—all hospital regularly employed persons—at that time *only* Dr. Stone was in command. . . . Under such circumstances, in my opinion, Dr. Kaplan could not be held liable upon any theory of respondeat superior and the judgment as to Dr. Kaplan should be reversed. . . .

## Case Discussion Questions

1    Whom was Dr. Jimenez working for? Who is/are the principal(s)?
2    How could Dr. Kaplan have exerted control? Dr. Stone?
3    What is the "captain of the ship" doctrine? Is it good public policy? Would the doctrine reach surgical nurses? Floor nurses? Physical therapists? Hospital janitors?

### "Within the Scope of Employment"

The second major issue in cases of *respondeat superior* is whether the servant was acting "within the scope of his or her employment" when the tort was committed. There are generally three requirements for determining whether an action is within the scope of employment: (1) The act must be of the kind that the servant was employed to do; (2) it must have occurred within "authorized time and space limits"; and (3) it must have been motivated, "at least in part, by a purpose to serve the master."[1] Liability is also imposed on the master for certain intentional acts such as fraud, bribery, and false representations, if they were either authorized or "apparently authorized" by the master.

**"Frolic" and "Detour"**    If servants take a **detour** from their employers' business, they will still be considered within the scope of their employment, and the employer will continue to be liable. The word *detour* generally means that a servant has departed from the authorized route or means to do the work but continues to work on the employer's behalf. Thus, if A is to drive a truck over a certain route but finds the road closed, he will still be within the scope of his employment by taking another route.

On the other hand, if servants are on a **frolic** of their own, they will not be considered to be within the scope of their employment, and an employer will not be liable for an agent's torts. The term *frolic* generally means that the servant's activities had some

---

1 *Restatement of Agency*, Sec. 228.

purpose other than the master's business. In such cases, of course, the servant remains liable for his own torts.

---

## Fiocco v. Carver

234 N.Y. 219, 137 N.E. 309 New York Court of Appeals (1922)

The defendants sent a truckload of merchandise from Manhattan to Staten Island by truck. The driver was required to bring the truck back to the garage but instead went to visit his mother some distance away. A neighborhood carnival was in progress, and several boys, dressed in a variety of costumes, asked the driver for a ride. The driver made a tour of the area with the boys aboard. He stopped the truck in front of a pool room to speak with a friend, and the plaintiff, an eleven-year-old boy, climbed aboard the truck with the others. The driver came back to the truck and ordered the boys off three separate times. On the third warning, the plaintiff began climbing down, but the truck started without warning and his foot was drawn into a wheel. The driver testified that it was then his purpose to go back to the garage. The injured boy brought this action against the employer. A jury found that the driver was in the scope of his employment at the time and held the employer liable as a result.

**Cardozo, J.**   We think the judgment may not stand. . . . We turn . . . to the driver's testimony to see whether anything there . . . gives support for the conclusion that the truck was engaged at the moment of the accident in the business of the master. All that we can find there, when we view it most favorably to the plaintiff, is a suggestion that after a temporary excursion in streets remote from the homeward journey, the servant had at last made up his mind to put an end to his wanderings and return to the garage. He was still far away from the point at which he first strayed from the path of duty, but his thoughts were homeward bound. Is this enough, in view of all the circumstances, to terminate the temporary abandonment and put him back into the sphere of service? We have refused to limit ourselves by tests that are merely mechanical or formal. Location in time and space are circumstances that may guide the judgment, but will not be suffered to control it, divorced from other circumstances that may characterize the intent of the transaction. The dominant purpose must be proved to be the performance of the master's business. Till then there can be no resumption of a relation which has been broken and suspended.

We think the servant's purpose to return to the garage was insufficient to bring him back within the ambit of his duty. He was indisputably beyond the ambit while making the tour of the neighborhood. . . . Neither the tour nor the stop was incidental to his service. Duty was resumed, if at all, when ending the tour, he had embarked upon his homeward journey. It was in the very act of starting that the injury was done. The plaintiff had climbed upon the truck while it was at rest in front of the pool room, still engaged upon an errand unrelated to the business. The negligence complained of is the setting of the truck in motion without giving the intruder an opportunity to reach the ground. The self-same act that was the cause of the disaster is supposed to have ended the abandonment and reestablished a relation which till then had been suspended. Act and disaster would alike have been avoided if the relation had not been broken. Even then, however, the delinquent servant did not purge himself of wrong. The field of duty once forsaken is not to be reentered by acts evincing a divided loyalty and thus continuing the offense.

[Reversed.]

## Case Discussion Questions

1   When did the driver leave the scope of employment? When, if ever, would the driver have reentered the scope of employment?

2    What evidence was there of the driver's intention? What evidence could there be?

3    Does the "scope of employment" rule make

sense? Who will pay for the little boy's injuries? Would the driver have injured the boy if he had not been employed by the defendant?

---

Some of the most important decisions regarding the "scope of employment" have to do with deviations from the authorized route by truck drivers. The various state jurisdictions have different rules to apply to such situations. For example, assume that a driver is instructed to drive directly from point A to point B in Figure 11.4 but instead decides to visit his sick grandmother at point C.

All states would hold that the driver left the scope of employment at point 1. Some states would hold that the driver is again within the scope of his employment when he begins his journey back on the employer's business, at point 2. Others would hold that he does not reenter the scope of his employment until he reaches the authorized route, at point 3. And still others would say that the driver *never* reenters the scope of employment, because he would never be on the same place on the authorized route that he would have been had he not deviated from it.

**The Borrowed Servant Rule**    A common problem arises when an employer "loans" an employee to someone else for a time. For example, P1 may permanently employ A, but may "loan" A to P2 for a time. If A then commits a tort, the question arises whether P1 or P2 is responsible under the doctrine of *respondeat superior*. In such cases, the courts generally ask which of the employers had the right to control the activities of the servant at the time of the tort. Other courts have found joint and several liability between the two employers, especially if the question of control cannot be easily answered.

**Liability for Intentional Acts**    Generally speaking, an intentional act can result in liability for the master if the act was performed within the scope of the employment, just like other torts. Whether a given act was within the scope of employment will depend on a variety of factors, including the purpose of the act. For example, store security personnel who falsely arrest and imprison people have committed an intentional tort for which the master is liable. If the same security guard unjustifiably strikes someone outside of store business, the employer may argue that such a beating was beyond the scope of employment, because such an action was not for the master's purpose. The issue is

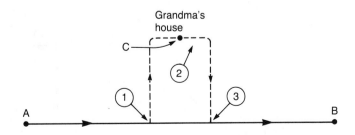

FIGURE 11.4    A "Frolic"

whether the commission of the wrongful act was the natural outgrowth of the nature of the work.

### Purposes of *Respondeat Superior*

The doctrine of *respondeat superior*, ancient as it is, continues to be questioned by lawyers and scholars alike. It is sometimes argued that *respondeat superior* is based on the employer's fault in selection or training of employees. But this theory does not explain why employers are not liable for the torts of their independent contractors, nor do they explain the existence of separate and distinct torts for negligent selection, training, and supervision of employees.

Upon close analysis, there seems to be little real reason for the rule aside from imposing liability upon the party who may be able to bear the financial burden. It is for this reason that the rule is sometimes called the **deep-pocket rule.** Many courts have concluded that the purpose of the rule is *risk shifting*, based on the idea that the innocent injured party should not bear the risk of injury, and the guilty servant may not have the financial resources to bear the loss. As a result, the law shifts the burden to the employer, perhaps with an eye to wider risk shifting in the form of higher prices for the employer's goods and services.

### CONTRACT LIABILITY

As a general rule, a principal is liable for contracts entered into by an authorized agent. Thus, if P authorizes A to make a contract on her behalf with T, and A makes such a contract, P will be liable to T on the contract (see Figure 11.5).

Whether the principal will be liable on the contract will depend on the authority he or she grants to the agent. Generally speaking, the principal will be liable for contracts that are authorized by *express authority, implied authority, apparent authority* or *agency by estoppel*. In addition, principals may be liable for contracts that are subsequently *ratified*, even though no express authority was granted. Students will quickly note that the authority to make contracts closely parallels the methods of creation of agencies (see p. 276).

The principal may place limits on the authority of an agent to make a contract. For example, P may give A authority to sell her property for $20,000. If A sells the

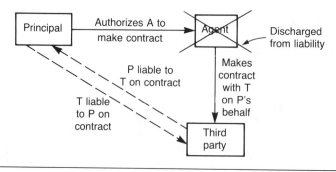

FIGURE 11.5    Contract Liability of Disclosed Principal

property for $19,000 to T, A has exceeded the authority granted. But since T may have no way of knowing of the limits on A's authority, the sale to T will stand because A had the apparent authority to act. A may be liable to P for the difference in price, however.

### Disclosed, Semidisclosed, and Undisclosed Principals

In dealing with third parties, agents sometimes fail to disclose the nature of their agency or the identity of their principals. This may be done for a variety of reasons such as bad personal relations between the principal and the third party or the possibility that the third party may demand a higher price if he knows that a particular principal was involved.

If the third party knows that the agent is dealing for someone else and also knows the identity of the principal, the principal is said to be **disclosed.** If the third party does not know that the agent is dealing for a principal at all, the principal is said to be **undisclosed.** And if the third party knows that the agent is dealing for someone else but does not know the identity of the principal, the principal is said to be **semidisclosed.**

If an agent makes a contract on behalf of a disclosed principal, the principal is liable to the third party, and the agent is discharged. The liability is said to "pass through" the agent to the principal. And this seems to make good sense, because the third party knows who the real party in interest in the case is and relies on the principal's reputation and credit, not the agent's.

On the other hand, if the agent makes a contract on behalf of either an undisclosed or a semidisclosed principal, *both* the principal and agent may be liable to the third party. The reason for imposing liability on the agent is simple: the third party cannot rely on the principal's credit and reputation because he or she does not know the identity of the principal. Therefore, the third party must rely on the agent's credit and reputation in making the contract (see Figure 11.6).

Once the third party learns the identity of the principal, the third party may *elect* between the principal and the agent and hold either (but not both) of them liable on the contract. In all three cases, the principal may bring an action to enforce the contract against the third party.

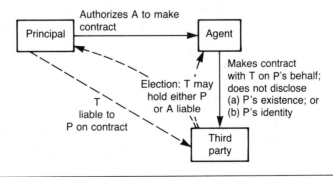

FIGURE 11.6   Contract Liability of Undisclosed and Semidisclosed Principals

### Disclosure of Agent's Capacity

An agent may be bound to a contract in one of two ways: (1) the agent was acting on behalf of an undisclosed or partially disclosed principal or (2) the agent actually intended to be bound, perhaps as a guaranty of performance by the principal. In order to avoid liability, the agent must disclose his or her capacity and cannot indicate that he or she intended to be bound to the contract in any way.

For example, assume that John Smith makes a contract with Mary Jones on behalf of the XYZ Company. If Smith simply signs the contract "John Smith," Smith will be bound to the contract, because the XYZ Company is neither named as a party to the contract nor is Smith's capacity as an agent disclosed. On the other hand, if Smith signs the contract "John Smith, as agent for XYZ Co.," the XYZ Company will be bound and Smith will not be liable, because the agency was clearly disclosed. If Smith signs "John Smith, Agent," a question of fact arises as to whether Mary Jones knew of Smith's agency for XYZ.

## DUTIES OF AGENT TO PRINCIPAL

The duties that an agent owes a principal arise from two principal sources: first, if a contract exists, that contract will establish certain duties on the part of the agent to the principal; and second, regardless of whether a contract exists, the agent will owe the principal certain **fiduciary duties** under the common law.

### Contractual Duties

If an agency contract exists, that contract will usually establish certain duties owed by the agent to the principal. Such contracts can take many forms, including (1) an employment contract between an employer and a principal; (2) a collective bargaining agreement between an employer and a labor union (see p. 413); or (3) a wide variety of agency contracts, such as a contract to act as a real estate or securities broker, an attorney, or an accountant.

Such contracts are enforceable contracts, and a breach of such contracts provides legally recognized remedies. Although the U.S. Constitution prohibits involuntary servitude in the thirteenth amendment and employers generally cannot force employees to work through the remedy of specific performance, the failure of agents to live up to their promises in such agreements may result in awards of damages. As noted earlier, an agent may have the right, but not the power, to terminate an employment contract.

### Fiduciary Duties

A **fiduciary relationship** is defined as a relationship of trust and confidence. Such fiduciary relationships may be found in any situation in which the courts find that one party should be able to rely on and have confidence in another. The two most common fiduciary relationships are agency situations and family relationships. Every agent is the fiduciary of the principal.

The opposite of a fiduciary relationship is an **arm's length relationship,** in which the parties can neither trust nor rely on each other in the absence of actual fraud. For example, the buyer in a contract to purchase an automobile has no right to rely on or have confidence in the seller, although the seller cannot use actual fraud.

If a person is found to be a fiduciary, he or she owes the other party to the relationship certain fiduciary duties. Those duties are generally known by the acronym COLAN, which stands for the five principal fiduciary duties: *care, obedience, loyalty,* to *account,* and *notice* (see Figure 11.7).

**The Duty of Due Care**   Every fiduciary owes his or her principal the duty to use *due care* in dealing with the property and affairs of the principal. This duty is identical to the duty that each person has to use due care and to refrain from negligent conduct. A fiduciary must use that degree of skill and care that would be expected of a reasonable and prudent person under like circumstances in dealing with the affairs and property of the principal.

**The Duty of Obedience**   It is the legal duty of the agent-fiduciary to *obey* the lawful instructions of his or her principal. The agent may be held liable to the principal if he or she fails to obey proper instructions and the principal is damaged as a result.

**The Duty of Loyalty**   Perhaps the most complex fiduciary duty is the obligation of *loyalty*. An agent cannot serve two principals involved in the same transaction without notifying both principals. For example, an attorney may not represent both sides in a lawsuit. Such problems of divided loyalty are known as *conflicts of interest*.

The vague duty of loyalty involves several more specific problems, including the duties (1) *not to compete with the principal,* (2) *not to make a secret profit,* (3) *not to appropriate business opportunities* belonging to the principal, and (4) *not to divulge secret information.*

*The Duty Not to Compete with the Principal*   As a general rule, an agent may not enter into competition with his or her principal. For example, if P is in the business of making computers and hires A as a salesperson (or any other capacity), A could not set up her own company to make or sell computers in competition with P, at least while A is still employed by P. At the termination of A's employment, and in the absence of a *covenant not to compete,* A could enter into competition with P.

---

**Care** of principal's property and business

**Obedience** of principal's directions

**Loyalty** to principal

**Account** for principal's property and money

**Notice** to principal of all material facts

---

FIGURE 11.7   The Fiduciary Duties

# Maryland Metals, Inc. v. Metzner

282 Md. 31, 382 A.2d 564 (1978) Maryland Supreme Court (1978)

Maryland Metals is engaged in the business of buying, processing, and selling scrap metal obtained from automotive, industrial, and miscellaneous sources. The business had been started by Harry Kerstein in the 1930's and was incorporated in 1955. In 1951 the business hired Sidney S. Metzner, a recent business administration graduate. With Metzner's help, the business grew rapidly, and Metzner was ultimately made executive vice-president. In 1970, upon Metzner's recommendation, the company hired George Sellers as operations manager and vice-president.

In November 1973, Metzner and Sellers asked for some equity in the business but were refused. In December of 1973 they told Kerstein of their intention to form their own company. In late May 1974, Metzner and Sellers resigned and formed their own company in direct competition with Maryland Metals.

It was clear from the evidence that Sellers and Metzner had made substantial arrangements to enter into such competition immediately after their request for an ownership interest was denied. They formed a corporation in December of 1973, purchased equipment in February of 1974, and borrowed money for the purchase of equipment in March. In May, Sellers was discharged, and Metzner quit in June, but even in the last few days of employment Metzner negotiated several beneficial contracts on behalf of Maryland Metals.

Maryland Metals brought this action for breach of fiduciary duties and requested an injunction against further operation of the new business, damages, and an accounting for profits. The trial court dismissed the action, and the plaintiff appealed.

**Levine, J.**    In this appeal we consider the extent to which officers and high-level managerial employees may, prior to termination of the employment relationship, make preparations to compete with their corporate employer without violating fiduciary obligations running to the corporation. . . .

Appellant's principal contention on appeal is that by deliberately failing to disclose in detail their preliminary arrangements to enter into competition with Maryland Metals, while serving as appellant's officers and employees, appellees committed a "gross breach of their fiduciary duty" of loyalty, thereby entitling appellant, as a matter of law, to an injunction restraining further operation of appellee's rival scrap metal processing business.

In defining the scope of the right of an employee or corporate officer to enter into competition with his former principal and in delimiting the countervailing right of an employer to restrain his agent's competitive endeavors both before and after termination of employment, the law seeks to harmonize two important and ofttimes conflicting policies. The first of these policy considerations is that commercial competition must be conducted according to basic rules of honesty and fair dealing. . . .

This concern for the integrity of the employment relationship has led courts to establish a rule that demands of a corporate officer or employee an undivided and unselfish loyalty to the corporation. . . . Thus we have read into every contract of employment an implied duty that an employee act solely for the benefit of his employer in all matters within the scope of employment, avoiding all conflicts between his duty to the employer and his own self-interest. . . .

A direct corollary of this general principle of loyalty is that a corporate officer or other high-echelon employee is barred from actively competing with his employer *during* the tenure of his employment, even in the absence of an express covenant so providing. . . . Thus, prior to his termination, an employee may not solicit for himself business which his position requires him to obtain for his employer. He must refrain from actively and directly competing with his employer for customers and employees, and must continue to exert his best efforts on behalf of his employer. . . .

Once the employment relationship comes to an end, of course, the employee is at liberty to solicit his former employer's business and employees, subject to certain restrictions concerning the misuse of his former employer's trade secrets and confidential information. . . .

The second policy recognized by the courts is that of safeguarding society's interest in fostering free and vigorous competition in the economic sphere. . . . Furthermore, courts have been receptive to the view that every person has or at least ought to have the right to ameliorate his socio-economic status by exercising a maximum degree of personal freedom in choosing employment. . . .

This policy in favor of free competition has prompted the recognition of a privilege in favor of employees which enables them to prepare or make arrangements to compete with their employers prior to leaving the employ of their prospective rivals without fear of incurring liability for breach of their fiduciary duty of loyalty. . . . Moreover, while an employee is under an obligation to be candid with his employer in preparing to establish a competing enterprise, . . . he is not bound to reveal the precise nature of his plans to the employer unless he has acted inimically to the employer's interest beyond the mere failure to disclose. . . .

The right to make arrangements to compete is by no means absolute and the exercise of the privilege may, in appropriate circumstances, rise to the level of a breach of an employee's fiduciary duty of loyalty. Thus, the privilege has not been applied to immunize employees from liability where the employee has committed some fraudulent, unfair or wrongful act in the course of preparing to compete. . . . Examples of misconduct which will defeat the privilege are: misappropriation of trade secrets, solicitation of employer's customers prior to cessation of employment, conspiracy to bring about mass resignation of employer's key employees [and] usurpation of employer's business opportunities. . . .

We hold that appellee's conduct here falls within the mere preparation privilege accorded employees contemplating termination of employment. Looking beyond the mere failure to disclose the details of their preparations, we have been unable to find in the record any evidence of such unfair, fraudulent, or wrongful conduct on the part of appellees as would entitle appellant to relief in the form of an injunction, damages, or an accounting for profits. . . .

[Affirmed.]

## Case Discussion Questions

1   What interest is Maryland Metals trying to protect? Why did they bring this suit?
2   What is the difference between actually competing with the principal and "mere preparations" to compete?
3   What social policies is the court protecting? Has the court drawn the line in an appropriate place?

*The Duty Not to Make a Secret Profit*   Closely related to the duty not to compete with one's principal is the duty not to make any secret profit arising from an agency. This generally means that an agent will be liable for any benefits received from third persons, even if the principal was not damaged.

For example, assume that X is an agent for ABC Corporation, and ABC makes a decision to build a factory on certain land. Before any offer is made to purchase the land, X (either personally or through someone else) acquires an interest in the land and thereby receives part of the purchase price when ABC ultimately purchases the property. That secret profit would belong to ABC, even if X could show that the price paid was no more than that which would have been paid if X was not an owner of the land. In an interesting application of the rule, one court found that illegal bribes accepted by a county official were actually the property of the county.[2]

_____

2 *County of Cook v. Barrett*, 344 N.E.2d 540 (Ill. App., 1975).

*The Duty Not to Appropriate Business Opportunities*    Another closely related portion of the duty of loyalty is the duty not to appropriate business opportunities that legitimately belong to the principal. If a principal has a legitimate interest in some opportunity, an agent cannot take that opportunity for himself. For example, if A is the agent for XYZ, and XYZ learns of oil-bearing land that it wishes to purchase, A may not purchase the land for himself, either personally or through someone else, unless the principal is unable or unwilling to take advantage of the opportunity.

*The Duty Not to Divulge Trade Secrets*    An agent cannot use or divulge trade secrets obtained from the course of the agency. A *trade secret* generally means any confidential information and has been defined as any "formula, patent, device, plan, or compilation of information which is used in one's business and which gives him an opportunity to obtain an advantage over competitors who do not know it."[3] One who discloses or uses another's trade secret is generally liable if the secret was improperly discovered and if the disclosure is a breach of a fiduciary duty. A person who discloses a trade secret may also be liable if he learned the secret from someone who discovered it improperly or was breaching a fiduciary duty, or even if he learned the secret by mistake if he had notice that it was in fact a secret.

**The Duty to Account**    A fiduciary also has the duty to *account* to his or her principal for all property or money entrusted to the agent's care. In the absence of some agreement, this means that the principal has the right at any time to learn the present status of his or her property. One common aspect of the duty to account is the rule that agents should not *commingle*, or mix, the property of the principal with the property of the agent. Lawyers, accountants, and others who commonly hold the property of others often set up special bank accounts to hold funds deposited with them, separate from their personal and business accounts.

**The Duty to Give Notice**    It is generally held that the knowledge of the agent is also the knowledge of the principal, and the principal can be held liable for facts known by the agent. For example, if P owns a car dealership, and A, her agent, sells a car that A knows is unsafe—a fact actually unknown by P—P might still be held liable to a person damaged by A's act, because A's knowledge is *imputed* (charged) to P. For this reason, an agent generally has a fiduciary duty to give *notice* to the principal of all material facts that come to the agent's attention and must do so as soon as reasonably possible.

## DUTIES OF PRINCIPAL TO AGENT

Because of the power that an agent has over a principal to bind the principal to contracts and to make the principal liable in tort under the doctrine of *respondeat superior*, the duties of an agent to a principal are generally far more extensive than the duties of a principal to an agent.

---

3 *Restatement of Torts*, Sec. 757.

### Contractual Duties

Most of the duties that a principal owes to an agent arise from a contract between them. The law has imposed some additional requirements on such contracts. For example, a principal may not act in a manner that impedes the performance of the contract by the agent, nor may the principal make demands on the agent that are unreasonable in relation to the contract.

### Common Law Duties of Principals

The common law imposes a few duties on the principal outside of employment contracts. These duties exist either *in place of* contractual duties, in the absence of contract, or *in addition to* the contractual duties. The common law duties may be varied by agreement between the parties.

**The Duty to Compensate**    Under an employment contract the employer will usually have the duty to pay an agreed amount of compensation, and failure to pay that amount may result in a civil lawsuit to collect the amount owed. If no amount of compensation is agreed, the employee has the right to be compensated a reasonable amount for his services, to be calculated by the court on the basis of quasi-contract (see p. 193).

A question in such cases is whether the agreement contemplated compensation at all. For example, if A were to drive his elderly mother to the grocery store every week, the courts would probably find that the parties did not intend an agreement for compensation and would deny recovery. On the other hand, if A were to do the same for a stranger, the court would probably find that the parties intended an agreement for compensation and would permit A to recover the reasonable value of his services.

**The Duty to Reimburse and Indemnify**    A principal is subject to a duty to reimburse an agent for certain payments made by the agent. Those payments include (1) payments authorized by the principal, (2) payments of damages to third persons which the agent is required to make on account of a action authorized by the principal, (3) expenses of defending lawsuits brought because of the agent's authorized performance, and (4) payments that benefit the principal where it would be inequitable not to require indemnity.

## AT-WILL EMPLOYMENT: THE DEVELOPING COMMON LAW OF AGENCY

In employment contracts where no term is expressed, the duration of employment depends on the intent of the parties. If no definite term exists, the agreement is usually considered to be *at will*, and either party may terminate the agreement at any time. Even a contract for "permanent employment" is considered to be a contract terminable at the will of either party.

Some federal and state statutes have modified the at-will employment doctrine somewhat. The National Labor Relations Act (see p. 395), the Federal Fair Labor Standards Act (see p. 432), and the Occupational Safety and Health Act (OSHA) (see

p. 427) all prohibit discharge of employees for exercising their rights under those acts. Antidiscrimination statutes also forbid discrimination based on certain protected categories, such as race, color, religion, national origin, sex, or age (see p. 455). And a variety of federal and state laws prohibit discharge for **whistle blowing,** or informing government authorities of employer violations of safety, consumer protection, and environmental protection laws.

Some courts are beginning to rethink the theory of at-will employment and provide for some remedies for abusive or retaliatory discharge as well. Several courts have found that ordinary at-will employment contracts contain an implied promise by the employer of good faith and fair dealing. Actions for wrongful discharge may be based on either this implied contract or in tort.

Courts have permitted recovery for wrongful discharge in three situations, all based on important public policies: (1) discharge of employees for performing an important public duty, such as voting or jury duty; (2) discharge of employees for whistle blowing; and (3) discharge of employees for exercising some protected legal right, such as bringing a worker's compensation claim against the employer.

---

## Kelsay v. Motorola, Inc.
74 Ill. 2d 172, 384 N.E.2d. 353 Supreme Court of Illinois (1979)

Marilyn Kelsay was injured while working for her employer, Motorola. She filed a worker's compensation claim (see p. 422) and was informed by the personnel manager that it was the corporation's policy to terminate employees who pursued worker's compensation claims. Kelsay proceeded with the claim and was discharged. She settled the injury claim and brought this action, claiming retaliatory discharge. The trial court rendered judgment for the plaintiff for $749 in compensatory damages (representing the lost wages until Kelsay found other employment) and $25,000 in punitive damages. Motorola appealed, and the appellate court reversed. Kelsay appealed to the Illinois Supreme Court.

**Ryan, J.**    We are not convinced that an employer's otherwise absolute power to terminate an employee at will should prevail when that power is exercised to prevent the employee from asserting his statutory rights under the Workmen's Compensation Act. As we have noted, the legislature enacted the workmen's compensation law as a comprehensive scheme to provide for efficient and expeditious remedies for injured employees. This scheme would be seriously undermined if employers were permitted to abuse their power to terminate by threatening to discharge employees for seeking compensation under the Act. We cannot ignore the fact that when faced with such a dilemma many employees, whose common law rights have been supplanted by the Act, would choose to retain their jobs, and thus, in effect, would be left without a remedy either common law or statutory. This result, which effectively relieves the employer of the responsibility expressly placed upon him by the legislature, is untenable and is contrary to the public policy as expressed in the Workmen's Compensation Act.

[The court affirmed the judgment, but held that the award of punitive damages should be prospective only and would not apply to the present case.—Ed.]

**Underwood, Justice, Concurring in Part and Dissenting in Part**    The employment contract in this case was terminable at the will of either party, as the majority concedes. But by the action it takes today, the majority transforms the contract . . . into tenured employment for every employee who files a compensation claim against an employer. . . . Henceforth, no matter how indolent, insubordinate or obnoxious an employee may be, if he has filed a compensation claim against an employer, that employer may thereafter discharge him only at the risk of being compelled to defend a suit for retaliatory discharge and unlimited punitive damages, which could well severely impair or destroy the solvency of small businesses.

Case Discussion Questions

1    Did the plaintiff have any guarantee that her employment would last for any length of time? Could the company have fired her at any time, for no reason at all?

2    Is this action brought in tort or contract? How can you tell?

3    What public policy is the court protecting? Does the dissent address that issue?

## SUMMARY AND CONCLUSIONS

An agency is defined as any relationship in which one party, the *agent*, acts for and on behalf of another party, the *principal*. Agency law is the basis of the law of partnerships and corporations and of the entire field of labor relations.

Agency law also determines whether the principal will be held liable for the actions of the agent. Under the doctrine of *respondeat superior*, a master is liable for the torts of his or her servants committed within the scope of the servant's employment. In contract law, a principal is liable for contracts made on his or her behalf by a duly authorized agent, or under the doctrines of apparent authority, agency by estoppel, or agency by ratification.

Agents generally have rather substantial duties to their principals, either under contract law or under the doctrine of fiduciary duties. Those duties include care, obedience, loyalty, the duty to account, and the duty to give notice. Principals have the duty to compensate agents, to reimburse agents for certain expenses, and, in some states, to continue employment.

## REVIEW QUESTIONS

1    In what ways may an agency be formed? In what ways may an agency be terminated?

2    What is a *consensual* relationship? Why is an agency considered to be a consensual relationship? It is said that a party to an agency generally has the *power* but not the *right* to terminate the agency. What does that mean?

3    Should the doctrine of *respondeat superior* be abolished? Consider the implications of abolishing that rule for employers, employees, injured persons, and insurers. Is *risk shifting* a valid basis for a legal policy?

4    Explain the concepts of express authority, implied authority, ratification, apparent authority, and agency by estoppel.

5    It has been argued that the fiduciary duties are the law's way of imposing ethical behavior on agents. Is that true? How do the fiduciary duties reflect ethical ideas?

6    Boffin owns a small candy store. One day his brother-in-law, Bob Glamour (who is not too bright) visited Boffin's store. Boffin wished to run an errand and asked Glamour to watch the store while he was gone, clearly stating, "Don't do *anything* while I am gone. Just watch the store." After Boffin left, Tootle, a sales representative for the Hexam Candy Company, visited the store and convinced Glamour to purchase 500 cases of Hexam Candy. Tootle believed Glamour to be the manager, but there was no

indication of authority of any sort. Upon arrival of the 500 cases of candy, is Boffin liable to Hexam? What kind of authority, if any, did Glamour have?

7    Leeford owed Bolters $100,000. To forestall a possible damaging lawsuit by Bolters, Leeford gave Bolters written authority to sell some land she owned. Leeford later changed her mind and wrote to Bolters revoking the right to sell. Bolters sold the property to Kags in spite of the revocation. Did Bolters have authority to sell?

8    Rokesmith, a grocery store clerk at Podsnap's Foods, confronted Whitrose and, in front of several customers, wrongfully accused him of shoplifting and then struck him in an effort to make him confess. Whitrose filed suit for assault, defamation, false imprisonment, and false arrest against both Rokesmith and Podsnap. May he recover? Would it make a difference if the same actions were taken by a janitor? By a security guard?

9    Burke, an employee of the Duane Jones Co. Inc., an advertising agency, planned to leave to start a new agency. While still employed by Jones, Burke persuaded two of Jones's clients to transfer their accounts to the new agency and convinced three fellow employees to leave Jones and join in the new agency. The new agency proved very successful, and Burke was able to induce two more clients and three more employees to join the new agency. Does Jones have any recourse? [*Duane Jones Co., Inc. v. Burke*, 306 N.Y. 172, 117 N.E.2d 237 (1954)].

10    Creakle had worked for Chillip for twenty-nine years, ten months. Chillip maintained a full-retirement program after thirty years of service. Chillip fired Creakle, stating no reason for the firing. Creakle had been an excellent employee for the entire time he had worked for Chillip. Does Creakle have a remedy at common law? (See p. 438 for non–common law developments.)

# CHAPTER 12

# The Law of Business Associations

*Corporations are invisible, immortal, and have no soul.*

ASCRIBED TO ROGER MANWOOD

Perhaps one of the most striking and least understood phenomena that grew out of the Industrial Revolution in the nineteenth century was the *organizational revolution*, which began about the same time. Although there had been large business enterprises for centuries, businesses prior to 1850 were generally small and were operated by their owners. But in the next century businesses became far more complex, until by the 1920s, large, sophisticated corporations controlled much of the nation's business.

This chapter is about the different ways in which businesses may organize. The chapter considers the principal forms of business organization in use today—the **sole proprietorship,** the **partnership,** and the **corporation,** as well as some of the more rare business forms and the major forms of **nonprofit associations.**

## THE CHOICE OF BUSINESS FORM

The choice of business form is one of the most crucial decisions in the life of any business and involves substantial legal consequences and effects. Businesses may choose to take several legal forms, such as sole proprietorships, partnerships, and corporations. But even if the parties fail to make a conscious choice, the law may impose certain consequences for failing to make a decision.

The effects of the choice of business form center on three areas. First, the choice of business form may affect *management* and *control* of the business. The organization and control of a business organized as a partnership or limited partnership differ sharply from that of a business organized as a corporation, for example.

Second, the type of business organization chosen may affect the *liability of parties.* The liabilities of general partners are substantially different from the liabilities of limited partners or corporate stockholders. Third, the *tax consequences* of various business forms may be substantial. Partnerships are taxed differently than corporations, for example.

There may be other reasons for choosing a particular business form over others. If a business has substantial capital needs, it may be easier to obtain investors for a corporation than for a partnership. The point is that the organizational needs of every business are different, and the choice of business form should be a conscious and deliberate decision, made after consultation with experts such as attorneys and accountants (see Table 12.1).

**Sole Proprietorships**    Perhaps the simplest business form is the *sole proprietorship*. Strictly speaking, a sole proprietorship is not a business "organization" at all, because it only involves one person, the owner. There are no formalities for the creation of sole proprietorship, nothing to file with the federal or state governments, and no agreements with others.

In a large sense, a sole proprietorship *is* the owner of the business, because the law makes no distinction between a businessperson and the business itself. If business debts are incurred, creditors may sue the proprietor personally and satisfy their claims from

TABLE 12.1    Sole Proprietorships, Partnerships, and Corporations Compared

|  | Sole Proprietorships | General Partnerships | Corporations |
|---|---|---|---|
| Formation | No formalities; licensing or registration under "assumed-name" laws; nominal fees | No formalities; may be created by agreement or implied; no fees | Filing and acceptance of articles of incorporation; may be relatively substantial fees and taxes |
| Legal Entity | Owner and business treated as one | For some purposes | Yes |
| Length of Existence | Until owner dies or decides to terminate | Until (1) any partner dies, withdraws, becomes insane, or is expelled; (2) partners agree to terminate | Perpetual |
| Liability | Owner liable for all business debts | All partners individually liable for all partnership debts | Shareholders liable only to extent of their investment |
| Property | Business property is owned by owner | Partnership property (all property brought into partnership or acquired with partnership funds) belongs to partnership | Corporate property owned by the corporation |
| Management | Owner manages | All gen'l partners have equal voice, decided by majority vote | Shareholders elect board of directors, who appoint officers |
| Taxation | All income taxed directly to owner | Income taxed to partners directly | Double taxation: income taxed to corporation, and distributed income (dividends) taxed to shareholders |

the proprietor's personal assets. Upon the death of the proprietor, the business dies as well, although the proprietor may give the assets of the business to another by will.

State and municipal laws and regulations often require licenses for certain types of businesses, such as restaurants, barber shops and taverns. Most states also require persons doing business under some name other than their own to register under an **assumed-name** statute, in order to protect and notify the public. Such statutes require registration of the tradename of the business and the names and addresses of the owner in some central filing place, such as the county clerk's office or the secretary of state.

**General Partnerships**    As discussed in more detail later in this chapter, a **general partnership** is a business operated by two or more co-owners for profit. Generally speaking, no formalities are required for the formation of a partnership, and partnerships may even be formed "by accident" (see p. 299). Typically, all partners are liable for the debts of the partnership, and any partner may bind the partnership to contracts or make the partnership liable for torts.

**Limited Partnerships**    A **limited partnership** is a form of partnership created entirely under state statutes. If the proper procedures are followed, a partnership may be established in which some partners are liable only to the extent of their investment. As a result, a limited partnership may act as an investment vehicle in a manner similar to a corporation.

**Joint Ventures**    A **joint venture** is a mutual undertaking by two or more persons, similar to a general partnership. In fact, general partnership law applies to joint ventures in most instances. Joint ventures are usually created for a limited purpose and often for a very specific duration. Two corporations may form a joint venture, as in the case of a joint venture between an American and a foreign auto manufacturer to produce a new car. Many speculative undertakings, such as drilling for oil or producing motion pictures, are organized as joint ventures. No formalities are required for the formation of a joint venture. Like a partnership, liability of joint venturers is unlimited, and in the absence of agreement, the parties have equal rights to control the affairs of the venture.

**Joint Stock Associations**    A **joint stock association** is in many ways a hybrid, somewhere between a partnership and a corporation. Many authorities believe it to be the forerunner of the modern corporation as well. In the nineteenth century such associations were quite common, because at the time it was difficult to create a corporation but relatively easy to create a joint stock association. Few such associations exist today, although a few large joint stock associations still exist.

In a joint stock association, potential investors pool their funds and receive stock certificates as evidence of their investments. The shareholders then appoint or elect a board of directors, which manages the affairs of the association. Profits and losses are shared proportionately, but each shareholder is personally liable for the debts of the association. Shares are transferrable, and such associations may have perpetual existence.

**Business Trusts**    **Business trusts,** sometimes called **Massachusetts trusts,** were also used in the early part of the twentieth century to obtain limited liability without using the corporate form. Business trusts are based on the law of trusts (see p. 245). Persons wishing to invest in a business give funds or property to a trustee or a board of trustees, which in turn use the property or funds for business purposes. The investors (beneficiaries) receive the benefits of the trust in the form of profits and receive certificates to prove their investments. The sole evidence of the trust is the trust agreement, which remains private. As a result, it is often difficult to learn the identity of the parties to the agreement. Trustees are usually personally liable to third parties but may seek indemnification from the shareholders.

**Corporations**   Almost all large businesses are organized as *corporations*. A corporation is a creature of statute and is created with certain very specific formalities. Once created, the corporation is considered a legal "entity" by the law and can sue or be sued in its own name; the shareholders have *limited liability*. The law of corporations is considered in greater detail later in this chapter.

## THE LAW OF PARTNERSHIPS

Forty-eight states have adopted the **Uniform Partnership Act** (UPA), a model act established in 1914 by the National Conference of Commissioners on Uniform State Laws. That act covers partnership law in considerable detail. There is also a common law of partnerships that preceded the UPA and which applies when the UPA is silent. In many ways, the UPA merely reflects that preexisting common law.

The UPA defines a partnership as "an association of two or more persons to carry on as co-owners a business for profit." This short definition is important for both what it says and what it does not say. First, it is clear that the UPA only applies in situations of *co-ownership* of a *business*, and second, the act also only applies to businesses run for the purpose of obtaining a *profit*.

### Formation of Partnerships

The UPA does *not* require a formal partnership agreement. It is possible that a partnership might be formed by oral agreement or even by an unexpressed understanding. In fact, it is possible for a partnership to be formed without the intention or even knowledge of the parties. The UPA takes a practical view of what constitutes a partnership and concentrates on whether the parties shared profits. The UPA provides:

> The receipt by a person of a share of the profits of a business is *prima facie* evidence that he is a partner in the business, but no such inference shall be drawn if such profits were received in payment:
> (a) As a debt by installments or otherwise,
> (b) As wages of an employee or rent to a landlord,
> (c) As an annuity to a widow or representative of a deceased partner,
> (d) As interest on a loan, though the amount of payment may vary with the profits of the business,
> (e) As the consideration for the sale of a good-will of the business or other property by installments or otherwise.

The UPA also makes it clear that simply holding property together, as in a joint tenancy, tenancy in common, or tenancy by the entireties or some other way (see p. 253) does not establish a partnership, even if the co-owners share the profits made by the use of the property. And the UPA provides that "the sharing of gross returns does not of itself establish a partnership," a phrase that is generally taken to mean that such sharing does not *conclusively* establish a partnership.

**Implied Partnerships**    The general partnership, as a creature of the common law, is a kind of "base" or "residual" category of business organization. That is, partnerships may be formed by attempting to form some other, more sophisticated business form and failing to do so. For example, if a group of people attempt to form a corporation but fail to file articles of incorporation properly (see p. 304) or otherwise do not comply with the strict requirements of state law, the law may treat the parties as general partners. This means that those parties have the same rights as partners and may be held personally liable for acts of the "partnership." Similarly, if parties attempt to form a limited partnership but fail to follow all of the formal rules of state law, a general partnership will be created.

**Agreement: Necessity and Form**    Although no written agreement is generally necessary for the formation of a partnership, a written agreement is preferable to avoid unnecessary disputes. In some instances the statute of frauds may apply as well, requiring evidence of certain transactions beyond an oral agreement. For example, both the transfer of property to a partnership and a partnership agreement that is to last more than one year should be in writing.

The following case discusses the formation of a partnership in a very informal manner, shown only through the sharing of profits.

---

## Cutler v. Bowen
543 F.2d 1349 (Utah, 1975)

Bowen leased a building that housed the Havana Club, a tavern in Salt Lake City, and also the equipment, furnishings, and inventory. He did not work in the club itself, however. In 1968 he made an oral arrangement with Cutler, who had been working for him as a bartender, to take over the management of the club. Cutler was to purchase supplies, pay bills, keep books, and hire and fire employees. Cutler and Bowen were each to take $100 per week from the tavern and split the net profits equally. In 1972, the city decided to take over the business as part of general redevelopment of part of the city and paid Bowen $10,000 to relocate the business. A suitable location could not be found, and the business was closed down. Cutler filed suit, claiming she was a partner, and asked for half the $10,000. The trial court ruled in her favor, and the defendant appealed.

**Crockett, J.**    One of the primary matters to consider in determining whether a partnership exists is the nature of the contribution each party makes to the enterprise. It need not be in the form of tangible assets or capital, but as is frequently done, one partner may make such a contribution, and this may be balanced by the other's performance of services and the shouldering of responsibility.

When parties join in an enterprise, it is usually in contemplation of success and making profits, and is often without much concern about who will bear losses. However when they so engage in a venture for their mutual benefit and profit, that is generally held to be a partnership, in which the law imposes upon them both liability for debts or losses that may occur. . . .

On the question whether profits shared should be regarded simply as wages, it is important to consider the degree to which a party participates in the management of the enterprise and whether the relationship is such that the party shares generally in the potential profits or advantages and thus should be held responsible for losses or liability incurred therein. . . .

It is not shown here that any occasion arose where the plaintiff's responsibility for debts or other liabilities of the business was tested. However throughout the four years in which she operated and managed the Club, apparently with competence and efficiency, it was her responsibility to see that all bills were paid, including the rental on the lease, employees' salaries, the costs of all purchases, licenses and other expenses of the business. During that time she saw the defendant Bowen only infrequently for the purpose of rendering an accounting and dividing the profits. It is further pertinent that the parties reported their income tax as a partnership.

Under the arrangement as shown and as found by the trial court, a good case can be made out that it was largely through the capability, experience, and efforts of the plaintiff that, in addition to the physical plant there existed a separate asset in the value of the "going concern and goodwill" of the business, which was being lost by its displacement. On the basis of what has been said we see nothing to persuade us to disagree with the view taken by the trial court: that the plaintiff's involvement in this business was such that she would have been liable for any losses that might have occurred in its operation and that, concomitantly, she was entitled to participate in any profits or advantages that inured to it. . . .

From the circumstances shown in evidence as discussed herein, there appears to be a reasonable basis for the trial court's view that, except for the physical assets, which belonged to the defendant and to which the plaintiff makes no claim, the further asset of the business: that is, the value of what is called going concern and goodwill, belonged to the two of them as partners in the enterprise; and that when the business could not be relocated, the $10,000 should properly be regarded as compensation for the loss . . . and that the partners having lost their respective equal shares in the going business concern, they should also share equally in the compensation for its loss. . . .

[Affirmed.]

## Case Discussion Questions

1    Did Cutler and Bowen intend the formation of a partnership?
2    Upon what evidence did the court base its finding that a partnership existed? If there had been a loss, would the parties have shared that loss equally? Which party would have argued that a partnership existed in that case?
3    How could the parties have avoided this problem at the beginning of their relationship?

## Partnerships as Legal Entities

One of the principal questions of partnership law is whether a partnership is a "legal person" or "entity." The short answer is that a partnership is an entity for some purposes and not for others, and that the answer will vary from state to state.

A partnership is not generally considered to be a legal "person" or entity, separate from its individual members, for purposes of liability, existence and duration, and taxation. Partners are generally personally liable for all of the debts of the partnership, and creditors may recover amounts due from the partnership from the partners individually. Similarly, a partnership "dies" whenever one of its partners dies, withdraws, or is expelled. Partnerships are not taxed directly. Federal taxes are levied against the individual partners for their share of partnership profits, even if those profits have not been distributed to the partners.

On the other hand, partnerships are considered to be "persons" in the eyes of the law for several purposes. Partnerships may hold and own property and can make contracts, and the assets of the partnership are considered separate from the assets of partners for some purposes. Whether a partnership can sue or be sued in its own name will depend on state procedural law.

## Liabilities of Partners

Generally speaking, a partnership is liable for every contract made with authority by any of its partners, and every partner is **jointly liable** for every contract for which the partnership is liable. Joint liability means that all of the partners must be sued together, and any judgment must be against all of the partners. On the other hand, a creditor may satisfy a judgment from the personal assets of any of the partners.

A partnership is liable for the torts of its partners under the theory of *respondeat superior* (see p. 279). Although partners are technically not "servants," the common law treats them as servants for purposes of *respondeat superior* and has had no trouble holding partnerships liable for the actions of partners. Partners are **jointly and severally liable** for the torts for which the partnership is liable, meaning that the plaintiff may sue any or all of the partners and recover judgments separately against the partners.

Partners have unlimited personal liability for the debts of the partnership. That means that if the assets of the partnership are insufficient to satisfy the claims of creditors, a creditor may proceed against the personal assets of any partner.

On the other hand, a partner's interest in a partnership is also considered a personal asset, and thus the personal creditors of individual partners have a right to proceed against a debtor-partner's interest in a partnership. Creditors may do so through a **charging order,** which is an order from a court against the debtor-partner's partnership interest, and by requiring that the partner's profits from the partnership be paid to the creditor. If the partner's profits are insufficient to pay off the creditor, the court may order the partner's interest in the partnership sold, which acts as a termination of the partnership. The partnership is not liable for personal claims against the partners in any other way, however.

If there are both partnership creditors and individual creditors, the courts generally follow the **jingle rule,** which provides that partnership creditors will be paid from partnership assets and individual creditors will be paid from individual assets. If partnership assets are insufficient to pay partnership creditors, they must wait until individual creditors have been paid before they proceed against individual assets of the partners. And if individual assets of a partner are insufficient to pay personal creditors, those creditors must wait until partnership creditors have been paid before they proceed against partnership assets (see Figure 12.1).

## Management, Control, and Operation of Partnerships

In the absence of an agreement to the contrary, all general partners have an equal voice in the management and control of a partnership. Most matters are determined by a majority vote of all the partners, but the UPA specifies some extraordinary matters that must be settled by a unanimous vote, such as bringing in a new partner or performing any act in violation of a formal partnership agreement.

A partnership always involves an agency among all of the partners. Each partner is the agent of the partnership, and any action by one partner will bind the partnership and all of the partners. The UPA provides a few exceptions to this rule, by providing that a partner may not confess a judgment, submit partnership claims to arbitration, as-

Assume the XYZ partnership, formed by X, Y, and Z, has assets of $20,000. Assume also that D, a partnership creditor, is owed $30,000.

|  | Personal Assets | Personal Liabilities | Net |
|---|---|---|---|
| X = | $20,000 | $ 5,000 (owed to A) | $15,000 |
| Y = | $50,000 | $ 8,000 (owed to B) | $42,000 |
| Z = | $ 5,000 | $10,000 (owed to C) | ($ 5,000) |

Under these circumstances, if all creditors (A, B, C, and D) sued, A and B would be paid from X and Y's assets. C would recover $5,000 from Z. D would receive all partnership assets ($20,000) and could proceed against X and/or Y for the remaining $10,000. C would not be able to recover the remaining $5,000 from the partners (X and Y) or the partnership.

FIGURE 12.1   The "Jingle Rule" Illustrated

sign partnership property for the benefit of creditors, or dispose of the goodwill of the business without the consent of all of the partners. In all other cases, the partnership is liable for any contract made on its behalf by any of the partners. Because each partner is the agent of the partnership and of all the other partners, the law also implies a *fiduciary relationship* between the partners.

## Partnership Property

The UPA creates a unique type of property, called **partnership property,** which is defined as *all property originally brought into the partnership stock or subsequently acquired by purchase or otherwise, on account of the partnership.* Included in the definition is any property acquired by partnership funds. It does not matter, however, how the property is titled. If X owns a store titled in his name and donates that store to a partnership business, that store may become partnership property. Upon X's death, the store may be sold to pay the partnership debts, and any surplus will be distributed to the surviving partners.

## Termination of Partnerships

A partnership is one of the most fragile creations of the law. Partnerships are technically **dissolved,** or terminated, whenever a partner is removed from or added to the firm. A partner's death, insanity, bankruptcy, withdrawal, or expulsion will cause the partnership to cease to exist, and the affairs of the partnership may be required to be *wound up.* The **winding up** procedure involves paying the debts of the partnership and distributing the remaining assets of the partnership to the surviving partners. In many cases, the remaining partners may form a new partnership to carry on business and assume the debts of the former partnership.

A partnership's fragility arises from the doctrine of **delectus personae,** or *choice of the person.* A partnership is a combination of persons, each bringing unique abilities and credit ratings to the business. Parties dealing with the firm may rely on the joint abilities and credit of the firm's members, and each partner relies on the abilities and credit of his or her partners as well. If a partner leaves the firm, that combination of abilities and credit has been changed. As a result, the creditors and remaining partners should be given the opportunity to reassess their relationships with the firm in light of the changed circumstances.

### Limited Partnerships

A **limited partnership** is entirely a creature of statute. Limited partnerships were unknown at common law and exist only under state laws that provide for them. Although still a partnership in form, the limited partnership permits some partners to have *limited liability*, instead of the unlimited personal liability found in general partnerships, upon certain conditions specified in the statute. In other words, parties may *invest* in the partnership.

The **Uniform Limited Partnership Act** (ULPA), also adopted by the National Conference of Commissioners on Uniform State Laws, has been adopted in over forty states. A firm must follow the requirements of that act closely in order to become a limited partnership in the states where it has been adopted. Those requirements include a formal agreement between the partners and registration with the state. In 1976 the ULPA was substantially revised. Few states adopted the revised version, in part because the Internal Revenue Service denied approval of some sections. That approval has now been given, and it is certain that many states will adopt the revised version of the ULPA in the near future.

Assuming the agreement and filing are proper, persons may invest in the firm as limited partners and will only be liable to the extent of their investment for debts and obligations of the partnership. In order to receive that preferred status, limited partners must give up the right to control or manage the partnership. Limited partners cannot exert any control over the affairs of the partnership and may be held personally liable for obligations of the partnership if they exert control.

Every limited partnership must have at least one **general partner,** and that general partner must manage the affairs of the partnership. The general partner will be personally liable for all debts of the partnership as well. Limited partners have the right to inspect the books and receive an accounting.

Unlike general partnerships, interests in limited partnerships are transferrable and assignable, although it is necessary to obtain the consent of all partners before a new party is made a partner. Withdrawal of a limited partner will not necessarily dissolve the partnership, but an amendment to the partnership agreement is necessary. Limited partners may withdraw their contributions on six months' notice, or any other time set by the agreement. If there is a full dissolution of a limited partnership, the creditors will be paid first, and then the limited partners will receive their shares and profits before the general partners receive any distribution. Under the revised ULPA, the claims on assets of limited and general partners are treated identically, unless the partnership agreement provides differently.

## CORPORATIONS

The corporate form was unknown at common law, and therefore all corporate law has its basis in statutes. The earliest corporations were formed by royal charter, granted by the king. Until the late nineteenth century, American corporations were generally formed by a special act of the state legislature or the federal Congress, often with special conditions and privileges. All states have now adopted **business corporation acts,** which are statutes providing a general method of incorporating within each state. Many states have adopted the **Model Business Corporation Act** of the Committee on Corporate Laws of the American Bar Association, in whole or in part. The discussion in this text is based on that act.

## Types of Corporations

A *close* corporation is generally considered to be one in which (1) there are a small number of stockholders; (2) there is no ready market for the stock of the corporation; and (3) the stockholders play a large role in the management and control of the corporation. A few states (notably Delaware) provide a statutory definition of close corporations, including a limit on the number of shareholders (Delaware's limit is thirty shareholders), but generally the term is a practical, vague concept without much legal significance. Control in such corporations is often a major problem.

The opposite of a close corporation is a *publicly owned* corporation, in which the shares are widely held and shareholders play very little part in the management and control of the company. The shares of such firms are often traded on one of the national or regional stock exchanges or in the over-the-counter market through stockbrokers (see Chapter 22).

Corporations may also be classed as *foreign* and *domestic*. A **domestic corporation** is chartered in the state in which it operates, and a **foreign corporation** is chartered in another state. Corporations chartered in other states may do business in any state but often must obtain permission to transact business in foreign states.

A final distinction lies between **business corporations, not-for-profit corporations,** and **municipal corporations.** Business corporations are, of course, out to make a profit, whereas not-for-profit corporations are usually organized for some charitable, religious, educational, or other "nonprofit" purpose. Not-for-profit corporations have no shareholders, and control is vested in a board of directors (or board of trustees in some states) usually made up of volunteers. A municipal corporation is a unit of local government, such as a city or county, chartered by the state.

## Creation and Powers of Corporations

Although corporation statutes vary from state to state, they seem to follow a common scheme for the formation of corporations. The idea for a corporation is hatched by the **promoters** of the corporation, who may make **preincorporation agreements** with third parties for supplies, leases of property, and so on. The promoters may also solicit **preincorporation stock subscriptions** from potential investors. The promoters then prepare and file an application for **articles of incorporation** from the state. If the application is granted, the **first meeting** of the incorporators is held, where the preincorporation agreements and stock subscriptions may be ratified, the **board of directors** elected, and the **by-laws** adopted (see Figure 12.2).

**The Articles of Incorporation**   Before a corporation may come into existence, the promoters or incorporators must apply for and receive **articles of incorporation** from the state. The articles, sometimes called the *corporate charter,* are written by the promoters

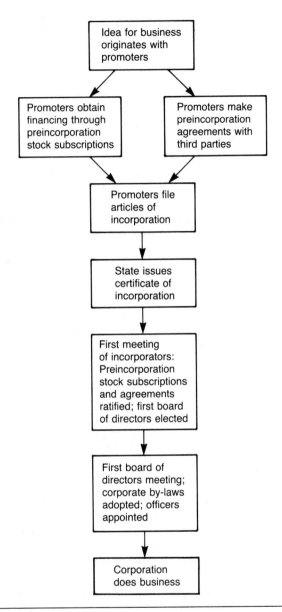

FIGURE 12.2    Formation of a Corporation

or incorporators and are filed with the secretary of state or some administrative agency charged with overseeing corporations. That state official approves the articles and issues a **certificate of incorporation.** The certificate, based on the articles, is the state's official permission to do business as a corporation. The articles include the corporate name, the powers and purposes of the corporation, the total number of shares of stock that may be issued, and the members of the first board of directors.

**The Powers of Corporations**    Each corporation has three sets of powers. First, it has authority to do those things that are specifically set out in the articles of incorporation. Those powers are applied for in the application for the articles and are supposed to be rather specific. In practice, most drafters prefer to state those powers as broadly as possible. Second, corporate powers are derived from the state business corporation act. The Model Act provides a number of specific powers shared by all corporations, including the right to maintain perpetual existence; to sue and be sued; to purchase, own, and sell real property; to make contracts; to lend money; and others. And third, corporations may have **implied powers,** based on a Model Act provision that any corporation has the power "to have and exercise all powers necessary and convenient to effect its purposes."

**The Doctrine of *Ultra Vires***    Although the powers granted to corporations are broadly worded under the Model Act and are broadly stated in the articles, the corporation must only do those acts that are within its powers. An action beyond those powers is said to be **ultra vires** and illegal. At one time the *ultra vires* doctrine was strictly construed in an attempt to restrict the influence and activity of corporations. The doctrine is far less influential than it once was, because the articles of incorporation may be amended rather easily to encompass most corporate acts, and the doctrine of implied powers permits many acts that are not specifically authorized.

In earlier times, the doctrine of *ultra vires* was also used as a defense to contract actions against the corporation on the theory that a contract that was beyond the powers of a corporation to make was void, and the corporation could not be held liable. Courts today tend to discard that theory and hold the corporation liable to the innocent party, especially if the corporation received any of the benefits of the contract. Similarly, a corporation may not escape liability for torts of agents on the grounds that such torts were *ultra vires*. In both instances shareholders may be able to hold the individual responsible for the contract or tort liable to the corporation.

## The Entity Theory

It is traditional to refer to a corporation as a legal *person*, which may sue and be sued, hold property, make contracts, lend money, hold the stock of other corporations, go bankrupt, and even be charged with a crime in its own name. Corporations are considered to be persons for the purpose of most statutes and constitutional enactments, unless the statute or constitutional provision obviously refers only to "natural persons." As a result, corporations generally are fully protected by the Constitution against unreasonable searches and seizures under the fourth amendment, and against deprivations of due process and equal protection under the fifth and fourteenth amendments.

## Limited Liability and "Piercing the Corporate Veil"

This separate corporate identity is also the source of **limited liability** for shareholders. Since the corporation is a separate person, it should be liable for its own debts, and the stockholders are only liable to the extent of the funds they have invested in the corporation. For example, if X has invested $5,000 in the ABC Corporation, and that corporation later loses everything, X's stock is worthless; but the creditors of ABC may not attempt to obtain further payment from X's personal assets.

The doctrine of **piercing the corporate veil** permits the courts to impose personal liability on the shareholders of a corporation if the corporate form has been used to defeat the public convenience, justify wrongs, or protect fraud or crime. The following case discusses the doctrine of piercing the corporate veil.

# Walkovszky v. Carlton

18 N.Y.2d 414, 276 N.Y.S.2d 585, 223 N.E.2d 6 (Ct. of Appeals of New York, 1966)

Walkovszky was severely injured in a traffic accident negligently caused by Marchese, a cab driver. Marchese worked for Seon Cab Company, a corporation whose stock was entirely owned by Carlton. Carlton owned all of the stock of ten cab companies. Each company owned two cabs and maintained the minimum auto insurance of $10,000 on each cab. The cabs were garaged together, and a single dispatcher handled all of the cabs. Walkovszky filed suit against Marchese and Seon; but Marchese was penniless, and the assets of Seon consisted of the two cabs and the minimum insurance—far less than the amount necessary to compensate Walkovszky. Walkovszky then sought in this action to "pierce the corporate veil" and impose personal liability on Carlton. Carlton filed a motion to dismiss, which was granted, but the Appellate Division reversed. Carlton appealed.

**Fuld, Judge.** The law permits the incorporation of a business for the very purpose of enabling its proprietors to escape personal liability . . . but, manifestly, the privilege is not without its limits. Broadly speaking, the courts will disregard the corporate form, or, to use the accepted terminology, "pierce the corporate veil," whenever necessary "to prevent fraud or to achieve equity." . . .

In the case before us the plaintiff has explicitly alleged that none of the corporations "had a separate existence of their own" and . . . all are named as defendants. However, it is one thing to assert that a corporation is a fragment of a larger corporate combine which actually conducts the business. . . . It is quite another to claim that the corporation is a "dummy" for its individual stockholders who are in reality carrying on the business in their personal capacities for purely personal rather than corporate ends. . . . Either circumstance would justify treating the corporation as an agent and piercing the corporate veil to reach the principal but a different result would follow in each case. In the first only a larger corporate entity would be held financially responsible while, in the other, the stockholder would be personally liable.

The individual defendant is charged with having "organized, managed, dominated and controlled" a fragmented corporate entity but there are no allegations that he was conducting business in his individual capacity. Had the taxicab fleet been owned by a single corporation, it would be readily apparent that the plaintiff would face formidable barriers in attempting to establish personal liability on the part of the corporation's stockholders. The fact that the fleet ownership has been deliberately split up among many corporations does not ease the plaintiff's burden in that respect. The corporate form may not be disregarded merely because the assets of the corporation, together with the mandatory insurance coverage of the vehicle which struck the plaintiff, are insufficient. . . .

[Reversed.]

## Case Discussion Questions

1   Why did Carlton organize his corporations as he did? Should that type of organization be against public policy?

2   What is the plaintiff's argument exactly? Did Carlton do anything wrong in this case?

3   What assets may Walkovszky recover as a result of this decision? Assume he suffered $200,000 in medical bills—who pays them?

The doctrine of piercing the corporate veil is not applied very often because, as the *Walkovszky* case indicates, it is perfectly permissible to incorporate for the sole purpose of avoiding liability. The modern trend is to apply the doctrine when the corporate form is used to perpetrate a fraud, where the corporation is undercapitalized, or where the corporation is found to be the "alter ego" of the shareholder, in the sense that the corporation is used as a mere front to conduct private business. In the latter case, the courts often look to see whether the shareholders themselves treated the corporation as a separate entity by actually holding shareholders' and directors' meetings, electing officers, and maintaining separate records and bank accounts.

### Corporate Organization and Structure

The organization of all corporations, from the smallest to the largest, is set by the state business corporation act, and except in those states that provide differences for close corporations, that organization is remarkably similar (see Figure 12.3).

The final authority in any corporation is its owners, or **stockholders.** Those shareholders come together at *annual meetings* or *special meetings* to determine major policy issues facing the corporation and to elect the **board of directors,** who manage the corporation on behalf of the stockholders. The board of directors in turn appoints the corporate **officers,** usually consisting of the president, vice-president, secretary, and treasurer, and sometimes other upper-level management as well. It has been argued that the real power in most large corporations resides in the officers, who manage the day-to-day

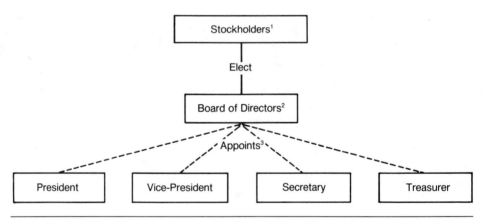

FIGURE 12.3    Traditional Corporate Organization

1 Each share of stock receives one vote. Most states permit a shareholder to vote for every director, or the votes may all be applied to one director under the concept of cumulative voting. In some states, some classes of stock may not have voting rights and, in others, holders of some kinds of debt securities may be given the right to vote.

2 The number of directors on the board may vary, though there must be at least one. That number is set in the Articles of Incorporation and may be changed by amending the articles. Amendment requires shareholder approval.

3 The Model Act uses the term *elect*, though it is clear that the officers serve at the pleasure of the Board of Directors. The board also has the authority to appoint other officers and, in many corporations, there is more than one vice-president pursuant to that authority.

affairs of the corporation and who can in many cases control the board of directors. Often the board of directors and the officers are referred to as **management.**

### Voting of Shares

Each share of stock is usually entitled to one vote, unless the articles of incorporation provide differently. But many articles of incorporation do provide differently, and voting rights, even in smaller corporations, tend to be quite complex. In addition to voting for members of the board of directors, shareholders must vote on any amendment to the articles of incorporation. Stockholders also have the right to vote on any merger, consolidation, or sale or exchange of all or substantially all of the corporate assets, except in the ordinary course of business.

**Straight voting** is the simplest form of voting and means that each share receives one vote for each issue and one vote for each seat on the board of directors. This means, of course, that minority interests would be outvoted on every issue and for every seat on the board of directors. As a result, some states require **cumulative voting,** which means that shareholders receive one vote for each seat on the board of directors, but they may distribute their votes in any way they see fit. A shareholder may use all of his or her votes for a single director, spread those votes out among all of the seats, or divide the votes between a few seats. In this way, owners of any substantial number of shares will be assured of representation on the board (see Figure 12.4).

The articles may also create **class voting,** also known as *series voting,* in which different classes of stock receive different voting rights. Sometimes the articles create different classes of directors and permit voting for one class of directors by one class of shares. Such voting configurations often require a majority of each class to pass certain propositions before the shareholders, rather than a mere majority of all of the shares. Perhaps the ultimate class voting is found in **nonvoting stock.** Most states permit nonvoting stock as long as at least one class of stock has voting rights. Some stock exchanges prohibit nonvoting stock.

---

The formula for determining the most effective use of cumulative votes is as follows:

$$X = \frac{Y \times N1}{N + 1} + 1$$

$X$ = number of shares needed to elect a given number of directors

$Y$ = total number of voting shares at meeting

$N1$ = number of directors desired to elect

$N$ = total number of directors to be elected

For example, assume that shareholder A desires to elect 3 directors of the RST Company, and that there are 8 directors to be elected at the next meeting. There are 15,000 shares expected to be voted at that meeting. The formula would then appear:

$$X = \frac{15,000 \times 3}{8 + 1} + 1 \quad \text{or} \quad X = \frac{45,000}{9} + 1$$

The result is that $X = 5{,}001$ shares. Thus, if A wishes to elect 3 directors, she will need 5,001 shares to do it.

---

FIGURE 12.4    How Cumulative Voting Works

Usually only those shares whose holders are present at a shareholders' meeting may be voted, although there is a tendency to permit voting by mail. Voting rights may be transferred by **proxy,** and management often tries to obtain proxies prior to the meeting to permit them to vote the shares and elect directors favorable to management. Sometimes minority shareholders will attempt to obtain proxies as well, and a *proxy contest* results. The federal securities laws and the regulations of the Securities and Exchange Commission provide rules to assure that those contests are run fairly (see p. 571). Proxies must be in writing and may be revoked by the shareholder prior to the meeting or if the shareholder attends the meeting.

## DISSENTERS' RIGHTS

In the event of a merger, consolidation, or sale or exchange of all or substantially all of the assets of a corporation, shareholders may choose not to take part in the corporation any longer. In those cases, the Model Act finds it unfair to hold dissenting shareholders in the corporation. As a result, the act provides that dissenters may obtain payment for their shares from the corporation, but dissenters must give notice of the decision before a vote and must abstain from voting on the action.

### Direct and Derivative Actions

Shareholders may generally file two types of lawsuits to enforce individual rights or rights of the corporation. A **direct action** is a suit by an individual shareholder to enforce rights as the owner of shares. Suits to recover dividends, to examine corporate books, or to enforce any other individual right of a shareholder may be brought as direct actions against the corporation or its management.

A **derivative action,** on the other hand, is filed by a single shareholder or a group of shareholders to redress an injury *to the corporation.* The real party in interest is the corporation, although the action is filed by the shareholders. The action is similar to a *class action* (see p. 76) and is often filed in federal court under the federal securities laws. Such actions are usually filed against officers or directors.

Derivative actions have four requirements: (1) The plaintiff must make a good-faith effort to convince the corporation to pursue the claim, (2) the plaintiff must make an effort to convince the shareholders to resolve the matter through internal procedures, (3) the plaintiff must have owned shares at the time the corporation suffered the injury, and (4) the plaintiff may be required to post security for the expenses of the case. In addition, the courts oversee and approve any settlement in order to avoid **strike suits.** The purpose of a strike suit is not to redress a corporate grievance but to obtain a settlement for the individual plaintiffs—a kind of legal blackmail.

### The Duties of Management

In most large corporations, shareholders do not take an active role in the management of the corporations in which they hold stock. Shareholders often do not attend shareholders' meetings and generally send the proxies requested by management. As a result, management often has the opportunity to operate the corporation relatively free from shareholder direction and control. Management, through its proxies, often can elect the board of directors, which in turn hires management.

Corporate managers, including the president, vice-president(s), secretary, and treasurer, are all *employees* of the corporation. The members of the board of directors, on the other hand, stand on slightly different footing, because they are elected by the shareholders. The officers of a corporation are considered *agents of the corporation*, whereas members of the board of directors are considered *agents of the shareholders*. In either event, both officers and directors are considered *fiduciaries*, although they owe duties to slightly different parties. In fact, the concept of fiduciary responsibilities (see p. 285) has reached its fullest flower in the law relating to the duties of corporate officers and directors.

**The Duty of Care**   Corporate officers and directors are subject to the duty of care, as are all fiduciaries. In an important early case, a New York court held that it is the duty of corporate directors to "exercise the same degree of care and prudence that men prompted by self interest generally exercise *in their own affairs*".[1] That duty has been further clarified by the Model Act to require a director to "perform his duties . . . in good faith, in a manner he reasonably believes to be in the best interests of the corporation, and with such care as an ordinary prudent person in a like position would use under similar circumstances."

**The Business Judgment Rule**   The **business judgment rule** provides that if the actions of the officers and directors were within the discretion given them by law, no breach of the fiduciary duty of care exists. Corporate officers and directors may manage the corporation within the bounds of the powers granted to them by law, and the courts will not interfere with their discretion except in cases of bad faith, fraud, or a dishonest purpose.

The common law and statutory duty of care seem to leave officers and directors of corporations at the mercy of shareholders who disagree with the actions of management, particularly if those actions turn out badly for the corporation. Shareholders could argue that almost any corporate act undertaken by management violates the duty of care if the corporation loses money. Even if such suits are unsuccessful, those actions may be embarrassing and expensive to defend. The following case considers the limits of the business judgment rule in the context of a corporate takeover attempt.

---

## *Treco, Inc. v. Land of Lincoln Savings and Loan*
749 F.2d 374 (7th Circ., 1984)

Treco, Inc., was part of group of West Coast investors who were attempting to gain control and take over Land of Lincoln Savings and Loan, an Illinois corporation, by purchasing stock. The group had obtained about 25% of the shares. The existing board of directors of Land of Lincoln then changed the by-laws of that corporation so that it would be extremely difficult to remove existing directors. Those changes in the by-laws required a 75% vote of the shares before an existing director could be removed, and

---

1 *Hun v. Cary*, 82 N.Y. 65 (Ct. of Appeals of New York, 1880).

such a vote could only be taken at a special meeting called for that purpose. Removal could only take place for cause.

Treco brought suit against Land of Lincoln and the board, alleging that the directors had acted carelessly in performing their duties and had acted out of a purpose to perpetuate themselves in office. The defendants argued that their actions were within their discretion and protected under the business judgment rule. The trial court held for the defendants, and the plaintiffs appealed.

**Cummings, Chief Judge**    [This appeal] really requires only that we determine what Illinois' common law business judgment rule is and whether it applies to this case. Plaintiffs' theory is that the Illinois business judgment rule insulates a director's action from scrutiny only when the action is solely in the interest of the corporation [because it] is a breach of duty for the directors to place themselves in a position where their personal interest would prevent them from acting for the best interest of those they represent. . . .

Under Illinois' common law business judgment rule, corporate directors, acting without corrupt motive and in good faith, will not be held liable for honest errors or mistakes of judgment, and a complaining shareholder's judgment will not be substituted for that of the directors. This statement [of the rule] is essentially a restatement of the common law business judgment rule generally applied in most states. The rule applies to protect directors who have performed diligently and carefully and have not acted fraudulently, illegally or . . . in bad faith. . . .

After reviewing the facts of this case . . . the district court found that (1) the directors reasonably believed the West Coast threat was serious, (2) the threat's implementation would be detrimental to Lincoln and its shareholders, (3) the defendants' amendments [to the by-laws] were adopted primarily to defend against the threat and on advice of counsel . . . , and (4) the directors' action was a reasonable exercise of business judgment. . . . [T]hese findings [are] accepted. . . .

Plaintiffs do contend, however, that the Illinois business judgment rule may be applied to protect only directors who exercise their best care, skill and judgment in the management of the corporate business *solely in the interest of the corporation*. The district court did not expressly find that Lincoln's directors acted solely in Lincoln's interest. Instead, without expressly determining whether the amendments were at all motivated by self-interest, the district court concluded that the directors were protected by the business judgment rule because self-interest was not shown to be the "sole or primary" reason the amendments were adopted. . . .

Courts that have encountered this issue generally have recognized that directors faced with such threats may be confronted with a difficult dilemma. If they determine in good faith that the threatened action is adverse to the corporation's interest, they have a duty to resist the action forcefully. But successful resistance will likely have the collateral effect of perpetuating the incumbent director's control, so that a director's self-interest in maintaining control may appear to be one of the purposes of the resistance. As a result, the courts generally have determined that the business judgment rule continues to apply to insulate directors' actions in challenge-to-control contexts, despite the directors' apparent self-interest, unless self-interest was the "sole or primary purpose" for the directors' resistance. . . .

[Affirmed.]

## Case Discussion Questions

1    What change in the by-laws was made? How did that change affect the ability of the West Coast investors to obtain control?

2    Was the change made for the benefit of the corporation or the directors? What theory do the plaintiffs advance?

3    Explain the business judgment rule in your own words.

**The Duty of Loyalty**    Cases involving the duty of loyalty are generally one of three types: (1) transactions between a director and his or her corporation (*self-dealing*), (2) transactions between two corporations in which the director has an interest or a position of authority (*interlocking directorates*), and (3) situations where the officer or director has taken advantage of a business opportunity belonging to the corporation (the *corporate opportunity doctrine*). Also related to the duty of loyalty is the issue of *majority oppression of minority shareholders*.

*Self-Dealing*    Self-dealing involves any kind of contract or transaction between a corporate director and the corporation. The danger in such transactions is potential unfairness to the corporation and its stockholders, because the corporate director is at once both an "adverse" party to the corporation and one of the persons who must make the decision whether to enter into the transaction. Although self-dealing is certainly suspect, many contracts between corporate directors and their corporations are in the best interests of the corporation. For example, many times the only place a corporation may obtain loans is from its own directors.

Although the decisions dealing with self-dealing are by no means consistent, several conclusions are possible. First, if a transaction is fair to the corporation, it will be upheld. Second, if the transaction involves fraud, waste of corporate assets, or overreaching on the part of the director, the transaction will be set aside. Third, if the transaction is in the "grey area" in between, the courts will uphold the transaction if it was ratified by a disinterested majority of the board of directors in which the interested director did not take part or was ratified by a majority of the shareholders. In either case, the interested director must make a full disclosure of all of the relevant facts to the rest of the board.

*Interlocking Directorates*    If an individual sits on the boards of directors of two corporations that deal with each other in some way, there is an opportunity for abuse similar to that found in cases of self-dealing, because the common director may "sell out" one corporation in favor of the other. In such cases, the courts look to see whether there is "manifest unfairness" to one company, and they may set aside transactions if such unfairness exists. The courts also look to the common director's involvement in the decision-making process in both corporations. If the common director was instrumental in convincing the board of the losing corporation to enter into the transaction, the courts will often set the transaction aside. **Interlocking directorates** may also be used to the benefit of both corporations, especially if the corporations are in need of communication links. That use of interlocking directorates is permissible unless the firms are competitors, in which case the interlock may be forbidden under the federal antitrust laws (see p. 516).

*The Corporate Opportunity Doctrine*    A corporate director or officer may not make a secret profit from corporate transactions, compete unfairly with the corporation, or take profitable business opportunities that belong to the corporation. For example, a corporate director who knows that his or her corporation is interested in acquiring certain mining property may not secretly purchase that property to resell it to the corporation at a higher price.

The first question in such cases is whether an opportunity is indeed a corporate opportunity. Most courts use a *line of business* test, which compares the types of business in which the corporation is engaged to the opportunity. If the opportunity is in the same or a similar line of business, it is considered a corporate opportunity and the directors and officers may not unfairly appropriate it.

This general rule does not preclude officers and directors from taking advantage of opportunities in all cases. If the corporation voluntarily gives up the opportunity after full disclosure, the officers and directors may take advantage of the opportunity. Directors and officers may also take advantage of such opportunities if the corporation is unable to do so, as in cases where the action would be illegal. Officers and directors may not take advantage of situations where the corporation merely lacks the funds to undertake an action, because directors might not exercise their best efforts to obtain funding for a project.

*Majority Oppression of Minority Shareholders*    Perhaps the murkiest application of the duty of loyalty deals with the duties of majority stockholders to minority interests. As noted by the U.S. Supreme Court, "The majority has the right to control; but when it does so, it occupies a fiduciary relation toward the minority. . . ."[2] The principal test in dealing with issues of oppression of minority stockholders appears to be one of basic fairness, but the situations in which such oppression may take place are so varied that it is difficult to distill a single rule from the cases. Often, these cases involve stock transactions or changes in stock designed to benefit the majority at the expense of the minority, and the courts, perhaps in frustration, tend to look simply at whether the transaction is fair.

**Statutory Duties of Officers and Directors**    In addition to the fiduciary duties imposed by the common law, state business corporation acts usually impose other duties and liabilities on directors and officers for certain types of transactions. State acts commonly impose such liability for paying dividends in violation of the act, stock repurchases in violation of the act, distributing assets of the corporation to stockholders upon liquidation without first paying corporate creditors, and allowing the corporation to loan money to an officer or director. Directors who wish to avoid such personal liability must vote against such actions. Those provisions often impose personal liability on directors for prohibited acts without regard to bad faith or unfairness.

## Corporate Financing

The financing methods of the smallest close corporation and the largest public corporation differ only in amounts invested. The basic types of financing remain the same. Initially, financing for a corporation comes from two sources: (1) investment in the firm, for which shares of stock are issued, and (2) borrowing by the firm, either in the form of direct loans from banks or other institutional lenders or by issuing bonds or other debt instruments. Investment is often termed **equity financing,** whereas issuance of bonds and other borrowing is often termed **debt financing.**

**Initial Funding: Preincorporation Stock Subscriptions**    Initially, capital funds of any corporation come from the investments of persons who have *subscribed for shares* prior to incorporation (see Figure 12.2). The promoters of a corporation will find persons willing to promise to buy shares when the corporation is formed. After the articles of

---

2 *Southern Pacific Co. v. Bogert,* 250 U.S. 483, 39 S. Ct. 533, 63 L. Ed. 1099 (1919).

incorporation are issued by the state, the corporation may accept those subscriptions and issue the shares when the amount promised is paid. Stock subscriptions are usually revocable until they are accepted by the board of directors at the first meeting.

**Authorized, Issued, and Treasury Shares**  The articles of incorporation specify how many shares of stock the corporation is authorized to issue without further state approval, and the classes and relative rights of each class of stock. These are the **authorized shares,** and additional shares may not be issued unless the articles are amended by vote of the shareholders. As a result, shareholders have some protection against **dilution** of their proportionate share interests and ownership rights.

The corporation is under no duty to issue all of the authorized shares, however. Those that are issued are called, logically, **issued shares,** and if they remain in the hands of stockholders, they may also be called **outstanding shares.** Issued shares that have been reacquired by the corporation are known as **treasury shares.** Treasury shares may not be voted, and state law may require such shares to be restored to the status of unissued shares on the corporate books.

**The Nature of Stock Interests**  Ownership of stock is a three-pronged interest in a corporation. Stockholders may have a right to *earnings* of the corporation, in the form of dividends; a right to *vote* on major issues facing the corporation and for members of the board of directors; and a right to a part of the *assets* of the corporation upon dissolution of the corporation. The term *dissolution* means termination and winding up of corporate affairs.

Not all shares of stock have equal rights regarding earnings, voting, and assets. Stock is often divided into different **classes,** and those classes may have different configurations of rights regarding earnings, voting, and assets. For example, a common configuration establishes two classes of stock, often called **preferred** and **common.** The preferred stock may have the right to receive dividends, often in a preestablished amount, before any dividends are paid to the common stock. But preferred stock may not be able to vote. The common stock may have the right to vote but must wait until all the holders of preferred stock are paid dividends before it shares in dividends. Because the amount is preestablished, preferred stock dividends may be lower than those paid on common stock. Preferred shares may be *preferred as to assets* as well as to dividends.

Stock **options,** the right to purchase shares in the future, are used to raise capital and provide employee incentives, and they sometimes serve as a control device. Stock subject to those options is not considered issued until the option is exercised. **Warrants** are transferrable options to acquire shares from the corporation at a specific price.

**Dividends**  The profits of a corporation may be accumulated within the corporation and used for corporate purposes, or they may be paid out to the shareholders in the form of **dividends.** There are limits imposed by the Internal Revenue Code on how much of the earnings may be held within the corporation without distribution in the form of the **accumulated earnings tax,** however. The decision whether or not to declare and pay a dividend rests almost entirely in the hands of the board of directors. Dividends may be payable in *cash,* in *kind* (in property or stock of other corporations), or in *stock* of the corporation. Most states prohibit giving a dividend if the corporation is insolvent at the time. The term *insolvent* is usually defined as being unable to meet debts as they come due.

Preferred dividends may be **cumulative, noncumulative,** or **partially cumulative.** If the directors fail to pay dividends in one year, they will be carried forward and paid in later years in the case of cumulative dividends, whereas noncumulative dividends are not carried forward if they are not declared. Partially cumulative dividends are usually cumulative to the extent of earnings, or a first claim on actual earnings only.

---

**PRO AND CON**

# Shareholder democracy: Do directors and managers represent shareholders adequately?

**Pro**    The corporate system is just as "democratic" as the American political system. Shareholders who wish to take part in corporate affairs have every opportunity to do so. They are invited to every shareholders' meeting, they may appear and vote their shares, and (subject to legal limitations) they may mount proxy battles and try to gain seats on the board of directors.

Most shareholders are interested only in profits. They have little interest in the social responsibilities of the corporations in which they invest or in the ethics that those corporations demonstrate. As long as profits remain up, those shareholders remain happy. And managers can keep those profits up much more easily if their personal positions are secure.

Shareholders who have some interest other than profits are free to attempt to convince other shareholders of their position. As in the American political system, officeholders and managers listen to those voters and shareholders who have power and who speak up. It would be dangerous and difficult to try to guess what the desires of shareholders (or voters) are. The silence of most shareholders is an excellent indication that they are happy with the way management is running the corporation.

Finally, shareholders have a great deal of legal protection. Shareholders may sue, either in direct or derivative actions. Federal law establishes proxy rules (see p. 310) to protect shareholders. State corporation laws require protections and disclosures, so that shareholders can learn how the corporation operates before they invest. And common law fiduciary duties assure that corporate managers will deal with shareholders fairly.

**Con**    Corporate directors and managers do a very poor job of representing their shareholders. Proxy voting, restrictive corporate by-laws, and permissive state and federal laws permit corporate directors and officers to run the corporation for their own benefit rather than for the benefit of the shareholders whom they represent.

Most shareholders do not take part in the governing of their corporations. Few shareholders attend shareholder meetings, and fewer still are active in promoting corporate policy. This lack of participation means that corporate managers can and do operate the corporation for their own benefit. Management solicits proxy votes from shareholders and votes for a slate of corporate directors that is friendly to current management.

The results are lucrative bonus plans, benefits, and "golden parachutes" for corporate executives. A golden parachute is a large severance bonus in the event the company is the subject of a corporate takeover. It is impossible for shareholders to challenge such activities under the business judgment rule, because such matters are ordinarily within the discretion of the board of directors.

Lack of shareholder democracy may also mean that corporations will not undertake certain unprofitable, but socially responsible or desirable, activities. Many, perhaps even most, shareholders would vote for safer products or more environmental protection. But in a mistaken belief that shareholders are interested only in profits, corporate managers refuse to undertake such activities.

The lack of shareholder democracy has another, more harmful result. Management is secure in most corporations if profits are high. But profits can be high in the short run by damaging the corporation for the long run. A company may maintain short-run profits by refusing to undertake research and development or by keeping wages low or by failing to undertake socially responsible actions. But those failures may result in long-term equipment obsolescence, demoralization of the work force, or loss of corporate goodwill in the consuming public. The result has been, at least in part, the creation of a crumbling American industrial base.

## Roundtable Discussion

1   What legal protections exist for shareholders? Are they enough? What other legal protections would you suggest?

2   Does shareholder silence indicate that the shareholders are happy with the way things are being run? Why or why not?

3   It has been suggested that the federal government charter corporations, rather than the individual states. Would that help shareholder democracy?

---

Preferred stock may also be **participating.** This means that after the preferred dividends are paid, the preferred stockholder also receives the dividend paid to the common stock. Typically, preferred stock is nonparticipating, however. Preferred shares may also be **convertible** into common stock at a specified price or ratio.

**Preemptive Rights**   By issuing new shares, a corporation may affect the existing financial and voting rights of preexisting shareholders, resulting in **dilution** of existing shareholders' rights. Assume that the XYZ corporation has ten shareholders, each owning ten shares of stock. Obviously, each stockholder has a 10% interest in dividends, assets, and voting rights. If the company were to issue twenty new shares to the ten existing shareholders equally, each shareholder would have twelve shares, but each would still have a 10% ownership interest in dividends, assets, and voting. But if the corporation issued those twenty shares to a new shareholder, the ten preexisting shareholders would no longer have a 10% interest but an 8.3% interest, resulting in a smaller proportion of dividends, assets, and voting rights.

To protect against such dilution of ownership, the common law developed the concept of **preemptive rights.** That concept permits existing shareholders to subscribe for their proportionate share of new shares to be issued by the corporation. Preemptive rights do not extend to authorized but unissued shares, treasury shares, or shares issued for property or services rather than for cash.

Modern corporation acts generally make preemptive rights permissive, rather than mandatory, and corporations are permitted to dispense with them entirely. Such statutes also provide that shares issued as a result of employee incentive plans are not subject to such rights. As a result, the doctrine of preemptive rights is less important than it once was.

**Debt Financing**   Corporations may obtain additional funds by borrowing money, usually by issuing debt securities, including **bonds, debentures,** and **notes.** A *bond* is secured by some type of mortgage or lien on corporate property, whereas a *debenture* is an unsecured obligation of the corporation. A *note* is usually issued for a shorter term than a bond and is made payable to the payee or his order, rather than to bearer, as in the case of many bonds. The term *bond* is often used in a generic sense to refer to all debt instruments. Debt instruments do not give any ownership interest in the corporation, although occasionally debt instruments are given the right to vote as further security for the payment of the debt. Upon dissolution of the corporation the debt instruments must be paid prior to any distribution of assets to shareholders.

Corporations usually reserve the right to *redeem* debt instruments, which means the corporation may call in such instruments and pay them, even before they are due. Many debt instruments require the corporation to set aside funds each year to pay off such instruments in **sinking funds.** Some debt securities may be convertible into equity securities at some predetermined ratio. Such securities include both *convertible bonds* and *convertible debentures.*

## NONPROFIT ORGANIZATIONS

*Nonprofit organization* is a term that covers a great deal of ground. Included in the term might be organizations formed for *charitable purposes,* including those organized for health, civic, educational, scientific, or religious goals; *social purposes,* including fraternal groups and other clubs; *trade purposes,* including labor unions, professional organizations, and business groups; and *political purposes,* such as political parties, interest groups, and political action committees.

Nonprofit organizations are divided into two categories: (1) *public-benefit organizations,* designed to aid the public or others outside of the organization, such as charities; and (2) *mutual-benefit organizations,* formed to aid the group and its members. Regardless of classification, some of the most powerful organizations in America are nonprofit organizations, including labor unions, foundations, political parties, hospitals, and church groups, to name a few.

### Structure of Nonprofit Organizations

Nonprofit organizations are usually organized as **associations, not-for-profit corporations,** or **foundations.** *Associations* closely resemble a partnership but are often treated as corporations for regulatory and tax purposes. They are rarely treated as separate entities for liability purposes, however, and there seem to be few advantages to this form except simplicity. Associations may or may not have a formal agreement and by-laws establishing the organization. Leadership is often hand-picked by the outgoing leadership.

The most popular form of organization for nonprofit organizations is a *not-for-profit corporation.* Such corporations, like their business counterparts, are treated as legal entities and must fulfill certain formalities before corporate status is granted by the state. Most states maintain a not-for-profit corporation act to regulate these organizations. If there is a membership, the members usually have the right to select the board of directors or other leadership.

A *foundation* is usually organized as a charitable trust (see p. 245). The creator of the trust, usually a philanthropist or group of charitable-minded citizens, will establish a board of trustees under a trust document and give a sum of money to that board to be used in accordance with specific directions in the trust document. Some foundations have been established by business corporations, although such a use of corporate funds has been criticized by regulatory bodies and stockholder interests.

### Liability of Nonprofit Organizations

The mere fact that an organization is nonprofit does not immunize it from suit. Although the common law had generally granted charities immunity from suits for torts, the doctrine of charitable immunity is now in full retreat and no longer exists in many states (see *Flagiello v. The Pennsylvania Hospital*, p. 25). Some states have provided specific statutes immunizing particular types of charities, such as hospitals, from certain kinds of torts. There never was an immunity from suits based on contracts made by charitable organizations, and nonprofit organizations other than charities are generally not immune from any kind of suit.

Perhaps the most important issue in the liability of nonprofit organizations is *who* is liable. If the organization is an entity, such as a not-for-profit corporation or a trust, the entity is liable in the same manner as business corporations and private trusts. If the organization is an unincorporated association, the common law rule was that all members of the association were jointly and severally liable for the obligations of the association, much like a business partnership. Some states have provided statutes holding the association primarily liable for such obligations, but if the assets of the association are insufficient to satisfy the judgment, the plaintiff may proceed against any member of the association for the balance. Such statutes also grant associations the right to sue in their own names, make contracts, and hold property.

### Tax Considerations

Nonprofit organizations organized for certain purposes have two distinct advantages under the federal tax laws: (1) Such organizations pay no taxes themselves, and (2) contributions to such organizations are deductible to the person making the contribution, if the organization is "qualified" and has received a proper letter from the Internal Revenue Service. Deductions are permitted for contributions to organizations that are organized and operated exclusively for religious, charitable, scientific, literary, or educational purposes or for the prevention of cruelty to children or animals.

### Duties of Officers and Leaders

The leadership of many nonprofit organizations, particularly public-benefit organizations, is "self-chosen." That is, since there is no "membership," the leadership is chosen by invitation by the existing leadership. As a result, no one oversees the activities of the leadership, as the stockholders do in a business corporation, and there is little accountability. Those leaders are still fiduciaries to the organization, but enforcement of those duties is difficult.

## SUMMARY AND CONCLUSIONS

Partnerships are formed whenever two or more persons conduct a business as co-owners, and they may be formed by formal agreement or by implication. All partners are individually liable for partnership obligations unless the firm has become a limited partnership. A variety of more exotic business forms, including joint ventures, joint stock associations, and business trusts, are based on partnership law as well.

Corporations are used to limit liability, obtain tax advantages, and encourage public investment. Corporations must be formed according to state law, beginning with an application for articles of incorporation. Corporations only have the power to do those things noted in their articles or permitted by state law.

Corporations are owned by their stockholders, who elect the board of directors. That board in turn appoints the corporate officers. Officers and directors have fiduciary duties to the corporation, which may be enforced by derivative actions filed by shareholders on behalf of the corporation.

Corporations are financed by selling stock, known as equity financing, or by borrowing money, known as debt financing. Stock may be divided into classes evidencing different claims of shareholders on earnings, assets, or voting rights.

Nonprofit organizations are usually organized as unincorporated associations, not-for-profit corporations, or foundations. Unincorporated associations have more problems of liability than other forms, but those problems have been resolved by recent state statutes. Leaders of such organizations have fiduciary duties as well, although enforcement is difficult.

## REVIEW QUESTIONS

1  Explain the principal differences between a sole proprietorship, a general partnership, a limited partnership, a joint venture, a joint stock association, a business trust, and a corporation.

2  What liabilities do general partners have for debts of the partnership? Limited partners? Corporate shareholders?

3  How may a partnership be formed? What steps must be taken to form a limited partnership? A corporation?

4  Explain the doctrine of *piercing the corporate veil*. When is the doctrine applied?

5  What is the difference between *equity* and *debt* financing in a corporation?

6  Williams was given the title "managing partner" of a restaurant and received a salary of $270 per week, plus 70% of gross sales, but was required to pay all employees' wages and make food purchases from that amount. Was a partnership formed? [*Williams v. Biscuitville, Inc.*, 253 S.E.2d 810 (N.C., 1979).]

7  Chicksey, Veneering, and Stobbles operated a furniture store as equal partners. At the time the business was formed, Chicksey contributed $15,000, Veneering contributed $5,000 and a truck worth $10,000, and Stobbles agreed to manage the business. Chicksey later loaned the business $5,000, which was not repaid. After substantial losses, the three partners agreed to dissolve the business. At that time, the business was worth $5,000. The business still owed Twemlow $20,000 and the Mortimer National Bank $15,000. Describe what will probably occur.

8  Monks and Barker decide to incorporate their amusement park. They consult Giles, an attorney, who files all of the necessary documents, including an application for articles of incorporation. Monks, Giles, and Barker are to be the board of directors, because state law requires three directors. Giles is to receive ten shares of stock for her work. No meetings are held, and the stock is never formally issued. Two days later, Gamfield falls from the roller coaster and is badly injured. May Gamfield sue the corporation? Monks and Barker? Giles?

9   There are 100 shares outstanding in the Sunbury Corporation. A owns 25 shares, B owns 31 shares, C owns 16 shares, D and E each own 10 shares, and F owns 8 shares. There are three seats on the board of directors up for election. How many directors will D, E and F, acting together, be able to elect if straight voting is used? If cumulative voting is used?

10   The directors of North Lane, Inc., a successful sportswear manufacturer, are fearful of any takeover bid, having heard rumors that certain investors might try to oust them from their positions. The directors pass an amendment to the by-laws requiring a unanimous vote of all of the shareholders for the election of any director. Is the by-law amendment legal? Explain.

# PART 3

# The Firm and Its Customers

To the businessperson, perhaps the most important of the eight relationships of the firm (see p. 12) is that between the firm and its customers. That relationship ultimately determines whether a business makes a profit or even survives.

The relationship between a firm and its customers is also subject to abuse, including fraud, false advertising, the sale of defective or unsafe products, and abusive and even fraudulent collection practices. On the other side of the coin, some consumers may defraud sellers, and others may not pay their bills when due.

Ethics and the law both restrain the relationship between consumers and the business firm. The most basic principles of honesty and fair play limit the methods by which products and services are sold. A fundamental principle of ethics forbids lying about products, in advertising or otherwise. Another fundamental principle requires that buyers get what they pay for, and sellers who sell dangerous products take responsibility for them. Principles of fairness say that harassment, threats, and other overbearing or fraudulent conduct have no place in the world of business, including the collection of debts.

But sometimes ethics are not enough. Throughout English and American history the common law has provided some basic limits on the sales transaction, but the protections of the common law have traditionally been somewhat narrow. During the 1960's and 1970's, consumers began to organize and approach the various units of government, demanding protection from a variety of selling practices. Many of the laws protecting consumers originated during that era of consumerism. But others, including federal regulation of advertising, have been with us for quite some time, as legacies from earlier consumer movements.

The following three chapters focus on the laws dealing with the relationship between the firm and its consumers. Chapter 13 deals with product safety, including both common law and regulatory protection. Chapter 14 considers the problems of false and misleading advertising, dealt with almost exclusively by federal law. And Chapter 15 covers the problems of the debtor-creditor relationship, including methods of collecting debts, government regulation of certain aspects of that relationship, and the ultimate consumer protection—bankruptcy.

# CHAPTER 13

# Products Liability and Product Safety

*I would give all my fame for a pot of ale, and safety.*

WILLIAM SHAKESPEARE, *HENRY V*, ACT III,
SCENE II

Consumer movements are by no means new to the American political and legal scene. In many ways, the creation of the Interstate Commerce Commission in 1887, the antitrust laws, various regulations of food and drug purity in the early twentieth century, and the regulation of securities and investments in the 1930's were all part of a continuing concern with the rights and security of "consumers." From the Populists and muckrakers of the turn of the century to the consumer advocates of the 1980's, consumerism has a long heritage in American politics.

In the 1960's and early 1970's the consumer movement reached a fever pitch. At the same time, related movements took place in environmental protection and worker safety. In many ways, President Kennedy identified the concerns of the movement in a speech to Congress when he stated the four basic rights of consumers: the right to *choose*, the right to *be informed*, the right to *safety*, and the right to *be heard*.

This chapter deals with the problems of products liability and product safety, including the common law of products liability, regulation of product warranties, the Consumer Product Safety Act, the Pure Food and Drug Act, and the Fair Packaging and Labeling Act. Chapter 14 discusses the problems of consumer advertising, and Chapter 15 considers the regulation of consumer financial transactions.

## PRODUCTS LIABILITY

Product defects can produce two types of injury: (1) a product may disappoint the purchaser by not living up to its expectations or the promises made about the product; and (2) a product may cause personal injuries, property loss, or economic loss. Both types of injury are addressed by the law of products liability.

### Theories of Recovery: Warranties, Negligence, and Strict Liability

Three separate theories of recovery have developed relating to products liability: (1) *contract liability* for breach of an express or implied warranty, (2) *negligence liability* in tort, and (3) *strict liability* in tort. All three theories were severely limited at the turn of

325

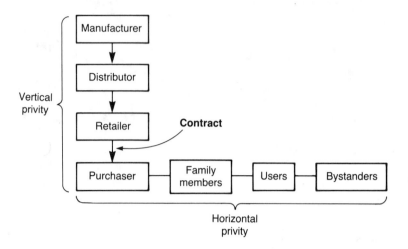

FIGURE 13.1    Privity of Contract

the century by common law defenses. But by judicial expansion, adoption of uniform state laws, and federal legislation, all three have grown into a vast body of law—the law of **products liability.**

Historically, it was quite difficult for a consumer to recover damages against a seller or manufacturer for damage caused by a dangerous or defective product. When a consumer purchased a product at common law, he or she entered into a private contract, and the rights to quality and to a safe product were determined solely by that contract. If the product was badly made or caused injury, the consumer had to resort to contract remedies. Remedies were also sharply limited by two common law doctrines: the rules of **privity of contract** and **caveat emptor.**

### The Common Law Defenses

**Privity of Contract**    For over a century, courts have recognized a defense by sellers of a product known as *privity of contract.* That defense held that a seller of goods was only liable for defects in the goods to a person with whom the seller had a *contract.* Thus, if A sold a wagon with a defective wheel to B, and the wheel later fell off and injured C, a passenger, or D, a bystander, neither C nor D could recover from A. According to the first case to apply that defense,[1] the purpose of the defense was to guard against "an infinity of actions," an early recognition that products could cause large numbers of injuries.

Privity of contract is often divided into two types. **Vertical privity** refers to the distribution chain for a product, from manufacturer to distributor to retailer to purchaser. **Horizontal privity** refers to those people who have some relationship to the purchaser and who may be injured by the product, such as family members or bystanders. The two types of privity are shown in Figure 13.1.

Many courts recognized actions within *vertical* privity far earlier and more readily than those within *horizontal* privity. The only contract involving an injured party that

---

1 *Winterbottom v. Wright,* 152 Eng. Rep. 402 (1842).

often exists is between the injured consumer and the retailer. The retailer often has a defense, because the defect was not caused by the retailer, and defects are often undetectable when the product reaches the retailer. At the same time, the manufacturer of the product probably caused the injury but had no contractual relationship with any of the injured parties.

Although the requirement of the existence of a contract between the injured purchaser and the seller of a defective product was generally followed, exceptions to the rule began to grow almost immediately in cases of products found to be *inherently dangerous*, such as explosives, firearms, or poisons. In 1916 the New York court ruled in *MacPherson v. Buick Motor Company* that privity was not required in products liability negligence actions. That landmark decision began a general rejection of the privity rule in most courts.

## MacPherson v. Buick Motor Company

217 N.Y. 382, 111 N.E. 1050 (1916)

The defendant, an automobile manufacturer, sold a car to a retail dealer who, in turn, sold the car to the plaintiff. While the plaintiff was in the car, one of the wooden wheels collapsed, throwing the plaintiff from the car and injuring him. Buick Motor Company had purchased the wheel from another firm, but there was evidence that a reasonable inspection of the wheel would have disclosed the defect in the wood that caused the accident. The plaintiff had won in the trial court and the defendant appealed.

The court began by reviewing a great number of earlier cases in which sellers of "inherently dangerous" goods, such as poisons, explosives, and firearms, might be held liable in negligence to any person injured, regardless of whether the injured party had a contract with the seller.

**Cardozo, J.**    We hold, then, that the principle . . . is not limited to poisons, explosives, and things of like nature to things which in their normal operation are implements of destruction. If the nature of the thing is such that it is reasonably certain to place life and limb in peril when negligently made, it is then a thing of danger. Its nature gives warning of the consequences to be expected. If to the element of danger there is added knowledge that the thing will be used by persons other than the purchaser, and used without new tests, then, irrespective of contract, the manufacturer of this thing of danger is under a duty to make it carefully. . . .

There is nothing anomalous in a rule which imposes upon A, who has contracted with B, a duty to C and D and others according as he knows or does not know that the subject matter of the contract is intended for their use. . . .

We think the defendant was not absolved from a duty of inspection because it bought the wheels from a reputable manufacturer. It was not merely a dealer in automobiles. It was a manufacturer of automobiles. It was responsible for the finished product. It was not at liberty to put the finished product on the market without subjecting the component parts to ordinary and simple tests. . . . The obligation to inspect must vary with the nature of the thing to be inspected. The more probable the danger, the greater the need of caution. . . .

[Affirmed.]

### Case Discussion Questions

1    What is "inherently dangerous" in this case?
2    Of what importance is the duty of inspection imposed on the manufacturer here?
3    What is the doctrine of privity? How did this case limit that doctrine?

Many state courts followed the *MacPherson* decision until the doctrine of privity had been almost totally rejected in negligence actions. The *MacPherson* decision only granted a cause of action to injured purchasers. Later cases extended the rule to a purchaser's employees, family, subsequent purchasers, and even casual bystanders.

**Caveat Emptor**    The second common law defense to products liability actions is *caveat emptor*, or "let the buyer beware." Under this theory, it is the duty of the purchaser of a product to determine whether there is any defect or danger. If the purchaser (1) failed to inspect the product or (2) inspected the product but did not find a defect that should have been found, the seller was not liable under any theory. The purchaser was even under a duty to hire experts to inspect the goods if necessary. The sole exceptions to this rule were fraud on the part of the seller or a latent (hidden) defect in the product.

As in the case of privity of contract, the strict application of *caveat emptor* resulted in substantial unfairness and pressure to change the law. Although *caveat emptor* technically remains the law, there have been so many exceptions and qualifications to the rule that the rule scarcely survives.

## Products Liability and the UCC: Breach of Warranty

A **warranty** is any statement or representation about goods made by the seller having to do with the goods' character, quality, or title. For example, if the seller were to state that "this item will last at least a year," the seller has effectively promised that it will last that long, and if the item fails to last that long, the buyer may recover damages in contract.

A warranty must be *material*, in the sense that the representation induces, or tends to induce, the purchaser to buy the goods. Warranties may be **express** or **implied** and may be oral or written. Warranties are a part of the basis for the bargain between the parties and become a part of the contract of sale of the product; and if the product does not live up to the warranties given, the purchaser may have an action for breach of contract against the seller.

Perhaps the most common form of *express* warranty is the written "guarantee" given with many consumer products. But any express statement or representation by the seller may also be an express warranty, including a salesperson's comments, models, demonstrations, price lists, and advertisements. The statement must be either a promise, an agreement, or a statement about the quality of the goods. A mere opinion will not constitute a warranty. Since 1975, express warranties have been closely regulated by the FTC (see p. 330).

Early in the history of the law of sales, courts began to enforce not only the express warranties given by a seller but also certain *implied* warranties, which the courts found even without an express statement by the seller. An implied warranty is a promise by the seller, supplied solely by the law, and existing solely because of the existence of a contract of sale. As an early case put it,

> [T]he purchaser has a right to expect a saleable article answering the description in the contract. Without any particular warranty, this is an implied term in every such contract. . . . [T]he intention of both parties must be taken to be, that it shall be saleable in the market. . . . The purchaser cannot be supposed to buy goods to lay them on a dunghill.

**Implied Warranties and the Uniform Commercial Code**   In the mid-twentieth century, the concept of implied warranties was substantially broadened by the Uniform Commercial Code (see p. 192). The UCC defines three types of implied warranties: the **implied warranty of title,** the **implied warranty of merchantability,** and the **implied warranty of fitness for a particular purpose.**

The *implied warranty of title* is a promise to the buyer that the seller has the right to transfer the goods, that the title is "good," and that there are no outstanding undisclosed liens or other claims on the goods. If A sells goods to B, and B later discovers A had no right to sell the goods, B may bring an action against A for breach of warranty, even if A made no express statement that she owned the goods. Sellers may make express warranties of title as well and may disclaim the implied warranty of title if it is done specifically and clearly.

The *implied warranty of merchantability* is often the buyer's best contract protection against defective or dangerous products. That warranty is only given by persons who are defined as **merchants** in the UCC. A merchant includes any person who regularly deals in goods of that kind, claims to be an expert in those goods, or employs a skilled agent in the sale. Under the implied warranty of merchantability, the seller implicitly promises that the goods are *merchantable,* a term given six meanings by the UCC (see below).

A breach of any of those six conditions is treated as a breach of contract and gives the buyer several remedies under the code, including a right to reject the goods and a right to sue for any damages, such as the price of the goods themselves and property damage or even personal injury caused by the goods. The purchaser and anyone who may be reasonably expected to use, consume, or be affected by the goods are protected by the implied warranty of merchantability. This section effectively abolishes the privity issue in warranty cases.

The *implied warranty of fitness for a particular purpose* is only given if the seller knew of the buyer's specific requirements for the goods and the buyer relied on the seller's skill and judgment in choosing the goods. For example, a restaurant owner may wish to buy a toaster for use in her place of business, where it will be used almost continuously. If she simply purchases a toaster from a retailer, she will receive only the

---

## UCC, 2–314(2)

Goods to be merchantable must be at least such as
(a) pass without objection in the trade under the contract description; and
(b) in the case of fungible goods, are of fair average quality . . . ; and
(c) are fit for the ordinary purposes for which such goods are used; and
(d) run, within the variations permitted by the agreement, of even kind, quality and quantity . . . ; and
(e) are adequately contained, packaged and labeled as the agreement may require; and
(f) conform to the promises or affirmations of fact made on the container or label if any.

implied warranty of merchantability; and if the toaster fails to fulfill her special needs, she will be without a remedy. But if she informs the seller of her needs and relies on the seller's expertise to select a "heavy-duty" toaster, the seller will have warranted that the toaster will fulfill those special needs. This warranty is given by both merchants and nonmerchants.

Remedies for breach of the warranty of fitness for a particular purpose are identical to those for breach of the implied warranty of merchantability, including a right to reject the goods and a right to sue for damages, including the price of the goods, and property damage or personal injury caused by the goods. The purchaser and anyone who may be reasonably expected to use, consume, or be affected by the goods are protected by the implied warranty of fitness for a particular purpose.

**Disclaimer and Modification of Warranties**   Either the implied warranty of merchantability or the implied warranty of fitness for a particular purpose may be modified or disclaimed by the seller. The seller must use the correct "magic words" to disclaim a warranty, such as *sold as is* or *with all faults*, or the term *merchantability* must be specifically mentioned in the disclaimer. A disclaimer of the warranty of merchantability may be oral, but a disclaimer of the warranty of fitness for a particular purpose must be written and conspicuous, although general language such as "no implied warranties given" may be used. In some circumstances a disclaimer may be "unconscionable," however (see p. 215).

After some experience with the UCC, sellers began to disclaim the implied warranties routinely. Almost every product came with a little note attached, usually giving the consumer some "limited" warranty but including a phrase such as the following: "This limited warranty is in lieu of all other warranties, expressed or implied, including warranties of merchantability and fitness for a particular purpose, and excludes all liability. . . . "

By the early 1970's, it had become obvious that the warranty provisions of the UCC, first seen as a protection for the consumer, were becoming less valuable as sellers became more sophisticated in the use of such disclaimers.

**Federal Regulation of Warranties: The Magnuson-Moss Warranty Act**   In 1975, Congress enacted the Magnuson-Moss Warranty Act. The act was aimed at four major problems: (1) Warranties were often written in "legalese," incomprehensible to most laypeople; (2) most warranties disclaimed the implied warranties; (3) warranties were often one-sided and unfair; and (4) in some cases, the sellers did not even live up to those one-sided warranties.

The Magnuson-Moss Act did not expand any of the remedies given by the common law or the UCC for breach of warranty. Instead, the act required disclosure of the terms of the warranty, established definitions and guidelines for "full" and "limited" warranties, prohibited many disclaimers of warranties, and gave the FTC authority to regulate warranties. The act only applies to consumer products.

*Disclosure Provisions*   The FTC hearings had found that many warranties were virtually incomprehensible to laypeople and did not provide enough information for the consumer to judge the worth of the warranty. To remedy these problems, the act required every written warranty to make thirteen separate disclosures.

1   The names and addresses of the persons making the warranty;

2   The parties to whom the warranty is extended;

3   The product or parts covered;

4   A statement of what the warrantor will do in the event of a defect or malfunction, the expense for such services, if any, and the duration of the warranty;

5   What the consumer must do and what expenses he must bear;

6   The exceptions and exclusions from the warranty;

7   The procedures that the consumer must follow in order to obtain performance of the warranty and an identification of the persons authorized to perform services or other obligations;

8   The legal remedies available to the consumer;

9   If informal dispute resolution procedures are available or are required prior to suit, a description of such procedures;

10   When the warrantor will perform warranty obligations;

11   The period of time within which the warrantor will perform any obligations under the warranty;

12   The characteristics or properties of the products or parts of the product that are not covered by the warranty;

13   Words or phrases that would not mislead a reasonable, average consumer as to the nature or scope of the warranty.

*Full and Limited Warranties*    Under the Magnuson-Moss Act, warranties are classified as either *full* or *limited*. If a warrantor (person giving a warranty) desires to call the warranty a **full warranty,** the warranty must meet several requirements: (1) The warrantor must remedy or repair the product within a reasonable time and without charge in the event of a defect, malfunction, or failure of the product to conform to the written warranty; (2) the warrantor may not limit the duration of any implied warranties; (3) unless the warrantor can remedy the defective product in "a reasonable number of attempts," the consumer has the option of either a refund or a replacement; and (4) the consumer need only notify the warrantor to obtain repair.

Any warranty that does not fulfill these requirements must be designated a **limited warranty.** If a limited warranty is given, or a service contract is made with the consumer within ninety days of the sale, the seller cannot disclaim the implied warranties of the UCC.

*Disclaimers of Warranties*    Striking at the heart of the problem, the act prohibited any warrantor from disclaiming or modifying any implied warranty if a limited warranty is made, or if the warrantor and the consumer enter into a service contract within ninety days of the sale. The implied warranties may be limited in time to the duration of a written warranty, if that length of time is reasonable. Such limitations must be "conscionable" and must be set forth in "clear and unmistakable language and prominently displayed on the face of the warranty." Disclaimers and modifications that violate the act are ineffective for the purposes of state law.

*Remedies*   The act declared that it was the policy of Congress to encourage informal dispute resolution procedures. The FTC has the authority to prescribe procedures or minimum standards for such procedures. Violation of the Magnuson-Moss Act or the rules is a violation of the FTC Act, and either the FTC or the U.S. Attorney General may sue for an injunction. Consumers may sue, and class actions are permitted.

## Products Liability and Negligence

Although many actions concerning defective products are brought under a contract theory of breach of warranty, traditional tort theory has always been an appealing alternative, particularly if the defective product injured the purchaser or some other person. Traditionally, it was almost impossible to recover for personal injuries resulting from a breach of contract. The rules of privity of contract and *caveat emptor* also stood in the way of such actions.

Every negligence action, as discussed in Chapter 9, requires proof of four elements: (1) a legally recognized *duty*, (2) a *breach* of that duty, (3) an *injury or damages*, and (4) a *proximate causal connection* between the breach of duty and the injury. Early products liability cases grafted certain *contract* duties onto this *tort* doctrine. The doctrine of privity of contract stated that the duties of a seller were established by contract; therefore, because the manufacturer of a defective product often had no contract with a person injured by the product, the manufacturer had no duty to provide safe products. As a result, the first element of negligence—a legally recognized duty—was missing.

The problem of privity of contract in negligence actions and the nature of the duty of manufacturers and sellers were considered in the *MacPherson* case discussed earlier. After that case, the doctrine of privity of contract as applied to negligence actions died a lingering death in the state courts.

Liability is determined by the "reasonable care" standard, just as in other negligence cases. If the defendant foresaw, or should have foreseen, that the plaintiff might be injured, the defendant is liable. The defendant may breach the duty of care in a variety of ways. Cases have held manufacturers or suppliers liable for negligent design, negligent inspection or testing, negligent failure to give proper warnings, negligent failure to provide safety devices, negligent assembly, and negligent manufacture. The duty is an ongoing one, and if a defect is discovered after a product is sold, the seller or manufacturer has a duty to seek out and warn the purchaser. The seller is normally not liable for misuse or abuse of the product, and contributory negligence and assumption of risk may be raised as defenses.

Products that are not "defective" but are dangerous in normal use, or from which the manufacturer can anticipate possible danger, can create liability as well. For example, failure to warn consumers that an oven cleaner is so caustic that it may burn skin in normal use would be negligence. Similarly, manufacturers ought to anticipate that small children might have access to medicines or chemicals and could be negligent for failure to provide child-proof caps or other safety devices.

**Negligence and the Doctrine of *Res Ipsa Loquitor***    Even with the decline of the privity rule and the availability of negligence theory in the consumer's arsenal, cases remained difficult to prove and win. Purchasers do not often have access to proof of how the defect arose, and that proof is essential to the plaintiff's case in any negligence action. It is extremely difficult for a plaintiff to prove just how a metal defect came to be in an automobile wheel or how a foreign object came to be in a sealed can, for example, but such defects do not ordinarily happen without negligence. In such cases the plaintiff may be able to rely on the doctrine of *res ipsa loquitor* to satisfy his burden of proof.

The doctrine of **res ipsa loquitor** ("the thing speaks for itself") provides that a plaintiff may satisfy the burden of proof by showing that the injury was caused by an instrumentality solely in the possession of the defendant, and that the injury is the sort that ordinarily does not take place in the absence of the defendant's negligence (see p. 238). Once the plaintiff has shown that the injury resulted from an instrumentality in the sole control of the defendant and that such injuries do not ordinarily occur without negligence, the burden of proof shifts to the defendant to show that it was *not* guilty of negligence.

**Limitation of Warranties and Negligence Cases**    In 1960 the New Jersey Supreme Court decided the case of *Henningsen v. Bloomfield Motors*,[2] a case with vast implications for the law of negligence-based product liability. In that case, Mr. Henningsen purchased a new Plymouth automobile through an independent dealer and was given an express warranty that disclaimed all other warranties and specifically excepted any physical injuries. Ten days later, while Mrs. Henningsen was driving the automobile, a defect in the steering mechanism caused her to crash into a brick wall. The court held that *contract* defenses, including the express warranty limitation on physical injuries, did not apply to *tort* actions. The *Henningsen* case has been almost uniformly followed by other states.

## Products Liability and Strict Liability

**Strict liability,** or liability without fault, has existed in tort law for centuries in the case of ultrahazardous activities (see p. 242). In the early twentieth century, this theory was extended to sellers of food and drink, following a national uproar over the problems of impure and unhealthy food. Slowly, the doctrine was extended to other "dangerous" products.

In 1962 the California court decided a case that forever changed the face of American tort law. *Greenman v. Yuba Power Products, Inc.*[3] involved a man who was injured by a power tool with a defective locking mechanism that permitted a piece of wood to be thrown out to hit him in the head. The tool had been purchased as a gift by his wife, and part of the warranty required the consumer to advise the seller of any defect within a short length of time, which had expired. The court held that (1) strict liability applied to any defective product, (2) privity of contract did not apply to strict liability cases, and

2 32 N.J. 358, 161 A.2d 69 (1960).
3 59 Cal. 2d 57, 27 Cal. Rptr. 697, 377 P.2d 897 (1962).

> ## Restatement of Torts (Second), Section 402A (1965)
>
> (1) One who sells any product in a defective condition unreasonably dangerous to the user or consumer or to his property is subject to liability for physical harm thereby caused to the ultimate user or consumer, or to his property, if
> (a) the seller is engaged in the business of selling such a product, and
> (b) it is expected to and does reach the user or consumer without substantial change in the condition in which it is sold.
> (2) The rule stated in Subsection (1) applies although
> (a) the seller has exercised all possible care in the preparation and sale of his product, and
> (b) the user or consumer has not bought the product from or entered into any contractual relation with the seller.

(3) contract defenses based on the warranty were of no effect. Many states followed the *Greenman* decision, resulting in an explosion in the law of strict products liability.

In 1965 the *Restatement of Torts* established the rules shown above governing strict liability in products liability cases, based on the *Greenman* decision. The *Restatement* rule has been adopted in many states.

Even in the face of *Greenman* and in the light of the *Restatement* rule, some products cases still seemed to show remnants of "fault" theory. Some cases excused liability if the manufacturer did not know of the defect or could not have known of the defect. Others seemed to excuse the manufacturer who did everything possible to prevent injury. A 1970 Illinois case, *Cunningham v. MacNeal Memorial Hospital*, laid those problems to rest in a decision that was followed in many other states.

---

# Cunningham v. MacNeal Memorial Hospital
47 Ill. 2d. 443, 266 N.E.2d 897 (1970)

The plaintiff, a patient in the defendant-hospital, contracted serum hepatitis from blood transfusions administered while she was a patient. She sued in tort, alleging negligence and strict liability theories. The hospital defended on the grounds that there is no way to tell the presence of serum hepatitis virus in whole blood. The trial court concluded that the hospital was without fault and not liable.

**Culbertson, Justice**   Whatever be the state of the medical sciences in this regard, we disagree with the defendant's conclusion. The Restatement provides in section 402A(2) (a) that "[t]he rule stated in subsection (1) applies although (a) the seller has exercised all possible care in the preparation and sale of his product." To allow a defense to strict liability on the ground that there is no way, either practical or theo-

retical, for a defendant to ascertain the existence of impurities in his product would be to emasculate the doctrine and in a very real sense would signal a return to a negligence theory. . . .

. . . [I]t is said that strict liability . . . "is strict in the sense that there is no need to prove that the manufacturer was negligent. If the article left the defendant's control in a dangerously unsafe condition

. . . the defendant is liable whether or not he was at fault in creating that condition or in failing to discover and eliminate it. . . . Thus, the test for imposing strict liability is whether the product was unreasonably dangerous, to use the words of the Restatement. . . . It has been suggested that this amounts to characterizing the product rather than the defendant's conduct. This is quite true, but it is easy to rephrase the issue in terms of conduct. Thus, assuming that the defendant had knowledge of the condition of the product, would he then have been acting unreasonably in placing it on the market? This, it would seem, is another way of posing the question of whether the product is reasonably safe or not. And it may well be the most useful way of presenting it." . . .

Defendant implicitly raises the *ad terrorem* argument that allowing a strict tort liability theory to obtain in this case will "open the flood gates" to disastrous litigation which will ultimately thwart the fulfillment of the hospital's worthy mission by drainage of their funds for purposes other than those intended. Our answer to this contention is that we do not be-

lieve in this present day and age, when the operation of eleemosynary hospitals constitutes one of the biggest businesses in this country, that hospital immunity can be justified on the protection-of-the-funds theory. The concept of strict liability in tort logically, and we think, reasonably, dictates that an entity which distributes a defective product for human consumption, whether for profit or not, should legally bear the consequences of injury caused thereby, rather than allowing such loss to fall upon the individual consumer who is entirely without fault.

[Reversed.][4]

## Case Discussion Questions

1   Was the hospital at fault in any way in this case? What else could it have done to protect the person receiving the blood?
2   Will this case "open the flood gates" for future litigation?
3   Does this case have any implications during the AIDS crisis? Is this case good public and social policy? Who should bear this risk?

---

**Defenses to Strict Products Liability in Tort**   There is substantial debate over the place of traditional tort defenses in strict liability actions. Generally speaking, *assumption of risk* is a complete bar to recovery, although a minority of states hold that it does not apply. Many courts require that the assumption of risk be "unreasonable" under the circumstances. This means that the plaintiff must at least be aware of the specific dangers of the product.

The *Restatement of Torts* and most courts take the position that *contributory negligence* does not apply in products cases based on strict liability, because if the defendant's negligence is not important, it would be inconsistent to give any weight to the plaintiff's negligence. With the adoption of comparative negligence, many state courts adopted the position that, because the harshness of the contributory negligence rule had been softened, they would apply the comparative negligence doctrine to strict tort products cases. Of course, comparing the plaintiff's "fault" with the strict liability of the defendant poses a major problem. It seems to be the majority rule at present that such comparisons will be made, and the plaintiff's recovery will be reduced to the extent that his or her fault contributed to the injuries.

One new defense that seems to be gaining ground is the **state-of-the-art** defense. If a product was designed twenty years ago, technology may have led the designers to believe that the product was as safe as possible *at the time*. But with advances in technol-

---

4 Soon after the *Cunningham* decision, the Illinois legislature acted to grant immunity from suit to charitable hospitals for blood transfusions.

ogy, products today may be much safer. It is not fair to apply standards for today's technology to yesterday's products, and the state-of-the-art defense says that juries should decide liability by the technology of the time the products were manufactured.

It is no defense that the actions of the seller were not negligent, or that those actions were somehow "reasonable." Those concepts belong to the law of negligence, not the law of strict liability, as the following decision points out.

## Berkebile v. Brantly Helicopter Corp.
462 Pa. 83, 337 A.2d 893 Supreme Court of Pennsylvania (1975)

[The facts are contained in the opinion.]

**Jones, Chief Justice**    Brantly manufactured the small, two-person, B-2 model helicopter. . . . [A]dvertising described the helicopter as "safe, dependable," not "tricky to operate," and one that "beginners and professional pilots alike agree . . . is easy to fly." Brantly had experienced some difficulties in designing its rotor blades and autorotation in the development stage and modified the system to some degree prior to its distribution. In January, 1962, Mr. Berkebile, a businessman, purchased the helicopter from defendant's distributor. Mr. Berkebile flew alone on July 9, and . . . the seven-foot outboard section of one of the three main rotor blades separated. The helicopter crashed . . . killing Mr. Berkebile.

[The trial court had given an instruction to the jury that they could consider the "reasonableness" of the seller's conduct. The jury found for the defendant, but the lower appellate court reversed the judgment and granted a new trial. The defendant appealed from that reversal, arguing that the instruction was proper. The issue in the case was whether "reasonableness" plays any part in a products liability case.—Ed.]

Plaintiff proposed four grounds for recovery. . . . (1) The design of the rotor system of the helicopter was defective because the average pilot had insufficient time to place the helicopter in autorotation in an emergency power failure in climbing flight; (2) The rotor blade was defectively manufactured and designed; (3) The defendant rendered the helicopter defective as a result of the inadequate warnings regarding the possible risks and inherent limitations of one of the systems of the helicopter; and (4) The defendant misrepresented the safety of the helicopter in its advertising brochures.

The defendant, denying the existence of any defective condition in its product, theorized that the helicopter's rotor blade had fractured due to an abnormal use brought about by power failure resulting from fuel exhaustion, followed by a failure on decedent's part to push down the collective pitch in time to go into autorotation and to effect a proper emergency landing. . . .

The law of products liability developed in response to changing societal concerns over the relationship between the consumer and seller of a product. The increasing complexity of the manufacturing and distribution process placed upon the injured plaintiff a nearly impossible burden of proving negligence where, for policy reasons, it was felt that a seller should be responsible for injuries caused by defects in his products. See Restatement (Second) of Torts Section 402A. . . . We [have] therefore held . . . that the seller of a product would be responsible for injury caused by his defective product even if he had exercised all possible care in its design, manufacture and distribution. We emphasized the principle of liability without fault most recently by stating that the seller is "effectively the guarantor of his product's safety." . . .

Our courts have determined that a manufacturer by marketing and advertising his product impliedly represents that it is safe for its intended use. We have decided that no current societal interest is served by permitting the manufacturer to place a defective article in the stream of commerce and then to avoid responsibility for damages caused by the defect.

Strict liability requires, in substance, only two elements of requisite proof: . . . that the product was defective, and . . . that the defect was a proximate cause of the plaintiff's injuries. Thus, the plaintiff cannot recover if he proves injury from a product absent proof of defect, such as developing diabetic shock from eating sugar or becoming intoxicated from drinking whiskey. Neither can plaintiff recover by proving a defect in the product absent proof of causation, as where plaintiff sustains eye injury while *not* wearing defective safety glasses. Also, plaintiff must prove that the defect causing the injury existed at the time the product left the seller's hands; the seller is not liable if a safe product is made unsafe by subsequent changes. . . .

The crucial difference between strict liability and negligence is that the existence of due care, whether on the part of the seller or consumer, is irrelevant. The seller is responsible for injury caused by his defective product "even if he has exercised all possible care in the preparation and sale of his product." Restatement (Second) of Torts, Section 402A (2)(a) . . . [T]he trial court here unnecessarily and improperly injected negligence principles into this strict liability case.

Section 402A recognizes liability *without fault* and properly limits such liability to defective products. The seller of a product is not responsible for harm caused by such inherently dangerous products as whiskey or knives that despite perfection in manufacture, design or distribution, can cause injury. . . . At first glance, however, it would appear that the section does impose a contradictory burden of proof in that the defect also be "unreasonably dangerous." An examination of [the comments to the Restatement] indicates that the purpose of the drafters of the clause was to differentiate those products which are by their very nature unsafe but not defective from those which can truly be called defective. The late Dean Prosser . . . has suggested that the only purpose for the clause was to foreclose any argument that the seller of a product with inherent possibilities for harm would become "automatically responsible for all the harm that such things do in the world." . . .

We hold today that the "reasonable man" standard in any form has no place in a strict liability case. . . . The plaintiff must still prove that there was a defect in the product and that the defect caused his injury; but if he sustains this burden, he will have proved that as to him the product was unreasonably dangerous. It is therefore unnecessary and improper to charge the jury on "reasonableness." . . .

[Affirmed.]

## Case Discussion Questions

1   Did the helicopter company use due care in this case? Does it matter?
2   Didn't the plaintiff assume the risk of injury in this case?
3   What is the purpose of strict liability in products cases? Does it make good social policy?

**The Parties: Who Is a "Seller?"**    The term *seller* in the *Restatement of Torts* and in judicial decisions interpreting the *Restatement* has been given a rather broad construction. The problem, of course, lies in whether persons further up the distribution chain, such as distributors, manufacturers of component parts, and manufacturers themselves, are also "sellers." It is clear that the *Restatement* definition includes everyone in the distribution chain, including manufacturers, wholesalers and distributors, and retailers.

It is important to note that **indemnification** is possible between sellers. For example, if a manufacturer makes a defective product, which is then sold to a retailer who sells it to a consumer who is injured, the consumer might sue the retailer as a "seller." The retailer, of course, was not responsible for the defect and may seek indemnification from the manufacturer if the retailer was not independently liable for failure to inspect the product for defects.

**The Parties: Who Is Protected?**    The *Restatement* definition clearly provides a remedy to "users or consumers" of the defective product. That phrase clearly includes the purchaser of the goods together with any person who can reasonably be foreseen to use or consume the goods. Thus, if A purchases food at a grocery store and provides it to a group of persons at a party, the seller will be liable to all who were invited to the party, because it clearly was foreseeable that the food might be eaten by someone other than the original purchaser. A more serious problem arises in the case of others who do not "use or consume" the product, such as the bystander or onlooker.

---

## PRO AND CON

# Does products liability law cost too much?

The explosion of products liability law since 1960, including the growth of warranty and strict liability theory and the virtual death of the privity and *caveat emptor* doctrines, has resulted in recovery for injured plaintiffs in many cases where it would not have been possible before. The question is whether this explosion has cost society more than it has benefited it.

**Pro**    Products liability law has caused tremendous dislocations in the American system of business. The increased numbers and amounts of jury verdicts associated with products liability have resulted in large increases in liability insurance premiums, which in turn have resulted in higher consumer prices. Products liability law, in that sense, is merely a method of passing on the cost of injury from the injured consumer to the consuming public.

Some businesses have been unfairly forced into bankruptcy as a result of products liability cases. In the early 1980's Johns-Manville sought protection from over 16,500 claims for injury caused by asbestos. The claims totaled over $2 billion, but the net worth of the company was just over $1 billion, not counting those claims. Most of the claims resulted from injuries caused twenty to forty years before the dangers of asbestos were known. Similar problems exist for the manufacturers of DDT and Agent Orange.

Tort law dealing with products liability is haphazard at best. The competing doctrines of negligence, warranty theory, and strict liability make it difficult, if not impossible, for a company to predict when it will be subjected to liability. Every product has some potential for harm. The possibility of products liability actions increases the costs of a product by forcing manufacturers to increase testing procedures, provide "fail-safe" mechanisms, and even withhold some products from the market. For example, very few firms continue to make ladders because of the frequency of products liability claims.

**Con**    Products liability law costs money, but it is worth it. Products liability law has been the single most significant incentive for American industry to supply safe products to the marketplace. In a time of increasing product complexity, it is impossible to rely on inspection by consumers as the sole method of preventing consumer injury from dangerous products.

For example, when granular Drano is combined with water, the chemical reaction creates tremendous pressure in a confined area. For years, the company used a screw-on cap on its cans, even after it learned of the hazard. Finally, after a housewife who was blinded by an exploding can received a $900,000 compensatory damage award and $10,000 punitive damage award, the company changed the design of its product. Numerous other examples exist of companies being forced to change or even withdraw their products after large damage awards. As one torts scholar put it, "defective products should be scrapped in the factory, not dodged in the home."

The fact that risk is shifted through tort liability is a virtue, not a vice. Why should the injured consumer be forced to bear the cost of injuries alone? A simple mechanism exists to shift that risk to the manufacturer and seller, and ultimately to those who purchase the product. That mechanism is the tort system.

## Roundtable Discussion

1    What are the costs of the products liability system? What are its benefits? Does one outweigh the other? Who ultimately pays those costs?

2   Should the products liability system be modified? For example, should we only provide remedies for dangers that are known? Would there be an effect on corporate research into product safety if we made that change?

3   Should products liability be based on strict liability? Doesn't that raise the costs to industry too much? Should products liability be based only on negligence and warranty theories? Would that solve the problem?

---

**Strict Liability: Reasons for the Rule**   Several reasons have been advanced for the adoption of strict liability in the products area. First, many argue that consumers ought to be given the maximum possible protection against defective products as a policy matter. Second, only the manufacturer can prevent defective and dangerous products. Third, the theory prevents numerous and duplicative lawsuits against retailers, distributors, and manufacturers by permitting the injured party to sue the manufacturer directly. Others argue that the manufacturer gets the benefit from the sale of the product and ought to bear the burdens as well. Finally, others simply argue that the manufacturer is financially better able to bear the burdens of the cost of injuries than are private consumers.

**Liability Based on Market Share**   One of the most far-reaching theories developed in the late 1970's to impose liability based on **market share.** If an entire industry has been producing defective products, and it is impossible to determine whether a particular manufacturer made the product that injured the plaintiff, the plaintiff may bring an action against *all* (or most) of the manufacturers and recover against them based on their respective shares of the market. The following leading case helped to establish the rule, although many states have not followed the doctrine.

---

## Sindell v. Abbott Laboratories

163 Cal. Rptr. 132, 607 P.2d 924 Supreme Court of California (1980)

Judith Sindell alleged that she developed a cancerous tumor and other physical injuries because her mother had taken diethylstilbestrol (DES). DES was prescribed to prevent miscarriages and had been manufactured by 200 different drug companies. Sindell brought suit against eleven market leaders, alleging that it was impossible to tell which company manufactured the drugs her mother had taken but that all DES caused that condition. The trial court dismissed the case and Sindell appealed to the Supreme Court of California.

**Justice Mosk**   [A]s a general rule, the imposition of liability depends upon a showing by the plaintiff that his or her injuries were caused by the act of the defendant. . . .

There are, however, exceptions to this rule. . . . Plaintiff places primary reliance upon cases which hold that if a party cannot identify which of two or more defendants causes an injury, the bur-den of proof may shift to the defendants to show that they were not responsible for the harm. This principle is sometimes referred to as the "alternative liability" theory. . . .

In our contemporary complex industrialized society, advances in science and technology create fungible goods which may harm consumers and which cannot be traced to any specific producer. The response of the courts can be either to adhere rigidly to prior doctrine, denying recovery to those injured by such products, or to fashion remedies to meet these changing needs. . . .

From a broader policy standpoint, defendants are better able to bear the cost of injury resulting from the manufacture of a defective product. . . . [T]he cost of injury and the loss of time or health may be an overwhelming misfortune to the person injured, and a needless one, for the risk of injury can be insured by the manufacturer and distributed among the public as a cost of doing business. The manufacturer is in the best position to discover and guard against defects in its products and to warn of harmful effects; thus, holding it liable for defects and failure to warn of harmful effects will provide an incentive to product safety. These considerations are particularly significant where medication is involved, for the consumer is virtually helpless to protect himself from serious, sometimes permanent, sometimes fatal, injuries. . . .

[W]e hold it to be reasonable in the present context to measure the likelihood that any of the defendants supplied the product which allegedly injured plaintiff by the percentage which the DES sold by each of them for the purpose of preventing miscar-

riage bears to the entire production of the drug sold by all for that purpose. . . .

If plaintiff joins in the action the manufacturers of a substantial share of DES which her mother might have taken, the injustice of shifting the burden of proof to the defendants to demonstrate that they could not have made the substance which injured plaintiff is significantly diminished. . . .

The presence in the action of a substantial share of the appropriate market also provides a ready means to apportion damages among the defendants. Each defendant will be held liable for the proportion of the judgment represented by its share of that market unless it demonstrates that it could not have made the product which caused plaintiff's injuries. . . .

[Reversed.]

## Case Discussion Questions

1   What proof existed that one of the eleven defendants manufactured the product taken by the plaintiff's mother? What proof existed that any one of them *did not* manufacture that product?
2   What is the alternative liability theory?
3   To what kinds of products should this rule be applied?

## GOVERNMENT REGULATION OF PRODUCT SAFETY

In addition to common law products liability and federal regulation of warranties, Congress adopted several statutes that regulate product safety. The vast majority of those statutes regulate the safety of specific products, such as food and drugs, firearms, tobacco, motor vehicles, and the like. But one, the **Consumer Product Safety Act,** regulates all consumer products.

### The Consumer Product Safety Act

The Consumer Product Safety Act of 1972 followed a study by the National Commission on Product Safety. That commission estimated that 20 million Americans were injured each year as a result of defective or dangerous products, including 30,000 fatalities and 110,000 permanent injuries, and an annual economic loss of $5.5 billion. The commission concluded that 20% of those injuries were preventable.

The act regulates only "consumer products" and defines those products as any article produced or distributed for "personal use, consumption or enjoyment, in a household, in school, or in recreation." The act excludes food and drugs, cosmetics, motor vehicles, insecticides, and other heavily regulated articles.

The act created an independent regulatory commission, the **Consumer Product Safety Commission (CPSC),** consisting of five members appointed by the President for staggered seven-year terms. The CPSC also was given authority over several existing product-safety laws, such as the Federal Hazardous Substances Act, the Flammable Fabrics Act, and the Poison Prevention Packaging Act.

The CPSC is authorized to develop consumer product-safety standards. If there is a hazard of injury, illness, or death, the CPSC is *required* to issue a standard, which is to be published in the *Federal Register*, if possible. If there is an unreasonable risk and no standard will provide adequate protection, the CPSC has the authority to completely ban the product. Interested parties must be given an opportunity to be heard, both orally and in writing. If the CPSC determines that "an imminently hazardous consumer product" is on the market or will be placed on the market, the commission may petition the federal court for an order to seize the product and call for recall, repair, replacement, or refund.

Manufacturers are required to test and certify that products meet the standards. The CPSC may require warning labels and may prescribe the form of the warnings; it also has broad authority to inspect products and books. Imported products are subject to the act as well. Some acts are made federal crimes, including failure to comply with standards and failure to furnish information. Civil penalties of up to $2,000 per violation may be assessed, and injunctions are available. Private parties have a right to sue in federal court if their damages exceed $10,000, and they may recover their attorneys' fees. The following decision considers the appropriateness of one of the CPSC's standards.

## Aqua Slide 'N' Dive Corp. v. Consumer Product Safety Commission
569 F.2d 831 (5th Cir., 1978)

In 1973, Aqua Slide 'N' Dive, a corporation that manufactured 95% of the swimming pool slides in the United States, requested the Consumer Product Safety Commission to establish a safety standard for swimming pool slides. Aqua Slide's admitted motive in doing so was to prevent a total ban of such products. The CPSC agreed to do so and accepted an offer by the National Swimming Pool Institute, a trade association, to develop the standard. The institute's proposed rule would have required that slides must impart a low angle of attack into the water, that manufacturers must include warning signs on new slides, and that installation of large slides must be limited to water more than four feet deep. The institute also recommended a ladder chain to warn children to stay off large slides.

The CPSC modified the institute's proposals in several ways. It rewrote the warning signs to include a specific mention of the danger of paralysis. It also decided it had no jurisdiction to regulate slide installation and therefore required that slides come with instructions that recommend certain installation depths. The ladder-chain provision remained in the standard, however.

Under the Consumer Product Safety Act, a manufacturer or other interested person may ask the courts to review new CPSC standards. The act provides that CPSC standards must be "reasonably necessary to prevent or reduce an unreasonable risk of injury associated with [a consumer] product." The act also provides that substantial evidence must appear on the record to support a new standard. Aqua Slide argued that no substantial evidence was present in two respects: first, the warning signs had not been tested and might not work; and second, the ladder chain might not be effective.

**Roney, Circuit Judge** The Act does not define the term "reasonably necessary," and apparently Congress intended the Commission and the courts to work out a definition on a case-by-case basis. . . .

In *Forester v. Consumer Product Safety Commission*, 559 F.2d 774 (1977), the D.C. Circuit defined "unreasonable risk" in the Federal Hazardous Substances Act as involving "a balancing test like that familiar in tort law: The regulation may issue if the severity of the injury that may result from the product, factored by the likelihood of the injury, offsets the harm the regulation itself imposes upon manufacturers and consumers." In this case, the legislative history specifies the costs to consumers that are to be considered: increases in price, decreased availability of a product, and also reductions in product usefulness implicit in this analysis is an understanding that the regulation is a feasible method of reducing the risk. Also, an important predicate to Commission action is that consumers be unaware of either the severity, frequency, or ways of avoiding the risk. If consumers have accurate information, and still choose to incur the risk, then their judgment may well be reasonable. . . .

. . . The Commission does not have to conduct an elaborate cost–benefit analysis. It does, however, have to shoulder the burden of examining the relevant factors and producing substantial evidence to support its conclusion that they weigh in favor of the standard.

In this case, the severity of the risk is so terrible that virtually any standard which actually promised to reduce it would seem to be "reasonably necessary." After surveying slide accidents, and considering the result of scientific studies of slide dynamics, the Commission identified a risk of "quadriplegia and paraplegia resulting from users (primarily adults using the swimming pool slide for the first time) sliding down the slide in a head first position and striking the bottom of the pool." The risk is greater than an inexperienced "belly slider" would anticipate, because improper head first entry can cause an uncontrollable "snap rotation of the body" that "allows the arms to clear the bottom prior to head impact." Also, a curved slide can disorient persons who are using it for the first time. Without question, paraplegia is a horrible injury.

The risk of paraplegia from swimming pool slides, however, is extremely remote. More than 350,000 slides are in use yet the Commission could find no more than 11 instances of paraplegia over a six-year period. . . . Given the severity of the injury, however, . . . it seems likely that a standard which actually promised to reduce the risk without unduly hampering the availability of the slides or decreasing their utility could render this risk "unreasonable." The question then is whether the specific provisions of the standard which Aqua Slide challenges have been shown to accomplish that task.

**A. Warning Signs** . . . [T]he record contains only the most ambiguous of indications that the warning signs would actually be heeded by slide users. The Commission did not test the signs. The only testing was done at the last minute by one Institute committee member who conducted experiments for two days. The letter describing the tests, although it concluded that the signs "would seem capable of effecting significant risk reduction," also indicated that the test subjects "claimed they understood the belly slide message, but this seemed questionable," the message was long, [and] few readers did more than glance at it. . . . In short, the Commission provided little evidence that the warning signs would benefit consumers.

In this case, the prime disadvantage to which Aqua Slide points is the warning's effect on the availability of slides. The Commission report indicated 20% of total sales would be lost over 6 years. . . .

Certainly, on this record, the economic finding is crucial. . . . We consequently hold that the Commission has failed to provide substantial evidence to demonstrate the reasonable necessity of the warning sign requirement. . . .

**B. Ladder-Chain** The one aspect of the standard which does promise to reduce the risk of paraplegia is the placement of large slides in deep water. . . . Deep water placement, however, presented the Commission with an increased risk of child drownings. . . .

The Commission took two steps to reduce the risk of drowning associated with deep water slides. It redrew the warning sign to include a drowning figure and it required all such slides to have a ladder chain. That warning sign, however, was never tested for effectiveness. The only tests performed on the ladder chain were done by [an] Institute consultant . . . who tried one out on his neighbors' children at a pool in his own back yard. . . .

This is not the stuff of which substantial evidence is made. . . . Because the Commission failed to produce substantial evidence to show the ladder chain and warning sign would work, its balance collapses and [the standard] must be set aside.

## C. Conclusion    . . . The Commission has failed to produce substantial evidence to support the warning sign and ladder chain requirements, and because

those requirements are integral parts of the standard's scheme for preventing paralytic injury, [the Commission's standard] must be set aside. . . .

### Case Discussion Questions

1   What standard exists to test whether a CPSC standard is appropriate?
2   Must the CPSC conduct a cost–benefit analysis of its rules? Explain.
3   Does this case represent a departure from the doctrine of *judicial deference* (see p. 159) to actions of administrative agencies? Explain. What evidence existed to back up the CPSC's claim that a rule was necessary?

## Federal Food and Drug Administration

The Federal Food and Drug Administration (FDA) was created in 1927 and has been given authority to administer several food and drug laws, including the **Federal Pure Food and Drug Act of 1906**; the **Federal Food, Drug and Cosmetic Act of 1938**; the **Drug Amendments of 1962**; and portions of the **Fair Packaging and Labeling Act of 1967**. The FDA has authority, under the various statutes, to prevent the sale and transportation of "adulterated" and "misbranded" food, drugs, and cosmetics. The FDA has the power to make rules; order examinations and investigations of the plants and records of food, drug, and cosmetic producers; seize and condemn adulterated and misbranded products; and administer "premarket clearance" of certain products.

In addition to testing and setting standards for drugs, the FDA also establishes standards for foods. The FDA has the authority to prohibit the sale of "impure" and "adulterated" foods. Because it is often technically or economically impossible to remove all impurities, the FDA has established "maximum standards" for poisons, pesticide residues, additives, filth, and decomposed matter that may be found in foods offered for sale.

In 1958 the Delaney Amendment was added to the Pure Food and Drug Act. That amendment provided that "no additive shall be deemed to be safe if it is found to induce cancer when ingested by man or animal, or if it is found, after tests . . . to induce cancer in man or animal." That amendment thus established a "zero tolerance" for carcinogens and has been invoked to ban cyclamates, saccharine, and other additives. The 1973 ban of saccharine caused a public outcry from diabetics, weight-conscious persons, and others. As a result, Congress reconsidered and passed a special bill permitting the sale of saccharine with a warning label.

## Federal Fair Packaging and Labeling Act

The 1967 Fair Packaging and Labeling Act made it unlawful to distribute any consumer commodity if the packaging or labeling failed to conform to the act's disclosure requirements. The act requires labels to disclose the identity of the product; the name of the manufacturer, distributor, or packer; the net quantity of contents expressed by some uniform method; and the net quantity of "servings" by some uniform method. The act applies to any "consumer commodity," including food, drugs, cosmetics, and "any other article, product or commodity" produced for retail sale, individual use, or individual consumption. Some heavily regulated products are exempt.

The FDA is authorized to issue regulations dealing with food, drugs, and cosmetics, and the FTC is authorized to make regulations dealing with "any other consumer commodity." Both agencies have made such regulations specifying standards for what may or must be disclosed on labels, including advertising. Failure to comply is either a violation of the Federal Food, Drug and Cosmetic Act or the FTC Act, depending on the nature of the product.

### National Traffic and Motor Vehicle Safety Act

The primary purpose of the **National Traffic and Motor Vehicle Safety Act of 1966** was to reduce motor vehicle accidents, injuries, and property damage. Administration of the act was given to the Department of Transportation. Under the act, manufacturers are required to notify purchasers of motor vehicles containing "a defect which relates to motor vehicle safety." The term *defect* has been defined as follows:

> We find that a vehicle . . . "contains a defect" if it is subject to a significant number of failures in normal operation, including failures either occurring during specified use or resulting from owner abuse (including inadequate maintenance) that is reasonably foreseeable (ordinary abuse), but excluding failures attributable to normal deterioration . . . as a result of age and wear. *U.S. v. General Motors.*[5]

The act sets minimum informational standards for the recall notices and requires manufacturers to provide repair services without charge. Violation of an order to make a recall may result in injunctions and civil penalties and may be the basis of private lawsuits.

### SUMMARY AND CONCLUSIONS

Consumer protection against dangerous or defective products involves the common law of *products liability* and a variety of government regulations designed to protect product safety. Products liability law involves three theories by which consumers may recover for product-related loss, including warranty theories, negligence, and the notion of strict liability in tort. Warranty theory is now established primarily through the Uniform Commercial Code and the Magnuson-Moss Warranty Act, though its origins were in the common law. The old common law doctrines of *privity of contract* and *caveat emptor* have been repudiated through case law. Modern law permits any person injured through a defective or dangerous product to recover for any loss.

The federal government has established several laws to regulate product safety directly. The most extensive statute is the Consumer Product Safety Act, which regulates most consumer products. The Federal Food and Drug Administration administers several acts dealing with food, drugs, and cosmetics. Requirements for package labeling are imposed by the Federal Fair Packaging and Labeling Act, and automobile safety is regulated by the National Traffic and Motor Vehicle Safety Act.

---

5  518 F.2d 420 (D.C. Cir., 1975).

## REVIEW QUESTIONS

1  What is "products liability"? Explain the warranty, negligence, and strict liability theories of recovery in a products case.

2  Given two morally innocent parties, the seller and the buyer, who should bear the loss if the buyer is injured by a defective or dangerous product? Why? Does either of those parties *in fact* bear the risk of loss? Or is it always passed along to the consumer in the form of higher prices? Should we somehow prevent sellers from passing the cost along?

3  *Caveat emptor* was established as a legal doctrine in a time when the most sophisticated piece of goods that a consumer might buy was a wheelbarrow. In the light of today's sophisticated consumer goods, such as home computers, all sorts of electronic gadgets, and powerful (and dangerous) automobiles, could *caveat emptor* still work?

4  Some experts claim that we could make a totally safe automobile. The vehicle would weigh several tons, maneuver like a tank, and guzzle huge amounts of fuel. Should we require it? Just how safe should products be? Totally safe? "Reasonably" safe? What criteria would you use?

5  What federal agencies protect product safety? What criteria does the Consumer Product Safety Commission use in evaluating a product? Are these criteria appropriate?

6  Brownfield purchased a new automobile from Brighton Motors, an independent dealer. The manufacturer of the automobile gave an express warranty but disclaimed "all other warranties, express and implied." The express warranty was printed on the back of the purchase order, along with the disclaimer, in very small print, and no one drew Brownfield's attention to it.

Ten days later, while Brownfield's daughter was driving the car, she heard a loud cracking sound from under the hood, the wheel spun out of her hand, and the car veered into another car driven by Felmley. The express warranty specifically excepted personal injuries. Brownfield brought suit for the value of the car, and his daughter and Felmley brought suit for personal injuries. The manufacturer defended on the basis of *caveat emptor*, privity of contract, and disclaimer of warranty. What result would you expect?

7  Green, a cigarette smoker, died of lung cancer. Under what theories, if any, may his estate sue the manufacturer of the cigarettes he smoked for forty years? [*Green v. American Tobacco Co.*, 409 F.2d 1166 (5th Cir., 1969).]

8  Escola was injured when a bottle of Coca-Cola exploded in her hand. She cannot prove why the bottle exploded. How will she prove her case, if at all? [*Escola v. Coca-Cola Bottling Co.*, 24 Cal. 2d 453, 150 P.2d 436 (1944).]

9  Midgley, age thirteen, purchased a telescope from K Mart. Some assembly was required. The telescope had been manufactured in Japan, and the instruction book had been written in English by persons who spoke English as a second language. The telescope contained a dark lens labeled "Sun." The instructions said: "CAUTION: Please refrain from looking up the sun without attaching the sun glass. Also the sun should not be seen through the finder-scope." There were no diagrams or pictures of proper installation. Midgley viewed the sun several times through the sun lens, but he had assembled the lenses incorrectly. He suffered irreparable damage to his vision and sued K Mart. What do you think was the result? [*Midgley v. S.S. Kresge Co.*, 55 Cal. App. 3d 67, 127 Cal. Rptr. 217 (1976).]

# Consumer Law: Deceptive Advertising

*The codfish lays ten thousand eggs,*
*The homely hen lays one.*
*The codfish never cackles*
*To tell you what she's done.*
*And so we scorn the codfish,*
*While the humble hen we prize,*
*Which only goes to show you*
*That it pays to advertise.*

ANONYMOUS

We live in an age of advertising. It is unlikely that a new product could become established or that an existing product could maintain its market position without substantial advertising. Advertising tends to attract some of the business world's most creative people, who spend their lives determining how best to present products to the consumer. New techniques of marketing are created almost daily, depending on consumer research and the most sophisticated psychological experimentation available.

And yet, as in all businesses, there are people at the fringe of the advertising world who insist on using misleading statements, unethical behavior, and outright lies to sell their products. Unprincipled and unethical advertising gives the entire industry a bad name and ultimately harms both consumers and competitors.

Controlling unethical advertising has proven to be a difficult task. Common law attempts have not been fruitful, and federal regulation may have indicted both the innocent and the guilty. This chapter is the story of how the judicial and administrative processes have dealt with deceptive advertising and marketing practices.

## WHO IS HARMED?

A common thread running through all of the law of deceptive trade practices is the issue of whom the law is trying to protect. On one hand, deception harms *consumers*, because they may purchase items that do not live up to the claims made for them. On the other hand, deception harms *competitors* of the unethical advertiser, because business is diverted from honestly presented products. The issue of whom the law should protect began in the common law, where competitors seemed to have more protection than consumers. The question arose again in the **Federal Trade Commission (FTC) Act,** which initially protected only competitors, and seemed to be settled with the passage of the **Wheeler-Lea Act of 1938,** which extended the reach of the FTC Act to protect consumers.

## COMMON LAW PROTECTIONS

The problem of misleading and deceptive advertising practices arose early in the history of the common law. The law had its origins with some trades, particularly silversmithing and similar arts, that were required by the king to mark their products with distinctive "trade-marks." Craftsmen often took advantage of this requirement and built substantial businesses on preferences for the products of a particular craftsman. Less scrupulous craftsmen sometimes copied a successful tradesman's mark in order to steal business. The common law lawsuits that resulted created the basis of the law of trademarks and the common law tort of *trademark infringement.* The same theories later resulted in the torts of **disparagement, passing off** and **product simulation, misappropriation,** and **malicious competition.**

### Competitor Torts: Common Law "Unfair Competition"

The ancient torts are still with us. The common law has provided protection to *competitors* against unethical conduct for hundreds of years. Those common law protections remain in place, even in light of contemporary regulation by the FTC and the creation of the antitrust laws (see Chapters 20 and 21).

**Common Law Trademark Infringement**    The earliest cases merely prohibited craftsmen from duplicating the "mark" of another craftsman in an effort to divert trade. This action was a claim that the property was being passed as another's work in order to obtain the benefits of the trademark owner's goodwill and established reputation. Often, the result was a judgment equal to all of the profits received as a result of the infringement, and injunctions were granted requiring the person infringing another's mark to cease the practice.

The first American trademark law, enacted by Congress in 1845, simply incorporated the common law doctrine. Trademarks were first registered with the federal government in 1870, and the present statute was enacted in 1947. In that year the **Lanham Trade-Mark Act** became law and protected all marks registered with the Trademark Office. Disputes are heard by the Trademark Trial and Appeal Board, and appeals may be taken to the U.S. Court of Appeals for the Federal Circuit.

In 1984, Congress passed the **Trademark Counterfeiting Act.** That law was aimed at deterring product piracy, which at that time cost American business an estimated $20 billion per year. Product piracy involves marketing goods under counterfeit trademarks or tradenames. The law permits companies to obtain a search warrant, based on probable cause and issued by a federal judge, to search for pirated merchandise and take away goods and business records. Those records and merchandise may then be used in subsequent civil or criminal proceedings under the Lanham Act. The search warrant is often served by private counsel with the aid of private detectives, although U.S. marshals often aid the search. Another provision of the law that permitted private attorneys to be named as special prosecutors has been held unconstitutional.

**Disparagement**    The common law tort of *disparagement* is a form of commercial slander, covering all false statements regarding the quality of another merchant's products or services. To be actionable, the statement must be false and must be made with "malice." Courts also require that there be proof of actual loss to the complaining party. One famous example of disparagement involved a car painted with lemons parked in front of a car dealership by a competing dealership. Consumers, competitors, or others may be sued for disparagement.

**"Passing Off" and Product Simulation**    Two closely related torts involve efforts to convince the public that a product is actually made by another manufacturer. *Passing off* involves some express representation that another manufacturer made the product. *Product simulation* is an intentional duplication of the physical characteristics of another's product. Duplicating the package design of a product might be product simulation, but putting the tradename of another manufacturer on the package would be passing off.

**Misappropriation**    The tort of *misappropriation* developed in the late nineteenth century. The tort is generally described as "reaping what one has not sown," because a product manufactured by another is passed off as one's own. It is a type of *product plagiarism*, because products of one manufacturer are presented to the public as one's own. (Note that passing off is a representation that the product is manufactured by another.)

**Malicious Competition**    Perhaps the most indefinite of all of the competitor torts is *malicious competition*, or "competing for a predatory purpose." Normal competitive activity is privileged, and it is expected that competitors will "play hardball" in an effort to win customers. But in some instances the courts have held that the activities of a competitor have gone beyond the bounds of normal competition and into the realm of unfairness. One example involved an action by a commercial trapper of wildfowl against a competitor who discharged guns over his traps in an effort to frighten animals away. Malicious competition requires proof of malice, or evil intent.

### Common Law Consumer Torts

From the beginning, consumers were not nearly as well protected as competitors from unethical conduct by merchants. The early common law recognized two consumer actions: actions for **fraud,** sometimes called *deceit* (see p. 212), and actions for **breach of warranty** (see p. 328). Neither was effective in protecting the consumer from misleading or deceptive advertising, although warranty protections have been greatly enlarged since the adoption of the Uniform Commercial Code (see p. 192).

### Inadequacies of the Common Law

Both consumers and competitors found it difficult to recover for the unethical business practices of businesspeople. The doctrines of **caveat emptor** and **privity of contract** (see

p. 326) resulted in recovery only in unusual cases of consumer fraud, misrepresentation, and false promise. Competitors were somewhat better off, but the difficulties of proving malice assured that many cases of competitive misbehavior would also go without a remedy.

The lack of effective remedies resulted in some outrageous claims for products, especially during the late nineteenth century. Manufacturers claimed that patent medicines would cure every disease known to man, that corsets charged with electricity would cure both "extreme fatness and leanness," and that products would last "forever." Such claims were made with little fear of legal action, because no effective remedy existed.

### State Statutes: The Beginnings of Regulation

The first real action against deceptive practices came in 1911, when *Printer's Ink*, a trade publication of the advertising industry, drafted a model state law dealing with the problems of false and deceptive advertising. It is important to emphasize that the force behind regulation of advertising was the advertising industry itself, because unethical advertisers had given the trade an extremely bad name. The *Printer's Ink* statute eventually became law in forty-four states, although several states made minor changes in the law. That statute prohibited any person, firm, or corporation from publishing in any way "an advertisement of any sort regarding merchandise, securities, service, or anything so offered to the public, which advertising contains any assertion, representation or statement of fact which is untrue, deceptive or misleading. . . . " Such acts were made criminal violations, punishable as misdemeanors in most cases.

Although the *Printer's Ink* statute is strongly worded, it is only randomly and unevenly enforced by the state courts and prosecutors. Some states have enacted more specific statutes in later years either to add to or replace the original law.

### FEDERAL REGULATION: THE FEDERAL TRADE COMMISSION

As originally enacted in 1914, the Federal Trade Commission Act had nothing to do with the problems of consumer protection and deceptive advertising. Instead, the act was part of an effort to improve the enforcement of the antitrust laws. The law created the FTC and declared that "Unfair methods of competition in commerce are hereby declared illegal." The FTC was given the authority to make rules to carry out the law and to enter orders of restraint, also called **cease and desist orders,** requiring violators to stop the unfair activity.

Some early decisions held that the FTC Act protected both competitors and consumers from such unfair methods, but a 1931 Supreme Court decision held that the term *methods of competition* in the FTC Act required the FTC to prove *injury to a competitor* before the act was violated. This requirement made it difficult to prove a violation in those industries where it was needed most. If there was no competitor, as in a monopolistic industry, or if every competitor was using unfair methods, there was no competitive injury. And the law no longer protected consumers.

The FTC approached Congress and requested an amendment to the act. The result was the Wheeler-Lea Act of 1938, which amended section 5 of the FTC Act to read as follows: "Unfair methods of competition in commerce, *and unfair or deceptive acts or practices in commerce*, are hereby declared unlawful." [Emphasis added.]

The new language in section 5 of the FTC Act gave the commission the authority to confront both competitive problems, as an extension of the antitrust laws, and consumer problems. The FTC now finds that it has two missions, that of *maintaining competition* and that of *protecting consumers*. The antitrust mission of the FTC is discussed in Chapter 20.

After the Wheeler-Lea Act, the FTC began making rules regarding a variety of consumer protection areas, including advertising practices, credit practices, service industries, marketing practices, and consumer warranties. Those rules may be found in the **Code of Federal Regulations.**

The "consumer protection mission" of the FTC is quite broad. Congress has also given the FTC specific authority to administer twenty-seven different statutes, including such diverse topics as cigarette labeling and advertising, fair credit reporting, importation of coin-collecting materials, petroleum marketing, electronic funds transfers, and energy-related matters. Some of these specific statutes are considered in later chapters. The balance of this chapter considers the knotty problem of deceptive advertising under the FTC Act.

### Informal Advice by the FTC: Trade Rules, Guides, and Advisory Opinions

The FTC has set out various types of rules and guides to aid businesspeople who wish to follow the law. The **Trade Practice Rules,** which apply to particular industries, are often the result of formal requests or conferences within the industry itself. The rules clarify what the law already prevents, and therefore industry members are required to follow the rules.

Another form of informal advice is found in the **FTC Guides.** Their purpose is to give the businessperson some idea of what the law requires in certain problem areas, but the guides are binding rules as well. Examples include the *Guides Against Deceptive Pricing, Guides Against Bait Advertising,* and *Guides Against Deceptive Advertising of Guarantees.* Other FTC Guides deal with advertising in particular industries, such as cigarettes and tires. The box on page 351 is an excerpt from perhaps the most widely known and important FTC Guide.

It is often difficult for businesspeople and corporate attorneys to determine whether a particular act is illegal under the FTC Act or other statutes the commission administers. The FTC will give **advisory opinions** on such points, but those opinions are not binding. The FTC will not give such opinions if (1) the conduct is already being followed; (2) similar action is currently under investigation by the Commission or by another government agency; or (3) the opinion would involve extensive investigation, clinical study, or testing.

### The Basics of Deception

More than almost any other area of the law, FTC handling of the area of deceptive advertising has been on a case-by-case basis. Few broad, overriding principles are applicable to every case. The problem is aggravated by the fact that there are very few U.S.

# Guides Against Deceptive Pricing (Excerpts)
FEDERAL TRADE COMMISSION

These Guides are designed to highlight certain problems in the field of price advertising which experience has demonstrated to be especially troublesome to businessmen who in good faith desire to avoid deception of the consuming public. Since the Guides are not intended to serve as comprehensive or precise statements of the law, . . . they will be of no assistance to the unscrupulous few whose aim is to walk as close as possible to the line between legal and illegal conduct. . . .

The basic objective of these Guides is to enable the businessman to advertise his goods honestly. . . . Price advertising is particularly effective because of the universal hope of consumers to find bargains. Truthful price advertising, offering real bargains, is a benefit to all. But the advertiser must shun sales gimmicks which lure consumers into a mistaken belief that they are getting more for their money than is the fact.

**Guide I. Former Price Comparisons**   One of the most commonly used forms of bargain advertising is to offer a reduction from the advertiser's own former price for an article. If the former price is the actual, *bona fide* price at which the article was offered to the public on a regular basis for a reasonably substantial period of time, it provides a legitimate basis for the advertising of a price comparison. . . . If, on the other hand, the former price being advertised is not bona fide but fictitious—for example, where an artificial, inflated price was established for the purpose of enabling the subsequent offer of a large reduction—the "bargain" being advertised is a false one; the purchaser is not receiving the unusual value he expects. In such a case, the "reduced" price is, in reality, probably just the seller's regular price.

Supreme Court decisions in the area. Most of the law has been made by the FTC itself in its orders, and in a few cases by the U.S. courts of appeal. It is possible to make a few generalizations about deceptive advertising, however.

**A Tendency to Mislead**   The basic question in all cases is whether the advertisement has a *tendency to mislead*. An outright lie has such a tendency, and an ad must be literally true. But even ads that are literally true may have a tendency to deceive and may run afoul of the commission's rules.

Intent and knowledge are not elements of deception. It does not matter whether the advertiser knew that the advertisement was false or had no intention to deceive consumers. The purpose of the FTC Act is to protect consumers, and therefore the burden is on the advertiser to present only truthful ads that do not mislead. Ads that have ambiguous meanings are interpreted strictly; that is, if the ad has two meanings, one of them legal and the other illegal, the ad will be interpreted to be illegal. The following classic case discusses the problems of ads that may have a "tendency to mislead."

# FTC v. Sterling Drug, Inc.

317 F.2d 669 (2d Circ., 1963)

In 1962 an article appeared in the *Journal of the American Medical Association* based on a study funded by the FTC, in which five pain relievers (Bayer Aspirin, St. Joseph's Aspirin, Bufferin, Anacin, and Excedrin) were studied as to both their pain-relieving effectiveness and their aftereffects. The conclusion of the article was that "[t]he data failed to show any statistically significant difference among any of the drugs." The researchers concluded, "Excedrin and Anacin form a group for which the incidence of upset stomach is significantly greater than is the incidence after Bayer Aspirin, St. Joseph's Aspirin, Bufferin, or the placebo. The rates of upset stomach associated with these last 4 treatments are not significantly different, one from the other."

Sterling, the manufacturer of Bayer Aspirin, quickly took out a large advertisement in *LIFE* magazine which read:

*Government-Supported Medical Team Compares Bayer Aspirin and Four Other Popular Pain Relievers*

Findings reported in the highly authoritative *Journal of the American Medical Association* reveal that the higher priced combination-of-ingredients pain relievers upset the stomach with significantly greater frequency than any of the other products tested, while Bayer Aspirin brings relief that is as fast, as strong, and as gentle to the stomach as you can get.

This important new medical study, supported by a grant from the federal government, was undertaken to compare the stomach-upsetting effects, the speed of relief and the amount of relief offered by five leading pain relievers, including Bayer Aspirin, aspirin with buffering, and combination-of-ingredients products. Here is a summary of the findings.

*Upset Stomach*

According to this report, the higher priced combination-of-ingredients products upset the stomach with significantly greater frequency than any of the other products tested, while Bayer Aspirin, taken as directed, is as gentle to the stomach as a plain sugar pill.

*Speed and Strength*

The study shows that there is no significant difference among the products tested in rapidity of onset, strength or duration of relief. Nonetheless, it is interesting to know that within just fifteen minutes, Bayer Aspirin had a somewhat higher pain relief score than any of the other products.

*Price*

As unreasonable as it may seem, the products which are most likely to upset the stomach—that is, the combination-of-ingredients products—actually cost substantially more than Bayer Aspirin. The fact is that these products, as well as the buffered product, cost up to 75% more than Bayer Aspirin.

The FTC brought an action to prevent the circulation of this ad on the grounds that it was false and misleading. The trial judge refused to grant an injunction, and the FTC appealed to the U.S. Court of Appeals.

**Kaufman, J.**    It is not difficult to understand the heartwarming reception [the] article received in the upper echelons of Sterling and its Madison Avenue colleagues; no sooner were the results of the study published . . . when Sterling Drug and its advertising agencies decided to make the most of them. This decision, we may fairly assume, did not surprise Sterling's competitors. The public had long been saturated with various claims proved by the study to be of doubtful validity. One of the products had boasted in its advertisements that it "works twice as fast as aspirin" and "protects you against the stomach distress you can get from aspirin alone," another that it "does not upset the stomach" and is better than aspirin and yet another, that it is "50% stronger than aspirin." Believing that the Judgment Day has finally arrived and seeking to counteract the many years of hard-sell by what it now believed to be the hard facts, Sterling and its co-defendants prepared and disseminated [the] advertising. . . .

The Commission alleged and sought to prove that the . . . advertising falsely represented directly and by implication: (a) that the findings . . . were endorsed and approved by the United States Government; (b) that the publication of the article . . . is evidence of endorsement and approval . . . by the medical profession; (c) that . . . Bayer Aspirin is not upsetting to the stomach and is as gentle thereto as a sugar pill; (d) that . . . Bayer Aspirin . . . affords a higher degree of pain relief than any other product tested. . . .

The legal principles to be applied here are quite clear. The central purpose of the provisions of the Federal Trade Commission Act under discussion is in effect to abolish the rule of *caveat emptor* which traditionally defined rights and responsibilities in the world of commerce. That rule can no longer be relied upon as a means of rewarding fraud and deception . . . and has been replaced by a rule which gives to the consumer the right to rely upon representations of facts as the truth. . . . In order best to implement the prophylactic purpose of the statute, it has been consistently held that advertising falls within its proscription not only when there is proof of actual deception but also when the representations made have a capacity or tendency to deceive, i.e., when there is a likelihood or fair probability that the reader will be misled. . . . For the same reason, proof of intention to deceive is not requisite to a finding of violation of the statute . . . ; since the purpose of the statute is not to punish the wrongdoer but to protect the public, the cardinal factor is the probable effect which the advertiser's handiwork will have upon the eye and mind of the reader. It is therefore necessary in these cases to consider the advertisement in its entirety and not to engage in disputatious dissection. The entire mosaic should be viewed rather than each tile separately. . . .

Unlike that abiding faith which the law has in the "reasonable man," it has very little faith indeed in the intellectual acuity of the "ordinary purchaser" who is the object of the advertising campaign.

The general public has been defined as "that vast multitude which includes the ignorant, and unthink-

ing and the credulous, who, in making purchases, do not stop to analyze but too often are governed by appearances and general impressions. The average purchaser has been variously characterized as not "straight thinking," subject to "impressions," uneducated, and grossly misinformed; he is influenced by prejudice and superstition; and he wishfully believes in miracles, allegedly the result of progress in science. . . . [Callman, *Unfair Competition and Trademarks*, 19.2 (a)(1) at 341–44(1950), and the cases there cited].

It is well established that advertising need not be literally false in order to fall within the proscription of the act. Gone for the most part, fortunately, are the days when the advertiser was so lacking in subtlety as to represent his nostrum as superlative for "arthritis, rheumatism, neuralgia, sciatica, lumbago, gout, coronary thrombosis, brittle bones, bad teeth, malfunctioning glands, infected tonsils, infected appendix, gallstones, neuritis, underweight, constipation, indigestion, lack of energy, lack of vitality, lack of ambition, and inability to sleep. . . ." See *FTC v National Health Aids, Inc.* . . . (1952). The courts are no longer content to insist simply upon the "most literal truthfulness," . . . for we have increasingly come to recognize that "Advertisements as a whole may be completely misleading although every sentence separately considered is literally true. This may be because things are omitted that should be said, or because advertisements are composed or purposefully printed in such a way as to mislead."

. . . There are two obvious methods of employing a true statement so as to convey a false impression. One is the half truth, where the statement is removed from its context and the nondisclosure of its context renders the statement misleading . . . ; a second is the ambiguity, where the statement in context has two or more commonly understood meanings one of which is deceptive. . . .

The Federal Trade Commission . . . concedes that none of the statements made therein is literally false, but it contends that the half-truths and ambiguities of the advertisement give it "reason to believe" that our hypothetical, sub-intelligent, less-than-careful reader will be misled thereby. Thus we are told that the reference . . . to a "Government-Supported Medical Team" gives the misleading impression that the United States Government endorsed or approved the findings. . . . Surely the fact that the word "supported" might have alternative dictionary definitions . . . is not alone sufficient. . . . Most words *do* have alternative dictionary definitions; if that in itself were a sufficient legal criterion, few advertisements would survive. Here, no impression is conveyed that the product itself has its source in or is being endorsed by the Government. . . .

The Commission's third objection deals with . . . the statement that "Bayer Aspirin, taken as directed, is as gentle to the stomach as a plain sugar pill." "Sugar pill," we are told, is misleading terminology; the advertisement should have used the word "placebo." Again, we are confronted by a simple problem of communication. For how can we expect our hypothetically slow-witted reader to react when he reads that "Bayer Aspirin is as gentle to the stomach as a placebo"! Most likely, he will either read on completely unaware of the significance of the statement, or impatiently turn the page. Perhaps he will turn to his neighbor, and in response to a request for a definition of the troublesome word be greeted with the plausible query, "A *what?*" (This assumes that the reader will have been able to muster the correct pronunciation of the word.) But, all this aside, the pill used as a control in this case was indeed constituted of milk sugar [and a cornstarch binder] and the use of the term "sugar pill" was neither inaccurate nor misleading.

The Commission relies heavily . . . upon *P. Lorillard Co. v FTC*. . . . There, *Reader's Digest* sponsored a scientific study of the major cigarettes. . . . It accompanied its conclusions with a chart which revealed that, although Old Gold cigarettes ranked lowest in [nicotine, tars, and resins], the quantitative differences between the brands were insignificant. . . . The tenor of the study is revealed by the cheery words to the smoker "who need no longer worry as to which cigarette can most effectively nail down his coffin. For one nail is just about as good as another." Old Gold trumpeted its dubious success, claiming that it was found lowest in nicotine, tars and resins. . . . The Court quite properly upheld a cease and desist order. . . . An examination of that case shows that it is completely distinguishable in at least two obvious and significant respects. Although the statements made by Old Gold were at best literally true, they were used in the advertisement to convey an impression diametrically opposed to that intended by the writer of the article. . . . Moreover as to the specifics of brand-comparison, it was found that anyone reading the advertisement would gain "the very definite impression that Old Gold cigarettes were less irritating to the throat and less harmful than other leading brands. . . . The truth was exactly the opposite. . . . " In the instant case, Sterling Drug can in no sense be said to have conveyed a misleading impression as to either the spirit or the specifics of the article published in the *Journal of the American Medical Association*.

[Affirmed.]

## Case Discussion Questions

1   Was the advertisement *true?* Were there any misstatements of fact in the advertisement?
2   Would a *reasonable person* believe that the advertisement implied (1) government sponsorship or endorsement of the study? (2) that Bayer is as gentle as a sugar pill? (3) that Bayer is more effective than other products? Would a large number of consumers believe those things?
3   Does this advertisement *hurt* consumers? Competitors?

**The Fool's Standard and the Reasonable Person**   Since at least the 1930's, the FTC Act was considered to be intended to protect the *general public*, which includes "the ignorant, the unthinking, and the credulous." This test, known as the **fool's standard,** has been replaced by a **reasonable person** standard before the FTC, but not before all courts.

Under the fool's standard, it did not matter that most of the consuming public would disbelieve a deceptive ad. As the Supreme Court noted:

> There is no duty resting on a citizen to suspect the honesty of those with whom he transacts business. Laws are made to protect the trusting as well as the suspicious. The best element of business has long since decided that honesty should govern competitive enterprises, and that the rule of *caveat emptor* should not be relied upon to reward fraud and deception.

The question was not whether the ad would deceive a reasonable person, an intelligent person, or a wise or suspicious person; the question was whether the ad would tend to deceive even the dullest and most trusting member of the public.

The fool's standard has been severely criticized and may be in retreat before the courts in cases like *Sterling Drug*. The standard presents problems when sales *puffery* is involved. Almost every advertisement claims its product is the *best* or is *perfect* or *easy to use* or *safe and simple*, all terms that, if considered objectively and from the standpoint of any person but "the ignorant, the unthinking and the credulous," simply cannot be true. In general, the FTC has permitted such puffery on the grounds that it cannot be taken literally. Even puffery may violate the act if a product cannot possibly fulfill the claims. For example, products that are purchased from junk dealers or are worn, dirty, or valueless cannot be "the best in the market."

In 1983, in a major policy change, the FTC announced a "Policy Statement on Enforcement of Deceptive Acts and Practices," which seems to overturn the fool's standard. Under the new policy, to be deceptive the representation must be likely to mislead "reasonable consumers under the circumstances." The test is whether the consumer's interpretation of the advertisement is reasonable, and the FTC will look to the effect of the practice on a reasonable number of consumers in the group to whom the advertisement is targeted. Under this standard the FTC will generally not bring actions based on subjective claims, such as taste, feel, appearance, or smell, or on correctly stated opinion claims. Opinion claims continue to be actionable if they are not honestly held, if they misrepresent the qualifications of the holder or the basis of his or her opinion, or if the recipient reasonably interprets them as implied statements of fact.

The FTC Policy Statement also added the requirement of *materiality* as an element of deception. Some statements are presumptively material: any express claims; omission of information that the seller knows, or should know, or that an ordinary consumer would need to evaluate the product or service; or any false claims. The FTC Policy Statement also considers claims or omissions of material if they significantly involve health, safety, or other areas of concern to a reasonable consumer.

## DECEPTIVE ADVERTISING TECHNIQUES

In the words of the House Conference Report on the Wheeler-Lea Act, "[T]here is no limit to human inventiveness in the field" of deceptive advertising. Although the general principles apply to every case, imaginative advertisers have developed unnumbered methods of deceiving the public. The FTC has been confronted with numerous forms of deceptive advertising in the past, and it is impossible to list all the advertising practices that have been held illegal.

Generally speaking, the FTC has placed a great deal of emphasis on **deceptive price claims,** primarily because the FTC believes that consumers are especially subject to claims that they are getting a bargain. A second area of concern in recent years has been **bait-and-switch** advertising, in which consumers are *baited* into a store with the promise of a bargain, only to be *switched* to another product by sales talk or product unavailability. The FTC has also been concerned with **deceptive nondisclosure** of important facts; **endorsements and testimonials; tests and surveys;** and various **lotteries, contests,** and **games.** Table 14.1 contains information about many of those advertising techniques and the FTC responses to them.

TABLE 14.1    Deceptive Advertising and FTC Rules

| Deceptive Technique | Description or Example | FTC Response |
| --- | --- | --- |
| I. Deceptive Price Claims | | |
| A. Comparison to Former Prices | "Was $10.00 — Now $7.50" | Former price must be "actual, bona fide, price at which the article was offered to the public on a regular basis for a reasonably substantial period of time." |
| B. "Comparable Value" Claims | "Price elsewhere—$10.00. Our price—$7.50." | The "price elsewhere" must be the prevailing price in the area. Items must be essentially similar. |
| C. "List" and "Suggested Retail" Prices | "List price—$10.00. Our price—$7.50." | "Suggested" and "list" prices must be the prevailing price in the area. |
| D. Special Deals | "Fire Sale," "Going out of Business Sale," or "Sale" | The event (fire, going out of business) must actually occur and be the cause of reduced price. A "sale" must be a significant price reduction. |
| E. Two-for-One Sales | "2-for-1," "Half-Price Sale," "Buy One, Get One Free" | Price for two items must be the usual and customary retail price for a single article in the recent, regular course of business. |
| II. "Bait-and-Switch" Tactics | | |
| A. Baiting and Switching | Customer "baited" in with offer of incredibly low price. Seller induces consumer to "switch" to higher-priced good by disparaging lower-priced product or saying the desired one is unavailable. | Technique is illegal. "Trading up," by making customer aware of other products, is permissible, without disparagement of lower-priced product. |
| B. Switch after Sale | Similar to bait and switch, but customer buys lower-priced good. When the product fails to work, seller offers to sell higher-priced good and give credit. | Illegal, as bait advertising. |

TABLE 14.1    Deceptive Advertising and FTC Rules *(continued)*

| Deceptive Technique | Description or Example | FTC Response |
|---|---|---|
| III. Deceptive Nondisclosure | | |
| A. Product Contents and Construction | Failure to tell consumers something important about the product | 1. Variety of laws require specific labeling, such as cigarettes and wool products. 2. Reprocessed, rebuilt, secondhand, or repossessed goods must be labeled as such. 3. Changes in existing goods must be disclosed (e.g., change of ingredients). 4. Fact of simulation ("simulated diamonds") must be disclosed. |
| B. Product Hazards | Failure to warn of hazards | 1. Specific statutes give FTC authority to require disclosures (e.g., Flammable Fabrics Act, Cigarette Labelling Act, Hazardous Substance Act) 2. FTC may require other disclosures if products are hazardous. |
| C. Foreign Origin | Failure to disclose foreign manufacture | Disclosure is required, unless there are no American-produced competitors. |
| IV. Endorsements and Testimonials | False or Nonexistent Testimonials | Testimonials must be made by endorser, and must be truthful and based on actual use. |
| A. Implicit Government Endorsement | "Backed by the U.S. Government" "U.S. Testing Co." | The U.S. Government does not endorse products. |
| B. Deceptive Private Endorsement | "Mayo Brothers' Vitamins" "Red Cross Ambulance Service" | Deceptive, unless actual endorsement is made by organization. |
| C. Solicited and Paid Testimonials | Failure to disclose an endorsement was solicited or paid for | Truthful testimonials need not disclose fact they were solicited or paid for. |

TABLE 14.1    Deceptive Advertising and FTC Rules *(continued)*

| Deceptive Technique | Description or Example | FTC Response |
|---|---|---|
| V. Tests and Surveys | Use of incomplete or erroneous scientific tests or opinion surveys | Tests must be truthful in comparison with available products; must make reference to standards and conditions of the test. Samples must be accurate and fairly state the results. |
| VI. Lotteries, Contests, and Games | | |
| | 1. Lotteries (purchase is necessary) | Illegal |
| | 2. Contest (which involves some skill) | Permissible, but rules must be fully disclosed and truthfully represented. Prizes must actually exist and their value be fairly represented. |
| | 3. Games of chance (no purchase is necessary) | Prizes must be awarded randomly, all prizes must actually be awarded, and game must be secure against tampering. Must make complete disclosure of odds of winning, number of game pieces or entries, and list of winners. |

It is important to note that many of the specific deceptive techniques forbidden by the FTC are quite common, at least for local advertisers. The FTC simply does not have the manpower to investigate every potentially deceptive ad and depends on consumer complaints for leads.

### Pictures and Illustrations

A picture may be worth a thousand words and, in advertising, may be worth millions of dollars. Simply put, photographs and illustrations must accurately portray the product advertised. A photo of one product, showing features not present on the product to be sold, is clearly deceptive.

A hotly debated area involves **collateral misrepresentation,** in which the presence of a picture implies a fact that is not true. A photo of a man who is wearing a white coat with a stethoscope around his neck and is holding up a bottle of a pain reliever could create the impression that the product was endorsed by physicians. Such ads have been considered misrepresentations in some cases. If trick photography, such as superimposition or time-lapse photography, is used, that fact must be disclosed.

## PRO AND CON

# Will the marketplace make federal regulation of advertising unnecessary?

**Pro**   False and misleading advertising is controlled by far more effective forces than pervasive federal regulation. First, consumers are becoming more intelligent. Many kinds of false claims can be detected by ever more sophisticated consumers, and as education becomes even more widespread, consumers will be able to detect even more deceptive claims.

Second, false claims are discouraged by the cost to the seller of developing a reputation for unethical conduct. If a business depends on repeat business, a policy of false advertising will force those sellers from the market in the long run.

Third, competition deters false advertising. Competitors of the false advertisers have an incentive either to refute the false ad in the marketplace or to sue the false advertiser. Industry groups may also "self-regulate" their markets, and such regulation is more effective, because the members of the industry know the limits and demands of their own industry.

Fourth, consumers who are injured by false advertising have a right to bring actions for fraud or misrepresentation. Those actions even permit punitive damages. The emergence of class actions even encourages suits when small claims are involved.

The combination of these factors means that extensive federal regulation of advertising is unnecessary. Such regulation results in a "chilling" of advertising, potentially violates first amendment freedoms, and simply costs too much.

**Con**   The market cannot regulate false advertising claims. Certainly there is *some* effect from market forces, but the market cannot regulate advertising in an effective way. For example, consumer sophistication cannot detect claims regarding the chemical composition or technical construction of goods. Similarly, comparison shopping of sophisticated services, such as life insurance, credit prices, and financial terms, is beyond the means of all but the best-educated consumers. Obtaining the information necessary to judge claims is beyond consumers' means in many industries as well.

Clearly, some competitors are harmed by a reputation for false advertising, but other sellers are not harmed by such a reputation, including sellers who do not depend on repeat business and sellers of products where false claims are not likely to be detected, such as medical services. Industry "self-regulation" may be expensive and nonenforceable and will always be undertaken *in the interests of the industry*. For example, it is doubtful that the cigarette industry will regulate itself effectively.

Competitors may sue false advertisers or refute false claims, *if there is competition in the industry*. Monopolistic or oligopolistic industries are rarely subject to such actions, simply because there is little competition. The costs of lawsuits may be too high as well, and in some industries the competitors may *all* advertise falsely. Similarly, consumer lawsuits require extensive proof, expense, and time. Recent limits on federal class actions also mean fewer such suits will be brought.

## Roundtable Discussion

1   Are there industries whose advertising need not be regulated through federal law? Are there others whose claims *must* be regulated through federal intervention?
2   Why do you suppose advertising regulation began as an effort *by the advertising industry*? Have conditions changed so that those reasons no longer exist?
3   Are market forces sufficient to deter false advertising? Are those forces sufficient to deter *misleading* advertising? Is there a difference?

## Television Advertising

Over the last thirty years, television advertising has become the principal method of marketing products and a principal area of FTC concern. Television permits a wide variety of techniques to the advertiser and involves some broad opportunities for deception. But the limitations of the small screen also present difficulties for the advertiser who, in good faith, wants to comply with the law, and for the FTC, which wants to eliminate deception in advertising. As noted in one opinion:

> Everyone knows that on television all that glitters is not gold. On a black and white screen white looks grey and blue looks white; the lily must be painted. Coffee looks like mud. Real ice cream melts much more quickly than the firm but false sundae. The plain fact is, except by props and mock-ups, some objects cannot be shown on television as the viewer, in his mind's eye, knows the essence of the object.

Many of the same concerns raised about still pictures may be raised regarding television. The product actually advertised must be pictured, and collateral misrepresentation is also controlled. The TV screen lends itself particularly to tests and demonstrations. Such tests should prove some *meaningfully relevant point about the product*. For example, one ad showed two separate razors, the advertised brand and a "nonsafety" variety, each "shaving" a boxing glove. The nonsafety razor left a long, ugly gash in the glove, whereas the advertised brand did no damage at all. The FTC said the demonstration was theatrical but proved nothing except that the advertised razor was better at shaving boxing gloves. The following decision considers the problem of television advertising in detail.

## FTC v. Colgate-Palmolive Co.
380 U.S. 374, 85 S. Ct. 1035, 13 L. Ed. 2d 904 (1965)

In the court's words, this case "arises out of an attempt by respondent Colgate-Palmolive Company to prove to the television public that its shaving cream, Rapid Shave 'outshaves them all'." At issue were three TV commercials designed to show that Rapid Shave could even shave sandpaper. An announcer told the audience that "To prove Rapid Shave's supermoisturizing power, we put it right from the can onto this tough, dry sandpaper. It was apply—soak—and off in one stroke." The camera showed the process while the announcer spoke.

In fact, sandpaper could not be shaved immediately following the application of Rapid Shave but required eighty minutes of soaking. And in fact, the substance was not sandpaper at all, but a simulated mock-up consisting of Plexiglas to which sand had been applied. The mock-up was used because TV signals would have made real sandpaper look like colored paper. Neither the moistening time nor the mock-up was disclosed to the viewing public. In fact, however, Rapid Shave could shave sandpaper, given sufficient moistening time.

The FTC held that the commercials were deceptive and issued a cease and desist order. The court of appeals affirmed but refused that part of the commission's order that forbade the future use of undisclosed simulations. The question before the court was the proper use of simulations and mock-ups. The company had not contested the holding that the commercial itself was a misrepresentation of the fact that Rapid Shave could *immediately* shave sandpaper. The FTC appealed.

**Mr. Chief Justice Warren Delivered the Opinion of the Court**  We granted certiorari to consider the Commission's conclusion that even if an advertiser has himself conducted a test, experiment or demonstration which he honestly believes will prove a certain product claim, he may not convey to television viewers the false impression that they are seeing the test, experiment or demonstration for themselves, when they are not because of the undisclosed use of mock-ups.

. . . The parties agree that §5 prohibits the intentional misrepresentation of any fact which would constitute a material factor in a purchaser's decision whether to buy. They differ, however, in their conception of what "facts" constitute a "material factor" in a purchaser's decision to buy. Respondents submit, in effect, that the material facts are those which deal with the substantive qualities of a product. The Commission, on the other hand, submits that the misrepresentation of *any* fact so long as it materially induces a purchaser's decision to buy is a deception prohibited by §5.

The Commission's interpretation of what is a deceptive practice seems more in line with the decided cases than that of respondents. This Court said . . . "[T]he public is entitled to get what it chooses, though the choice may be dictated by caprice or by fashion or perhaps by ignorance." . . .

Respondents claim that [prior] cases are irrelevant to our decision because they involve misrepresentations related to the product itself and not merely to the manner in which an advertising message is communicated. This distinction misses the mark for two reasons. In the first place, the present case is not concerned with a mode of communication, but with a misrepresentation that viewers have objective proof of a seller's product claim over and above the seller's word. Secondly, all of the above cases, like the present case, deal with methods designed to get a consumer to purchase a product, not with whether the product, when purchased, will perform up to expectations. . . .

We agree with the Commission, therefore, that the undisclosed use of plexiglass in the present commercials was a material deceptive practice. . . . Respondents claim that it will be impractical to inform the viewing public that it is not seeing an actual test, experiment or demonstration, but we think it inconceivable that the ingenious advertising world will be unable, if it so desires, to conform to the Commission's insistence that the public not be misinformed. If, however, it becomes impossible or impractical to show simulated demonstrations on television in a truthful manner, this indicates that television is not a medium that lends itself to this type of commercial, not that the commercial must survive at all costs. Similarly unpersuasive is respondents' objection that the Commission's decision discriminates against sellers whose product claims cannot be "verified" on television without the use of simulations. All methods of advertising do not equally favor every seller. If the inherent limitations of a method do not permit its use in the way a seller desires, the seller cannot by material misrepresentation compensate for those limitations. . . .

The Court of Appeals has criticized the reference in the Commission's order to "test, experiment, or demonstration" as not capable of practical interpretation. It could find no difference between the Rapid Shave commercial and a commercial which extolled the goodness of ice cream while giving viewers a picture of a scoop of mashed potatoes appearing to be ice cream. We do not understand this difficulty. In the ice cream case the mashed potato prop is not being used for additional proof of the product claim, while the purpose of the Rapid Shave commercial is to give the viewer objective proof of the claims made. If in the ice cream hypothetical the focus of the commercial becomes the undisclosed potato prop and the viewer is invited, explicitly or by implication, to see for himself the truth of the claims about the ice cream's rich texture and full color, and perhaps compare it to a "rival product," then the commercial has become similar to the one now before us. Clearly, however, a commercial which depicts happy actors delightedly eating ice cream that is in fact mashed potatoes or drinking a product appearing to be coffee but which is in fact some other substance is not covered by the present order. . . .

[Reversed.]

## Case Discussion Questions

1  What harm did the advertisement cause? Who was hurt?

2  Under what circumstances must an advertiser disclose the fact that a simulation is being used?

3  What remedy did the FTC obtain? What good does that remedy do? Hasn't the damage already been done?

## FTC REMEDIES FOR DECEPTIVE ADVERTISING

### Cease and Desist Orders and Civil Penalties

For most of its history, the FTC was restricted to issuing cease and desist orders to offenders. In 1975 the remedies were broadly expanded in the Federal Trade Commission Improvements Act. Under that act, the FTC may bring an action in its own name to recover civil penalties from offenders. A civil action may be brought against any advertiser directly in federal court, and the penalty for violation is a civil fine of up to $10,000 for each violation.

### Retroactive Advertising

One recent technique used by the FTC is **retroactive advertising,** which is a type of cease and desist order that requires an advertiser to correct the mistaken impression left by the misleading scheme. Retroactive, or *corrective*, advertising has become a popular method of remedying deceptive advertising, as described in the following case.

# *Warner-Lambert Co. v. FTC*
562 F.2d 749 (D.C. Circuit, 1977)

Warner-Lambert, the manufacturer of Listerine mouthwash, advertised that Listerine "kills germs by million on contact" on its label and claimed in its television ads that Listerine cured colds. At a hearing it was shown that Listerine in fact "has no efficacy in the prevention of colds, sore throats or in the amelioration of colds symptoms, including sore throats." Following the hearing, the FTC issued a cease and desist order, which ordered the firm to:

(1) cease and desist from representing that Listerine will cure colds or sore throats, prevent colds or sore throats, or that users of Listerine will have fewer colds than nonusers;
(2) cease and desist from representing that Listerine is a treatment for, or will lessen the severity of colds or sore throats; that it will have any significant beneficial effect on symptoms of colds, or that the ability of Listerine to kill germs is of medical significance in the treatment of colds or sore throats or their symptoms;
(3) cease and desist from disseminating any advertisement for Listerine unless it is clearly and conspicuously disclosed in each such advertisement, in the exact language below, that: "Contrary to prior advertising, Listerine will not help prevent colds or sore throats or lessen their severity." This requirement extends only to the next ten million dollars of Listerine advertising.

Warner-Lambert appealed the order to the U.S Circuit Court of Appeals.

**J. Skelly Wright, Circuit Judge**    Petitioner contends that even if its advertising claims in the past were false, the portion of the Commission's order requiring "corrective advertising" exceeds the Commission's statutory power. The argument is based upon a literal reading of section 5 of the Federal Trade Commission Act, which authorizes the Commission to issue "cease and desist" orders against violators and does not expressly mention any other remedies. The Commission's position, on the other hand, is that the affirmative disclosure that Listerine will not prevent colds or lessen their severity is absolutely necessary to give effect to the prospective cease and desist order; a hundred years of false cold claims have built up a large reservoir of erroneous consumer belief which would persist, unless corrected, long after petitioner ceased making the claims.

. . . [T]he threshold question is whether the Commission has the authority to issue such an order. We hold that it does. . . .

. . . [I]t is clear that the Commission has the power to shape remedies which go beyond the simple cease and desist order. Our next inquiry must be whether a corrective advertising order is for any reason outside the range of permissible remedies. Petitioner . . . argue[s] that it is because (1) legislative history precludes it, (2) it impinges on the First Amendment, and (3) it has never been approved by any court.

**A. Legislative History**    Petitioner relies on the legislative history of the 1914 Federal Trade Commission Act and the Wheeler-Lea amendments to it in 1938 for the proposition that corrective advertising was not contemplated. In 1914 and in 1938 Congress chose not to authorize such remedies as criminal penalties, treble damages, or civil penalties, but that fact does not dispose of the question of corrective advertising. . . . [P]etitioner's construction of [the statute] runs directly contrary to the congressional intent as expressed in a later subsection: "Nothing in this section shall be construed to affect any authority of the Commission under any other provision of law." ,

[In the next section, the Court rejected the claim that corrective advertising was barred by the first amendment. Later, Warner-Lambert raised the issue once again on rehearing, basing its arguments on *Virginia State Board of Pharmacy v. Virginia Citizen's Consumer Council* (see p. 123). The Court found that "[u]ntruthful speech, commercial or otherwise, has never been protected for its own sake" and that the FTC could restrict and correct such speech.—Ed.]

The concept [of corrective advertising] is well established. It is simply that under certain circumstances an advertiser may be required to make affirmative disclosure of unfavorable facts.

One such circumstance is when an advertisement that did not contain the disclosure would be misleading. For example, the Commission has ordered the sellers of treatments for baldness to disclose

that the vast majority of cases of thinning hair and baldness are attributable to heredity, age, and endocrine balance (so-called "male pattern baldness") and that their treatment would have no effect whatever on this type of baldness. It has ordered the promoters of a device for stopping bed wetting to disclose that the device would not be of value in cases caused by organic defects or diseases. And it has ordered the makers of Geritol, an iron supplement, to disclose that Geritol will relieve symptoms of tiredness only in persons who suffer from iron deficiency anemia, and that the vast majority of people who experience such symptoms do not have such a deficiency.

Having established that the Commission does have the power to order corrective advertising in appropriate cases, it remains to consider whether use of the remedy against Listerine is warranted and equitable. We have concluded that part 3 of the order should be modified to delete the phrase "Contrary to prior advertising." With that modification, we approve the order.

The Commission has adopted the following standard for the imposition of corrective advertising:

> [I]f a deceptive advertisement has played a substantial role in creating or reinforcing in the public's mind a false and material belief which lives on after the false advertising ceases, there is clear and continuing injury to competition and to the consuming public as consumers continue to make purchasing decisions based on the false belief. Since this injury cannot be averted by merely requiring respondent to cease disseminating the advertisement, we may appropriately order respondent to take affirmative action designed to terminate the otherwise continuing ill effects of the advertisement.

We think this standard is entirely reasonable. It dictates two factual inquiries: (1) did Listerine's advertisements play a substantial role in creating or reinforcing in the public's mind a false belief about the product? and (2) would this belief linger on after the false advertising ceases? It strikes us that if the answer to both questions is not yes, companies everywhere may be wasting their massive advertising budgets. Indeed, it is more than a little peculiar to hear petitioner assert that its commercials really have no effect on consumer belief. . . .

[W]e believe the preamble "Contrary to prior advertising" is not necessary. It can serve only two purposes: either to attract attention that a correction follows or to humiliate the advertiser. The Commission claims only the first purpose for it, and this we think is obviated by the other terms of the order. The second purpose, if it were intended, might be called for in an egregious case of deliberate deception, but this is not one. . . .

Accordingly, the order, as modified, is affirmed.

## Case Discussion Questions

1  Under what circumstances will the FTC order corrective advertising?

2  Why did the Court delete the phrase "Contrary to prior advertising" from the required disclosure?

3  How long should the corrective ads run?

## SUMMARY AND CONCLUSIONS

Deceptive and misleading advertising is regulated by the common law, state statutes, and the Federal Trade Commission Act. Common law theories of regulation included fraud and warranty theories, both of which are difficult to prove and less than satisfactory to control misleading advertising. Common law protections of competition are somewhat more satisfactory, but the torts of trademark infringement, disparagement, passing off and simulation, misappropriation, and malicious competition are also difficult to prove.

In the 1914 Federal Trade Commission Act, "unfair methods of competition" were prohibited. A 1938 amendment, the Wheeler-Lea Act, extended the protections of the FTC Act to consumers and enabled the FTC to reach deceptive or misleading advertising.

In considering such misleading or deceptive advertising, the FTC has generally required an act to be literally true, and even a tendency to deceive in a literally truthful advertisement will be considered misleading. The standard applied by the courts is the so-called fool's standard, in which the question is whether the ad would deceive the most ignorant and unthinking consumer. The fool's standard has been abandoned by the FTC, however. The deception need not be intentional or even made with knowledge of its falsity, and ambiguous ads will be construed to violate the statute.

Under these strict standards, the FTC has developed rules and guidelines covering a large number of specific forms of deception. Generally, the courts have found that a commission determination, if based on the evidence, should stand.

## REVIEW QUESTIONS

1  Do the *FTC Guides* really help the average businessperson? How many of the retailers in your hometown do you think have read them? Should the FTC advertise the guides? How?

2  What is the fool's standard? Should it be changed? To what? What level of education would you pick? If you picked the average level of education or intelligence, does that mean it is

permissible to deceive half the population? Whom are we trying to protect, anyway?

3  Should ads directed at children be treated differently? In what ways?

4  The FTC may prohibit truthful ads that have only a tendency to deceive the most ignorant and credulous consumer. It need not prove intent or knowledge, and it now may sue for

damages, civil penalties, and restitution and order retroactive advertising. Even in light of the *Virginia Pharmacy* case discussed in Chapter 5, doesn't all this violate the first amendment?

5 Explain the nature of FTC regulation of price comparisons, bait and switch, testimonials, and the use of simulations and mock-ups on TV.

6 Clairol hair coloring was advertised as coloring the hair permanently. Obviously, since hair grows, this cannot be the case. Has Clairol violated the FTC Act? [*Gelb v. FTC*, 144 F.2d 580 (2d Cir., 1944).]

7 Wonder Bread was advertised with a television sequence that showed a human-looking figure magically "grow" in the background, while an announcer stated that "Wonder Bread builds strong bodies twelve ways," and made other statements which implied that the product was responsible or helpful in the growth of children. The bread did contain extra vitamins, but there was no proof that the bread had any effect on children's growth. What result would you expect? Does the result change at all if the commercials are run on a children's cartoon show? [*In Re ITT Continental Baking Co.* 83 FTC 947 (1973).]

8 Sly owns a patent medicine company that advertises Sly's Tonic, a concoction of various vitamins, as a cure-all for baldness, gout, debilitation, and the common cold. Petruchio, who is not very bright, believes the ad and purchases the tonic, although virtually no one else believes the representation. Has Sly violated the FTC Act? Would he be prosecuted?

9 Helena, the owner of an appliance store, advertises a Rousillon Electric Range at a price of $350, with the representation that the price is "one-third off of our regular price, $100 under list, and $75 under comparable values in this area." In fact, Helena had never sold Rousillon ranges before, and no one else in 50 miles sold such ranges. The "list" price was indeed $450, but no one ever charged that price. What result would you anticipate?

10 Audrey, a famous author, was asked to endorse Le Beau wine in a magazine advertisement. Audrey was in fact a teetotaler and had never drunk Le Beau wine or any other kind. The money offered for the ad was too good, however, and Audrey took one sip of wine before the ad was published. The ad quoted Audrey as saying Le Beau was "the best wine I ever tasted." Is the ad deceptive?

# C H A P T E R  1 5

# Consumer Law: Debtor-Creditor Relations

The American economy is built on credit. Our economic system probably could not have been built without borrowed funds. Consumer credit rose dramatically in the 1950's and 1960's and in large measure fueled the economic revival of those decades. Installment payments and credit cards became a way of life for many consumers, running directly against the "cash only" practices of their Depression-oriented parents.

With the increased availability of credit came increased abuse of the credit system by creditors and consumers alike. As Chief Justice Burger noted in *Mourning v. Family Publications Service*[1]

> From the end of World War II to 1967, the amount of . . . credit outstanding had increased from $5.6 billion to $95.9 billion, a rate of growth more than 4 1/2 times as great as that of the economy. Yet, as . . . congressional hearings [on the Truth-in-Lending Act] revealed, consumers remained remarkably ignorant of the nature of their credit obligations and of the cost of deferring payments. Because of the divergent, and at times fraudulent, practices by which consumers were informed of the terms of the credit extended to them, many consumers were prevented from shopping for the best terms available and, at times, were prompted to assume liabilities they could not meet. . . .

Sellers of goods and creditors usually have the upper hand in most transactions, if for no other reason than that they know their business, whereas consumers are sometimes remarkably ignorant of the transactions into which they enter. Consumers were unable to shop for credit because different creditors advertised their credit terms differently ("10% per year," "3% per quarter," "1 and 1/2% per month," etc.). Abusive collection techniques, including misrepresentation, threats, and calls to employers, were commonplace. Credit reports, created by private companies for profit, were often wrong, misleading, or available to anyone willing to pay for them. Bills came haphazardly and were often erroneous or incomprehensible. Collection techniques permitted by the law, such as confession of judgment clauses and wage assignments, clearly favored creditors, even when the debt was not owed. The only recourse to many consumers was bankruptcy, and some consumers abused that right by filing as often as the law allowed and running up large debts just before filing.

In the 1960's, consumer groups began lobbying state and federal authorities for

---

1 411 U.S. 356, 93 S. Ct. 1652, 36 L. Ed. 2d 318 (1973).

changes in the credit system. Those changes resulted in major federal and state statutes. As a result of those statutes, consumers now have substantial protection against abuses by creditors. Those protections are the subject of this chapter.

This chapter considers several problems in the debtor-creditor relationship. First, we briefly examine some of the ways in which the law aids creditors in the collection of debts. The chapter then discusses the federal and state regulations imposed on creditors and collection practices, including the federal Truth-in-Lending Act, the federal Fair Credit Reporting Act, the Fair Debt Collection Practices Act, and others. The chapter concludes with a discussion of bankruptcy, perhaps the ultimate consumer protection law.

## COLLECTION PROCEDURES

A person who owes another is called a **debtor,** and the person to whom a debt is owed is known as a **creditor.** If a debtor fails to pay a debt, the creditor has the right to bring a legal action against the debtor and obtain a judgment. That judgment permits the creditor to use the power of the law to collect the debt through procedures like **writs of execution, citations to discover assets, attachments** of property, **foreclosures** of liens, or **garnishments** of wages (see Figure 15.1). Limits on the amounts that a creditor may receive are imposed through state laws, including limitations on garnishments and the **homestead exemption.** In addition, a creditor may **repossess** secured property, either through a court proceeding known as **replevin** or in some cases through **self-help.** It is important to note at the outset that procedures vary widely from state to state. Debtors often pay judgments voluntarily as well.

### Writs of Execution

A **writ of execution** is a legal demand for payment of a judgment. Once a final judgment has been entered, the owner of the judgment, known as the **judgment creditor,** may have a writ of execution served on the party owing the debt, known as the **judgment debtor.** The judgment debtor may pay the debt by simply paying the officer who delivers the writ. In many cases the writ is *unsatisfied* (unpaid), however. In many states an unsatisfied writ of execution is required before other collection procedures may be used.

### Discovery of Assets

**Discovery of assets** is not strictly a collection proceeding, but rather a procedure to learn the nature and location of the judgment debtor's property and income. After a judgment is rendered, the successful judgment creditor may have a document served upon the judgment debtor, ordering the judgment debtor to appear in court to answer questions under oath concerning the location of assets and the nature of income available to pay the judgment. In some states that document is known as a **subpoena to discover assets** or a **citation to discover assets.** The debtor must answer the questions or face contempt of court. In many states the plaintiff may call other witnesses in the citation proceeding as well. The citation may also order the debtor to bring records to court.

At this hearing, the court may issue an order to the defendant to pay the creditor, either completely or in installments. This order is sometimes called a **charging order.** If the debtor fails to pay as ordered, the court may order the debtor to show cause why he

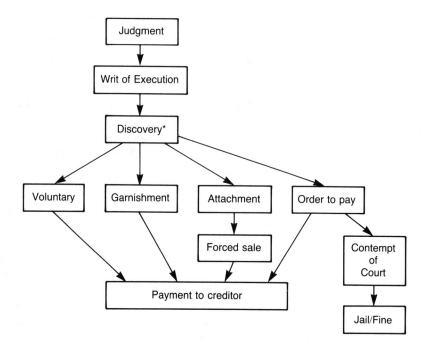

*Discovery is not essential; in some states a subpoena or citation is used to discover assets.

FIGURE 15.1   The Collection Process

or she should not be punished for contempt of court. Almost as importantly, the creditor obtains knowledge of the debtor's employer and the location of bank accounts, securities, real estate, and other assets.

### Attachments

An **attachment** is the act of taking "legal custody" of property. Attachments, which may issue against property in the hands of the debtor or third persons, are effectively court orders requiring the person holding property to turn it over to the creditor or to the court. For example, if A owes B $1,000 on a judgment, and A has an account in the XYZ Bank, B may have an attachment served on the bank, ordering the bank to turn over up to $1,000 to B or to the court. Property other than cash may be sold at public auction. The costs of sale are usually subtracted from the proceeds before they are turned over to the creditor. If the sale yields a surplus over the amount of the debt, that amount is paid to the debtor.

### Garnishments

A **garnishment** is a proceeding directed toward a third person requiring the third person to turn over assets belonging to a debtor. The procedure is most often used in the case of wages, although, strictly speaking, any attachment of property in the hands of third persons is a garnishment.

For example, if A has a judgment for $5,000 against B, and B is employed by the LMN Company, A may file a garnishment against LMN, claiming any wages owed by LMN to B. The employer must often answer **interrogatories** about the amounts owed and is ordered to retain those sums for a period of time. The creditor may then request **execution** (payment) on the sums held by the employer. If the employer fails to respond to interrogatories or fails to withhold wages, it may be held in contempt of court, or may, in some states, become liable for the amounts that should have been withheld, or even for the entire debt.

Most states and the federal government impose limits on the amount that may be withheld from an employee's wages. The Federal Wage Garnishment Act limits that amount and gives some protection from dismissal to employees whose wages have been garnished.

## Foreclosures

The remedy of **foreclosure** is limited to situations in which the creditor has some **lien**, or legal claim, on a particular piece of property. For example, if a creditor has loaned money to purchase a house and has taken a mortgage on that house, the creditor may foreclose the mortgage if the debtor fails to live up to the terms of the mortgage agreement. State statutes grant a variety of liens in other circumstances as well. For example, many states give a **mechanic's lien** to people who have provided labor or materials to a piece of real estate. If the owner of the property fails to pay for the labor or materials, the lien may be foreclosed and the property sold to pay the debt.

State law imposes a variety of limits and procedures on foreclosures. Ordinarily, a very specific type of lawsuit must be filed, usually preceded by notice of default and an opportunity to pay the debt. If judgment is rendered in favor of the creditor, the debtor again receives some time to pay the debt, followed by a foreclosure sale, usually at public auction. The purchaser at the sale pays the debt, and the debtor again has the opportunity to **redeem** from the sale for a period of time by paying the purchaser the amount he or she paid. Those periods during which the debtor may pay the debt and keep the property are known as **periods of redemption** and vary widely in length, from a few days to a year or more. Foreclosure procedure varies widely from state to state.

## Repossession and Replevin

If personal property is used as security for a debt, the creditor may *repossess* the property if the debtor fails to pay or otherwise breaches the agreement. Many creditors use *self-help*, by simply taking the property, but that technique is filled with danger, both legal and otherwise. The right of repossession is created by agreement between the parties.

The creditor may also file a **replevin** action to obtain the property. A replevin action is a specific form of lawsuit requiring notice and perhaps involving a redemption period similar to a foreclosure. Such actions result in court orders to turn over the property. If a debtor fails to turn over the property, he or she may be subject to contempt of court. Creditors may be able to take possession of the property before the case is heard, but many states require the creditor to post a bond.

### State Limits on Collection Procedures

All states impose limits on the amount of property or income that may be taken in collection proceedings. Most statutes provide a list of certain kinds of property that cannot be taken to satisfy a debt, including items like the family Bible, personal clothing, tools, and medical supplies. The debtor may often choose other personal property up to a certain dollar limit (commonly $500 or $1,000) that will be exempt.

Most states also provide a **homestead exemption,** which permits debtors to protect a certain amount or value of real estate from the claims of creditors. For example, a state statute may provide a homestead exemption of $5,000, which means that real property up to the value of $5,000 is exempt from creditors. If A has a judgment against B for $20,000, and B owns a piece of real estate worth $15,000, the property may be sold, but B will receive $5,000 from the proceeds of the sale. A will receive $10,000 from those proceeds to apply to the debt.

Finally, most states provide that garnishments cannot take all of a person's wages for any period. Often the law permits the debtor to receive some amount of those wages each pay period, so that the debtor and the debtor's family have something on which to live during the garnishment period. Those laws often provide a sliding scale varying with the size of the debtor's family. If there is not enough money to satisfy a debt, the judgment remains outstanding for a period of years (often seven years), until it lapses by law. The creditor may renew the judgment for an additional period of time and may use any collection proceedings at any time.

## FEDERAL REGULATION OF CREDIT

To stop some of the possible abuses of the debtor-creditor relationship, the federal government has imposed a variety of regulations, including the federal Truth-in-Lending and Truth-in-Leasing acts; the Fair Credit Reporting, Fair Credit Billing, Fair Debt Collection Practices, and Electronic Funds Transfer acts; the Real Estate Settlement Procedures Act; the Equal Credit Opportunity Act; and a variety of Federal Trade Commission rules. State governments have also imposed a variety of similar laws, as discussed in the next section.

### Federal Truth-in-Lending Act

The federal **Consumer Credit Protection Act,** also known as the **Truth-in-Lending Act,** attempts to provide remedies for credit abuses through disclosure of credit terms to consumers and prospective consumers. The House Committee Report on this law stated that "[b]y requiring all creditors to disclose credit information in a uniform manner . . . the American consumer will be given the information he or she needs to compare the cost of credit and to make the best informed decision on the use of credit."

The Truth-in-Lending Act is a *disclosure* law. It does not impose many specific requirements for credit itself but depends instead on the marketplace. The purposes of the act are to provide consumers with information so that they may shop for the best credit deal available and to require that the information disclosed by *all* creditors be in similar form.

The act applies to any individual or firm that extends or arranges for consumer credit, including financial institutions, stores, credit card issuers, and finance companies; and it reaches all extensions "of credit for personal, family, household or agricultural purposes." The act does not apply to personal loans over $25,000, business and commercial loans, transactions involving an SEC-registered securities or commodities broker, and some public utility charges made by regulated companies. Home mortgages, regardless of amount, are covered.

Authority to administer the act was given to the Federal Reserve Board, and in 1969 the board issued specific regulations, known as **Regulation Z,** to implement the act. In addition to the Federal Reserve, nine other government agencies administer portions of the act. The most important of these is the Federal Trade Commission (FTC), which is responsible for all general retailers, consumer finance companies, and all other creditors not regulated by other agencies. If a credit practice is not covered by the act, the FTC may still find the practice "deceptive or unfair" under the general provisions of the FTC Act (see p. 503).

**Disclosure Requirements**    A *closed-end* credit transaction involves only a single credit transaction, such as a consumer loan payable over time. In such closed-end transactions, the creditor is required to make eighteen separate disclosures to the consumer before the transaction is completed. Those disclosures include the amount financed, the "finance charge" as computed under the act, the annual percentage rate (APR), the payment schedule, the total of payments, the total sale price (including the finance charge), prepayment options, late-payment penalties, security interests, security interest charges, and others.

Creditors in *open-end transactions*, such as revolving charge accounts and credit cards, must make an *initial disclosure* including the finance charge, other charges that may be imposed, security interests, and a statement of the consumer's billing rights. Such plans must also provide a *periodic statement* that shows the previous balance; identifies all new transactions; shows any credits; and discloses the periodic rates, the balance of which finance charges are computed, and the amount of the finance charge and other charges; identifies the closing date of the billing cycle; and shows an address to be used for notice of billing errors. Forms to be used for many of the disclosures are contained in the regulation, and creditors must use those forms.

**Advertising of Credit**    Regulation Z provides that if an advertisement of credit states that specific credit terms are available, it shall state only those terms *actually* available. If an advertisement states a finance charge, it must be stated in terms of the APR, or *annual percentage rate*, which must be stated on an annual basis and include many "hidden" credit charges, such as carrying costs, points, and loan or assumption fees. If the interest rate may change, the advertisement must disclose that fact. As a general rule, if an advertisement states *any* figures, it must disclose *all* of the figures.

General statements in an advertisement, such as "easy credit," "charge accounts available," "all major credit cards honored," and others do not call for disclosure. But once specific figures are mentioned or statements such as "no money down," "pay only $7 per week," and the like are made, disclosures are required. Broad statements such as "liberal credit" and "easy credit" must mean what they say, and their use may result in liability under the FTC Act but not require truth-in-lending disclosures.

---

## Advertising of Terms That Require Additional Disclosures
REGULATION Z, SECTION 226.4(c)

1 If any of the following terms is set forth in an advertisement, the advertisement shall meet the requirements of paragraph (2) of this section:

   i    The amount or percentage of any down payment.
  ii    The number of payments or period of repayment.
 iii    The amount of any payment.
 iv    The amount of any finance charge.

2 An advertisement stating any of the terms in paragraph (1) of this section shall state the following terms, as applicable:

   i    The amount or percentage of the down payment.
  ii    The terms of repayment.
 iii    The "annual percentage rate," using that term, and, if the rate may be increased after consummation, that fact.

---

**Right of Rescission**     One of the chief concerns of Congress when it passed the Truth-in-Lending Act was the fast-talking salesperson who induces a homeowner to make a purchase or loan secured by a second mortgage on the debtor's home. The act provides a special **right of rescission** in such cases, which gives the debtor the right to void the transaction within three business days.

The debtor must be informed in writing of the right of rescission, and the three-day period does not start until the written disclosure of the right of rescission is made. The consumer must give notice of rescission in writing, but that notice must be prepared and attached to the notice given the debtor. The form of the notice is prescribed by Regulation Z. The right to rescind may be waived only in emergency situations.

**Remedies**     Both civil and criminal penalties are provided under the Truth-in-Lending Act. A debtor may bring a civil action for double the amount of the finance charge, from a minimum of $100 to a maximum of $1,000, plus attorneys' fees and costs. Criminal penalties for willful violations include a fine of up to $5,000 and/or a year in jail.

### Federal Truth-in-Leasing Act

In 1976 the Consumer Credit Protection Act was amended by the **Consumer Leasing Act,** sometimes called the *Truth-in-Leasing law.* Congressional concerns included the trend toward long-term leasing of consumer goods and the lack of adequate disclosure to consumers. The act covered any lease of personal property for a total contract value under $25,000 to be used for personal, family, or household purposes. The act applied regardless of whether the lessee had an option to purchase the property.

The act required eleven different disclosures, including a description of the property; the "down payment"; the amount of license fees, taxes, and other official fees; the amount of other charges; the number, amount, and due dates of payments and the total amount of the payments; the cost of the lease on expiration; and statements of warranties and conditions of termination.

Advertisements of leases may not state the amount of any payment, down payment or the number of payments unless the advertisement clearly discloses the fact that the transaction is a lease; the amount of the down payment; the number, amount, due date, and total of payments under the lease; and the fact that the lessee may be liable for the difference between the fair market value and the actual value of the leased property at the termination of the lease, if the lessee is to be held liable for that amount.

If the lease transaction is through a bank or other financial institution, the Federal Reserve has the authority to administer the law. Virtually all other transactions fall within the authority of the FTC. Remedies include a private civil action for 25% of the total of the monthly payments, but not less than $100 or more than $1,000, plus costs and attorneys' fees. If an advertisement violates the law, the consumer may sue for his or her actual damages. Willful violations may result in criminal penalties of a up to $5,000 and/or a year in jail.

## Federal Fair Credit Reporting Act

Credit reports are used by businesses as background checks on people who have applied for credit. These reports are often made by private, profit-making companies that maintain records on all people with credit in a particular area. The reports may also be used as background checks for applications for employment or insurance.

In 1970, Congress passed the **Fair Credit Reporting Act** to remedy some abuses in the credit-reporting system, to ensure the accuracy of credit reports, and to secure the consumer's right to privacy. Consumers were given an absolute right to review any file maintained on them by a consumer credit reporting agency. If credit is denied, access is free. If not, a reasonable fee may be imposed. If a discrepancy is found, consumers are given the right to dispute information, and agencies are required to reinvestigate the disputed information. Later reports must show the dispute; and if the original information is found to be in error, the report must be corrected. If such a dispute is not resolved, consumers have the right to file a statement of not more than 100 words regarding the dispute. Those statements must be included in later reports.

If a report is to be used for credit, insurance, or employment purposes, the person who is the subject of the report must be informed that such an investigative report will be prepared or used. If the consumer is denied credit, insurance, or employment because of a report, the user of the report must give the consumer the name and address of the party preparing the report, or at least state that the consumer has a right to such information. The act contains civil and criminal penalties, provides private civil liability, and authorizes FTC enforcement.

## Federal Fair Credit Billing Act

The **Fair Credit Billing Act of 1974,** another amendment to the Truth-in-Lending Act, is aimed at the problems of billing errors, the responsibilities of credit card issuers, and the degree of control that credit card companies may exert over retailers who accept their credit cards.

All creditors—that is, persons who regularly extend or arrange credit (including all credit card issuers)—must acknowledge any complaint or inquiry about a billing error within thirty days and must either correct or explain the alleged error within ninety days of the receipt of the complaint. Open-end credit accounts cannot be restricted or closed for failure to pay alleged billing errors until the account has been investigated and explained or corrected. Failure to comply results in forfeiture of the disputed amount up to a maximum of $50.

Credit card issuers must credit a consumer's account when notified that a retailer has accepted return of the merchandise or has forgiven payment for any reason. Credit card issuers that are also banks or savings and loans may not use funds on deposit to offset credit card charges without a prior written authorization from the consumer. Credit card issuers may not prevent sellers from offering "discounts for cash," nor may issuers require *tie-in* purchases as a condition of participating in the credit card plan, such as requiring holders of gasoline credit cards to purchase ten gallons of gasoline every month as a condition of holding the card.

## Federal Fair Debt Collection Practices Act

Concern over debt collection tactics resulted in the **Fair Debt Collection Practices Act of 1977.** The act applies to attorneys and independent collection agencies, and not to creditors attempting to collect debts owed directly to them. Abusive collection techniques are prohibited, including threats of violence, obscene language, publication of the names of debtors, false and misleading representations, and harassment. Collectors may not contact debtors at unusual or inconvenient hours.

If a debtor requests in writing that a collector cease contact, the creditor can only contact the debtor to inform him or her that a specific action will be taken (e.g., filing of a lawsuit) and then only if the action is actually taken. Within five days of the first contact, the debtor must be sent a written notice detailing the debt. The collector may contact others, including employers, but only to find out where the consumer lives or works; the collector may not inform any other person of the debt. Generally, other persons may only be contacted once. Collectors may be liable for the actual damages caused by their actions in violation of the act, plus a civil penalty of up to $1,000, attorneys' fees, and costs. The FTC is charged with administration of the act.

## Federal Electronic Funds Transfer Act

The development of a large variety of electronic funds transfer techniques, including automated tellers, computer funds transfers, and pay-by-phone systems, gave rise to potential consumer problems. These potential problems resulted in passage of the **Electronic Funds Transfer Act of 1978.** This act requires that creditors using such systems provide a monthly statement of transactions to the consumer. After the consumer receives the statement, he or she has sixty days in which to report an error, after which the creditor has the duty to investigate and report to the consumer within ten days. Errors must be corrected, and creditors are liable for all actual damages caused by failure to make a transfer properly.

The act also limits consumers' liabilities in the event of a lost or stolen credit card to $50 if the issuer is notified within two days after the consumer learns of the loss or theft. After the two-day period, the consumer's liability rises to $500 for the next sixty days. After sixty days, the consumer's liability is unlimited if the issuer can show that prompt notice would have prevented the loss, and the consumer knew or should have known of the theft or loss. The Federal Reserve has provided specific regulations in its **Regulation E.**

In addition to actual losses, an issuer may be liable for a civil penalty of $100 to $1,000, plus costs and attorneys' fees. Criminal penalties of up to a $5,000 fine, a year in jail, or both are provided for "knowing" or "willful" violations.

### Real Estate Settlement Procedures Act (RESPA)

The federal **Real Estate Settlement Procedures Act of 1974** was aimed at specific abuses in transactions for the purchase of homes. The act requires disclosure of *closing costs* prior to the sale of a home or the granting of a mortgage on a home. Closing costs are the expenses related to a real estate transfer, including attorneys' fees, title insurance, inspection fees, and other related costs. The act also prohibits kickbacks between various settlement service providers and requires the use of a standardized settlement form disclosing many hidden costs. All prospective mortgage applicants must be given an information booklet entitled, "Settlement Costs and You," and all purchasers are given the right to select their own title insurer, attorney, or other service provider. The act applies to all federally related mortgage transactions.

### Federal Equal Credit Opportunity Act

The **Equal Credit Opportunity Act of 1974,** an amendment to the Consumer Credit Protection Act, prohibits discrimination in giving credit on the basis of race, creed, color, religion, age, national origin, income derived from public assistance, sex, or marital status. Virtually all creditors except individuals are covered, including banks, retailers, and credit card issuers.

The act gives a credit applicant the right to a decision on the application within thirty days. In the event of a denial, the creditor must state its reasons in writing, along with the basic provisions of the act and the name and address of the federal agency administering compliance. Credit applications may request all information that will permit the creditor to make a reasoned judgment about the applicant's ability to repay, but such applications may not request information regarding the "suspect categories." For example, information regarding marital status is usually irrelevant, unless the debtor's spouse will use the property or be liable for the debt, the applicant is relying on income from the spouse to pay the debt, or the property to be purchased may become community property under state law.

An applicant may sue for actual and punitive damages not to exceed $10,000 plus attorneys' fees and costs. The act also provides for class actions, and the FTC is given authority to oversee compliance and make regulations.

### Federal Trade Commission Rules

The FTC Act, as discussed in Chapter 20, authorizes the Federal Trade Commission to make rules regarding "unfair and deceptive trade practices." Under this general authority, the FTC has made several rules directly affecting the debtor-creditor relationship.

For example, one of those FTC rules imposes a **three-day cooling-off period** on door-to-door sales, during which a consumer has a right to rescind transactions over the value of $25. The FTC has also imposed detailed rules regulating mail-order sales.

One of the most far-reaching FTC regulations was adopted in 1984. That regulation touches on several common creditor practices and outlaws **confession of judgment clauses,** most **wage assignments,** and some types of **security interests.** In addition, the regulation imposes a disclosure requirement on the obligations of a **cosigner.**

**Confession of Judgment Clauses**    A *confession of judgment clause* in a credit contract permits a creditor to avoid most of the procedural protections given defendants in civil cases. Normally, such clauses permit *any* attorney to confess judgment on behalf of the debtor, which means that the creditor's attorney may ask any other lawyer (and in many states even nonlawyers) to sign a document that acknowledges the debt and consents to the entry of a judgment against the debtor. Confession of judgment clauses often waive service of process and notice of the hearing. As a result, a debtor may not receive notice of the court proceeding until after judgment is entered. Unless the debtor can convince a judge to set the judgment aside, there is no trial and no opportunity to raise a defense. The 1984 regulation[2] prohibits all such confession of judgment clauses or any waiver of notice and the opportunity to be heard.

**Wage Assignments**    A *wage assignment* is an agreement by a debtor that the creditor may go directly to the debtor's employer and receive payment of the debt out of the debtor's paycheck. Many states prohibited such clauses or limited the amounts that the creditor could demand from the debtor's wages. The FTC regulation outlawed all wage assignments unless the assignment is revocable at will by the debtor or the assignment only applies to wages already earned at the time of the assignment.

**Security Interests**    A *security interest* is a lien or claim on property, which permits the creditor to repossess the property in the event of default. Some credit contracts included a provision that gave the creditor a security interest in *all* of the debtor's property, not just the property purchased on credit. Some credit card or "revolving charge" agreements also gave the creditor a security interest in all goods purchased since the account was opened, not just the most recent purchases or those for which payment had not been received. The FTC regulation outlaws all security interests in household goods other than *purchase money security interests* (for amounts used to pay for the secured property).

**Cosigners**    Some creditors also may insist on a *cosigner* of a loan or credit agreement. A cosigner is liable on the debt, even if the creditor does not attempt to collect the debt from the delinquent debtor, but many cosigners neither know this nor understand the nature of the agreement they are signing. The FTC regulation provides that cosigners must be informed of their obligations under the agreement by providing a printed form as a separate document that states as follows:

---

2  16 C.F.R. 444.2.

## Notice to Cosigner

You are being asked to guarantee this debt. Think carefully before you do. If the borrower doesn't pay the debt, you will have to. Be sure you can afford to pay if you have to, and that you want to accept this responsibility. You may have to pay up to the full amount of the debt if the borrower does not pay. You may also have to pay late fees or collection costs, which increase this amount. The creditor can collect this debt from you without first trying to collect from the borrower. The creditor can use the same collection method against you that can be used against the borrower, such as suing you, garnishing your wages, etc. If this debt is ever in default, that fact may become a part of *your* credit record. This notice is not the contract that makes you liable for the debt.

**Late Charges**   Finally, the regulation also prohibits "pyramiding late charges." That means that a creditor may not assess a late charge on a late charge, if the debtor has made what would otherwise be a full payment.

## STATE AND COMMON LAW CONSUMER PROTECTION

The development of federal statutes protecting consumer interests was accompanied by similar state laws. Although consumer protection statutes vary widely between the states, four major developments deserve attention: the UCC doctrine of **unconscionability**, the **Uniform Consumer Credit Code** (UCCC) and the related **Retail Installment Sales Acts** (RISAs), **state consumer protection agencies**, and **usury laws**.

### Unconscionability

One of the most important changes made by the Uniform Commercial Code was found in the new concept of *unconscionability*, as discussed in Chapter 8. As noted in that chapter, the UCC does not define the term *unconscionability*, even though the rule applies to all sales of goods, including virtually every consumer transaction in personal property. Court decisions have interpreted the term generally to mean *grossly unfair*, and courts often require a finding of inequality of bargaining position between the parties to a contract. The unconscionability doctrine has been applied with substantial success in consumer transactions in which the consumer did not bargain on equal terms with the seller. Although the UCC doctrine applies only to transactions in *goods*, some court decisions have applied the doctrine to other transactions, including services and the sale of land.

### Uniform Consumer Credit Code (UCCC) and RISAs

In 1968 the National Conference of Commissioners on Uniform State Laws approved the final draft of the *Uniform Consumer Credit Code* (UCCC). Only a few states have totally adopted the law, but many states have used this uniform or "model" act as a guide for state legislation. The UCCC was meant to dovetail with the federal Truth-in-Lending Act of the same year.

The UCCC requires certain written notices to the buyer in any credit transaction, similar to those required under truth-in-lending provisions, but goes much further by establishing a uniform set of rules governing all aspects of consumer credit. The act sets maximum interest rates, governs door-to-door sales, and regulates the use of credit-line insurance. The act also prescribes the method of rebating finance charges in the event of prepayment of the debt.

Although only a few states have adopted the UCCC, virtually all states have enacted *Retail Installment Sales Acts* (RISAs). Such acts are similar in form to the UCCC but only cover installment sales of personal property. RISAs generally require advance disclosure and regulate billing practices, and they may go much further, depending on the state.

### State Consumer Protection Agencies

Virtually every state has established some type of consumer protection agency. Those agencies vary considerably in their power and jurisdiction. Some of the state agencies are little more than mediators, taking complaints from consumers and forwarding them to sellers. Others have a great deal of power, including the right to initiate administrative or criminal proceedings and arbitrate consumer disputes.

### Usury Statutes

Perhaps the first government regulation of business was a **usury statute** that set the maximum rate of permissible interest in ancient Rome. Every state has a usury statute of some sort, although the methods of setting the maximum rate of interest and the penalties for violation vary considerably. During the interest rate escalations of the late 1970's many of those laws were "suspended" or preempted by federal regulations, because in many instances the enforcement of the state usury statute would have eliminated any lending whatsoever.

### BANKRUPTCY

Perhaps the ultimate consumer protection law is the **Federal Bankruptcy Act.** Under the Constitution, article 1, section 8, clause 4, "Congress shall have the power . . . to establish . . . uniform laws on the subject of bankruptcies throughout the United States." The first bankruptcy act was passed in 1800, although that law applied only to "traders." Such acts were passed and repealed several times in the nineteenth century, but since 1898 a federal bankruptcy act has existed. The current act was amended substantially in 1984.

The purpose of bankruptcy is to permit debtors to make a fresh start. It is possible for anyone to get into financial difficulty through business reverses, medical or marital problems, lawsuits, employment layoffs, and simple overextension in an atmosphere of easy credit. Such difficulties result in the need to fend off creditors, collection agencies, and lawyers at every turn. Bankruptcy exists to give such debtors a second chance.

Three basic types of bankruptcy are available under the federal law: (1) **liquidation proceedings,** commonly known as *straight bankruptcy* or *Chapter 7 proceedings*; (2) **ad-**

justment of debts, or *wage earner plans* or *Chapter 13 proceedings* for individuals with regular income who wish to pay off their debts over time; and (3) **business reorganizations,** sometimes called *Chapter 11 proceedings,* used by businesses in financial trouble.

## Liquidation Proceedings: Straight Bankruptcy

The most common and best-known procedure is *straight bankruptcy,* which is available to any individual, partnership, or corporation. Such cases may be filed by the debtor (a *voluntary* petition) or by the creditors of the debtor (an *involuntary* petition), but less than 1% of all cases are initiated by creditors. The law does not require that the person filing be insolvent or unable to pay his or her debts, but only that he or she be a *debtor.*

A debtor must file a series of rather complex disclosure forms and a *petition for a discharge in bankruptcy.* The petition must list all of the assets, liabilities, and creditors of the debtor and must disclose the location of all assets, books, and records. At this time, all of the debtor's property is in the technical legal possession of the court, and creditors need court permission to proceed against the debtor. All creditors are notified and given an opportunity to object to the discharge or to make claims. An *automatic stay* of all lawsuits prohibits proceeding in any case against the debtor.

After the petition is filed, the U.S. Bankruptcy Court then appoints a **trustee** to take over the debtor's property and business. The trustee may be elected by the creditors or, as in the usual case, may be appointed by the court. The trustee may sue and be sued on behalf of the debtor and may move to set aside **fraudulent transfers** (transfers of property for less than full value by the debtor within one year of filing the petition). The bankruptcy court holds a **meeting of creditors** shortly after the petition is filed for the purpose of electing or appointing the trustee and examining the debtor. A date is also set at that meeting for the discharge of the debtor. (See Figure 15.2.)

**Claims of Creditors and Exemptions**    The assets of the debtor, less the exemptions permitted by law, are then distributed to the creditors who have filed claims, according to their priority as established in the act (see Figure 15.3). Under the Bankruptcy Act, the debtor may elect between two sets of exemptions: the exemptions permitted by the law of the state in which he or she is domiciled (see p. 69), *or* the exemptions permitted by federal law under the Bankruptcy Act. States may *require* debtors to use the state exemptions, however. Under the 1984 amendments, if a husband and wife file a joint bankruptcy petition, they each receive separate exemptions, but both must choose either the state exemptions or the federal exemptions.

The following property is exempt from the claims of creditors:

1   The debtor's homestead interest in a residence, up to $7,500;

2   The debtor's motor vehicle, up to $1,200 in value;

3   The debtor's interest in household furnishings and other personal property for personal, family, or household use, up to $200 per item up to a maximum of $4,000 of total exemptions;

4   The debtor's interest in jewelry for personal, family, or household use, totalling $500 in aggregate value;

5   The debtor's interest in other property, up to $400, plus any unused portion of the homestead exemption up to $3,750;

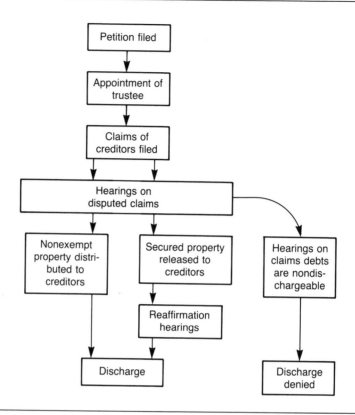

FIGURE 15.2    Bankruptcy Procedure

1    Creditors with claims resulting from the costs of administering and preserving the bankrupt's estate (accountants, attorneys, etc.);

2    Creditors with claims occurring in the ordinary course of the debtor's business after the bankruptcy petition is filed;

3    Employees owed wages earned within 90 days, or employee benefits earned within 180 days of the petition, up to $2,000;

4    Consumers who have paid deposits or other prepayments for undelivered goods or services, up to $900;

5    Government taxes;

6    Other claims (general creditors).

FIGURE 15.3    Priority of Creditors in Bankruptcy

6   The debtor's interest in tools, professional books, and implements;

7   Unmatured life insurance policies;

8   Health aids prescribed by a physician or other health professional;

9   The debtor's right to receive government benefits, such as social security;

10   The debtor's right to receive certain private payments, such as alimony, child support, and private pensions.

If all of the debtor's property may be brought within the federal exemptions or the exemptions permitted by state law, there will be no property to distribute to the creditors. Many cases fall within that category and are termed **no asset cases,** because there are no assets to distribute to creditors.

Even if property is exempt, a creditor that has a lien or security interest on the property is entitled to the property. For example, if debtor A has a home worth $50,000 but has a mortgage of $48,000 on the property, the lending institution or other creditor holding the mortgage would have the right to foreclose the mortgage. The debtor's interest of $2,000 would be claimed under the homestead exemption, and the debtor could claim up to $3,750 of other property (see item 5 in the preceding list). Similarly, if the debtor owned a car worth $5,000 with a $4,500 lien to a lender, the lender would have a right to the car, and if the car were sold for $5,000 the debtor could claim $500 (see item 2 in the list). The trustee may set aside security interests in some property, however.

**Reaffirmation**   Since secured creditors have a right to their property under any circumstances, debtors often attempt to save property by making a new agreement to pay the creditor. That means that after the bankruptcy petition is filed, the debtor makes a **reaffirmation** agreement with the creditor to pay certain amounts, in return for the creditor's promise not to take back the goods.

At one time, such reaffirmation agreements could be entered into without court approval, which resulted in a great deal of abuse by both debtors and creditors. Under a 1978 amendment, the Bankruptcy Court must determine whether such reaffirmations are in "the best interests of the debtor." The following case, which arose prior to the 1984 amendments, shows the problems inherent in such reaffirmation agreements.

## In Re Jenkins
United States Bankruptcy Court, E.D., Va. 1980 (4 B.R. 651)

**Hal J. Bonney, Jr., Bankruptcy Judge**   Once more into the breach! Again the Court must express an opinion as to what it considers to be—or not to be—in the best interest of a debtor. Indeed, an awesome thing. Shall the Court interposition itself when both the debtor and the creditor seek approval of an agreement which, in effect, would reaffirm an indebtedness of $792.76 on $200 worth of furniture?

The application for approval of the agreement was filed by the creditor, Carolina Furniture Outlet. At stake are a three piece living room suite and a complete bed.

Faithful to its statutory duty . . . at the appropriate hearing the Court heard the debtor testify to his desire to reaffirm the entire debt since he wished to retain the property. It also heard the creditor recite that the agreed amount was the outstanding balance on the debtor's discharged account, $792.76. But what was the chattel worth? The Court directed an appraisal and this came in for $200.

The issue burns: Is it in the best interest of the debtor to be permitted to become so obligated?

A knowledge of the legislative antecedents of the Bankruptcy Code readily reflects the clear intent of Congress for courts to scrutinize debtor agreements and applications for revival of debts with the utmost care. . . .

The initial draft of the legislation [the 1978 amendments] prohibited any and all agreements by debtors and creditors to revive pre-bankruptcy debts. There had been such a sordid history of the reaffirmation of debts that the fresh start envisioned by the Congress had been cast away by many bankrupts. The process which would have restored them to the marketplace [society], to their families and to themselves as more useful citizens was thwarted. Indeed, it is clear from this bench that the chief cause of "repeaters" in bankruptcy is reaffirmation of debts.

We can take judicial notice of the fact that in the past many bankrupts almost immediately returned to financial difficulty after discharge because they reaffirmed discharged debts. For some it was a matter of conscience. "I want to repay you as soon as I can." "Good. Sign here." Or the fellow needs a loan and his usual source says, "Sure, sign up again for the old debt and we'll let you have some additional money," knowing that he could not declare straight bankruptcy again for six years.

Some Congressional draftsmen wanted to ban all reaffirmations. Others said there might be, in some cases, genuine *need* to reaffirm. The compromise was close scrutiny by the Court. We are to look them over in an exceedingly fine manner. . . .

The Congress has made a test of that scrutiny. The agreement (i) [must] not impos[e] an[y] undue hardship on the debtor or a dependent of the debtor; and (ii) [it must be] in the best interest of the debtor. . . .

No hardship is anywhere evident. But what of the debtor's best interest?

The Court notes that the best-interest-of-the-debtor test is largely, though not exclusively, an eco-nomic inquiry given a specific factual setting. Simply put, either the debtor is entering into a mutually beneficial agreement or he is not. . . .

It is inconceivable that the debtor could not strike a better bargain than the one presented here. Carolina Furniture makes much of the fact that no interest is accruing over the 25 odd months of the proposed agreement. That is of no moment in light of the incontroverted fact that the parties are applying to the Court for authorization to pay nearly $800 for $200 worth of furniture. What will this furniture be worth in six, twelve, or eighteen months? And should untoward events transpire in the interim, the debtor is bound by a legally enforceable obligation.

The Court will not approve this agreement. It is not in the debtor's best interest to do so.

We find reflected here a factual situation emblematic of the mistakes people make who are likely candidates for bankruptcy. A significant part of the profile is this matter of entering into unfortuitous agreements. In a word, they make poor bargains. And they are prone to take the line of least resistance. "You can keep the stuff if you sign up for it again."

What could this debtor have done which would be in his better interest?

(1) He could redeem the furniture for $200.[3]

(2) He could have sought a better bargain with the creditor for some figure between $200 and $792. It is apparent from the record that no effort at all was directed toward this end.

(3) He could allow the creditor to recover or reclaim the property and then purchase not necessarily new but replacement furniture.

The post-bankruptcy period is a time for leanness. Debtor Jenkins would be surprised at what he can purchase, on credit, if need be, for two or three hundred dollars.

Debtor Jenkins has previously been in bankruptcy. His schedules reveal recent purchases of such luxuries as a piano, watch and a tape recorder as well as $1,000 cash on his Mastercharge. He apparently has not learned a great deal; perhaps he is not too astute as to what is in his own best interest.

He won't obtain approval of a complete reaffirmation from this Court. Frankly, we do not anticipate that this firm hand on the part of the Court will

---

3 Section 722 of the Bankruptcy Act empowers debtors to extinguish liens on certain property by paying the holder of the secured claim an amount equal to the value of the encumbered property—Ed.

rehabilitate him, but in this small sphere of influence the Congressional intent shall be followed.

And what of the creditor? Are its rights trampled upon? Naturally, it would like to have its $792.76. However, while it is a "secured creditor," it is secured only to the extent of the value of its collateral. Since this is a no asset case and the debt a dischargeable one, the most it would otherwise receive is what can be realized on its collateral. If it can obtain approval of the proposed agreement—and note that it and not the debtor filed the application—it would realize its unsecured portion, $596.76 in full; the other unsecured creditors will receive nothing.

Under the agreement as proposed, the creditor would receive nearly $600 *more* for allowing the debtor to retain the furniture. This cannot be; it is too high a premium.

. . . Just as we wish people did not become ill or did not become criminals or did not have troubles we wish people paid their just debts. But they don't always do so. That is the way it is. We wish they didn't need a doctor; we wish they didn't need bankruptcy. Yet through their own hands [extravagance] or through adverse winds that blow over which they have no control [illness, inflation], they require a cure. You must understand that the Congress—and

responsible governments throughout history, from Biblical times—is trying to help these people. An effort is being made to restore these people with a fresh start so that they might return to the marketplace as viable, useful citizens. The philosophy of bankruptcy requires no explanation or defense among knowledgeable men and it is not our purpose here to defend it. We have noted over the years, however that only about 5% of the bankrupts-debtors ever return. One could conclude that the vast majority benefit and learn from the process.

The debtor will not be permitted to give nor the creditor receive $800 on $200 of what is now second-hand furniture. The application for approval of the agreement is hereby denied. IT IS SO ORDERED.

## Case Discussion Questions

1  What benefit will the creditor get from a reaffirmation? What benefit will the debtor receive?
2  What business does the court have in telling these parties how to run their lives? Is there a valid public policy behind the court's decision?
3  Is there a hardship on the debtor by having the furniture repossessed? Under what circumstances might a court find a hardship?

---

In addition, the 1984 amendments provide that the debtor may rescind such agreements at any time up to discharge or within sixty days, whichever is later, and requires that the agreement represent a fully informed and voluntary agreement on the part of the debtor and does not impose an undue hardship on the debtor.

**Discharge**    A **discharge** is granted in the vast majority of cases. A discharge means that the debtor is released from liability for all prefiling debts that are properly scheduled. Once granted, the discharge *relates back* to the date the petition was filed. For example, if a petition is filed on July 1 and the discharge is granted on November 1, the discharge will be treated as existing from July 1. Creditors are prevented from attempting to collect discharged debts, both through the nature of a discharge itself and by means of a federal court injunction. If a debtor is sued on such a debt in state courts, the discharge in bankruptcy will act as a complete defense to the action.

**Bars to Discharge**    There are situations in which the Bankruptcy Court may not grant a discharge, including the following:

1    If the debtor has received a discharge in bankruptcy within six years of the filing of the bankruptcy petition;
2    If the debtor has intentionally concealed or transferred assets to evade creditors, has

concealed, destroyed, falsified, or failed to keep business records without a reasonable explanation, or has failed to explain adequately a loss of assets;

**3**    If the debtor has refused to obey an order of the bankruptcy court;

**4**    If the debtor has made any fraudulent statements or claim in connection with the bankruptcy.

These bars to bankruptcy are not automatic. Some creditor or other person with standing to complain must object to the discharge before the court will refuse to grant the discharge.

**Nondischargeable Debts**    Some types of debts are also **nondischargeable.** This does not mean that the entire discharge is barred, but only that those specific debts will not be discharged. Nondischargeable debts include claims for alimony and child support (both past and current), federal taxes incurred within three years, claims for willful or malicious torts, and student loans less than five years old, unless hardship can be shown.

The 1984 amendments added a new and controversial section for consumer debts. That section provided that consumer debts owed to a single creditor for more than $500 worth of "luxury goods or services" incurred within forty days of discharge are not dischargeable. Similarly, cash advances over $1,000 are nondischargeable if made under an open-end credit plan within twenty days of the discharge. The creditor in both instances must ask the court for a determination of dischargeability, and if the court finds that the creditor was not justified in asking for such a determination, the court may order the creditor to pay court costs and attorneys' fees.

The 1984 amendment also provides that the court may, on its own motion or at the request of a creditor, dismiss a petition for straight bankruptcy filed by an individual debtor if the debts are primarily consumer debts and if the court finds that the discharge would be "a substantial abuse" of the Bankruptcy Act.

**Straight Bankruptcy and Employment**    The 1984 amendments also made some important changes in the employment relationships of bankrupts and debtors. A private employer may not terminate the employment of, or discriminate against, an individual who is or has been a debtor under any provision of the Bankruptcy Act, or has been associated with such a person. The act also prohibits employment termination or discrimination if a person is or has been "insolvent" prior to filing under the act, or has not paid a dischargeable debt that was later discharged under the act.

## Adjustment of Debts: Wage Earner Plans

Chapter 13 of the Bankruptcy Act provides a real alternative for debtors who find themselves in financial difficulty but who do not wish to use the extreme remedy of straight bankruptcy. Such Chapter 13 petitions are often referred to as **wage earner plans.**

Under Chapter 13, any "individual with regular income" and who has less than $100,000 in unsecured debts and less than $350,000 in secured debts may file a *Petition for Adjustment of Debts.* That petition will contain a plan to pay off the debts over a certain period of time. A certain portion of the debtor's income is paid to the trustee on a monthly basis, and the trustee in turn makes payments under the plan to the creditors. Only the debtor may file a petition, and there is no such thing as an involuntary petition under Chapter 13.

If either the trustee or an unsecured creditor objects to the plan, the court may not approve the plan unless (1) the debt will be fully paid under the plan, or (2) the plan provides that all of the debtor's projected disposable income for the next three years will be applied to make payments on the plan. In the case of secured creditors, the court may not confirm the plan unless one of three things happens: (1) the secured creditor accepts the plan; (2) the proposed payments to the secured creditor have a current value that at least equals the value of the collateral, and the lien remains in place on the collateral; or (3) the collateral is surrendered to the secured party.

A wage earner plan may be converted to a straight bankruptcy at any time, which provides a substantial incentive to creditors to accept such plans. After completion of the plan, the debtor receives a discharge. The only debts not discharged are (1) certain long-term obligations specifically set out in the plan itself; and (2) child support and maintenance payments and alimony payments.

### Business Reorganizations

Using Chapter 11 of the Bankruptcy Act, businesses may request **reorganization,** although creditors may also file such petitions. The purpose of such petitions is to continue the business and to pay off the debts of the business over time, in much the same manner as a wage earner plan, although business reorganizations are often far more complex. Generally, the prior management is retained and continues to run the business (a "debtor in possession"), although a trustee or a committee of creditors may be appointed by the court as well. A plan is filed, either by the debtor or by the creditors, that will pay off the debts over a fixed period of time. The plan is confirmed by majority vote of the creditors and accepted by two-thirds of the shareholders voting on the plan.

### SUMMARY AND CONCLUSIONS

Creditors have a variety of legal techniques available to collect debts. Once a judgment is rendered, the creditor may learn the location of assets and other information through a citation to discover assets. An attachment may be issued to obtain property, and a garnishment may be issued to obtain wages or other property held by third persons.

Because of abuses in credit and collection practices, both federal and state legislatures have passed statutes restricting the granting of credit as well as a variety of collection practices. The Federal Truth-in-Lending Act requires disclosures prior to granting credit and in advertising of credit. The Truth-in-Leasing Act performs a similar function in leasing transactions. The Federal Fair Credit Reporting Act regulates the credit reporting industry, and the Federal Fair Credit Billing Act places restrictions on billing and billing errors. The Federal Fair Debt Collection Practices Act prohibits a variety of abusive collection practices, and the Electronics Funds Transfer Act regulates electronic funds and credit cards. Other federal laws deal with equal credit opportunity and real estate settlement procedures, and FTC rules augment those laws through a variety of administrative regulations.

Perhaps the most important "consumer protection" law is the federal Bankruptcy

Act. That law permits some debtors to obtain a complete discharge of their debts. Certain debts are not dischargeable, and debtors may be denied a discharge under some circumstances. Some debtors may be eligible to file petitions for wage earner plans, in which the debtor pays off his or her debts over an extended period of time. Corporations may file for corporate reorganization.

## REVIEW QUESTIONS

1    The number of functionally illiterate American adults has been estimated at 23 million (!) Do "disclosure" laws such as the Truth-in-Lending Act and RESPA help those people at all? Aren't those persons the very people the law is trying to help?

2    One criticism of the consumer legislation passed in the last two decades is that it results in a great deal of unnecessary paperwork. Name all of the consumer legislation that requires such extra paperwork. Is that a good enough reason to do away with the legislation, as some advocate?

3    Why does the law insist on protecting those who fail to pay their bills? Does their behavior justify any harassment or ill treatment that a creditor cares to inflict?

4    What do you think has been the overall effect on the price paid for consumer goods from the various consumer laws discussed in this chapter and the previous two chapters? Are you willing to pay higher prices for the goods you purchase (if that is the effect you found) in return for the safeguards of these laws?

5    Sheehan purchased a car financed by the Ford Motor Credit Company, then moved several times and became delinquent in his payments. One of Ford's collection employees phoned Sheehan's mother, identified herself as an employee of a hospital, told her that one of Sheehan's children had been injured in an auto accident and requested that Sheehan call a specific number. Sheehan's mother supplied information regarding Sheehan's home address, business, and home phone numbers as well. The following day Sheehan's car was repossessed.

Does Sheehan have a remedy? [*Ford Motor Credit Union v. Sheehan*, 373 So. 2d 956 (Fla., 1979).]

6    Martin gave his American Express card to an associate, instructing him orally that only $500 should be charged. Martin later received a bill for $5,300, which he refused to pay. Is he liable? [*Martin v. American Express, Inc.*, 361 So. 2d 597 (1978).]

7    Mercutio purchased a set of encyclopedias from Tybalt, a door-to-door salesperson. The price of the books was $700, payable at $50 per month. Tybalt forgot to give the "truth-in-lending" statement to Mercutio, so he delivered it six days later. The day after Mercutio received the statement, Mercutio decided that he could not afford the books after all and sent a letter to Tybalt telling him to cancel the sale. Has the sale been effectively cancelled?

8    Williams maintained a charge account for the purpose of purchasing furniture from the Walker-Thomas Furniture Co. The initial contract for the charge account said that the customer did not own any of the furniture as long as any balance remained on the charge account, and that all payments would be applied pro rata to all purchases. From 1957, when the contract was signed, until 1962, Williams purchased over $1,800 worth of furniture and made payments totalling over $1,400. In 1962, Williams became unable to make payments, because she had been forced to go on public aid and was supporting herself and seven children on $218 per month. Walker-Thomas brought an action to repossess everything Williams had purchased

since 1957. Does Williams have a defense? [*Williams v. Walker-Thomas Furniture Co.*, 350 F.2d 445 (D.C. Cir., 1965).]

9 Balthazar, an employee of Pedro, purchased furniture from Dogberry's Furniture Store. In the contract was a confession of judgment clause and a wage assignment. (a) If Dogberry attempts to enforce the wage assignment against Pedro, what is Balthazar's remedy? (b) If Dogberry obtains a judgment by confession, what is Balthazar's remedy? (c) How may Dogberry get her money?

10 LaFue had run up a number of debts, including $3,000 in back alimony to his ex-wife Violenta, $5,000 in student loans to Rousillon College five years earlier, $2,000 in past due taxes, and $8,000 in credit card charges. LaFue also had a car which he had purchased for $12,000 (and on which he owed $9,000, and now worth about $7,500) and a house worth $60,000 (on which he owed $55,000). LaFue earned $55,000 per year. (a) Is he eligible for straight bankruptcy? What will be the result if he files for straight bankruptcy? (b) Is he eligible for a wage earner plan? What kind of plan would be workable for him? (c) If LaFue files for straight bankruptcy, should the court permit him to reaffirm the debt on the car?

# PART 4

# The Firm and Its Employees

The common law of agency created a large number of duties owed by employees and agents to employers, but provided very little in the way of duties to employees by employers (see Chapter 11). Agency principles were based on the wrongs that employees could do to their employers, and not the other way around. With the Industrial Revolution of the nineteenth century came a whole host of employee abuses: Sweatshops, child labor, unsafe working conditions, and meager pay seemed the rule in the late nineteenth century.

Public revulsion at such employer practices led to changes in the law, which in turn led to a changing view of the relationship of the firm to its employees. Consequently, the definition of "fair" labor practices has changed substantially over the years, and the predominant ethical principles have become a sense of fairness and a mutual sense of loyalty for employers and employees. Thus, both ethics and the law have regulated the relationship of the firm to its employees.

The two chapters in this section reflect two different streams of labor law. Chapter 16 deals with federal labor-management relations law. Chapter 17 covers a variety of federal and state laws dealing with "specific evils" in the workplace. Federal labor-management relations is based on the notion that if the bargaining power of the firm and its employees can be equalized, usually through unionization, most labor problems can be dealt with through collective bargaining. For that reason, this approach is sometimes called the **market approach.** So-called **specific evil laws** are aimed directly at specific problems, such as unsafe working conditions, employee security, or wages and hours. Both streams of labor law come from a single source, however—concern for the individual worker.

# CHAPTER 16

# Labor Law: Labor-Management Relations

*If capital and labor ever do get together, it's good night for the rest of us.*

FRANK MCKINNEY HUBBARD (1930)

Almost every major employer in the nation must deal with labor unions. Organized labor continues to be a potent political and economic force, revered by many and feared and hated by some. Although some argue that labor unions no longer have the influence that they had in earlier years, unions continue to represent millions of workers and exert tremendous political, economic, and social power.

Yet this was not always so. Employees had no right even to belong to unions in many states until 1935. It took a series of sweeping federal laws to give labor such power, power that grew so quickly that other federal laws were passed to limit its use. In a large sense, federal labor law is a "power balancer," stabilizing the power of labor and business to produce a rough equilibrium. Much of the controversy over labor law is whether such a balance has been reached.

This chapter provides an overview of federal regulation of labor-management relations. After a consideration of the history of the labor movement, we discuss the federal labor laws in broad strokes. The problems of unionization, unfair labor practices, negotiation, enforcement of collective bargaining agreements, and the relationship of members to their own unions are considered in some detail. The chapter ends with a discussion of the newest area of controversy, unionization of public employees.

## THE EVOLUTION OF THE LABOR MOVEMENT

Labor and management were not always antagonistic. Until the middle of the nineteenth century employees and employers generally shared a harmonious and mutually profitable relationship. Although there were glaring exceptions in the cases of slavery and indentured servants, most employers were craftsmen who worked shoulder-to-shoulder with their employees. The opening frontier beckoned to any dissatisfied worker, so labor was in short supply and wages were high. Employer and employee often shared the workshop, so working conditions were generally good. Daily contact led to lasting personal relationships. And perhaps most importantly, employers and employees did not consider themselves to be "natural enemies."

Wrenching social and economic changes in the middle of the nineteenth century destroyed the craft system forever. Factories and assembly lines replaced the workshop. Anonymous corporations replaced individual owners. Businesses grew rapidly, and the number of industrial workers grew even faster. As costs became a prime concern, working conditions deteriorated and wages fell, forced down even further by immigration from Europe. The personal relationships of the craft system were replaced by steely animosity and antagonism between employer and employee.

### The Common Law Employer-Employee Relationship

The legal relationship between employer and employee was based on the law of agency, contracts, and (in the case of slaves) property. The law of contracts assumed that all employment relationships were mutually negotiated agreements, like any other contract. But that assumption depends on equality of bargaining position between the parties. Those assumptions may in fact have been valid under the craft system, but the increasing industrialization of the nineteenth century produced a buyer's market in favor of employers. Unskilled laborers, often illiterate and faced with an oversupply of competing laborers, found employment on a "take it or leave it basis." As noted by the Supreme Court in 1921,

> A single employee was helpless in dealing with an employer. He was dependent ordinarily on his daily wage for the maintenance of himself and his family. If the employer refused to pay him the wages that he thought fair, he was nevertheless unable to leave the employ and to resist arbitrary and unfair treatment. Union was essential to give laborers an opportunity to deal on equality with their employer.[1]

### The Rise of Unionism

Trade unions can be traced back hundreds of years, to the guilds and associations of craftsmen created for the betterment of the trade and for social functions. Such groups formed the nucleus of the trade union movement, which began in earnest immediately following the Civil War, as a result of the Industrial Revolution.

Employees soon recognized that their sole weapon was the **strike,** or work stoppage, and that their goal must be joint negotiation, or **collective bargaining,** of labor contracts. During the late nineteenth century, many such organizations rose and fell, usually defeated by a combination of employer opposition and economic depression. It was not until the creation of the American Federation of Labor (AFL) in 1886 that a lasting labor organization was formed. That organization supported social and labor legislation but relied on collective bargaining as its principal tool to achieve its objectives. Under the leadership of Samuel Gompers, such agreements were reached in the building trades, stove and glass container industries, and later in the coal mines. By 1903, almost 1.5 million persons claimed membership in the AFL. Perhaps most surprisingly, the AFL seemed able to withstand economic depressions.

---

1 *American Steel Foundries v. Tri-City Council*, 257 U.S. 184, 42 S. Ct. 72, 66 L. Ed. 189 (1921).

### Employer Opposition and Tactics

The free-swinging entrepreneurs of the Gilded Age were not about to sit back and permit labor to chip away at their profits and power. Those men began their own campaign against unions, using a variety of tactics. The employers' arsenal included various self-help techniques, public opinion, and a variety of legal weapons.

The nineteenth-century capitalists were quite able to help themselves in the conflict with labor. Often they would hire **strikebreakers,** or simply thugs who broke both strikes and strikers. **Scabs** would be hired to take striking laborers' jobs. **Labor spies** would be used to infiltrate labor organizations to learn the identity of leaders, who would soon be fired and placed on a **blacklist,** which was circulated to all employers. Often the employers would simply close a plant in a **lockout,** a kind of reverse strike designed to starve workers into submission.

While the American labor organizations were developing, some European labor groups were pursuing far more sinister and extreme tactics. Groups like the Molly McGuires and the Wobblies (Industrial Workers of the World) used violence, riots, and even murder to achieve their goals and succeeded in exporting a small part of their violence to the United States. These groups, taken together with the fearsome call for worldwide revolution by Karl Marx, convinced many Americans that all labor movements were somehow "evil." It was easy for American businessmen and the newspapers they controlled or influenced to convince the American public that the domestic labor movement should be repudiated as well.

The most potent weapons of businessmen were legal ones. Many labor organizers were jailed under **criminal conspiracy statutes,** which prohibited agreements to strike or even organize in many states. Even in the face of the first amendment's freedom of assembly clause, courts ruled that there was no constitutional right to strike or even to organize. Many workers were forced to sign **yellow dog contracts,** which required workers to renounce union membership as a condition of employment. And most importantly, businessmen were often able to convince the courts to issue **injunctions** against labor activity. Once an injunction was granted, businessmen could seek the aid of the police or even the army to suppress labor activity by force.

In 1890 the federal **Sherman Act** was passed, and employers gained a new weapon. That law is an antitrust statute aimed at unfair combinations of businesses (see Chapter 20). But by outlawing all "contracts, combinations or conspiracies . . . in restraint of trade," the act could also be applied to labor unions without too much judicial stretching. The theory was that a labor union was nothing more than an agreement between competing workers to set prices and restrain competition for employment. The results were federal court injunctions against labor activity and federal indictments of labor organizers. In *Loewe v. Lawlor,*[2] sometimes known as the *Danbury Hatters' Case,* the U.S. Supreme Court held that the Sherman Act should be applied to both labor and business, and held federal court injunctions could be issued against labor activity on the authority of the Sherman Act.

---

2 208 U.S. 274, 28 S. Ct. 301, 52 L. Ed. 488 (1908).

## The Turnabout: Federal Labor Legislation

Even in the face of employer opposition and staggering legal disadvantages, labor made strong inroads into American public opinion. Harsh employer actions in the Pullman strike and the anthracite coal confrontation hurt the employers' cause deeply. By the time Woodrow Wilson became President, public sentiment strongly favored federal intervention on the side of workers. Between 1914 and 1935 there came a steady stream of federal labor legislation, first encouraging and later virtually requiring collective bargaining. That stream included two key sections of the **Clayton Act** of 1914, the **Railway Labor Act** of 1926, the **Norris-LaGuardia Act** of 1932, and the **National Labor Relations Act,** including the **Wagner Act** of 1935, later amended by the **Taft-Hartley Act** of 1947 and the **Landrum-Griffin Act** of 1959 (see Table 16.1).

**The Clayton Act**   The first major federal labor law was the *Clayton Act* of 1914, another antitrust law discussed in detail in Chapters 20 and 21. Two sections of the act were hailed by Samuel Gompers as an "industrial Magna Charta." Section 6 of the Clayton Act provides that "the labor of a human being is not a commodity or article of commerce. Nothing contained in the antitrust laws shall be construed to forbid the existence and operation of labor . . . organizations. . . . " This section meant that the Sherman Act could no longer be used against labor activity.

Section 20 of the Clayton Act bars federal injunctions "in any case between an em-

TABLE 16.1   The Federal Labor Laws

| Statute | Date | Purpose |
|---------|------|---------|
| Clayton Act | 1914 | Eliminated some federal injunctions; held Sherman Act could not be used against labor |
| Railway Labor Act | 1926 | Established collective bargaining for railroads; acted as a model for later laws |
| Norris-LaGuardia Act | 1932 | Outlawed federal antilabor injunctions; outlawed yellow dog contracts |
| Wagner Act (National Labor Relations Act [NLRA]) | 1935 | Created NLRB; gave right to organize; established majority rule and voting for unions; created 5 "employer" unfair labor practices |
| Taft-Hartley Act (amended NLRA) | 1947 | Created 6 "union" unfair labor practices; established employer's right to free speech; created Mediation and Conciliation Service; made election procedures more specific; created "National emergency strikes"; established right of employees *not* to join a union; gave states right to outlaw union shops |
| Landrum-Griffin Act (amended NLRA) | 1959 | Required registration of unions, union members' bill of rights; required democratic elections; outlawed blackmail picketing and hot-cargo agreements |

ployer and employees" involving a dispute concerning terms and conditions of employment, and it specifically prohibits injunctions against activities such as quitting work or persuading others to do so.

But even in the light of the Clayton Act, state-court injunctions continued to issue on the basis of the common law. The Supreme Court later permitted federal injunctions against labor activity, if that activity was not directed against the employees' direct employer. As a result, the Clayton Act did not have a major effect on federal injunctions against labor activity.

**The Railway Labor Act**    Because of possible interruptions in rail service during World War I, the federal government operated the nation's railroads between 1917 and 1920 and, in the process, encouraged collective bargaining in that industry. When the railroads were transferred back to private hands, Congress passed the *Railway Labor Act* of 1926. That act emphasized collective bargaining and mediation by a federal board in the event of disputes and declared the right of the parties to designate representatives (unions) without interference, influence, or coercion. The act became a model for later, more encompassing federal labor legislation.

---

### PRO AND CON

# Have unions outlived their usefulness?

**Pro**    The power of organized labor is declining steadily. Unions are losing membership, many recent contracts have involved "take-backs," and labor has lost much of its political clout. Unions have not only outlived their usefulness, they were never very useful at all.

Unions are in fact highly inefficient from an economic standpoint. They are actually "horizontal price fixing arrangements," in antitrust terminology (see p. 508), and result in higher labor prices than would otherwise be charged in a totally unrestricted economy. The result is higher prices for goods and inflationary pressures, along with featherbedding and nonsensical work rules.

In fact, many of the functions of unions have been taken over by government. Federal laws like OSHA, Fair Labor Standards, and ERISA (see Chapter 17) have displaced union functions in many areas and protect *all* workers, not just those who belong to a union. The result is less need for organized labor.

Finally, corporate America has learned that it is important to play fair with its workers. Corporate personnel departments spend a great deal of time and money on employee morale. The end result of all of these pressures is less need for labor organizations.

**Con**    Unions continue to be a vital force for change in employee-employer relationships. Certainly organized labor has lost members in the manufacturing sector, but it has gained huge numbers of members in the service and public sectors. Although take-backs occurred in recessionary times, those take-backs are being reevaluated, and new pressure for wage gains exists during good economic times.

The government has indeed begun to protect workers through laws like OSHA, the Fair Labor Standards Act, and ERISA, but those laws came about as a result of political pressure *by organized labor*. Organized labor lobbies for all working people, and in fact for other important causes, such as education, civil rights, and environmental and consumer protection. Organized labor has been one of the most potent forces for social change in American history.

Although wage increases do affect inflation, the full effect must be reviewed. Nonunion wage increases often follow union wage increases, so that all workers benefit from union wage demands. And, most importantly, all workers are also *consumers* and most consumers are also workers. This means that wage increases result in increased demand for the goods and services produced by American business. In fact, the American economy probably could not have developed without the increased standard of living caused by union wage pressures.

## Roundtable Discussion

1    Could the American economy have progressed as far as it has without labor unions? Are they still necessary? What changes in our society and economy since 1935 have had an effect on whether unions are still workable?

2    Is the "power-balancing" approach taken by the federal labor laws appropriate? Would a different approach create a less adversarial labor-management environment? What approach would you suggest? Is a less adversarial environment really desirable?

3    Would laws like OSHA, workers' compensation, social security, and others that protect *all* workers have come into existence without organized labor? Which approach—that of the NLRA, or that of specific laws aimed at all employees—intrudes more on the marketplace?

---

**The Norris-LaGuardia Anti-Injunction Act**    Even though section 20 of the Clayton Act had little effect in controlling injunctions against labor, unions continued to battle the court injunction in Congress. Finally, in 1932, Congress passed the *Norris-LaGuardia Act*, which provided that yellow dog contracts were unenforceable in federal courts and prohibited the issuance of any injunction by a federal court "in a case involving or growing out of a labor dispute."

In a broad sense, the Norris-LaGuardia Act ushered in an era of industrial *laissez faire*. That is, although the federal government did not take an active role in promoting the interests of labor, it did not actively promote the interests of employers either. Prior to the act, the federal courts had taken a clear proemployer stand, but the Norris-LaGuardia Act instructed the courts to take a hands-off attitude.

But a hands-off attitude was not enough. The Depression, like all economic downtrends, produced a huge oversupply of labor resulting in a buyer's market for labor. Employers could—and did—insist on having nonunion employees. State courts continued to be adverse to the interests of labor and granted injunctions against organizing, strikes, and other labor activity. The U.S. Supreme Court held both federal and state labor laws unconstitutional under the commerce clause, the contracts clause, or under the doctrine of substantive economic due process (see Chapter 4). It was obvious that more positive measures were needed.

At first the "New Deal" Congress tried a form of voluntary compliance in the *National Industrial Recovery Act* of 1933, which established codes of fair competition in various industries. Those codes were required to contain a guarantee of the employees' right to organize and bargain collectively. That act was held unconstitutional by the Supreme Court in 1935.[3] It did not seem possible for the federal government to pass any labor law under the Court's reading of the commerce clause.

**The Wagner Act**    As described in Chapter 3, Congress did pass a sweeping labor law in 1935. The *National Labor Relations Act* (NLRA), also known as the *Wagner Act*, forced the Supreme Court's hand through the famous **court-packing plan**. Not long after, the Supreme Court announced its decision in *NLRB v. Jones & Laughlin Steel* (p. 107). That decision not only held the Wagner Act constitutional but also vastly widened

---

3 *Schecter Poultry Corp. v. U.S.*, 295 U.S. 495, 55 S. Ct. 837, 79 L. Ed. 1570 (1935).

federal authority over interstate commerce and set the stage for many other federal regulations.

The basic policy of the Wagner Act was to support unionization by establishing a right to organize and encouraging collective bargaining. The act promoted those objectives in several ways: (1) it established the *right to organize* and to become a member of a labor organization; (2) it established a *method of election* by which employees might choose a union and the principle of majority rule; (3) it specified five *unfair labor practices* on the part of employers, generally prohibiting activity that hampered the right to organize, and provided remedies for their violation; and (4) it created a new independent regulatory commission, the *National Labor Relations Board (NLRB)*, with the authority to make rules, hold elections, and hear unfair labor practice charges. Many of the specific provisions of the NLRA were later amended by the Taft-Hartley Act of 1947 and the Landrum-Griffin Act of 1959.

**The Taft-Hartley Act**    Between 1935 and 1947, organized labor gained vast power as union membership grew from 3 million in 1935 to 15 million in 1947, with two-thirds of all manufacturing employees covered by labor contracts. This rapid growth, along with crippling strikes in key industries, labor corruption, and heavy-handed tactics by some unions, resulted in pressure for reform of the labor laws.

The result of this pressure was the 1947 *Taft-Hartley Act*, an amendment to the Wagner Act passed over the veto of President Truman. It was aimed at an imbalance in the Wagner Act, which had been designed solely to protect labor. The new law was created, at least according to its sponsors, to provide balance between labor and management.

The act is long and involved, making many technical changes in the Wagner Act. Among its more important sections are (1) the creation of six *union* unfair labor practices; (2) establishment of the right of employers to express their views publicly, as long as there is no threat of reprisal or promise of economic benefit; (3) establishment of the federal **Mediation and Conciliation Service** as an independent agency; (4) creation of specific requirements for union elections; (5) creation of a procedure for dealing with strikes during a "national emergency," including a forced "eighty-day cooling off period"; (6) establishment of the right of an employee *not* to join a union, except in the case of a **union-shop agreement;** and (7) permission to the states to outlaw compulsory union membership (state right-to-work laws).

**The Landrum-Griffin Act**    During the 1950's, a series of congressional investigations disclosed that some labor unions had been tainted by corruption and undemocratic procedures. To remedy the situation, Congress passed the *Landrum-Griffin Act*, also known as the *Labor-Management Reporting and Disclosure Act* of 1959. That act required labor unions to register with the Secretary of Labor; adopt constitutions, by-laws, and democratic voting procedures; supply annual reports to the Secretary of Labor; and grant their members certain rights as union members, known as the **Union Member's Bill of Rights.** Embezzlement of union funds was made a federal crime, and the act specified two more union unfair labor practices—*blackmail picketing* and *hot cargo agreements* (see p. 411).

## THE NATIONAL LABOR RELATIONS ACT

Virtually all of the federal law dealing with labor-management relations is found in the National Labor Relations Act (NLRA). That act includes the Wagner Act, as amended by the Taft-Hartley and Landrum-Griffin acts. The NLRA provides a basic right to organize, prohibits unfair labor practices, prescribes the processes by which employees may choose a union, regulates the process of collective bargaining, and provides limits on the activities of unions in dealing with their own members. The act authorizes the National Labor Relations Board (NLRB) to make rules to enforce the act.

### Coverage of the NLRA

The NLRA was based on commerce clause authority; thus, all cases must involve activities that "affect commerce." However, as discussed in Chapter 4, commerce clause authority is very broad, so that almost any employer is covered by the act except the smallest exclusively local business. The NLRB has established self-imposed limits for exercising its authority, however.

The NLRB will generally not involve itself in disputes involving (1) retail enterprises, unless the total annual volume of business is over $500,000; (2) nonretail businesses with under $50,000 per year in direct sales to consumers (outflow), or $50,000 in purchases (inflow); (3) newspapers with under $200,000 in total annual volume of business; or (4) colleges and universities with under $1 million in gross revenues. Certain employees are exempt from the act as well, including agricultural laborers, domestic servants, persons employed by their parents or spouses, independent contractors, persons subject to the Railway Labor Act, government employees, and supervisors.

Under the act the term *supervisor* includes any person who has the authority to hire, transfer, suspend, lay off, promote, discharge, assign, reward, or discipline another, or who has the authority to direct other employees or adjust grievances, as long as the authority results from independent judgment. It also includes persons whose opinion carries substantial weight with management in hiring, firing, and related decisions. That term has created a number of problems of interpretation.

### The Right to Organize

Perhaps the most important part of the Wagner Act is section 7 (see the box on p. 398), which established the rights of employees to organize and join labor unions and to join in concerted action for the purpose of collective bargaining. The act also provided that employees had the right to refrain from joining unions or engaging in such concerted behavior.

In the few words of section 7, all of the prior debate over the legality of unions and collective bargaining, the problems of criminal conspiracy laws and the misapplication of the antitrust laws, and the question of federal court injunctions against union activity were answered. Section 7, especially when read together with section 1 (see Appendix B), clearly established a national policy favoring collective bargaining as the principal means of resolving disputes between labor and management.

Establishing a national policy favoring collective bargaining is one thing; enforcing it is quite another. The National Industrial Recovery Act (NIRA) of 1933 had contained

> ## Section 7 of the NLRA
>
> **Rights of Employees.** Employees shall have the right to self-organization, to form, join, or assist labor organizations, to bargain collectively through representatives of their own choosing, and to engage in other concerted activities for the purpose of collective bargaining or other mutual aid or protection, and shall also have the right to refrain from any or all of such activities except to the extent that such right may be affected by an agreement requiring membership in a labor organization as a condition of employment as authorized in section 8(a)(3).

a similar expression of policy, but that law was largely unenforceable and was ruled unconstitutional by the Supreme Court. The Wagner Act was different, however, because it was held constitutional in 1937 in the *Jones and Laughlin Steel* decision (p. 107), and because the Wagner Act contained real "teeth" in the form of the National Labor Relations Board (NLRB) and the concept of unfair labor practices.

### The National Labor Relations Board (NLRB)

The NLRB is a five-member independent regulatory commission. The members of the Board are appointed by the President for staggered five-year terms and are assisted by the General Counsel, who is also appointed by the President, but for a four-year term. The NLRB also has established thirty-two regional offices and a number of field offices, which are supervised by the General Counsel.

The NLRB has four principal functions under the act: (1) it may make rules to carry out the act; (2) it must conduct representation elections; (3) it must act to prevent unfair labor practices; and (4) it may conduct investigations. The vast majority of the NLRB's activities involve elections and unfair labor practices.

### Unfair Labor Practices

The Wagner Act introduced the concept of "unfair labor practices" by listing five types of conduct by *employers* that were prohibited by the act. The Taft-Hartley and Landrum-Griffin acts later created seven *union* unfair labor practices. Taken together, these sections—sections 8(a) and 8(b) of the NLRA—provide the principal means of enforcing the act. The NLRB enforces the unfair labor practices provisions. (See Table 16.2)

**Section 8(a): Employer Unfair Labor Practices**    Five employer unfair labor practices were identified by the Wagner Act:

1    *Section 8(a)(1): Interference, Restraint or Coercion of Employee Rights.* Examples include physical violence and economic or physical threats, including threats of discharge if employees vote for a union, spying, or even questioning employees about

TABLE 16.2    Unfair Labor Practices (ULPs)

| §8a: Employer ULPs | §8b: Union ULPs |
| --- | --- |
| Interference, restraint, or coercion of employee rights | Restraint or coercion of employees or employers |
| Company-dominated unions | Causing or attempting to cause discrimination |
| Discrimination against employees for union (or nonunion) membership | Refusal to bargain in good faith |
| | Certain strikes and boycotts prohibited |
| Discrimination for NLRB activities | Excessive or discriminatory membership fees |
| Refusal to bargain in good faith | Featherbedding |
| | Organizational and recognitional picketing by noncertified unions |

union activities. *Interference* also includes granting benefits to employees during union organizing activities.

**2**    *Section 8(a)(2): Company Dominance or Financial Support of a Union.* This section was aimed at the practice of forming "company unions" dominated by the employer, which do not have the same independence or power as labor organizations unrelated to the employer.

**3**    *Section 8(a)(3): Discrimination Against Employees.* This section requires employers to deal even-handedly with both union and nonunion employees. Examples of prohibited conduct include discharge or discipline of union members for union activities, or of any employee because of his or her union *or* nonunion status. Employers may discriminate against an employee for failure to pay union dues.

**4**    *Section 8(a)(4): Discrimination for NLRB Activities.* This section guards the right of employees to take action under the act and preserves the integrity of the NLRA by prohibiting action against employees who make use of the act's provisions.

**5**    *Section 8(a)(5): Refusal to Bargain in Good Faith.* This section, together with section 8(b)(3), imposes a duty to bargain in good faith (but not to agree) about certain subjects, including "wages, hours and other terms and conditions of employment."

**Section 8(b): Union Unfair Labor Practices**    Seven union practices were prohibited by the Taft-Hartley and Landrum-Griffin acts:

**1**    *Section 8(b)(1): Restraint or Coercion of Employees or Employers.* This section prohibits unions from forcing persons to join unions or join in union activities. A major exception exists if the employer and the union have formed a *union-shop agreement*, in which all employees must be members of the union. This section also prohibits threats and acts of violence, mass picketing, and similar activities. Section 8(b)(1)(B) prohibits unions from restraining or coercing *employers* in the selection of a bargaining representative, regardless of whether the union is the choice of the majority of employees. Legal strikes and picketing are not considered coercion.

**2**  *Section 8(b)(2): Causing or Attempting to Cause Discrimination.* This section prohibits unions from pressuring employers to discriminate against nonunion employees in the absence of a union-shop contract. This section dovetails with section 8(a)(3).

**3**  *Section 8(b)(3): Refusal to Bargain in Good Faith.* This section imposes the same duty to bargain on unions as imposed on employers by section 8(a)(5).

**4**  *Section 8(b)(4): Prohibited Strikes and Boycotts.* This section prohibits certain strikes and boycotts to accomplish certain purposes or objects. Prohibited actions include compelling membership in an employer or labor organization, requiring execution of a **hot-cargo agreement** or compelling a **secondary boycott** (see p. 411), compelling recognition of an uncertified union, compelling recognition of a union if another union has been certified, and requiring assignment of certain work to certain employees.

**5**  *Section 8(b)(5): Charging Excessive or Discriminatory Membership Fees.* The purpose of this section is to prohibit entry barriers to new employees.

**6**  *Section 8(b)(6): Featherbedding.* This section prohibits a union from compelling an employer to hire employees who are not needed or paying for work not actually done.

**7**  *Section 8(b)(7): Organizational and Recognitional Picketing by Noncertified Unions.* Picketing by a *noncertified* union is prohibited if it is done for purposes of obtaining recognition by an employer or obtaining members for the union in three instances: (1) when the employer has already recognized another union and no representation election is possible; (2) when a valid NLRB election has been held within the last twelve months; and (3) when a "representation petition" is not filed within thirty days.

**Enforcement of Unfair Labor Practices**   The NLRB enforces the unfair labor practice provisions of the NLRA. One of the parties must file a charge with the NLRB. Unfair labor practices are heard initially by an NLRB Administrative Law Judge, who makes findings and recommendations to the board. Based on those recommendations, the board may issue an order requiring a party to **cease and desist** from such practices and may order some action, such as reinstatement of an employee, or may grant a **bargaining order** requiring the parties to bargain over an issue.

If an employer or a union fails to comply with an NLRB order, the board may petition the U.S. court of appeals for a court decree enforcing the order of the board. Likewise, either party may appeal the order to the court of appeals. The court may enforce the order, remand it to the NLRB for reconsideration, change it, or set it aside entirely. Failure to comply with the court order enforcing a board order is punishable by fine or imprisonment for contempt of court. In some cases the board may even recognize the union without an election, as in the following case.

# NLRB v. Gissel Packing Co.
395 U.S. 575, 89 S. Ct. 1918, 23 L. Ed. 2d 542 (1969)

In three virtually identical cases, a union waged an organizational campaign and succeeded in having a majority of the employees sign **authorization cards.** An authorization card is not a membership card but merely a statement that the employee wants the union to request an election on the question of union representation. Signing an authorization card in no way indicates that the employee will vote for the union once the election is held.

All three unions demanded recognition on the basis of the authorization-card majority, and all three employers refused to bargain with the unions. Instead, all three employers embarked on vigorous antiunion campaigns, including some actions that gave rise to unfair labor practice charges against the employers, such as the discharge of workers who had been active in organizing the union.

In the case of one employer (Gissel Packing Co.), the union did not seek an election but filed unfair labor practice charges for refusal to bargain, coercion, and intimidation of employees. In the second case (involving Heck's Inc), an election was sought but never held because of nearly identical unfair labor practices. And in the third case (involving General Steel Products), an election was won by the employer but later set aside by the NLRB because of unfair labor practices. In each case, the NLRB issued a bargaining order to the employer, requiring the employer to recognize the union, and ordered the companies to cease and desist from future unfair labor practices and to offer reinstatement with back pay to employees who had been discriminatorily discharged. The companies appealed, and the Court of Appeals rejected the NLRB's order and refused to enforce the order to bargain. The NLRB appealed to the Supreme Court.

The Court first considered at length whether an "authorization-card majority" was sufficient to impose a duty to bargain on an employer. The Court held that the language of the Taft-Hartley Act provided more than one means of choosing a bargaining representative, and as long as the representative was chosen by the majority of the employees, the employer had a duty to bargain. The Court also found that such authorization cards, while "admittedly inferior" to a secret election, were not so "inherently unreliable indicators of employee desires" that they could not establish a majority and impose a duty to bargain.

**Mr. Chief Justice Warren Delivered the Opinion of the Court**   Remaining before us is the propriety of a bargaining order as a remedy for a §8(a)(5) refusal to bargain where an employer has committed independent unfair labor practices which have made the holding of a fair election unlikely or which have in fact undermined a union's majority and caused an election to be set aside. We have long held that the Board is not limited to a cease-and-desist order in such cases, but has the authority to issue a bargaining order without first requiring the union to show that it has been able to maintain its majority status. . . . And we have held that the Board has the same authority even where it is clear that the union, which once had possession of cards from a majority of the employees, represents only a minority when the bargaining order is entered. . . . We see no reason now to withdraw this authority from the Board. If the Board could enter only a cease-and-desist order and direct an election or a rerun, it would in effect be re-

warding the employer and allowing him to "profit from [his] own wrongful refusal to bargain," . . . while at the same time severely curtailing the employees' right freely to determine whether they desire a representative. The employer could continue to delay or disrupt the election processes and put off indefinitely his obligation to bargain; and any election held under these circumstances would not be likely to demonstrate the employees' true, undistorted desires.

The employers argue that the Board has ample remedies, over and above the cease-and-desist order, to control employer misconduct. The Board can, they assert, direct the companies to mail notices to the employees, to read notices to employees during plant time and to give the union access to employees during working time at the plant, or it can seek a court injunctive order . . . as a last resort. In view of the Board's power, they conclude the bargaining order is an unnecessarily harsh remedy that needlessly prejudices employees' §7 rights solely for the purpose of punishing or restraining an employer. Such an argument ignores that a bargaining order is designed as much to remedy past election damage as it is to deter future misconduct. If an employer has succeeded in undermining a union's strength and destroying the laboratory conditions necessary for a fair election, he may see no need to violate a cease-and-desist order by further unlawful activity. The damage will have been done. . . . There is, after all, nothing permanent in a bargaining order, and if, after the effects of the employer's acts have worn off, the employees clearly desire to disavow the union, they can do so by filing a representation petition. . . .

We emphasize that under the Board's remedial power there is still a . . . category of minor or less extensive unfair labor practices, which, because of their minimal impact on the election machinery, will not sustain a bargaining order. There is, the Board says, no *per se* rule that the commission of any unfair labor practice will automatically result in a §8(a)(5) violation and the issuance of an order to bargain.

[Reversed].

## Case Discussion Questions

1    What is a bargaining order? Under what circumstances will the NLRB issue a bargaining order *without* an election?

2    Are there any other remedies available that will remove the "taint" from an election following employer unfair labor practices?

3    Are authorization cards a reliable indicator of employee preferences?

Just what type of unfair labor practices will result in the imposition of a **Gissel remedy** seems unclear. The remedy is clearly applicable in cases involving the grant of significant benefits to the employees and in cases of repeated violations of section 8(a)(3), such as discharge of employees with union affiliations.

**Contemporary Dimensions: The Problem of the "Runaway Shop"**    One answer to continuing union pressure is to simply shut down a plant or move operations to a more friendly location, such as a state where unions are less active or to a state with a right-to-work law (see p. 406). But if the move arises from antiunion sentiment, it may be an unfair labor practice, as discussed in the following case.

## *Textile Workers Union v. Darlington Manufacturing Co.*
380 U.S. 263, 85 S. Ct. 994, 13 L. Ed. 2d 827 (1965)

Darlington Manufacturing Company operated a single textile mill. But a majority of Darlington's stock was held by a New York firm, which in turn was controlled by Roger Milliken. Milliken and his family controlled seventeen different textile mills, all operated as separate corporations.

In 1956, the Textile Workers Union began an organizational campaign in the Darlington plant which the company resisted vigorously. The union won the election on September 6. On September 12, Milliken called a meeting of the board of directors, which voted to close the mill and liquidate the corporation. The purpose of the closing was found to be to avoid unionization. The union filed unfair labor practice charges with the NLRB on the basis of sections 8(a)(1), 8(a)(3), and 8(a)(5). The NLRB found a violation of section 8(a)(3) and ordered back pay until the employees obtained substantially equivalent work. The court of appeals set aside the order and denied enforcement. The union appealed.

**Mr. Justice Harlan Delivered the Opinion of the Court**   We hold that so far as the National Labor Relations Act is concerned, an employer has the absolute right to terminate his entire business for any reason he pleases, but [we] disagree with the Court of Appeals that such right includes the ability to close part of a business no matter what the reason. . . .

We consider first the argument . . . that an employer may not go completely out of business without running afoul of the [National] Labor Relations Act if such action is prompted by a desire to avoid unionization. Given the Board's findings on the issue of motive, acceptance of this contention would carry the day for the Board's conclusion that the closing of this plant was an unfair labor practice. . . . A proposition that a single businessman cannot choose to go out of business if he wants to, would represent such a startling innovation that it should not be entertained without the clearest manifestation of legislative intent or unequivocal judicial precedent so construing the Labor Relations Act. We find neither. . . .

The AFL-CIO suggests in its *amicus* brief that Darlington's action was similar to a discriminatory lockout, which is prohibited "because designed to frustrate organizational efforts, to destroy or undermine bargaining representation, or even the duty to bargain." One of the purposes of the Labor Relations Act is to prohibit the discriminatory use of economic weapons in an effort to obtain future benefits. The discriminatory lockout designed to destroy a union, like a "runaway shop," is a lever which has been used to discourage collective employee activities in the future. But a complete liquidation of a business yields no such future benefit for the employer, if the termination is bona fide. It may be motivated more by spite against the union than by business reasons, but it is not the type of discrimination which is prohibited by the Act. The personal satisfaction that such an employer may derive from standing on his beliefs and the mere possibility that other employers will follow his example are surely too remote to be considered dangers at which the labor statutes were aimed. Although employees may be prohibited from engaging in a strike under certain conditions, no one would consider it a violation of the Act for the same employees to quit their employment en masse, even if motivated by a desire to ruin the employer. The very permanence of such action would negate any future economic benefit to the employees. The employer's right to go out of business is no different.

We are not presented here with the case of a "runaway shop," whereby Darlington would transfer its work to another plant or open a new plant in another locality to replace its closed plant. Nor are we concerned with a shut down where the employees, by renouncing the union, could cause the plant to reopen. Such cases would involve discriminatory employer action for the purpose of obtaining some benefit from the employees in the future. We hold here only that when an employer closes his entire business, even if the liquidation is motivated by vindictiveness toward the union, such action is not an unfair labor practice. . . .

The closing of an entire business, even though discriminatory, ends the employer-employee relationship; the force of such a closing is entirely spent as to that business when termination of the enterprise takes place. On the other hand, a discriminatory partial closing may have repercussions on what remains of the business, affording employer leverage for discouraging the free exercise of §7 rights among remaining employees of much the same kind as that found to exist in the "runaway shop" and "temporary closing" cases. . . . Moreover, a possible remedy open to the Board in such a case, like the remedies available in the "runaway shop" and "temporary closing" cases, is to order the reinstatement of the discharged employees in other parts of the business. No such remedy is available when an entire business has been terminated. . . . [W]e are constrained to hold . . . that a partial closing is an unfair labor practice under §8(a)(3) if motivated by a purpose to chill unionism in any of the remaining plants of the single employer and if the employer may reasonably have foreseen that such closing would likely have that effect.

[The Court referred the case back to the NLRB to determine the purpose and effect of the plant closing on employees in other mills operated by Milliken—Ed.]

## Case Discussion Questions

1   How does the conduct of the employer violate section 8(a)(3), as the NLRB found?

2   If you were an employee of one of the other corporations run by Milliken, would you want to start any unionization activities?

3   Should the NLRB have the power to act in these circumstances? What other alternatives are available to the employees?

The problem of the "runaway shop" remains. As the *Darlington* case indicates, an employer has an absolute right to close down a business for any reason, but simply closing down *part* of a business is an entirely different matter, especially if the courts find that the closing was done to "chill unionism." Students are invited to compare *Darlington* with *First National Maintenance Corp. v. NLRB*, pp. 408–409, in which the court considered the issue further.

Plant closings and runaway shops pose substantial difficulties for employers, employees, and local communities. On one hand, employers own their businesses and ought to have the right to close or move their businesses. On the other hand, shutting down a business creates massive problems for employees, who lose their jobs, and for the local community, where the economic effect of a plant closing may be disastrous.

Several states have enacted laws requiring employers considering closing down a business to notify both employees and the local community in advance of the closing. Most other nations have such plant-closing laws as well. In 1988, Congress passed a federal plant-closing law covering firms with 100 or more full-time employees. Such firms must give sixty days' advance notice to their employees of plant closings and mass layoffs. Faltering firms and shutdowns or layoffs occurring because of unforeseeable business circumstances or natural disasters are exempt. Violators are required to pay damages to employees equal to their pay and benefits for each day that the notice would have applied. Local communities must also be given notice, and they may receive up to $500 per day in damages if not properly notified. President Reagan refused to sign the measure but did not veto it. As a result, the bill became law.

## The Process of Unionization

Most union-organizing efforts begin when a group of employees contacts a union, usually because of some deep-rooted dissatisfaction or some unsettling development on the job. The initial meeting is usually followed by the creation of an "inside" organizing committee, demonstrating local control and providing greater access to the employees. Often the drive is initially kept secret from the employer out of fear of reprisal, although the union may announce its intention right away in order to obtain a list of employee names and addresses, to which it is entitled under NLRB rules.

**The Election Process**   The National Labor Relations Act requires that 30% of the employees sign authorization cards in order to hold an election regarding representation. (A card *majority* of 51% may be used to obtain bargaining rights without an election, or even despite an election loss, if the employer commits unfair labor practices considered by the NLRB to have had a substantial impact on the vote under the *Gissel doctrine*. See p. 400.) When enough authorization cards have been signed, the union organizer will write a **recognition letter** to the company president, informing the company that the union has signed up a majority of the employees and requesting that the employer bargain with the union (see Figure 16.1).

While an employer may simply enter into collective bargaining, it may also insist that the union win an election. Employers usually refuse the demand for recognition. The union's response is usually to file a petition for an election with the NLRB. The NLRB can only hold such an election if a petition has been filed requesting one. In

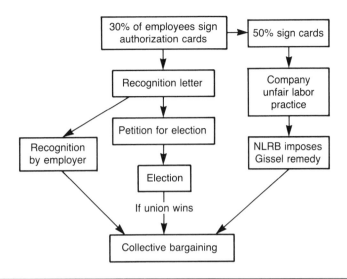

FIGURE 16.1   The Process of Unionization

some circumstances, employers may file such a petition if more than one labor organization has made a claim for recognition as the representative of the same employees.

Once a labor organization has been *certified* by the NLRB as the bargaining unit for a particular group of employees, that unit will become the **exclusive bargaining agent.** The employer may not deal with individual employees or any other group for the purpose of setting wages or working conditions, nor may the employer make changes in those areas without first bargaining with the union.

The act also provides that **decertification elections** may be held after a petition is filed by employees or someone acting on their behalf to determine whether the current bargaining representative should be retained. Petitions for **union-shop deauthorization elections** may be filed if signed by 30% of the employees to determine whether to withdraw the authority of their representative to continue a union-shop agreement. Upon receipt of a petition, the NLRB must investigate the petition, hold a hearing if necessary, and direct an election if it finds that a question of representation exists.

Elections are by secret ballot, and employees are given the choice between one or more bargaining representatives or no representatives at all. To be certified, the organization must receive a majority of all ballots cast. The election may be held by agreement between the parties as to time and place, the choices on the ballot, and the method of determining eligibility to vote. If the parties cannot agree, the NLRB will hold a hearing to determine such matters.

To be entitled to vote, an employee must have worked in the unit during the "eligibility period" set by the NLRB, which is generally set at the employer's payroll period just before the date on which the election was directed. Ordinarily, elections are held thirty days after they are directed, although different dates may be set to obtain fairer representation of employees.

An election may be set aside by the NLRB if the election was accompanied by conduct that the Board feels tended to interfere with the employee's free choice. Threats of loss of jobs or benefits, misstatements of important facts, discharge of employees, incitement of racial or religious prejudice, the use or threat of physical force, or the delivery of campaign speeches on company time within twenty-four hours of the election have all resulted in elections being set aside.

**The Appropriate Bargaining Unit**    One vital issue is the determination of the **appropriate bargaining unit.** The NLRB determines that issue, within limits set by the NLRA. Any group of two or more employees who share common employment interests and conditions may be a bargaining unit, but various employees, particularly managerial and supervisory employees, cannot participate. The unit may consist of all employees of a particular employer, all members of a particular craft or trade, or just employees of a particular plant or facility. Often employees of two or more employers constitute an appropriate bargaining unit. The board is required to consider any history of collective bargaining, the desires of the employees, and the extent to which the employees are already organized.

**Union Shops, Open Shops, and Agency Shops: State Right-to-Work Laws**    The Taft-Hartley Act provided that states were free to adopt laws prohibiting *union shop* agreements. Such laws are called **right-to-work laws** and have been adopted in about half of the states, mostly in the West and South. Those laws are among the most controversial aspects of modern American labor law.

    **Union-shop** arrangements (sometimes called *union security agreements*), which require all employees to join a union as a condition of employment, are considered essential by organized labor. An **open shop** exists if employees are free to join or not join the union. Since employers are prohibited from discriminating against nonunion employees, such employees must receive the same benefits as union employees in an open shop. Thus, although the union negotiates the collective bargaining agreement, nonunion employees receive the same benefits as union employees but do not pay union dues. Such nonunion employees are known as **free riders.** Therefore, no incentive exists for an individual employee to join the union and pay the dues. Union membership goes down, and the power to negotiate from a position of strength declines.

    Advocates of right-to-work laws respond by stressing the individual's right *not* to join a "voluntary" association. While granting the free-rider problem, these advocates would also point to some employees who do not wish to join unions as a matter of principle. Others point to the power of organized labor and assert that the power of labor can only be controlled through such legislation. Those advocates also argue that the union shop tends to permit one union to remain in power indefinitely, resulting in stagnation and corruption.

    One answer has been permitted in some cases—the **agency shop,** in which employees are not required to join the union but must, as a condition of employment, pay a "service fee" to the union. Such a fee eliminates the economic incentive of not joining a union and pays the union for the benefits the employees receive from the union's collective bargaining activities. Union fees not related to collective bargaining, such as those for political action, cannot be assessed against nonmembers. Some union contracts provide for a "conscientious objector" status for employees and require payment of an amount equal to the service fee to some charitable organization. The agency shop may be prohibited by state law as well.

Union-shop agreements cannot require that all applicants for employment be members of the union in order to be hired. At most, such agreements may require all employees in the group covered by the agreement to become members of the union within a certain period of time, not less than thirty days, except in the building and construction industries. In those industries a shorter grace period of seven full days is permitted. A union-shop agreement that provides a shorter grace period is invalid, and any employee discharged because of nonmembership is entitled to reinstatement.

## The Duty to Bargain in Good Faith

Both employers and unions are required to bargain collectively under the provisions of sections 8(a)(5) and 8(b)(3) of the NLRA. Whereas the original Wagner Act only required collective bargaining on the part of employers and did not define the term, the Taft-Hartley Act imposed that obligation on unions as well and defined the term more clearly. That act required bargaining "with respect to wages, hours, and other terms and conditions of employment" *in good faith.*

It is difficult to understand how the law may require the parties to a labor dispute to negotiate but not require that the negotiations bear fruit. The idea behind the requirement is that if parties sit down to talk, they will probably find some common ground. One court defined the term *good faith bargaining* as "an obligation . . . to participate actively in the deliberations so as to indicate a present intention to find a basis for agreement." Bad faith has been found from disruptive negotiating tactics of the parties and from refusals to make substantive proposals.

**Subjects of Collective Bargaining**    The second issue involving the duty to bargain is to define the subjects about which the parties must negotiate. As the law developed, there are two categories of collective bargaining subjects: (1) **mandatory bargaining topics,** including "wages, hours and other terms and conditions of employment," and (2) **permissive bargaining topics,** which are those matters not mentioned in the statute. There are also prohibited topics, such as hot-cargo agreements, secondary boycotts, and discrimination against persons who are not union members.

Mandatory bargaining topics include (1) wages, including pensions, fringe benefits, profit sharing, and all other forms of compensation; (2) work rules dealing with seniority, workloads, and discipline; (3) union status problems, such as the recognition clause and union-shop problems; and (4) conditions of employment, a grey area of other problems such as technological change, production volume, and plant location. Permissive bargaining topics include all other subjects.

Parties *must* bargain over mandatory subjects and *may* bargain over permissive topics. But insistence on bargaining on a permissive topic may itself be an unfair labor practice. Failure to bargain over a mandatory subject is a clear unfair labor practice under either section 8(a)(5) or section 8(b)(3). But the mandatory topics are defined in such vague terms that it is sometimes difficult to tell whether a particular issue is mandatory or merely permissive. The following case considers whether closing a part of the employer's business is a mandatory bargaining topic.

# First National Maintenance Corp. v. NLRB
452 U.S. 666, 101 S. Ct. 2573, 69 L. Ed. 2d 318 (1981)

First National Maintenance (FNM) operated a housekeeping, cleaning, and maintenance business in the New York City area. One of its contracts was with Greenpark Care Center, and the agreement provided for "cost plus $250 per week" in fees to FNM. FNM found this to provide too small a profit for an operation in which thirty-five of its employees were engaged, so FNM notified Greenpark that it intended to terminate the contract unless its fees were raised to cost plus $500 per week. Greenpark failed to respond, and FNM gave final notice of termination of the contract effective August 1, 1976.

During FNM's problems with Greenpark, the National Union of Hospital and Health Care Employees, Retail, Wholesale and Department Store Union, AFL-CIO (Union) conducted an organization campaign of FNM's employees. An election was held, and the union won. On July 12, 1976, the president of the union notified FNM that it wished to negotiate a contract.

On July 28, FNM notified all of the employees working in the Greenpark facility that they would be discharged on August 1 because of the termination of the Greenpark contract. The union president requested a delay to negotiate and requested that the parties bargain over the matter. The company refused, and the union filed an unfair labor practice charge, alleging violations of sections 8(a)(1) and (5). The Board found for the union, and the court of appeals affirmed. FNM appealed.

**Justice Blackmun Delivered the Opinion of the Court**    Must an employer, under its duty to bargain in good faith "with respect to wages, hours, and other terms and conditions of employment," . . . negotiate with the certified representative of its employees over its decision to close a part of its business? . . .

Some management decisions, such as choice of advertising and promotion, product type and design, and financing arrangements, have only an indirect and attenuated impact on the employment relationship. . . . Other management decisions, such as the order of succession of layoffs and recalls, production quotas, and work rules, are almost exclusively "an aspect of the relationship" between employer and employee. . . . The present case concerns a third type of management decision, one that had a direct impact on employment, since jobs were inexorably eliminated by the termination, but had as its focus only the economic profitability of the contract with Greenpark, a concern under these facts wholly apart from the employment relationship. This decision involving a change in the scope and direction of the enterprise is akin to the decision whether to be in business at all. . . . Cf. *Textile Workers v. Darlington*. . . . At the same time, this decision touches on a matter of central and pressing concern to the union and its member employees: the possibility of continued employment and the retention of the employees' very jobs. . . .

With this approach in mind we turn to the specific issue at hand: an economically-motivated decision to shut down part of a business.

A union's interest in participating in the decision to close a particular facility or part of an employer's operations springs from its legitimate concern over job security. . . .

Management's interest in whether it should discuss a decision of this kind is much more complex and varies with the particular circumstances. If labor costs are an important factor in a failing operation and the decision to close, management will have an incentive to confer voluntarily with the union to seek concessions. . . . At other times, management may have great need for speed, flexibility, and secrecy in meeting business opportunities and exigencies. It may face significant tax or securities consequences that hinge on confidentiality, the timing of a plant closing, or a reorganization of the corporate structure. . . . The employer also may have no feasible alternative to the closing, and even good faith bargaining over it may be both futile and cause the employer additional loss. . . .

We conclude that the harm likely to be done to an employer's need to operate freely in deciding whether to shut down part of its business purely for economic reasons outweighs the incremental benefit that might be gained through the union's participation in making the decision, and we hold that the decision itself is *not* part of §8(d)'s "terms and conditions," over which Congress has mandated bargaining.

The judgment of the Court of Appeals . . . is reversed. . . .

**Justice Brennan, with Whom Justice Marshall Joins, Dissenting**    As this Court has noted, the words "terms and conditions of employment" plainly cover termination of employment resulting from a management decision to close an operation. . . . In the exercise of its congressionally-delegated authority and accumulated expertise, the Board has determined that an employer's decision to close part of its opera-

tions affects the "terms and conditions of employment" within the meaning of the Act and is thus a mandatory subject for collective bargaining. . . . Nonetheless, the Court today declines to defer to the Board's decision on this sensitive question of industrial relations, and on the basis of pure speculation reverses the judgment of the Board and of the Court of Appeals. I respectfully dissent.

The Court bases its decision on a balancing test. . . . I cannot agree with this test, because it takes into account only the interests of *management*; it fails to consider the legitimate employment interests of the workers and their union. . . .

## Case Discussion Questions

1    What is the definition of a *mandatory bargaining topic?* What criteria are used to determine whether a bargaining topic is permissive or mandatory?
2    Does this decision further the idea that management and labor should work together towards the best interests of both?
3    Did this case overrule the *Darlington* case (p. 402)?

---

In 1983 the NLRB ruled that transfer of operations from union plants to nonunion facilities was not a violation of a collective bargaining agreement, unless the contract contained a **work-preservation clause.** A work-preservation clause requires the employer to provide jobs at a particular location. The board ruled that such transfers do not disturb the wages and benefits provisions of the contract, even though the facility may be shut down. Many unions now insist on work-preservation clauses as a result of the ruling. Such clauses require bargaining before transfers may be made.

### Strikes, Picketing, and Boycotts

Section 7 of the Wagner Act provides in part that employees shall have the right to strike as part of the term "other concerted activities" (see p. 398). Section 13 of the act also provides that "Nothing in this Act . . . shall be construed so as either to interfere with or impede or diminish in any way the right to strike. . . ."

**Economic Strikers and Unfair Labor Practice Strikers**    If, as during initial contract negotiations, the object of a strike is to obtain some economic concession from an employer, such as higher pay or better working conditions, the strikers are **economic strikers.** Such strikers cannot be discharged, but they can be replaced; and if the employer has hired bona fide replacements, they are not entitled to reinstatement. But if the strikers do not obtain regular and substantially equivalent employment, they are entitled to be recalled when openings occur if they have made an unconditional request for reinstatement.

**Unfair labor practice strikers** strike to protest some employer unfair labor practice. Such strikers cannot be discharged or permanently replaced, and they are entitled to their jobs at the end of the strike. In either case, the NLRB may order back pay if the employer unlawfully denies reinstatement.

Both economic and unfair labor practice strikers may lose their protected status if they engage in serious misconduct. Violence, threats, sitdown strikes that deprive the owner of the use of his property, and attacks on property are all "serious misconduct."

**Limits on Striking and Unlawful Strikes**    Strikes may be illegal if undertaken for illegal objectives, such as imposing secondary boycotts, compelling recognition of the union in certain circumstances, or compelling work assignments to specific workers. Strikes in support of any union unfair labor practice are also prohibited. If a strike is unlawful, employees who participate may be discharged and need not be reinstated.

**Strikes and Picketing During the Organizational Process**    Section 8(b)(4) provides that strikes, boycotts, and work stoppages are prohibited if their purpose is to compel recognition of an uncertified union where the employees are already represented. Picketing an employer is also prohibited for the purposes of obtaining recognition by an employer or gaining acceptance by employees (1) if the employer has already recognized another union and an election is barred by NLRB rules, (2) if a valid NLRB election has been held in the last twelve months, or (3) if a representation petition is not filed within a reasonable period of time, and not more than thirty days from the beginning of the picketing. If such picketing takes place, the NLRB may order an expedited election. The period cannot exceed thirty days and may be considerably shorter if the picketing is accompanied by violence or there are other indications that an expedited procedure is necessary.

**Informational picketing** is permitted by noncertified unions in some cases, however. The purpose of informational picketing is to inform the public that a particular employer does not have a union contract. Whether particular picketing is informational or is designed to obtain certification is a question of proof of the intention of the union, as disclosed by matters such as the language used on picket signs.

**No-Strike Clauses**    Collective bargaining agreements often contain **no-strike** provisions prohibiting strikes during the contract term. Such agreements usually provide for arbitration of disputes that arise. A strike in violation of such an agreement is called a **wildcat strike** and is illegal. Some walkouts are permitted, such as those caused by unsafe working conditions. No-strike clauses are found in most collective bargaining agreements, often together with a *no-lockout* clause.

**Strikes at the End of the Contract Period**    Most strikes occur when the collective bargaining agreement terminates and a new agreement is to be negotiated. The NLRA requires that parties desiring to terminate an existing agreement must notify the other party sixty days prior to the agreement's expiration and must notify the federal Mediation and Conciliation Service within thirty days of the notice to the other party. Any person who engages in a strike before the end of the notice period loses the protections of the NLRA.

**Picketing and Refusal to Cross Picket Lines**   Like the right to strike, the right to picket is also not absolute. Generally, if a strike is lawful, picketing in support of that strike is also lawful, although the number and placement of those pickets may be restricted by the NLRB. As noted earlier, recognitional picketing is unlawful under certain circumstances, although informational or publicity picketing is permissible. And the employer has the right to try to get its work done by finding someone willing to cross the picket lines.

**Hot-Cargo Agreements**   A **hot-cargo agreement** is a part of a labor contract which provides that employees are not required to handle or work on goods or materials going to or coming from an employer designated by the union as "unfair." Such agreements were quite common in the construction trades and transportation industries prior to the Landrum-Griffin Act. Strikes or other union action to obtain such agreements are unfair labor practices, and entering into such an agreement is an unfair labor practice by both unions and management under section 8(e) of the NLRA (see Table 16.2). There are limited exceptions from the hot-cargo prohibition in the construction and garment industries. (See Figure 16.2.)

**Secondary Boycotts**   A **secondary boycott** occurs when a union has a dispute with Company A and causes Company B to cease doing business with Company A to put pressure on Company A. In such a case, Company A is the *primary employer*, and Company B is the *secondary employer*. For example, urging employees of a building contractor not to install doors made by a manufacturer with whom a union is having a dispute might be a secondary boycott. Strikes or picketing to obtain such a boycott by the building contractor is an unfair labor practice. (See Figure 16.3.)

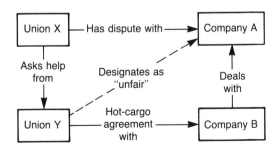

Union X, in its dispute with Company A, asks Union Y for help. Union Y, as part of its collective bargaining agreement with Company B, has a "hot cargo" clause whereby union employees of B need not handle goods going to, or coming from, a firm the union designates as "unfair." As a result, Company B cannot ship goods to, or receive goods from, Company A.

FIGURE 16.2   Hot-Cargo Agreements

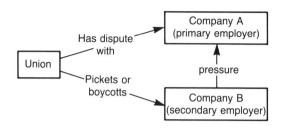

FIGURE 16.3    Secondary Boycotts

The act does not protect an employer from the "incidental" effects of union activities against the primary employer, however. As a result, picketing a **common situs,** where both employers do business, is generally not an unfair labor practice, as in the case of picketing a construction site where both the primary and secondary employers are doing business. Picketing at such a common site is generally limited by the courts to (1) times when the employees of the primary employer are working and when the primary employer is carrying on its normal business, and (2) places where the primary employer is carrying on its business. Picketing must be conducted in a manner, including wording of signs, that indicates that the dispute is with the primary employer and not with the secondary employer. It is also possible for a secondary boycott to involve consumers, as the following case illustrates.

## DeBartolo Corp. v. Florida Gulf Coast Building and Construction Trades Council
56 U.S.L.W. 4328 (1988)

Florida Gulf Coast Building and Construction Trades Council ("union") had a dispute with the H.J. High Construction Co., claiming that High paid substandard wages and fringe benefits. High had a contract to construct a department store in a shopping mall for the H.J. Wilson Company, which in turn had an agreement to rent space from DeBartolo, the owner of the mall. There were eighty-five other mall tenants.

The union distributed handbills asking mall customers not to shop at any of the stores in the mall until "the Mall's owner publicly promises that all construction at the Mall will be done using contractors who pay their employees fair wages and fringe benefits." The handbills clearly stated that the union was seeking only a consumer boycott against the other mall tenants, not a secondary strike by their employees. No picketing took place.

DeBartolo filed a complaint with the NLRB, claiming a secondary boycott. The NLRB held the activity was illegal, but the court of appeals denied enforcement of the order. DeBartolo appealed to the Supreme Court.

**Justice White Delivered the Opinion of the Court**    We agree with the Court of Appeals and respondents that . . . this case poses serious questions of the validity of Section 8(b)(4) under the First Amendment. . . . Had the union simply been leafletting the public generally, including those entering every shopping mall in town, pursuant to an annual educational effort against substandard pay, there is little doubt that legislative proscriptions of such leaflets would pose a substantial issue of validity under the First Amendment. . . . That a labor union is the leafletter and that a labor dispute was involved does not foreclose this analysis. . . .

This case turns on whether handbilling such as involved here must be held to "threaten, coerce, or restrain any person" to cease doing business with another, within the meaning of Section 8(b)(4)(ii)(B). . . . There is no suggestion that the leaflets had any coercive effect on customers of the mall. There was no violence, picketing, or patrolling and only an attempt to persuade customers not to shop in the mall.

The Board nevertheless found that the handbilling "coerced" mall tenants and explained . . . that "[a]ppealing to the public not to patronize secondary employers is an attempt to inflict economic harm on the secondary employers by causing them to lose business. . . . [S]uch appeals constitute economic retaliation and are therefore a form of coercion." Our decision in *NLRB v. Fruit Packers*, 377 U.S. 58 (1964) (the *Tree Fruits* case), however, makes untenable the notion that *any* kind of handbilling, picket-

ing, or other appeals to a secondary employer involved in a labor dispute is "coercion" . . . if it has some economic impact on the neutral. . . .

In *Tree Fruits*, we could not discern . . . that Congress intended to proscribe all peaceful consumer picketing at secondary sites. There is even less reason to find in the language of Section 8(b)(4)(ii) . . . any clear indication that handbilling, without picketing, "coerces" secondary employers. The loss of customers because they read a handbill urging them not to patronize a business, and not because they are intimidated by a line of picketers, is the result of mere persuasion, and the neutral who reacts is doing no more than what its customers honestly want it to do. . . .

[Affirmed.]

## Case Discussion Questions

1   What is a secondary boycott? What is the purpose of such a boycott?
2   Is labor union activity protected by the first amendment? What kinds of activity?
3   Why does the court make a distinction between handbilling and picketing? Is handbilling coercive? Is picketing *always* coercive?

---

If a company establishes a *reserved gate* to its premises for the exclusive use of an outside contractor, that gate may not be picketed by employees involved in a dispute with the company. Such picketing would be considered as a secondary boycott, unless the gate was used by both the company and the contractor for whom the gate was reserved.

**The Role of the Federal Mediation and Conciliation Service**   The Taft-Hartley Act established the **Federal Mediation and Conciliation Service** as an independent agency, headed by a director appointed by the President. It is the duty of this agency, "in order to prevent or minimize interruptions of the free flow of commerce growing out of labor disputes, to assist parties to labor disputes . . . to settle such disputes, through conciliation and mediation." The agency has no authority to impose settlements on parties, but rather offers a neutral third party to present suggestions and attempt to direct the proceedings.

### Content and Enforcement of Collective Bargaining Agreements

The ultimate result of collective bargaining is, in most cases, an agreement between the company and the union. In a very few cases, of course, agreement is never reached; the union stays out on strike indefinitely; and the company goes out of business, moves from the community, or hires an entirely new work force. But such changes are drastic and expensive, and the usual result is a **collective bargaining** agreement.

**Common Provisions of Collective Bargaining Agreements**    Labor contracts vary among industries and even among firms in the same industry, but some generalizations are possible. First, it is important to realize that the labor contract is a *contract* establishing enforceable legal rights and duties.

Most labor contracts include a **recognition clause,** in which the company recognizes the union as the exclusive bargaining agent for the employees and promises not to interfere with the rights of the employees to become union members. Often that clause will contain a promise that only union members will be hired, the so-called union-shop provision.

**Wage and benefits clauses** set the wage scales for all covered employees, including cost-of-living adjustments, overtime premiums, and wage increases during the contract term. All benefits, such as insurance, hospitalization, vacations, sick leave, pension plans, personal leave days, and many others, are specifically spelled out. Wage and benefit increases were an accepted way of life for many years, but recent trends during economic recessions introduced the idea of company "take-backs" of previously granted benefits or wages.

Two other important provisions set the *hours of work* and *seniority* of laborers. The hours provision generally provides the overtime premium, perhaps a guarantee of a certain number of hours of overtime, and provides for the distribution of overtime among the employees. The seniority provision generally assures that promotional opportunity and job security should increase in proportion to length of service. It is important to realize that employers almost always retain the right to discharge employees for cause, regardless of seniority, and may lay off workers in the event their services are not needed, usually in order of seniority.

One of the most important provisions sets the **grievance procedure.** The purpose of the clause is to establish the orderly resolution of differences between employees and employers. Normally, the grievance procedure involves several steps, including consultation with the foreman, the superintendent, a consultation with the grievance committee of the union and plant representatives, and ultimately, **arbitration.** Arbitration is a binding judgment by a neutral third party.

**Suits to Enforce Collective Bargaining Agreements**    One of the more important provisions of the Taft-Hartley Act gave both employers and unions the right to sue for violations of contracts, without regard to diversity of citizenship or the jurisdictional amount. Cases have interpreted that section to mean that employers may sue unions, but not individual employees, for damages of violations of collective bargaining agreements. Injunctions may also be granted against labor organizations by the federal courts, even in the face of the Norris-LaGuardia Act, if the collective bargaining agreement contains a no-strike clause and requires arbitration of disputes.

### Relationship of Union Members to Their Union

One of the more controversial areas of labor law deals with the rights of union members and other employees in relation to their union. During the mid-1950's, a series of congressional investigations found that some unions had become corrupt and that union leaders were abusing their power in a variety of ways. Since the federal law was in part responsible for the power of these officials, Congress acted by passing the Labor-Management Reporting and Disclosure Act of 1959, known as the Landrum-Griffin Act.

**The Landrum-Griffin Requirements**    The election of officers is the key to union democracy. But the congressional hearings found that many unions had constructed the rules of elections so that only a small group of persons was eligible to be elected and had provided little or no relief to union members injured by union actions. The act dealt with such problems by requiring (1) certain organizational procedures for all unions; (2) disclosure of union affairs to the Secretary of Labor and to the public; (3) the establishment of a union members' bill of rights; and (4) the designation of some new federal crimes, including embezzlement of union funds.

**Organizational and Reporting Requirements**    Under the act, unions were required to have a constitution and by-laws establishing the rules of election, and those documents were to be filed with the Secretary of Labor. Current information regarding union financial affairs, leadership, and potential areas of conflict of interest must be filed annually. Elections at the local level are required at least every three years and at the national level at least every five years.

**Union Members' Bill of Rights**    The act also established certain rights of union members in relation to their own unions, including the right to nominate candidates, vote in elections, attend membership meetings, have a voice in business transactions, vote on dues increases, and sue and testify against the union. Members are also guaranteed the right to free expression in union meetings and the right to receive a written, specific notice of charges and a fair hearing in union disciplinary actions. Each union member also has a right to a copy of the collective bargaining agreement.

**The Duty of Fair Representation**    Unions stand in a unique position in relation to the members, whom they represent at many critical stages in the employment relationship, from general contract negotiations to grievance procedures. From time to time unions may be tempted to represent employees in some unfair manner.

The national labor laws do not expressly require *fair representation* from unions. But over the years, the courts have found that right in the general duties of unions under section 7 of the Landrum-Griffin Act and the bargaining representative's implied duty of fair representation from its status as bargaining representative. A union must represent *all* of its members "without hostility or discrimination toward any, to exercise its discretion with complete good faith and honesty, and to avoid arbitrary conduct."[4] The

---

4 *Vaca v. Sipes*, 386 U.S. 171, 87 S. Ct. 903, 17 L. Ed. 2d 842 (1967).

duty of fair representation has been used in a number of ways, including racial discrimination suits against unions by employees.

**Union Discipline of Its Members**   The Landrum-Griffin Act provides that before a union disciplines one of its members, a member is entitled to a "full and fair hearing." Furthermore, it provides that certain types of conduct, such as expression of views in a union meeting, cannot be the subject of union disciplinary proceedings. A union member aggrieved by such discipline may bring suit in federal court, but not before he or she has exhausted all of the internal union remedies. The act does not set out the type of conduct that may be used to justify discipline.

## UNIONS AND THE PUBLIC SECTOR

The national labor laws treat the relationship of labor and management as an essentially private problem in need of rules to prevent disagreements from harming the parties and the public. Although labor disputes and collective bargaining agreements may injure the public by stopping the free flow of commerce and by inflating the economy, the laws do not address these problems except to provide methods by which disputes may be settled peacefully and quickly.

Two aspects of labor disputes do have rather severe public consequences, however. First is the problem of strikes in crucial industries during a national emergency, such as a steel strike in the middle of a war. Second is the problem of the unionization of public employees, such as firemen, policemen, and teachers.

### National Emergency Strikes

A President who believes that an actual or threatened strike or lockout imperils the national health or safety is authorized to appoint a board to inquire into the issues. Upon receipt of the report of that board, the President may direct the Attorney General to petition a district court for an injunction against the strike or lockout. If the strike affects all or a substantial part of an industry engaged in commerce, and if the court finds such peril as well, an injunction *must* issue.

Parties to the dispute must make every effort to settle their differences, but no party is required to accept any settlement proposal. A report is compiled by the Mediation and Conciliation Service, and the employees must vote by secret ballot whether to accept the final offer of the employer. At the end of an eighty-day *cooling-off period*, the injunction must be dissolved.

In 1959, President Eisenhower used these procedures in a steel strike involving a half million steelworkers and ninety-seven companies. An injunction was granted, and the unions appealed to the Supreme Court. In a very short opinion, the Court upheld the procedures of the Taft-Hartley Act.[5] The provisions have been used a few other times in the coal, atomic energy, maritime, and telecommunications industries.

**Public Employee Unions**   Until 1950, unions and collective bargaining agreements between public employees and units of government were extremely rare. Courts initially

---

5 *United Steelworkers of America v. U.S.*, 361 U.S. 39 (1959).

treated any attempt to organize or bargain as an invasion of governmental sovereignty or a threat to public safety, and usually enjoined such action.

But during the 1960's, the movement to organize public employees and grant them rights similar to those of employees in the private sector increased. Several reasons existed for this movement. The number of public employees grew rapidly in this period, which increased the number of persons affected and opened a fertile field for union organizers. Public salaries generally could not keep pace with those in the private sector, which was experiencing extraordinary growth, resulting in job dissatisfaction among public employees. The public became aware that there was more at issue in collective bargaining than wages and hours, including grievance procedures and job security. And government activities reached into new areas, belying the notion that all government services were crucial or essential. There seemed little difference, for example, between a strike of public school teachers and a strike of private school teachers, or between a strike of employees of a municipally owned utility and those of a privately owned utility.

Public employees remain outside of the protection of the National Labor Relations Act. But many states passed laws giving public employees certain rights to bargain collectively and, in a few instances, a limited right to strike. Most of those state laws have been copied almost verbatim from the National Labor Relations Act, although most do not grant the right to strike and instead substitute various *impasse resolution* procedures. Many of the laws are limited to certain classes of employees, such as teachers or municipal employees.

**The Duty to Bargain**    Generally, the state laws are of two types: (1) those requiring **collective negotiation** and (2) the so-called **meet and confer laws.** The former impose a duty to bargain similar to that imposed by the federal law for the private sector. The latter require discussions prior to adoption of policies by a governmental body—an advisory function, limited sharply by the legislative right to make laws. Many states adopt a model somewhere in between, such as the duty to "meet and confer in good faith." Of course, the basic problem with collective bargaining with public bodies is that often the public bodies do not have the final authority over budget matters and must await an appropriation by a legislature which may not feel bound by the previous negotiations.

**Impasse Resolution Procedures**    Instead of a right to strike, most state statutes provide for at least one of four **impasse resolution techniques:** (1) *mediation*, or neutral aid in achieving a solution; (2) *fact finding*, which involves mediation followed by public airing of the dispute by the mediator if an impasse is not resolved, potentially exposing both sides to bad publicity; (3) *voluntary arbitration*, or a binding decision by a neutral party, entered into by agreement of both parties; or (4) *compulsory arbitration*, or a binding decision by a neutral third party, required by law.

**Public Employee Strikes**    Historically, public employees have not had the right to strike. The theory, of course, was that essential services provided by government, such as fire and police protection, must be provided at all times. Most courts and legislatures continue to adopt that view and outlaw all strikes by public employees. A few states have permitted employee strikes if there is no adverse effect on the public health or safety,

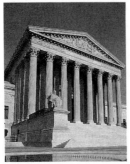

PROFILE

# The Air Traffic Controllers' Strike

The Civil Service Reform Act of 1978 provides the statutory basis for collective bargaining between the federal government and federal employee unions. The Professional Air Traffic Controllers Organization (PATCO) had formulated a collective bargaining agreement with the Federal Aviation Administration in the early 1970s. That agreement expired in 1981, and PATCO began negotiations early that year for a new contract. A tentative agreement was reached in June, but it was overwhelmingly rejected by the PATCO rank and file. PATCO announced a strike deadline of August 3, 1981. No agreement was reached, and a strike was called that morning.

Only 2,038 of the 9,034 controllers reported for work that morning. During the first five days of the strike, the FAA cancelled 26,000 air flights and operated at 69% capacity. That first morning, President Reagan gave the striking controllers forty-eight hours to return to work or forfeit their jobs. Those who did not return to work on their first scheduled shift after 11:00 A.M. on August 5 were terminated. The federal government also withdrew PATCO's certification as a bargaining representative for the controllers. That action was approved by the court in *PATCO v. Federal Labor Relations Authority*, 110 LRRM 2676 (U.S. Court of Appeals for the District of Columbia, 1982).

and there seems to be a trend toward such legislation, although the exact content varies widely.

Yet prohibiting strikes by law and preventing them as a practical matter are two totally separate considerations. "Job actions," "blue flu," and outright strikes have increased dramatically in recent years, even in the face of no-strike legislation. Economic strikes often turn into strikes for amnesty, and as a practical matter government employers must deal with strikers because replacing skilled workers is often impossible.

The courts have held that although there is no constitutional right to strike, there is a constitutionally protected right to join in labor organizations and to express one's opinion under the first amendment. It appears that public sector labor law will become the legal frontier of labor relations for the foreseeable future.

## SUMMARY AND CONCLUSIONS

The federal labor policy may be viewed as a balancer between the conflicting interests of labor and management. With the coming of the Industrial Revolution, organized labor was extremely weak and state laws placed labor at a severe disadvantage. An attempt to create a hands-off policy by outlawing injunctions against labor activity in the Norris-LaGuardia Act was not sufficient to give labor any real power.

It was not until Congress passed the Wagner Act in 1935 that labor obtained significant power. That act created the National Labor Relations Board (NLRB), established the right of employees to organize, and outlawed certain employer unfair labor practices. The law did not regulate union activities, however; and as a result, the strength of labor grew enormously.

In order to counter that power, Congress passed the Taft-Hartley Act in 1947. That act established certain union unfair labor practices, established detailed procedures for holding union elections, and provided a right *not* to join a labor union. In 1959, in response to charges of corruption in labor unions, the Landrum-Griffin Act was passed to regulate the internal procedures of unions.

The end result of the unionization process is the collective bargaining agreement, a voluntary contract between an employer and its organized employees. Whereas the private purpose of such agreements is to negotiate the best terms possible, the public purpose is to resolve labor disputes quickly and without disruption. To that end, the organization and negotiation processes are subject to a variety of regulations in the form of unfair labor practices. The theory behind collective bargaining is, of course, to equalize the bargaining power of the two sides.

Contemporary problems in labor relations involve the continuing debate over right-to-work laws, which are state statutes prohibiting union-shop contracts, and the controversy over the right of public employees to organize, bargain, and strike. Both areas promise to remain in the forefront of the development of American labor-management relations law.

## REVIEW QUESTIONS

**1**  Is the balance of power between business and labor equal today? If not, what *specific* changes would you make to equalize the power? Are those changes politically possible?

**2**  What are the *employer* unfair labor practices? What are the *union* unfair labor practices? Explain each in detail.

**3**  Explain the process of unionization. What unfair labor practices might occur during that period? What remedies exist for such unfair labor practices?

**4**  Explain the differences between a union shop, an open shop, and an agency shop.

**5**  What is a hot-cargo agreement? A secondary boycott? Why are secondary boycotts illegal? What about hot-cargo agreements?

**6**  A union representation election was held among certain employees of Savair Manufacturing Co. Prior to the election, the union circulated "recognition slips" among the employees. An employee who signed the slip before the election became a member of the union and would not have to pay the initiation fee to join the union. If the union was voted in, those who had not signed a recognition slip would have to pay. The employer refused to bargain after the union won the election, and the union filed an unfair labor practices charge against Savair. What do you think was the result? [*NLRB v. Savair Mfg. Co.*, 414 U.S. 270, 94 S. Ct. 495, 39 L. Ed. 2d 495 (1974).]

**7**  Fiberboard Paper Products decided that it could save a great deal of money by "contracting out" its maintenance work to an independent firm. Fiberboard had a collective bargaining agreement with a union representing its current maintenance employees. At the expiration of the agreement, Fiberboard notified the union that it had made a contract with the independent firm and would not bargain with the union. All current maintenance employees of the firm were discharged. The union filed a series of unfair labor practice charges against the firm. What do you think the outcome was? [*Fiberboard Paper Products Corp. v. NLRB*, 379 U.S. 203, 85 S. Ct. 398, 13 L. Ed. 2d 233 (1964).]

8   The contract that the XYZ Union had with the ABC Company expired. At the first meeting to resolve differences between the company and the union, the union raised the following issues: (a) changes in the company retirement plan; (b) whether employees with seniority should be given preference for overtime work; (c) whether a union representative should sit on the board of directors of the company; (d) changes in the grievance procedures; (e) how much employees will be docked for tardiness; (f) whether certain jobs will be phased out in favor of mechanization; (g) increased vacation time; (h) whether a union-shop agreement will be instituted; (i) whether the company may use a nonunion printer to print materials for the company; and (j) whether the company will close a facility and move part of its operations to another state. The

company refused to bargain on each of these issues. How many unfair labor practices has the company committed?

9   At most universities, faculty members have responsibilities beyond teaching and research, such as making recommendations regarding tenure, promotion, discharge, and other concerns. Are such full-time faculty members "supervisors" and therefore outside the protection of the NLRA? [*NLRB v. Yeshiva Univ.*, 444 U.S. 672, 100 S. Ct. 856, 63 L. Ed. 2d 115 (1980).]

10   A provision in the constitution of the United Steelworkers of America limits eligibility for local union office to members who have attended at least one-half of the regular meetings of the local for three years previous to the election, unless prevented by union activities or working hours. Among the members of Local 3489, 96.5% were ineligible under this provision. The Landrum-Griffin Act, however, provides that all members in good standing may be candidates, subject to "reasonable qualifications." The Secretary of Labor brought an action to invalidate a union election, claiming the provision in the union's constitution violated the act. What was the result? [*Local 3489, United Steelworkers of America v. Usery*, 429 U.S. 305, 97 S. Ct. 611, 50 L. Ed. 2d 502 (1977).]

# Labor Law: Worker Safety, Wages, and Security

American labor law can be viewed as two streams running from a single source. The source is a public concern with the welfare of individual workers. The first stream, discussed in the preceding chapter, might be called the *market approach*, because it is based on a national policy to enhance the bargaining power of workers by legalizing labor organizations and collective bargaining, and then permit market forces to protect workers through bargained agreements.

The second stream, sometimes called the *specific evil* approach, involves direct regulation of specific problems. Such specific regulations existed long before the NLRA or other collective bargaining laws, and in a sense were the first American labor laws.

The emphasis of specific evil labor legislation has always been in three areas: (1) protection of workers from unsafe working conditions; (2) protection of workers' pay, chiefly through minimum wage laws; and (3) protection of employees' security, both from penniless retirement and from unemployment. A fourth and more recent area of concern, that of protection from employment discrimination, is discussed in Chapter 18.

Specific regulations of labor have a long and checkered history. Late in the nineteenth century, several states passed laws dealing with abuses of labor, usually in the form of child labor acts, minimum wage laws, and laws prohibiting hiring women for certain dangerous occupations. Because of the restrictive definitions given the commerce clause and the broad definitions given the contracts clause and the due process clause, such laws were often found to be beyond the power of both the states and the federal government (see Chapter 4). It was not until after the watershed decisions of the Supreme Court in 1937 that the constitutionality of such laws was assured (see *West Coast Hotel v. Parrish*, p. 113).

## REGULATION OF WORKER SAFETY

One of the prime concerns of American labor law has always been worker safety and decent working conditions. Nineteenth-century factories were often extremely hazardous, resulting in large numbers of injured and disabled workers. The law provided little relief for such injuries, and states began adopting **worker's compensation laws.** Later, similar concerns would result in the Occupational Safety and Health Act of 1970 (OSHA).

### Common Law Remedies for Work-Related Injuries

At common law, work-related injuries were always considered under the tort system (see Chapter 9), which required the injured worker to prove that the employer was negligent. Employers had certain duties to protect workers, even under the common law, including the duty to provide a safe place to work, the duty to provide safe tools and equipment, the duty to give instructions and warnings to employees regarding unsafe conditions, the duty to provide suitable fellow employees, and the duty to make and enforce suitable rules to keep the workplace safe.

But employees still found it difficult to recover for work-related injuries. Employers had three defenses under the common law which barred recovery in many cases. Those defenses were **assumption of risk, contributory negligence,** and the **fellow-servant rule.**

**Assumption of Risk**    *Assumption of risk* is a traditional common law defense against negligence of all kinds (see p. 240). The rule says that a person cannot recover for injuries resulting from risks that are voluntarily accepted. Many courts held that workers assumed the risks of employment simply by accepting a job, even though the alternative was either starvation or accepting another equally dangerous job.

**Contributory Negligence**    *Contributory negligence* is another traditional tort defense that had special application to cases against employers (see p. 238). Any negligence on the part of a worker would act as a complete bar to recovery for injuries caused by the employer's negligence, even if that contributory negligence involved only a momentary lapse during a long workday.

**The Fellow-Servant Rule**    The *fellow-servant rule* was a rule that developed specifically within the context of employer torts. That rule says that an employee cannot recover against an employer for injuries caused by the torts of other employees. Technically, it is an exception to the rule of *respondeat superior*, which imposes liability on the master for the torts of his servants committed in the scope of the servant's employment (see p. 279).

**The Effect of the Common Law Defenses**    It is not accurate to say that employees were never able to recover for an employer's torts. But the three common law defenses did prohibit recovery in a great many cases. In addition, judges were generally probusiness and made it difficult for employees to recover, and attorneys' fees and costs often took up much of the proceeds of the few successful lawsuits.

Employees who were severely injured or disabled were no longer able to perform their duties and were often fired. Even if a recovery was obtained, it was often too little and too late to maintain that employee for the rest of his or her life or until other employment was obtained. Injured employees often became burdens on their family and friends or sought shelter in the nineteenth century's version of public welfare, the workhouse.

### Worker's Compensation Statutes

The first *worker's compensation statutes* were passed in Europe in the late nineteenth century. The first American law was passed in 1902 in Maryland, but that act was held unconstitutional. The first state statute to be upheld was passed in Wisconsin in 1911. All states now have some type of worker's compensation statute, although the content of those laws varies widely.

An early federal law protecting railroad workers, the **Federal Employer's Liability Act,** provided a model for many state worker's compensation acts. The FELA imposes liability on railroads operating in interstate commerce for any injury resulting from a violation of safety rules. The act virtually eliminates the defenses of assumption of risk and contributory negligence in such actions and completely eliminates the fellow-servant rule. Contributory negligence will not bar recovery but will reduce the employee's recovery proportionately. Actions may be brought in any state or federal court having venue. A 1920 amendment, the Jones Act, extended the same protections to seamen.

The underlying theory of worker's compensation statutes is that "the cost of the product should bear the blood of the workman." In other words, injuries to workers should be treated as a cost of doing business, like tools that break or goods that are wasted. The financial burden is lifted from the worker's shoulders and shifted to the employer. The employer is expected to obtain liability insurance to spread the risk of such injuries, and the premiums for that insurance are included in the price of the goods produced. Often liability insurance is made compulsory by state law to guarantee risk spreading.

**Common Worker's Compensation Provisions**    The typical worker's compensation law is *compulsory*, although a large minority of states permit some employers or some employees to make an election of coverage. Most state laws exempt certain industries or trades, but those exemptions are for industries or trades with other forms of protection for injured workers. Commonly, farm workers, domestic servants, and employees of very small businesses are also not covered by worker's compensation laws. Most state laws apply to both *injuries* and *industrial diseases*.

**"Arising from Employment"**    Most state statutes are *no fault* in nature. That is, the worker need not prove that the employer was "at fault" in causing the injury. Usually employees have a right to recover if the injury *arose from employment*. This broad language is usually interpreted to mean that the injury was caused by the employment, with no requirement of proof of fault. Commonly, the traditional tort defenses of assumption of risk, contributory negligence, and the fellow-servant rule are abolished in such cases.

As a result, the worker has a very light burden of proof. Even if the injury resulted from the worker's own carelessness, or if the employer was completely blameless in the matter, the injured employee still has a right to recover. The issue is not whether the employer caused the injury, but whether the employment *resulted in* the injury.

---

## Murray v. Industrial Commission of Illinois
516 N.E.2d 1039 (Ill. App., 3d Dist., 1987)

David Murray, a garageman for Commonwealth Edison Company, was standing in front of his supervisor's desk, when a co-worker (Baker) approached him from behind and hit him in the back of the knees. Murray's knees buckled, and because of oil on the floor he could not catch himself. His entire weight fell on his right knee. An operation to repair some of the damage was successful, but a doctor testified that ligaments in the knee were torn, and the knee would always be unstable and subject to arthritis.

Murray brought this action before the Industrial Commission on the theory that the injury "arose out of and in the course of employment." The Industrial Commission arbitrator found for Murray and awarded him medical benefits, temporary total disability in the amount of $186.20 (two-thirds of his gross weekly wage) for eleven weeks, and seventy additional weeks of compensation at the same rate for permanent partial disability for a 35% loss of his right leg.

The full Industrial Commission reversed the arbitrator's decision on the ground that this was an *assault*, and under Illinois law Murray had to show

> that a fellow employee assaulted [claimant] for no apparent reason, and the failure to show that the assault was in any way occasioned by or related to the performance of his duties as a garageman or that his employment was such as to particularly subject him to the hazard of attack by fellow employees. . . . [quoted from commission order].

Murray appealed to the courts, and the trial court held that this incident was *horseplay* and not an assault, and found for Murray. Commonwealth Edison appealed.

**Justice McNamara Delivered the Opinion of the Court** . . . Illinois permits the non-participating victim of horseplay to recover worker's compensation benefits. . . . An assault is not compensable unless it arises out of the work environment.

It is within the province of the Commission to weigh the evidence and resolve conflicts in the testimony, and this court will not reject permissible inferences drawn by the Commission or substitute its judgment for that of the Commission on such matters unless its findings are contrary to the manifest weight of the evidence.

In the present case, the record is completely devoid of any evidence which might indicate that Baker assaulted claimant. Both claimant and Baker agree that they had never argued or disagreed. Baker testified that he did not intend to harm claimant, and had previously been reprimanded for inappropriate horseplay. The foreman's report found that the cause of

the accident was horseplay. We conclude that the Commission's finding that claimant was assaulted by a co-worker is against the manifest weight of the evidence.

Judgment affirmed. . . .

## Case Discussion Questions

1   Did the employer *cause* the injury to the plaintiff? Why didn't the plaintiff sue Baker, who really caused the injury?

2   Why should an employer be liable under worker's compensation for horseplay, but not for an assault? What is the difference? Would this have been an assault under a common law tort theory?

3   What evidence existed that this was horseplay, not an assault? What administrative law rule (see Chapter 6) does this case illustrate?

---

The broad language of the usual worker's compensation statute has given rise to numerous other problems as well. Some of the most difficult areas have involved workers who suffer some *mental injury*, workers who are injured on the way to work or on the way home, and workers who contract cancer or other diseases as a result of prolonged exposure to substances on the job. All three types of cases have resulted in conflicting decisions among the state courts.

**Mental Injury**    *Mental injury* refers to several types of cases that have caused some difficulty in worker's compensation practice. First, all courts have provided recovery for a mental illness caused by a physical injury. For example, a worker who is injured as a result of a fall from a building may develop a fear of heights, and the courts have generally compensated both the physical and mental injuries. Courts have also granted compensation when a physical injury results from a mental shock, such as a heart attack resulting from the fear caused by a sudden noise, a robbery, or a fire. Courts have had more difficulty with physical injuries caused by long periods of job stress, such as a heart attack caused by years of intense pressure. For example, an Illinois worker's compensation arbitrator received a substantial award for a heart attack caused by years of deciding dozens of important cases every day. In those cases, most jurisdictions will permit recovery if proof exists that the stress caused the physical injury.

**Injuries on the Way to Work**    As a general rule, employees will not be compensated for injuries that happen on the way to work or on the way home. Employers are generally not liable for injuries that result from "common risks" that all of us run, such as traffic accidents. On the other hand, if the employee does not have fixed hours or a place of employment, such as a salesperson or truck driver, the employer will be liable. Many courts draw the line at the employer's property, and accidents that happen in the employer's parking lot will be compensable. Employees who travel are generally considered to be protected continuously by worker's compensation.

**Occupational Diseases**    All states maintain some kind of **occupational diseases** statute, providing compensation for diseases caused by employment. Recovery is similar to that provided by worker's compensation, but many state occupational disease laws provide fewer benefits than under worker's compensation. The employee must show that the disease was caused by the employment, which is sometimes not an easy task. Cancer, lung disease, allergies, and hearing loss have all been compensated under such acts.

**"Within the Scope of Employment"**    Some states use language in their statutes to the effect that injuries must arise "within the scope of employment" before they are compensable by worker's compensation. While state court decisions are not consistent, such language seems to indicate a more narrow view of the kinds of injuries that will be compensated. That language seems to indicate that the employee must be actually performing duties related to his or her employment when the injury occurs, whereas the "arising out of employment" language seems to mean that there need only be a causal connection between the employment and the injury.

**Worker's Compensation Benefits**    Benefits available under the state worker's compensation laws and the methods of computing those benefits vary widely. Almost all state acts provide for *medical expenses* resulting from the injury, usually for the life of the worker. Most laws also require payment for a part of the worker's *lost earnings*, both temporarily if he or she must stop working to recuperate, and permanently if he or she is disabled. Most states require employers to assist in any *rehabilitation* of the injured worker and to offer some form of *death benefit* for workers killed on the job. (See Figure 17.1.) Some states provide for as little as six months' income for widows, widowers, and

Assume that Joe Smith, a carpenter, earns $400 per week on the average. One day Joe fell from scaffolding while erecting a house for his employer, the XYZ Construction Company. Joe broke his arm and was hospitalized for two days. In addition, Joe was off work for a period of six weeks while the arm mended. A physician stated that Joe's arm will always be a little weaker than before, and he may be subject to arthritis in the arm later on.

Because this accident happened in Illinois, Joe's benefits would be as follows.

**1**  *Medical Costs.* All medical bills resulting from the injury would be paid for the rest of Joe's life.

**2**  *Temporary Total Disability.* Joe would receive pay for the time he is off work. In order to determine how much, we must determine Joe's *rate*. In Illinois, a worker's rate is found by multiplying the worker's average weekly wage (in this case $400) times 2/3, up to certain maximums and above certain minimums. (Rates in other states may be as low as 1/4 or as high as 3/4.) Joe's rate would be $400 × 2/3, or $267. Joe would receive $267 per week for the entire time he is temporarily totally disabled, or in this case, $1,602.

**3**  *Permanent Partial Disability.* Joe's arm is permanently injured, although the injury is slight in this case. Statutes provide a certain number of weeks of compensation for each member or part of the human body—for example, in Illinois a leg is worth 200 weeks, a hand is worth 180 weeks, and an arm is worth 235 weeks. Thus, in this case Joe's arm would be worth 235 weeks times Joe's rate, or $267. Thus, if Joe's arm were 100% disabled, it would be worth 235 × $267, or $62,745.

But in this case, the permanent injury to Joe's arm is slight—perhaps 5% or 10%. The figure finally selected would either result from a compromise or be imposed by the arbitrator—under Illinois law no physician can testify as to the percentage of disability. Assuming that the arbitrator found a 10% disability in Joe's arm, Joe would receive 10% × $62,745, or $6,275.

FIGURE 17.1    Example of Worker's Compensation Calculation

orphans, whereas others provide for as many as twenty years of support. Perhaps the most controversial of the worker's compensation benefits are the payments for *temporary and permanent disability.*

**Insurance**    Benefits vary widely between states, causing large differences in the amount of insurance premiums paid by employers to obtain coverage. Thus, in a state where the benefits are high, the insurance premiums are also high. Generally, those rates are highest in the northeastern and midwestern industrial states, and some have argued that high insurance premiums in those states have contributed to the exodus of industry to other states.

Most state laws require employers to maintain insurance to cover losses under the worker's compensation laws, although some states will permit larger employers to become **self-insurers** (pay claims out of a reserve fund maintained by the company), if they can demonstrate the financial ability to do so. Some states operate a state fund, either to augment private insurance or to replace it. Most states expressly permit employers to pass on the costs of such insurance to consumers in the form of increased prices.

**Worker's Compensation as the Exclusive Remedy**    Most worker's compensation statutes provide that the worker's compensation benefits are the *exclusive remedy* available to employees. This means that, as a general rule, an employee may not bring both a worker's compensation action and a common law tort action. Courts have recently provided a number of exceptions to this rule, including situations where the employer *intentionally* injures a worker, where the employee sues the manufacturer of a product (e.g., a machine on which the employee is working) that injures the employee, or where the employee sues a third party for negligence.

For example, if A, a truck driver for XYZ Company, is injured by B, the driver of another car, A may sue B in tort. If an injured employee receives worker's compensation and then files a common law tort action against some third party for causing the injury, the employer may have a right to indemnification for the amounts paid under worker's compensation.

**Administration and Enforcement**    In most states an administrative agency, often known as the Industrial Commission or the Worker's Compensation Commission, is charged with the administration of the law. Normally, an injured worker must file with the agency a claim, which is quickly heard by an **arbitrator** appointed by the agency. Employers are normally required to pay temporary disability after the first week of injury, or even earlier, and must seek commission approval before terminating those payments. Decisions of the arbitrator may be appealed to the full agency and then to the courts. A few states simply permit private lawsuits brought in the state courts instead of using an administrative agency.

## The Occupational Safety and Health Act of 1970 (OSHA)

Worker's compensation acts provide a remedy for injuries *after* they occur. But other laws, notably the federal **Occupational Safety and Health Act (OSHA)**, take a different approach—that of trying to *prevent* injuries before they occur. The approach is quite simple: Establish safety standards and punish employers who do not meet those standards.

In 1969, Congress began holding hearings on injuries in the workplace. The evidence showed that 2.2 million persons were disabled and 14,500 persons were killed in on-the-job accidents each year. The number of disabling injuries actually was going up, as much as 20% higher than it had been twelve years before. The economic waste attributed to such injuries was staggering, amounting to $1.5 billion in lost wages and an annual loss to the GNP of $8 billion in 1969 dollars.

The result of the hearings was the passage of the Occupational Safety and Health Act of 1970. The act established a new administrative agency, the **Occupational Safety and Health Administration,** and gave that agency the authority to make rules and enforce the act. The act covers any employer whose work *affects commerce*—the same criterion used in the *Heart of Atlanta Motel* case (p. 108). As a result, very few, if any, employers escape coverage under the law.

**Employer Duties**    The act imposes two principal duties on employers. First, the act includes the so-called **general duty clause**, which provides that "each employer . . . shall furnish . . . employment and a place of employment which are free from recognized hazards that are causing or are likely to cause death or serious physical harm to his employees." Second, the Secretary of Labor may make specific *rules* promoting employment health and safety. The act imposes some *ancillary duties*, such as keeping records, reporting injuries, and telling employees of their rights under the act.

The act sets up four major categories of violations: (1) *willful or repeated violations*; (2) *serious violations*, from which "death or serious physical harm could result . . . unless the employer did not, and could not with the exercise of reasonable diligence, know of the presence of the violation"; (3) *nonserious violations*; and (4) *de minimus* (technical and minor) *violations*. Civil penalties may be imposed in all cases except *de minimus* violations, and criminal penalties may be imposed by the courts for willful violations that result in death, for false reporting, and for advance warnings of an inspection. The Secretary of Labor may seek injunctions against dangerous conditions, but there is no private right of action for persons injured as a result of OSHA violations.

**OSHA Organization**    The Occupational Safety and Health Administration is a part of the Department of Labor, headed by an Assistant Secretary of Labor for OSHA. The nation is divided into ten geographical regions, each of which contains several area and district offices and field stations. Each area office is under an Area Director, who is in charge of scheduling and conducting inspections and issuing citations and proposed penalties.

The rule-making function is delegated to the Secretary of Labor and the Secretary of HEW. Originally, the Secretary of Labor was given authority to adopt standards for industry without elaborate rule-making procedures. Those interim standards gave way to formal *notice and comment rule making* (see p. 152) in 1973, and such procedures must be followed except in emergency situations. Emergency standards may only exist for six months before a formal rule is adopted. The Administrative Procedures Act applies to the adoption of OSHA standards.

Much of the background research for the standards is done by the National Institute for Occupational Safety and Health (NIOSH). NIOSH has no authority to make standards but conducts research and makes recommendations to the Secretary. A private organization, the American National Standards Institute (ANSI) also works closely with OSHA and with private firms to draft the OSHA standards.

The judicial function of OSHA is delegated to another agency, the **Occupational Safety and Health Review Commission.** That body consists of three members appointed by the President for staggered six-year terms. The Review Commission appoints hearing examiners to hear cases prior to record review by the full commission. If OSHA issues a citation, the party to whom it is issued may contest the citation before the commission. A hearing examiner will hear the case and forward a report to the commission, which either adopts or rejects the examiner's decision. Either party may appeal to the U.S. courts of appeal.

**OSHA Enforcement**    OSHA is required by the act to inspect workplaces to determine compliance. The administration has adopted a "worst-first" inspections priorities system. The first to be inspected are cases of imminent danger, followed by catastrophe and fatality investigations, employee complaints, and finally "special emphasis" program inspections. The act forbids advance notice of an inspection and provides criminal penalties for persons giving such notice. A search warrant is required for such inspections, but such warrants may be issued on an **ex parte** (one-party) basis and without a showing of probable cause (see *Marshall v. Barlow's, Inc.*, p. 161). Inspectors, known as Compliance Safety and Health Officers, or *COs*, usually have an engineering background and are required to undergo specialized training before beginning work. The actual inspection consists of three stages: (1) an *opening conference* in which the inspector discusses the procedures for conducting the inspection, (2) a *walkaround* tour of the facility, and (3) a *closing conference* at which the inspector issues any citations and makes other safety and health suggestions. Employers have a right to know the nature of any employee complaints, but they do not have a right to know the name of the complaining employee.

Employers may claim certain areas off-limits because of trade secrets, but inspectors have a right to ask for a hearing to determine whether or not the claim is justified. Such hearings are held in secret by the Review Commission. At the closing conference, the inspector will issue any citations and propose penalties. If the employer accepts the penalty, there will be no further review. Contests of such penalties take place before the OSHA Review Commission.

It was initially argued that OSHA procedure deprived parties of their right to a jury trial and imposed criminal-like penalties without due process of law. The following decision considered the first of those arguments and also contains one of the best summaries of OSHA enforcement techniques.

## *Atlas Roofing Co. v. Occupational Safety and Health Review Commission*

430 U.S. 442, 97 S. Ct. 1261, 51 L. Ed. 2d 464 (1977)

**Mr. Justice White Delivered the Opinion of the Court**    The issue in this case is whether, consistent with the Seventh Amendment, Congress may create a new cause of action in the Government for civil penalties enforceable in an administrative agency where there is no jury trial.

After extensive investigation, Congress concluded, in 1970, that work-related deaths and injuries had become a "drastic" national problem. Finding the existing state statutory remedies as well as state common law actions for negligence and wrongful death to be inadequate to protect the employee population from death and injury due to unsafe working conditions, Congress enacted the Occupational Safety and Health Act of 1970. . . . The Act created a new statutory duty to avoid maintaining unsafe or unhealthy working conditions, and empowers the Secretary of Labor to promulgate health and safety standards. Two new remedies were provided—permitting the Federal Government, proceeding before an administrative agency, (1) to obtain abatement orders requiring employers to correct unsafe working conditions and (2) to impose civil penalties on any employer maintaining any unsafe working condition. . . .

Under the Act, inspectors, representing the Secretary of Labor, are authorized to conduct reasonable safety and health inspections. . . . If a violation is discovered, the inspector, on behalf of the Secretary, issues a citation to the employer fixing a reasonable time for its abatement and, in his discretion, proposing a civil penalty. . . . Such proposed penalties may range from nothing for *de minimus* and nonserious violations, to not more than $1,000 for serious violations, to a maximum of $10,000 for willful or repeated violations. . . .

If the employer wishes to contest the penalty or the abatement order, he may do so by notifying the Secretary of Labor within 15 days, in which event the abatement order is automatically stayed. . . . An evidentiary hearing is then held before an administrative law judge of the Occupational Safety and Health Review Commission. The Commission consists of three members, appointed for six-year terms, each of whom is qualified to adjudicate contested citations and assess penalties "by reason of training, education, or experience." . . . At this hearing the burden is on the Secretary to establish the elements of the alleged violation and the propriety of his proposed abatement order and proposed penalty, and the judge is empowered to affirm, modify, or vacate any or all of these items giving due consideration in his penalty assessment to "the size of the business of the employer . . . the gravity of the violation, the good faith of the employer, and the history of previous violations." The judge's decision becomes the Commission's final and appealable order unless within 30 days a Commissioner directs that it be reviewed by the full Commission.

If review is granted, the Commission's subsequent order directing abatement and the payment of any assessed penalty becomes final unless the employer timely petitions for judicial review in the appropriate court of appeals. . . . The Secretary similarly may seek review of Commission orders . . . but, in either case, "[t]he findings of the Commission with respect to questions of fact, if supported by substantial evidence on the record considered as a whole, shall be conclusive." . . . If the employer fails to pay the assessed penalty, the Secretary may commence a collection action in a federal district court in which neither the fact of the violation nor the propriety of the penalty assessed may be retried. . . . Thus, the penalty may be collected without the employer ever being entitled to a jury determination of the facts constituting the violation.

[In this case petitioners] were separately cited by the Secretary and ordered immediately to abate pertinent hazards after inspections of their respective work sites conducted in 1972 revealed conditions that assertedly violated a mandatory occupational safety standard. . . . In each case an employee's death had resulted. . . . [Each argued that OSHA procedure deprived them of the right to a trial by jury as guaranteed by the Seventh Amendment—Ed.]

The Seventh Amendment provides that "in Suits at common law, where the value in controversy shall exceed twenty dollars the right of trial by jury shall be preserved." The phrase "suits at common law" has been construed to refer to cases tried prior to the adoption of the Seventh Amendment in courts of law

in which jury trial was customary as distinguished from courts of equity or admiralty in which jury trial was not. . . .

Petitioners claim that a suit in federal court by the Government for civil penalties for violation of a statute is a suit for a money judgment which is classically a suit at common law . . . and that the defendant therefore has a Seventh Amendment right to a jury determination of all issues of fact in such a case. . . . Petitioners then claim that to permit Congress to assign the function of adjudicating the Government's rights to civil penalties for violation of the statute to a different forum—an administrative agency in which no jury is available—would be to permit Congress to deprive a defendant of his Seventh Amendment jury right. We disagree. At least in cases in which "public rights" are being litigated—e.g., cases in which the Government sues in its sovereign capacity to enforce public rights created by statutes within the power of Congress to enact—the Seventh Amendment does not prohibit Congress from assigning the factfinding function and initial adjudication to an administrative forum which the jury would be incompatible.

[H]istory and our cases support the proposition that the right to a jury trial turns not solely on the nature of the issue to be resolved, but also on the forum in which it is to be resolved. Congress found the common law and other existing remedies for work injuries resulting from unsafe working conditions to be inadequate to protect the Nation's working men and women. It created a new cause of action, and remedies therefor, unknown to the common law, and placed their enforcement in a tribunal supplying speedy and expert resolutions of the issues involved. The Seventh Amendment is no bar to the creation of new rights or to their enforcement outside the regular courts of law.

The judgments below are affirmed.

## Case Discussion Questions

1  Are the OSHA procedures fair? Do they provide procedural due process to employers charged with violations?

2  If jury trials were permitted in OSHA cases, what would be the effect on court workloads? Would juries have the expertise to rule in such cases?

3  Are the OSHA procedures too complex? Could they be simplified?

| De minimus violations | $0 |
| Nonserious violations | $0–1,000 |
| Serious violations | $1–1,000 |
| Repeated violations | $0–10,000 |
| Willful violations | $0–10,000 |
| Failure to abate violations | $0–1,000 per day |

FIGURE 17.2    Penalties for OSHA Violations

**Penalties**    The act provides for a wide range of penalties, depending on the severity of the offense (see Figure 17.2). The amount of the penalty assessed will depend on two factors: (1) the *gravity* (seriousness) of the violation; and (2) whether the violator was acting in *good faith*. Gravity is composed of three factors: (1) the likelihood that an injury would result from the violation; (2) the severity of any resulting injuries; and (3) the extent to which a standard has been violated, e.g., the amount of employee exposure. Good faith may be demonstrated by four factors: (1) the employer's overall safety program; (2) actual attempts to comply with the standard; (3) employer cooperation with the CO; and (4) prompt abatement of violations. The act also provides that the size of a business and the employer's history of compliance should be considered in determining the penalty. The commission retains the authority to either raise or lower the penalty proposed by the CO, but the authority to raise the penalty has been used sparingly.

**Refusal of Employees to Work**    While it is clear under the Taft-Hartley Act that an employee may walk off the job if the work becomes unreasonably hazardous, the issue quickly arose under OSHA whether employees could protect themselves by refusing to work. In *Whirlpool Corp. v. Marshall*[1] the Supreme Court upheld an OSHA regulation that permits employees to refuse to work if they have a "reasonable apprehension of death or serious injury coupled with a reasonable belief that no less drastic alternative is available."

**State Enforcement**    One of the purposes of the original act was to encourage the adoption of state standards and procedures to protect worker safety. For that reason, the act permitted the states to adopt their own standards; and once such standards are adopted and approved, the state governs the area. Those standards must be at least as effective as the federal standards, and the enforcement procedures must be "workable." About half the states have adopted such standards and secured the approval of the Secretary of Labor to implement those plans.

## REGULATION OF WAGES

Some states had passed minimum wage and maximum hours laws in the late nineteenth and early twentieth centuries, but those laws were often held unconstitutional under the economic due process doctrine (see p. 112). After the 1937 *Jones & Laughlin Steel* de-

---

1 445 U.S. 1, 100 S. Ct. 883, 63 L. Ed. 154 (1980).

cision (p. 107) widened the authority of Congress to regulate commerce, Congress passed its own minimum wage law: the federal Fair Labor Standards Act of 1938.

### The Federal Fair Labor Standards Act (FLSA)

The Fair Labor Standards Act has five principal parts: (1) It requires that employers keep payroll records on all employees; (2) it requires employers to pay men and women "equal pay for equal work"; (3) it requires payment of at least the minimum wage to all covered employees; (4) it requires payment of "overtime," or one and one-half times the ordinary wage, for work over forty hours in one week; and (5) it prohibits employers from oppressively employing child labor.

Initially, the FLSA only covered *employees* who were directly engaged in interstate commerce. This restriction resulted in situations in which two employees, both working for the same employer and doing identical work, might be paid different rates, if one was engaged in interstate commerce and the other was not. In later years the act was changed to cover any *enterprise* engaged in commerce. The act also exempted many categories of employees, but many of those exemptions have been removed. Agricultural workers, domestic servants, and some government workers have been covered under later amendments.

### Minimum Wage–Maximum Hours Provisions

The key provision of the FLSA provides a federal minimum wage for certain classes of employees and required premium pay, or *overtime*, for all hours over a statutory maximum, usually forty hours. Contrary to common belief, the law does not permit employees to refuse to work over forty hours, but only requires the payment of "overtime" for such work. The original minimum wage was 25¢ per hour, but there have been numerous increases since that time. Some states have also imposed minimum wage laws, and employers must pay either the state or federal minimum wage, whichever is higher. Employers or employees not subject to the federal law may be covered under state law.

Only "employees" are covered by the act, and some employers have attempted to create employment relationships that are traditionally treated as some nonemployment relationship (such as an independent contractor) by the common law, either to avoid the effect of the FLSA or for other reasons. The following decision considers whether a scheme to establish "independent" businesses to hire migrant workers defeated the coverage of the act.

---

## Hodgson v. Griffin and Brand of McAllen, Inc.
471 F.2d 235 (5th Cir., 1973)

The defendant owned a large fruit- and vegetable-packing firm in Texas, and conducted farming operations as well. There was no doubt that its produce ended up in interstate commerce, and many of the laborers were migrant workers. Griffin and Brand dealt with so-called crew leaders, who secured the migrant workers and transported them to the work site. The crew leader was paid a weekly sum from which he paid the migrant workers. An employee of the defendant in turn supervised the crew leaders. The defendant also withheld social security, because it believed that the crew leaders were incapable of doing the calculations.

It was clear that the crew leaders violated the FLSA in several respects, including paying less than the minimum wage, not paying overtime, and hiring children. The Secretary of Labor brought this action under the FLSA, claiming the migrant workers were the defendant's "employees." The District Court found that the defendant had violated the act, and the defendant appealed on the grounds that the employees were not "employees" within the meaning of the act. The district court granted an injunction against future violations. The defendant appealed to the U.S. circuit court of appeals.

**Thornberry, Circuit Judge** The independent contractor status of the crew leaders, if they are independent contractors, does not as a matter of law negate the possibility that Griffin and Brand may be a joint employer of the harvest workers. There may be independent contractors who take part in production or distribution who would alone be responsible for the wages and hours of their own employees, . . . but independent contractor status does not necessarily imply the contractor is solely responsible under the Fair Labor Standards Act. Another employer may be jointly responsible for the contractor's employees. . . .

Whether appellant is an employer of the harvest workers does not depend on technical or isolated factors, but rather on the circumstances of the whole activity . . . it depends not on the form of the relationship but on the "economic reality." . . . This court has summarized the proper approach to be taken and some important factors to be regarded as follows:

Whether a person or corporation is an employer or joint employer is essentially a question of fact. . . . In considering whether a person or corporation is an "employer" or "joint employer," the total employment situation would be considered with particular regard to the following questions: (1) Whether or not the employment takes place on the premises of the company?; (2) How much control does the company exert over the employees?; (3) Does the company have the power to fire, hire, or modify the employment condition of the employees?; (4) Do the employees perform a "specialty job" within the production line?; and (5) May the

employee refuse to work for the company or work for others? . . .

We do not think the district court's conclusion in this case that appellant was a joint employer was clearly erroneous; on the contrary, we find that it was amply supported by the evidence. Of course, the work necessarily took place on appellant's premises. The testimony that appellant's field supervisors supervised the harvest work tends to indicate an employment relationship. The fact that appellant effected the supervision by speaking to the crew leaders, who in turn spoke to the harvest workers, rather than speaking directly to the harvest workers, does not negate a degree of apparent on-the-job control over the harvest workers. The fact that appellant set the rate of pay of the harvest workers, decided whether crew leaders would pay a piece rate or an hourly rate in a given instance, and handled the social security contributions for the harvest workers also tends to indicate an employment relationship. Viewing the total work arrangement, we agree with the district court that appellant was a joint employer and thus responsible for the violations of the Fair Labor Standards Act. . . .

[Affirmed.]

## Case Discussion Questions

**1** Why did the employer choose to organize the business in this way? Isn't it rather clumsy?

**2** Why does the court look to the "economic reality" of the arrangement, rather than to the names which the parties call the relationship?

**3** To what factors does the court look to determine whether a true employment relationship exists?

Some employees remain outside the protections of the act, including executive, managerial, and professional employees; employees of certain seasonal amusement firms and some small newspapers; casual babysitters and companions to the elderly; and persons in individually or family owned small businesses. State law may be more extensive than the FLSA.

**Child Labor Provisions**    Both state and federal laws impose restrictions on the employment of children. Most of the federal law regarding child labor is found in the FLSA, but that act exempts several categories of child labor from the act, including newspaper delivery, modeling, acting, nonhazardous farm work when school is not in session, farm work on a farm owned or operated by the child's parent, and other nonhazardous employment for the child's parent or guardian. Most regulation of child labor is done under state law.

The FLSA prohibits children, other than those in an exempt category, from working if they are under the age of fourteen. Children between fourteen and sixteen may work outside of school hours, provided they work no more than eight hours a day and forty hours a week during school vacation periods and three hours a day and eighteen hours a week while school is in session. Such children may not work between 7 P.M. and 7 A.M. (9 P.M. when school is not in session). In addition, the Secretary of Labor has established certain categories of hazardous employment in which children cannot be employed. Children between sixteen and eighteen years of age may work in any nonhazardous employment.

**Equal Pay**    In 1963 the federal Equal Pay Act was added as an amendment to the Fair Labor Standards Act. The act required that "equal work be rewarded with equal wages." Women cannot be paid less than men "for equal work on jobs the performance of which requires equal skill, effort and responsibility, and which are performed under similar working conditions." Different payment is permissible in four instances: (1) a seniority system, (2) a merit system, (3) a system that measures earnings by quantity or quality of production (e.g., piecework), and (4) a differential that measures earnings based on any factor other than sex. Remedies may include an order to pay back wages and injunctions against continued violation. The Secretary of Labor has the authority to file such actions. Sex discrimination in employment is discussed further in Chapter 18.

**Enforcement and Remedies**    Administrative responsibility for FLSA enforcement is vested in the Wage and Hour Division of the Employment Standards Administration of the Department of Labor. That division brings compliance actions to force the payment of wages that should have been paid either under the minimum wage or overtime provisions. Most of those actions are for small amounts and are settled for the amount due immediately after an inspection.

The division may refer the matter to the Solicitor of Labor, a kind of general counsel for the Department of Labor, who may begin litigation in the name of the Secretary. The Solicitor may issue a **subpoena duces tecum** (see p. 83) to obtain information and secure records indicating lack of compliance. The Secretary may bring damage actions or may sue for injunctive relief, including mandatory injunctions barring employers from "continuing to withhold unpaid wages." Willful violations are criminal violations carrying a fine of $10,000. The prosecution is not required to prove an "evil" motive, but only that the violation is deliberate, voluntary, and intentional.

**Labor Standards Affecting Federally Related Contracts**   Aside from the direct regulation of wages and hours under the FLSA, several other federal statutes require payment of higher wages to employees working on federal projects or projects funded by federal dollars in whole or in part. Those four statutes include the Walsh-Healey Public Contracts Act, the McNamara-O'Hara Service Contract Act, the Davis-Bacon Act, and the Contract Work Hours Standards Act.

All four laws generally require that employees working on federal projects or on projects funded by federal money must be paid the **prevailing wage** in the area for similar work, but not less than the federal minimum wage. Thus, if a construction worker on a private project would receive $8.00 an hour, a worker on a federal project would receive the same amount. Each act applies to different types of contracts, and each contains exceptions for smaller contracts of varying amounts. Overtime pay is also required. Such laws are generally enforced by private lawsuits to collect the back amounts of such wages.

In 1972 Congress passed the Government Employee's Prevailing Rate Systems Act, which requires that federal hourly employees be paid according to the prevailing rate for similar labor in their area. The law does not affect employees under collective bargaining agreements.

## REGULATION OF EMPLOYMENT SECURITY

In the absence of collective bargaining agreements or an individual employment contract, an employee may generally be discharged for any reason or for no reason at all. This rule is known as the **at will employment doctrine,** and it was discussed at length in Chapter 11 (pp. 291–293). The insecurity of employment has resulted in attempts by the federal and state governments to provide some basic security for the working people of the nation. That security has taken three important forms: (1) the federal Social Security Act, (2) unemployment compensation laws, and (3) regulation of private pension funds.

### The Social Security Act

Almost all workers become less "marketable" as they grow older. Only a very few escape the decision whether to retire, and often that decision is made by company policy, illness, or physical inability to do the work.

Few workers make adequate provision for old age. It is tempting to argue that such a lack of foresight, while regrettable, is the workers' "fault," and workers should be left to their own devices. Such a hands-off attitude by government would encourage private savings and private sector involvement and would eliminate a large part of government's activities in providing entitlements to the public.

But such an argument may beg the question. First, those workers who do not provide for their old age may become a burden on family or friends, or become eligible for some form of public welfare. Second, for most workers it is extremely difficult to set back sufficient amounts of money to care for themselves over an indeterminate period of time. There may not be enough money available to maintain a reasonable standard of living and to set aside money for retirement out of the same paycheck. Third, many of the people most in need of help do not have the sophistication necessary to set up such retirement plans. The result of these factors was, in the heart of the Depression of the 1930's, a great number of elderly persons—more than half of those over age sixty-five in 1935, for example—were dependent on friends, relatives, or the meager public aid measures of that time. It appears that the choice may not be between social security and private systems, but rather between social security and welfare.

**Overview and Constitutionality of Social Security**    The federal Social Security Act was passed in 1935 to remedy the problems of retiring and elderly persons. The original act provided one kind of benefit—*old-age insurance*—and covered only a limited number of employees. Employees covered by the act were required to make contributions out of their pay to the Treasury, which used those contributions as a basis for paying benefits. The plan was never "fully funded," and contributions have never equalled payments. The act has been amended to add other kinds of insurance, notably benefits for some wives, children, and survivors, disabled persons, and self-employed persons; and in 1965 the Medicare amendments were added to provide health insurance for the elderly.

The constitutionality of the Social Security Act was challenged in 1937, at the same time that the *Jones & Laughlin Steel* case came before the Court and the "court-packing plan" was before Congress (see pp. 102–103). In *Helvering v. Davis*,[2] the Court held the social security system constitutional against a series of claims based on economic due process and the right of Congress to regulate commerce.

**Employees Covered**    The 1935 act was fairly restrictive in its coverage of employees, generally sheltering only workers in industry and commerce. A series of amendments since that time have expanded the coverage substantially to include three separate categories of workers: (1) any "employee" according to a common law test, namely whether the employer has the right to direct and control the result, details, and means of accomplishing the employee's work; (2) officers of corporations, which may not be covered under the common law test, are specifically included; and (3) four kinds of "service employees," which may not be covered under the common law test, including agent drivers and commission drivers, life insurance agents, homeworkers, and traveling salespeople, all of whom generally work on a commission basis.

The act provides for nineteen specific exempt categories of workers, including some types of agricultural and domestic labor, family employment, ministers, employees of tax-exempt organizations, newspaper deliverers, employees of colleges, employees of international organizations, sharecroppers, employees of communist governments, and the largest category of all, employees of local, state, and federal governments. Some of those employees or their employers may elect to be covered.

Since 1950, self-employed persons may be covered by social security as well. A tax

---

2 301 U.S. 619, 57 S. Ct. 904, 81 L. Ed. 1307 (1937).

is levied on *self-employment income*, which is defined as the net earnings from self-employment up to certain maximums. That amount must be paid with the individual's federal income tax, either quarterly or annually.

**Insured Status**   **Insured status** is required before an individual is eligible to receive benefits of any kind. There are three types of insured status: *fully insured, currently insured*, and *insured for disability benefits*. An individual's status is generally determined by the number of **quarters of eligibility** that he or she has accumulated. For example, a person is generally considered fully insured after accumulating forty quarters (quarters of a year) under the social security system. Currently insured status requires six quarters of coverage in the preceding thirteen quarters, and disability status requires twenty quarters during the preceding forty quarters. Each type of benefit requires some form of insured status before payment can be made (see Table 17.1).

**Administration and Enforcement of Social Security**   The **Social Security Administration** is part of the Department of Health, Education and Welfare. Branch offices are maintained in major cities across the country. In order to be eligible for any benefit, an individual usually must file a claim with the local office, and the determination of eli-

TABLE 17.1   Social Security Benefits

| Type of Benefit | Eligibility | Nature of Benefit |
| --- | --- | --- |
| Old-Age Benefits | Age 62, if fully insured; benefits increase if filing delayed to age 65; persons between 62 and 70 may earn wages up to certain maximums, no restriction on wages over age 70. | Monthly pension, based on formula using individual's monthly wage over a 7-year period; wives, children and divorced spouses may be entitled to benefits as well. |
| Survivor's Insurance | Minor dependent children (under 18, disabled or full-time student); spouses over 60 (50 if disabled); married for at least 9 months before death. | Monthly payment, based on decedent's wages. |
| Disability Benefits | Be disabled as defined in act; 5 month waiting period; under age 65. | Same monthly benefit as would be received under old-age benefits. |
| Medicare | Eligibility under old-age benefits | *Part A*: In-patient hospital care and later post-hospital extended care<br>*Part B*: Supplemental medical insurance, providing physician services, out-patient care, and other services; part B is voluntary and financed by insurance premiums. |

gibility is made by the local office. An initial determination becomes final unless reconsideration is requested within six months. The final review is a civil action in the U.S. district court.

## Unemployment Compensation

Part of the original Social Security Act provided for a federal tax on employers to finance a system of unemployment compensation. The system was to be state-run, however, and amounts paid to state unemployment compensation systems may be credited against the federal tax. The federal government makes grants to the states to pay the administrative costs of such programs and advances funds to states to pay benefits when state funds run low.

States usually make payments to unemployed workers for a specific number of weeks, during which the unemployed worker is usually required to look for work. State plans are similar because of the requirements attached to the federal grants.

Typical state laws impose several eligibility requirements, including (1) that a claimant have worked in covered employment for an appropriate "base period"; (2) that a claimant register for work through the public employment service; and (3) that the claimant be able and available to work. The weekly benefit amount is typically based on the taxable earnings of the claimant during the base period. Every state provides for weekly minimums and maximums and often provides increments if the claimant has dependents. Benefits are usually payable for a maximum of twenty-six weeks, although it may be as high as thirty-six. A person who has exhausted the "regular benefits" may be eligible for payments under the Federal State Extended Unemployment Compensation Program established in 1970, which provides for up to an additional thirteen weeks per extension. Most states do not provide benefits if a claimant leaves work voluntarily or is fired for misconduct.

Under the **Trade Act of 1974,** Congress sought to lessen the problems of workers who had been displaced from their employment as a result of economic dislocations caused by foreign imports. Workers may receive compensation on the basis of their prior weekly wages, employment services, training, a job-search allowance, and relocation allowances. The Secretary of Labor must certify that employees are eligible, after a finding that workers are being threatened with separation from employment.

## Regulation of Pension Plans: ERISA

A pension plan is an arrangement whereby an employer can provide for retirement benefits for employees in recognition of their service to the company. No federal law requires that employers supply a pension plan for their employees. Many employers do supply such plans, of course—some as a result of collective bargaining, and others as a method of attracting skilled employees.

The use of such plans grew tremendously between 1940 and 1970, but despite the increase in the use of such plans, some employees who expected to receive benefits upon retirement did not receive those payments. In some cases, employers terminated underfunded plans; in others, plan participants quit or were fired with few or no vested rights. Some plan administrators made bad investments or used assets for personal purposes.

The **Employee Retirement Income Security Act of 1974 (ERISA)** was adopted to regulate such abuses. ERISA applies to all plans established by sponsors engaged in interstate commerce, except government plans, church plans, and a few other minor exceptions. The act establishes certain fiduciary duties; participation, vesting, and funding rules; reporting and disclosure requirements; and other miscellaneous rules.

**Fiduciary Responsibilities**    A *fiduciary* is defined in the act as any person who exercises discretionary control over a plan, gives investment advice for a fee, or has any discretion in the administration of the plan. The act imposes six rules on such fiduciaries. Such fiduciaries must

1    Manage assets solely in the interest of participants and beneficiaries;

2    Act with the care that a prudent person in like circumstances would exercise;

3    Diversify investments in order to minimize the risk of large losses;

4    Invest no more than 10% of the fair market value of plan assets in a combination of qualifying employer securities and qualifying employer real property;

5    Not transfer assets outside the United States unless specifically permitted by the Secretary of Labor; and

6    Be liable for those acts or omissions of cofiduciaries that constitute breaches of their fiduciary responsibilities.

**Participation Requirements**    Prior to ERISA, some plans did not permit employees to take part in the plan for long periods of time. A plan may not impose age and service requirements for participation by employees that are stricter than one year of service and age twenty-five, or in the alternative, age twenty-five with a three-year waiting period with 100% vesting thereafter (see the following discussion). Thus, most employees will be eligible for such plans rather quickly after beginning work.

**Vesting Requirements**    *Vesting* means that an employee has an absolute right to the funds in the plan, even if he or she leaves employment. The ERISA vesting rules (see Figure 17.3) are designed to assure that employees will have an absolute right to the funds after a set period of time. If an employee's rights are vested, he or she has a right to the funds in the event employment is terminated for any reason.

**Funding Requirements**    The funding rules require that an employer's contributions cover (1) the normal costs of the plan; (2) all interest on unfunded amounts; and (3) a portion of unfunded original past service liability. All other amounts may come from employee contributions. The purpose of these requirements is to assure sufficient contributions to fund the plan.

**Reporting and Disclosure Requirements**    ERISA requires that several reports must be made to government agencies, including the Internal Revenue Service, if the employer claims a deduction for the contributions to the plan. The act also requires disclosure of information to participants, including annual reports prepared by independent accountants. Participants have a right to receive a full copy of the plan upon request.

ERISA provides four alternative vesting rules, any of which might be adopted by a plan:

1    *Graded vesting*, with at least 25% vesting after five years and at least 5% each year thereafter for five years, and 10% each year thereafter. The whole plan would therefore be vested no later than the fifteenth year.

2    *Cliff vesting*, or 100% vesting after ten years, with no vesting before the end of the tenth year.

3    *Rule of 45 vesting*, in which accrued benefits of employees with five or more years of service must be at least 50% vested when the sum of his or her age and years of service equals 45, with 10% additional vesting for each year of service thereafter. A participant with ten years of service must be at least 50% vested and vest thereafter at a rate not less than 10% per year.

4    *Forty percent vesting*, in which 40% must be vested after four years of service and incrementally each year thereafter until the plan is 100% vested after eleven years of service. This final category *must* be used unless the employer can demonstrate a rank-and-file employee turnover rate of less than 6% per year.

FIGURE 17.3    ERISA Vesting Rules

**Miscellaneous Provisions**    ERISA also requires that if a plan provides for a retirement annuity for married participants, it must also provide a survivor annuity for the support of a surviving spouse, in an amount not less than one-half of the annuity payable to the participant. The act further requires plan administrators to pay annual termination insurance premiums to the Pension Benefits Guaranty Corporation, a government corporation, to guarantee that benefits will be received even if the plan is terminated.

**Penalties and Remedies**    The act permits civil actions by participants or beneficiaries to recover lost benefits, and excise taxes may be imposed for delinquent contributions. Failure to comply with the reporting and disclosure requirements may lead to fines up to $100,000 plus fines of up to $100 per day per participant or beneficiary.

## SUMMARY AND CONCLUSIONS

The second "stream" of American labor law embraces specific regulations of worker safety, wages, and security. Such laws are meant to provide protections to the majority of American workers who are not covered by collective bargaining agreements, although many of the specific protections apply to union workers as well.

Common law protections of worker safety were subject to the employer defenses of assumption of risk, contributory negligence, and the fellow-servant doctrine, which resulted in many uncompensated workplace injuries. Around the turn of the century, many states enacted state worker's compensation statutes to provide a remedy for injured workers. Direct regulation of employee safety was not accomplished until 1970 with the Occupational Safety and Health Act (OSHA).

The principal protection of workers' wages is found in the federal Fair Labor Standards Act (FLSA), which requires payment of a minimum wage, provides for overtime, requires payment of equal pay for equal work, and prohibits much child labor. Most states also have similar laws that apply to intrastate businesses.

The future economic security of employees is protected by the federal Social Security Act, unemployment compensation, and the Employees Retirement Income Security Act (ERISA). Those laws attempt to assure that retirement and unemployment do not become economic catastrophes for most workers.

## REVIEW QUESTIONS

1  Does the "market" approach, as exemplified by the Wagner Act, or the "regulatory" approach, as discussed in this chapter, make more sense? Which is more consistent with our economic system? Can we rely on only one approach?

2  Does the common law provide an adequate remedy to injured workers? Why or why not?

3  Describe the typical worker's compensation statute. A few states provide that workers may not recover under worker's compensation for injuries resulting from the worker's reckless conduct or intoxication. Are such qualifications consistent with the purposes of the system?

4  OSHA is considered by many businesspeople to be the most objectionable of all the federal regulations of business and is usually the system of regulation pointed to as an example of government "overreaching" and "overregulation." Could we do without the act entirely? What changes should be made in the act?

5  Does the Fair Labor Standards Act (or any other labor law, for that matter) protect illegal aliens? Should they be protected?

6  Describe the basic provisions of the Social Security Act. Is the Social Security Act a "welfare" law? Which would you prefer to receive when you retire, public welfare or social security? Why? Which system permits retiring workers to maintain their dignity? Is dignity an appropriate consideration for a government program?

7  It has been argued that in the long run OSHA and ERISA may well prove to be the most important federal labor laws. Why? Do you agree?

8  Hattaway, an employee of Mississippi State University, reported to work at 7:30 A.M. and began welding on a water tank. After about five minutes, he went to his supervisor's office and reported that the burning paint had made him nauseated. He rested a short while, then died. A physician testified that he could not explain Hattaway's death. No autopsy was performed. Hattaway's wife and children brought a worker's compensation action. Did Hattaway's death "arise out of" his employment? [*Mississippi State University v. Dependents of Hattaway,* 191 So. 2d 418 (Miss., 1966).]

9  Smith, an employee of National Realty, rode the running board of a front-end loader at a construction site. The loader's engine stalled while going down an earthen ramp and swerved off the ramp. Smith jumped from the loader, but the loader toppled off the ramp and fell on top of him. At the time, no specific OSHA standards related to riding on machinery. An OSHA inspector nevertheless found the company guilty of a "serious violation" and levied a fine of $300. The company appealed. What do you think was the result? [*National Realty and Construction Company, Inc. v. Occupational Safety and Health Review Commission,* 489 F.2d 1257 (U.S. App. D.C., 1973).]

10  Thomas, a Jehovah's Witness, terminated his employment when he was transferred to a department that produced turrets for military tanks. He claimed his religious beliefs prevented him from participating in the production of war materials. The Indiana Employment Security Division refused him unemployment compensation because Indiana law does not permit payment unless an employee is involuntarily terminated or terminates voluntarily "with good cause." What outcome would you expect? [*Thomas v. Review Board of the Indiana Employment Security Division,* 450 U.S. 707, 101 S. Ct. 1425, 67 L. Ed. 2d 624 (1981).]

# PART 5

# The Firm and the Public

The law not only *regulates* relationships but also sometimes *creates* them. Usually this happens because the ethics of society demand that the law regulate certain activity, forcing the law to recognize new legal relationships where none existed before.

Some public responsibilities of business have been regulated for a long time. For example, the law of public nuisance clearly established a relationship between the individual and the anonymous "public" and required that individuals' behavior not violate that public's rights. Similarly, the antitrust laws (see Chapters 20 and 21) protect the public's right to *competition* in the abstract, and not specific competitors.

The two chapters in this section deal with some recently created public rights. Chapter 18 deals with the right of the public to be free from discrimination, and Chapter 19 considers the public's right to environmental protection.

The law of discrimination reflects an ethical judgment of society that our nation cannot accept legal classifications or business decisions based on irrelevancies such as race, color, religion, national origin, or sex. The law of discrimination also has an impact on two other relationships of the business firm: (1) the relationship of the firm to its employees, in the form of laws against employment discrimination, and (2) the relationship of the firm to its customers, in the form of laws prohibiting discrimination in the provision of certain services or the sales of certain property.

The law of environmental protection reflects a similar ethical judgment that our natural resources deserve protection. Those laws protect our air, water, wildlife, and wilderness areas from damage. In both cases, the ethics of society, in the form of the civil rights movement and the environmental movements of the 1960s and 1970s, led to major changes in the law.

443

# CHAPTER 18

# The Law of Discrimination

*[I]n view of the Constitution, in the eye of the law, there is in this country no superior, dominant ruling class of citizens. There is no caste here. Our Constitution is color-blind, and neither knows nor tolerates classes among citizens.*

MR. JUSTICE HARLAN
Dissenting in *Plessy v. Ferguson* (1896)

The Declaration of Independence proclaimed to all the world that "all men are created equal," but it is clear that the slave owners who signed that document did not have their human property in mind. This chapter is about the bizarre ability of many Americans since that time to defend the cause of freedom while denouncing other U.S. citizens because of race, sex, age, or a hundred other irrelevancies. On another level, this chapter concerns the often halting and grudging efforts of government to limit discrimination and the weighty issues and conflicts that affect that effort.

Whenever a legislative body enacts a law, it must inevitably *classify*. A judgment of a legislature about who is to be taxed or who is to receive benefits singles out some groups for special treatment. A crucial question is whether the basis of such classifications is permissible under the Constitution, especially under the equal protection clause of the fourteenth amendment. That issue was discussed in Chapters 4 and 5 and will be further considered in this chapter.

A more difficult problem exists when discrimination results from *private* conduct. Long ago, the Supreme Court held that the fourteenth amendment does not prohibit *private* discrimination, but only forbids discriminatory **state action.** A major issue is whether, and under what circumstances, state or federal governments ought to step in to outlaw discrimination by private individuals in employment, housing, public accommodations, or other areas. The largest part of this chapter will consider the instances in which the government has done so.

## EQUAL PROTECTION: CONSTITUTIONAL LIMITS ON DISCRIMINATION

The fourteenth amendment provides in part that no state shall "deny to any person within its jurisdiction the equal protection of the laws." Theoretically *any* classification

444

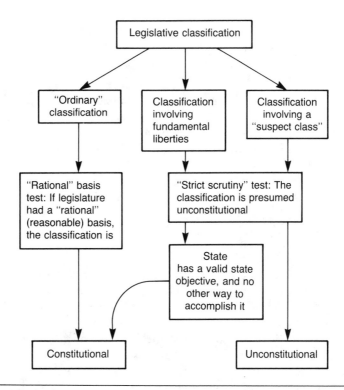

FIGURE 18.1    The "Reasonable Basis" and "Strict Scrutiny" Tests Under the 14th Amendment

in a statute treats some people differently than others, but clearly the equal protection clause cannot mean that all classification schemes are unconstitutional.

The courts have traditionally adopted two tests to determine whether a law violates the fourteenth amendment's equal protection clause. The first, known as the **reasonable basis test,** permits a classification scheme if the legislature had a "reasonable basis" for making the classification (see p. 137). The second test, sometimes called the **strict scrutiny test,** prohibits a classification scheme unless the legislature can demonstrate that a valid state objective (that is, one within the police power of the state) could not be accomplished any other way (see Figure 18.1).

The reasonable basis test is used to determine the constitutionality of most laws. That test is used unless the classification scheme involves either (1) **fundamental rights,** such as those protected by the Bill of Rights, or (2) a **suspect classification.** State laws classifying on the basis of race and national origin have generally been subjected to strict scrutiny. Laws classifying on the basis of indigence or age have been subjected to a reasonable basis test. And laws classifying on the basis of sex and illegitimacy have received a mixed reaction from the courts.

The determination of whether a particular group belongs in the suspect class category depends on three factors: (1) whether membership "carries an obvious badge, such as race or sex do"; (2) whether treatment of members of the group has been historically severe and pervasive; and (3) whether members of the class have been subjected to the "absolute deprivation" of benefits available to nonmembers.

## The Problem of State Action

The earliest cases interpreting the fourteenth amendment, the *Civil Rights Cases of 1883*,[1] held that the fourteenth amendment prohibited discriminatory *state* action but had no effect on discriminatory *private* action. In 1948 the Court again considered the problem of discrimination arising from private action in the following landmark decision.

---

## Shelley v. Kraemer

334 U.S. 1, 68 S. Ct. 836, 92 L. Ed. 1161 (1948)

The creator of a subdivision in St. Louis placed a condition in documents creating the subdivision that lots in the development could not be sold to persons of "the Negro or Mongolian race." Shelley, a black person, purchased one of the lots. Kraemer, a resident of the same subdivision, sued to restrain Shelley from taking possession of the property. The Missouri courts held the condition valid, concluding that it violated no rights guaranteed by the U.S. Constitution, and issued the injunction against Shelley. Shelley argued that the condition violated the Civil Rights Act of 1866, which is quoted in the body of the case. Kraemer contended that the Civil Rights Act of 1866 could not affect "private action," because that act, like the fourteenth amendment, only prohibited discriminatory "state action."

**Mr. Chief Justice Vinson Delivered the Opinion of the Court**  Whether the equal protection clause of the Fourteenth Amendment inhibits judicial enforcement by state courts of restrictive covenants based on race or color is a question which this Court has not heretofore been called upon to consider. . . .

It cannot be doubted that among the civil rights intended to be protected from discriminatory state action by the Fourteenth Amendment are the rights to acquire, enjoy, own and dispose of property. Equality in the enjoyment of property rights was regarded by the framers of that Amendment as an essential precondition to the realization of other basic civil rights and liberties which the Amendment was intended to guarantee. Thus, [§1982] . . . of the Civil Rights Act of 1866 which was enacted by Congress while the Fourteenth Amendment was also under consider-

ation, provides:

> All citizens of the United States shall have the same right, in every State and Territory, as is enjoyed by white citizens thereof to inherit, purchase, lease, sell, hold, and convey real and personal property.

It is likewise clear that restrictions on the right of occupancy of the sort sought to be created by the private agreements in these cases could not be squared with the requirements of the Fourteenth Amendment if imposed by state statute or local ordinance. . . .

But the present case . . . [does] not involve action by state legislatures or city councils. Here the particular patterns of discrimination and the areas in which the restrictions are to operate are determined, in the first instance, by the terms of agreements among private individuals. Participation of the State

---

1 109 U.S. 3, 3 S. Ct. 18, 27 L. Ed. 835 (1883).

consists in the enforcement of the restrictions so defined. The crucial issue with which we are confronted is whether this distinction removes these cases from the operation of the . . . Fourteenth Amendment. . . .

We hold that in granting judicial enforcement of the restrictive agreements in these cases, the States have denied petitioners the equal protection of the laws and that, therefore, the action of the state courts cannot stand. We have noted that freedom from discrimination by the States in the enjoyment of property rights was among the basic objectives sought to be effectuated by the framers of the Fourteenth Amendment. That such discrimination has occurred in these cases is clear. . . .

[Reversed.]

Case Discussion Questions

1    Why do you suppose the fourteenth amendment is restricted to *state action?* What problems did the people who wrote the fourteenth amendment have in mind in 1868, three years after the Civil War?

2    What policy does the 1866 law demonstrate in this case? Did the Missouri court violate the letter of the fourteenth amendment or the 1866 act? What of the spirit of those laws?

3    Should private individuals be able to use their own property in any way they see fit, including how the property will be transferred later on? How is the action in this case considered to be "state action?"

Later decisions held that conviction of black persons under "trespass" ordinances for violating a store policy of segregated lunch counters was also **state action.** But other cases held that the mere fact that a private club possessed a liquor license issued by the state, or that a public utility was closely regulated by state law, was not a sufficient "tie" to the state to constitute state action. It appears that the state must take some discretionary action to constitute state action.

The state-action doctrine is crucial to an understanding of later cases. For example, a central question in affirmative action cases is whether a *state* has imposed reverse discrimination. Plans imposed by state or local government may be held unconstitutional under the fourteenth amendment (see p. 449); but a plan imposed by *private* action, such as by agreement between an employer and a labor union, cannot be unconstitutional (see p. 462).

### The Curious Doctrine: The Rise and Fall of "Separate but Equal"

In the latter part of the nineteenth century, some states tried to evade the spirit of the fourteenth amendment by passing laws requiring "equal but separate" treatment of blacks and whites. In 1896, in the notorious decision of *Plessy v. Ferguson,*[2] the Supreme Court approved such statutes, because they required equal facilities for both races. Justice John Harlan (1833–1911) presented an impassioned dissent calling for a "color-blind" interpretation of the Constitution.

Following the Court's decision, the **separate but equal doctrine** was used to justify all sorts of segregationist statutes, generally known as **Jim Crow laws.** Those laws required separation of the races in almost every aspect of life, from separate washrooms and drinking fountains to separate facilities in restaurants and public beaches. Perhaps

2 163 U.S. 537, 16 S. Ct. 1138, 41 L. Ed. 256 (1896).

the most notorious and, in the long run, the most damaging of those laws required separate schools for black students from kindergarten through graduate school.

Slowly, the Supreme Court began to chip away at the separate but equal doctrine. In 1954, in the towering decision of *Brown v. Board of Education*, the Supreme Court finally overruled the doctrine completely in the context of public schools.

---

# *Brown v. Board of Education of Topeka*
347 U.S. 483, 74 S. Ct. 686, 98 L. Ed. 873 (1954)

This case arose from common facts in several cases arising in Kansas, South Carolina, Virginia, and Delaware. In each case, the local school board or state statute required that black students attend "black" schools and white students attend "white" schools. In each case there were in essence two separate school systems, one for each race, and students were prohibited from attending the other school system. The school boards attempted to justify the system on the basis of the separate but equal doctrine of *Plessy v. Ferguson*. In each case black students sought and were denied admission to the "white" school system.

**Mr. Chief Justice Warren Delivered the Opinion of the Court**   The plaintiffs contend that segregated public schools are not "equal" and cannot be made "equal," and that hence they are deprived of the equal protection of the laws. . . .

In the first cases in this Court construing the Fourteenth Amendment, decided shortly after its adoption, the Court interpreted it as proscribing all state-imposed discriminations against the Negro race. The doctrine of "separate but equal" did not make its appearance in this Court until 1896 in the case of *Plessy v. Ferguson*. . . . American courts have labored with the doctrine for over half a century. . . .

In approaching this problem, we cannot turn the clock back to 1868 when the Amendment was adopted, or even to 1896 when *Plessy v. Ferguson* was written. We must consider public education in the light of its full development and its present place in American life throughout the Nation. Only in this way can it be determined if segregation in public schools deprives these plaintiffs of the equal protection of the laws. . . .

We come then to the question presented: Does segregation of children in public schools solely on the basis of race even though the physical facilities and other "tangible" factors may be equal deprive the children of the minority group of equal educational opportunities? We believe that it does.

In *Sweatt v. Painter* . . . (1950) in finding that a segregated law school for Negroes could not provide them equal educational opportunities, this Court relied in large part on "those qualities which are incapable of objective measurement but which make for greatness in a law school." In *McLaurin v. Oklahoma State Regents* . . . (1950) the Court, in requiring that a Negro admitted to a white graduate school be treated like all other students, again resorted to intangible considerations ". . . his ability to study, to exchange in discussions and exchange views with other students, and, in general, to learn his profession." Such considerations apply with added force to children in grade and high schools. To separate them from others of similar age and qualifications solely because of their race generates a feeling of inferiority as to their status in the community that may affect their hearts and minds in a way unlikely ever to be undone. The effect of this separation on their educational opportunities was well stated by a finding in the Kansas case by a court which nevertheless felt compelled to rule against the Negro plaintiffs:

Segregation of white and colored children in public schools has a detrimental effect upon the colored children. The impact is greater when it has the sanction of the law; for the policy of separating the races is usually interpreted as denoting inferiority of the Negro group. A sense of inferiority affects the motivation of a child to learn. Segregation with the sanction of law, therefore, has a tendency to [retard] the educational and mental development of Negro children and to deprive them of some of the benefits they would receive in a racial[ly] integrated school system.

Whatever may have been the extent of psychological knowledge at the time of *Plessy v. Ferguson*, this finding is amply supported by modern authority [citing numerous psychological studies]. Any language in *Plessy v. Ferguson* contrary to this finding is rejected.

We conclude that in the field of public education the doctrine of "separate but equal" has no place. Separate educational facilities are inherently unequal.

Therefore, we hold that the plaintiffs . . . are, by reason of the segregation complained of, deprived of the equal protection of the laws guaranteed by the Fourteenth Amendment. . . .

## Case Discussion Questions

1  What is the effect of "separate but equal" on schoolchildren? Don't separate but equal schools deprive *both* blacks and whites of the equal protection of the law, because it also limits the education of whites?

2  Why is desegregation of schools so important? Why did so much of the early effort in desegregation concentrate on the schools, rather than other aspects of life?

3  What must a school district do, following *Brown v. Board?* Is bussing required by the decision?

---

The following year, the Court announced a further decision in the case *(Brown II),*[3] sometimes called the **Implementation Decision.** In that case, the Court left it to the local school boards to solve the "varied local school problems," with the condition that it should be done "with all deliberate speed."

Seventeen years later, the Court found that in many instances local school boards were dragging their feet and held that local federal district courts should supervise desegregation plans under their general equity powers. The same decision held that bussing may be, in appropriate circumstances, a "reasonable, feasible and workable" solution.[4]

Perhaps the most difficult question yet to be resolved is whether **de facto segregation** is included within the ban of *Brown v. Board.* De facto segregation (segregation "in fact") is segregation arising from housing patterns, as contrasted with **de jure segregation,** which is segregation required by law, including dual school systems as in *Brown,* gerrymandered school districts (district boundaries drawn to encourage segregation), or "private" schools created to replace a closed public school system. Strictly *de facto* segregation has not been treated by the courts, but any official action encouraging or taking advantage of *de facto* segregation is strictly prohibited.

### Affirmative Action and Equal Protection

*Brown v. Board* could easily be read to require only Justice Harlan's color-blind Constitution, outlawing official discrimination but stopping short of any positive steps to "set the record straight." *Brown* appears, on its face, simply to forbid the use of racial criteria in statutes.

---

3  349 U.S. 294, 75 S. Ct. 753, 99 L. Ed. 1083 (1955).
4  *Swann v. Charlotte-Mecklenburg Board of Education,* 402 U.S. 1, 91 S. Ct. 1267, 28 L. Ed. 2d 554 (1971).

But racial criteria may be used to *cure* the effects of historic segregation as well. Racial classifications may be used to benefit minority races and to make up for centuries of racial abuse and intolerance. New sensitivity to the problems of minorities developed following *Brown v. Board* and the civil rights activity of the 1960's and 1970's, resulting in the creation of **affirmative action** plans in many areas of society. Affirmative action plans are positive efforts to eliminate the effects of past racial or sexual discrimination, including special efforts to hire minorities, provide education, or provide benefits to minorities that had been withheld. Sometimes those programs include *racial quotas* in employment or education. Two federal Executive Orders, signed by Presidents Johnson and Nixon, *require* affirmative action in many companies that deal with the federal government (see p. 463).

But affirmative action plans, by providing special advantages for minorities, may discriminate against members of the majority race or sex as well. In 1978 the Supreme Court confronted the issue of whether the "reverse discrimination" caused by an affirmative action plan violated the fourteenth amendment in *Regents of the University of California v. Bakke.*[5] The plan in that case was created by *state action* in the form of an admissions plan established by the University of California Medical School, a state institution.

The plan set aside 16 of 100 positions in its entering class for disadvantaged and minority students. Students who were found to be disadvantaged or members of specific minorities received special consideration, including waiver of a grade point requirement. The result was that a number of students who did not meet the ordinary criteria for entrance were admitted, and a number of students who did meet the criteria were "bumped" to make room for the disadvantaged and minority students. Bakke, a white male, had better credentials than any of the minority students admitted under the program, but he was twice denied admission. A state judge found that the special procedures constituted "reverse discrimination," and the state supreme court agreed, ordering Bakke admitted. The university appealed to the U.S. Supreme Court.

The decision by the U.S. Supreme Court was confused at best. Four Justices (Chief Justice Burger and Justices Rehnquist, Stewart, and Stevens) decided that the special admissions program violated federal civil rights statutes. Four Justices (Brennan, White, Marshall, and Blackmun) argued that racial classifications were permitted by the fourteenth amendment if they served important governmental interests, such as remedying the effects of past social discrimination. Justice Powell agreed with *both* groups, and argued that although the program violated federal law and Bakke must be admitted, under certain circumstances "race or ethnic background" may be deemed a "plus" in a particular applicant's file.

Later cases indicate that *Bakke* might be restricted to the special facts found in that case, specifically, an affirmative action plan required by *state action*. For example, a 1980 decision held that a congressional act requiring that 10% of federally supported public works contracts go to minority-owned businesses was constitutionally permitted.[6] Similarly, a 1979 decision held that a private, voluntary, affirmative action program im-

---

5 438 U.S. 265, 98 S. Ct. 2733, 57 L. Ed. 2d 750 (1978).
6 *Fullilove v. Klutznick*, 448 U.S. 448, 100 S. Ct. 2758, 65 L. Ed. 2d 902 (1980).

posed by a collective bargaining agreement did not violate either the Constitution or the federal Civil Rights Act of 1964.[7] In 1986 the Court held that race-conscious affirmative action plans may be used as a remedy by a court confronted with past discrimination by a public body.[8] In 1986 the Supreme Court again confronted the issue in the following case.

# Wygant v. Jackson Board of Education
476 U.S. 267, 106 S. Ct. 1842, 90 L. Ed. 2d 260 (1986)

A collective bargaining agreement between the Jackson Board of Education and a teachers' union provided that if it became necessary to lay off teachers, those with the most seniority would be retained, except that at no time would there be a greater percentage of minority teachers laid off than the current percentage of minority teachers employed at the time of the layoff.

It later became necessary to lay off teachers. In accordance with the plan, some minority teachers were retained and some nonminority teachers with greater seniority were laid off. This case was filed by some of the nonminority teachers who were laid off, arguing that racial preferences violated the fourteenth amendment. The district court dismissed the case, and the court of appeals affirmed. The displaced teachers appealed to the U.S. Supreme Court.

**Justice Powell Delivered the Opinion of the Court, Joined by the Chief Justice (Burger), Justice Rehnquist, and Justice O'Connor . . .** Petitioners' central claim is that they were laid off because of their race in violation of the Equal Protection Clause of the 14th Amendment. . . . This Court has consistently repudiated distinctions between citizens solely because of their ancestry as being odious to a free people whose institutions are founded upon the doctrine of equality. Racial and ethnic distinctions of any sort are inherently suspect and thus call for the most exacting judicial examination [citing *Bakke*].

The Court has recognized that the level of scrutiny does not change merely because the challenged classification operates against a group that historically has not been subject to governmental discrimination. Any preference based on racial or ethnic criteria must necessarily receive a most searching examination to make sure that it does not conflict with constitutional guarantees. There are two prongs to this ex-

amination. First, any racial classification must be justified by a compelling governmental interest. Second, the means chosen by the State to effectuate its purpose must be narrowly tailored to the achievement of that goal.

The Court of Appeals . . . held that the Board's interest in providing minority role models for its minority students, as an attempt to alleviate the effects of societal discrimination, was sufficiently important to justify the racial classification embodied in the layoff provision. The court discerned a need for more minority faculty role models by finding that the percentage of minority teachers was less than the percentage of minority students.

This Court never has held that societal discrimination alone is sufficient to justify a racial classification. Rather, the Court has insisted upon some showing of prior discrimination by the government unit involved before allowing limited use of racial classifications in order to remedy such discrimination. . . .

[T]he role model theory employed by the Dis-

7 *United Steelworkers v. Weber*, 443 U.S. 193, 99 S. Ct. 2721, 61 L. Ed. 2d 480 (1979).
8 *Local No. 93, International Assoc. of Firefighters v. City of Cleveland*, ——— U.S. ———, 106 S. Ct. 3063, 92 L. Ed. 2d 405 (1986).

trict Court has no logical stopping point. The role model theory allows the Board to engage in discriminatory hiring and layoff practices long past the point required by any legitimate remedial purpose. . . .

Moreover, because the role model theory does not necessarily bear a relationship to the harm caused by prior discriminatory hiring practices, it actually could be used to escape the obligation to remedy such practices by justifying the small percentage of black teachers by reference to the small percentage of black students. Carried to its logical extreme, the idea that black students are better off with black teachers could lead to the very system the Court rejected in *Brown v. Board of Education.* . . .

We have recognized, however, that in order to remedy the effects of prior discrimination, it may be necessary to take race into account. As part of this Nation's dedication to eradicating racial discrimination, innocent persons may be called upon to bear some of the burden of the remedy. . . .

Here, . . . the means chosen to achieve the Board's asserted purposes is that of laying off nonminority teachers with greater seniority in order to retain minority teachers with less seniority. . . . In cases involving valid *hiring* goals, the burden to be borne by innocent individuals is diffused to a considerable extent among society generally. Though hiring goals may burden some innocent individuals, they simply do not impose the same kind of injury that layoffs impose. Denial of a future employment opportunity is not as intrusive as loss of an existing job. . . .

While hiring goals impose a diffuse burden, often foreclosing only one of several opportunities, layoffs impose the entire burden of achieving racial equality on particular individuals, often resulting in serious disruption of their lives. That burden is too intrusive. We therefore hold that, as a means of accomplishing purposes that otherwise may be legitimate, the Board's layoff plan is not sufficiently narrowly tailored. Other, less intrusive means of accomplishing similar purposes—such as the adoption of hiring goals—are available.

[Reversed.]

**Justice White, Concurring in the Judgment**    I cannot believe that in order to integrate a work force, it would be permissible to discharge whites and hire blacks until the latter comprised a suitable percentage of the work force. . . . The layoff policy in this case

. . . has the same effect and is equally violative of the Equal Protection Clause. . . .

**Justice Marshall, with Whom Justice Brennan and Justice Blackmun Join, Dissenting**    The general practice of basing employment decisions on relative seniority may be upset for the sake of other public policies. For example, a court may displace innocent workers by granting retroactive seniority to victims of employment discrimination. Further, this Court has long held that employee expectations arising from the seniority system agreement may be modified by statutes furthering a strong public interest. And we have recognized that collective bargaining agreements may go further than statutes in enhancing the seniority of certain employees for the purpose of fostering legitimate interests. . . .

**Justice Stevens, Dissenting**    We should not lightly approve the government's use of a race-based distinction. History teaches the obvious dangers of such classifications. Our ultimate goal must, of course, be to eliminate entirely from government decisionmaking such irrelevant factors as a human being's race. In this case, however, I am persuaded that the decision to include more minority teachers in the . . . school system served a valid public purpose and that it was adopted with fair procedures and given a narrow breadth, that it transcends the harm to petitioners, and that it is a step toward that ultimate goal of eliminating entirely from governmental decisionmaking such irrelevant factors as a human being's race. . . .

## Case Discussion Questions

1    What is the plaintiff's argument? Is there anything in the law that *requires* seniority to be used as a basis for making employment decisions? Which is more important—seniority, or remedying the effects of historic segregation? Why?

2    The Court makes a distinction between affirmative action in *hiring* and affirmative action in *layoffs.* Is the distinction valid?

3    What is the position of the four dissenters? Would you classify the majority opinion as restraintist, neutralist, or activist? Why? What about the dissenters' opinions?

## PRO AND CON

# Are affirmative action plans justified?

**Pro**   Affirmative action plans are essential to eliminate the effects of past discrimination. Perhaps the principal reason for the need for affirmative action is the difference in education received by black and white children. Because of the existence of segregated schools as late as the 1970's in some parts of the country, many black students received substandard education from the primary grades on. Many black students were unable to go on to higher education because of that substandard education, and many others were unable to compete for the best jobs.

The result was, and is, that many black people find themselves in jobs that pay less, or with no job at all. Family pressure to obtain education, and even to succeed at work, is lost in the cycle of hopelessness that was created over centuries of slavery and discrimination. Role models are rare, and overt discrimination still exists in some areas. As President Lyndon Johnson said, "To be black in a white society is not to stand on level and equal ground. While the races may stand side by side, whites stand on history's mountain and blacks stand in history's hollow. Until we overcome unequal history, we cannot overcome unequal opportunity."

The cycle of hopelessness, poverty, lack of education, and real discrimination can only be broken by *positive* or *affirmative* steps. It may be necessary to establish quotas or require favorable treatment to assure that the legal segregation of yesterday does not become the *practical* segregation of tomorrow.

**Con**   Certainly the government ought to prohibit direct discrimination against individuals. Affirmative action programs promote *group* justice and *individual* injustice. Racial quotas may be fair from the standpoint of blacks or women as a whole, but individual members of minorities receive more than their share, while individual members of the majority are made to suffer for injuries that they did not cause and possibly did not favor.

For example, Allan Bakke did not have anything to do with the harm that had been visited upon generations of minority aspirants to a medical career. Yet he was not given the chance he had earned, at least until the Supreme Court admitted him to the medical school.

Affirmative action programs violate the whole notion of a nation built on *individual* worth and dignity. They mean deep government intrusions into vital and personal areas, such as education and employment. And they undermine the very nature of a democratic society.

Finally, affirmative action programs manage to destroy the very idea that they are intended to create. The notion of a society built without reference to color or sex cannot survive long if quotas based on race or sex are permitted to exist. The result is reverse discrimination; and discrimination, however practiced, is destructive of individual liberty and human dignity.

## Roundtable Discussion

**1**   Are affirmative action plans justified as long as the effects of segregated schools are still felt? Does that mean that affirmative action plans will become unnecessary at some time in the future?

**2**   Are there differences between different *types* of affirmative action plans, such as between (a) strict racial quotas and (b) efforts to hire members of the minority if everything else is equal?

**3**   Should the law be concerned with *individual* justice or *group* justice? Can the two be separated?

## OVERVIEW OF FEDERAL CIVIL RIGHTS LEGISLATION

### The Authority of Congress to Regulate Discrimination

The authority of Congress to pass laws designed to end private discrimination has been challenged in several cases. One aspect of that problem was considered in the *Heart of Atlanta Motel* decision (p. 108), where the Court held that Congress had the authority to pass such laws under the authority of the commerce clause. Congress may also have such authority under the thirteenth, fourteenth, and fifteenth amendments, all of which were passed shortly after the close of the Civil War. The thirteenth amendment prohibits slavery, and later cases gave Congress the right to legislate against "badges of servitude" under that amendment.

In 1968 the Supreme Court held that Congress had the right to legislate against private discrimination under the thirteenth amendment in the landmark decision of *Jones v. Alfred H. Mayer Co.*,[9] a decision that involved the same section of the Civil Rights Act of 1866 described in *Shelley v. Kraemer* (see p. 446). Said Justice Stewart in that case,

> Negro citizens, North and South, who saw in the Thirteenth Amendment a promise of freedom—freedom to go and come at pleasure and to buy and sell when they please—would be left with a mere paper guarantee if Congress were powerless to assure that a dollar in the hands of a Negro will purchase the same thing as a dollar in the hands of a white man. At the very least, the freedom that Congress is empowered to secure under the Thirteenth Amendment includes the freedom to buy whatever a white man can buy, the right to live wherever a white man can live. If Congress cannot say that being a free man means at least this much, then the Thirteenth Amendment made a promise the Nation cannot keep.

The fifteenth amendment prohibited discrimination in voting rights "because of race, color, or previous condition of servitude." Although some voting rights acts were passed during Reconstruction, the first modern federal voting rights act was not passed until 1957.

### History of Federal Antidiscrimination Legislation

The first federal civil rights act was the **Civil Rights Act of 1866,** passed even before the fourteenth amendment was ratified. The act guaranteed property rights as discussed in *Shelley v. Kraemer* (p. 446) and also provided criminal penalties for depriving persons of their rights "under color of law." Additional civil rights legislation was passed in 1870, 1871, and 1875 and outlawed threats and intimidation. Both civil and criminal penalties were provided. Most of those laws remain on the books, and the 1866 and 1870 acts continue to be prime sources of litigation. The 1866 act is simple in form and contains no exceptions, as contrasted with later federal acts. (See Table 18.1.)

---

9 392 U.S. 409, 88 S. Ct. 2186, 20 L. Ed. 2d 1189 (1968).

TABLE 18.1   Federal Civil Rights Laws

| Title | Purpose |
|---|---|
| Civil Rights Act of 1866 | • Guaranteed property and contract rights<br>• Provided criminal penalties to those depriving another of rights "under color of law" |
| Civil Rights Acts of 1870, 1871, 1875 | • Prohibited violence, threats, and intimidation |
| Civil Rights Act of 1957 | • Federal protection of voting rights<br>• Established Commission on Civil Rights |
| Civil Rights Act of 1960 | • Plugged loopholes in 1957 act |
| Equal Pay Act of 1963 | • Eliminated sex-based wage differences |
| Civil Rights Act of 1964 | • Omnibus act prohibiting discrimination in employment, public accommodations, public facilities, federally assisted programs, and education<br>• Created EEOC |
| Executive Order 11246 | • Prohibits discrimination by federally related employers; some affirmative action required |
| Voting Rights Act of 1965 | • Comprehensive voting rights act |
| Age Discrimination in Employment Act of 1973 | • Prohibits age discrimination |
| Civil Rights Act of 1968 | • Prohibits discrimination in sale or rental of housing |
| Executive Order 4 | • Requires affirmative action in federal projects |
| Equal Employment Opportunity Act of 1972 | • Amended Title VII extensively |
| Rehabilitation Act of 1973 | • Prohibits discrimination based on handicap in federal projects |
| Pregnancy Discrimination Act of 1978 | • For purposes of employment defines "sex discrimination" to include pregnancy |

After the Reconstruction legislation there was little activity in the area of civil rights until 1957. In that year the federal **Voting Rights Act** was passed, to be amended in 1960. Another voting rights act was passed in 1965 to expand the rights granted by the earlier laws.

Perhaps the most ambitious federal law was the **Civil Rights Act of 1964,** an *omnibus* (all-inclusive) law that deals with discrimination in employment, public accommodations, federally assisted programs, public facilities, and public education. The act is concerned with discrimination on the basis of race, color, religion, national origin, and sex.

Another ambitious law, the **Civil Rights Act of 1968**, prohibited discrimination in the sale or rental of housing. The law contained numerous exemptions, and as a result, most housing discrimination cases are brought under the Civil Rights Act of 1866.

In 1963, Congress passed the **Equal Pay Act** as an amendment to the Fair Labor Standards Act. That law prohibits employers from making sex-based wage differentials for similar work. The **Age Discrimination in Employment Act (ADEA) of 1967** prohibits some discrimination based on age, the **Rehabilitation Act of 1973** prohibits discrimination in federal projects based on handicap, and the **Pregnancy Discrimination Act of 1978** prohibits employment discrimination based on pregnancy.

Federal law generally regulates discrimination in six areas: employment, housing, public accommodations, credit, voting rights, and education. This chapter discusses the areas of employment, housing, public accommodations, and credit, because those are of prime importance to business.

### Discriminatory Classifications

To many Americans, the term *discrimination* automatically conjures up images of racial segregation. And it is true that a great deal of the political and legal activity in the law of discrimination has taken place in the context of racial discrimination. But other classifications may be illegal as well. The federal civil rights acts passed in the 1960s generally prohibit discrimination on the basis of *race, color, religion, sex,* and *national origin,* and other federal laws deal with discrimination on the basis of *age* and *handicap.*

But even those classifications do not exhaust the possible categories of discrimination. State laws often protect other groups from discriminatory action as well. The Illinois Human Rights Act, for example, prohibits discrimination on the basis of race, color, religion, national origin, ancestry, age, sex, marital status, handicap (either physical or mental), or unfavorable discharge from military service. Political pressures continue for the inclusion of still other groups into the "protected" category. Two of the more controversial pressures, for example, are to include minority language groups and homosexuals in the protected category. Such pressures exist at two levels: first, such groups may petition Congress or state legislatures to be included in the various antidiscrimination statutes; and, second, such groups may argue that their rights are being violated under the federal equal protection clause.

### DISCRIMINATION IN EMPLOYMENT

The principal legislation dealing with discrimination in employment is found in **Title VII** of the Civil Rights Act of 1964, as amended by the Equal Employment Opportunity Act of 1972. Additional laws are found in the Equal Pay Act, the Age Discrimination in Employment Act, the Rehabilitation Act, and the Pregnancy Discrimination Act of 1978.

### Title VII of the Civil Rights Act of 1964

The 1964 Civil Rights Act devoted an entire section, or "title," to the problems of discrimination in employment. The act created the concept of "unlawful employment practices," or categories of prohibited discriminatory acts, and established a new independent regulatory commission, the **Equal Employment Opportunity Commission (EEOC)**, to administer the act. The act also prohibited discrimination in federal employment or in federally related projects.

**Coverage of the Act and Exemptions**  Title VII covers employers, employment agencies, and labor organizations, as defined in the act. An *employer* is defined as a person engaged in an "industry affecting commerce," who has fifteen or more employees for each working day in each of twenty or more calendar weeks in the current or preceding year. An *employment agency* is defined as any person undertaking to procure employees for an employer, as defined in the act, with or without compensation. A *labor organization* is defined as a labor organization in an industry affecting commerce, organized for the traditional purposes of such labor organizations, such as collective bargaining. The act does not apply to employers employing aliens outside of the United States, religious groups, religious educational institutions, or religious societies.

**Unlawful Employment Practices**  The act prohibits discrimination on the basis of *race, color, religion, sex,* or *national origin*, and specifies six different types of unlawful employment practices:

1  For an *employer* to fail or refuse to hire or to discharge any individual, or to otherwise discriminate in the "compensation, terms, conditions or privileges of employment" on the basis of any of the prohibited categories, or to limit, segregate or classify employees or applicants for employment in any way which would tend to deprive an individual of employment opportunities or "otherwise adversely affect his status as an employee";

2  For an *employment agency* to fail or refuse to refer for employment, or to otherwise discriminate against individuals because of the prohibited categories;

3  For a *labor organization* to exclude or expel from membership, or to otherwise discriminate against an individual, or to limit, segregate or classify members or applicants, on the basis of any of the prohibited categories;

4  For an *employer, labor organization,* or *joint labor-management committee* to discriminate against any individual in any apprenticeship or training program on the basis of the prohibited categories;

5  For an *employer, labor organization,* or *joint labor-management committee* to discriminate against an individual in any way because the individual has opposed any practice, made an unlawful employment practice, or because the individual has made a charge, testified or assisted in any Title VII proceeding;

6  For an *employer, labor organization,* or *joint labor-management committee* to print or publish any advertisement indicating any preference based on the prohibited categories.

The act contains several exceptions from these six practices. Classification on the basis of *religion, sex,* or *national origin* (but not race or color) is permissible if religion, sex, or national origin is a "bona fide occupational qualification (bfoq) reasonably necessary to the normal operation of that particular business or enterprise" (see p. 461).

Schools and universities affiliated with religious groups may restrict hiring to persons of that particular religion. Discrimination against communists and other subversives is permitted, and employers need not shelve "national security" requirements because of the act. Employers may establish different compensation systems for persons who work in different parts of the country. The act expressly *permits* affirmative action plans in favor of native Americans, but does not *require* affirmative action or quota plans in any instance.

**The Equal Employment Opportunity Commission (EEOC)**    Title VII created the Equal Employment Opportunity Commission (EEOC), a five-member independent regulatory commission. Members are appointed by the President for staggered five-year terms, and no more than three members may be from the same political party. The EEOC, which is charged with enforcement of Title VII, may also establish guidelines for equal employment.

Charges may be brought before the EEOC by any person, and notice is to be served to the accused party within ten days. The commission must investigate the charge, and if it finds reasonable cause to believe a violation has occurred, it must attempt conciliation of the dispute by informal methods. If such methods are unsuccessful, the EEOC may refer the case to the Attorney General, in the case of a charge against a unit of government, or may bring a civil action in federal court in its own name, against private parties. The courts have jurisdiction to issue injunctions, order reinstatement or hiring, and order back pay, and they may grant any other equitable relief. If the EEOC fails to act within 180 days, private parties may sue in their own names. The EEOC may also establish administrative rules dealing with discrimination in employment.

**EEOC Rules: Sexual Harassment**    One of the most volatile issues with which the EEOC has dealt in recent years has been sexual harassment in the workplace. Many women argued that they were sexually victimized at work by crude jokes, physical abuse, propositions of job advancement for sexual favors, and even rape.

In 1978 the EEOC passed a broad rule prohibiting unwelcome sexual advances, requests for sexual favors, and other verbal or physical conduct of a sexual nature if (1) submission to such conduct is a condition of employment; (2) submission to or rejection of such conduct is used as a basis for employment decisions; or (3) such conduct has the purpose or effect of unreasonably interfering with an individual's work performance or creates an intimidating, hostile or offensive work environment.

**The Definitions of Discrimination**    Although Title VII generally makes discrimination in employment illegal, the act does not define the term *discrimination*. In the relatively

---

## Meritor Savings Bank v. Vinson
477 U.S. 57, 106 S. Ct. 2399, 91 L. Ed. 2d 49 (1986)

Mechelle Vinson was hired by Sidney Taylor, vice-president of Meritor Savings, as a teller trainee at the bank, and she worked at the same branch for four years. Vinson alleged that shortly after her probationary period was over, Taylor invited her out to dinner and later suggested sexual relations. At first she refused, but later agreed out of fear of losing her job. After that, Taylor made numerous advances, and the two had intercourse forty or fifty times. Taylor also fondled her in front of other employees, exposed himself to her, and forcibly raped her on several occasions. Taylor denied all of these allegations. Vinson never reported the harassment to any of Taylor's supervisors and never attempted to use the bank's complaint procedure. Instead, she brought this action under Title VII of the Civil Rights Act against the bank itself. The district court denied relief, but the Court of Appeals reversed. The bank appealed.

**Justice Rehnquist Delivered the Opinion of the Court**   Since the [EEOC] guidelines were issued, courts have uniformly held, and we agree, that a plaintiff may establish a violation of Title VII by proving that discrimination based on sex has created a hostile or abusive work environment. Surely, a requirement that a man or woman run a gauntlet of sexual abuse in return for the privilege of being allowed to work and make a living can be as demeaning and disconcerting as the harshest of racial epithets. . . .

[T]he fact that sex-related conduct was "voluntary," in the sense that the complainant was not forced to participate against her will, is not a defense to a sexual harassment suit. . . . The correct inquiry is whether respondent by her conduct indicated that the alleged sexual advances were unwelcome, not whether her actual participation in sexual intercourse was voluntary.

Although the District Court concluded that respondent had not proved a violation of Title VII, it nevertheless went on to consider the question of the bank's liability. Finding that "the bank was without notice" of Taylor's alleged conduct, and that notice to Taylor was not the equivalent of notice to the bank, the court concluded that the bank therefore could not be held liable for Taylor's alleged actions. The Court of Appeals took the opposite view, holding that an employer is strictly liable for a hostile environment created by a supervisor's sexual advances, even though the employer neither knew nor could have known of the alleged misconduct. . . .

The EEOC . . . contends that courts formulating employer liability rules should draw from traditional agency principles. Examination of those principles has led the EEOC to the view that where a supervisor exercises the authority actually delegated to him by his employer, by making or threatening to make decisions affecting the employment status of his subordinates, such actions are properly imputed to the employer whose delegation of authority empowered the supervisor to undertake them. Thus, the courts have consistently held employers liable for the discriminatory discharges of employees by supervisory personnel, whether or not the employer knew, should have known, or approved of the supervisor's actions.

[Since Vinson was not permitted to present some evidence, we] decline . . . to issue a definitive rule on employer liability, but we do agree with the EEOC that Congress wanted courts to look to agency principles for guidance in the area. . . . [We do not hold] that employers are always automatically liable for sexual harassment by their supervisors. For the same reason, absence of notice to an employer does not necessarily insulate that employer from liability.

Finally, we reject petitioner's view that the mere existence of a grievance procedure and a policy against discrimination coupled with respondent's failure to invoke that procedure, must insulate petitioner from liability. While those facts are plainly relevant, the situation before us demonstrates why they are not necessarily dispositive. . . . Since Taylor was the alleged perpetrator, it is not altogether surprising that respondent failed to invoke the procedure and report her grievance to him.

[Reversed.]

## Case Discussion Questions

1   Is an employer liable for the sexual harassment of its employees?
2   Was Vinson's sexual relationship with Taylor voluntary? Does it make a difference?
3   Why didn't Vinson use the established complaint procedures at the bank?

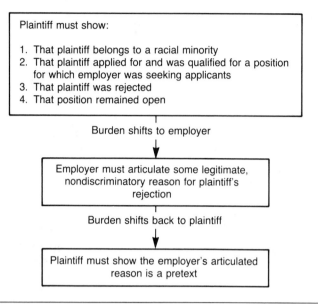

Plaintiff must show:

1. That plaintiff belongs to a racial minority
2. That plaintiff applied for and was qualified for a position for which employer was seeking applicants
3. That plaintiff was rejected
4. That position remained open

Burden shifts to employer

Employer must articulate some legitimate, nondiscriminatory reason for plaintiff's rejection

Burden shifts back to plaintiff

Plaintiff must show the employer's articulated reason is a pretext

FIGURE 18.2    Plaintiff's Proof in a Disparate Impact Discrimination Case

short history of Title VII, the courts have supplied two different meanings for the term. The first, called **disparate treatment,** involves overtly different treatment of individuals because of race, color, religion, sex, or national origin. The second, called **dispropor-tionate impact,** involves employment policies that are neutral on their face but in fact have a discriminatory effect on members of the protected categories.

**Disparate Treatment**    Disparate treatment clearly includes employment policies expressly based on race, color, religion, sex, or national origin. For example, a company policy refusing to hire members of a particular minority or providing that members of a particular minority must receive different treatment involves disparate treatment.

A major issue in such cases is the amount and type of evidence necessary to prove discrimination. It is clearly not enough simply to prove that an individual is a member of a minority and that the individual did not get a job. In a series of cases in the mid-1970's the Supreme Court outlined the order and type of proof necessary to show disparate treatment in hiring or other employment practices (see Figure 18.2). In *McDonnell Douglas v. Green*[10] the Court held that

> The complainant in a Title VII trial must carry the initial burden under the statute of establishing a prima facie case of racial discrimination. This may be done by showing (i) that he belongs to a racial minority; (ii) that he applied and was qualified for a job for which the employer was seeking applicants; (iii) that, despite his qualifications, he was rejected; and (iv) that, after his rejection, the position remained open and the employer continued to seek ap-

---

10 411 U.S. 792, 93 S. Ct. 1817, 36 L. Ed. 2d 668 (1973).

plicants from persons of complainant's qualifications. . . . The burden then must shift to the employer to articulate some legitimate, nondiscriminatory reason for the employee's rejection. . . . [The applicant must be] afforded a fair opportunity to show that [the employer's] stated reason for . . . rejection was in fact pretext.

Later decisions by the Court make it clear that the employer need not *prove* that its reasons for not hiring the applicant were legitimate and nondiscriminatory. The employer need only *articulate* such reasons, and then the burden shifts back to the applicant to show that the reasons were a pretext. The basic method of proof described in *McDonnell Douglas v. Green* has been adopted in a large number of areas, including age discrimination and pregnancy discrimination, as well as in Title VII cases.

**Disproportionate Impact**    Employment policies that are neutral on their face may have a *disproportionate impact* on certain groups of individuals. For example, a requirement that all employees must have a college education is neutral on its face, but the proportion of persons who complete college is smaller among some minority groups than among whites. The issue then becomes whether the requirement of a college education is related to the employment requirements necessary for the job involved. If so, even though the requirement has a disproportionate impact on minorities, the employment practice is permissible. If not, the practice may be discriminatory.

Title VII considers at length the problems of tests and testing for employment. The act specifically provides that it is not an unlawful employment practice "for an employer to give and act upon the results of any professionally developed ability test provided that such test, its administration or action upon the test is not designed, intended or used to discriminate. . . . "

In *Griggs v. Duke Power Co.*[11] the Court held that neither a standardized intelligence test nor a requirement of a high school diploma was permissible unless such a requirement had a "demonstrable relationship to successful performance of the job. . . . " On the other hand, it is permissible to impose reasonable strength requirements for firefighters or police officers, even though such requirements have a disproportionate impact on women, because strength may be an important factor for such jobs. One of the more difficult areas has been height and weight requirements, because such requirements clearly discriminate against women. Such requirements may be valid if height and weight have a demonstrable relationship to job performance.

**The Problem of Bona Fide Occupational Qualifications**    Title VII specifically permits discrimination on the basis of national origin, sex, or religion if the classification is a **bona fide occupational qualification,** or **bfoq.** That is, if national origin, sex, or religion is a real qualification for a job, discrimination on those bases is permitted. The act does *not* provide a bfoq exception in the case of race or color.

It is of course the exceptional situation in which even national origin, sex, or religion is a bfoq. Obviously, Catholic priests must be Catholic, rabbis must be Jewish, and ministers must be members of the churches in which they serve. But aside from such obvious situations, the bfoq exception has been very narrowly construed by the Courts.

---

11 401 U.S. 424, 91 S. Ct. 849, 28 L. Ed. 158 (1971).

In *Dothard v. Rawlinson*[12] the Supreme Court upheld a state rule that prison guards in men's prisons must be male, but the case made it clear that the bfoq rule provides only the "narrowest of exceptions to the general rule requiring equality of employment." In fact, the *Dothard* case is the *only* Supreme Court decision to approve a bfoq on account of sex.

**Affirmative Action Under Title VII**    The language of Title VII, particularly the words used in Sections 703(a) and (d), seem on their face to prohibit *any* type of discrimination in employment based on race, color, religion, sex, or national origin. Those sections also could be construed to prohibit private, voluntary, affirmative action plans by employers or by employers and unions working together.

Following the *Bakke* decision (see p. 450), it seemed clear that reverse discrimination caused by *state action* was unconstitutional, but the case did not deal with *private* discrimination. In 1979, in *United Steelworkers of America v. Weber*[13] the Court held that private affirmative action plans did not violate the fourteenth amendment equal protection clause. That case also held that the provisions of Title VII did not prohibit private affirmative action programs.

In 1986 the Court held in *Local 28 of the Sheet Metal Worker's Internat'l Assoc. v. EEOC*[14] that a federal district court may *order* a labor union to adopt a race-conscious affirmative action program to remedy past violations of Title VII by the union. In that case the union had previously been found guilty of discriminating against nonwhite workers in recruitment, selection, training, and admission to the union, and the Court ordered the union to admit a strict percentage of nonwhite members (29.23%) to mirror the available work force.

## Other Employment Discrimination Legislation

A variety of other statutes condemn discriminatory practices in employment as well. The first modern statute to consider sex discrimination was the **Equal Pay Act of 1963,** which generally prohibited differentials in pay between employees of different sexes performing "equal work." That statute was discussed in Chapter 16.

**Age Discrimination in Employment Act**    The Age Discrimination in Employment Act (ADEA) of 1967 generally follows the form of Title VII, including its applicability to employers, labor organizations, and employment agencies, and generally prohibits the same types of discrimination as prohibited by Title VII. The prohibitions against discrimination are limited to individuals over the age of forty. Mandatory retirement before seventy is generally banned but is permitted at sixty-five if the individual is employed in a "bona fide executive or a high policy-making position" and will obtain a pension or other deferred compensation benefits of at least $27,000 per year. The act also contains a bfoq exception identical to that found in Title VII. The EEOC also administers this act.

---

12  433 U.S. 321, 97 S. Ct. 2720, 53 L. Ed. 2d 786 (1977).
13  443 U.S. 193, 99 S. Ct. 2721, 61 L. Ed. 2d 480 (1979).
14  478 U.S. 421, 106 S. Ct. 3019 92 L. Ed. 2d 344 (1986).

**The Rehabilitation Act of 1973**    The Rehabilitation Act of 1973 protects handicapped individuals from discrimination in two instances: (1) the act requires "affirmative action" to hire the handicapped if a firm has a federal contract over $2,500; and (2) the law prohibits discrimination against the handicapped in federal grants and programs. The term *handicapped* includes both physical and mental impairments, but alcoholism and drug abuse are specifically excepted. All remedies provided by Title VII are available.

**The Pregnancy Discrimination Act of 1978**    In 1978, Congress amended Title VII to further define sex discrimination to include discrimination on account of pregnancy. The amendment provided that "women affected by pregnancy, childbirth, or related medical conditions shall be treated the same for all employment-related purposes, including receipt of benefits under fringe benefit programs, as other persons not so affected but similar in their ability or inability to work. . . . " The total impact of that law has not yet been assessed, particularly in problems relating to abortion, health insurance, and *paternity* leave.

**Executive Order 11246**    In the unlikely event an employer is not covered by Title VII, the firm may well be covered under Executive Order 11246, issued by President Johnson in 1965. That order requires all employers involved in federal contracts or in any employment situation involving federal funds not to discriminate in employment, to seek out qualified applicants from disadvantaged groups, to provide special training to members of such groups, and to hire preferentially from minority groups if qualifications of applicants are roughly equal. The order may also apply to firms that deal with firms with government contracts.

**Executive Order 4 and Affirmative Action**    Executive Order 4, issued by President Nixon in 1971, is the basis of most affirmative action programs in employment. Any firm with a nonconstruction contract with the federal government must file a written affirmative action program with the Office of Federal Contract Compliance. That program must contain a statement of good-faith efforts to achieve equal employment opportunity, an analysis of deficiencies in the use of minorities, and a timetable for correcting such deficiencies. Failure to develop such a program can lead to cancellation of existing contracts and elimination from consideration for future contracts. It is important to note that only *failure to develop* a program, and not failure to meet its goals, may lead to problems.

## DISCRIMINATION IN HOUSING

Discrimination in employment obviously is important to many businesses, but it is also important for businesspeople to have an understanding of the laws affecting housing discrimination. Many businesses and businesspeople are involved in real estate transactions, including real estate brokers, banks and other lending institutions, and rental agencies; and they are directly affected by federal and state fair-housing laws. Other individuals may invest in real estate and be affected by the fair-housing laws. And many students will find a knowledge of those laws helpful in personal transactions.

The history of discrimination in housing is unique and contradictory. The Civil

Rights Act of 1866, discussed in *Shelley v. Kraemer* (see p. 446), clearly covered some forms of housing discrimination. That act was held not to apply to *private* discrimination in 1883, and it lay dormant for over eight decades. In 1968, Congress passed a very specific and detailed law regulating private discrimination in housing. A few weeks later the Court held in *Jones v. Alfred H. Mayer Co.* (see p. 454) that the 1866 law did in fact apply to private discrimination. The result is that *both* the Civil Rights Act of 1866 and the Civil Rights Act of 1968 may apply to housing discrimination.

### The Civil Rights Act of 1968

Exactly one week after the assassination of Dr. Martin Luther King, Jr., Congress passed the Civil Rights Act of 1968, also known as the Federal Fair Housing Act. The law became known as **Title VIII** because it was an amendment to the 1964 Civil Rights Act. The statute is a comprehensive attempt to end private discrimination in housing and related fields.

**Unlawful Housing Practices**    The Civil Rights Act of 1968 prohibited a variety of discriminatory housing practices on the basis of the five protected categories: race, color, religion, sex, and national origin. In 1988 the protections of the act were extended to handicapped persons and families with young children. Illegal practices include

1    Refusal to sell, rent, or negotiate on the basis of the prohibited categories;

2    Discrimination in the terms, conditions, or privileges of sale or rental;

3    Advertising a preference or limitation based on the prohibited categories;

4    Falsely representing that a dwelling is unavailable because of the prohibited categories (sometimes called **steering**);

5    Inducing a person to sell or rent by making representations concerning the entry of persons of a particular race, color, religion, or national origin into an area (called **blockbusting**);

6    Denying loans or discriminating in their terms because of the prohibited categories; and

7    Denying real estate brokers' services or membership in brokers' organizations because of the prohibited categories.

**Exceptions from Coverage**    The act contains several exceptions. The law generally does not apply to owners who sell their own homes, but that exception does not apply if

1    The owner owns or has an interest in three or more properties at the time;

2    The owner uses a broker in the transaction;

3    The owner advertises a preference; or

4    The owner does not reside in the home and is not the most recent resident in the home, in which case the exemption may only apply once in a twenty-four-month period.

The Act also does not apply in rental situations if the rental property contains four or fewer units and the owner resides in one unit. Discrimination *in favor* of members of a particular religion is permitted in the case of housing operated by religious organizations.

**Enforcement and Remedies**    Persons injured by a practice made unlawful under the act may file a complaint with the Secretary of Housing and Urban Development (HUD). HUD is required to send a copy of the complaint to the person charged and must investigate the charge. After the investigation, HUD may attempt private conciliation or refer the case to the U.S. Attorney General.

In 1988, Congress passed an amendment to the Civil Rights Act of 1968, simplifying enforcement procedures substantially. Under that amendment, unless one of the parties asks to have the enforcement proceeding heard in federal court, it will be heard by an Administrative Law Judge attached to HUD. The Administrative Law Judge may award actual damages, grant injunctive and equitable relief, and impose civil penalties of up to $50,000 for repeat offenders. The bill also extends the protections of the 1968 act to make it illegal to discriminate in the sale or rental of housing to handicapped persons or to families with young children.

### The Civil Rights Act of 1866

The first American "fair housing act" was the Civil Rights Act of 1866, commonly known as *section 1982*. Because of the state-action doctrine discussed in *Shelley v. Kraemer* (see p. 446), section 1982 was not applied to *private* discrimination in housing between 1883 and 1968. In 1968 that ruling was reversed in *Jones v. Alfred H. Mayer Co.* (see p. 454).

The provisions of section 1982 are simple and straightforward. Almost from the beginning, the section was held to apply only to *racial* discrimination, but otherwise its wording is broad enough to cover almost any type of housing discrimination. The act is enforced by a lawsuit brought by the plaintiff in federal court. The complex enforcement procedures and exemptions found in the 1968 act are not found in the simple provisions of the 1866 law. Parties injured by racial discrimination usually have a choice between the two laws.

Section 1982, and a similar broad provision of the Civil Rights Act of 1870 known as section 1981,[15] have been applied to a number of discriminatory acts. For example, the Court has held that people who sprayed anti-Semitic symbols on a synagogue were liable under section 1982 for interfering with property rights.[16] The Court has also held that section 1981 prohibits a private college from refusing to grant tenure on the basis of Arabian ancestry.[17]

---

15 Section 1981 provides: "All persons within the jurisdiction of the United States shall have the same right . . . to make and enforce contracts, to sue, be parties, give evidence, and to the full and equal benefit of all laws and proceedings for the security of persons and property as is enjoyed by white persons, and shall be subject to like punishment, pains, penalties, taxes, licenses, and exactions of every kind, and no other."

16 *Shaare Tefile Congregation v. Cobb,* ——— U.S. ———, 107 S. Ct. 2019, 95 L. Ed. 2d 594 (1987).

17 *Saint Francis College v. Al-Khazraji,* ——— U.S. ———, 107 S. Ct. 2022, 95 L. Ed. 2d 594 (1987). The case also gave a very broad definition to the term *race*.

### State and Local Fair Housing Laws

In addition to section 1982 and the 1968 act, many states and some local governments have enacted fair housing statutes or ordinances. Often those statutes parallel the terms of the 1968 act, but occasionally the terms of those statutes or ordinances are broader and include other categories of discrimination, including marital status, age, and handicap.

## DISCRIMINATION IN PUBLIC ACCOMMODATIONS

It is also vital that businesspeople have an understanding of the law dealing with discrimination in public accommodations. Any person who deals in the entertainment or travel industries will be directly affected by this section of the law. And this law illustrates the conflict between private rights and public responsibilities of business.

**Title II** of the Civil Rights Act of 1964, known as the *Public Accommodations* section, generally prohibits discrimination between customers of certain businesses. Title III of the act also protects "equal utilization of any public facility," such as public parks and beaches. The constitutionality of Title II was established in the *Heart of Atlanta Motel* decision (see p. 108).

The public accommodations section was probably the most controversial aspect of the Civil Rights Act of 1964. Opponents of the law argued that private businesses ought to be able to sell, or refuse to sell, to whomever they chose as an incident to the right to own private property; that the law was an attempt to legislate morality; and that it constituted an unwarranted extension of government power. Proponents of the bill argued that racial discrimination is the link between personal prejudice and segregation; that businesses are in business to make money, not to discriminate; and that it should make no difference whether that money comes from a black or a white customer. Proponents also argued that the right to own property is never absolute and is subject to other restrictions, such as zoning laws or licensing requirements, and that Title II is simply another such restriction.

### Forbidden Discrimination and Coverage of the Law

The principal section of Title II provides that "[a]ll persons shall be entitled to the full and equal enjoyment of the goods, services, facilities, privileges, advantages, and accommodations of any place of public accommodation, as defined in this section, without discrimination or segregation on the ground of race, color, religion or national origin."

Four categories of establishments were specifically made "places of public accommodation" under the act: (1) inns, hotels, motels, or other lodging establishments with more than five rooms for rent; (2) restaurants and gasoline stations; (3) motion picture theaters, concert halls, sports arenas, and stadiums; and (4) any establishment physically located within the premises of any establishment covered by the act that holds itself out as serving patrons of such covered establishment. All such establishments must "affect commerce" under the commerce clause, although under *Heart of Atlanta Motel*, the amount of contact with interstate commerce may be minimal. Discrimination supported by state action is also forbidden. The act expressly exempts action by a "private club or other establishment not in fact open to the public."

### Remedies and Enforcement

The act permits actions for injunctions by either private persons aggrieved by a violation, or by the U.S. Attorney General in the case of persons "engaged in a pattern or practice of resistance to the full enjoyment of any of the rights" established by the act. Attorneys' fees and costs may be assessed against a violator. The act does not provide for damages, although damages may be available under state law.

Actions under section 1982 (the Civil Rights Act of 1866) are also possible, and damages are available under that section. The court may refer cases brought under Title II to the *Community Relations Service* to obtain voluntary compliance before issuing an injunction. The Community Relations Service was established by the Civil Rights Act of 1964 as a mediation and conciliation body.

## DISCRIMINATION IN CREDIT

The Equal Credit Opportunity Act of 1974 prohibits discrimination against credit applicants on the basis of race, creed, color, religion, age, national origin, income derived from public assistance, sex, or marital status (see p. 375). In addition, the Civil Rights Act of 1968 prohibits lenders from discriminating in real estate loans because of race, color, religion, or national origin.

Many of the regulatory agencies charged with overseeing the various financial institutions in the country have also adopted rules, guidelines, and regulations requiring equal credit opportunity. For example, the Federal Home Loan Bank Board requires that federally chartered savings and loan associations evaluate "each loan applicant's credit worthiness . . . on an individual basis without reference to presumed characteristics of a group." Other regulations prohibit discounting of an employed wife's income. Similar regulations restricting various types of discrimination have been issued by the Federal Housing Authority (FHA), the Veteran's Administration (VA), the Federal Deposit Insurance Corporation (FDIC), the Federal National Mortgage Association (FNMA), the Federal Home Loan Mortgage Corporation (FHLMC), and others.

Several states have also passed statutes prohibiting discrimination in the granting of credit, although the "prohibited categories" vary between states. Many such statutes specifically permit creditors to consider an applicant's ability to repay but prohibit consideration of other factors.

## SUMMARY AND CONCLUSIONS

Although the law relating to discrimination developed in the context of racial segregation, other groups are discriminated against as well, including religious, national, and sexual minorities. The fourteenth amendment broadly prohibits state action that deprives individuals of the equal protection of the laws, and the thirteenth and fifteenth amendments are also relevant to a consideration of racial discrimination. The state action requirement has been narrowly interpreted, although for decades the requirement operated to prohibit federal action against private discrimination. Congressional authority to regulate private discrimination was not firmly established until 1968. The fourteenth amendment was also interpreted for the first half of the twentieth century to permit separate but equal treatment of racial minorities. That curious doctrine was overturned in 1954 in the landmark *Brown v. Board* decision, discussed earlier.

In the 1960s, Congress passed several laws dealing with the problems of discrimination. The Civil Rights Act of 1964 contained separate titles, dealing with discrimination in public accommodations, public facilities, education, and employment. The Civil Rights Act of 1968 prohibited discrimination in the sale or rental of real estate. Other statutes prohibited sex-based discrimination in pay for equal work, age discrimination, discrimination against the handicapped, and discrimination on account of pregnancy.

Even in the light of the 1960s legislation, discrimination remains an unresolved problem in contemporary America. Two of the most controversial areas are affirmative action, particularly in the context of claims of reverse discrimination, and the problems of implementing school desegregation in the context of a society that continues to maintain racially segregated housing patterns, not as the result of law but as a result of habit and personal bias. Those problems point to the ever-present problem of attempting to legislate the moral feelings of the nation.

## REVIEW QUESTIONS

1   Is the Constitution color-blind? Should it be color-blind? Are there instances in which the law should take race into account? If so, when?

2   Explain the difference between disparate treatment and disproportionate impact. Isn't a high school education a reasonable requirement for every job, even in light of the disproportionate impact doctrine? If discrimination in education is ever totally ended, would a high school education become a reasonable requirement for all jobs?

3   If you thought you were being discriminated against, how would you prove it? How would you prove that an employer's articulated reasons for not giving you a job were a mere pretext for discrimination?

4   After you graduate, you are made supervisor over several other people. You find one of the people working for you very attractive, and you want to ask that person for a date. After the *Meritor* case, may you do so?

5   What is a bfoq? Name five jobs for which sex is a bfoq. Now do the same for religion and national origin. Why do you suppose race or color is not a bfoq? Can you think of any jobs for which race or color might arguably be a bfoq?

6   Wilson and 100 other males applied for positions as flight attendants and ticket agents with Southwest Airlines, but all were turned down. An advertising agency had suggested that Southwest adopt a "sexy" image for its flight attendants and agents in order to attract customers, based on the slogan "At Last There Is Somebody Else Up There Who Loves You." Southwest contended that its requirement that flight attendants and ticket agents be female is a bona fide occupational qualification. What do you think the result was? [*Wilson v. Southwest Airlines Co.*, 500 F. Supp., 292 (N.D. Texas, 1981).]

7   Somerset University, a publicly supported institution, designed an affirmative action program in which a point system was established for admission. Points were awarded for a student's high school grade point average, scores on standardized tests, high school activities, and race. Edmund, a white student, and George, a black student, had precisely the same scores for all of the criteria except race. Because George received more "points" for his race, he received the last position to be awarded for admission to Somerset. Does Edmund have a complaint?

8   Hermione wanted to become a firefighter. In order to do so she had to pass both an intelli-

gence test and a physical stamina test, and she had to weigh over 140 pounds and stand five feet six inches. Hermione was five feet three inches and weighed 125 pounds. Does she have a remedy? Are the intelligence and physical stamina tests permissible?

9 The Holofernes Company, an American corporation, maintains offices around the world. Recently, several applicants were turned down for several positions in those offices. Jaquenetta was turned down for a position in a Latin American country because the people in that country would not deal with a woman. Anthony, a black man, was turned down for a position in South Africa because of that nation's racial policies. Henry, who is Jewish, was turned down for a position in Iran because of that nation's policies. And Maria was turned down for a position in the New York office because the manager of that office had a reputation with women and a jealous wife. Which of those people had a valid claim of discrimination?

10 Conrade is the manager of a loan company with ultimate responsibility for determining to whom loans are made. To which of the following persons may he refuse to grant credit: (a) a divorced person; (b) a person who is unemployed; (c) a person who receives welfare; (d) a person newly arrived in the United States; (e) a person with a low-paying job; (f) a person with a large number of debts?

C H A P T E R   1 9

# Environmental Law

*Universe to each must be*
*All that is, including me.*
*Environment in turn must be*
*All that is, excepting me.*

R. BUCKMINSTER FULLER
*Synergetics* 2, sec. 100.12. (1979)

*We have met the enemy and he is us.*

POGO (WALT KELLY CARTOON CHARACTER)

Interest in the environment was not new to the 1960's and 1970's, when most of the environmental regulations developed. Concern with dirty air and foul water can be seen at least as early as the middle of the nineteenth century. But in a time when economic "progress" and industrialization were the principal values of society, such concerns could not become part of public policy. Environmental pollution and misuse of resources were viewed as unfortunate but necessary costs of industrial development.

Some environmental problems had been addressed by ancient common law theories of *nuisance, trespass,* and *strict liability,* although not very well. During the 1950's, feeble attempts to control air and water pollution began at the federal level, but those attempts relied on enforcement by the states. Such an approach was bound to fail, because each state must protect its own industries, and because air and water pollution are interstate or even international problems.

Grassroots pressure for effective laws to protect the environment continued throughout the 1960's, and in 1969, Congress passed the most important of the environmental protection laws, the National Environmental Policy Act (NEPA). That same year, President Nixon issued an Executive Order creating the Environmental Protection Agency (EPA) to centralize authority over environmental matters in one agency. During the 1970's, Congress also passed strong new laws or amended old ones concerning air and water pollution, solid waste disposal, toxic wastes, and preservation of wilderness and wildlife.

The same period saw a growing concern with the problems of conserving energy resources and the development of nuclear and other alternative energy sources. That concern resulted in a series of statutes designed to encourage energy conservation and development of energy sources.

In the 1980's a new international arena for environmental concern has developed from the recognition that pollution does not respect national boundaries. Pollution of a river flowing through Switzerland has caused severe economic distress in Austria and

France. Air pollution from American smokestacks has created acid rain that threatens Canada's forests. And perhaps most devastating of all, a radioactive cloud from the Chernobyl nuclear disaster has resulted in health hazards throughout most of Western Europe. The law is only beginning to deal with the international implications of pollution and environmental hazards.

## COMMON LAW ENVIRONMENTAL PROTECTION

Until the 1950's, the sole method of dealing with environmental problems was through private lawsuits filed by persons injured by the actions of others and through the concept of *public nuisance*, a common law crime. The principal theories by which injured persons might recover are **private nuisance, trespass,** and **strict liability.** All are common law torts and are enforced by private lawsuits.

### Private Nuisance

The tort of *private nuisance* is an ancient and ambiguous doctrine. Nuisance requires proof of an intentional (or sometimes negligent) interference with another's right to use and enjoy the ownership of land. The tort has been applied to smoke or dust settling on a landowner's property, excessive noise, noxious odors, sewage percolating into someone's basement, and a wide variety of other objectionable occurrences.

Nuisance cases inevitably involve a balancing of interests. Generally, a landowner has the right to use his or her property in any lawful manner, but the doctrine of nuisance says that such use may not interfere with the rights of another landowner to use and enjoy land. The question then becomes *which* landowner's rights are to be protected.

The usual private nuisance case involves a landowner whose use of land results in smoke, dust, or some other irritant. Proof in such cases is often quite difficult, because there are often several polluters in the same area. Proof of damages is also often quite difficult. The term *nuisance* is broad, as discussed in the following "right to sunlight" case.

---

## *Prah v. Maretti*
108 Wisc. 2d 223, 321 N.W.2d 182 (1982)

The plaintiff, Prah, built the first home in a subdivision and established a solar energy system to partially heat the home. The defendant, Maretti, purchased the lot next to the plaintiff's and began construction of his home on the lot. The plaintiff informed the defendant that if the defendant's home was located as originally planned, the plaintiff's solar collectors would be shaded, resulting in inefficiencies in the system and possibly damaging the collectors. The defendant refused to change the location of the house, and the plaintiff filed suit, asking for an injunction to stop Maretti from blocking the collectors. The trial court dismissed the complaint, and the plaintiff appealed.

**Abrahamson, Justice**   This state has long recognized that an owner of land does not have an absolute or unlimited right to use the land in a way which injures the rights of others. The rights of neighboring landowners are relative, the uses by one must not unreasonably impair the uses or enjoyment of the other. . . . When one landowner's use of his or her property unreasonably interferes with another's enjoyment of his or her property that use is said to be a private nuisance. . . .

The private nuisance doctrine has traditionally been employed in this state to balance the conflicting rights of landowners, and this court has recently adopted the analysis of private nuisance set forth in the Restatement (Second) of Torts. . . . The Restatement defines private nuisance as "a nontrespassory invasion of another's interest in the private use and enjoyment of land." . . .

Although the defendant's obstruction of the plaintiff's access to sunlight appears to fall with the Restatement's broad concept of a private nuisance as a nontrespassory invasion of another's interest in the private use and enjoyment of land, the defendant asserts that he has a right to develop his property in compliance with statutes, ordinances and private covenants without regard to the effect of such development upon the plaintiff's access to sunlight. In essence, the defendant is asking this court to hold that the private nuisance doctrine is not applicable in the instant case and that his right to develop his land is a right which is *per se* superior to his neighbor's interest in access to sunlight. This position is expressed in the maxim *cujus est solum, ejus est usque ad coelum et an infernos,* that is, the owner of land owns up to the sky and down to the center of the earth. The rights of the surface owner are, however, not unlimited. . . .

Many jurisdictions in this country have protected a landowner from malicious obstruction of access to light (the spite fence cases) under the common law private nuisance doctrine. If an activity is motivated by malice, it lacks utility and the harm it causes others outweighs any social values.

This court's reluctance in the nineteenth and early part of the twentieth century to provide broader protection for a landowner's access to sunlight was premised on three policy considerations. First, the right of landowners to use their property as they wished as long as they did not cause physical damage to a neighbor was jealously guarded. . . . Second, sunlight was valued only for aesthetic enjoyment or as

illumination. Since artificial light could be used for illumination, loss of sunlight was at most a personal annoyance which was given little, if any, weight by society. Third, society had a significant interest in not restricting or impeding land development. . . .

[But t]his court repeatedly emphasized that in the growth period of the nineteenth and early twentieth centuries change is to be expected and is essential to property and that recognition of a right to sunlight would hinder property development. The court expressed this concept as follows:

> As the city grows, large grounds appurtenant to residences must be cut up to supply more residences. . . . The cistern, the outhouse, the cesspool, and the private drain must disappear in deference to the public waterworks and the sewer; the terrace and the garden, to the need for more complete occupancy. . . . *Miller v. Hoeschler.* . . . (1905).

These three policies are no longer fully accepted or applicable. They reflect factual circumstances and social priorities that are now obsolete.

First, society has increasingly regulated the use of land by the landowner for the general welfare. . . . Second, access to sunlight has taken on a new significance in recent years. In this case the plaintiff seeks to protect access to sunlight, not for aesthetic reasons or as a source of illumination but as a source of energy. Access to sunlight as an energy source is of significance both to the landowner who invests in solar collectors and to a society which has an interest in developing alternative sources of energy. Third, the policy of favoring unhindered private development in an expanding economy is no longer in harmony with the realities of our society. . . . The need for easy and rapid development is not as great today as it once was while our perception of the value of sunlight as a source of energy has increased significantly.

Private nuisance law, the law traditionally used to adjudicate conflicts between private landowners, has the flexibility to protect both a landowner's right of access to sunlight and another landowner's right to develop land. . . .

We therefore hold that private nuisance law, that is, the reasonable use doctrine as set forth in the Restatement, is applicable to the instant case. . . .

[Reversed.]

Case Discussion Questions

1    What are Prah's interests in the land in this case? What are Maretti's interests? Which interest is more important?
2    What is the doctrine of private nuisance? What is the doctrine of *cujus est solum, ejus usque ad coelum et an infernos?* How are those two doctrines in conflict in this case?
3    How have changes in society contributed to the change in the law caused by this case?

## Public Nuisance

The common law crime of **public nuisance** has become a part of the criminal statutes in many states. Such laws are often broadly worded to prohibit "maintaining a public nuisance" and have been applied to everything from houses of prostitution to being a common scold. These laws may also be applied to a variety of environmentally related activities, including smoke, dust, and odors. Often the laws are so broad that they invite challenge on constitutional due process grounds. Persons who are "specially injured" may have the right to bring a private civil lawsuit based on violation of the criminal statute as well. Prosecutors and plaintiffs face problems of proof similar to those in private nuisance cases.

## Trespass

One of the most ancient torts is **trespass to land,** which is an unauthorized entry onto land. The common law tort of *trespass* gave a right of action for all such entries, including intentional, negligent, and even accidental ones. This tort was in fact a strict liability action, because it was not necessary to prove any mental element.

Since a personal invasion of property is not necessary, the tort may be committed when physical objects are caused to come in contact with another's land. As a result, successful actions have been maintained based on pollutants, such as smoke particles, which settle on the land of another. Again there are substantial difficulties of proof, particularly in showing the damages caused by such actions. Both damages and injunctions may be awarded.

## Strict Liability

The concept of *strict liability*, or liability without fault, gives a right of action to persons damaged by an ultrahazardous or abnormally dangerous activity that causes an unreasonable risk of harm to others or to the property of others (see p. 241). Some modern pollution-generating activities may be within the requirements of strict liability, such as discharging poisons into a water supply or releasing radioactive materials into the atmosphere.

## Limits of the Common Law in Controlling Environmental Damage

The traditional torts of nuisance, trespass, and strict liability proved quite ineffective in controlling pollution and other environmental damage. Only landowners could recover for nuisance and trespass, reflecting the concern of the common law with the rights of property. But clearly others besides landowners were injured by environmental damage, including the public.

The common law torts also required that the plaintiff suffer some *special damage*, or injury different or greater than that suffered by the general public. In many cases the damage suffered, although real, was small and difficult to prove, and polluters were willing to spend large amounts to defend such cases in order to prevent precedents from being set.

Perhaps most importantly, the common law torts were designed to remedy *individual* injuries, whereas the damage done by pollution is to the *public as a whole*, or even to *nonhuman elements* of the ecological system. Wildlife, after all, has no standing to bring a lawsuit. The result was that the remedies of common law were of little effect in protecting the environment.

## FEDERAL ENVIRONMENTAL PROTECTION—NEPA

In retrospect, federal concern with the environment came extremely late, after the nation and its people had been subjected to filthy air, dirty water, and the refuse of industrial society for decades, and after some of the effects of pollution may have become irreversible. But the blissful ignorance of our legislators only mirrored the blissful ignorance of society itself.

It was not until refined scientific testing procedures became available in the 1960's that the true extent of environmental damage became known. The ravages of pollution were pointed out to the public in several well-known books, such as Rachel Carson's *Silent Spring*,[1] and a grassroots movement placed pressure on Congress to take steps to remedy environmental damage. The first and most important result was the **National Environmental Policy Act of 1969 (NEPA)**.

NEPA had three major aspects: (1) it established a national policy of preventing environmental damage; (2) it established the **Council on Environmental Quality (CEQ)**; and (3) it required the filing of **Environmental Impact Statements (EIS)** by federal agencies undertaking "major federal actions significantly affecting the quality of the human environment."

The crucial effect of NEPA is on federal administrative agencies. The purpose of the requirement of filing Environmental Impact Statements, described later, is to force every federal agency to consider environmental factors in their decision-making processes. NEPA requires each agency to take a hard look at environmental concerns and to consider environmental matters before undertaking agency actions.

### The Council on Environmental Quality (CEQ)

The *Council on Environmental Quality* is a three-member board appointed by the President with the advice and consent of the Senate. The purpose of the CEQ is to coordinate programs and activities that "affect, protect and improve environmental quality" and to assist and advise the President on environmental matters. The CEQ does not enforce laws; instead, it acts as a mediator between other agencies of government in-

---

1 Boston: Houghton Mifflin, 1962.

volved in interagency disputes involving environmental matters. The CEQ may simply mediate such disputes or may pass them on to the President, with its advice, for final resolution. The CEQ also acts as a central filing point for Environmental Impact Statements.

## Environmental Impact Statements

The most important effect of NEPA lies in the requirement that *Environmental Impact Statements (EIS)* be filed by federal agencies. An EIS is required "in every recommendation or report on proposals for legislation and other *major Federal actions significantly affecting the quality of the human environment* [emphasis added]. . . . "

The EIS must contain a detailed statement by the responsible official on (1) the environmental impact of the proposed action; (2) any unavoidable adverse environmental effects of the project; and (3) alternatives to the proposed action. The EIS must be quite detailed but should not run more than 150 pages. NEPA requires federal agencies to prepare a detailed explanation of the environmental effects of their actions and make the report available to Congress, other agencies, and the public.

It is important to note that it is the *agency's* responsibility to prepare the EIS, and that responsibility cannot be delegated to private individuals or firms involved in the project. The agency may seek the help of such individuals or firms in preparing the EIS, but the ultimate responsibility for preparation of the document is the agency's.

**Use of the EIS**    The primary purpose of the EIS is to provide information to decision makers and other agencies. Disputes between agencies may be referred to the CEQ for resolution by a written *referral* by one agency and a written *response* by another. The CEQ must act within twenty-five days and has several options: It may decide that the referral and response have settled the matter, it may act as mediator, it may hold public meetings or hearings, it may decide that the matter lacks national significance, or it may publish its findings and recommendations and submit them to the President for action.

For example, if the Defense Department is considering the construction of a new air force base, it will file an EIS with the CEQ. The Environmental Protection Agency and perhaps other agencies will review the EIS and comment on it. If the EPA finds some potential environmental damage, it may make a referral to the CEQ, and the Defense Department may make a response. The CEQ may mediate the matter, hold hearings, and finally submit the matter to the President for determination (see Figure 19.1).

NEPA provides no judicial remedies for enforcement of the EIS provisions. NEPA was meant to provide an additional administrative hurdle for federal projects, forcing agencies to consider the environmental effect of their actions. But a determined agency with little environmental conscience could, under that view, force an environmentally dangerous project through the decision-making process. Such events would not occur frequently, because public pressure would undoubtedly be brought to bear on such agencies, but such actions could occur.

The following landmark case established the rule that courts may review agency consideration of an EIS and hold that an agency has given insufficient consideration to environmental factors in its decision making. The case also includes a discussion of the policy behind NEPA and the EIS requirement.

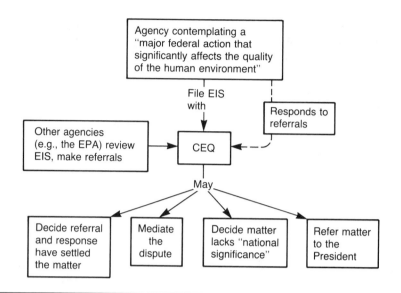

FIGURE 19.1   The EIS Process

# Calvert Cliffs Coordinating Committee v. A.E.C.
449 F.2d 1109 (D.C. Circ., 1971)

The Atomic Energy Commission[2] adopted procedural rules to comply with the EIS requirements. The rules adopted seemed to comply *technically* with NEPA but were clearly designed to avoid the real purposes of that act. The AEC included rules which (1) stated that environmental factors need not be considered by the AEC hearing board unless raised by outside parties or staff members; (2) prohibited any party from raising most environmental issues prior to a date well after the adoption of AEC rules; (3) prohibited the AEC hearing board from considering environmental factors if other agencies certify that their own environmental standards are satisfied by the proposed action; and (4) prohibited the consideration of environmental factors in nuclear power facility cases until the time of the issuance of the operating license, a time long after plants have been constructed.

Petitioners, a private group concerned with nuclear power, brought suit claiming that the AEC rules did not live up to the requirements of NEPA. The AEC, on the other hand, claimed that the broadness of NEPA permitted those rules. The case reached the U.S. court of appeals.

**J. Skelly Wright, Circuit Judge**   These cases are only the beginning of what promises to become a flood of new litigation—litigation seeking judicial assistance in protecting our natural environment. Several recently enacted statutes attest to the commitment of the Government to control, at long last, the

---

2 The AEC was disbanded in 1974. Most of its functions went to the new Nuclear Regulatory Commission, and others went to the Department of Energy.

destructive engine of material "progress." But it remains to be seen whether the promise of this legislation will become a reality. Therein lies the judicial role. In these cases we must for the first time interpret the broadest and perhaps most important of the recent statutes: the National Environmental Policy Act of 1969 (NEPA). We must assess claims that one of the agencies charged with its administration has failed to live up to the congressional mandate. Our duty, in short, is to see that important legislative purposes, heralded in the halls of Congress, are not lost or misdirected in the vast hallways of the federal bureaucracy.

We begin our analysis with an examination of NEPA's structure. . . . The relevant portion of NEPA is Title 1, consisting of five sections. Section 101 sets forth the Act's basic substantive policy: that the federal government "use all practicable means and measures" to protect environmental values. Congress did not establish environmental protection as an exclusive goal; rather, it desired a reordering of priorities, so that environmental costs and benefits will assume their proper place along with other considerations. . . .

NEPA . . . makes environmental protection a part of the mandate of every federal agency and department. The Atomic Energy Commission, for example, had continually asserted, prior to NEPA, that it had no statutory authority to concern itself with the adverse environmental effects of its actions. Now, however, its hands are no longer tied. It is not only permitted, but compelled, to take environmental values into account. . . .

Of course, all of these duties are qualified by the phrase "to the fullest extent possible." We must stress as forcefully as possible that this language does not provide an escape hatch for footdragging agencies; it does not make NEPA's procedural requirements somehow "discretionary." Congress did not intend the act to be such a paper tiger. Indeed, the requirement of environmental consideration "to the fullest extent possible" sets a high standard for the agencies, a standard which must be rigorously enforced by the reviewing courts. . . .

We conclude, then, that NEPA mandates a particular sort of careful and informed decisionmaking process and creates judicially enforceable duties. The reviewing courts probably cannot reverse a substantive decision on its merits, unless it be shown that the actual balance of costs and benefits that was struck was arbitrary or clearly gave insufficient weight to envi-ronmental values. But if the decision was reached procedurally without individualized consideration and balancing of environmental factors—conducted fully and in good faith—it is the responsibility of the courts to reverse. . . .

In the cases before us now, we do not have to review a particular decision by the Atomic Energy Commission granting a construction permit or an operating license. Rather we must review the Commission's recently promulgated rules which govern consideration of environmental values in such individual decisions. The rules were devised strictly in order to comply with the NEPA procedural requirements—but petitioners argue that they fall far short of the congressional mandate. . . .

We believe that the Commission's crabbed interpretation of NEPA makes a mockery of the Act. What possible purpose could there be in the [NEPA] requirement [that the "detailed statement" accompany proposals through agency review processes] if "accompany" means no more than physical proximity—mandating no more than the physical act of passing certain folders and papers, unopened, to reviewing officials along with other folders and papers? What possible purpose could there be in requiring the "detailed statement" to be before hearing boards, if the boards are free to ignore entirely the contents of the statement? NEPA was meant to do more than regulate the flow of papers in the federal bureaucracy. . . . It must, rather, be read to indicate a congressional intent that environmental factors, as compiled in the "detailed statement," be *considered* through agency review processes. . . .

We believe the Commission's rule is in fundamental conflict with the basic purpose of the Act. NEPA mandates a case-by-case balancing judgment on the part of federal agencies. In each individual case the particular economic and technical benefits of planned action must be assessed and then weighed against the environmental costs; alternatives must be considered which would affect the balance of values. . . . The magnitude of possible benefits and possible costs may lie anywhere on a broad spectrum. Much will depend on the particular magnitudes involved in particular cases. In some cases, the benefits will be great enough to justify a certain quantum of environmental costs; in other cases, they will not be so great and the proposed action may have to be abandoned or significantly altered so as to bring the benefits and costs into a proper balance. . . .

We hold that . . . the Commission must revise

its rules governing consideration of environmental issues. . . .

Remanded for proceedings consistent with this opinion.

Case Discussion Questions

1    Did the AEC rules comply with the *letter* of the law in NEPA? Did they comply with the *spirit* of the law? What reasons could there be for such a "crabbed interpretation" by the AEC?

2    According to the court, what is the purpose of NEPA? What procedures does NEPA establish to reach that goal?

3    What is the effect of this decision on the workload of federal agencies? Is the cost worth it?

**The Threshold Requirements for an EIS: "Major Federal Actions"**    NEPA requires an EIS in the case of any "major federal action significantly affecting the quality of the human environment." In most cases, the "major federal action" requirement is no problem if a federal agency is undertaking or contracting directly for a project. Slightly more difficult problems exist if the agency only approves or licenses private action. Generally, if a federal agency has the authority to control the action, it is considered a federal action.

There is also no real problem in determining whether a federal action is *major*. Any project that involves a substantial commitment of resources or funds is considered major, and the issue has not resulted in much litigation. Some argue that no project that involves a significant environmental impact could ever be considered anything but "major."

**The Threshold Requirements for an EIS: "Significant Environmental Effect"**    A more difficult problem involves whether a proposed federal action "significantly affects the quality of the human environment." To the uninitiated, the term *environment* includes only nature—wild areas, forests, beaches, and the like. But the act had broader concerns in mind, such as preserving cultural and historic areas, enhancing the quality of renewable resources, and achieving a balance between population and resource use. The following case involves the question of how Congress intended the term *human environment* to be interpreted in the context of the Three Mile Island incident.

## *Metropolitan Edison Co. v. People Against Nuclear Energy*
460 U.S. 766, 103 S. Ct. 1556, 75 L. Ed. 2d 534 (1983)

On March 29, 1979, one of the nuclear reactors (TMI-2) owned by Metropolitan Edison at Three Mile Island near Harrisburg, Pennsylvania, suffered a serious accident that damaged the reactor. Although no dangerous radiation was released, the accident caused widespread concern, and the Governor of Pennsylvania recommended an evacuation of pregnant women and small children. Many area residents left their homes for several days. At the time of the accident, a second reactor (TMI-1) owned by Metropolitan at the same location had been shut down for refueling and was not operating.

After the accident, the Nuclear Regulatory Commission ordered Metropolitan to keep TMI-1 shut down until it had an opportunity to determine whether the plant could be operated safely. A citizens' group, People Against Nuclear Energy (PANE), intervened before the NRC, claiming that reopening TMI-1 would cause substantial *psychological* harm to the people who resided around the Three Mile Island plant, and that the NRC must consider that psychological harm as a "significant environmental effect" under NEPA.

The NRC refused to take evidence regarding the psychological impact of restarting TMI-1, and Metropolitan was permitted to restart TMI-1. (TMI-2 was closed completely.) PANE appealed to the Court of Appeals, which held that the NRC improperly failed to consider the psychological harm to the residents of the surrounding area. Metropolitan appealed to the Supreme Court.

**Justice Rehnquist Delivered the Opinion of the Court**  All the parties agree that effects on human health can be cognizable under NEPA and that human health may include psychological health. The Court of Appeals thought these propositions were enough to complete a syllogism that disposes of the case: NEPA requires agencies to consider effects on health. An effect on psychological health is an effect on health. Therefore, NEPA requires agencies to consider the effects on psychological health asserted by PANE. . . . Although these arguments are appealing at first glance, we believe they skip over an essential step in the analysis. They do not consider the closeness of the relationship between the change in the environment and the "effect" at issue. . . .

To paraphrase the statutory language [of NEPA] in light of the facts of this case, where an agency action significantly affects the quality of the human environment, the agency must evaluate the "environmental impact" and any unavoidable adverse environmental affects of its proposal. The theme [of the Act] is sounded by the adjective "environmental": NEPA does not require the agency to assess *every* impact of its proposed action, but only the impact or effect on the environment. If we were to seize the word "environmental" out of its context and give it the broadest possible definition, the words "adverse environmental effects" might embrace virtually any consequence of a governmental action that someone thought "adverse." But we think the context of the statute shows that Congress was talking about the physical environment—the world around us, so to speak. NEPA was designed to promote human welfare by alerting governmental actors to the effect of their proposed actions on the physical environment. . . .

PANE argues that the psychological health damage it alleges "will flow directly from the risk of [a nuclear] accident." . . . But a risk of an accident is not an effect on the physical environment. A risk is, by definition, unrealized in the physical world. In a causal chain from renewed operation of TMI-1 to psychological health damage, the element of risk and its perception by PANE's members are necessary middle links. We believe that the element of risk lengthens the causal chain beyond the reach of NEPA. . . .

Time and resources are simply too limited for us to believe that Congress intended to extend NEPA as far as the Court of Appeals has taken it. We do not mean to denigrate the fears of PANE's members, or to suggest that the psychological health damage they fear could not, in fact, occur. Nonetheless, it is difficult for us to see the differences between someone who dislikes a government decision so much that he suffers similar anxiety and stress, someone who fears the effects of that decision so much that he suffers anxiety and stress and someone who suffers anxiety and stress that "flow directly" . . . from the risks associated with the same decision. It would be extraordinarily difficult for agencies to differentiate between "genuine claims of psychological health damage and claims that are grounded solely in disagreement with a democratically adopted policy. . . ."

For these reasons, we hold that the NRC need not consider PANE's contentions. . . . The judgment of the Court of Appeals is reversed. . . .

## Case Discussion Questions

1  According to PANE, what sort of injury may occur if TMI-1 is permitted to restart? Is this an "environmental effect"?

2  What sort of effects are covered by the EIS requirement?

**3** Following the Three Mile Island problem, property values have dropped by a large amount in the surrounding area, several businesses have gone bankrupt, and hundreds of people have been put out of work. Is that a "significant environmental effect"? Should it be?

## FEDERAL ENVIRONMENTAL PROTECTION: THE EPA

The **Environmental Protection Agency (EPA)** was created as part of an executive reorganization plan submitted to Congress by President Nixon in 1970. It was given powers originally delegated to fifteen separate agencies or executive departments, such as the Department of Interior, Bureau of Solid Waste Management, and the Department of Agriculture. The EPA is headed by a single Administrator, appointed by the President. The agency is an "independent" agency, but it is not an "independent regulatory commission" in the sense described in Chapter 6, because its administrator serves at the pleasure of the President. The EPA is a part of the executive branch.

Congress has, from time to time, delegated additional power to the EPA to enforce new legislation in the environmental area, as in the Clean Air Amendments of 1970. The EPA's enforcement powers vary with the area considered, as in air pollution, water pollution, or solid waste management, for example.

## REGULATION OF AIR POLLUTION

The term *pollution* simply means "dirt or contamination," and the term is far too broad to be used meaningfully in any law. A basic problem throughout the fight for clean air has been finding some workable definition of air pollution.

A second problem is, of course, that the air is a common sea, and it is extremely difficult to control one small part of that sea without controlling the entire ocean. Pollution in one area affects the quality of the air in all other areas. The same problem makes air pollution extremely dangerous, because we all live at the bottom of that sea.

In 1955, when Congress first attempted to deal with the problems of air pollution in the **Air Pollution Control Act,** it failed to consider both problems. That act contained no definition of air pollution, and it left enforcement of the law to voluntary efforts by the states. Initially the law merely provided technical and financial assistance to the states.

Slowly the federal law acquired more teeth, and in 1963 federal agencies were authorized to move against interstate air pollution in the **Clean Air Act.** That act did not define air pollution either. In 1965 the act was amended to set standards for emissions by new cars. Throughout this period, the primary emphasis was on state control of air pollution. In 1967 a further amendment required the states to establish *air quality standards* and to adopt *state implementation plans*, but the nature of those standards and implementation plans was left up to the states.

Real teeth were finally put in the federal law with the **Clean Air Amendments of 1970.** Those amendments gave authority over the act to the EPA and required the Administrator of the EPA to make regulations dealing with air quality, but the amendments continued to assert that "[E]ach state shall have the primary responsibility for assuring air quality within the entire geographic area comprising such State. . . . "

### The Definition of Air Pollution

The 1970 amendments resolved the problem of defining the term *air pollution* by requiring the Administrator of the EPA to issue a list of *air pollutants* that have an adverse effect on public health or welfare. Initially, the Administrator's list included six such pollutants: sulfur dioxide ($SO_2$), particulates, carbon monoxide (CO), photochemical oxidants (nitrogen oxide and ozone), hydrocarbons, and nitrogen dioxide ($NO_2$). In 1977 lead was added, and in 1982 hydrocarbons were removed from the list.

### National Ambient Air Quality Standards (NAAQSs)

For each pollutant, the Administrator was also required to establish **National Ambient Air Quality Standards (NAAQSs),** which are the maximum amounts of each pollutant that will be permitted. For each such pollutant there are two standards: **primary standards,** those necessary to protect human life and health, and **secondary standards,** those necessary to protect nonhuman elements, such as buildings, animals, and crops. EPA regulations define the secondary standards as "necessary for human welfare." The NAAQSs are phrased in micrograms per cubic meter or parts per million over a period of time. The NAAQSs are essentially the maximum limits of pollutants that the air may legally carry.

**State Implementation Plans (SIPs)**    After the Administrator established the NAAQSs, states were required to establish **State Implementation Plans** (SIPs) to enforce the primary standards as "expeditiously as practicable but . . . in no case later than three years from the date of approval of such plan." States were required to meet the secondary standards within a reasonable time specified in the plan itself. The original dates for meeting the primary standards ranged from 1975 to 1977, but nowhere were those goals met. As a result, the deadlines were extended by a series of amendments.

**Existing Stationary Sources of Pollution**    Emission standards for *existing stationary sources* of pollution, such as factories or power plants that existed before the adoption of the 1970 amendments, are found in the state implementation plans. In areas in which pollution concentrations exceed the NAAQSs, the act requires that the state plans impose at least "reasonably available control technology" on such sources. The federal EPA Administrator may amend the state plans to reach those goals. States may adopt implementation plans that exceed the NAAQSs, however.

Economic cost and technological feasibility cannot be taken into account by the EPA Administrator in approving a state implementation plan, but such issues may be raised before the state agency or in the state courts. Many states have set up a procedure for "hardship variances," which take technological feasibility and economic cost into account.

In 1977 the Clean Air Act was amended when it became obvious that the primary standards would not be met. The 1977 amendments contained a delayed schedule for compliance and provided relief to individual sources unable to meet the NAAQSs because present facilities are being retired, because of investment in innovative facilities with the promise of better pollution reduction, or because of requirements to convert to coal because of the energy crisis (see *Profile*, p. 490). Such sources may obtain *delayed compliance orders* from state or federal EPAs.

**State Failure to Attain Air Quality Standards**   If a state does not meet the NAAQS standards, the principal sanction is a moratorium on construction and operation of new or modified stationary sources. Another possible remedy is denial of federal grants, including federal grants for highway construction. In 1977 the Clean Air Act was amended to authorize postponement of the date for compliance with the primary standards until 1983, or 1987 in the case of oxidants and carbon monoxide. Early in 1983 the EPA designated over a hundred counties nationwide as "probable noncompliance areas."

**Offsets and Bubbles**   In **nonattainment areas,** or places in which the NAAQS standards have not been met, new sources of air pollution must obtain permits from the EPA. Permits may be issued only if the total allowable emissions from the new source are less than the total emissions from existing sources under the state implementation plan. In other words, the permit will only be allowed if the new emissions are **offset** by a reduction in old emissions. Thus, the owner may have to shut down an old facility in order to open a new one or reduce existing emissions by adding new control facilities to old plants.

Offsets are also permitted within a single source, under the so-called **bubble doctrine.** All of the parts of a single industrial plant are treated as a single source, and offsetting increases and decreases in emission from different parts of the facility are permitted as long as the end result is no net increase in total emissions.

---

# Chevron, U.S.A., Inc. v. Natural Resources Defense Council
467 U.S. 837, 104 S. Ct. 2778, 81 L. Ed. 2d 694 (1984)

**Justice Stevens Delivered the Opinion of the Court**   In the Clean Air Amendments of 1977, Congress enacted certain requirements applicable to the States that had not achieved the national air quality standards established by the Environmental Protection Agency (EPA) pursuant to earlier legislation. The amended Clean Air Act required these "nonattainment" States to establish a permit program regulating "new or modified major stationary sources" of air pollution. Generally, a permit may not be issued for a new or modified major stationary source unless several stringent conditions are met. The EPA regulation promulgated to implement this permit requirement allows a State to adopt a *plantwide* definition of the term "stationary source." Under this definition,

an existing plant that contains several pollution-emitting devices may install or modify one piece of equipment without meeting the permit conditions if the alteration will not increase the total emissions from the plant. The question presented by these cases is whether EPA's decision to allow States to treat all of the pollution-emitting devices within the same industrial grouping as though they were encased within a single "bubble" is based on a reasonable construction of the statutory term "stationary source."[3]

In the 1950s and the 1960s Congress enacted a series of statutes designed to encourage and to assist the States in curtailing air pollution. The Clean Air Amendments of 1970 sharply increased federal authority and responsibility in the continuing effort to

---

3 The National Resources Defense Council had originally brought the action to review the EPA rules. Chevron, Inc., and other companies were granted leave to intervene and argue in support of the rule—Ed.

combat air pollution, but continued to assign primary responsibility for assuring air quality to the several States. Section 109 of the 1970 Amendments directed the EPA to promulgate National Ambient Air Quality Standards (NAAQSs) and Section 110 directed the States to develop plans (SIPs) to implement the standards within specified deadlines. In addition, Section 111 provided that major new sources of pollution would be required to conform to technology-based performance standards; the EPA was directed to publish and to establish new source performance standards (NSPS) for each. Section 111(e) prohibited the operation of any new source in violation of a performance standard.

Section 111(a) defined the terms that are to be used in setting and enforcing standards of performance for new stationary sources. It provided: "For purposes of this section: . . . . (3) The term 'stationary source' means any building, structure, facility, or installation which emits or may emit any air pollutant. . . ."

[The EPA had issued rules that interpreted that statute to envision the "bubble doctrine," in which all parts of a plant would be considered to be a single source.—Ed.]

In these cases, the Administrator's interpretation represents a reasonable accommodation of manifestly competing interests and is entitled to deference: the regulatory scheme is technical and complex, the agency considered the matter in a detailed and reasoned fashion, and the decision involves reconciling conflicting policies. . . .

We hold that the EPA's definition of the term "source" is a permissible construction of the statute which seeks to accommodate progress in reducing air pollution with economic growth. The Regulations which the Administrator has adopted provided what the agency could allowably view as an effective reconciliation of these twofold ends. . . .

## Case Discussion Questions

1 Does the "bubble doctrine" aid in the fight against pollution?

2 What interest does business have in promoting the bubble doctrine?

3 Is this case merely another example of judicial deference to administrative rulings?

---

Offsets are permitted because of reductions by others as well, and some owners have gone so far as to pay an owner of a nearby facility to shut down or control an existing facility. Since 1979, the EPA has permitted "banking" of unused emission credits for future offset and the trading and sale of such unused credits. The total equation must represent "reasonable progress" toward reaching the NAAQSs, however.

**New Stationary Sources of Pollution** The Administrator was also required to establish federal standards of performance for *new* sources of pollution. A "new source" is one constructed or modified after the effective date of the permanent regulations, and a "standard of performance" is defined as a limit on emissions of pollutants. Such limits must use the "best system of emission reduction . . . taking into account the cost of achieving such reduction. . . ."

**Hazardous Pollutants** There are, of course, pollutants other than those for which NAAQSs have been established, and the Clean Air Act directs the Administrator to publish a list of *hazardous air pollutants*. A hazardous air pollutant is defined as a pollutant for which no NAAQS has been established but which may cause or contribute to an increase in mortality or in serious illness. The Administrator must also prescribe a national emission standard for each such pollutant with "an ample margin of safety to protect the public health."

### New Motor Vehicle Standards

Under the 1970 amendments, beginning with model year 1975, automobiles must have reduced their exhaust emissions of hydrocarbons and carbon monoxide by at least 90% from the levels permissible in 1970. The act contained an escape clause, permitting manufacturers to apply for a one-year suspension if technology was not available to achieve timely compliance. The act was later amended once again to delay compliance to 1983.

### International Problems of Air Pollution

Air pollution presents one of the most severe challenges to international law. Even the simplest example, that of a smokestack blowing pollution across a national border, presents major problems to the international system. International law seems to be following an ancient rule of both Roman and common law—that one should use one's property so as not to injure that of another. In 1972 the United Nations adopted the so-called **Stockholm Declaration,** which seems to use a strict liability principle to judge whether one nation should pay reparations to another for environmental damage. Such claims may be brought before the International Court of Justice, if the nations involved have agreed to be bound by its decisions and by the Stockholm Declaration.

In the United States acid rain remains a major problem between the United States and Canada. Pollution from industrial sources or automobiles reacts with water vapor to form sulfuric and nitric acid, which falls to earth with rainwater. Forests in Canada and the United States are dying, and even buildings and monuments are slowly being eaten away. A similar problem exists throughout Europe and the Soviet Union. Canadians have been putting diplomatic pressure on the U.S. government to enforce its laws more rigorously, but lawsuits have not been successful.

## REGULATION OF WATER POLLUTION

Control of pollution of waters and waterways involves totally different problems and concerns from those involved in air pollution. But like air pollution concerns, federal water pollution policies began evolving during the 1950's and left enforcement up to the states. In 1972, federal water pollution policy became more effective with major amendments to the **Federal Water Pollution Control Act (FWPCA).**

### The Nature of Water Pollution

The national water policy focuses on three principal concerns: (1) *aquatic ecology,* or the nature of the relationships between aquatic plants and animals; (2) *recreational and aesthetic concerns,* centering on the inability to use America's waters for fishing, swimming, and boating because of pollutants; and (3) *contamination of the water supply.*

Water pollutants fall into five major classes: (1) *organic wastes,* principally human sewage; (2) other *nutrients,* such as those found in agricultural fertilizers; (3) *toxic chemicals* and other hazardous substances, such as pesticides, acids, and alkaline substances; (4) *sediment,* or particulate matter that settles to the bottom of lakes and streams; and (5) *heated water,* discharged from industrial sources and nuclear power plants.

Water pollution, like air pollution, poses a number of international problems. Rivers often form the boundaries between countries or flow from one country into another, and many nations border on seas and oceans. Pollution control efforts in one country often have little effect if other nations do not impose similar controls. The Stockholm Declaration (see p. 484) appears to cover some aspects of water pollution as well as air pollution.

For example, in 1986 hazardous chemicals caught fire in a warehouse in Basel, Switzerland, and water used by the firefighters carried thirty metric tons of toxic pollutants into the Rhine River. Those poisons washed into France, West Germany, Luxembourg, Belgium, and the Netherlands, causing massive fish kills and pollution of drinking water for 20 million people. France alone has presented a bill for $32 million to Switzerland, and the Swiss have agreed to pay all just claims.

### The Federal Water Pollution Control Act (FWPCA)

Before 1972, water pollution control was left up to state enforcement in much the same way that air pollution control had been left to the states. Often the states could only regulate parts of a body of water (for example, Lake Michigan), and enforcement did not begin until the quality of the entire body of water deteriorated below those standards.

In 1972 the FWPCA was amended, and a totally different philosophy was adopted. Those amendments established two "goals": (1) to make the nation's waters *safe for fishing and swimming* by 1983 and (2) to eliminate completely *all pollutant discharges* into navigable waters by 1987. The act generally imposed a system of gradually increasing strictness, including discharge standards, permits, and enforcement, in order to reach those goals. The amendment permitted enforcement by the states, but federal authorities had the right to enforce the laws as well. Like the Clean Air Act, the FWPCA was again amended in 1977 to permit extensions from the 1983 deadlines on a case-by-case basis. Other amendments in 1987 continued the same practice.

**Point Source Standards**    The FWPCA requires all **point sources** (such as a pipe) of pollution to reflect the **best available technology (BAT)** that is economically achievable. BAT use is required as expeditiously as possible, and in no case later than March 31, 1989. The technology used must result in reasonable progress toward eliminating the discharge of all pollutants. The EPA may impose rules prohibiting all discharge of pollutants if the Administrator finds that such elimination is technologically and economically achievable for any class or category of point sources. The federal act has complex rules for determining different classes of point sources and pollutants, and provides especially strict rules for *toxic* pollutants.

**The Permit System**    The FWPCA also created a permit system, known as the National Pollutant Discharge Elimination System (NPDES). Under that system, *any* point discharge is unlawful unless the polluter has a permit issued by the EPA or by the states. Permits must include any conditions and a schedule of compliance to meet the deadlines.

**Sanctions and Penalties Against Individual Polluters**    Criminal penalties against *negligent* offenses may include fines up to $25,000 per day of violation or one year in prison or both for the first offense and fines up to $50,000 per day of violation or two years in prison, or both, for subsequent offenses. Penalties for *knowing* violations may include fines up to $50,000 per day of violation or three years' imprisonment or both, and fines of $100,000 per day or up to six years in jail, or both, for subsequent offenses. Knowingly endangering another's life through water pollution may result in penalties up to $250,000 in fines or 15 years in jail, or both. Corporations may be fined up to $1,000,000. Penalties are doubled for subsequent offenses.

A civil penalty of up to $25,000 per day of violation may also be assessed, and injunctions against continued violations may be issued. Any person may bring a civil lawsuit for violation. If such a suit is successful, the courts may order the polluter to pay attorneys' fees and costs as well as actual damages. In addition, federal agencies may not enter into government contracts with persons convicted of any offense under the act.

## PRO AND CON

# Issue: Should cost–benefit analysis be applied to environmental law?

**Pro**    In February 1981, President Reagan issued an Executive Order that required all agencies to conduct cost–benefit analyses of new rules and regulations before proposing them. That Executive Order required that the costs of any new regulation must be balanced against its benefits, and that agencies "refrain from regulatory action unless potential benefits outweigh potential costs to society." The measuring criterion was to be in *dollars*.

Applying those principles to the environmental area, it is clear that some measurement and control are necessary. An environmental regulation that requires adoption of expensive pollution control equipment that puts a major employer out of business is ludicrous. A regulation that leaves an entire region without cheap power because the construction of a dam threatens a small and useless fish is simply absurd.

Certainly, environmental protection is important. But sentimental attachment to wilderness or oversensitivity to small amounts of pollution come at the expense of other major values, including jobs, economic progress, and technological innovation. For example, at a time when oil resources are dwindling, it seems counterproductive to stop oil drilling in wilderness areas or near coastlines useful only for their beauty.

There is simply no other measure but dollars. Congress is unwilling to make that measurement, and therefore it must be made by a tough-minded, politically neutral, and politically insulated administrator. Only in this way will proper choices be made.

**Con**    Cost–benefit analysis, in environmental law and elsewhere, is already being done, but on a larger scale and with all of the factors—not just dollars—built into the system. That is the function of Congress and other elected officers. Those people conduct precisely the kind of balancing envisioned by cost–benefit analysis but do so intuitively by considering the conflicting claims of business, environmentalists, and others when they vote for a law. It is important to realize that cost–benefit analysis is *policymaking* in its purest sense and should be done by elected policymakers.

In environmental areas, the costs are obvious, but the good that comes from environmental laws is often subjective and indefinable. For example, the costs of not building a dam are obvious and measurable. But the benefits of saving a little fish are subjective, aesthetic, and not subject to measurement. But that does not mean they are no less real. There are many who find that the world is a better place because the snail darter, the grizzly bear, the California condor, and the bald eagle are protected. There are many who would willingly trade a dam or a pipeline for that protection. And there are many who would willingly trade some economic progress for cleaner air or water.

Measurements here must be made by human beings. Somewhere there is a bureaucrat deciding the dollar value of the California condor or of clean air. A great deal depends on that person's view of the world—for example, does he or she value clean air a great deal or not at all? It seems much more logical that those decisions be made by politically accountable representatives.

## Roundtable Discussion

1   Weigh the costs and benefits of an environmental regulation that requires pollution control equipment, but that puts some businesses into bankruptcy.

Assign dollar values, as best you can, to all of the factors. Now compare your analysis with that of one of your classmates. Why are they different?

2   Should these decisions be made by political groups, such as Congress, or by administrative agencies? Why?

3   Is there a difference between long-run and short-run costs in assessing costs for this kind of analysis?

## REGULATION OF TOXIC SUBSTANCES AND SOLID WASTE

Unlike air and water regulation, there is no comprehensive federal statute dealing with the problems of toxic chemicals. Instead, several statutes deal with different parts of the problem: the **Federal Insecticide, Fungicide and Rodenticide Act**, the **Resource Conservation and Recovery Act**, and the **Toxic Substances Control Act.**

### Regulation of Pesticides and Other Poisons

The *Federal Insecticide, Fungicide and Rodenticide Act (FIFRA)*, originally enacted in 1947 and substantially amended in 1978, regulates poisons used to control a variety of pests. Poisons must be registered with the EPA before being sold and must be labelled with directions for use. The EPA must approve the registration and may only approve the product if there are not unreasonably adverse effects on the environment. States may also certify persons to apply such products.

### Regulation of Solid Wastes

The *Resource Conservation and Recovery Act (RCRA)*, with its controversial "superfund," is aimed at solid waste disposal, including disposal of toxic substances. The act classifies solid waste generators, transporters, and disposal sites and gives authority to the EPA to prescribe standards for each. Solid waste generators (i.e., persons or firms "creating" solid waste such as trash, by-products, or liquids) are required to file reports, keep records, label materials, and use appropriate containers. Solid waste transporters must keep accurate records of where they pick up waste and where they dispose of it. Disposal sites must have a permit, and the EPA is given broad inspection powers and the power to issue compliance orders, seek an injunction, or ask for the imposition of criminal penalties.

**The Superfund**   In 1980 the act was amended to include the controversial **superfund** found in the **Comprehensive Environmental Response, Compensation and Liability Act.** That act authorized the President to require cleanup of releases of toxic materials and to establish a national contingency plan to clean up such releases. The superfund was reauthorized in 1986. As of June 1986, 888 toxic-waste sites had been identified (see Figure 19.2).

The act also makes owners of facilities or contaminated land liable for government cleanup costs. The act does not impose liability for injuries to private persons. Finally,

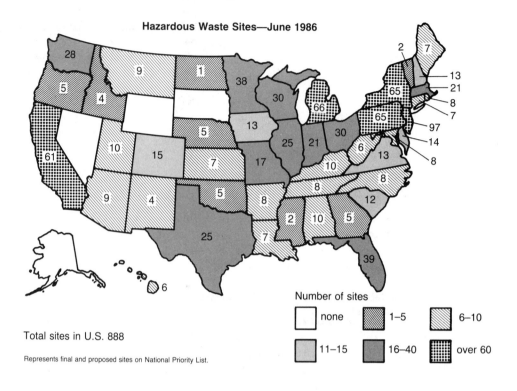

FIGURE 19.2    Hazardous Waste Sites—June 1986

the act creates a fund financed by a tax on the production of toxic chemicals. The fund is to be used to pay cleanup and other costs, including the expense of the national contingency fund and the government's cost of restoring the natural resources injured by toxic chemicals.

### Regulation of Toxic Substances

The *Toxic Substances Control Act of 1976* is concerned with the manufacture and processing of toxic substances. The act applies to any substance that creates an unreasonable risk of danger to health or to the environment and requires manufacturers to test products for their effect on health and the environment. Such manufacturers must give notice to the EPA before manufacturing any new chemical substance, and the EPA may apply administrative restrictions or apply for an emergency injunction to stop "imminent hazards."

### PROTECTION OF WILDLIFE AND WILD PLACES

While a great deal of environmental law focuses on pollution control, another branch of environmental law seeks to preserve the natural resources and natural beauty of our world. This goal of environmental policy is difficult to justify under traditional cost–

benefit analysis. Although the economic and social costs of pollution may be measured and weighed against the benefits of the industrialization causing such pollution, it is impossible to place a value on having wild places in the world or of maintaining a species of wild animal that, at least for now, is economically useless. Some economists would argue that wildlife and wilderness are public goods, much like fire protection and national defense, which do not fit neatly into cost–benefit analysis. Others argue that wilderness and wild things may acquire value in the future and thus must be saved in the present. And others simply argue that the world is a better place because of the existence of wilderness and wild things. The result is that both the public and Congress have chosen a national policy of preserving wilderness areas and wildlife through a series of federal statutes (see Table 19.1).

## STANDING: WHO MAY COMPLAIN?

One of the problems in environmental cases is who has **standing** to complain. Standing means the right to bring a lawsuit, and standing depends on the existence of a legally recognized injury (see p. 65). The Supreme Court has held that standing in such cases has two requirements: (1) an "injury in fact" and (2) an interest "within the zone of interests to be protected or regulated" by the statute alleged to have been violated. The "injury in fact" may be as simple as an injury to one's aesthetic sensibilities, and the

TABLE 19.1    Federal Statutes Protecting Wildlife and Wild Places

| Statute | Purpose |
| --- | --- |
| Endangered Species Act of 1978 | • Prohibits any federal agency from taking *any* action that would jeopardize the continued existence of any *endangered species*, as defined by the Secretary of Interior, including the destruction or modification of habitat<br>• Prohibits taking, killing, or selling of any endangered species<br>• Prohibits import or export of any endangered species or products made of such species |
| Wilderness Act of 1964 | • Prohibits *any permanent activity* in areas formally designated as "wilderness." No commercial activity or permanent road may be built or undertaken. Hydroelectric dams, transmission lines, and livestock grazing are permitted. |
| Endangered American Wilderness Act of 1978 | • Immediately declared certain wilderness areas immune from development |
| Wild and Scenic Rivers Act of 1968 | • Made certain waterways immune from development, including hydroelectric power projects |

"interest" requirement may be satisfied by showing that the plaintiff has almost any special claim so that court action will help the plaintiff.

In one case, for example, the fact that some members of the Sierra Club had hiked a trail in the past and would be foreclosed from doing so in the future if a proposed resort were built, was enough to confer standing on the Sierra Club.[4] Generally, the standing requirement is liberally construed by the Court, as a recognition that the injury resulting from environmental mischief affects the interests of large numbers of persons in countless important ways.

## FEDERAL ENERGY POLICIES

Like the environment, the existence of an adequate supply of energy was taken for granted by many Americans until the OPEC oil embargo of the mid-1970's (see *Profile:*

PROFILE

# The OPEC Oil Crisis

The Organization of Petroleum Exporting Countries (OPEC) is a cartel of nations that trade oil with other nations. Its purpose is to set a common price and selling policy for petroleum in hopes of gaining higher prices and not undercutting each other. The member nations are overwhelmingly Middle Eastern Arab states, although some African and South American nations also participate.

In the early 1970's world demand for petroleum increased sharply, and Western nations depended heavily on imported oil. In 1973, during the Arab-Israeli war, OPEC nations reduced exports to other nations drastically, especially to the United States and other nations that supported Israel. In the winter of 1973–74, many people predicted an acute shortage, but thanks to a mild winter and conservation measures, the shortage was not as bad as originally anticipated. Long, frustrating lines for gasoline greeted motorists, however, and the price of petroleum products doubled in a few months.

Through the mid-1970's, OPEC members forced the price of oil up sharply. Some argued it was part of the Arab war effort, and others simply argued that the OPEC nations had a right to as high a profit as possible before oil ran out. The real results were massive conservation efforts in Europe and the United States, transition to more plentiful coal reserves where possible, and oil exploration in the United States. Many of the American laws dealing with energy conservation can be traced directly to the oil embargo and OPEC's pricing policies.

---

4 *Sierra Club v. Morton*, 405 U.S. 727, 92 S. Ct. 1361, 31 L. Ed. 2d 636 (1972).

*The OPEC Oil Crisis*). That crisis made obvious what many experts had been arguing for years: Energy resources were in fact limited, and dependence on foreign energy resources was dangerous and misplaced. Although Congress had shown sporadic concern with energy in the past, the oil crisis was the crucial factor in the creation of the twin energy policies of the federal government. Those policies were (1) conservation of existing resources of traditional fuels, such as oil and coal, and (2) development and control of alternative energy sources, including nuclear power.

Energy and the environment cannot be viewed as isolated categories but are instead closely related. Operation of new oil refineries and burning of high-sulfur coal may be important to our national energy policy, but they also result in greater air pollution. Oil pipelines may be necessary to transport fuel cheaply, but they leave lasting scars on wilderness areas. Offshore oil development is important but defaces coastlines and risks

TABLE 19.2   Federal Energy Statutes

| *Statute* | *Purpose* |
|---|---|
| National Energy Act | ▪ Requires electric power plants and other major fuel-burning installations to switch from gas and oil to coal |
| Outer Continental Shelf Lands Act of 1978 | ▪ Requires oil leases for offshore drilling<br>▪ Makes owner and operator of offshore facilities and vessels liable for oil spills, up to $250,000 for vessels and $35 million for facilities; limits not applicable for willful acts, gross negligence, or violation of federal rules |
| Clean Water Act | ▪ Makes owners of vessels strictly liable for cleanup of oil spills, unless caused by act of God, war, act or omission of third parties, or negligence of federal government, up to $125,000 for inland oil barges and $250,000 for other vessels |
| Surface Mining Control and Reclamation Act of 1977 | ▪ Requires states to adopt policies to protect environment from strip mining. Plans generally require restoration of land to original condition and contour, preservation of topsoil, and revegetation. |
| Clean Air Act (1977 Amendments) | ▪ Permits EPA to set variable limits on air pollution to take coal-burning requirements of National Energy Act into account |
| Clean Air Act (1978 Amendments) | ▪ Permits President, on application of a state governor, to prohibit use of fuels other than coal, if necessary to prevent or minimize economic disruption or unemployment |

dangerous oil spills. Development of nuclear energy is an attractive solution to energy problems but results in the release of large amounts of superheated water into reservoirs and runs the risk of radiation release. Everywhere, it seems, concern with the environment must be balanced with concern with energy (see Table 19.2).

## REGULATION OF NUCLEAR ENERGY

Perhaps the most controversial form of energy is nuclear power. Originally, the federal government retained a monopoly over nuclear energy and gave control of nuclear power in all forms to the Atomic Energy Commission (AEC) through the **Atomic Energy Act of 1946.** In 1954 that act was amended to permit licensing of private nuclear power generating facilities. In 1974 the Atomic Energy Commission was reorganized, and most of its functions were given to the **Nuclear Regulatory Commission (NRC).**

The NRC is responsible for licensing all private nuclear facilities (including nuclear power plants), and for regulating nuclear health and safety. Under that authority, the NRC develops research in all phases of nuclear energy, inspects nuclear facilities, and investigates accidents. Major controversies exist over plant safety and location and disposal of nuclear waste.

### Plant Licensing: Safety and Location

In the aftermath of the Three Mile Island incident in 1979 and an awakening public concern with the safety of nuclear power plants, the NRC tightened its procedures for licensing and plant-safety requirements. (See *Metropolitan Edison Co. v. PANE*, p. 478.)

Upon an application for a permit, the NRC conducts a review of the construction plans, safety procedures, and environmental impact of a new nuclear facility. That review includes the preparation of an Environmental Impact Statement under the NEPA requirements, and those documents are usually reviewed by the EPA, state EPAs, and local zoning boards. Under the *Calvert Cliffs* decision (p. 476), the environmental effects must be considered at every stage of the decision-making process.

Following the Three Mile Island incident, Congress toughened the procedures relating to licensing and authorized funds for additional federal inspectors. The NRC was ordered to develop a plan for agency response to future accidents and to develop new population limits for the area surrounding a licensed nuclear power plant. The NRC was directed to develop a plan for improving the technical capabilities of employees in such plants. The agency has also begun including a discussion of the environmental risks of *class 9 accidents* in the EIS. A class 9 accident, the most serious kind, involves a breach of the reactor and exposure of radiation to the atmosphere. Each violation of NRC regulations carries a civil penalty of up to $100,000.

Under NEPA, consideration of the environmental impact of a plant, including consideration of alternative sites, must *precede* the issuance of a construction permit. The NRC has followed a practice of permitting utility companies to begin site development of the proposed plant before the Commission issues the construction permit. As a result, the site chosen by the utility will often be "superior" to other sites because of the money already spent to develop that site. Other sites will be less favorable, because the utility would be required to start over.

### Disposal of Nuclear Waste

Operation of a nuclear power facility involves the creation of tons of radioactive waste. Some of that waste can be reprocessed into usable fuel and might constitute a significant energy source, whereas other waste must be disposed of in some manner. Nuclear waste is generally considered either *low level*, which is generally not considered particularly dangerous and may be incinerated, buried, or deposited at sea, or *high level*, which is extremely dangerous and may remain toxic for 250,000 years. A related problem deals with how to dismantle and dispose of worn-out nuclear power plants, because portions of the plants themselves become radioactive.

The NRC has taken the position that, although science has not yet resolved how to dispose of high-level nuclear waste completely, that problem will be resolved someday, and in the meantime those wastes should be kept at the power plants. The commission has concluded that "the environmental effects of the uranium fuel cycle have been shown to be relatively insignificant."

Congress has adopted a solution requiring deposit of nuclear waste in a bedded salt repository several hundred meters underground. States are responsible for low-level nuclear wastes, and the federal government coordinates regional plans for burial at three sites.

## STATE ENVIRONMENTAL PROTECTION

All states have adopted some form of environmental protection statute, often based closely on the federal model. State environmental protection agencies, often closely duplicating the federal agency, have authority to enforce many of the federal environmental laws, including the Clean Air and Clean Water acts, but state legislatures have often gone further than the federal requirements. Many states include noise pollution and odors in the statutory scheme, along with more traditional concerns of air, water, and wilderness control. In addition, many states impose direct limits on fishing, hunting, and trapping as both conservation measures and game-management techniques.

### Zoning Statutes

All states have some kind of *zoning statute*, as well, to regulate the use of land. Often authority to enforce those statutes is delegated to units of local government, which must classify land use and require that uses of land that do not conform to the classifications be terminated. Zoning statutes must be reasonable and nondiscriminatory, and there must be some rational basis for the classification system.

The usual zoning ordinance classifies land uses into several major classifications, and each classification will be broken down into several subclassifications. A common breakdown is found in Figure 19.3. **Nonconforming uses,** that is, uses of property inconsistent with the zoning laws, are permitted if they existed before the laws went into effect. If the nonconforming use is discontinued or abandoned, the right to continue the

R-1: Residential, low-density, single-family housing

R-2: Residential, low-density, duplexes and triplexes

R-3: Residential, high-density apartments and condominiums

C-1: Commercial, single-story nonpolluting retail stores

C-2: Commercial, several-story retail stores

C-3: Commercial, including warehousing and distributing

I-1: Light industrial, nonpolluting manufacturing

I-2: Medium industrial

I-3: Heavy industrial, with no limits on noise or pollution

Some zoning ordinances are *cumulative,* so that in a C-3 classification, for example, all of the classes *above* C-3 are permitted. Others are *noncumulative,* so that in a C-2 classification, *only* C-2 uses are permitted, for example.

FIGURE 19.3    A Common Zoning Classification

nonconforming use is lost. The zoning board may permit **variances** in individual cases of hardship.

Perhaps the most controversial of all land-use statutes are the *no-growth ordinances* in place in a few cities. Those cities place a limit on the number of building permits that may be issued, often tying that number to the number of demolition permits, in order to limit the amount of growth of a community.

## SUMMARY AND CONCLUSIONS

A national commitment to environmental protection did not arise until the 1960's, when the damage to the environment caused by air and water pollution and disposal of hazardous wastes became clear. The complex and interwoven nature of the environment has led to development of a series of specific statutes, each designed to deal with one phase of the environmental problem. That complex and interwoven nature also creates conflicts between competing environmental and energy policies, because improvement in one area often comes at the expense of another.

The common law provided limited remedies to persons injured by actions of others affecting the environment. Those remedies, including the actions of nuisance, trespass, and strict liability, and the common law crime of public nuisance, are difficult to prove and provide a remedy only under certain strict conditions. They have not proven very useful in protecting the public interest.

The broadest environmental protection statute is the National Environmental Policy Act of 1969. That act requires federal agencies to take a "hard look" at environmental considerations before undertaking "major federal actions significantly affecting the quality of the human environment" and requires the filing of Environmental Impact Statements.

Specific federal pollution control statutes include the Clean Air Act, the Federal Water Pollution Control Act, and a variety of laws dealing with toxic substances and solid wastes. Wildlife and wild places are also protected under a series of federal statutes.

With the oil crisis of the mid-1970's, Congress began considering the problems of energy and centered on two major policies: (1) conservation of traditional fuels and development of new sources of such fuels and (2) encouragement of alternative energy sources. Problems of nuclear energy have centered on plant-licensing procedures and disposal of nuclear waste.

State agencies also protect the environment, often by statutes that closely mirror the federal laws. State laws also regulate land use through zoning ordinances and other statutes.

## REVIEW QUESTIONS

1   Explain the differences between *nuisance*, *trespass*, and *strict liability* actions in environmental cases. Are the common law actions sufficient to protect the environment? Why or why not?

2   What is NEPA? How does NEPA protect the environment? Why do you suppose NEPA only deals with *government* actions? Why don't we require an EIS in cases of major *private* actions significantly affecting the human environment? Could we do so? Should we do so?

3   Compare the federal laws dealing with air pollution, water pollution, toxic substances, and solid waste. Is there a better way to address these problems?

4   Doesn't each property owner have the right to use his or her property in any way he or she sees fit? Aren't the environmental protection laws a substantial interference with the rights of private property? Then again, aren't laws prohibiting operating gambling houses or "houses of ill repute" also substantial invasions of private property rights? Is there a difference?

5   One argument holds that since there is a limited amount of wilderness available, if we continue to grant exceptions to wilderness preservation statutes "just one more time," ultimately there will be no wilderness left. Is the argument sound? Of what possible use is wilderness, anyway?

6   Who should pay to clean up oil and toxic chemical spills? Should corporations be permitted to pass those costs on to their customers?

How would you stop them from passing such costs on to customers? Should shareholders bear these costs?

7   Abergavenny's home is in a rather exclusive subdivision. Unfortunately, he has some rather interesting hobbies that his neighbors find objectionable. Those hobbies include (a) blacksmithing, which requires a rather large, smoky forge; (b) taxidermy, which requires that he dry smelly pelts and animal parts in the sun; and (c) playing the bagpipes on his patio on summer evenings. Assuming that Abergavenny's hobbies violate no local criminal laws, do his neighbors have a remedy?

8   Cornwall Construction Company has several projects on the drawing board at the moment, including (a) building a new office building for a private investor; (b) building a new post office on the outskirts of town; (c) repairing a federal highway; (d) building a new federal highway; (e) remodeling the interior of an existing federal courthouse. For which of the projects is an Environmental Impact Statement required?

9   Blanche owned a home near the Three Mile Island plant during its "accident" in 1979. After the incident, she found herself so fearful of future incidents that she moved to another state. Now a utility company is considering construction of a nuclear power plant three miles from Blanche's new home. Does she have any recourse?

10   Bianca recently purchased a lot in Florida on which she intended to build a home after her

retirement as a schoolteacher in Massachusetts. The land was previously owned by Curtis Development Company, a real estate developer. A year after Bianca purchased the property, Curtis went out of business. Unknown to Bianca, the Sly Chemical Company had been secretly using the lot for years to dump polychlorinated biphe- nyls (PCBs), a toxic contaminant, and contin- ued to do so for the first year or two Bianca owned the property. Sly also went out of busi- ness. Bianca received a bill from the federal gov- ernment for $218,000, the estimated cost of the cleanup of her property. Must she pay?

# PART 6

# The Firm and Its Competitors

Almost every firm has competitors. From the earliest common law cases the legal system has imposed restrictions on the ways in which competitors may deal with each other. It is part of the ethics of Anglo-American history that competitors deal with each other fairly. In fact, a number of early torts deal with the problems of unfair competition.

A part of the ethic of individualism is the economic theories of Adam Smith and his followers. The most efficient economic system is based on competition between firms. "Perfect competition is thought to lead to low prices and high output to the benefit of all society. But unlimited competition has its dangers and may even tend to destroy itself."

The antitrust laws that are the subject of the next two chapters represent an attempt to *control* competition in order to *preserve* competition and, in the process, regulate the relationship between the firm and its competitors, and to a lesser extent, with the firm's suppliers and customers. They attempt to balance the benefits of competition to the community with the individual's freedom to conduct business. The choice made represents a middle ground between total freedom and total control.

The antitrust laws also represent an effort to enforce some personal ethical standards, particularly in the Federal Trade Commission Act. Those portions of the antitrust laws provide a rather comprehensive "code of ethics" for business.

# CHAPTER 20

# Antitrust Law: Regulation of Conduct

*People of the same trade seldom meet together, even for merriment and diversion, but the conversation ends in a conspiracy against the public, or in some contrivance to raise prices.*

ADAM SMITH
*The Wealth of Nations,* 1776

The term *antitrust* is used to describe a group of four federal statutes that attempt to control competitive practices and market structures in American business. Those laws include the **Sherman Antitrust Act of 1890,** the **Clayton Act** and **Federal Trade Commission (FTC) Act,** both enacted in 1914, and the **Robinson-Patman Act of 1936.**

The term *antitrust* is an anachronism. The laws developed at a time when one of the chief public fears involved a form of collusive business arrangement known as a *trust.* That business form is virtually nonexistent today, but the term *antitrust* remains as a legacy. Although the term is antiquated, the antitrust laws themselves remain vital and important. The laws are a unique attempt to regulate business in a *general* way and as a result continue to be highly controversial a century after the first such law was enacted.

Students should be cautioned that the antitrust laws are entirely *statutory.* The main provisions of those laws are included in Appendix B, and students can only understand those laws if they *read the statutes.* It is extremely important that students become familiar with the language found in these laws, probably more so than in most other areas of the law.

### Structure and Conduct: A Word About Organization

A continuing debate exists in antitrust theory between those who would control business *conduct* and those who would regulate business *structure.* Those who concentrate on conduct prefer to regulate outward signs of competitive misbehavior, such as price fixing or group boycotts. Those who would concentrate on regulation of structure prefer to deal in long-term trends and market patterns, primarily those resulting from monopolization and mergers, and argue that controlling conduct alone is treating the symptom, and not the disease. Even though the antitrust laws are old, that debate rages today, perhaps with even more heat than a century ago.

Chapters 20 and 21 mirror that debate. This chapter deals with antitrust regulation of business conduct. The next chapter considers matters of structure, including regulation of monopolization under section 2 of the Sherman Act and mergers under section 7 of the Clayton Act.

## THE PURPOSES AND GOALS OF ANTITRUST

The main purpose of antitrust is to legislate classical economic theory based on "perfect" competition. But from the beginning, the antitrust laws involved secondary purposes as well. Those purposes involved the *political* and *social* consequences of big business and business practices. It is also clear that parts of the antitrust laws, notably the Federal Trade Commission (FTC) Act, were aimed at imposing *ethical* rules of business behavior.

### Economic Goals of Antitrust

Most observers agree that the main purpose of the antitrust laws is to encourage *pure competition*. The laws were designed to remove obstacles to competition and to prohibit or discourage the effects of *imperfect competition*. As one observer noted:

> The American antitrust laws are essentially conservative in nature. Their purpose is to maintain free competition by insuring that such competition is fair. They seek to prevent giant aggregations of economic power from being built unfairly, because the use of such power necessarily stifles the opportunities competitors will have to compete meaningfully. The antitrust laws seek to prevent conduct which weakens or destroys competition.[1]

To many laypersons, the analysis of antitrust as an effort to encourage free competition is contradictory. Antitrust seems to be just another example of government overregulation and interference with business. Much of the public misunderstanding of the antitrust laws stems from the meaning of the term *competition*. When an economist uses the term, he or she means something far different from the everyday meaning of the term, that of sharp business practices and rivalry between firms. The economist has in mind a specific ideal state from which flow important economic consequences.

**The Traditional Theory of Competition**    According to Adam Smith, the founder of classical economics, the ideal economic system is one of perfect or *pure* competition. Perfect competition demands markets that are made up of a large number of buyers and sellers, each with perfect knowledge of market conditions. Each firm must be free to enter or leave the market, must sell identical (homogeneous) products, and be motivated by a desire to maximize its own welfare.

Traditional economic theory holds that if such a system did exist, the benefits would be substantial. The two principal benefits of such a system are that the prices

---

1 Earl W. Kintner, *An Antitrust Primer*, 2d Ed. (New York: Macmillan Company, 1973) p. 15.

charged consumers for the product would be the lowest possible, and that the amount of the product supplied would be at its greatest point. But perfect competition rarely, if ever, exists in the real world.

**Imperfect Competition**    The opposite of perfect competition is a pure **monopoly,** in which a single firm is the sole supplier of a product for which there are no close substitutes. The monopolist succeeds in doing something that is impossible under perfect competition—determining the price to be charged for its goods. In perfect competition, all sellers are "price takers" from the market, because they cannot influence that price. Under monopoly conditions, prices are higher and output lower than under perfect competition. It is also argued that monopolies are less efficient than firms operating under the pressure of competition.

Pure monopoly is almost as rare as perfect competition, perhaps existing only in isolated examples (the only general store in a resort town, for example) or in government-granted monopolies, such as public utilities. Far more common is the case of **oligopoly,** where there is more than one seller but fewer than the number necessary for perfect competition. Almost all industries reflect this form to a greater or lesser extent.

At first glance, oligopolistic markets seem to be highly competitive and in the beginning are often marked by bitter price warfare. But oligopolists soon learn that price warfare hurts all market participants. The result is often a "shared monopoly," in which several participants coexist and behave as a single monopolist would act. Again, output is lower and prices are higher than under perfect competition. Those results are obtained by cooperation between the firms, perhaps by outright agreement, covert conspiracy, or perhaps by **price leadership,** in which all participants simply follow the lead of one firm in determining prices.

**Workable Competition**    The benefits of perfect competition and the imperfections of monopoly and oligopoly are, of course, theoretical. Many, though not all, argue that Smith's model of perfect competition can never really exist. Certainly, the rigorous assumptions are most difficult to fulfill. Some economists and policymakers use more practical definitions of competition, such as the concept of **workable competition,** as a basis for antitrust policy.

The concept of workable competition is a practical one, looking to the effects of market conduct rather than to the precise assumptions of the model of perfect competition. A market is generally considered workably competitive if market forces provide the drive for technological innovation, efficient allocation of resources, and equitable distribution of income.

Modern economists tend to concentrate on three criteria for judging the effectiveness of competition in a market: (1) the *structure* of the market; (2) the *conduct* of firms within the market; and (3) the *performance* of the market in terms of prices, output, and efficiency. The basic question is not whether Adam Smith's model exists, but how well the market works.

### Political and Social Goals of Antitrust

It is clear from the history of the antitrust movement at the close of the nineteenth century that antitrust had goals other than economics. Many of the proponents of antitrust

ANTITRUST LAW: REGULATION OF CONDUCT

laws felt that democratic society was being threatened by the accumulation of wealth and size of some business units. It appeared that there was a direct relationship between the wealth of business and its political power. As Senator John Sherman, sponsor of the Sherman Antitrust Act, noted, "The popular mind is agitated with . . . the inequality of condition, of wealth, and opportunity that has grown within a single generation out of the concentration of capital into vast combinations."

Aside from simple fear of business and wealth and its influence, two other political goals of antitrust policy have been identified. First, it is clear that some of the Congressmen who supported the antitrust statutes did so out of fear of socialism and communism. They believed that if the evils of monopoly became too severe, the public might desert free enterprise and support the various socialist, Marxist, and anarchist groups that abounded at the turn of the century.

Second, it has been argued that the inevitable alternative to the antitrust laws is direct government intervention in business. Whenever a monopoly is formed, it seems, the government steps in to control prices and output directly. In public utilities, for example, monopolies exist, but they are closely regulated by government at all levels. Broad antitrust laws to prevent the formation of monopolies were preferable to close regulation after monopolies had formed.

### Ethical Goals of Antitrust

The antitrust laws also create a code of ethical conduct for businesspersons. The FTC Act in particular prohibits "unfair trade practices" and requires the Federal Trade Commission to make rules that govern various aspects of trade and competition. The act is aimed at protecting ethical businesspersons from competitive disadvantage suffered because of the actions of unfair competitors, and it was amended in 1938 to protect customers from being victimized by unscrupulous businesspersons as well. The Clayton Act and Robinson-Patman Act also contain several sections that prohibit business practices that might be considered unethical or unfair.

The courts further this ethical goal of the antitrust laws by treating deliberate and knowing conduct more harshly. If a businessperson attempts in good faith to comply with the law and the law is still technically violated, that person may expect more sympathetic treatment from the courts than the businessperson who consciously flouts the law.

---

**PRO AND CON**

## Are the antitrust laws still relevant?

**Pro**  The antitrust laws are vital to both the American economy and the American political system, and that will remain true for the foreseeable future. Antitrust removes the "frictions" of capitalism. The conduct offenses of the Sherman, Clayton, and Robinson-Patman acts deter conduct that would hurt both the competitive system and competitors, contribute to ethical business conduct, and assure a level playing field to all competitors. The structure offenses of the

Sherman, Clayton, and FTC acts guarantee that the market structure will remain open to new competitors in the future and assure that corporate influence does not move beyond its proper sphere.

For example, if two competitors agree to set prices, the results will probably be (1) higher consumer prices; (2) lower output to the market; (3) a channel of communication between the competitors to allow them to keep other competitors from the market; (4) a general lowering of ethical standards within that market; (5) a lowering of efficiency, since the two producers are not prodded by competition; and (6) potentially, a "shared monopoly." Certainly the size of the competitors may result in some economies of scale, but at what price?

The antitrust laws also work to guarantee the future of democratic institutions. Corporate bigness and wealth are directly related to corporate political power. If a few large corporations control the market, they also have political power inconsistent with democratic ideals. By deterring monopolization and uncompetitive conduct, we are also deterring inordinate corporate wealth and political power.

**Con**    The antitrust laws have not worked, nor could they hope to work. The federal budget devoted to antitrust is less than that devoted to the Fish and Wildlife Service and about half that needed to construct one B-1 bomber. Members of Congress and former members of the administration lobby in individual cases to defeat the efforts of antitrust enforcers. For a multinational corporation the penalties are no more severe than a parking ticket would be. There is in fact little deterrent effect from the antitrust laws.

Perhaps more importantly, the antitrust laws are based on faulty economics. Business *size* often means business *efficiency*. The measuring principle of an efficient economic system is lower consumer prices,

and large firms can usually supply lower prices because of economies of scale. The remote dangers of business size and conduct must be balanced against the very real efficiencies of larger firms and controlled markets.

Other markets involve international competitors, often subsidized by foreign governments and not bound by antitrust conduct requirements. American businesses faced with such competition are handicapped, because they may be charged with antitrust laws in the domestic environment for conduct that is perfectly legal and accepted in the international environment. We simply cannot handicap our businesses through antitrust laws.

## Roundtable Discussion

**1**    Is the sole purpose of antitrust to produce lower consumer prices? Is there a "sole" goal of antitrust?

**2**    Should we determine antitrust policy based on what other nations do? Wouldn't this produce a "lowest common denominator" of business and ethics?

**3**    Are the antitrust laws working? Can we tell how much monopolization has *not* taken place because of the antitrust laws? Should we make the antitrust penalties more harsh, increase the amount of money devoted to federal antitrust enforcement, and strengthen the laws against lobbying?

## THE ANTITRUST STATUTES

### The Sherman Antitrust Act

In 1890, Senator John Sherman of Ohio introduced the first federal antitrust legislation, later named in his honor. Antimonopoly sentiment was so high at the time, that the act passed both houses of Congress with only one dissenting vote. This relatively simple act contains two principal sections: Section 1 prohibited "every contract, combination in the form of trust or otherwise, or conspiracy, in restraint of trade . . ."; and section 2 made it a criminal offense to "monopolize" or "attempt to monopolize" any part of interstate commerce. Section 1 offenses are discussed later in this chapter, and section 2 matters are covered in Chapter 21.

### The Clayton Act

In 1911 the Supreme Court announced its decision in the *Standard Oil* case, discussed in detail later (see p. 108), in which the Court limited the application of the Sherman Act to only *unreasonable restraints of trade*. The Sherman Act was also criticized from many quarters, from businesspeople who felt it was too vague to reformers who felt it did not go far enough.

Finally, in 1914, came the enactment of the *Clayton Act*, which amended the Sherman Act. That law made several specific types of business practices illegal, such as interlocking directorates, exclusive dealing arrangements, and certain mergers. In part, the Clayton Act closed several "loopholes" created by the *Standard Oil* case. Unlike the Sherman Act, the Clayton Act is very specific in the types of activities prohibited. With the exception of mergers, the Clayton Act is dealt with in this chapter.

### The Federal Trade Commission Act

Also in 1914, Congress presented the nation with another broad antitrust law, the *Federal Trade Commission Act (FTC)*, which generally prohibited *unfair methods of competition*. Other aspects of that act were discussed in Chapters 14 and 15, dealing with advertising and consumer protection. The FTC Act also created an administrative agency, the **Federal Trade Commission,** to make rules to enforce the antitrust laws and define the term *unfair methods of competition*. Because of its broad nature, the FTC Act and its antitrust uses are discussed in Chapter 21.

### The Robinson-Patman Act

One type of conduct specifically prohibited by the Clayton Act was **price discrimination;** that is, charging different prices to different purchasers of the same product. In 1936, Congress passed the *Robinson-Patman Act*, a long and technical amendment to the Clayton Act to clarify the policy of the law toward price discrimination. That act is discussed later in this chapter.

### Exemptions from the Antitrust Laws

Some types of businesses and other organizations are exempt from the operation of the laws. Most of these businesses are regulated in other ways, either through specific statutes dealing with an industry or by state or local authorities. Those exemptions include agricultural commodities; railroads, trucking, and urban transit; shipping; airlines; pipelines; electricity; telephone and telegraph; radio and television broadcasting; commercial banking; insurance; crude oil; natural gas production; and the anthracite coal industry.

One of the earliest exemptions came in section 6 of the Clayton Act. Early decisions of the courts had indicated that labor unions constituted a "combination . . . in restraint of trade" within the meaning of the Sherman Act, and all labor activity might be illegal. The Clayton Act specifically exempted labor unions from the reach of the antitrust laws (see p. 393).

The courts have also created a variety of exemptions from the antitrust laws. One of the most interesting and questionable decisions was that which exempted major league baseball (but not football or basketball) from the reach of the statutes.[2]

## ANTITRUST ENFORCEMENT PROCEDURES

Antitrust is unique in that *two* agencies of the federal government, the *Department of Justice* and the *Federal Trade Commission (FTC)*, have overlapping and concurrent ju-

---

2 *Flood v. Kuhn*, 407 U.S. 258, 92 S. Ct. 2099, 32 L. Ed. 2d 728 (1972).

risdiction to enforce the antitrust laws. The Department of Justice generally enforces the Sherman Act and parts of the Clayton Act through civil and criminal proceedings, including actions for injunctions against illegal activity.

The FTC may also enforce portions of the Clayton Act, together with the FTC Act itself. The FTC was one of the first independent regulatory commissions (see p. 143) created by Congress. Five commissioners are appointed by the President for staggered seven-year terms. Only three commissioners may be from the same political party, and one of the commissioners is designated as chairman by the President. The FTC is empowered to make rules that define "unfair or deceptive" trade practices.

Other agencies of government, such as the Interstate Commerce Commission, have authority to enforce some portions of the law or exempt persons or businesses from its application. Recent amendments also permit *state attorneys general* to institute antitrust actions (known as *parens patriae* cases) in the name of their citizens. Private citizens may bring suits under the laws for injunctive relief and for damages as well.

## Antitrust Remedies

The antitrust laws are extremely flexible, both in the possible interpretations under the broad wording of the statutes and in the administration and enforcement of those statutes. One aspect of that flexibility is the wide variation in remedies available under the antitrust laws, which allows remedies to be tailored to the circumstances of each case.

**Criminal Penalties**    Criminal penalties, for the most part, are available only under the Sherman Act. It has generally been the policy of the Department of Justice to ask for criminal sanctions only in cases involving clearcut **per se** violations of the act (see p. 507).

The penalties for violation of the Sherman Act are a $1 million fine for corporations and a fine of $100,000 or three years in prison, or both, for individuals. Those penalties were increased from much lower figures in 1974. Very few persons have served jail terms under the antitrust laws, resulting in criticism of antitrust enforcement policies. Criminal actions under the antitrust laws are tried as are other criminal matters in federal court.

**Injunctive Relief**    The Justice Department also may go to court to ask for an *injunction* requiring the defendant to stop its illegal activity. This is the most common method of enforcement by the Justice Department and is used to enforce both the Sherman and Clayton acts.

The nature of injunctions permits those orders to be carefully crafted to meet the needs of the parties and the case. Perhaps the most complicated decrees come in merger cases under section 7 of the Clayton Act, in which one of the primary methods of forcing compliance is **divestiture,** a procedure in which a merged company is ordered to divide into two or more companies. Divestiture is far less important since *premerger notification* was adopted in 1976 (see p. 526).

**Commission Orders**    Under the FTC Act, the Federal Trade Commission has the authority to issue *commission* orders after appropriate hearings. An administrative law judge initially hears the case and decides the matter. Appeals may be taken to the full commission, which has wide discretion to fashion appropriate orders. Violations of FTC orders and rules may result in fines of $10,000 per offense or $10,000 per day in the case of a continuing offense. The commission may also institute actions to benefit consumers by obtaining rescission or reformation of specific contracts, refunds of money, or payment of appropriate damages for violation of its rules or orders.

**Private Suits and Defenses**    Private persons may use and enforce the antitrust laws in three ways: (1) Injured persons, including competitors, customers, licensees, and suppliers, may bring private lawsuits in federal court for **treble damages,** that is, three times the actual amount lost as a result of violations; (2) such persons may also sue for *injunctive relief* to stop ongoing or threatened violations; and (3) under certain circumstances, parties sued by violators may raise violations of the laws as a defense.

***Parens Patriae* Actions**    Any state attorney general may bring a civil action, known as a **parens patriae** suit, in the name of the state and on behalf of residents to obtain damages for such persons. Persons injured may petition for part of that money, in a manner similar to class actions, or the money may be retained by the state as a civil penalty, at the discretion of the trial judge. The federal Attorney General is required to cooperate with the state attorneys general in such cases.

**Consent Decrees**    Both the Justice Department and the FTC make extensive use of **consent decrees,** or negotiated settlements of antitrust cases. Companies that are the subject of antitrust actions by either the Justice Department or the FTC generally prefer such negotiated settlements to full trials for three reasons: (1) antitrust cases are extremely expensive and time-consuming for both sides; (2) a consent decree cannot be used as *prima facie* evidence of violation in a private action, whereas a judgment in a criminal or injunction case may be used as evidence in private suits; and (3) most companies prefer the relative privacy of consent decrees to a public exposure of a courtroom airing of their misdeeds.

## SECTION 1 OF THE SHERMAN ACT

The first and most basic antitrust statute is the Sherman Act of 1890. The simple words of that statute have resulted in some of the most complex lawsuits in American legal history (see the box on the following page).

### The Problem of "Agreement"

One person acting alone cannot violate section 1 of the Sherman Act. The terms *contract*, *combination*, and *conspiracy* require some kind of *agreement* between two or more persons. Often the courts use the term *concerted action* to refer to the kind of joint activity condemned by section 1.

Clearly, formal agreements such as contracts are covered by section 1. Formal agreements are usually **overt**, which means clear and unconcealed, and are fairly rare. Formal market arrangements, called *cartels*, are even more rare. Such cartel arrangements, such as the OPEC oil cartel of the 1970's and 1980's, try to set prices restrict a market through formal agreements between the parties. Some formal ag

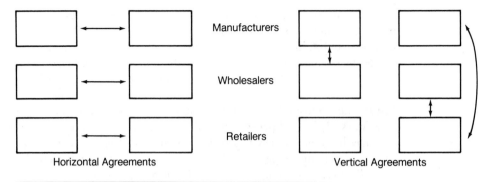

FIGURE 20.1    Horizontal and Vertical Agreements

ments may be **covert,** or concealed. Both overt and covert agreements may violate section 1.

**Horizontal and Vertical Agreements**    One important classification of agreements is between **horizontal** and **vertical agreements** (see Figure 20.1). *Horizontal agreements* are between two firms operating at the same level of the distribution process, such as two manufacturers or two distributors or two retailers. *Vertical agreements* are between firms at different levels of the same process, such as an agreement between a manufacturer and a distributor, or between a distributor and a retailer or between a manufacturer and a retailer.

Whether the agreement is horizontal or vertical may be crucial to the outcome of an antitrust case. For example, *horizontal* price-fixing agreements, that is, agreements between competitors to set the prices, are considered one of the *worst* violations of the Sherman Act and have traditionally been treated very harshly. On the other hand, *vertical* price-fixing agreements, such as requirements that a retailer sell products at a price set by the manufacturer, were legal under many circumstances for a long time.[3] Both

---

## The Sherman Act, Section 1

Every contract, combination in the form of trust or otherwise, or conspiracy, in restraint of trade or commerce among the several States, or with foreign nations, is hereby declared to be illegal. Every person who shall make any such contract or engage in any such combination or conspiracy shall be deemed guilty of a felony, and, on conviction thereof, shall be punished by a fine not exceeding one million dollars if a corporation, or, if any other person, one hundred thousand dollars or by imprisonment not exceeding three years, or by both said punishments in the discretion of the court.

---

**3** Vertical price fixing is now considered *per se* illegal. See p. 513.

horizontal and vertical agreements may violate the Sherman Act, but the method of analysis and the legal results may differ sharply.

**Parallel Action and Price Leadership**    Some agreements are never expressed, even in covert conversations between the parties. Such "agreements," known as **parallel action,** are merely tacit understandings that certain practices will be followed, resulting in identical or similar competitive moves. One example is **price leadership,** in which one firm, usually the dominant firm in the market, sets its price and all other firms in the market follow its lead. The economic and competitive effect of price leadership is identical to the impact of a pricing cartel, but without express agreement. The courts generally take the position that parallel action is *evidence* of an agreement, but is not conclusive proof.[4]

**Intraenterprise Conspiracy**    Another problem area concerns agreements within a single firm. On one hand, a corporation is a single "person," and a conspiracy or agreement requires two or more persons. On the other hand, a corporation is made up of many individuals, all of whom are capable of agreeing with others involved in the corporation.

The Supreme Court has held that a conspiracy among the officers and directors of a corporation may violate section 1 of the Sherman Act. Shareholders also may conspire with their corporation, because a corporation is considered a separate entity from its shareholders. A corporation may not conspire with its officers and directors, however, because the corporation may only act through those officers and directors. In 1984 the Supreme Court held that an "agreement" could not exist between a parent corporation and its wholly owned subsidiary corporations,[5] and it has been the law for some time that a corporation cannot "agree" with its unincorporated divisions.

A related problem deals with *joint enterprises*, which are multiparty business arrangements. An example might be a professional football league, which consists of a number of separately incorporated teams but depends on joint scheduling, similar ticket prices, a common media broadcast policy, and similar contracts with players. The issue in all such cases is whether the participants in a joint enterprise should be treated as separate parties, and therefore be capable of agreement under section 1, or as a single enterprise. The answer to that question depends on many factors, including the legal nature of the association, the desirability of the practices, whether the practices are "predatory" or "coercive," and the practicality of other arrangements to accomplish the otherwise valid objectives of the organization. The courts have not provided any other guidelines to judge such enterprises.

### The Rule of Reason and the *Per Se* Violations

Although on its face the Sherman Act prohibits *every* agreement that restrains trade, as a practical matter Congress could not have meant the statute to be applied in so strict and uncompromising a manner. Many common business practices involve some manner of

---

4 *Theatre Enterprises, Inc. v. Paramount Film Distributing Corp.*, 346 U.S. 537, 74 S. Ct. 257, 98 L. Ed. 273 (1954).
5 *Copperweld Corp. v. Independence Tube Corp.*, 467 U.S. 752, 104 S. Ct. 2731, 81 L. Ed. 2d 628 (1984)

cooperation and result in some restraint of trade. For example, even partnership agreements restrain trade, at least between the partners.

Within a few years after the Sherman Act became law, the courts retreated from such a strict and literal application of the Sherman Act. In 1911 the Supreme Court adopted a practical view of the Sherman Act in the landmark case of *U.S. v. Standard Oil of New Jersey*.[6] The *Standard Oil* decision has been called "the real starting point of modern antitrust law."[7]

The *Standard Oil* decision is long and involved, and its language is less than memorable. The result of the decision was the announcement of the so-called **rule of reason,** which holds that only *unreasonable* restraints of trade would be considered illegal under the Sherman Act. Thus, if a restraint of trade is *reasonable*, it is legal and permitted. The courts must decide which restraints of trade are reasonable or unreasonable.

Determining whether a particular restraint of trade is reasonable is a long and complex job involving in-depth economic analysis of the industry and markets in the case. Almost from the beginning, certain kinds of trade restraints were viewed as *always* unreasonable: " . . . [T]here are certain agreements or practices which, because of their pernicious effect on competition and lack of any redeeming virtue, are conclusively presumed to be unreasonable and therefore illegal without elaborate inquiry as to the precise harm they have caused or the business excuse for their use."[8]

Those practices, termed the **per se violations** (*per se* means "of itself"), include *horizontal price fixing, geographic division of markets, tying contracts, group boycotts,* and *vertical price fixing.*

The *per se* categories are not the only ways in which the Sherman Act may be violated. Other forms of conduct may be illegal under the act but are subject to the rule of reason. Those cases require the courts to conduct, in the Supreme Court's terms, "incredibly complicated and prolonged economic investigation into the entire history of the industry, as well as related industries," resulting in trials that may last for years. Consequently, antitrust prosecutors and private plaintiffs prefer to file the simpler *per se* cases.

The *per se* categories were established only after long experience and substantial economic analysis under the Sherman Act. Even in *per se* cases the defendant may try to show **special industry facts** that set the specific case apart from the general *per se* rule. Thus, the *per se* categories are not automatic convictions in every case, but the burden of proving special industry facts is on the defendant and is very heavy. If a case is considered *per se*, the government need *not* prove an anticompetitive effect: that effect is *presumed* from the nature of the agreement.

### Horizontal Price Fixing

*Horizontal price-fixing conspiracies*, or agreements between competing firms to set prices, are considered to be the worst antitrust violation. Such agreements have absolutely no economic benefit to the public. The problem in price-fixing cases is not that

---

6 221 U.S. 1, 31 S. Ct. 502, 56 L. Ed. 619 (1911).
7 Earl W. Kintner, *An Antitrust Primer*, 2d Ed. (New York: Macmillan, 1973), p. 18.
8 *Northern Pacific Railway Co. v. U.S.*, 356 U.S. 1, 78 S. Ct. 514, 2 L. Ed. 2d 545 (1958).

the prices set are unreasonable, but that the power to fix prices exists at all. As noted in one case:

> The aim and result of every price-fixing agreement, if effective, is the elimination of one form of competition. The power to fix prices, whether reasonably exercised or not, involves power to control the market and to fix arbitrary and unreasonable prices. The reasonable price fixed today may through economic and business changes become the unreasonable price of tomorrow.[9]

The only thing the government need prove in a price-fixing case is the existence of an agreement to set prices. It need not prove that the prices were too high or that anyone was harmed. The basic problem is proving the existence of an agreement, as discussed in the following case.

# U.S. v. Container Corporation of America
393 U.S. 333, 89 S. Ct. 510, 21 L. Ed. 2d 526 (1969)

The defendants, manufacturers of about 90% of the corrugated cardboard containers in the United States, had agreed to share price information between themselves on request. Any participant could request price lists or other price data from any other participant. There was no agreement to set prices at any level.

Purchasers of corrugated containers base virtually all decisions on price, because all containers are identical or are made to specifications of the purchaser. The defendants therefore did not exceed the prices charged by competitors. The result of this agreement was that prices were either extremely stable or slowly declining. The district court had found no violation, and the government appealed.

**Mr. Justice Douglas Delivered the Opinion of the Court**    The exchange of price information seemed to have the effect of keeping prices within a fairly narrow ambit. Capacity has exceeded the demand . . . and the trend of corrugated container prices has been downward. Yet despite this excess capacity and the downward trend of prices, the industry has expanded. . . .

The result of this reciprocal exchange of prices was to stabilize prices though at a downward level. Knowledge of a competitor's price usually meant matching that price. The continuation of some price competition is not fatal to the Government's case. The limitation or reduction of price competition brings the case within the ban, for . . . interference with the setting of price by free market forces is un-

lawful *per se*. Price information exchanged in some markets may have no effect on a truly competitive price. But the corrugated container industry is dominated by relatively few sellers. The product is fungible and the competition for sales is price. The demand is inelastic, as buyers place orders only for immediate, short-run needs. The exchange of price data tends toward price uniformity. For a lower price does not mean a larger share of the available business but a sharing of the existing business at a lower return. Stabilizing prices as well as raising them is within the ban of section 1 of the Sherman Act. . . . [T]he inferences are irresistible that the exchange of price information has had an anticompetitive effect in the industry chilling the vigor of price competition. . . . Price is too critical, too sensitive a control to allow it

---

9 U.S. v. Trenton Potteries, 278 U.S. 392, 47 S. Ct. 377, 71 L. Ed. 700 (1927).

to be used even in an informal manner to restrain competition.

[Reversed.]

**Marshall, J., with Whom Harlan, J., and Stewart, J., Join, Dissenting**    I agree with the Court's holding that there existed an agreement among the defendants to exchange price information whenever requested. However, I cannot agree that the agreement should be condemned, either as illegal *per se*, or as having had the purpose or effect of restricting price competition. . . . In this market, we have a few sellers presently controlling a substantial share of the market. We have a large number competing for the remainder of the market, also quite substantial. And total demand is increasing. In such a case, I think it is just as logical to assume that the sellers, especially the smaller and new ones, will desire to capture a larger market share by cutting prices as it is that they will acquiesce in oligopolistic behavior. The likelihood that prices will be cut and that those lower prices will have to be met acts as a deterrent to setting prices at an artificially high level in the first place. Given the uncertainty about the probable effect of an exchange of price information in this context, I would require that the Government prove that the exchange was entered into for the purpose of, or that it had the effect of, restraining price competition.

## Case Discussion Questions

1   Assume that you are asked to bid on a contract to make containers under this arrangement. The cost to make each box is 27¢, but your competitors are charging 58¢. What price do you charge? Under pure competition, what price should you charge?

2   May a retailer visit his or her competitors' stores to see what prices are being charged? Is that conduct illegal under section 1 of the Sherman Act? What is the difference between that and the conduct in this case?

3   Why do the *per se* categories exist? Does that reasoning apply in this case? What happens when the courts start to make exceptions to *per se* rules?

Trade associations, or voluntary associations of competitors, often can create the type of communication necessary for an agreement under the act. The Supreme Court has held that meetings between competitors in trade associations, as well as the gathering and dissemination of statistics about an industry by associations, do not, of themselves, constitute a violation of the Sherman Act. But if those associations reach agreements respecting the price of their goods, the act has been violated. Professional organizations, including pharmacist and bar associations, violate the act if minimum fee schedules are prescribed for members.

### Group Boycotts

Sellers have the right to choose to whom they sell their goods. This basic doctrine, part of a generally respected "freedom of alienation of property," is one of the fundamental tenets of Anglo-American law. Yet *agreements* to boycott a seller or a buyer are *per se* violations of the Sherman Act. A *group boycott* is an agreement between two or more sellers not to sell to a buyer, or between two or more buyers not to buy from a seller (see Figure 20.2).

Group boycotts act as a "clog on competition" by eliminating access to markets or access to supplies needed to compete. In extreme cases, the boycotted firm can be forced out of business, or at least be greatly restricted in its ability to compete with non-boycotted firms. Like all *per se* violations, there is no excuse for a boycott or any defense that may be raised. An example might involve an agreement between retail lumber dealers to refuse to purchase lumber from lumber wholesalers who also sold lumber to retail customers at wholesale prices for the purpose of driving up the price charged by wholesaler-retailers.

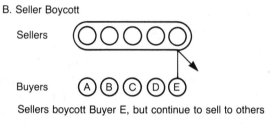

A. Buyer Boycott

Buyers boycott Seller 5, but continue to purchase from others

B. Seller Boycott

Sellers boycott Buyer E, but continue to sell to others

FIGURE 20.2    Group Boycotts

### Horizontal Geographic Market Division

**Horizontal geographic market division** means competitors divide a market into distinct geographic territories. The effect of such divisions is the creation of regional monopolies, each with the power to set prices and withhold supply in its assigned territory. One of the earliest antitrust decisions[10] held that territorial divisions between competitors were illegal under the Sherman Act. The "almost inevitable" result of horizontal territory divisions is the avoidance of price competition, because there is no competition within the territories.

### Tie-in Contracts

Assume that you are the manufacturer of the world's greatest automobile tire. Through technological breakthroughs, whether patented or not, you are able to produce a tire that will wear for 200,000 miles and that can be produced and sold at a price equal to that of other tires on the market. Assume also that you produce the world's worst automobile battery, plagued by high prices, constant leakage, and a very short life span. A most logical marketing strategy under those circumstances would be to refuse to sell tires to wholesalers and retailers who do not purchase the batteries. The purchase of the batteries is "tied" to the purchase of the tires. Such **tie-in sales** (or "tying" sales) are *per se* illegal under the Sherman Act. In such a case, the *tying* product is tires, and the *tied* product is batteries. The following case discusses the need for "market power" in the market for the tying product.

---

10 *U.S. v. Addystone Pipe & Steel Co.*, 85 Fed. 271 (6th Circ., 1898).

# Jefferson Parish Hospital District No. 2 v. Hyde
466 U.S. 2, 104 S. Ct. 1551, 80 L. Ed. 2d 2 (1984)

East Jefferson Hospital had a contract with Roux & Associates [Roux], in which Roux would provide all anesthesiologist services in the hospital. The contract provided that the hospital would provide all necessary space, equipment, and personnel; and the hospital agreed to restrict the use of its anesthesia department to Roux, with no other persons performing such services for five years. Any person who chose to have an operation at East Jefferson could not employ any other anesthesiologist, and no other anesthesiologist could practice at East Jefferson.

East Jefferson was located in the New Orleans area, and there were about twenty other hospitals in the area. About 70% of the patients living in Jefferson Parish, the area immediately surrounding the hospital, went to hospitals other than East Jefferson.

Hyde, a certified anesthesiologist, applied for admission to the medical staff at East Jefferson but was refused because of the exclusive contract with Roux. Hyde brought this action for a declaratory judgment and an injunction declaring the contract in violation of the Sherman Act. The district court found that the hospital did not possess significant "market power" in New Orleans, and therefore this contract was not *per se* illegal. The court of appeals found the hospital had market power in the area surrounding the hospital and reversed the district court's decision. The hospital appealed.

**Justice Stevens Delivered the Opinion of the Court**    It is far too late in the history of our antitrust jurisprudence to question the proposition that certain tying arrangements pose an unacceptable risk of stifling competition and therefore are unreasonable "per se." The rule was first enunciated in [1947] and has been endorsed by this Court many times since. . . .

Our cases have concluded that the essential characteristic of an invalid tying arrangement lies in the seller's exploitation of its control over the tying product to force the buyer into the purchase of a tied product that the buyer either did not want at all, or might have preferred to purchase elsewhere on different terms. When such "forcing" is present, competition on the merits in the market for the tied item is restrained and the Sherman Act is violated.

*Per se* condemnation—condemnation without inquiry into actual market conditions—is only appropriate if the existence of forcing is probable. Thus, application of the *per se* rule focuses on the probability of anticompetitive consequences. Of course, as a threshold matter there must be a substantial potential for impact on competition in order to justify *per se* condemnation. If only a single purchaser were "forced" with respect to the purchase of a tied item,

the resultant impact on competition would not be sufficient to warrant the concern of antitrust law. . . . Similarly, when a purchaser is "forced" to buy a product he would not have otherwise bought even from another seller in the tied product market, there can be no adverse impact on competition. . . .

Once this threshold is surmounted, *per se* prohibition is appropriate if anticompetitive forcing is likely. For example, if the government has granted the seller a patent or similar monopoly over a product, it is fair to presume that the inability to buy the product elsewhere gives the seller market power. . . . Thus, the sale . . . of a patented item on condition that the buyer make all his purchases of a separate tied product from the patentee is unlawful. . . .

In sum, any inquiry into the validity of a tying arrangement must focus on the market in which the two products are sold, for that is where the anticompetitive forcing has its impact. Thus, in this case our analysis of the tying issue must focus on the hospital's sale of services to its patients, rather than its contractual arrangements with the providers of anesthesiological services. In making that analysis, we must consider whether petitioners are selling two separate products that may be tied together, and, if so, whether they have used their market power to force their patients to accept the tying arrangement. . . .

Unquestionably the anesthesiological component of the package offered by the hospital could be provided separately and could be selected either by the individual patient or by one of the patient's doctors if the hospital did not insist on including anesthesiological services in the package it offers to its customers.

The question remains whether this arrangement involves the use of market power to force patients to buy services they would not otherwise purchase. Respondent's only basis for invoking the *per se* rule against tying and thereby avoiding analysis of actual market conditions is by relying on the preference of persons residing in Jefferson Parish to go to East Jefferson, the closest hospital. . . .

Seventy percent of the patients residing in Jefferson Parish enter hospitals other than East Jefferson. . . . Thus East Jefferson's "dominance" over persons residing in Jefferson Parish is far from overwhelming. The fact that a substantial majority of the parish's residents elect not to enter East Jefferson means that the geographic data does not establish the kind of dominant market position that obviates the need for further inquiry into actual competitive conditions. The Court of Appeals acknowledged as much; it recognized that East Jefferson's market share alone was insufficient as a basis to infer market power, and buttressed its conclusion by relying on "market imperfections" that permit petitioners to charge noncompetitive prices for hospital services: the prevalence of third party payment for health care reduces price competition, and a lack of adequate information renders consumers unable to evaluate the quality of the medical care provided by competing hospitals. . . . While these factors may generate "market power" in some abstract sense, they do not generate the kind of market power that justifies condemnation of tying.

[Reversed.]

## Case Discussion Questions

1 What is the effect of the agreement in this case on Hyde? What is the effect on hospital patients? What prices do you suppose Roux charges for its services? Are they higher or lower than those that would have been charged if Hyde had been permitted to practice in the hospital?

2 Do consumers ask for price information about anesthesiological services before they are admitted to the hospital? Is this a "market imperfection" in this case?

3 Are tie-in contracts still *per se* illegal after this case? Would the result have been the same if the hospital had been located in the middle of Montana, fifty miles from another hospital?

## Vertical Price Fixing

*Vertical price fixing*, or *resale price maintenance*, involves requirements by manufacturers or other "upstream" sellers that dealers charge certain minimum prices set by firms higher in the distribution chain. For example, Firm A manufactures an item and sells it to Firm B, a wholesaler, who resells it to Firm C, a retailer. Resale price maintenance might include either a condition imposed by A that B's price to C, or C's price to the consumer, be at or above a certain level.

On the surface, resale price maintenance makes little sense. It would appear that A would wish to sell as much of its product as possible, and supply and demand would seem to indicate that firm A would want its distributors and retailers to sell for as *low* a price as possible. But A might wish to impose minimum prices on its products for several good reasons. Retailers who make more money on a product will probably promote it with more intensity. Greater profits at the retail level may also permit dealers to increase the number of outlets and, consequently, increase the amount of the product sold. Finally, some products actually sell better at higher prices because consumers often equate "price" with "quality." Resale price maintenance virtually eliminates price competition between retailers of the affected product.

Early cases found vertical price fixing to be as evil as horizontal price fixing and held those restrictions *per se* illegal under the Sherman Act. In 1919 a limited exception, termed the **Colgate doctrine**,[11] recognized the right of manufacturers to simply "refuse to deal" with those who failed to charge a price set by the manufacturer. But any activity going beyond a simple refusal to deal, such as enlisting the aid of distributors in enforcing or policing prices, constituted an agreement under the Sherman Act and remained illegal *per se*.

Between 1937 and 1975, resale price maintenance was legal under certain circumstances under an exemption passed in the **Miller-Tydings Act of 1937**. In 1975, Congress repealed the Miller-Tydings Act, making vertical price fixing *per se* illegal once again. It had been statistically shown in several studies that resale price maintenance not only resulted in higher consumer prices by eliminating horizontal price competition among retailers but also enhanced the monopoly or oligopoly power of the manufacturers.

Today, manufacturers have the option of outright refusals to deal under the Colgate doctrine or of providing "suggested retail prices," which are in no way binding upon retailers. In the auto industry, the **Automobile Information Disclosure Act of 1958** requires any firm using suggested retail prices on automobiles to post those prices on the cars, and such prices do not violate the antitrust laws if the word *suggested* is clearly displayed.

## OTHER "CONDUCT" VIOLATIONS

Aside from the *per se* categories, conduct violations may be found in other areas of the antitrust laws. First, section 1 of the Sherman Act is not restricted to the *per se* categories. *Any* business conduct that unreasonably restrains trade may be illegal. Second, the Clayton Act also prohibits certain types of business conduct. And third, the Robinson-Patman Act, perhaps the most specific of the antitrust laws, prohibits price discrimination.

### The Rule of Reason and Vertical Restraints

Perhaps the most common rule-of-reason cases involve **vertical territory limitations**. Manufacturers and franchise companies often want to create exclusive territories for their retailers, distributors, and franchisees as well, arguing that imposition of such territorial restrictions ensures maximum sales within an area and those granted exclusive territories will not neglect the home market in favor of greener pastures.

*Horizontal* territorial divisions have been *per se* illegal for decades (see p. 508), but the legal status of *vertical* territorial divisions was not decided until late in the history of antitrust and may not yet be settled. In 1963 the Supreme Court ruled that there was simply not enough economic information about the effects of such vertical territorial divisions. In 1967, in a somewhat confusing decision,[12] the Court held that such divisions were *per se* illegal. Ten years later that rule was overturned in *Continental T.V.,*

---

11 The doctrine originated in *U.S. v. Colgate & Co.*, 250 U.S. 300 (1919).
12 *U.S. v. Arnold, Schwinn & Co.*, 388 U.S. 350, 87 S. Ct. 1847, 18 L. Ed. 2d 1238 (1967).

*Inc. v. GTE Sylvania, Inc.*[13] In that case, the court held that vertical territory divisions may hurt *intrabrand* competition (competition within the same brand) but may help *interbrand* competition (competition between brands). As a result, the Court refused to find them *per se* illegal.

Vertical territory limitations are not the only kind of vertical restraints on competition that may be imposed. In 1988 the Court decided the following case dealing with vertical agreements to terminate other dealers. The case may have implications far beyond its facts, extending to every nonprice vertical restraint.

## Business Electronics Corp. v. Sharp Electronics Corp.
— US. —, 108 S. Ct., 1515, —L. Ed. — (1988).

In 1968, Business Electronics became the exclusive retailer in the Houston, Texas, area for the sale of electronic calculators manufactured by Sharp Electronics. At the time, electronic calculators were primarily sold to business customers at prices of up to $1,000. In 1972, Sharp appointed Hartwell as a second retailer in the same area.

Sharp published a list of suggested retail prices, but the written dealership agreements between Sharp and both retailers did not require them to follow the suggested prices. Business Electronics' prices were generally lower than both the suggested prices and Hartwell's prices.

In June 1973, Hartwell gave Sharp an ultimatum that Hartwell would terminate his dealership unless Sharp terminated Business Electronics' dealership. Sharp terminated its relationship with Business Electronics. Business Electronics brought this suit, alleging that Sharp and Hartwell had conspired to terminate its dealership, and that such a conspiracy was *per se* illegal under section 1 of the Sherman Act. A jury found for Business Electronics in the amount of $600,000, which the Court trebled.

The U.S. court of appeals reversed, holding that to render *per se* illegal a vertical agreement between a manufacturer and a dealer to terminate a second dealer, the first dealer "must expressly or impliedly agree to set its prices at some level, though not a specific one. The distributor cannot retain complete freedom to set whatever price it chooses." Business Electronics appealed to the Supreme Court.

**Justice Scalia Delivered the Opinion of the Court**    Although vertical agreements on resale prices have been illegal *per se* since *Dr. Miles Medical Co. v. John D. Park & Sons Co.*, 220 U.S. 373 (1911), we have recognized that the scope of *per se* illegality should be narrow in the context of vertical restraints. In *Continental T.V. Inc. v. GTE Sylvania, Inc.*, we refused to extend *per se* illegality to vertical nonprice restraints, specifically to a manufacturer's termination of one dealer pursuant to an exclusive territory agreement with another. . . . We concluded that vertical nonprice restraints had not been shown to have such a "pernicious effect on competition" and to be so "lacking in redeeming value" as to justify *per se* illegality. Rather, we found, they had real potential to stimulate interbrand competition, the primary concern of antitrust law:

> [N]ew manufacturers and manufacturers entering new markets can use the restrictions in order

---

[13] 433 U.S. 36, 97 S. Ct, 2549, 53 L. Ed. 2d 568 (1977).

to induce competent and aggressive retailers to make the kind of investment of capital and labor that is often required in the distribution of products unknown to the consumer. Established manufacturers can use them to induce retailers to engage in promotional activities or to provide service and repair facilities necessary to the efficient marketing of their products. . . .

Moreover, we observed that a rule of *per se* illegality for vertical nonprice restraints was not needed or effective to protect *intrabrand* competition. First, so long as interbrand competition existed, that would provide a significant check on any attempt to exploit intrabrand market power. . . . Second, the *per se* illegality of vertical restraints would create a perverse incentive for manufacturers to integrate vertically into distribution, an outcome hardly conducive to fostering the creation and maintenance of small businesses. . . .

There has been no showing here that an agreement between a manufacturer and a dealer to terminate a "price cutter" without a further agreement on the price or price levels to be charged by the remaining dealer, almost always tends to restrict competition and reduce output. Any assistance to cartelizing that such an agreement might provide cannot be distinguished from the sort of minimal assistance that might be provided by vertical nonprice agreements like the exclusive territory agreement in *GTE Sylvania* and is insufficient to justify a *per se* rule. Cartels are neither easy to form nor easy to maintain. Uncer-

tainty over the terms of the cartel, particularly the prices to be charged in the future, obstructs both formation and adherence by making cheating easier. Without an agreement with the remaining dealer on price, the manufacturer both retains its incentive to cheat on any manufacturer-level cartel (since lower prices can still be passed on to consumers) and cannot as easily be used to organize and hold together a retailer-level cartel. . . .

In sum, economic analysis supports the view, and no precedent opposes it, that a vertical restraint is not illegal *per se* unless it includes some agreement on price or price levels.

[Affirmed. Justice Stevens and Justice White dissented.]

## Case Discussion Questions

1   Is the Court's economic analysis correct? Might there be other economic analyses that are just as correct? Should economics be the basis of Supreme Court opinions?
2   Why did Hartwell insist that Sharp terminate Business Electronics' dealership? What benefit did Hartwell get from the termination? What do you suppose happened to consumer prices for calculators in Houston following the termination of Business Electronics' dealership?
3   Which is more important—interbrand or intrabrand competition? Is the Court's requirement of an agreement about price in *every* case justified?

### Clayton Act Violations: Exclusive Dealing Agreements

An **exclusive dealing contract** may be attacked under either section 1 of the Sherman Act or section 3 of the Clayton Act. An exclusive dealing arrangement is a vertical agreement in which a purchaser agrees not to purchase any products that compete with those purchased from the seller. For example, a cosmetic company may sell its products to a department store on the condition that no competing lines of cosmetics are sold. The major anticompetitive effect of exclusive dealing contracts is that the market is foreclosed to the seller's competitors (see Figure 20.3). Buyers may, of course, decide on their own to buy only one seller's products, but in such circumstances there is no *agreement* and therefore no violation.

If an exclusive dealing arrangement is to be attacked under the Clayton Act, new requirements are added for a finding of guilt, primarily the necessity of proving that "the effect of such . . . contract for sale . . . may be to substantially lessen competition or tend to create a monopoly in any line of commerce." That language, familiar in other

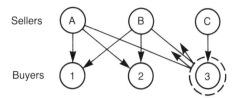

A and B cannot sell to 3. C may or may not be free
to sell to 1 and 2.

FIGURE 20.3    Exclusive Dealing Agreements

antitrust statutes, provides the requirement of a **relevant market** within which the anticompetitive effect must take place.

The concept of relevant market is considered at length in the context of other antitrust statutes in Chapter 21. For this discussion it is sufficient to define it as "the area of
effective competition." That is, the exclusive dealing contract must have some *substantial anticompetitive effect* on *some competing product line* and in *some definable geographic region*. The statute also requires proof of the lessening of competition or a tendency to create a monopoly. As a result, section 3 of the Clayton Act requires what the
Sherman Act does not require in *per se* cases—proof that an anticompetitive effect will
probably take place.

*Requirements contracts* are agreements by a purchaser to buy all of its requirements
of a certain product from a certain manufacturer. Requirements contracts are really
nothing more than exclusive dealing contracts and are treated as such. Some courts
have treated requirements contracts more leniently than pure exclusive dealing contracts, because there may be more business justification for such agreements, in the
form of assured supply, lower costs, and protection against rising prices.

A common form of exclusive dealing contract is found in many franchise arrangements. A company that owns a trademark, the main subject of any franchise arrangement, may wish to protect the quality associated with that trademark by prohibiting the
franchise owners from purchasing products elsewhere. Such restrictions may be permissible if the arrangement does not go beyond what is necessary to protect quality control.

### Clayton Act Violations: Interlocking Directorates

The Clayton Act also prohibited **interlocking directorates.** In the early 1900's the boards
of many corporations saw familiar faces at the directors' meetings, and those interlocks,
in which one person served on several boards, resulted in substantial anticompetitive
conduct.

The Clayton Act generally prohibits directors of firms in banking, banking associations, and trust companies from serving on the board of more than one such corporation. The act also prohibits interlocking directorates if one of the firms has more than $1
million in capital, surplus, and undivided profits. The firms must deal in interstate
commerce, and the two firms must compete with each other in some area. The act does
not prohibit other relationships, as in a case where an officer of one corporation serves

as a director of another corporation. Actions may be brought against either corporation or the common director and may result in cease and desist orders.

### Price Discrimination and the Robinson-Patman Act

It has been said that "[t]he Robinson-Patman Act is sometimes praised, sometimes abused, much interpreted, little understood, and capable of producing instant arguments of infinite variety."[14] This act, which amended the Clayton Act in 1936, generally prohibits the practice of charging different prices to different purchasers of the same goods.

The act is sometimes called the *Chain Store Act* because it was aimed at the giant grocery chains that had emerged by the 1930's. Those chains were able to obtain favored prices from suppliers through high-volume purchases. Those price reductions were generally passed on to the consumer; and they placed independent grocery stores in an unfavorable competitive position, because the independents could not obtain price concessions. Pressure from the independents and large-scale public support produced the Robinson-Patman Act in 1936.

Section 2(a) of the act generally prohibits *suppliers* from *granting* price concessions, although section 2(f) also prohibits *receiving* a discriminatory price. Disguised price discrimination, in the form of brokerage fees, commissions, services, and facilities, is also prohibited.

The Robinson-Patman Act applies by its wording to sellers "engaged in commerce." This is a narrower concept than that found in the Sherman Act, for example, which applies to matters both *in* interstate commerce and that *affect* interstate commerce. Thus, local sales within a state, even those that affect interstate commerce, are not covered by the act. Many states have laws similar to the Robinson-Patman Act that prohibit intrastate price discrimination.

Later judicial interpretation of the act has required *two (or more) reasonably contemporaneous sales* of a product to different purchasers at different prices. The requirement of two sales is necessary for comparison purposes to prove the discrimination. The requirement that the sales be reasonably contemporaneous takes into account the effect of time on the price charged for an item. What will be considered "reasonably contemporaneous" must vary with the circumstances of each case. It is also important that the transactions are *sales*—a sale to one buyer and an outright refusal to deal with another is not covered by the act, nor is a sale to one buyer and a consignment or agency transaction with another buyer.

The law applies only to "commodities of like grade and quality." The term *commodities* refers to tangible personal property only, although discrimination in the sale of services may be illegal under section 5 of the FTC Act as an "unfair method of competition." The requirement that the commodities be of like grade and quality may be satisfied by the sale of the same product under a prominent trademark and under a private label, as well as by the sale of identical products.

**Methods of Price Discrimination**   Price discrimination may be either *direct* discrimination, as in the case of charging two different prices for the same commodity, or *indi-*

---

14 Earl W. Kintner, *An Antitrust Primer*, 2d Ed. (New York: Macmillan, 1973), p. 61.

*rect* discrimination, in which the same price is charged but the terms and conditions of the sale are different for different purchasers of the same commodity.

A seller can favor one customer over another in many ways: advertising and promotional aids, special packaging, payment of transportation expenses, return privileges, display and storage facilities, warehousing facilities and fees for storage, and kickbacks and brokerage commissions, to name a few. Congress was aware of the possibility of indirect price discriminations and provided that such favors be "available on proportionally equal terms to all other customers competing in the distribution of such products or commodities."

The requirement that the favor be available means more than providing the favor on request; the seller must make all competing purchasers *aware* that the favor is available. The requirement that it be available to all competing sellers depends on the actual competition between the purchasers. For example, a manufacturer may make a favor available to all the purchasers on the East Coast but not to those on the West Coast, if those purchasers do not compete with each other.

Similarly, the favor must not be tailored to apply only to some firms. For example, if a seller develops a promotional assistance plan that provides large-scale aid useful only to huge chains and department stores, the plan is indirect price discrimination because it is not useful to small purchasers.

The requirement that the favors must be made available on "proportionally equal terms" means that they are available to each according to his or her worth as a retailer. Some plans, based on a percentage of dollar volume of goods purchased or on the quantity of goods purchased over a period of time, are probably valid. Volume discounts are especially suspect, however.

**The Requirement of Competitive Injury**    Price discrimination is illegal if any of three types of anticompetitive effect are present: (1) a substantial lessening of competition, (2) a tendency to create a monopoly, or (3) an injury to competition by specific persons. The first two anticompetitive effects take a great deal more effort to prove, and as a result, most of the cases involve specific injuries to competitors.

*Primary-Line Injury to Competition*    **Primary-line** injury is nothing more than injury to the *seller's competitors*. Thus, in Figure 20.4, Seller 1 and Seller 2 compete in Illinois, and Seller 1 sells in Wisconsin as well. If Seller 1 were to charge lower prices to Illinois purchasers than to those in Wisconsin in order to obtain more of the market from Seller 2, the result would be primary-line injury.

Primary-line injury usually occurs in cases of geographic or territorial discrimina-

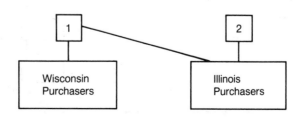

FIGURE 20.4    Primary-Line Injury

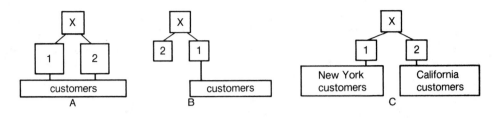

FIGURE 20.5    Secondary-Line Injuries

tion, but it isn't confined to that form. Primary-line injuries might also arise if a supplier cuts his or her prices to a competitor's customers while selling at higher prices to his or her own customers in the same area.

*Secondary-Line Injury to Competition*    A discrimination scheme that injures *competitors of the buyer* is a **secondary-line injury.** In Figure 20.5A, Seller X discriminates in price between buyers 1 and 2. Buyer 2, who does not receive the lowered price, may be less able to compete with Buyer 1 because of the price discrimination. However, discrimination between buyers may not result in competitive injury. Two examples are shown in Figure 20.5, parts B and C. In Figure 20.5B, Buyer 1 is a retail gasoline dealer and Buyer 2 the owner of a trucking company. If X, a refiner-supplier of gasoline, sells to Buyer 2 at a lower price than to Buyer 1, there is no anticompetitive effect. Likewise, in Figure 20.5C, Buyer 1 sells only to retailers in California, whereas Buyer 2 sells only to retailers in New York. Since they are not competitors, there is no violation.

*Third-Line and Fourth-Line Injury to Competition*    Courts and commentators have also identified competitive injuries that take place even further down the distribution line. **Third-line injury** involves injuries to customers in competition with customers of the supplier's favored buyer. **Fourth-line injuries** are suffered by customers in competition with a customer of a customer of the supplier's favored customer. As shown in the Figure 20.6, the injury in both instances would be suffered by C1, and the discriminatorily lower price will have been given by M to C2.

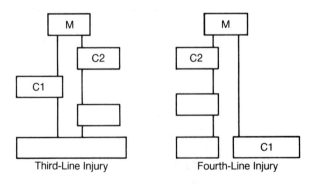

FIGURE 20.6    Injuries Further down the Distribution Line

In both instances, a lower price is given to C2 because C2 is a wholesaler or jobber of some sort. But there is no rational reason to favor C2. Thus, to stay within the Robinson-Patman Act, M must charge both C1 and C2 the same price.

### Defenses to Charges of Price Discrimination

*Cost Justification*    Some buyers are cheaper to sell to than others. A host of factors account for the differences, including savings in shipping costs, reduced sales expenses, and the buyer's purchasing practices. The Robinson-Patman Act permits sellers to pass on such *actual* differences in costs to the purchaser. A mere quantity discount does not meet the standards, unless it can be shown that the quantity sold to a particular purchaser resulted in actual cost savings equal to the discount.

*Meeting Competition*    Lowering one's price to meet a price offered by a competitor is an effective defense to a Robinson-Patman Act claim. The defense is not popular with antitrust enforcers, and legislation has been proposed to abolish it. The defense is difficult to prove as well: it is not available if the competitor's price is unlawful under the Robinson-Patman Act. The price must be a temporary measure to meet competition, not a permanent price schedule resulting in systematically charged discriminatory prices; the price must be given for like quantities as offered by the competitor; the price must *meet*, not *beat*, the competitor's price; and the price must be limited to meeting a specific individual competitor's price to specific customers.

*Other Defenses*    Other types of sales are also exempted from the act. Those exemptions include actual or imminent deterioration of perishable goods; distress sales under court order; obsolescence of seasonal goods; and sales in good faith in the course of discontinuing business in the goods concerned. Generally speaking, those sales are examples of the general defense of "changing conditions affecting the market for or the marketability of the goods concerned." Other legislation has exempted purchases by schools, colleges, and universities; public libraries; churches; hospitals and charitable institutions; and local, state, and federal governments.

## SUMMARY AND CONCLUSIONS

The federal antitrust laws include the Sherman Act of 1890, the Clayton Act and Federal Trade Commission Act, both of 1914, and the Robinson-Patman Act of 1936. Those laws developed in response to business activities that threatened the economic, political, and social structure of the country. The primary purpose of those laws is to preserve, so far as possible, the attributes of classical economics, and to bring the economy as close as possible to the requirements of perfect competition.

The antitrust laws are jointly administered by the Department of Justice and the Federal Trade Commission. The Justice Department administers the Sherman Act and portions of the Clayton Act through traditional criminal actions and actions for injunctions in the federal courts. The FTC administers the Clayton, Robinson-Patman, and FTC acts through administrative proceedings.

Section 1 of the Sherman Act prohibits all "contracts, combinations and conspiracies . . . in restraint of trade." That section has been interpreted to reach all concerted action, but action by a single party is not covered.

The rule of reason was announced in 1911 in order to make only *unreasonable* restraints of trade illegal under section 1 of the Sherman Act. Some restraints, such as horizontal and vertical price fixing, group boycotts, horizontal market divisions, and tie-in sales, have been held to be "so pernicious" that a *per se* rule will be applied; that is, such restraints are never justifiable except under the most unusual circumstances, and the courts are relieved of the burden of conducting a massive inquiry into the reasonableness of the restraint. All other restraints are analyzed under the rule of reason.

The Clayton Act also prohibits certain types of conduct, including exclusive dealing and interlocking directorates. A very specific amendment to the Clayton Act, the Robinson-Patman Act, prohibits price discrimination, or charging different prices for the same commodity to different purchasers. The Robinson-Patman Act provides a series of exceptions and defenses as well.

## REVIEW QUESTIONS

**1** What are the reasons for antitrust? Should government policy ever be based on an unsubstantiated theory, even one as generally accepted as Adam Smith's theory of perfect competition? Is Smith's argument still only a theory?

**2** One of the hallmarks of antitrust is its flexibility, both in the broadness of the statutes and in its administration. Why do you suppose Congress built this type of flexibility into the law?

**3** Is "parallel action" the same thing as "concerted action?" What does the term *agreement* really mean?

**4** What is the *rule of reason?* What are the *per se* categories? Why were the *per se* categories established?

**5** Explain the *economic effects* of horizontal and vertical price fixing, group boycotts, horizontal and vertical geographic market allocation, tying contracts, exclusive dealing, interlocking directorates, and price discrimination.

**6** The Goldfarbs contracted to buy a home in Virginia, and the mortgage company which was to lend them the money for the purchase required a title examination before the deal was closed. Only a licensed attorney could conduct such an examination. The Goldfarbs contacted thirty-six lawyers, and every one indicated that the fee would be the recommended fee for such services as described by the state bar association. Habitually charging lower than the recommended fees was grounds for disciplinary action against lawyers. The Goldfarbs sued, claiming a section 1 violation. What do you think the result was? [*Goldfarb v. Virginia State Bar*, 421 U.S. 773, 95 S. Ct. 2004, 44 L. Ed. 2d 572 (1975).]

**7** Klor's, Inc., and Broadway-Hale are two appliance dealers operating stores next door to each other in San Francisco. Both sell the same sort of merchandise and directly compete in several lines. Broadway-Hale is a chain, however, and Klor's is a small independent store. None of the large manufacturers of appliances will sell to Klor's, although they sell to many other independents in the San Francisco area. Klor's charges a violation of section 1. (a) Is there sufficient evidence of an agreement? (b) What type of violation is this? (c) Does it make a difference that Klor's is a small store, whose destruction will not affect the economy? [*Klor's, Inc. v. Broadway-Hale Stores, Inc.*, 359 U.S. 207, 79 S. Ct. 705, 3 L. Ed. 2d 741 (1959).]

**8**  Chicken Delight, Inc., licensed Siegel and others under its franchise plan. It charged no franchise or royalty fees but required Siegel and the other franchisees to purchase a specified number of cookers and fryers and to purchase packaging supplies and mixes exclusively from Chicken Delight, in return for the right to use the Chicken Delight trademark. Siegel was not given an exclusive territory, but Chicken Delight endeavored to restrict the number of franchises in a given area. The prices charged by Chicken Delight for its equipment and food materials were substantially higher than those charged by competing suppliers for similar products. Siegel brought a private treble damage action to recover the price difference. What was the result? [*Siegel v. Chicken Delight, Inc.*, 448 F.2d 43 (9th Cir., 1971).] Does your conclusion mean all franchises are illegal?

**9**  Jerrold Electronics manufactured the first community master television antenna for use in communities with poor television reception but sold the system only if the community also entered into a service contract, because they felt only they had the technical expertise to main- tain the system. A part of that contract provided that the purchaser would also purchase from Jerrold "at the then prevailing prices, whatever additional Jerrold Equipment may be necessary. . . ." Communities also agreed not to purchase any other equipment except that provided by Jerrold. Is the contract *per se* illegal? What kind of contract is it? [*U.S. v. Jerrold Electronics Corporation*, 187 F. Supp. 545 (E.D.Pa., 1960), aff'd *per curiam*, 365 U.S. 567, 81 S. Ct. 755, 5 L. Ed. 2d 806 (1961).]

**10**  Morton Salt Company had established a "quantity discount" plan for purchases of its table salt. It charged $1.60 per case in less than carload purchases, $1.50 per case for carload purchases, $1.40 per case for more than 5,000 cases, and $1.35 per case for more than 50,000 cases purchased in twelve months. Only five purchasers—all national grocery chains—were able to take advantage of the lowest prices and were therefore able to sell salt at lower prices than other retailers. Has Morton violated the Robinson-Patman Act? [*FTC v. Morton Salt Co.*, 334 U.S. 37, 68 S. Ct. 822, 92 L. Ed. 1196 (1948).]

CHAPTER 21

# Antitrust: Regulation of Structure

*Nobody cheers for Goliath.*

ATTRIBUTED TO WILT CHAMBERLAIN

Almost a century after the passage of the Sherman Act the debate between *structure* and *conduct* still rages. A 1981 comment by Attorney General William French Smith that "bigness does not necessarily mean badness" signified a changing view of antitrust by some that new trends, particularly in international trade, make traditional antitrust regulation of monopolization and mergers obsolete.

Other people remain concerned about the inefficiency, monopolistic behavior, and political power of large corporations. Those who favor regulation of business structure argue that the size of business units and concentration of whole industries results in economic inefficiency, unjust distribution of resources and income, and political and social power in the hands of a few people or firms. Those persons see large business size and concentration as contrary to free enterprise and democracy.

This chapter discusses the traditional areas of regulation of structure, notably **mergers** and **monopolization.** The chapter also contains a discussion of the broadest antitrust law of all, the Federal Trade Commission Act, and some of the problems of antitrust in an international environment.

## MERGERS

One of the concerns of antitrust law has traditionally been **corporate integration,** or the joining together of two firms. The purposes of the antimerger provisions of the antitrust laws are based on purposes similar to the purposes of the other antitrust laws (see p. 499). Mergers increase *market concentration* by reducing the number of participants in an industry, possibly creating a monopolistic or oligopolistic market. Mergers can also increase the *market power* of firms, which can result in the foreclosure of markets or in predatory pricing. Both market concentration and market power are directly related to the preservation of competition and to the political and social power of business.

### Methods of Corporate Integration

Integration between business firms can be accomplished in a variety of ways, including **true mergers, consolidations, purchases of stock, purchases of assets,** and **joint ventures** (see Figure 21.1). All five forms are commonly referred to (somewhat erroneously) as "mergers," and all five forms are subject to regulation by the antitrust merger statutes.

A *true merger* takes place when one firm acquires and absorbs another. The acquired firm ceases to exist, and the acquiring firm remains. In a *consolidation*, two firms join together and form a new, third company, and both of the original firms cease to exist.

In a *purchase of stock*, one company buys controlling interest in another firm, thereby gaining the right to elect the board of directors of the acquired firm and obtaining operational control of the company. The acquired firm becomes a subsidiary of the acquiring firm and has an independent existence only in a technical sense. A *purchase*

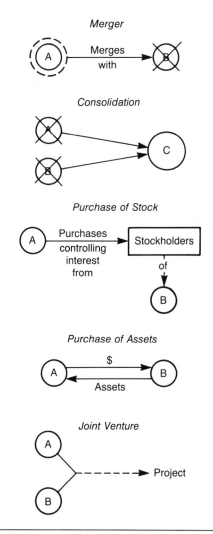

FIGURE 21.1    Types of Corporate Integration

*of assets* involves an exchange of cash for the assets of the acquired company. The assets of the acquired firm, including capital, personnel, and markets, become a part of the acquiring firm, and the acquired firm consists of only the cash received, which usually must be distributed to shareholders.

A *joint venture* is a partnership, usually temporary, between two other business entities for joint participation in a project. Both firms continue to exist but join forces for the purposes of a transaction. Many oil-drilling endeavors and motion pictures are put together as joint ventures of two or more business firms. The law of partnerships generally regulates such relationships (see p. 298).

The most fashionable new form of integration is the **tender offer.** Tender offers are nothing more than a purchase-of-stock acquisition, but usually without the consent and against the wishes of the acquired firm. The acquiring company makes a public offer to purchase the shares of the target company at a price higher than the price of the shares on the stock market, up to the number of shares necessary to obtain control of the target company. If stockholders sell their shares, the acquiring company obtains control and the target company becomes a subsidiary. The management of the target company may resist the tender offer, because new management is usually installed if the takeover is successful.

## The Antimerger Statutes

Mergers were first addressed by the antitrust laws under section 1 of the Sherman Act. Because of doubts created by the 1911 *Standard Oil* decision (see p. 508), Congress enacted section 7 of the Clayton Act in 1914 (see below). In 1950, Congress moved to close certain loopholes in the Clayton Act by enacting the **Celler-Kefauver Anti-Merger Act.**

In 1976 the Clayton Act was amended once again by the **Hart-Scott-Rodino Antitrust Improvement Act,** which allowed the FTC to adopt a **premerger notification** requirement. If the merging parties reach certain size limitations and the acquisition involves 15% or $15 million of assets or stock in the acquired corporation, the parties must notify both the Justice Department and the FTC of the impending merger. Once the firms have notified these agencies, there is a thirty-day waiting period before the merger may be consummated. The time limit may be extended, and the Justice Depart-

---

## Section 7 of the Clayton Act, as Amended

That no corporation engaged in commerce shall acquire, directly or indirectly, the whole or any part of the stock or other share capital and no corporation subject to the jurisdiction of the Federal Trade Commission shall acquire the whole or any part of the assets of another corporation engaged also in commerce, where in any line of commerce in any section of the country, the effect of such acquisition may be substantially to lessen competition, or to tend to create a monopoly.

ment or the FTC may file injunction actions to stop the merger during this time. Failure to file the appropriate premerger notification may result in a civil fine of up to $10,000 per day.

### Remedies: Unscrambling the Egg

The same remedies apply to violations of the merger statutes as to the other antitrust statutes, including private civil actions for treble damages, *parens patriae* actions, and actions for injunctions filed by the government.

One form of injunctive relief unique to merger problems is **divestiture.** The merging companies may be required, under an order of divestiture, to "unmerge"; that is, to divide into separate companies as best as possible. Divestiture orders often require the "acquiring" firm to support the newly re-created firm in a variety of ways, including the purchase of goods from the new company or other forms of financial support. Because of the difficulty of sorting out the assets of the acquired and acquiring firms, divestiture is sometimes called *unscrambling the egg.*

### Merger Analysis

Mergers are classified into three general types: **horizontal, vertical,** and **conglomerate.** Conglomerate mergers are subdivided into three subtypes: the **market extension, product extension,** and **pure conglomerate** forms.

Mergers between any of the firms operating on the same distribution level—such as a merger between Firm A and Firm C or Firm V and Firm Y or Firm 2 and Firm 5 in Figure 21.2—would be a *horizontal merger.* Any merger between firms at different levels of the distribution process is considered to be a *vertical merger,* such as a merger between Firm B and Firm X or Firm Y and Firm 7 or Firm C and Firm 4 (see Figure 21.2). Horizontal and vertical mergers involve different effects on competition among the firms and on competition in general and are subjected to different analyses under the antitrust laws.

In order to analyze *conglomerate mergers,* we must add some facts to our assumptions. If firms X and Y sell the same product, but Firm X operates exclusively in California and Firm Z operates solely in New York State, then a merger between the two

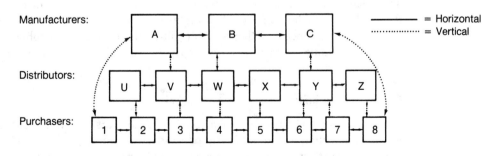

FIGURE 21.2    Horizontal and Vertical Mergers

would not be considered a horizontal merger at all, but a *market extension merger*, because the firms were not "in competition" before the merger and such integration would involve somewhat different effects on competition than would a horizontal merger.

Likewise, if Firm B were to merge with a firm that manufactures a different but similar and related product, the merger would be viewed as a *product extension merger*, because it has entered a similar and related industry with which it had no prior competition.

Finally, if one of the firms merges with a firm in a totally different and unrelated industry, the merger would be a *pure conglomerate*. Pure conglomerate mergers present some of the most far-reaching issues for the antitrust laws and are the only type of merger that has never been held illegal under section 7.

Much of the recent trend toward merger has been in the pure conglomerate form, perhaps because the courts have yet to rule that a pure conglomerate merger can have anticompetitive effects within the meaning of the antitrust statutes. Supreme Court decisions hold that all of the other forms of mergers, including horizontal, vertical, product extension, and market expansion mergers, may violate section 7 under certain circumstances.

## Relevant Market

Under section 7, the anticompetitive effect must take place within a "line of commerce," which has been interpreted to mean the **relevant product market.** The issue is whether the products of the competing firms are reasonably interchangeable. In more sophisticated economic terms, the question is the **cross-elasticity of demand** for the products, that is, whether an increase in price for one product will shift demand to the other product.

For example, if a merger is proposed between a manufacturer of plastic wrap and a manufacturer of aluminum foil, the courts might determine that the two products do not compete and each product is a separate relevant market. On the other hand, the courts might determine that the appropriate relevant market is flexible wrapping materials, in which case the two products are competing. In the first instance, the merger would be considered as a *product extension merger*. In the second case, the merger would be considered *horizontal*.

The anticompetitive effect must also appear in some **relevant geographic market.** That market has been defined as the *area of effective competition*, or the places where the products actually compete. If firms manufacture the same product and actually compete in some location, that location will be the relevant geographic market. If the firms sell the same product in entirely separate locations, a merger would be considered as a *market extension merger*.

## Anticompetitive Effect

In order to hold that a merger violates section 7, the court must find that the acquisition lessens competition within both the product market and the geographic market. The **anticompetitive effect** of a merger may take many forms. The only requirements are that the effect be *substantial* and that it take place within the relevant product and geographic markets.

Although each case is unique, the courts have focused on some classic anticompetitive effects of each of the forms of merger. Horizontal mergers always involve the *removal of a competitor* from the market and result in further *concentration of the market*. Vertical mergers often involve *barriers to entry* to competitors, such as access to supplies or markets. Market extension and product extension mergers may involve the reduction of *potential competition* (see p. 535). Such mergers may also involve *reciprocity* (see p. 538), which is the practice of purchasing from a subsidiary of a company to which one sells. All forms of merger involve the enhancement of *market power* through increases in size and the possibility of *cross-subsidization* of a smaller firm by a larger firm's "deep pocket," thereby enhancing the ability of the smaller firm to compete.

### The Merger Guidelines

Because of the vagueness of section 7, businesspeople often have a difficult time predicting whether a particular acquisition will be challenged by the Justice Department or the FTC. In order to remedy the "predictability gap," the Justice Department issued the first **Merger Guidelines** in 1968. In 1982 the Justice Department issued an entirely new set of guidelines and revised them in 1984. The new guidelines eliminated all references to conglomerate mergers and introduced the **Herfindahl-Hirschmann Index of Industrial Concentration (HHI)** (see Figure 21.3), a mathematical method of determining the concentration of a market.

The Merger Guidelines are not law. In no way are they binding on the courts or even on the Justice Department itself. The 1968 guidelines were ignored by some administrations, and it is likely that the new guidelines will meet a similar fate. Taken together with the premerger notification rules, they may be helpful to business in deciding whether to merge, however.

### The *Brown Shoe* Decision

In 1962 the Supreme Court decided the case of *Brown Shoe v. U.S.*,[1] the most important merger decision in the law. The case was the first to reach the court after the Celler-Kefauver Amendment to section 7, and it established far-reaching doctrines regarding relevant markets and vertical mergers, along with some vital basic policies behind all of merger law. *Brown Shoe* has been called a "textbook on mergers," and the case is cited in virtually every merger case.

**Merger Policy and the *Brown Shoe* Case**   In *Brown Shoe*, the Court announced the **incipiency doctrine.** According to this doctrine, mergers that might harm competition may be challenged *at the outset*, before any anticompetitive effects have become visible, because Congress intended to give the FTC and the courts the power to challenge further concentration of the American economy "at its outset and before it gathered momentum."

The Court also found that legislative history indicated that Congress's concern was

---

1 370 U.S. 294, 82 S. Ct. 1502, 8 L. Ed. 2d 510 (1962).

Assume a market contains five firms, A, B, C, D, and E. Assume also that Firm A has 30% of the market, Firm B has 25% of the market, firms C and D each have 20% of the market, and Firm E has 5% of the market. Under these circumstances the HHI would be figured as follows:

| Firm | Market Share | Individual Market Share Squared |
|---|---|---|
| Firm A | 30% | 900 |
| Firm B | 25% | 625 |
| Firm C | 20% | 400 |
| Firm D | 20% | 400 |
| Firm E | 5% | 25 |
| | | Total HHI of the market = 2350 |

This industry has a premerger HHI of 2350, and thus any merger will fall under Section 3.1c of the Merger Guidelines, which says:

The general standards for horizontal mergers are as follows:

(a) *Post-Merger HHI Below 1000.* . . . The Department will not challenge mergers falling in this region except in extraordinary circumstances.
(b) *Post-Merger HHI Between 1000 and 1800.* . . . The Department . . . is unlikely to challenge a merger producing an increase in the HHI of less than 100 points. The Department is *likely* to challenge mergers in this region that produce an increase in the HHI of more than 100 points. . . .
(c) *Post-Merger HHI Above 1800.* . . . The Department is unlikely . . . to challenge mergers producing an increase in the HHI of less than 50 points. The Department is likely to challenge mergers in this region that produce an increase in the HHI of more than 50 points. . . .

**3.12 Leading Firm Proviso**
[T]he Department is likely to challenge the merger of any firm with a market share of at least 1 percent with the leading firm in the market, provided the leading firm has a market share that is at least 35 percent. . . .

If Firm D were to merge with Firm E, the HHI would be recalculated as follows:

| Firm | Market Share | Individual Market Share Squared |
|---|---|---|
| Firm A | 30% | 900 |
| Firm B | 25% | 625 |
| Firm C | 20% | 400 |
| Firm D (merged with Firm E) | 25% | 625 |
| | | Total postmerger HHI = 2550 |

This merger between the two smallest firms in the market creates a change in the HHI of 200 points, and thus under Section 3.1c of the Merger Guidelines, the Department is likely to challenge the merger.

FIGURE 21.3    Using the Herfindahl-Hirschmann Index (HHI)

with *probabilities*, not *certainties*. That meant that courts were called upon to forecast the probable anticompetitive effects of a merger, and that they could look to *trends toward concentration* in the industry as proof of an anticompetitive effect. Finally, the Court made a very telling remark when it said that Congress was concerned with "protection of *competition*, not *competitors*. . . . " This oft-quoted remark means that the purpose of the act—and indeed all of antitrust law—is to protect competitive conditions in the market, not individual competitors.

**The Facts of *Brown Shoe***    *Brown Shoe* involved the acquisition of Kinney Shoe Company, the largest shoe retailer in the country, by Brown Shoe Company, the nation's fourth-largest shoe manufacturer. Kinney was also the twelfth-largest shoe manufacturer in the country, and Brown already owned many retail outlets. As a result, the merger was *vertical*, between Brown as manufacturer and Kinney as retailer, and *horizontal* on two levels, both manufacturing and retailing. Although Brown and Kinney were both major participants in the shoe market, their relative market shares were very small. Brown accounted for 4% of the shoes manufactured in the United States, and Kinney accounted for only .5%. Kinney sold 2% of the nation's shoes, and Brown sold less than 1%.

The Court spent considerable time reviewing the *trends* in the shoe industry, including a trend among shoe manufacturers to acquire retail outlets, a trend for the parent manufacturing firms to supply an ever-increasing percentage of the retail outlets' needs (thereby "drying up" the available outlets for independent shoe manufacturers), and a decrease in the number of firms manufacturing shoes. The Court also found that Brown was a "moving factor" in these industry trends through its acquisition of retail outlets and its acquisition of seven other manufacturers through merger.

**The Relevant Market Issues**    A major issue in the case was that of the *relevant market*. Brown made two arguments: (1) that Kinney stores were primarily *suburban*, whereas Brown stores sold shoes *downtown*, and therefore the stores did not compete; and (2) Kinney sold lower-priced shoes and Brown sold higher-priced shoes, and therefore the stores were not in competition.

The court rejected both of Brown's arguments. The relevant geographic market was found to be any city in which both Brown and Kinney sold shoes, and the relevant product market was found to be divided into three submarkets—men's shoes, women's shoes, and children's shoes. The "price/quality" divisions that Brown presented were rejected on the basis that shoes selling below some arbitrary price in fact compete with more expensive shoes. As the Court said, it is important "to recognize competition where, in fact, competition exists. . . . "

**The Horizontal Aspects of *Brown Shoe***    Finally, the Court viewed the *effect* of the horizontal aspects of the merger:

> The market share which companies may control by merging is one of the most important factors to be considered when determining the probable effects of the combination on effective competition in the relevant market. In an industry as fragmented as shoe retailing, the control of substantial shares of the trade in a city may have important effects on competition.

If a merger achieving 5% control were now approved, we might be required to approve future merger efforts by Brown's competitors seeking similar market shares. . . .

Other factors to be considered in evaluating the probable effects of a merger in the relevant market lend additional support to the District Court's conclusion that this merger may substantially lessen competition. One such factor is the history of tendency toward concentration in the industry. . . . By the merger in this case the largest single group of retail stores still independent of one of the large manufacturers was absorbed into an already substantial aggregation of more or less controlled retail outlets. As a result of this merger, Brown moved into second place nationally in terms of retail stores directly owned. . . . We cannot avoid the mandate of Congress that tendencies toward concentration in industry are to be curbed in their incipiency, particularly when those tendencies are being accelerated through giant steps striding across a hundred cities at a time. In the light of the trends in this industry we agree with the Government and the court below that this is an appropriate place at which to call a halt.

**The "Failing-Company" and "Small-Company" Defenses**    While the horizontal aspects of the merger were found illegal, the Court said that in future cases it would consider some mitigating factors. Those factors have resulted in the two principal defenses in horizontal merger cases. The **failing-company defense** permits any firm to merge with a company that is failing in order to keep its resources and personnel employed. The **small-company defense** permits smaller companies to merge if it will help them compete with larger firms.

**The Vertical Aspects of _Brown Shoe_**    Even though the horizontal aspects of the merger were held illegal, the court went on to consider the _vertical_ aspects of the merger between Brown as manufacturer and Kinney as retailer. This was the first vertical merger case to reach the Supreme Court, and the Court provided substantial guidance for future cases.

The Court first defined a vertical merger as an economic arrangement "between companies standing in a supplier-customer relationship" and held that "the primary vice of a vertical merger . . . is that, by foreclosing the competitors of either party from a segment of the market otherwise open to them, the arrangement may act as a "clog on competition" . . . which deprives rivals of a fair opportunity to compete. . . . " The Court said that the determination of whether a particular foreclosure of competition would be illegal would depend on the size of the market share foreclosed, the purpose of the merger, and future trends in the market. The Court found that the trend toward vertical integration in the shoe market justified holding the merger illegal.

## Horizontal Mergers

A horizontal merger, or a merger between competitors, is considered to be the worst type of merger from an antitrust standpoint. Such mergers _always_ involve some anti-competitive effect in the form of a reduction in the number of competitors (see Figure 21.4). The only defenses that have been permitted in horizontal merger cases were established in _Brown Shoe_. A merger with a _failing company_ is permissible in order to keep its resources active in the marketplace, and a merger between _small companies_ is permissible to allow them to compete with larger firms.

The legality of the merger will depend on the relative size of the firms and the con-

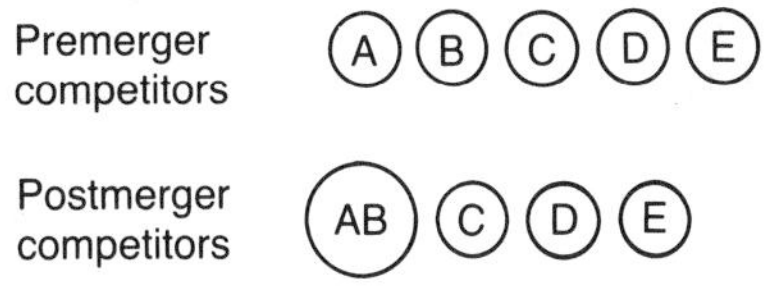

Premerger competitors (A) (B) (C) (D) (E)

Postmerger competitors (AB) (C) (D) (E)

FIGURE 21.4   Reduction of Competitors in Horizontal Mergers

centration of the market. In Figure 21.4, if firms A and B are the smallest in the market, they may well be able to compete more effectively with giant firms C, D, and E. If A and B are the largest firms in the market, the market will become much more concentrated and the merger would be prohibited. A merger in a market with a large number of firms hinders competition less than a merger in a market with only a few firms.

**The Relevant Product Market**   The determination of the appropriate "line of commerce" (or relevant product market) under section 7 depends for the most part on questions of substitutability of products, or more technically, the **cross-elasticities of demand** for the products of the merging firms. In *Brown Shoe*, for example, Brown argued that its medium-priced shoes did not compete with the lower-priced shoes sold by Kinney and, therefore, that they were not in the same product market. In later cases, the Supreme Court held that tin cans and glass bottles were in the same relevant product market, because there was a high degree of interchangeability of use of such containers.[2]

In such cases the defendant will often argue that the relevant product market is either broader or narrower than the market proposed by the government. If the market is found to be broader than that proposed by the government, the anticompetitive effect is lessened because more firms will be considered as competitors. If the market is found to be narrower than that proposed by the government, the merger may not be horizontal at all but may be analyzed as a **product extension merger,** a type of merger that receives much different treatment from the courts (see p. 537).

**The Relevant Geographic Market**   The question of the relevant geographic market is just as crucial as the determination of the relevant product market. The issue is whether the merging firms competed in some "section of the country." If the firms operate in different areas, the merger is not a horizontal merger but will be analyzed as a **market extension merger,** described later in this chapter.

The section of the country need not be a very large area. In *Brown Shoe* the relevant geographic market was defined as those cities where Kinney and Brown already had competing stores. In subsequent cases the relevant geographic market has been determined to be as small as the city of Los Angeles[3] or the four counties around Philadelphia,[4] for example.

Again the defendant may argue that the relevant geographic market is either larger or smaller than the market proposed by the government. If the area is larger, then more firms will be considered as competitors, and the effect of the merger on competition will

2 *U.S. v. Continental Can Co.,* 378 U.S. 441, 84 S. Ct. 1738, 12 L. Ed. 2d 953 (1964).
3 *U.S. v. Von's Grocery Co.,* 384 U.S. 270, 86 S. Ct. 1478, 16 L. Ed. 2d 555 (1966).
4 *U.S. v. Philadelphia National Bank,* 374 U.S. 321, 83 S. Ct. 1715, 10 L. Ed. 2d 915 (1963).

be less. If the area is smaller, the merging firms may not be competitors at all, and the merger will be considered as a **market extension merger** rather than as a horizontal merger (see p. 536).

### Vertical Mergers

**Vertical mergers** involve integration between firms operating at different levels of the distribution process for the same product. Mergers between a manufacturer and a supplier, a manufacturer and a distributor, or a distributor and a retailer are all examples of vertical mergers. Many of the concerns of horizontal mergers are also matters of importance in vertical mergers, such as relevant product and geographic markets and anticompetitive effect, although the analysis of each is somewhat different in vertical merger cases.

The principal anticompetitive effect of a vertical merger involves *foreclosure of markets* or *foreclosure of supplies*. If a supplier and a purchaser merge, other suppliers are cut off from selling to the purchaser, and other purchasers may be cut off from buying from the supplier (see Figure 21.5). Whether this effect is substantial will depend on a number of factors, including whether the market is already highly vertically integrated, the size of the merged firms, and the number of firms in the market.

Vertical integration may involve other anticompetitive effects as well. For example, if the entire industry, or most of it, is vertically integrated, new entrants into the market will have to enter at *both levels*, thereby increasing the barriers to entry to the market (see Figure 21.6). Vertical integration may also be used to evade section 1 prohibitions against vertical price fixing, eliminate buyers who disrupt collusive agreements between suppliers, and evade rate regulations on public utilities. In the latter case, a public utility may merge with a nonregulated supplier (e.g., of natural gas) and charge itself high

1. "Clog" of the Purchasing Market

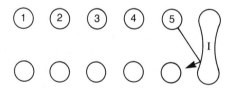

Firms 1–5 cannot sell to vertically-integrated Firm I

2. "Clog" of the selling market

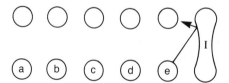

Firms a–e cannot buy from vertically-integrated Firm I

FIGURE 21.5    "Clogs" on Competition

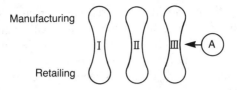

Firm A will have to enter the market at *both* levels

FIGURE 21.6    Barriers to Entry Through Vertical Integration

prices for its supplies, permitting an argument before the regulatory bodies that its rates should be increased because its costs have gone up.

### Conglomerate Mergers

Conglomerate mergers, or mergers between firms in unrelated industries or different geographical markets, are perhaps the most difficult of all merger cases. At first glance, such mergers often seem to have no anticompetitive effect and seem not to fall within the Clayton Act. Yet on closer analysis some anticompetitive effects are found, and the courts have held some forms of conglomerate mergers to be in violation of section 7.

As noted earlier, conglomerate mergers are divided into three basic forms: (1) *product extension mergers*, or mergers between firms dealing in similar but noncompeting products; (2) *market extension mergers*, or mergers between firms dealing in identical products in different sections of the country; and (3) *pure conglomerate mergers*, which involve totally unrelated firms. The anticompetitive effects of conglomerate mergers center around the *potential competition doctrine*, *reciprocity*, and the *"deep-pocket" theory*.

**The Potential Competition Doctrine: The "Wings" Effect**    Whenever an existing firm wants to enter a new market, it may do so in one of three ways: (1) build its own facilities and develop its own markets, thereby adding a new competitor to the market (**de nova entry**); (2) acquire one of the smaller competitors in the market and help that competitor become more effective through an infusion of capital (a **toehold acquisition**); or (3) acquire one of the larger competitors in the market (a **major merger**). It is generally agreed that both *de nova* entries and toehold acquisitions *aid* competition, because either the number of competitors increases, or the competitive abilities of one of the smaller competitors increases.

But the very existence of a potential competitor "waiting in the wings" to enter the market may sharply alter the competitive behavior of firms already in a market. Firms in the market may decide to keep prices low to discourage the potential competitor. If the potential competitor enters the market, its effect on the behavior of firms already in the market is lost. If the potential competitor enters the market through *de nova* entry or a toehold acquisition, there is a net gain in competition, even though the "wings effect" has been lost. But if the potential competitor enters the market through a major merger, an even larger competitor has been substituted for one of the market leaders, producing an even more concentrated market and a net decrease in competition.

**Potential Competition and Market Extension Mergers**    Market extension mergers involve firms dealing in the same product in different geographical areas. Such mergers may involve the loss of potential competition from the acquiring firm. Other firms in the market perceive the acquiring firm as a potential competitor who will enter the market through internal expansion if profits become large. As a result, such firms alter their competitive behavior by keeping prices low. The following decision established the basic law to be applied to market extension mergers.

# U.S. v. Falstaff Brewing Corp.

410 U.S. 526, 93 S. Ct. 1096, 35 L. Ed. 2d 475 (1973)

In 1965, Falstaff Brewing Corporation acquired Narragansett Brewing Company. At the time of the acquisition, Falstaff was the fourth-largest brewer in the United States, accounting for 5.9% of the nation's beer production. Falstaff sold beer in thirty-two states but sold none in New England. Narragansett was the largest seller of beer in New England at the time of the acquisition, accounting for approximately 20% of the market. The Justice Department brought this action for divestiture under section 7.

The evidence showed that Falstaff faced significant competition from four other brewers who sold in all fifty states. National brands are able to advertise on a nationwide basis, their beers have greater prestige than regional products, and they are less affected by weather and labor problems. The proof also disclosed that while beer sales in New England had increased approximately 9.5% in the four years preceding acquisition, the eight largest sellers had increased their share of the beer market from 74% to 81%, and that the number of brewers in New England had declined from eleven in 1957 to six in 1964. The evidence also showed that New England had the highest beer consumption of any region of the country. The District Court held for Falstaff, and the government appealed.

**Mr. Justice White Delivered the Opinion of the Court**    Before the acquisition was accomplished, the United States brought suit alleging that the acquisition would violate section 7. . . . This contention was based on two grounds: because Falstaff was a potential entrant and because the acquisition eliminated competition that would have existed had Falstaff entered the market *de nova* or by acquisition and expansion of a smaller firm, a so-called "toehold" acquisition. . . .

[T]he acquisition by a competitor not competing in the market but so situated as to be a potential competitor and likely to exercise substantial influence on market behavior [is suspect]. Entry through merger by such a company, although its competitive conduct in the market may be the mirror image of the acquired company, may nevertheless violate section 7 because the entry eliminates a potential competitor exercising present influence on the market. . . .

In the case before us, Falstaff was not a competitor in the New England market nor is it contended that its merger with Narragansett represented an entry by a dominant market force. . . . The District Court, however, relying heavily on testimony of Falstaff officers, concluded that the company had no intent to enter the New England market except through acquisition, and that it therefore could not be considered a potential competitor in that market. Having put aside Falstaff as a potential *de nova* competitor, it followed for the District Court that entry by a merger would not adversely affect competition in New England.

The District Court erred as a matter of law. The error lay in the assumption that because Falstaff, as a matter of fact, would never have entered the market *de nova*, it could in no sense be considered a potential competitor. More specifically, the District Court failed to give separate consideration to whether Falstaff was a potential competitor in the sense that it was so positioned on the edge of the market that it exerted a beneficial influence on competitive conditions in that market.

The specific question with respect to this phase of the case is not what Falstaff's internal company decisions were but whether, given its financial capabilities and conditions in the New England market, it would be reasonable to consider it a potential entrant into that market. . . . This does not mean that the testimony of company officials about actual intentions of the company is irrelevant or is to be looked upon with suspicion; but it does mean that theirs is not necessarily the last word in arriving at a conclusion about how Falstaff should be considered in terms of its status as a potential entrant into the market in issue.

. . . We leave for another day the question of the applicability of section 7 to a merger that will leave competition in the marketplace exactly as it was, neither hurt nor helped, and that is challengeable under section 7 only on grounds that the company could, but did not, enter *de nova* or through "toe-hold" acquisition and that there is less competition than there would have been had entry been in such a manner.

[Reversed.]

## Case Discussion Questions

1  Assume you are the owner of a medium-sized brewery in New England. How do you view Falstaff before the merger? Do you change your competitive behavior in any way because you think Falstaff may enter the market if it becomes attractive enough? After the merger with Narragansett takes place, how do you act?

2  Why doesn't it matter that Falstaff would never have entered through *de nova* entry or a toehold acquisition?

3  If Falstaff had entered through *de nova* entry or a toehold acquisition, what would have been the effect on competition?

**Potential Competition and Product Extension Mergers**    Product extension mergers involve acquisitions between firms that stand at the edge of a product market, in much the same manner that market extension mergers involve firms that stand at the edge of a geographic market. The potential competition doctrine is applicable to product extension mergers in exactly the same way that it applies to a market extension merger.

For example, in *FTC v. Procter & Gamble Co.*,[5] Procter wished to move into the household-bleach market. At the time, Procter was the largest producer of soaps and other household products but did not produce bleach. The bleach market was unique, in the sense that Clorox had 49% of the market, Purex had 16% of the market, 3 other firms had 25%, and the remaining 10% of the market was divided between 200 small producers. Procter was the most likely "potential competitor," and it was clear that the participants in the bleach market feared Procter's entry, primarily because Procter had a huge advertising budget and volume discounts from television networks.

Procter could have entered *de nova* or through a toe-hold merger with any of the smaller bleach producers and probably could have created a much more competitive market for bleach. Instead, it chose to merge with Clorox. The Supreme Court held the merger illegal on the grounds that (1) Procter was no longer a potential competitor and (2) Procter had merged with Clorox, creating an even more concentrated market for bleach.

---

5  386 U.S. 568, 87 S. Ct. 1224, 18 L. Ed. 2d 303 (1967).

**The Limits of Potential Competition**    The "new antitrust majority," formed by the appointments to the Court by Presidents Nixon, Ford, and Reagan, has cast some doubt on the future of the potential competition doctrine. The court imposed three requirements on the theory of potential competition in 1974:[6] (1) The target market must be concentrated, (2) an alternative method of entry must be available to the acquiring firm, and (3) that method must offer a prospect of competitive improvement.

**Reciprocity**    In its simplest terms, *reciprocity* means "I'll buy from you if you will buy from me." Although reciprocity may be good business, the emergence of giant conglomerates greatly complicates the issue and introduces possible anticompetitive effects to the practice. Such firms often have complex and far-reaching effects in markets not their own. If a merger promotes reciprocity or is undertaken to promote reciprocity, the merger may be challenged.

For example, in *FTC v. Consolidated Foods Corp.*,[7] a major distributor of food products was a major purchaser from food processors. Consolidated merged with Gentry, a manufacturer of dehydrated spices. Consolidated then informed the food processors from whom it purchased food that it expected them to purchase Gentry spices, with the implied threat that Consolidated would withhold purchases from processors who failed to "reciprocate."

**The Deep-Pocket Theory: Is "Bigness" Bad?**    No antitrust case has held that the size of a firm is itself a reason to deny a merger. Mergers must contain some definable anticompetitive effect before the courts will hold them illegal. Many theorists argue that size has such anticompetitive effects, however. The principal effect of size and diversification is described by the **deep-pocket theory,** in which a firm may subsidize one branch of its business with monopoly profits from other branches. The firm may undercut the prices of competitors to the subsidized branch and drive those competitors from the market through **predatory pricing,** ultimately achieving a monopoly. Once a monopoly is attained in that branch, the firm may charge monopoly prices for that branch's products and subsidize other branches of the firm.

Although the deep-pocket theory has been argued in academic circles for years, no court has held a pure conglomerate merger unlawful. In 1969 the Justice Department moved against International Telephone & Telegraph (ITT), charging it with a violation of section 7 because of its acquisitions in various industries—hotels, insurance, finance, rental cars, baking, and many others. The government's case was based on several theories, including reciprocity, foreclosure of competition, and sheer financial power. The trial court ordered divestiture of a few firms where it found reciprocity, but it denied full divestiture on the basis of the deep-pocket theory.

> The alleged adverse effects of economic concentration brought about by merger activity, especially merger activity by large, diversified corporations such as ITT, arguably may be such that, as a matter of social and economic policy, the standard by which the legality of a

---

6 *U.S. v. Marine Bancorporation, Inc.*, 418 U.S. 602, 94 S. Ct. 2856, 41 L. Ed. 2d 978 (1974).
7 380 U.S. 592, 84 S. Ct. 1220, 14 L. Ed. 2d 95 (1965).

merger should be measured under the antitrust laws is the degree to which it may increase economic concentration—not merely the degree to which it may lessen competition. If the standard is to be changed, however, in the opinion of this court it is fundamental under our system of government that that determination be made by the Congress and not by the courts. . . . "[8]

---

## PRO AND CON

# Is business bigness bad?

**Pro** As John R. Kuhlman explains,

I have never been in a lifeboat with an elephant and furthermore, I never *want* to be in a lifeboat with an elephant. In my imagination, anyway, I can see the elephant trying to make himself comfortable. As he moves forward, the aft portion of the boat rises out of the water. As he moves from side to side, I scramble to keep from falling out of the boat. In short, a lifeboat with one very large passenger and one very small passenger has to be an unstable platform and it has to be more unstable than would a lifeboat with the same total amount of weight distributed equally over a large number of passengers. My "ideal society" also consists of a large number of small units. Just as I don't know whether I could coexist with an elephant in a lifeboat, neither am I sure that I can coexist with a small number of very large units in the social system. . . . [9]

The analogy of an elephant in a lifeboat poses the central problem of big business in a democratic society. Power—whether economic, social, or political—*cannot* be centralized in a democracy. The definition of a democratic system (and of a competitive system) requires a *diffusion* of power, so that no one person or group can determine public policy (or price or output).

Just as a dictatorship is an "efficient" form of government, big business claims that it is more "efficient" than many small producers. But economies of scale only bring about efficiency *to a point*. Otherwise, the most efficient form of farm would be one large farm, or the most efficient auto producer would

be one large company. The problem is, no one knows—or can know—just where that point is. Since we have to determine policy, it is better to err on the side of democracy, competition, and small business units.

**Con** All of the arguments against big business, including the economic ones, are based on supposition and assumption. In fact, there has been very little increase in the aggregate concentration ratio in the last thirty years.

The political arguments against big business are, in the words of one critic, "pure intellectual mush." There is absolutely no proof that political power increases with wealth or with corporate size, and even if there could be, the proper response should be through laws restricting campaign contributions and political ethics, not through economic laws such as antitrust.

The economic arguments against big business simply do not prove true. For example, the so-called "deep-pocket" theory makes no sense, because a firm is better off to drop an unprofitable line than to divert returns from a profitable activity to bolster the unprofitable one. It has been shown that if a firm has projects that promise favorable returns, the capital will be forthcoming. The result is that "bigness" does not deter new entrants, so the market is always changing. Certainly, economies of scale have their place as well.

If the choice is between restrictive laws and big business, we should err on the side of economic freedom. After all, economic freedom is essential to political freedom.

---

8 Chief Judge Timbers in *U.S. v. International Telephone & Telegraph Corp.*, 306 F. Supp. 766 (1969).
9 Dr. John M. Kuhlman, "In a Lifeboat with an Elephant: The Problem of Corporate 'Bigness,'" *Antitrust Law & Economics Review*, Vol. 12, No. 1 (1980), pp. 41–42, by permission of Antitrust Law & Economics Review, Inc., P.O. Box 3532, Vero Beach, FL 32964.

Roundtable Discussion

1   What are the advantages of big business? What are its disadvantages?

2   Is there such a thing as "economic freedom" in the American economy? Does the term refer only to political freedom?

3   Should we (and can we) place a "cap" on the size of business? Is business bigness bad?

## SECTION 2 OF THE SHERMAN ACT: MONOPOLIZATION

Perhaps the most vague of the antitrust laws is section 2 of the Sherman Act (see below). The act does not make possession of a monopoly illegal. Mere possession of monopoly power is not enough; the monopolist must have *used* this power in some way. As one of the few Supreme Court decisions dealing with section 2 noted:

> The offense of monopoly under section 2 of the Sherman Act has two elements: (1) the *possession of monopoly power* in the relevant market, and (2) the *willful acquisition or maintenance of that power* as distinguished from growth or development as a consequence of a superior product, business acumen, or historic accident."[10] [Emphasis added.]

### The Need for "Conduct": Early Cases and Predatory Practices

From the beginning the courts have required proof of *conduct* along with proof that an industry *structure* was monopolistic. The nature of that conduct and the amount of "monopoly power" that must be held have formed the twin issues in every monopolization case.

In the early cases some type of **predatory conduct** was required before a conviction could be obtained. The courts identified several types of predatory conduct.

1   *Predatory pricing.* Cutting prices below cost in certain regions or in certain product lines to force competitors out of business, and subsidizing such price cuts with monopoly profits obtained in other areas or from other products.

---

## Section 2 of the Sherman Act

Every person who shall monopolize, or attempt to monopolize, or conspire with any other person or persons to monopolize, any part of the trade or commerce among the several states, or with foreign nations, shall be deemed guilty of a felony, and, on conviction thereof, shall be punished by fine not exceeding one million dollars if a corporation, or, if any other person, one hundred thousand dollars or by imprisonment not exceeding three years, or by both said punishments, in the discretion of the court.

---

10 *U.S. v. Grinnell Corp.*, 384 U.S. 563, 86 S. Ct. 1698, 16 L. Ed. 2d 778 (1966).

**2**  *Predatory advertising and promotion.* Heavily promoting specific products or brands (sometimes called *fighting brands*) or "bogus independent" firms in order to force competitors out of business, again subsidizing the extra expense by monopoly profits in other lines.

**3**  *Advantages and rebates.* Exacting special favors from suppliers or service firms, such as railroads, resulting in cost advantages over competitors unable to exact the same favors.

**4**  *Physical violence.* Use of actual violence against competitors, customers of competitors, or competitors' products.

**5**  *Misuse of patents, copyrights and trademarks.* Use of legal monopolies to exert pressure in other markets.

**6**  *Section 1 violations.* Such tactics as refusals to deal, tie-in sales, and exclusive dealing arrangements.

As noted in a 1920 landmark decision, size alone is not illegal: "The law . . . does not make mere size an offence or the existence of unexerted power an offence. The law requires overt acts and trusts to its prohibition of them and its power to repress or punish them. It does not compel competition nor require all that is possible."[11]

In the early years, prosecutors found it far easier to challenge predatory practices under section 1 than to file monopolization charges under section 2. The requirement of proving predatory conduct in order to show monopolization resulted in two decades of dormancy for section 2. In 1945 all that changed.

### The Retreat of Predatory Practices: The *Alcoa* Case

Just as merger law is based on the *Brown Shoe* case, the law surrounding section 2 cases is based on one case, *U.S. v. Aluminum Company of America (ALCOA).*[12] The case arose in 1945 and involved some very strange procedural facts. After a three-year trial, the government's case against Alcoa was dismissed by the trial judge, who felt that mere size, without proof of predatory practices, was insufficient to prove a violation of section 2. On direct appeal, the Supreme Court could not hear the case because four justices had previously participated in the case in some way and another justice was ill. The U.S. Circuit Court of Appeals for the Second Circuit was designated the court of last resort for the case. A congressional act later made the decision of the Second Circuit "binding precedent." As a result, the decision seems to have the status of a U.S. Supreme Court decision, and it is arguable that even a Supreme Court decision could not reverse the case.

Alcoa had been originally assigned a patent on the process of manufacturing aluminum in 1889 by the inventor of the process. Until that patent and others assigned to Alcoa expired in 1909, Alcoa had either a complete monopoly of the manufacture of aluminum or of the process, which eliminated all practical competition. During the period when the patents were effective, Alcoa made agreements with electric companies that prohibited the utilities from selling electricity to any other manufacturer of alumi-

---

11  *U.S. v. U.S. Steel,* 251 U.S. 417, 40 S. Ct. 293, 64 L. Ed. 343 (1920).
12  148 F.2d 416 (2d Cir., 1945).

num. Since electricity is essential in the manufacture of aluminum, these agreements also practically eliminated all competition. Alcoa also entered into agreements with foreign manufacturers by which those foreign manufacturers agreed not to export aluminum to the United States.

**_Alcoa_ and the Problem of Relevant Market**    Part of the _Alcoa_ case dealt with the problem of the relevant product market. Alcoa alone manufactured aluminum from ore. But such "virgin" aluminum had some competition in the form of "secondary" aluminum, that is, aluminum recycled from aluminum already used, such as scraps from plants using aluminum to fabricate items, or from used items, such as kitchen utensils. If all aluminum was defined as the market, including secondary aluminum and such foreign aluminum as existed outside of the cartels, Alcoa had only 33% of the market. But if the market was defined as only virgin aluminum, Alcoa had 91% of the market. The court held that since all "secondary" aluminum had once been "virgin" aluminum, Alcoa could control that market through the "virgin" market, and it found that Alcoa had monopoly power.

**"Good Trusts" and "Bad Trusts"**    Alcoa also argued that it had not obtained "extortionate" profits, because its profits had averaged only 10%. To this, the Court replied, in an oft-quoted remark,

> But the whole issue is irrelevant anyway, for it is no excuse for "monopolizing" a market that the monopoly has not been used to extract from the consumer more than a "fair" profit. The Act has wider purposes. . . . Many people believe that possession of unchallenged economic power deadens initiative, discourages thrift and depresses energy; that immunity from competition is a narcotic, and rivalry is a stimulant, to industrial progress; that the spur of constant stress is necessary to counteract an inevitable disposition to let well enough alone. . . . Congress . . . did not condone "good trusts" and condemn "bad" ones, it forbad all. Moreover, in so doing it was not necessarily actuated by economic motives alone. . . .

**_Alcoa_ and the Need for Conduct Revisited**    The Court then considered the knotty problem of the need for some kind of _conduct_ as required by the old cases. All of Alcoa's conduct, while ethically suspect, was _legal_ at the time it was done. The question was whether Alcoa's _use_ of monopoly power violated section 2. The Court, in several memorable phrases, said that it had.

The Court argued that monopoly itself is illegal only if it is "thrust upon" a company. "The only question is whether [Alcoa] falls within the exception established in favor of those who do not seek, but cannot avoid, the control of the market." The Court gave several examples of the **thrust-upon** defense, including markets that are too small or capital requirements that are too large to support more than one producer, or declining markets, driving all but one producer from the market.

Perhaps the most questionable exception reserved by the Court was for "a single . . . survivor out of a group of active competitors, merely by virtue of his superior skill, foresight and industry." The Court said that "the successful competitor, having been urged to compete, must not be turned upon when he wins."

Having said that, the Court concluded that Alcoa had indeed monopolized the aluminum market.

> It was not inevitable that it should always anticipate increases in the demand for ingot and be prepared to supply them. Nothing compelled it to keep doubling and redoubling its capacity before others entered the field. It insists that it never excluded competitors; but we can think of no more effective exclusion than progressively to embrace each new opportunity as it opened, and to face every newcomer with new capacity already geared into a great organization, having the advantage of experience, trade, connections and the elite of personnel.

Alcoa had also argued that the government had not proven an "intent to monopolize." But the Court disregarded the question of intent:

> In order to fall within §2, the monopolist must have both the power to monopolize, and the intent to monopolize, To read the passage as demanding any "specific" intent makes nonsense of it, for no monopolist monopolizes unconscious of what he is doing. So here, "Alcoa" meant to keep and did keep, that complete and exclusive hold upon the ingot market. . . .

The *Alcoa* decision did not do away with the need for some type of conduct to go along with proof of monopoly power, but the decision radically changed the definition of that conduct. No longer would the courts require predatory or abusive conduct; instead, they would require proof of a general intent to monopolize, which may be proven, as in *Alcoa*, by proof of *legal* actions taken to maintain or obtain that power.

The *Alcoa* decision has never been reversed by the Supreme Court, but it has never been expressly adopted either. In 1966 the Supreme Court decided *U.S. v. Grinnell Corporation*, quoted at the beginning of this section, and seemed to reach similar results in the portion quoted. Some observers believe that *Grinnell* did away with the thrust-upon defense found in *Alcoa*, because under the quoted language even monopoly lawfully achieved may be maintained unlawfully. The point remains unclear.

After the *Alcoa* decision, the law respecting monopolization did not change to any extent. Few section 2 cases are filed. Although the language of *Alcoa* would seem to give antitrust prosecutors substantial weapons with which to attack the giants of American industry, those attacks have not come. Part of the reason is that section 2 cases are among the largest and most complex legal actions in American law. Another reason is the language of *Alcoa* itself. As a court of appeals decision noted, "[T]he cryptic *Alcoa* opinion is a litigant's wishing well, into which, it sometimes seems, one may peer and find nearly anything he wishes."[13]

## Relevant Market in Section 2 Cases

Section 2 also requires that the monopolization be of "any part of the trade or commerce among the several States, or with the foreign nations." If a business has a large enough share of a market, it is presumed to have monopoly power over that market. But

---

13 Kaufman, J., in *Berkey Photo, Inc. v. Eastman-Kodak Co.*, 603 F.2d 263 (2d Cir., 1979).

a central question is the definition of the *market* over which it has such power. This crucial concept of the relevant market is identical to the determination of relevant market in merger cases under section 7 of the Clayton Act. Monopolization must occur in some *relevant geographic market* and in some *relevant product market*, just as in merger cases.

## The Problem of Monopoly Power

After the relevant market has been defined, the next question is whether, within that relevant market, a firm has monopoly power. The term *monopoly power* has been defined as *the power to control prices or exclude competition*. The existence of such monopoly power may usually be inferred from the market share of the defendant. A firm need not be the sole occupant of a market, but its market share must be so predominant that it may unilaterally affect prices or exclude competitors. The Supreme Court has not fastened on any clear percentage of the market that would automatically confer market power on a firm.

Most section 2 cases have involved market shares in excess of 75%, but at least one case involved a market share of exactly 50%, and several cases have involved shares of 50% to 75%. Judge Learned Hand wrote in the *Alcoa* decision that any percentage over ninety "is enough to constitute a monopoly; it is doubtful whether sixty . . . would be enough; and certainly thirty-three percent is not."

## The Theory of Shared Monopoly

Section 2 also outlaws *conspiracy* to monopolize. In 1945 a Supreme Court decision applied that portion of the act to an oligopolistic industry. The issue is whether section 2 reaches an industry in which a few giant firms control the industry and use similar pricing, advertising, or other competitive actions.

In *American Tobacco Company v. U.S.*,[14] the government charged the three largest tobacco companies with conspiracy to monopolize under section 2. The evidence showed no agreement between the firms, but rather a "clear course of dealing," the Court's term for parallel action. The Supreme Court affirmed the convictions entered in the lower court, and in doing so stated:

> A correct interpretation of the statute and/or the authorities makes it the crime of monopolizing, under §2 of the Sherman Act, for parties, as in these cases, to combine or conspire to acquire or maintain the power to exclude competitors from any part of the trade or commerce . . . provided they also have such a power that they are able, *as a group*, to exclude actual or potential competition from the field and provided that they have the intent and purpose to exercise that power. [Emphasis added.]
>
> It is not the form of the combination or the particular means used but the result to be achieved that the statute condemns. It is not of importance whether the means used to accomplish the unlawful objective are in themselves wholly innocent acts. Yet, if they are part of the sum of the acts which are relied upon to effectuate the conspiracy which the statute forbids, they come within its prohibition. No formal agreement is necessary to constitute an unlawful conspiracy.

---

14 328 U.S. 781, 66 S. Ct. 1125, 90 L. Ed. 1575 (1945).

The *American Tobacco* case has had little impact. Even though the case contains language that would clearly make most oligopolies illegal if applied to its fullest, the case was never followed and was generally ignored as precedent. It has also never been reversed.

During the early 1970's, the FTC brought two cases against the major participants in the oil and cereal industries under the theory of **shared monopoly,** based on the *American Tobacco* case. That theory involves possession of massive market shares by a few firms and **parallel action** by the firms in setting prices or other competitive behavior. The oil case was quickly dismissed, but the cereals case lingered until 1982, when the FTC dismissed the action. Even in the light of the *American Tobacco* case, shared monopoly remains only a theory.

## Contemporary Application of Section 2

Following *Alcoa* it seemed clear that otherwise legal conduct might be wrongful under section 2, if coupled with sufficient monopoly power. But the 1970's saw, if not a retreat from that position, at least a standstill. Several private actions resulted in similar judgments by several different U.S. courts of appeal, all of which limited the use of legal actions by monopolists as proof of a violation of section 2.

The first series of cases were filed by several computer firms complaining of the actions of IBM. Allegedly, IBM had manufactured central computers (CPUs) that were incompatible with peripherals, such as disc drives, printers, and tapes, manufactured by competitors. IBM's purpose was alleged to be to make sure that purchasers of IBM computers would buy peripherals manufactured by IBM as well. At least four separate cases were filed against IBM by manufacturers of peripherals driven from the market, and the Justice Department filed an action as well. All of the private cases resulted in judgments in favor of IBM. The government action was dismissed by the Justice Department after six years of trial. As one court noted, "[IBM] was under no duty to help [competitors] survive or expand."

The second action bore some striking similarities to the IBM cases. That case involved a private action against Eastman-Kodak Company over introducing a new camera and new film together in such a way that purchasers had to buy the new camera in order to use the new film. The U.S. Circuit Court of Appeals for the Second Circuit held that Kodak's activities did not violate section 2:

> In sum, although the principles announced by the §2 cases often appear to conflict, this much is clear. The mere possession of monopoly power does not *ipso facto* condemn a market participant. But, to avoid the proscriptions of §2, the firm must refrain at all times from conduct directed at smothering competition. This doctrine has two branches. Unlawfully acquired power remains anathema even when kept dormant. And it is no less true that a firm with a legitimately achieved monopoly may not wield the resulting power to tighten its hold on the market.
>
> . . . [A]s we have indicated, a large firm does not violate §2 simply by reaping the competitive rewards attributable to its efficient size, nor does an integrated business offend the Sherman Act whenever one of its departments benefits from association with a division possessing a monopoly in its own market. So long as we allow a firm to compete in several fields, we must expect it to seek the competitive advantages of its broad-based activity — more efficient production, greater ability to develop complementary products, reduced transaction

costs, and so forth. These are gains that accrue to any integrated firm, regardless of its market share, and they cannot by themselves be considered uses of monopoly power.[15]

## THE FEDERAL TRADE COMMISSION (FTC) ACT

The Federal Trade Commission (FTC) Act, enacted in 1914 to deal in part with the problems caused by the rule of reason, prohibits all *unfair methods of competition*. The FTC Act was originally intended by Congress to act as an antitrust law. Congress established the Federal Trade Commission as an independent regulatory commission and gave it the power to enforce its rules through administrative orders (see p. 152).

A major issue in interpreting the FTC Act is whether the broad phrase *unfair methods of competition* is the same as, is different from, or overlaps with the coverage of the antitrust laws. For example, horizontal price fixing clearly violates section 1 of the Sherman Act. But horizontal price fixing might also be an "unfair method of competition" under the FTC Act. The following case considers the relationship of the FTC Act and the other antitrust laws.

---

# FTC v. Indiana Federation of Dentists
476 U.S. 574, 106 S. Ct. 2009, 90 L. Ed. 2d 445 (1986)

Since the 1970's, dental health insurers have limited payment of benefits to the cost of the "least expensive yet adequate treatment." In order to make such judgments, insurers often request dentists to submit X-rays for evaluation prior to payment of a claim. The members of the Indiana Federation of Dentists, a state association of dentists, agreed among themselves to refuse to submit X-rays to insurers on the grounds that (1) nondentists who evaluated the X-rays were not competent to do so and (2) the plans posed a threat to the economic well-being of dentists.

The FTC issued a complaint against the federation, alleging that the refusal was an "unfair method of competition." After a hearing before an Administrative Law Judge, the commission issued a cease and desist order directed at the federation. The federation appealed to the U.S court of appeals, which reversed the commission's order. The FTC appealed.

**Justice White Delivered the Opinion of the Court** The issue is whether the Commission erred in holding that the Federation's policy of refusal to submit X-rays to dental insurers for use in benefits determinations constituted an "unfair method of competition," unlawful under . . . the FTC Act. . . . The standard of "unfairness" under the FTC Act is, by necessity, an elusive one, encompassing not only practices that violate the Sherman Act and other antitrust laws, but also practices that the Commission determines are against public policy for other reasons. . . . In the case now before us, the sole basis of the FTC's finding of an unfair method of competition was the Commission's conclusion that the Federation's collective decision to withhold X-rays from insurers was an unreasonable and conspiratorial restraint of trade in violation of §1 of the Sherman Act. . . .

Application of the Rule of Reason to these facts is not a matter of any great difficulty. The Federa-

---

**15** *Berkey Photo, Inc. v. Eastman Kodak Co.*, 603 F.2d 263 (2d Cir., 1979).

tion's policy takes the form of a horizontal agreement among the participating dentists to withhold from their customers a particular service that they desire—the forwarding of X-rays to insurance companies. . . . A refusal to compete with respect to the package of services offered to customers, no less than a refusal to compete with respect to the price term of an agreement, impairs the ability of the market to advance social welfare by ensuring the provision of desired goods and services to consumers at a price approximating the marginal cost of providing them. Absent some countervailing procompetitive virtue—such as, for example, the creation of efficiencies in the operation of a market or the provision of goods and services—such an agreement limiting consumer choice by impeding the "ordinary give and take of the market place" cannot be sustained under the Rule of Reason. [The Court found no such "countervailing procompetitive virtue".—Ed.]

[Reversed.]

### Case Discussion Questions

1   Could the actions of the dentists have been challenged under section 1 of the Sherman Act?
2   What is "unfairness" under the FTC Act?
3   Why does the Court apply the rule of reason in this case? What does that standard mean here?

---

The FTC Act covers not only *all* of the ground covered by the other antitrust laws but also matters that lie between, or outside of, those laws. The coverage of the FTC Act is described in Figure 21.7.

## INTERNATIONAL ASPECTS OF ANTITRUST

One of the principal arguments against traditional antitrust analysis is that domestic American producers are placed at a disadvantage by restrictive antitrust enforcement, because foreign firms may not be subject to antitrust laws in their own countries. In fact, many nations have antitrust laws, many modeled on the American antitrust system. The activities of *American* firms abroad are subject to the antitrust laws, but some special defenses have arisen, such as the legality of cartels in certain nations or the need to come to an agreement with a foreign competitor in order to enter a foreign market. In addition, the *American* activities of foreign firms are clearly subject to American antitrust laws.[16] The biggest problem deals with the *foreign* activities of *foreign* firms. The following case discusses that problem.

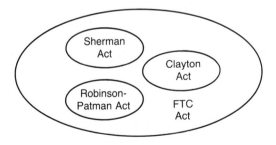

FIGURE 21.7    Coverage of the FTC Act

---

16 *BOC International v. FTC*, 557 F.2d 24 (2d Cir., 1977).

## Matsushita Electric Industrial Co., Ltd. v. Zenith Radio Corp.

475 U.S. 574, 106 S. Ct. 1348, 89 L. Ed. 2d 538 (1986)

Zenith and other American firms alleged that over a twenty-year period, several Japanese corporations had engaged in a course of conduct to drive American firms from the consumer electronic products market, especially the market for TVs. The scheme involved a price-fixing agreement *in Japan* to set prices high, thereby permitting the firms to charge *low* prices for goods shipped to the United States. The agreements in Japan included (1) formal agreements arranged through Japan's Ministry of International Trade and Industry (MITI) to fix certain *minimum* prices, or "check prices" for products exported to the United States; and (2) agreements to distribute their products in the United States according to a "five-company rule," which provided that each Japanese producer was permitted to sell to only five American distributors. Zenith also alleged an agreement to illegally undercut the "check prices" in violation of the formal MITI agreements.

Zenith charged that these agreements violated sections 1 and 2 of the Sherman Act, the Robinson-Patman Act, and a variety of other laws. The district court granted summary judgment in favor of the Japanese firms, but the court of appeals reversed. The Japanese firms appealed.

**Justice Powell Delivered the Opinion of the Court**    We begin by emphasizing what respondents' claim is *not*. Respondents cannot recover antitrust damages based solely on an alleged cartelization of the Japanese market, because American antitrust laws do not regulate the competitive conditions of other nations' economies. Nor can respondents recover damages for any conspiracy by petitioners to charge higher than competitive prices in the American market. Such conduct would indeed violate the Sherman Act, but it could not injure respondents: as petitioners' competitors, respondents stand to gain from any conspiracy to raise the market price. . . . [F]or the same reason, respondents cannot recover for a conspiracy to impose nonprice restraints that have the effect of either raising market price or limiting output. Such restrictions, though harmful to competition, actually *benefit* competitors. . . . Thus, neither petitioners' alleged supracompetitive pricing in Japan, nor the 5-company rule that limited distribution in this country, nor the check prices insofar as they established minimum prices in this country, can by themselves give respondents a . . . claim against petitioners for antitrust damages.

Respondents nevertheless argue that these supposed conspiracies . . . are circumstantial evidence of another conspiracy . . . to monopolize the Amer-

ican market by means of pricing below the market level. The thrust of respondents' argument is that petitioners used their monopoly profits from the Japanese market to fund a concerted campaign to price predatorily and thereby drive respondents . . . out of business. Once successful, according to respondents, petitioners would cartelize the American . . . market, restricting output and raising prices above the level that fair competition would produce. . . . The issue in this case thus becomes whether respondents adduced sufficient evidence. . . .

[The Court found that there was no direct evidence of a conspiracy to monopolize through predatory pricing, and that it could not infer such an agreement because predatory pricing is "inherently implausible." Predatory pricing requires a firm to forgo present profits for speculative future profits, and the Court would not presume such a potentially irrational motivation. The Court reversed, but Justices White, Brennan, Blackmun, and Marshall dissented.—Ed.]

Case Discussion Questions

1    If the Japanese firms had undertaken these activities in the United States, could they be challenged under section 1 of the Sherman Act?

**2**  Is it really so unreasonable to suppose that firms will forgo short-run profits for long-run profits by undercutting competitors? Is such behavior irrational?

**3**  Is this "dumping" under federal antidumping statutes? (See p. 184.) If such behavior is so irrational, why do we have antidumping statutes?

## BUSINESS STRUCTURE IN THE YEAR 2000: TRENDS AND ENFORCEMENT POLICIES

With the election of President Reagan in 1980 came both hopes and fears that merger and monopolization enforcement policies would be relaxed. Critics of antitrust enforcement had argued that enforcement of the law emasculated American business in the face of international competition. Even Douglas Fraser, former president of the United Auto Workers, finds that "the problem of monopolistic practices" has become "a completely moot question now in the auto industry because you have the fierce competition with the Japanese. You don't have to break up General Motors; they've got all they can handle from foreign competition. Even if GM would gobble up Chrysler and Ford now, the competition is so stiff from the Japanese that it wouldn't be a tragedy anymore."[17] Fraser believes the mergers between giant firms are beneficial if they strengthen companies and save the jobs of workers in the industry. Other critics have found antitrust enforcement outmoded in the new competitive atmosphere.

The 1980's also saw the rise of the so-called *Chicago School* of economics and antitrust. According to the Chicago School, the sole reason for antitrust law was "consumer welfare," and economies of scale usually meant that larger firms charged lower consumer prices, at least in the short run. The Chicago School—named for the University of Chicago, where many of its proponents were educated—had a huge influence on the Reagan Administration's antitrust policies. Proponents of the Chicago School include economist Milton Friedman, Supreme Court Justice Antonin Scalia, and unsuccessful Supreme Court nominees Robert Bork and Douglas Ginsburg.

The critics' hopes and the proponents' fears were justified. Several moves took place in the early 1980's that indicated a relaxed attitude toward business size among the enforcing authorities. Attorney General William French Smith held that "[b]igness does not necessarily mean badness." The 1984 merger guidelines eliminated references to reciprocity completely and made only vague references to conglomerate mergers. Funding for FTC enforcement of the antitrust laws was almost eliminated entirely. And the Justice Department permitted, after premerger notification, many of the largest mergers in American history.

Proponents of antitrust enforcement point not only to the economic power of such large firms in their respective markets, but also to the political and social power of such firms. Such critics point to the bureaucratic hazards of large institutions, complacency toward innovation, and general corporate "arteriosclerosis." Young people entering careers in such corporations have less choice of employers and a much longer climb up the corporate ladder. Such critics also point to probable loss of community responsibility and the ability of such corporate giants to influence both political events, through their lobbying efforts, and political attitudes, through "advocacy advertising."

---

17 Quoted in *The Wall Street Journal*, July 8, 1981.

Perhaps the largest problem in antitrust enforcement is the attitude of Americans toward corporate size. As several experts have pointed out, the American public is schizophrenic about business size. On the one hand, we admire corporate bigness and those who run huge firms. On the other hand, we fear such size and the power it brings. Perhaps the antitrust dilemma cannot be resolved until our attitudes toward size are resolved.

## SUMMARY AND CONCLUSIONS

The antitrust laws regulate mergers through section 7 of the Clayton Act. All types of integration of firms are covered by the statute, including mergers, consolidations, purchases of stock, purchases of assets, and joint ventures. The purpose of the regulation of mergers is to protect competition by outlawing any merger that "substantially lessens competition."

The prohibitions of section 7 extend to horizontal, vertical, and some types of conglomerate mergers. The prime anticompetitive effect of a horizontal merger is the removal of a competitor from the market. The major impact of vertical mergers involves the barriers to entry to the market and the necessary difficulty competitors have in reaching the market or source of supplies of the firms involved. The principal anticompetitive effects of conglomerate mergers are reciprocity and the potential competition doctrine.

Every merger case involves a determination of the relevant product market and the relevant geographic market. Relevant product market refers to the line of commerce in which the anticompetitive effect is felt, whereas the relevant geographic market refers to the physical area in which the impact is felt. Current debate centers around the proper sphere of conglomerate mergers, particularly the dimensions of the potential competition doctrine and the place of pure size in antitrust theory.

Section 2 of the Sherman Act prohibits *monopolization*, and the act's wording has given rise to the argument between advocates of structure alone as proof of a violation of the act and advocates of conduct, who would require some use of monopoly power before a conviction could be obtained. The courts require two elements to prove monopolization: "(1) the possession of monopoly power in the relevant market, and (2) the willful acquisition or maintenance of that power. . . . " Usually that means a fairly large market share and some conduct to show an "intent to monopolize" by attaining or maintaining a monopoly position. Thus, some form of conduct is required for conviction, but that conduct need not be illegal. Traditionally, some form of predatory or abusive conduct has been required.

## REVIEW QUESTIONS

1   Is business concentration inevitable? Is antitrust simply fighting a holding action against the necessary growth in concentration that comes with economic success?

2   Explain the concept of relevant market in the context of both mergers and monopolization.

3   Explain the differences between horizontal,

vertical, product extension, market extension, and pure conglomerate mergers. How is each treated by the antitrust laws?

**4** What is monopolization? Explain the concepts of monopoly power, predatory practices, and willful acquisition or maintenance of monopoly power.

**5** Calculate the HHI of the following markets: (a) a four-firm market, with market shares of 30%, 30%, 20%, and 20%; (b) a one-firm market with 100% of the market; (c) a ten-firm market, each with 10% of the market; (d) a ten-firm market, one firm with 55% of the market, the rest with 5% each; (e) seventy-one firms, one with 30% of the market, the rest with 1% of the market each. Rank them in competitiveness.

**6** Should competition from foreign countries dictate our domestic policy toward business? Always? Aren't the antitrust laws an anachronism in the new international business environment? Explain how other countries might have a competitive advantage because of the antitrust laws. Aren't there other reasons why the antitrust laws may still be necessary or desirable?

**7** Von's Grocery Company, the third-largest retail grocery chain in Los Angeles, merged with Shopping Bag Food Stores, the sixth-largest food chain in the same area. Von's operated 27 stores, and Shopping Bag had 34. The two chains together had 7.5% of the retail grocery market in Los Angeles. There were over 3,000 independent grocers in the city, although the number was declining, and 150 other "chains," which were growing. A chain is defined as at least two stores owned by the same firm. What is the relevant geographic market? What impact does this merger have on competition? Does this merger violate section 7? [*U.S. v. Von's Grocery Company*, 384 U.S. 270, 86 S. Ct. 1478, 16 L. Ed. 2d 555 (1966).]

**8** Following the *Falstaff* case, assume that Bardolph Brewing Company is acquired by the Falstaff company. Bardolph Brewing is the second-largest brewer in New England, after Narragansett, with 12% of the market, and has provided stiff competition for Narragansett for years. What result would you expect? What if Falstaff were to merge instead with Pym Brewing Company, one of the smallest brewers in the area, with only 2% of the market?

**9** Grinnell Corporation, a manufacturer of plumbing and fire sprinkler systems, owns controlling interest in ADT, which provides burglary and fire-protection services; AFA, which provides only fire-protection services; and Holmes, which provides only burglary-protection services. Each provides "central station service," which means that in the event of a fire or break-in, electronic signals are received by the station and guards or fire equipment are dispatched. ADT has 73% of the market for both services, AFA has 12.5% of the fire business, and Holmes has 2% of the burglary business. Grinnell argued that the relevant market should include night guards, guard dogs, and other services or should be divided into fire and burglary sectors. What result would you expect under §2 of the Sherman Act? [*U.S. v. Grinnell Corp.*, 384 U.S. 563, 86 S. Ct. 1698, 16 L. Ed. 2d 778 (1966).]

**10** Are the automobile, oil, computer, TV broadcasting, rubber, farm equipment, soft drink, beer, distilling, or banking businesses illegal under the *shared monopoly* theory?

# The Firm and Its Investors

The relationship between the firm and its investors is odd indeed. On one hand, the investors are the owners of the business and, therefore, should exert control over the business and its dealings. But on the other hand, investors are often more like customers of a business, buying and selling interests in the business for a profit, often not caring about the control they might exercise.

Legal controls on the firm-investor relationship are quite new, dating back a mere half-century (a twinkling of the legal eye). Those controls grew out of a storm of protests over unethical conduct by investors and securities professionals that many believed caused, or helped to cause, the Great Depression of the 1930's.

In a large sense, securities laws provide the clearest example of the regulation of ethical conduct by the law. First, those laws are disclosure laws and require persons selling securities to inform potential investors fully of the nature of the securities they are purchasing. And second, those laws provide some of the clearest expressions of the ethical standards of society in their "antifraud" provisions, which outlaw insider trading and related conduct.

# C H A P T E R  2 2

# Securities Law

> *Publicity is justly commended as a remedy for social and industrial diseases. Sunlight is said to be the best of disinfectants; electric light the most efficient policeman.*
>
> LOUIS D. BRANDEIS
> *Other People's Money* (1932)

The health of the American economy depends on the ability of business to obtain money from private investors. That money may flow either through the capital markets, such as the various stock exchanges, or through private financing and direct investment of funds in business. Although the New York Stock Exchange has existed continuously since 1792, most capital was invested directly until after the Civil War.

During the 1920's, capital flowed into the stock market in ever-increasing amounts. The market crash of 1929 impoverished many Americans and resulted in a demand for government control of the stock markets. The result was federal regulation of the securities industry and the creation of the **Securities and Exchange Commission** (SEC) to regulate the securities markets.

## THE CAPITAL MARKETS

If it was difficult to buy or sell securities, many potential investors would find other places to invest their money, and firms would be deprived of needed capital. Two sets of markets for securities have developed to make securities freely transferable. Those markets are known as the **exchange markets** and the **over-the-counter (OTC) markets.** The exchange markets consist of the two national exchanges, the *New York Stock Exchange (NYSE)* and the *American Stock Exchange (AMEX)*, and several regional exchanges located in major cities. All of the exchanges have adopted strict rules concerning which stocks may be listed and traded on those exchanges. In addition, the **National Association of Securities Dealers (NASD)**, a private association of securities dealers, imposes rules regarding the securities they trade. Together the rules of the exchanges and the NASD form a rather effective system of self-regulation.

The over-the-counter (OTC) market has no physical location. The OTC market is the exchange of securities not listed on any national or regional stock exchange. Unlisted securities include stocks or debt securities of small local companies and those of large nationwide firms that have chosen not to list their securities on any of the exchanges. Such stock may be available directly from the company in the case of smaller firms, or from stockbrokers registered with the SEC.

In 1975, Congress instructed the SEC to "facilitate the establishment" of a national market system linking the exchanges and OTC markets. A consolidated system for reporting volume and price information was installed between the NYSE and the AMEX in 1976, and a uniform quotation system for all securities was introduced in 1978.

**The Role of Underwriters**   Securities issued by a firm may be sold by the firm directly to the public, instead of through the exchanges or other markets. Such direct sales are often complex and beyond the expertise of the company itself. To avoid those difficulties, a securities issuer will usually enlist the aid of an **underwriter,** who renders financial advice and serves as manager of the issue. Such underwriters are often **investment bankers,** as distinguished from more traditional commercial bankers. Investment bankers do not accept deposits from the public and generally specialize in the marketing of securities. They are experts in setting the price of securities and exploring the ways securities may be marketed.

**The Role of Securities Professionals**   The intermediaries in the capital markets are the securities professionals, classified by the federal law as **brokers, dealers,** and **investment advisers.** A *broker* is a person engaged in the business of making transactions in securities for the account of others, whereas a *dealer* is engaged in the business of buying and selling securities for its own account. Often a single firm or individual will be able to transact both kinds of business and will be known as a **broker-dealer.** An *investment adviser* is a person who advises others regarding securities for compensation. All three types of professionals must register with the SEC and are subject to regulation.

### Stock Market Abuses and the Great Depression

The most influential events in the history of securities law were the stock market crash of 1929 and the Great Depression of the 1930's which followed the crash. By one estimate, over 55% of all personal savings in the late 1920's was invested in corporate stocks, usually through the exchange markets. The aggregate value of all stocks in 1929 was $89 billion, but by 1932 that value had plummeted to $15 billion. The resulting loss of savings, unemployment, and general misery directly caused the election of President Franklin D. Roosevelt in 1932, the implementation of the New Deal, and vast changes in government. One of those changes was federal regulation of securities.

In Senate hearings in 1932 and 1933, large securities traders and dealers were found to have been involved in a series of stock practices and manipulations that played a large part in bringing about the crash and the Depression. Those practices included market manipulation, insider trading, fraud, excess margin trading, and underwriting practices.

**Market Manipulation**   Large traders and dealers may manipulate the price of stock through a variety of techniques. One of the most useful is **wash sales.** Some investors judge a stock in part by its volume (how many shares are traded during a given length of time) on the assumption that active stocks will rise. Large traders can affect the value of a stock by artificially inflating the number of shares traded by buying and selling matched orders of a stock. The price will then go up, and the trader can sell remaining shares in the company at a profit.

**Insider Trading and Fraud**   Corporate officers and other **insiders** were often able to take advantage of developments within their own companies, sometimes by delaying the announcement of oil strikes, research, mergers, or financial gains and losses while the "insiders" bought or sold stock in their firm. Officers, large traders, and brokers also sometimes indulged in actual fraud to encourage investment in a particular company. One Senate report found that most of the stocks made worthless by the 1929 crash had been sold in transactions marked by fraud.

**Margin Trading**   Many investors entered the market on credit, or on **margin,** during the 1920's. There was no limit to the amount of credit that might be extended by a broker-dealer at that time, and some investors purchased stock with as little as 5% or 10% down. There was no problem as long as the market continued to go up. But if the market went down, the broker would insist on partial payment for the stock, at least to make up the difference between the new lower price and the borrowed amount. If a broker "called the margin," the investor might have to sell other stock to pay the margin. This in turn resulted in price declines and margin calls in other stocks. Once a general decline in the market began, it was difficult to stop.

**Commercial Bank Underwriting and Investing**   During the 1920's, many commercial banks (banks that accepted deposits and made loans to the general public) established subsidiary firms specializing in underwriting securities issues. Underwriters often traded heavily in the shares of their clients, and so did the commercial banks.

After the market began to decline in 1929, the banks began to lose money on their investments and were unable to meet their depositors' demands for their cash. This resulted in both bank closings and demands by the banks for full payment of outstanding loans, including mortgages on homes and farms, and resulted in a huge number of foreclosures on the homes and farms.

**The Call for Regulation**   Following Senate hearings in 1932 and 1933, it became clear that stock market abuses were a major cause of the Depression of the 1930's. It was also clear that state regulation had been ineffective. The result was an immediate call for federal regulation. Before we discuss the resulting federal statutes, it is necessary to consider briefly the state laws regulating the securities industry.

## State Blue Sky Laws

The first state regulation of securities was adopted in Kansas in 1911, to be followed quickly by similar regulations in many other states. Such laws are generally called **blue sky laws,** because in the words of an early court decision,[1] such laws prohibited "schemes that have no more basis than so many feet of blue sky."

State regulation of securities generally follows one of three basic forms: (1) *state brokerage-licensing laws;* (2) *antifraud statutes,* forbidding misrepresentation in the sale or purchase of securities; and (3) *registration and disclosure laws,* which require securities to be listed with the state and which require companies to provide certain information

---

1 *Hall v. Geiger-Jones,* 242 U.S. 539 (1917).

about the stock to state authorities and investors. State registration and disclosure laws sometimes require some state agency to determine whether a securities offering is "fair" or "equitable" to the public before it is made. In that sense, those state laws are more strict than federal securities laws, which do not require a finding of fairness.

State regulation of securities, while strict on its face, never proved effective. Some states did not regulate at all, and some laws were enforced inconsistently. Persons who could not sell stock in one state had only to move to another state where regulation was lax. Many state laws contained broad exemptions, and those who were prosecuted often found it easy to avoid punishment by offering to pay back the defrauded investors on condition that charges be dropped.

The **Uniform Securities Act** is intended to mesh with the federal securities laws and has been at least partially adopted in at least thirty states. The law imposes civil liability on sellers, broker-dealers, officers, and directors, and any person who "materially aids in the sale" of securities in violation of the act. Such persons may be liable to defrauded investors for the purchase price of the security or for other damages, subject in some cases to the defense of *due diligence*. That means that if officers, directors, accountants, attorneys, or others use "due diligence" to prevent fraud, they will not be liable.

## FEDERAL REGULATION OF SECURITIES

Federal regulation of securities began with the Securities Act of 1933 and the Securities and Exchange Act of 1934 and later resulted in several secondary acts applying to certain industries or actions. The most detailed regulations are found in the rules of the Securities and Exchange Commission.

### The Federal Securities Statutes: An Overview

**The Securities Act of 1933**    The **Securities Act of 1933** requires registration and disclosure of information and contains broad antifraud prohibitions. It is important to note that the registration and disclosure provisions apply only to *new issues* of securities, whereas the antifraud provisions apply to *all* sales of securities. The act does not guarantee the accuracy of the information disclosed but provides penalties for giving false or misleading information. The act in no way guarantees that an issue of securities is "fair"; instead, it is intended only to provide information to investors and to punish actual misconduct in the sale of securities.

Certain categories of offerings are exempt from registration and disclosure, including **private offerings** and offerings by governmental bodies, but the exemptions do not apply to the antifraud provisions of the act. The Federal Trade Commission was initially given authority to administer the act, but the SEC was created, and authority to administer the 1933 act was transferred to that agency in 1934.

**The Securities Exchange Act of 1934**    The **Securities Exchange Act of 1934** performs six major functions: (1) It requires *registration and disclosure* by corporations whose securities are listed on any national securities exchange; (2) it created the *Securities and Exchange Commission* (SEC), an independent regulatory commission with authority to make rules regarding the securities industries; (3) it regulates *solicitation of proxies* (rights to vote stock); (4) it requires *registration of all securities exchanges and broker-dealers* operating in interstate commerce; (5) it generally prohibits and regulates *insider trading*; and (6) it requires the SEC to conduct *market surveillance* of the securities markets. In 1964 the registration and disclosure provisions were amended to include firms whose securities are traded on the over-the-counter markets, which have assets of over $3 million and over 500 shareholders. Certain types of issuers are exempt from the registration and disclosure provisions if they are subject to comparable state regulations.

A variety of other federal laws regulate other aspects of the securities business as well, including the Public Utility Holding Company Act, the Trust Indenture Act, the Investment Company Act, the Federal Investment Advisers' Act, the Williams Act, and others (see Table 22.1).

**SEC Rules**    Most of the details of federal securities laws are found in the rules made by the Securities and Exchange Commission (SEC). Most of the federal laws dealing

TABLE 22.1    The Federal Securities Laws

| Act | Purposes |
| --- | --- |
| Securities Act of 1933 | <ul><li>Requires registration of *new* issues</li><li>Antifraud provisions apply to *all* securities</li></ul> |
| Securities Exchange Act of 1934 | <ul><li>Created SEC</li><li>Requires registration and disclosure by corporations</li><li>Regulates solicitation of proxies</li><li>Prohibits insider trading</li><li>Requires registration of securities exchanges and broker-dealers</li></ul> |
| Public Utility Holding Company Act of 1935 | <ul><li>Permits SEC to request dissolution of corporate "shells" if they have no useful purpose (the corporate "death sentence" provision)</li></ul> |
| Trust Indenture Act of 1939 | <ul><li>Regulates underlying security of stock issues by requiring security for debt securities and regulating contracts with independent trustees</li></ul> |
| Investment Company Act of 1940 | <ul><li>Requires investment companies to register with SEC; requires "honest and unbiased" management, reporting, and disclosure</li></ul> |
| Federal Investment Adviser's Act of 1940 | <ul><li>Regulates investment advisers, prohibits fraudulent practices</li></ul> |
| Williams Act of 1968 | <ul><li>Regulates tender offers; requires disclosure of information to shareholders of target company</li></ul> |
| Securities Investor Protection Act of 1970 | <ul><li>Provides protection against cash losses from broker-dealers</li></ul> |
| Foreign Corrupt Practices Act of 1977 | <ul><li>Prohibits most foreign bribery</li><li>Requires detailed record keeping</li></ul> |

with securities gave authority to the SEC to make rules regarding securities matters, and the SEC has adopted detailed regulations in most fields. Some of those rules have had important effects on the accounting profession as well, because they dictate the practices that must be followed by corporations issuing stock or other securities to be traded publicly.

## The Definition of a "Security"

Clearly the term *security* refers to corporate stocks and bonds, but the term includes many other types of transactions. The 1933 Securities Act defines a *security* as:

> . . . any note, stock, treasury stock, bond, debenture, evidence of indebtedness, certificate of interest or participation in any profit-sharing agreement, collateral-trust certificate, preorganization certificate or subscription, transferable share, investment contract, voting-trust certificate, certificate of deposit for a security, fractional undivided interest in oil, gas, or other mineral rights, or in general, any interest or instrument commonly known as a "security," or any certificate of interest or participation in, temporary or interim certificate for, receipt for, guarantee of, or warrant or right to subscribe to or purchase, any of the foregoing. (Section 2[1]).

Although the language of the statute is quite specific, some problems remain. Three major areas of controversy are (1) instruments that are not in the form of traditional stocks or bonds but are, in fact, investments; (2) matters that are called *shares of stock* or some other name used in the statute, but that are issued for noninvestment purposes; and (3) financial instruments issued by financial institutions, such as "shares" in a credit union or "certificates" of deposit.

***De Facto* Securities**   The definition of securities in the federal law is broad enough to include investment schemes that do not fit into the traditional meanings of the term *security*. The federal acts cover "investment contracts" and "certificates of interest or participation in any profit-sharing agreement," terms that cover almost every form of investment that might be devised.

The basic test was established in 1946 in the case of *SEC v. W.J. Howey Co.*,[2] where the court said that the question is whether the investor puts money "in a common enterprise and is led to expect profits from the efforts of the promoter or a third party." That case involved the sale of individual rows of orange trees, together with a service contract in which the seller agreed to care for and market the crop. The court held the sale to be a "security" for purposes of the federal securities laws and required registration and disclosure.

**Noninvestment "Stock"**   Just because something is called a *stock* does not make it one. It is a dangerous game to label something by one of the names used in the statute; but according to the courts, "[F]orm should be disregarded for substance and the emphasis should be on economic reality," as noted in *United Housing Foundation v. For-*

---

2 328 U.S. 293, 66 S. Ct. 1100, 90 L. Ed. 2d 1244 (1946).

*man.*[3] In that case, the court held that "shares of stock" in a cooperative housing project were not "securities" even in spite of their name. The test appears to be whether the investor or lender has contributed "risk capital" to the venture.

**Instruments Issued by Financial Institutions**    Many of the instruments issued by financial institutions, such as certificates of deposit, credit union shares, and others, are specifically exempt from the federal laws. But if such institutions issue instruments on which the rate of return varies with the profitability of the financial institution or with the profitability of a specific portfolio of securities, the instruments will be considered as securities under federal law.

## REGISTRATION AND DISCLOSURE REQUIREMENTS

At first, the 1933 and 1934 acts provided two separate disclosure systems, one for *new* securities in the 1933 act, and one for issuers of *existing* securities under the 1934 act. The dual system resulted in inefficiency and duplication of effort, and in the 1970's, Congress and the SEC decided to create an **integrated disclosure system** for all registration and disclosure requirements. That system is still evolving.

The purpose of registration and disclosure is to provide information to would-be investors about the stocks or other securities they may purchase. The SEC does *not* guarantee that a particular security is "fair" or a "good deal." That is for the individual investor to determine, using the information in the registration and disclosure statements.

### Registration and Disclosure Under the 1933 Act: "Going Public"

The 1933 act provides that before a security may be offered for public sale, it must be registered with the SEC. In order to meet that requirement, a firm that wants to issue a security for public sale must file with the SEC a **registration statement** containing certain required information. In addition, investors must be furnished with a **prospectus,** or selling circular, containing certain relevant information from the registration statement. The law does not guarantee the accuracy of the information in those documents, but the act not only prohibits false and misleading information under penalty of fine or imprisonment but also provides for a civil action by injured parties against any party providing false or misleading information.

In general, the registration statement must contain (1) a description of the registering firm's business and property; (2) a description of the security to be offered for sale and its relationship to the registering firm's other securities; (3) information about the management of the registering firm; and (4) financial statements prepared by independent public accountants.

**The Registration Process**    The SEC staff is available for **prefiling conferences** with firms that have questions about the registration process, although such conferences are not required. After consultation with its attorneys, accountants, and underwriters, the

---

3 421 U.S. 837, 95 S. Ct. 2051, 44 L. Ed. 2d 621 (1975).

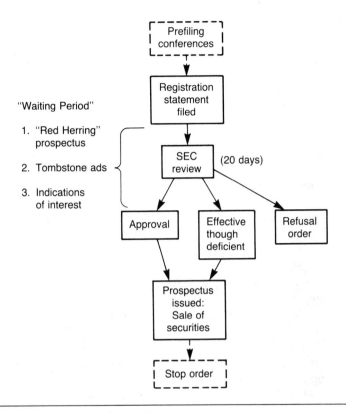

"Waiting Period"

1. "Red Herring" prospectus

2. Tombstone ads

3. Indications of interest

FIGURE 22.1    Registration of New Securities

company will prepare the registration statement. The accuracy of the statement is the responsibility of the company and its officers, the underwriters, and the independent public accountants who must audit and certify the financial documents. The statement is then delivered to the SEC. (See Figure 22.1.)

The SEC has prepared guidelines for accountants for determining whether data is "false or misleading." Those guidelines have had a massive impact on the accounting profession by supplying rules of practice that must be followed in any situation involving a public corporation.

**SEC Review and the Effective Date**    The statute provides that the **effective date** of the registration statement is twenty days after it is filed, but that date may be delayed by the SEC or accelerated at the request of the registering firm. During that period, the SEC reviews the registration statement and sends a **letter of comments** to the company. Amendments are permitted, and if amendments cannot be made within twenty days, the SEC usually requests a **delaying amendment.**

In the event of deficiencies in the registration statement, and if the firm does not amend its original statement, the SEC has three alternatives: (1) permitting the statement to become **effective though deficient** and advising the company that it may be civilly liable for actions arising from misleading information; (2) issuing a **refusal order** and scheduling a hearing within ten days after the filing date; or (3) issuing a **stop order**, either before or after the effective date, which stops further consideration of the statement before the effective date and stops further trading in the security after the effective date. Such drastic action is rarely needed, because most firms prefer to amend the statement. Because of increasing pressure on the staff of the SEC, the agency has adopted a policy of *selective review*, concentrating on areas of highest priority.

**Waiting Period Activities: Indications of Interest**     During the **waiting period** between initial filing and the effective date, the company may solicit **indications of interest** from potential investors and dealers. No contract of sale may be executed during the waiting period. An indication of interest does not obligate a party to purchase a security. An indication of interest is usually obtained in one of three ways: *oral communication* with a prospective investor; a *preliminary* or **"red herring" prospectus**; or a **tombstone ad.**

A *preliminary*, or *red herring*, *prospectus* is a circular given to potential customers similar to a *final prospectus* (see the next paragraph), but it omits information regarding the offering price, dealer commissions, and other price matters. The term *preliminary prospectus* must be stamped in red ink across the front page, and the document must contain a statement that registration is not yet effective and the securities may not yet be sold.

*Tombstone ads* are circulars or advertisements that list sources from which a prospectus may be obtained and by whom orders will be executed. Such ads commonly appear in major financial publications and must indicate that the announcement is not an offer to sell or a solicitation of offers to buy.

**The Prospectus Requirement**     The 1933 act requires every issuer subject to the act to make a **final prospectus** available not later than the delivery of a security or a confirmation of sale of a security. A *prospectus* is defined as a written communication that "offers any security for sale or confirms the sale of any security."

The prospectus must contain all of the information required in the registration statement, together with the price of the security, information about commissions to be paid by the company relating to the sale of the security, and other information relevant to the price. The **confirmation** is a piece of paper sent to a customer by a broker to confirm the transaction. The confirmation complies with the "writing" requirement of the Statute of Frauds (see p. 207).

**Exemptions**     The 1933 act exempts several types of securities from registration and disclosure: (1) private offerings, generally to private investors who have access to the kinds of information disclosed in the registration statement and prospectus and who do not intend to redistribute the securities; (2) totally intrastate offerings; (3) securities of municipal, state, and federal governments; (4) small issues not in excess of specified amounts set by the SEC; and (5) offerings of "small business investment companies."

The **small-issues** exemption, sometimes known as the **Regulation A** exemption, exempts issues up to $5 million from the general registration and disclosure requirements; but the SEC requires a simplified **offering circular,** similar to a prospectus, and the filing of a simplified *notification* to the SEC, similar to a registration statement.

## Registration and Disclosure Under the 1934 Act: Being Public

While the 1933 act requires disclosure and registration of *new issues* of securities, the 1934 act requires registration of *firms* that make public offerings of securities. Registration and disclosure are required of four types of companies: (1) firms that are listed on a national securities exchange; (2) firms whose securities are traded over the counter, if the firm's total assets exceed $3 million or if the firm has over 500 shareholders; (3) firms that elect to comply with the act; and (4) firms with over 500 shareholders of a class of securities registered under the 1933 act.

Annual reports and quarterly reports are required, and if certain events take place, a current report must be filed as well. The annual report, also known as a 10-K Report, must contain audited financial reports for the last two fiscal years; a summary of earnings and management analysis for the past five fiscal years; a brief description of the business; a "line of business" or "product line" report for the last five fiscal years; identification of directors and officers; identification of the principal market(s) in which securities are traded; and the range of market prices and dividends for each quarter of the last two fiscal years.

The quarterly report, also known as a 10-Q Report, updates the annual report at the close of each quarter and contains the same information as the annual report, reduced to quarterly segments. Legal proceedings, changes in securities, defaults, and other information must also be included in all reports. Current reports, known as 8-K Reports, may be required anytime, if certain events take place, including changes in control, acquisitions or sales of major assets, bankruptcy, changes in accountants, resignation of directors, and others.

## Shelf Registration

Beginning in 1982, SEC rules permitted companies to submit a single comprehensive disclosure statement describing the company and its long-term financing plans. If such a comprehensive plan is filed, companies may issue new securities without filing a new report or prospectus, in order to take advantage of rapid market changes. The SEC rule does not permit shelf registration by companies with less than $150 million in stock held by investors not connected with the company, but that restriction does not apply to employee stock ownership plans, dividend reinvestment plans, and similar transactions.

## Impact on the Accounting Profession

Much of the work in preparing disclosure and registration materials under both the 1933 and 1934 acts is done by accountants. The financial reports must be certified by an independent public accountant, and underwriters and firms issuing securities often require a comfort letter from an independent accountant stating that the reports do not include any false or misleading information. If false or misleading information is included, the accountant may be sued in many instances, although accountants have the defense of due diligence. That defense is available if the required tasks were performed according to generally accepted accounting standards and with proper care. Accountants may also be censured by the SEC.

Under both the 1933 and 1934 acts, the SEC is given authority to prescribe accounting rules and procedures within the context of the various reports filed with the commission. Many of those standards have evolved from dialogues between the SEC and professional accounting associations. The SEC standards have, in many instances, influenced general accounting principles and practices.

## ANTIFRAUD PROVISIONS

Many of the federal and state securities laws contain important **antifraud provisions.** Such provisions generally prohibit fraud, deceit, and other more specific practices. Two types of antifraud provisions exist: (1) **Rule 10b-5** regulation, derived from the Securities Act of 1934, and (2) **Non-10b-5** regulation, based on provisions of other acts.

### Rule 10b-5

Perhaps the most important "antifraud" provision in the federal securities laws is section 10(b) of the 1934 act, which provides that it is unlawful "[t]o use or employ, in connection with the purchase or sale of any security . . . any manipulative or deceptive device or contrivance in contravention of such rules and regulations as the Commission may prescribe. . . ."

The act makes nothing illegal unless the SEC adopts a rule prohibiting a practice. In 1942 the SEC adopted the famous *Rule 10b-5,* which provides the basis for much of the SEC's antifraud activity (see the box on the following page).

There are no exemptions in either the rule or the act, and Rule 10b-5 applies whether or not the securities are registered with the SEC. Court decisions have required a further element in the proof of "10b-5" violations, that of **scienter,** or "guilty knowledge." The scienter requirement does not mean that alleged violator knew that he or she was violating the law, but instead that the violator intended to defraud or deceive someone. A reckless or negligent act cannot violate the rule.

Violations of Rule 10b-5 may result in both civil and criminal liability. Private civil actions to recover amounts lost to deceptive schemes are permitted, and the SEC may bring injunctive actions. Criminal violations are possible but are reserved for the most serious cases.

A variety of practices have been held illegal under Rule 10b-5, including *market manipulations, insider* and *tippee trading, misstatements* on registration and disclosure statements or elsewhere, and several types of *corporate mismanagement.*

**Market Manipulation**　Section 10(b) of the 1934 act prohibits any "manipulative . . . device." This provision has been used against wash sales or matched orders and similar devices that artificially inflate the price of a stock. Later concerns have dealt with the effect of large block orders by institutional investors. Not all manipulations are illegal, because the SEC permits "stabilizing" purchases or sales of securities during periods of rapid price changes. Since 1968 the SEC has regulated corporate repurchases of stock and has acted against fraudulent schemes when corporations have been involved in transactions in their own stock.

**Insider Trading and Tippees**　Rule 10b-5 generally prohibits trading by persons who have access to *inside information* about a firm. Such persons have a duty to disclose that

> # Rule 10b-5
>
> It shall be unlawful for any person, directly or indirectly, by the use of any means or instrumentality of interstate commerce, or of the mails, or of any facility of any national securities exchange (1) to employ any device, scheme, or artifice to defraud, (2) to make any untrue statement of a material fact or to omit to state a material fact necessary in order to make the statements made, in the light of circumstances under which they were made, not misleading, or (3) to engage in any act, practice, or course of business which operates or would operate as a fraud or deceit upon any person, in connection with the purchase or sale of any security.

they have such information to the persons with whom they deal. For example, the officers of an oil company about to announce the discovery of a new oil field must disclose that fact before they buy stock in their company. Similarly, if such persons disclose confidential corporate information to another, known as a **tippee,** the tippees are subject to the same duty of disclosure as the insider tippers.

The obligation to disclose extends beyond corporate directors and officers and includes employees, attorneys, and accountants for the company, and any other person receiving confidential information from a corporate source. The information used must be confidential and material. Inside information may not be used until after it is made public and until the news may be circulated. In other words, an investment cannot be made at the instant news is announced. Civil actions by persons dealing with insiders and tippees are permitted, along with actions by the company or stockholders acting on its behalf. The following case discusses the problem of tippees in the notorious "Equity Funding" case, but from a slightly different perspective.

## Dirks v. SEC
452 U.S. 490, 101 S. Ct. 2478, 69 L. Ed. 2d 185 (1983)

Dirks was an officer of a broker-dealer firm that specialized in investment analysis of insurance company securities for institutional investors. In 1973 he received information from Secrist, a former officer of Equity Funding of America, that the assets of Equity Funding were vastly overstated as the result of fraudulent corporate practices. Secrist urged Dirks to verify the fraud and disclose it publicly. Dirks interviewed several employees of Equity Funding who corroborated the allegations.

During this time, Dirks openly discussed the allegations with a number of clients and investors. Some of these persons sold their holdings in Equity Funding, including five investment advisers who liquidated holdings of more than $16 million. As a result, the price of Equity Funding stock fell from $26 per share to less than $15 per share. The New York Stock Exchange stopped all trading in Equity Funding securities as a result. Shortly thereafter, California authorities found evidence of fraud. Dirks had also contacted the *Wall Street Journal*, which refused to print any information, and the

SEC, which refused to issue a complaint. After the California authorities publicized their findings, the *Journal* printed its story and the SEC filed a complaint against Equity Funding. The SEC also issued a complaint against Dirks, charging "tippee trading."

The SEC found that Dirks had aided and abetted violations of the 1934 securities act, concluding that "[W]here 'tippees'—regardless of their motivation or occupation—come into possession of material information that they know is confidential and know or should know came from a corporate insider, they must either publicly disclose that information or refrain from trading." The SEC recognized that Dirks had played an important role in bringing the Equity Funding fraud to light and imposed only a censure. Dirks appealed to the court of appeals, which affirmed the censure. Dirks sought relief from the Supreme Court.

**Justice Powell Delivered the Opinion of the Court**  In *Chiarella v. United States*, 445 U.S. 222, 100 S. Ct. 1108, 63 L. Ed. 2d 348 (1980) we accepted the two elements . . . for establishing a Rule 10b-5 violation "(i) the existence of a relationship affording access to inside information intended to be available only for a corporate purpose and (ii) the unfairness of allowing a corporate insider to take advantage of that information by trading without disclosure." . . . [T]he Court found that there is no general duty to disclose before trading on material nonpublic information, and held that "a duty to disclose under §10(b) does not arise from the mere possession of nonpublic market information." . . . Such a duty arises rather from the existence of a fiduciary relationship. . . .

Not all breaches of fiduciary duty in connection with a securities transaction, however, come within the ambit of Rule 10b-5. . . . There must be "manipulation or deception." . . . In an inside-trading case this fraud derives from the "inherent unfairness involved where one takes advantage" of "information intended to be available only for a corporate purpose and not for the personal benefit of anyone." . . . Thus, an insider will be liable under Rule 10b-5 for inside trading only where he fails to disclose material nonpublic information before trading on it and thus makes "secret profits." . . .

. . . [T]here can be no duty to disclose where the person who had traded on inside information "was not [the corporation's] agent, . . . was not a fiduciary, [or] was not a person in whom the sellers [of the securities] had placed their trust and confidence. . . ." This requirement of a specific relationship between the shareholders and the individual trading on inside information has created analytical difficulties for the SEC and courts in policing tippees

who trade on inside information. Unlike insiders who have independent fiduciary duties to both the corporation and its shareholders, the typical tippee has no such relationships. In view of this absence, it has been unclear how a tippee acquires the . . . duty to refrain from trading on inside information.

The SEC's position . . . is that a tippee "inherits" the . . . obligation to shareholders whenever he receives inside information from an insider. . . .

In effect, the SEC's theory of tippee liability . . . appears rooted in the idea that the antifraud provisions require equal information among all traders. This conflicts with the principle set forth in *Chiarella* that only some persons, under some circumstances, will be barred from trading while in the possession of material nonpublic information. . . .

Imposing a duty to disclose or abstain solely because a person knowingly receives material nonpublic information from an insider and trades on it could have an inhibiting influence on the role of market analysts, which the SEC itself recognizes is necessary to the preservation of a healthy market. It is commonplace for analysts to "ferret out and analyze information" . . . and this often is done by meeting with and questioning corporate officers and others who are insiders. And information that the analysts obtain normally may be the basis for judgments as to the market worth of a corporation's securities. . . .

The conclusion that recipients of inside information do not invariably acquire a duty to disclose or abstain does not mean that such tippees always are free to trade on the information. The need for a ban on some tippee trading is clear. Not only are insiders forbidden by their fiduciary relationship from personally using undisclosed corporate information to their advantage, but they may not give such information to an outsider for the same improper purpose. . . .

Similarly, the transactions of those who knowingly participate with the fiduciary in such a breach are "as forbidden" as transactions "on behalf of the trustee himself." . . . [A] contrary rule "would open up opportunities for devious dealings in the name of the others that the trustee could not conduct in his own." . . . Thus, the tippee's duty to disclose or abstain is derivative from that of the insider's duty. . . .

Thus, some tippees must assume an insider's duty to the shareholders not because they receive inside information, but rather because it has been made available to them *improperly.* . . . Thus, a tippee assumes a fiduciary duty to the shareholders of a corporation not to trade on material nonpublic information only when the insider has breached his fiduciary duty to the shareholders by disclosing the information to the tippee and the tippee knows or should know that there has been a breach. . . .

In determining whether a tippee is under an obligation to disclose or abstain, it thus is necessary to determine whether the insider's "tip" constituted a breach of the insider's fiduciary duty. All disclosures of confidential corporate information are not inconsistent with the duty insiders owe to shareholders. In contrast to the extraordinary facts of this case, the more typical situation in which there will be a question whether disclosure violates the insider's . . . duty is when insiders disclose information to analysts. . . . In some situations, the insider will act consistently with his fiduciary duty to shareholders, and yet release of the information may affect the market. . . . [T]he test is whether the insider personally will benefit, directly or indirectly, from his disclosure. Absent some personal gain, there has been no breach of duty to stockholders. And absent a breach by the insider, there is no derivative breach. . . .

Under the insider-trading and tipping rules set forth above, we find that there was no actionable violation by Dirks. It is undisputed that Dirks himself was a stranger to Equity Funding, with no preexisting fiduciary duty to its shareholders. He took no action, directly or indirectly, that induced the shareholders or officers of Equity Funding to repose trust or confidence in him. There was no expectation by Dirks' sources that he would keep their information in confidence. Nor did Dirks misappropriate or ille-

gally obtain the information about Equity Funding. Unless the insiders breached their . . . duty to shareholders in disclosing the nonpublic information to Dirks, he breached no duty when he passed it on to investors as well as to the *Wall Street Journal.*

It is clear that neither Secrist nor the other Equity Funding employees violated their . . . duty to the corporation's shareholders by providing information to Dirks. The tippers received no monetary or personal benefit for revealing Equity Funding's secrets, nor was their purpose to make a gift of valuable information to Dirks. As the facts of this case clearly indicate, the tippers were motivated by a desire to expose the fraud. . . . In the absence of a breach of duty to the shareholders by the insiders, there was no derivative breach by Dirks. . . .

[Reversed.]

**Justice Blackmun, with Whom Justice Brennan and Justice Marshall Join, Dissenting** The Court today takes still another step to limit the protections provided investors by §10(b). . . . The device employed in this case engrafts a special motivational requirement on the fiduciary duty doctrine. This innovation excuses a knowing and intentional violation of an insider's duty to shareholders if the insider does not act from a motive of personal gain. . . .

The fact that the insider himself does not benefit from the breach does not eradicate the shareholder's injury. . . . It makes no difference to the shareholder whether the corporate insider gained or intended to gain personally from the transaction; the shareholder still has lost because of the insider's misuse of nonpublic information. The duty is addressed not to the insider's motives, but to his actions and their consequences on the shareholder. Personal gain is not an element of the breach of this duty.

## Case Discussion Questions

1   Did Secrist violate any fiduciary duties by giving Dirks the information in this case? Is that important?
2   What is the *Chiarella* test? Does that case, or Rule 10b-5, mention motivation?
3   If Dirks had not told his clients about Equity Funding's problems, would he have violated his fiduciary duties to those clients?

In 1987 the Supreme Court affirmed the conviction of R. Foster Winans, a columnist for the *Wall Street Journal,* and others for violating section 10b of the Securities Exchange Act.[4] Winans wrote an influential column known as "Heard on the Street," which was based on information received from corporate executives. Although no inside information was used, the column affected the price of stocks that it featured. The *Journal* did not permit the disclosure of that information prior to publication, but Winans entered into a scheme with representatives of a brokerage firm to give advance information about the timing and contents of the column and to share the proceeds from investments made prior to the publication of the columns. Over a four-month period the conspirators made $690,000.

The lower court held that the deliberate breach of the *Journal's* confidentiality rule was a fraud on the *Journal,* and that although the *Journal* was not a buyer or seller of the stocks, the fraud was "in connection with" a purchase of stock, within the meaning of the statute. The court of appeals affirmed. The decision was affirmed by an equally divided Supreme Court. The courts all made it clear that Rule 10b-5 is not restricted to frauds on persons who have an interest in the securities traded.

---

**PRO AND CON**

# Should insider trading be controlled?

**Pro**   Insider and tippee trading must be prohibited out of a simple sense of fairness. Investors should deal on a level playing field. It is simply unfair to permit those with material nonpublic information to use that information at the expense of those to whom the information is not available.

If insider trading was permitted, the integrity of the stock markets would quickly be called into question. Those markets depend for their very existence on the assumption that all investors start from similar positions. If insider information becomes commonplace, many investors will simply refuse to invest, depriving the economy of needed capital.

Finally, insider trading provides opportunities for abuse and unethical behavior that will infect all of American business. In the Ivan Boesky case, for example, evidence showed that Boesky bribed stockbrokers involved in merger negotiations for other companies to give him inside information about the pending mergers, so that he could invest in those firms. The unethical behavior of Boesky and those stockbrokers has created a bad impression for all of American business, both at home and abroad. The bribery and corruption that resulted have called into question the ethics of the entire securities industry. If such practices were commonplace, more unethical conduct would result.

**Con**   The rules against insider and tippee trading create an artificial market environment that fails to recognize the true reality of securities trading. Every investor bases his or her decisions on information. Giant publications such as the *Wall Street Journal* have made fortunes on providing information to the public. The rules against insider trading create artificial divisions, telling investors that decisions cannot be made on the basis of some information. Court decisions make that situation even worse by drawing artificial lines around certain investors, and not others. Managers cannot share their information, even with friends and relatives. A printer who is able to determine the parties to a merger is not an insider, but one who is told who the parties are is an insider. Those distinctions make no sense.

Capitalism and free enterprise are based on the idea of a competitive edge. In the case of insider trading, we are depriving investors of precisely that kind of competitive edge and depriving those who run

---

4 *Carpenter v. U.S.,* ——— U.S. ———, 108 S. Ct. 316, 98 L. Ed. 2d 275 (1987).

American business of an incentive to run it efficiently. A manager who creates profits cannot take advantage of those profits by investing in his or her own firm, at least until the information is made public. And finally, truly efficient markets adjust to new information so quickly that no one is benefitted, including the insider. If an insider acts, that information is reflected in the stock price very quickly, and inside information in fact *aids* in the creation of efficient markets.

Finally, it seems far more appropriate to punish bribery and corruption directly than to approach it through insider trading. The activities of stockbrokers who sell information can be controlled through the market quickly, because few firms would use a broker that disclosed secret information. Controls through the marketplace are far more consistent with free enterprise than additional government regulation.

## Roundtable Discussion

1    Is the use of inside information unfair? Who is hurt when such information is used? Is a true "level playing field" really possible?

2    If insider trading was permitted, would you invest the stock market? Why or why not? What dangers do you see?

3    Will market forces control insider trading? In the long run? In the short run? Should we depend on market forces to regulate such conduct?

**Corporate Misstatements**    The provisions of section 10(b) and Rule 10b-5 have been applied to any misleading corporate statement, including registration and disclosure statements, prospectuses, or any other statements made "in connection with the purchase and sale of securities." Such statements must be misleading to the reasonable investor, made with "scienter," or "guilty knowledge," that the statements were false or misleading, and made with intent to defraud or deceive.

## Basic Incorporated v. Levinson
——— U.S.,——— 108 S. Ct. 978,——— L. Ed. 2d——— (1988)

Basic was a publicly traded corporation in the business of manufacturing chemical refractories for the steel industry. For several years Combustion Engineering had expressed an interest in acquiring Basic and began meetings with Basic's officers and directors. Those meetings lasted throughout 1977 and 1978. On December 18, 1978, Basic asked the New York Stock Exchange to suspend trading in its shares because it had been "approached by another company" concerning a merger. On December 20, Basic announced its approval of Combustion's tender offer for all outstanding shares.

Rumors of the merger continued to surface from time to time, and prices of Basic stock fluctuated wildly. On October 21, 1977, a news release said that "no negotiations were under way with any company for a merger." On September 25, 1978, in response to an inquiry from the New York Stock Exchange, Basic issued another release that said that "management is unaware of any present or pending company development that would result in the abnormally heavy trading activity and price fluctuation." And on November 6, 1978, Basic issued a report to its shareholders that "we remain unaware of any present or pending developments which would account for the high volume of trading and price fluctuations."

This was an action brought by investors who had sold Basic stock prior to the formal announcement of the merger, alleging material misrepresentations had been made, causing them to sell before the announcement. The district court held that the statements were not material and that there was no proof that the investors relied on the misleading statements in their decision to sell the stock. The Court of Appeals reversed, and Basic appealed.

**Justice Blackmun Delivered the Opinion of the Court**    The 1934 Act was designed to protect investors against manipulation of stock prices. Underlying the adoption of extensive disclosure requirements was a legislative philosophy: "There cannot be honest markets without honest publicity. Manipulation and dishonest practices of the marketplace thrive upon mystery and secrecy." This Court repeatedly has described the fundamental purpose of the Act as implementing a philosophy of full disclosure. . . .

The Court . . . explicitly has defined a standard of materiality under the securities laws, concluding . . . that "an omitted fact is material if there is a substantial likelihood that a reasonable shareholder would consider it important. . . . Acknowledging that certain information concerning corporate developments could well be of "dubious significance," the Court was careful not to set too low a standard of materiality; it was concerned that a minimal standard might bring an overabundance of information within its reach, and lead management simply to bury the shareholders in an avalanche of trivial information—a result that is hardly conducive to informed decision-making. . . .

The application of this materiality standard to preliminary merger discussions is not self-evident. Where the impact of the corporate development on the target's fortune is clear, the materiality definition admits straightforward application. Where, on the other hand, the event is contingent or speculative in nature, it is difficult to ascertain whether the "reasonable investor" would have considered the omitted information significant at the time. Merger negotiations, because of the ever-present possibility that the contemplated transaction will not be effectuated, fall into the latter category.

Whether merger discussions in any particular case are material . . . depends on the facts. Generally, in order to assess the probability that the event will occur, a factfinder will need to look to indicia of interest in the transaction at the highest corporate levels. Without attempting to catalog all such possible factors, we note by way of example that board resolutions, instructions to investment bankers, and actual negotiations between principals or their intermediaries may serve as indicia of interest. To assess the magnitude of the transaction to the issuer of the securities allegedly manipulated, a factfinder will need to consider such facts as the size of the two corporate entities and of the potential premiums over market value. No particular event or factor short of closing the transaction need be either necessary or sufficient by itself to render merger discussions material. . . .

We turn to the question of reliance and the "fraud-on-the-market" theory. Succinctly put:

"The fraud on the market theory is based on the hypothesis that, in an open and developed securities market, the price of a company's stock is determined by the available material information regarding the company and its business. . . . Misleading statements will therefore defraud purchasers of stock even if the purchasers do not directly rely on the misstatements. . . . The causal connection between the defendant's fraud and the plaintiff's purchase of stock in such a case is no less significant than in a case of direct reliance on misrepresentation." . . .

The presumption of reliance employed in this case is consistent with, and, by facilitating Rule 10b-5 litigation, supports, the congressional policy embodied in the 1934 Act. In drafting that Act, Congress expressly relied on the premise that securities markets are affected by information, and enacted legislation to facilitate an investor's reliance on the integrity of those markets. . . .

The presumption is also supported by common sense and probability. Recent empirical studies have tended to confirm Congress' premise that the market price of shares traded on well-developed markets reflects all publicly available information, and, hence, any material misrepresentation. It has been noted that "it is hard to imagine that there is a buyer or seller who does not rely on market integrity. Who would knowingly roll the dice in a crooked crap game?"

[The Court vacated the judgment of the Court of Appeals and remanded the case for further evidence on the issue of materiality. Justices White and O'Connor dissented from the "fraud-on-the-marketplace" theory, on the grounds that such a theory makes the corporation virtually an insurer of stock losses.—Ed.]

Case Discussion Questions

1   How would a company know if its merger discussions were material enough to justify making a public announcement? What might be the effects of a premature announcement?

2   What is the "fraud-on-the-marketplace" theory?

Did the investors in this case rely on the announcements that no merger was planned? How do you know?

3   Would the result in this case have been different if the company had said *nothing*, rather than denying that a merger was being discussed?

**Corporate Mismanagement**    Management may make transactions in the shares of a company in a variety of ways, including mergers and acquisitions, reorganizations, and the sale of controlling interests. Management may be liable under Rule 10b-5 if such stock transactions are fraudulent. Many actions under this rule are brought by injured shareholders, or by shareholders on behalf of the corporation. The courts generally require that the plaintiff be either a "purchaser" or "seller" of the security.

## Non-10b-5 Regulation

Aside from the general prohibitions of Rule 10b-5, several other regulations apply to publicly held corporations, including *proxy-solicitation rules*, regulation of *tender offers*, and rules relating to *short-swing profits*.

**Proxy-Solicitation Rules**    A **proxy** is an authorization by a shareholder to another to vote the shareholder's stock. State corporation acts generally permit shareholders to give proxies to others to vote their shares at stockholders' meetings. Proxies are often solicited by management, but sometimes other groups of stockholder insurgents try to obtain proxies in an attempt to oust the present management, resulting in *proxy fights*. Proxies are generally revocable at any time by the shareholders giving them.

The 1934 act requires that any proxy solicitation, whether by management or by insurgents, be accompanied by a **proxy statement.** That statement is a disclosure to shareholders of all of the material facts regarding matters that will be voted on at the meeting and gives the shareholders the opportunity to register their preference in the proxy. If there is to be a contest for the control of the corporation, the names and interests of all participants in the proxy contest must be disclosed. If securities are registered in a broker's "street name," the parties soliciting the proxies must inquire as to the real owners of the securities, furnish enough copies for each such owner to the broker, and pay the reasonable expenses of distributing the statement.

Proxy statements must be filed with the SEC at least ten days before they are sent to shareholders, and the SEC may require changes in those statements. In an attempt to bring about **shareholder democracy,** the SEC rules also require that proposals by shareholders be included in the proxy statement if they are presented to management a reasonable time before the statements are sent. This rule permits discussion of such items as management compensation, shareholder voting rights, and conduct of the annual meeting—items that management often tries to keep off of the agenda of the annual meeting. Shareholder proposals relating to personal claims or grievances, matters not significantly related to the company's business, and nominations of candidates for the board of directors need not be permitted. The SEC has the authority to determine whether shareholder proposals must be included in the proxy request.

**Tender Offers**    As discussed in Chapter 12, a **tender offer** is a general offer to all of the shareholders of a corporation to purchase their shares at a specified price, often subject to a minimum or maximum number of shares that the offeror will accept. Such offers are usually communicated to the shareholders through a newspaper advertisement or through a general mailing to all shareholders. The purpose of the offeror is to obtain enough stock to elect a majority of the board of directors and obtain control of the corporation. Tender offers are often bitterly contested by the management of the target corporation, because management will probably be replaced if the bid is successful.

During the 1960's, tender offers were often marked by claims and countercharges on both sides, efforts to manipulate the market, and confusing and sometimes coercive approaches to existing stockholders. In an effort to counter those problems, the **Williams Act** was passed by Congress in 1968 as an amendment to the 1934 act. The purpose of the Williams Act was to require disclosure to shareholders of all important information they need to decide whether to sell their shares.

The Williams Act requires any person or group that becomes the owner of 5% or more of any class of securities registered under the 1934 act, or who makes a tender offer to acquire more than 5% of such shares, to file a disclosure statement with both the SEC and the issuer of such securities within ten days. That statement must include the background of the persons acquiring the stock; the source of the funds used for the acquisition; the purpose of the acquisition; the number of shares owned; and any contracts, arrangements, or understandings regarding the acquisition.

Shareholders who have decided to sell their shares may withdraw their shares during the first seven days of the offer and any time following sixty days after the beginning of the offer. If the tender offer is for less than all of the outstanding shares, and more than the requested number of shares are tendered, the offeror must take the shares on a pro rata basis during the first ten days of the offer to decrease the pressure on shareholders when the offeror makes its offer on a first-come, first-served basis. Finally, if the offered price increases during the course of an offer, all tendering shareholders must receive the additional consideration, even if they tendered their stock before the price increase was announced.

The act also contains a broad antifraud section, making it illegal to make any untrue statement of a material fact, to fail to state any material fact, or to engage in fraudulent, deceptive, or manipulative acts or practices in connection with a tender offer. The Williams Act is enforced by SEC orders, injunctions, and civil actions by injured shareholders.

**Short-Swing Profits**    In order to provide an additional protection from insider trading, another provision effectively prohibits certain insiders from profiting from short-term gains on the securities of their firms. The provision generally applies to officers, directors, and persons owning more than 10% of a class of equity (ownership) securities registered under the 1934 act. Such persons must file a report with the SEC when they become officers, directors, or 10% shareholders, and must file another report at the end of any month in which they acquire or dispose of any of the company's equity securities. The company, or any shareholder suing on behalf of the company, may sue such persons. Any profit realized from the purchase and sale, or sale and purchase, of any equity security within a six-month period may be recovered and will go to the corporation.

## REGULATION OF SECURITIES PROFESSIONALS

The 1934 act also requires brokers and dealers to register with the SEC, and investment advisers are required to register with the Commission under the Investment Advisers Act. The 1934 act regulates *broker-dealer selling practices*, requires a certain degree of *financial responsibility* on the part of broker-dealers, authorizes the Federal Reserve Board to establish *margin requirements*, and places *restrictions on trading by broker-dealers*.

### Broker-Dealer Selling Practices

The 1934 act and the SEC rules regulate broker-dealer selling practices by prohibiting conflicts of interest between the broker-dealer and the customer and by requiring a factual basis for recommendations by broker-dealers to their customers.

Generally, *conflicts of interest* are controlled under the so-called **shingle theory**, which holds that a securities professional who "hangs out his shingle" represents to the public that he or she is an expert in securities transactions and will act in the best interests of the customer. This means in part that a securities professional will violate the antifraud provisions of the act if he or she does not disclose all conflicts of interest prior to a customer's investment decision.

Two potential conflicts of interest involve **churning** a customer's account by making rapid and unnecessary transactions solely to earn commissions and **scalping,** or recommending that customers purchase securities in which the broker-dealer has personally invested in order to make the price of the stock go up. The SEC has also taken the position that it is a violation of the antifraud provisions for a broker-dealer to recommend the purchase of a security unless the broker-dealer has enough reliable information to form a basis for a recommendation.

### Broker-Dealer Financial Responsibility

In order to protect customers from the acts of unscrupulous broker-dealers, the securities laws and SEC rules provide three financial responsibility requirements. Since 1972 broker-dealers have been required to keep the net cash due to their customers in special accounts, called *special reserve accounts*. An SEC rule requires broker-dealers to maintain at least $25,000 in net capital and provides that the aggregate indebtedness of broker-dealers may not exceed 1,500% of its net capital. Finally, the nonprofit Securities Investor Protection Corporation maintains a fund from which investors who have suffered cash losses by the acts of broker-dealers may be reimbursed. The act does not cover ordinary investment losses. Funds are obtained by mandatory contributions from all registered brokers and dealers.

### Margin Requirements

The 1934 act authorized the Federal Reserve Board to limit the amount of credit that may be extended on any security. The Federal Reserve Board has issued several regulations of such credit applying to broker-dealers, banks, and others.

The Federal Reserve's **margin requirements** specify the maximum loan value of securities. The Federal Reserve changes those requirements from time to time, in response to changes in the amount of speculative activity and the availability of credit. Thus, if the margin requirement is 50%, a customer will have to pay at least half the value of a security before it can be purchased. The Federal Reserve does not require additional margin if the value of stocks declines, but several of the securities exchanges impose such **margin maintenance** rules. The margin rules only apply to equity securities.

Loans by broker-dealers to their customers are specifically exempt from the Truth-in-Lending Act (see p. 370), but the SEC has established disclosure rules for such transactions. Those rules require broker-dealers to disclose the rate and method of computing interest on such indebtedness and the nature of the broker-dealer's interest in the customer's securities.

### Broker-Dealer Trading Restrictions

Because broker-dealers can affect the price of a security through their actions, and because broker-dealers have many of the characteristics of insiders, the 1934 act permits the SEC to regulate the trading activities of such persons for their own accounts. The act generally prohibits any trading by broker-dealers unless the SEC provides an exception, but there are some major exceptions to the rule. The purpose of such regulations is to prohibit manipulations of prices by securities professionals.

## REMEDIES, SANCTIONS, AND CIVIL LIABILITY

A variety of sanctions and remedies are available under the federal acts, including criminal penalties, civil injunctions, and administrative remedies. In addition, the federal laws may be used in many instances as the basis for civil lawsuits by injured parties.

### Criminal Sanctions

If fraud or other willful violations of the federal laws are present, the SEC may refer the case to the Justice Department for criminal prosecution. The usual penalty under the federal laws is a fine of up to $10,000 or five years' imprisonment, or both. Criminal action is reserved for the most outrageous cases.

### SEC Injunction Actions

The SEC may apply to a federal district court for an injunction against practices that violate the federal statutes or the SEC rules. Although such injunctions were routinely granted in earlier years, courts have become reluctant to grant injunctions unless the defendant is likely to continue to violate the law or is a "continuing menace" to the public. Courts may order additional or "ancillary" relief in an injunction action, such as requiring a defendant to turn over the profits from an illegal transaction.

### Administrative Remedies

The SEC may, after an investigation and hearing, issue orders suspending or expelling members from exchanges or over-the-counter dealer associations; denying, suspending, or revoking broker-dealer registrations; or barring individuals from employment with a registered firm, temporarily or permanently. As noted, the commission may also issue a stop order, which terminates trading of an issue as well. Such orders may be appealed to the U.S. courts of appeal.

## Civil Liability

Perhaps the most important deterrent to violation of the federal securities laws is the possibility of a civil lawsuit. Injured parties, including corporations or shareholders suing on behalf of a corporation, may file lawsuits under two possible theories: *express liability*, which arises under a specific statute granting injured persons the right to sue, and *implied liability*, which arises from interpretation of the federal law.

**Express Liability**   Several sections of the federal laws provide expressly for private civil lawsuits. For example, the 1933 Securities Act gives purchasers of securities sold in violation of the disclosure and registration requirements the right to sue the issuer and the individuals responsible. Similarly, corporations and shareholders suing on behalf of the corporation may sue officers, directors, and major shareholders who profit from short-swing profits. The 1934 act expressly gives persons who purchase or sell securities due to misleading statements a right to sue for their loss.

**Implied Liability**   Some parts of the federal law do not grant an express right to sue but do affect private legal relationships, such as provisions in which contracts in violation of the law are made void. The courts generally grant private civil actions to enforce the rights created by those sections of the securities laws.

Many provisions of the federal law simply make a particular act or transaction unlawful. The courts have generally applied traditional tort principles in such cases and have implied a private right of action on behalf of injured persons who are in the class of persons the statute was designed to protect. This rule has been applied most extensively in cases involving the general antifraud provisions and the proxy-solicitation rules.

## SUMMARY AND CONCLUSIONS

Although the securities markets have been regulated by state laws since 1911, it was not until the stock market crash and the Depression of the 1930's that federal regulation was found necessary. The state blue sky laws only regulated intrastate offerings of securities and were often subject to exemptions and lax enforcement. Stock market abuses during the 1920's, such as market manipulation by large traders, insider trading, excessive margin purchases, and investment by commercial banks and their subsidiaries, contributed substantially to the market crash of 1929 and to the pressure for reform and regulation.

Federal securities regulation is found in two major statutes, the Securities Act of 1933 and the Securities Exchange Act of 1934, a series of secondary acts regulating specific transactions or businesses, and the rules of the Securities and Exchange Commission (SEC). The SEC is an independent regulatory commission created by the 1934 act and has authority to make rules pursuant to both the 1933 and 1934 acts.

Federal law requires that new issues of securities be registered under the 1933 act and disclosure be made to prospective investors in a prospectus. The 1934 act requires registration and disclosure by most publicly traded corporations and others described in the act. The purpose of registration and disclosure is to provide information to prospective investors, who are free to make up their own minds about an investment. Federal law does not guarantee that any investment is fair or a "good deal."

In addition to the registration and disclosure provisions, the federal statutes also include antifraud provisions, which prohibit fraud, deceit, and manipulative practices. The most important such provision is found in SEC Rule 10b-5, through which insider trading, corporate misstatements, and corporate mismanagement are controlled. Other sections of the federal law regulate proxy solicitation and tender offers and prohibit short-swing profits.

The federal laws also regulate the securities business by regulating the selling practices of broker-dealers, imposing financial responsibility on broker-dealers, imposing margin requirements, and restricting the trading practices of broker-dealers.

Remedies for violation of the federal securities laws include criminal penalties, injunctions, and administrative sanctions by the SEC, but perhaps the most important remedy is found in the variety of express and implied civil causes of action found in the federal statutes.

## REVIEW QUESTIONS

1   How did excessive margin trading, market manipulation, fraud and insider trading, and the involvement of commercial banks in the underwriting process contribute to the stock market crash of 1929 and the Great Depression of the 1930's? Can another Great Depression occur in the light of federal securities laws?

2   Explain the key differences between the 1933 and 1934 federal securities acts.

3   If an investor fails to take advantage of registration and disclosure statements, do the federal securities laws afford him or her any protection against a "bad deal"?

4   What is Rule 10b-5? What does it prohibit?

5   An insider who knows "special information" and desires to purchase stock must disclose that information to the seller before the purchase. (a) How can he or she disclose that information to the unknown public investors from whom the stock is purchased through the exchange markets? (b) If he or she in fact discloses that information without permission from the company, what results would you expect?

6   Which of the following must be registered under the Securities Act of 1933: (a) shares of limited partnership in a cattle ranch; (b) individual rows of orange trees, with a management contract; (c) a bank certificate of deposit; (d) shares in a mutual fund?

7   Gross advertised for "purchaser-investors" to raise earthworms. Each purchaser would have his or her own "worm ranch," and Gross would supply the initial breeding worms. Gross agreed to repurchase all bait-sized worms for $2.25 a pound, ostensibly for sale as bait, although "ranchers" were free to sell to anyone. Gross represented that the worms bred twenty times per year. In fact, the worms bred eight times per year, and the only market at $2.25 per pound was Gross himself, who used the worms repurchased as "breeders" for new worm ranchers. Smith sued Gross, claiming that the scheme should have been registered under the 1933 act and that a violation of Rule 10b-5 had occurred. What do you think was the result? [*Smith v. Gross*, 604 F.2d 292 (9th Circ., 1979).]

8   Smith learns that the ABC Company is going to make a public offering of stock after the

SEC clears its registration statement. Smith is a current investor in ABC and has been very pleased with the performance of ABC stock. Wanting to purchase more stock, Smith calls his broker and offers to make a contract promising to purchase 1,000 shares of the stock when it is issued. May the broker or the ABC Company accept the offer?

9    Accidental Oil Company obtains geologist reports that there may be a large untapped field of oil under the Mojave Desert. Accidental acquires land and begins drilling, but it is impossible to "keep the lid on" the possible discovery and rumors are rampant throughout the industry. There are no firm results from the test wells yet, but Accidental stock begins fluctuating wildly with each successive rumor. Is Accidental under a duty to make any statement? What sort of statement should it make?

10    First Securities, a brokerage house, and its president, Nye, had been involved for some time in a scheme to defraud investors. The scheme involved false escrow accounts of customers' money. Ernst & Ernst, an accounting firm, had audited First Securities' books for many years but was unaware of the fraud. Nye committed suicide and left a note confessing all. Customers of First Securities brought an action against Ernst & Ernst, claiming that the firm should have discovered the irregularities, and that the firm's failure to do so was a violation of Rule 10b-5. What was the result? [*Ernst & Ernst v. Hochfelder*, 425 U.S. 185, 96 S. Ct. 1375, 47 L. Ed. 2d 668 (1976).]

11    Chiarella was a printer in the offices of an independent firm that prepared financial documents, stock certificates, and other materials dealing with securities. Although the names of firms and participants were kept secret until the last possible moment, Chiarella was able to ascertain that a large tender offer was about to be made, and he and some relatives made large purchases of stock in the company about to be purchased. Was he guilty of "insider trading?" [*Chiarella v. U.S.*, 445 U.S. 222, 100 S. Ct. 1108, 63 L. Ed. 2d 348 (1980). Hint: See the references to *Chiarella* in *Dirks v. SEC*, p. 566.]

# Appendix A
# The Constitution of the United States (Unabridged)

## PREAMBLE

We the People of the United States, in Order to form a more perfect Union, establish Justice, insure domestic Tranquility, provide for the common defence, promote the general Welfare, and secure the Blessings of Liberty to ourselves and our Posterity, do ordain and establish this Constitution for the United States of America.

## Article I

**Section 1.** All legislative Powers herein granted shall be vested in a Congress of the United States, which shall consist of a Senate and House of Representatives.

**Section 2.** (1) The House of Representatives shall be composed of Members chosen every second Year by the People of the several States, and the Electors in each State shall have the Qualifications requisite for Electors of the most numerous Branch of the State Legislature.

(2) No Person shall be a Representative who shall not have attained to the Age of twenty five Years, and have been seven Years a Citizen of the United States, and who shall not, when elected, by an Inhabitant of that State in which he shall be chosen.

(3) Representatives and direct Taxes shall be apportioned among the several States which may be included within this Union, according to their respective Numbers, which shall be determined by adding to the whole Number of free Persons, including those bound to Service for Term of Years, and excluding Indians not taxed, three fifths of all other Persons. The actual Enumeration shall be made within three Years after the first Meeting of the Congress of the United States, and within every subsequent Term of ten Years, in such manner as they shall by Law direct. The Number of Representatives shall not exceed one for every thirty Thousand, but each State shall have at Least one Representative; and until such enumeration shall be made, the State of New Hampshire shall be entitled to choose three, Massachusetts eight, Rhode Island and Providence Plantations one, Connecticut five, New York six, New Jersey four, Pennsylvania eight, Delaware one, Maryland six, Virginia ten, North Carolina five, South Carolina five, and Georgia three.

(4) When vacancies happen in the Representation from any State, the Executive Authority thereof shall issue Writs of Election to fill such Vacancies.

(5) The House of Representatives shall choose their Speaker and other Officers; and shall have the sole Power of Impeachment.

**Section 3.** (1) The Senate of the United States shall be composed of two Senators from each State, chosen by the Legislature thereof, for six Years; and each Senator shall have one Vote.

(2) Immediately after they shall be assembled in Consequence of the first Election, they shall be divided as

equally as may be into three Classes. The Seats of the Senators of the first Class shall be vacated at the Expiration of the Second Year, of the second Class at the Expiration of the fourth Year, and of the third Class at the Expiration of the sixth Year, so that one third may be chosen every second Year; and if Vacancies happen by Resignation, or otherwise, during the Recess of the Legislature of any State, the Executive thereof may make temporary Appointments until the next Meeting of the Legislature, which shall then fill such Vacancies.

(3) No Person shall be a Senator who shall not have attained to the Age of thirty Years, and been nine Years a Citizen of the United States, and who shall not, when elected, be an Inhabitant of that State for which he shall be chosen.

(4) The Vice President of the United States shall be President of the Senate, but shall have not Vote, unless they be equally divided.

(5) The Senate shall choose their other Officers, and also a President pro tempore, in the Absence of the Vice President, or when he shall exercise the Office of President of the United States.

(6) The Senate shall have the sole Power to try all Impeachments. When sitting for that Purpose, they shall be on Oath or Affirmation. When the President of the United States is tried, the Chief Justice shall preside: And no Person shall be convicted without the Concurrence of two thirds of the Members present.

(7) Judgment in Cases of Impeachment shall not extend further than to removal from Office, and disqualification to hold and enjoy any Office of honor, Trust or Profit under the United States: but the Party convicted shall nevertheless be liable and subject to Indictment, Trial, Judgment, and Punishment, according to Law.

**Section 4.** (1) The Times, Places and Manner of holding Elections for Senators and Representatives, shall be prescribed in each State by the Legislature thereof; but the Congress may at any time by Law make or alter such Regulations, except as to the Places of choosing Senators.

(2) The Congress shall assemble at least once in every Year, and such Meeting shall be on the first Monday in December, unless they shall by Law appoint a different day.

**Section 5.** (1) Each House shall be the Judge of the Elections, Returns, and Qualifications of its own Members, and a Majority of each shall constitute a Quorum to do Business; but a smaller Number may adjourn from day to day, and may be authorized to compel the Attendance of absent Members, in such Manner, and under such Penalties as each House may provide.

(2) Each House may determine the Rules of its Proceedings, punish its Members for disorderly Behavior, and, with the Concurrence of two thirds, expel a Member.

(3) Each House shall keep a Journal of its Proceedings, and from time to time publish the same, excepting such Parts as may in their Judgment require Secrecy; and the Yeas and Nays of the Members of either House on any

question shall, at the desire of one fifth of those Present, be entered on the Journal.

(4) Neither House, during the Session of Congress, shall, without the Consent of the other, adjourn for more than three days, nor to any other Place than that in which the two Houses shall be sitting.

**Section 6.** (1) The Senators and Representatives shall receive a Compensation for their Services, to be ascertained by Law, and paid out of the Treasury of the United States. They shall in all Cases, except Treason, Felony and Breach of the Peace, be privileged from Arrest during their Attendance at the Session of their respective Houses, and in going to and returning from the same; and for any Speech or Debate in either House, they shall not be questioned in any other Place.

(2) No Senator or Representative shall, during the Time for which he was elected, be appointed to any civil Office under the Authority of the United States, which shall have been created, or the Emoluments whereof shall have been increased during such time; and no Person holding any Office under the United States, shall be a Member of either House during his Continuance in Office.

**Section 7.** (1) All Bills for raising Revenue shall originate in the House of Representatives; but the Senate may propose or concur with Amendments as on other bills.

(2) Every Bill which shall have passed the House of Representatives and the Senate, shall, before it becomes a Law, be presented to the President of the United States; If he approve he shall sign it, but if not he shall return it, with his Objections to the House in which it shall have originated, who shall enter the Objections at large on their Journal, and proceed to reconsider it. If after such Reconsideration two thirds of that House shall agree to pass the bill, it shall be sent together with the Objections, to the other House, by which it shall likewise be reconsidered, and if approved by two thirds of that House, it shall become a Law. But in all such Cases the Votes of Both Houses shall be determined by yeas and Nays, and the Names of the Persons voting for and against the Bill shall be entered on the Journal of each House respectively. If any Bill shall not be returned by the President within ten Days (Sundays excepted) after it shall have been presented to him, the Same shall be a Law, in like Manner as if he had signed it, unless the Congress by their Adjournment prevent its Return in which Case it shall not be a Law.

(3) Every Order, Resolution, or Vote, to Which the Concurrence of the Senate and House of Representatives may be necessary (except on a question of Adjournment) shall be presented to the President of the United States; and before the Same shall take Effect, shall be approved by him, or being disapproved by him, shall be repassed by two thirds of the Senate and House of Representatives, according to the Rules and Limitations prescribed in the Case of a Bill.

**Section 8.** (1) The Congress shall have Power To lay and collect Taxes, Duties, Imposts and Excises, to pay the Debts and provide for the common Defence and general

Welfare of the United States; but all Duties, Imposts and Excises shall be uniform throughout the United States;

(2) To borrow money on the credit of the United States;

(3) To regulate Commerce with foreign Nations, and among the several States, and with the Indian Tribes;

(4) To establish an uniform Rule of Naturalization, and uniform Laws on the subject of Bankruptcies throughout the United States;

(5) To coin money, regulate the Value thereof, and of foreign Coin, and fix the Standard of Weights and Measures;

(6) To provide for the Punishment of counterfeiting the Securities and current Coin of the United States;

(7) To Establish Post Offices and Post Roads;

(8) To promote the Progress of Science and useful Arts, by securing for limited Times to Authors and Inventors the Exclusive Right to their respective Writings and Discoveries;

(9) To constitute Tribunals inferior to the supreme Court;

(10) To define and punish Piracies and Felonies committed on the high Seas, and Offenses against the Law of Nations;

(11) To declare War, grant Letters of Marque and Reprisal, and make Rules concerning Captures on Land and Water;

(12) To raise and support Armies, but no Appropriation of Money to that Use shall be for a longer Term than two Years;

(13) To provide and maintain a Navy;

(14) To make Rules for the Government and Regulation of the land and naval forces;

(15) To provide for calling forth the Militia to execute the Laws of the Union, suppress Insurrections and repel Invasions;

(16) To provide for organizing, arming, and disciplining the Militia, and for governing such Part of them as may be employed in the Service of the United States, reserving to the States respectively, the Appointment of the Officers, and the Authority of training the Militia according to the discipline prescribed by Congress;

(17) To exercise exclusive Legislation in all Cases whatsoever, over such District (not exceeding ten Miles square) as may, by Cession of particular States, and the Acceptance of Congress, become the Seat of the Government of the United States, and to exercise like Authority over all Places purchased by the Consent of the Legislature of the State in which the Same shall be, for the Erection of Forts, Magazines, Arsenals, dock-Yards, and other needful Buildings;—And

(18) To make all Laws which shall be necessary and proper for carrying into Execution the foregoing Powers, and all other Powers vested by this Constitution in the Government of the United States, or in any Department or Officer thereof.

**Section 9.** (1) The Migration or Importation of Such Persons as any of the States now existing shall think proper to admit, shall not be prohibited by the Congress prior to the Year one thousand eight hundred and eight, but a Tax or duty may be imposed on such Importation, not exceeding ten dollars for each person.

(2) The privilege of the Writ of Habeus Corpus shall not be suspended, unless when in Cases of Rebellion or Invasion the public Safety may require it.

(3) No Bill of Attainder or ex post facto Law shall be passed.

(4) No Capitation, or other direct, Tax shall be laid, unless in Proportion to the Census or Enumeration herein before directed to be taken.

(5) No Tax or Duty shall be laid on Articles exported from any State.

(6) No Preference shall be given by any Regulation of Commerce or Revenue to the Ports of one State over those of another; nor shall Vessels bound to, or from, one State be obliged to enter, clear, or pay Duties in another.

(7) No money shall be drawn from the Treasury, but in Consequence of Appropriations made by Law; and a regular Statement and Account of the Receipts and Expenditures of all public Money shall be published from time to time.

(8) No Title of Nobility shall be granted by the United States: And no Person holding any Office of Profit or Trust under them, shall, without the Consent of Congress, accept any present, Emolument, Office, or Title, of any kind whatever, from any King, Prince, or foreign State.

**Section 10.** (1) No State shall enter into any Treaty, Alliance, or Confederation; grant Letters of Marque and Reprisal; coin Money; emit Bills of Credit; make any Thing but gold and silver Coin a Tender in payment of Debts; pass any Bill of Attainder, ex post facto Law, or Law impairing the Obligation of Contracts, or grant any Title of Nobility.

(2) No State shall, without the Consent of the Congress, lay any Imposts or Duties on Imports or Exports, except what may be absolutely necessary for executing it's inspection laws: and the net Produce of all Duties and Imposts, laid by any State on Imports or Exports, shall be for the Use of the Treasury of the United States; and all such Laws shall be subject to the Revision and Controul of the Congress.

(3) No State shall, without the Consent of Congress, lay any Duty of Tonnage, keep Troops, or Ships of War in time of Peace, enter into any Agreement or Compact with another State, or with a foreign Power, or engage in War, unless actually invaded, or in such imminent Danger as will not Admit of Delay.

# Article II

**Section 1.** (1) The executive Power shall be vested in a President of the United States of America. He shall hold his Office during the Term of four Years, and, together with the Vice President, chosen for the same Term, be elected, as follows:

(2) Each State shall appoint, in such Manner as the Legislature thereof may direct, a Number of Electors, equal to the whole Number of Senators and Representatives to which the State may be entitled in the Congress; but no Senator or Representative, or Person holding an Office of Trust or Profit under the United States, shall be appointed an Elector.

(3) The Electors shall meet in their respective States, and vote by Ballot for two Persons, of whom one at least shall not be an Inhabitant of the same State with themselves. And they shall make a List of all the Persons voted for, and of the Number of Votes for each; which List they shall sign and certify, and transmit sealed to the Seat of the Government of the United States, directed to the President of the Senate. The President of the Senate shall, in the Presence of the Senate and House of Representatives, open all the Certificates, and the Votes shall then be counted. The Person having the greatest Number of Votes shall be the President, if such a Number be a Majority of the whole Number of Electors appointed; and if there be more than one who have such Majority, and have an equal Number of Votes, then the House of Representatives shall immediately choose by Ballot one of them for President; and if no Person have a Majority, then from the five highest on the List the said House shall in like Manner choose the President. But in choosing the President, the Votes shall be taken by States the Representation from each State having one Vote; A quorum for this Purpose shall consist of a Member or Members from two thirds of the States, and a Majority of all the States shall be necessary to a Choice. In every Case, after the Choice of the President, the Person having the greater Number of Votes of the Electors shall be the Vice President. But if there should remain two or more who have equal Votes, the Senate shall choose from them by Ballot the Vice President.

(4) The Congress may determine the Time of choosing the Electors, and the Day on which they shall give their Votes; which Day shall be the same throughout the United States.

(5) No person except a natural born Citizen, or a Citizen of the United States, at the time of the Adoption of this Constitution, shall be eligible to the Office of President; neither shall any Person be eligible to that Office who shall not have attained to the Age of thirty-five Years, and been fourteen Years a Resident within the United States.

(6) In case of the removal of the President from Office, or of his Death, Resignation or Inability to discharge the Powers and Duties of the said Office, the Same shall devolve on the Vice President , and the Congress may by Law provide for the Case of Removal, Death, Resignation or Inability, both of the President and Vice President, declaring what Officer shall then act as President, and such Officer shall act accordingly, until the Disability be removed, or a President shall be elected.

(7) The President shall, at stated Times, receive for his Services, a Compensation, which shall neither be increased nor diminished during the period for which he shall have been elected, and he shall not receive within that Period any other Emolument from the United States, or any of them.

(8) Before he enter on the Execution of his Office, he shall take the following Oath or Affirmation: "I do solemnly swear (or affirm) that I will faithfully execute the Office of President of the United States, and will to the best of my Ability, preserve, protect, and defend the Constitution of the United States."

**Section 2.** (1) The President shall be Commander in Chief of the Army and Navy of the United States, and of the militia of the several States, when called into the actual Service of the United States; he may require the Opinion, in writing, of the principal Officer in each of the Executive Departments, upon any Subject relating to the Duties of their respective Offices, and he shall have Power to grant Reprieves and Pardons for Offenses against the United States, except in Cases of Impeachment.

(2) He shall have Power, by and with the Advice and Consent of the Senate to make Treaties, provided two thirds of the Senators present concur; and he shall nominate, and by and with the Advice and Consent of the Senate, shall appoint Ambassadors, other public Ministers and Consuls, Judges of the supreme Court, and all other Officers of the United States, whose Appointments are not herein otherwise provided for, and which shall be established by Law; but the Congress may by Law vest the Appointment of such inferior Officers, as they think proper, in the President alone, in the Courts of Law, or in the Heads of Departments.

(3) The President shall have power to fill up Vacancies that may happen during the Recess of the Senate, by granting Commissions which shall expire at the End of their next Session.

**Section 3.** He shall from time to time give to the Congress Information of the State of the Union, and recommend to their Consideration such Measures as he shall judge necessary and expedient; he may, on extraordinary Occasions, convene both Houses, or either of them, and in Case of Disagreement between them, with Respect to the Time of Adjournment, he may adjourn them to such Time as he shall think proper; he shall receive Ambassadors and other public Ministers; he shall take Care that the Laws be faithfully executed, and shall Commission all the Officers of the United states.

**Section 4.** The President, Vice President and all civil Officers of the United States, shall be removed from Office on Impeachment for, and Conviction of, Treason, Bribery, or other high Crimes and Misdemeanors.

# Article III

**Section 1.** The judicial Power of the United States, shall be vested in one supreme Court, and in such inferior Courts as the Congress may from time to time ordain and establish. The Judges, both of the supreme and inferior Courts, shall hold their offices during good Behaviour, and shall, at stated Times, receive for their Services a Compensation, which shall not be diminished during their Continuance in Office.

## Section 2.

(1) The judicial Power shall extend to all Cases, in Law and Equity, arising under this Constitution, the Laws of the United States, and Treaties made, or which shall be made, under their Authority;—to all Cases affecting Ambassadors, other public Ministers and Consuls;—to Controversies to which the United States shall be a Party;—to Controversies between two or more States;—between a State and Citizens of another State;—between Citizens of different States;—between Citizens of the same State claiming Lands under the Grants of different States, and between a State, or the Citizens thereof, and foreign States, Citizens or Subjects.

(2) In all Cases affecting Ambassadors, other public Ministers and Consuls, and those in which a State shall be a Party, the supreme Court shall have original Jurisdiction. In all the other Cases before mentioned, the supreme Court shall have appellate Jurisdiction, both as to Law and Fact, with such Exceptions, and under such Regulations as the Congress shall make.

(3) The trial of all Crimes, except in Cases of Impeachment, shall be by Jury; and such Trial shall be held in the State where the said Crimes shall have been committed; but when not committed within any State, the Trial shall be at such Place or Places as the Congress may by Law have directed.

## Section 3.

(1) Treason against the United States, shall consist only in levying War against them, or, in adhering to their Enemies, giving them Aid and Comfort. No Person shall be convicted of Treason unless on the Testimony of two Witnesses to the same overt Act, or on Confession in open Court.

(2) The Congress shall have Power to declare the Punishment of Treason, but no Attainder of Treason shall work Corruption of Blood, or Forfeiture except during the Life of the Person attainted.

# Article IV

## Section 1.

Full Faith and Credit shall be given in each State to the public Acts, Records, and judicial Proceedings of every other State. And the Congress may by general Laws prescribe the Manner in which such Acts, Records and Proceedings shall be proven, and the Effect thereof.

## Section 2.

(1) The Citizens of each State shall be entitled to all Privileges and Immunities of Citizens in the several States.

(2) A Person charged in any State with Treason, Felony, or other Crime, who shall flee from Justice, and be found in another State, shall on demand of the executive Authority of the State from which he fled, be delivered up, to be removed to the State having Jurisdiction of the Crime.

(3) No Person held to Service or Labour in one State, under the Laws thereof, escaping into another, shall, in Consequence of any Law or Regulation therein, be discharged from such Service or Labour, but shall be delivered up on Claim of the Party to whom such Service or Labour may be due.

## Section 3.

(1) New States may be admitted by the Congress into this Union; but no new State shall be formed or erected within the Jurisdiction of any other State; nor any State be formed by the Junction of two or more States, or Parts of States, without the Consent of the Legislatures of the States concerned as well as of the Congress.

(2) The Congress shall have Power to dispose of and make all needful Rules and Regulations respecting the Territory or other Property belonging to the United States; and nothing in this Constitution shall be so construed as to Prejudice any Claims of the United States, or of any particular State.

## Section 4.

The United States shall guarantee to every State in this Union a Republican Form of Government, and shall protect each of them against Invasion; and on Application of the Legislature, or of the Executive (when the Legislature cannot be convened) against domestic Violence.

# Article V

The Congress, whenever two thirds of both Houses shall deem it necessary, shall propose Amendments to this Constitution, or, on the Application of the Legislatures of two thirds of the several States, shall call a Convention for proposing Amendments, which, in either Case, shall be valid to all Intents and Purposes, as part of this Constitution, when ratified by the Legislatures of three fourths of the several States, or by Conventions in three fourths thereof, as the one or the other Mode of Ratification may be proposed by the Congress; Provided that no Amendment which may be made prior to the Year One thousand eight hundred and eight shall in any Manner affect the first and fourth Clauses in the Ninth Section of the first Article; and that no State, without its Consent, shall be deprived of its equal Suffrage in the Senate.

# Article VI

(1) All Debts contracted and Engagements entered into, before the Adoption of this Constitution shall be as valid against the United States under this Constitution, as under the Confederation.

(2) This Constitution, and the Laws of the United States which shall be made in Pursuance thereof; and all Treaties made, or which shall be made, under the Authority of the United States, shall be the supreme Law of the Land; and the Judges in every State shall be bound

thereby, any Thing in the Constitution or Laws of any State to the Contrary notwithstanding.

(3) The Senators and Representatives before mentioned, and the Members of the several State Legislatures, and all executive and judicial Officers, both of the United States and of the several States, shall be bound by Oath or Affirmation, to support this Constitution, but no religious Test shall ever be required as a Qualification to any Office or public Trust under the United States.

## Article VII

The Ratification of the Conventions of nine States shall be sufficient for the Establishment of this Constitution between the States so ratifying the Same.

## AMENDMENTS

## Amendent I (1791)

Congress shall make no law respecting an establishment of religion, or prohibiting the free exercise thereof; or abridging the freedom of speech, or of the press; or the right of the people peaceably to assemble, and to petition the Government for a redress of grievances.

## Amendment II (1791)

A well regulated Militia, being necessary to the security of a free State, the right of the people to keep and bear Arms, shall not be infringed.

## Amendment III (1791)

No soldier shall, in time of peace be quartered in any house, without the consent of the Owner, nor in time of war, but in a manner to be prescribed by law.

## Amendment IV (1791)

The right of the people to be secure in their persons, houses, papers, and effects, against unreasonable searches and seizures, shall not be violated, and no Warrants shall issue, but upon probable cause, supported by Oath or affirmation, and particularly describing the place to be searched, and the persons or things to be seized.

## Amendment V (1791)

No person shall be held to answer for a capital, or otherwise infamous crime, unless on a presentment or indictment of a Grand Jury, except in cases arising in the land

or naval forces, or in the Militia, when in actual service in time of War or public danger; nor shall any person be subject for the same offence to be twice put in jeopardy of life or limb; nor shall be compelled in any criminal case to be a witness against himself, nor be deprived of life, liberty, or property, without due process of law; nor shall private property be taken for public use, without just compensation.

## Amendment VI (1791)

In all criminal prosecutions, the accused shall enjoy the right to a speedy and public trail, by an impartial jury of the State and district wherein the crime shall have been committed, which district shall have been previously ascertained by law, and to be informed of the nature and cause of the accusation; to be confronted with the witnesses against him; to have compulsory process for obtaining witnesses in his favor, and to have the Assistance of Counsel for his defence.

## Amendment VII (1791)

In Suits at common law, where the value in controversy shall exceed twenty dollars, the right of trial by jury shall be preserved, and no fact tried by jury, shall be otherwise re-examined in any Court of the United States, than according to the rules of the common law.

## Amendment VIII (1791)

Excessive bail shall not be required, nor excessive fines imposed, nor cruel and unusual punishments inflicted.

## Amendment IX (1791)

The enumeration in the Constitution, of certain rights, shall not be construed to deny or disparage others retained by the people.

## Amendment X (1791)

The powers not delegated to the United States by the Constitution, nor prohibited by it to the States, are reserved to the States respectively, or to the people.

## Amendment XI (1798)

The Judicial power of the United States shall not be construed to extend to any suit in law or equity, commenced or prosecuted against one of the United States by Citizens of another State, or by Citizens or Subjects of any Foreign State.

## Amendment XII (1804)

The Electors shall meet in their respective states and vote by ballot for President and Vice-President, one of whom, at least, shall not be an inhabitant of the same state with themselves; they shall name in their ballots the person voted for as President, and in distinct ballots the person voted for as Vice-President, and they shall make distinct lists of all persons voted for as President, and of all persons voted for as Vice-President, and of the number of votes for each, which lists they shall sign and certify, and transmit sealed to the seat of government of the United States, directed to the President of the Senate;—the President of the Senate shall, in the presence of the Senate and House of Representatives, open all the certificates and the votes shall then be counted;—The person having the greatest number of votes for President, shall be the President, if such number be a majority of the whole number of Electors appointed; and if no person have such majority, then from the persons having the highest numbers not exceeding three on the list of those voted for as President, the House of Representatives shall choose immediately, by ballot, the President. But in choosing the President, the votes shall be taken by states, the representation from each state having one vote; a quorum for this purpose shall consist of a member or members from two-thirds of the states, and a majority of all the states shall be necessary to a choice. And if the House of Representatives shall not choose a President whenever the right of choice shall devolve upon them before the fourth day of March next following, the Vice-President shall act as President, as in the case of the death or other constitutional disability of the President.—The person having the greatest number of votes as Vice-President, shall be the Vice-President, if such number be a majority of the whole number of Electors appointed, and if no person have a majority, then from the two highest numbers on the list, the Senate shall choose the Vice-President; a quorum for the purpose shall consist of two thirds of the whole number of Senators, and a majority of the whole number shall be necessary to a choice. But no person constitutionally ineligible to the office of President shall be eligible to that of Vice President of the United States.

## Amendment XIII (1865)

**Section 1.** Neither slavery nor involuntary servitude, except as punishment for a crime whereof the party shall have been duly convicted, shall exist within the United States, or any place subject to their jurisdiction.

**Section 2.** Congress shall have power to enforce this article by appropriate legislation.

## Amendment XIV (1868)

**Section 1.** All persons born or naturalized in the United States, and subject to the jurisdiction thereof, are citizens of the United States and of the State wherein they reside. No State shall make or enforce any law which shall abridge the privileges or immunities of citizens of the United States; nor shall any State deprive any person of life, liberty, or property, without due process of law; nor deny to any person within its jurisdiction the equal protection of the laws.

**Section 2.** Representatives shall be apportioned among the several States according to their respective numbers, counting the whole number of persons in each state, excluding Indians not taxed. But when the right to vote at any election for the choice of electors for President and Vice President of the United States, Representatives in Congress, the Executive and Judicial officers of a State, or the members of the Legislature thereof, is denied to any of the male inhabitants of such State, being twenty-one years of age, and citizens of the United States, or in any way abridged, except for participation in rebellion, or other crime, the basis of representation therein shall be reduced in the proportion which the number of such male citizens shall bear to the whole number of male citizens twenty-one years of age in such State.

**Section 3.** No person shall be a Senator or Representative in Congress, or elector of President and Vice President, or hold any office, civil or military, under the United States, or under any State, who having previously taken an oath, as a member of Congress, or as an officer of the United States, or as a member of any State legislature, or as an executive or judicial officer of any State, to support the Constitution of the United States, shall have engaged in insurrection or rebellion against the same, or given aid or comfort to the enemies thereof. But Congress may by a vote of two-thirds of each House, remove such disability.

**Section 4.** The validity of the public debt of the United States, authorized by law, including debts incurred for payment of pensions and bounties for services in suppressing insurrection or rebellion, shall not be questioned. But neither the United States nor any State shall assume or pay debt or obligation incurred in aid of insurrection or rebellion against the United States, or any claim for the loss or emancipation of any slave; but all such debts, obligations and claims shall be held illegal and void.

**Section 5.** The Congress shall have power to enforce, by appropriate legislation, the provisions of this article.

## Amendment XV (1870)

**Section 1.** The right of citizens of the United States to vote shall not be denied or abridged by the United States or by any State on account of race, color, or previous condition of servitude.

**Section 2.** The Congress shall have power to enforce this article by appropriate legislation.

## Amendment XVI (1913)

The Congress shall have power to lay and collect taxes on incomes, from whatever source derived, without apportionment among the several States, and without regard to any census or enumeration.

## Amendment XVII (1913)

(1) The Senate of the United States shall be composed of two Senators from each State, elected by the people thereof, for six years; and each Senator shall have one vote. The electors in each State shall have the qualifications requisite for electors of the most numerous branch of the State legislatures.

(2) When vacancies happen in the representation of any State in the Senate, the executive authority of such State shall issue writs of election to fill such vacancies: Provided, That the legislature of any State may empower the executive thereof to make temporary appointments until the people fill the vacancies by election as the legislature may direct.

(3) This amendment shall not be so construed as to affect the election or term of any Senator chosen before it becomes valid as part of the Constitution.

## Amendment XVIII (1919)

**Section 1.** After one year from the ratification of this article, the manufacture, sale, or transportation of intoxicating liquors within, the importation thereof into, or the exportation thereof from the United States and all territory subject to the jurisdiction thereof for beverage purposes is hereby prohibited.

**Section 2.** The Congress and the several States shall have concurrent power to enforce this article by appropriate legislation.

**Section 3.** This article shall be inoperative unless it shall have been ratified as an amendment to the Constitution by the legislatures of the several States, as provided in the Constitution, within seven years from the date of the submission hereof to the States by the Congress.

## Amendment XIX (1920)

[1] The right of citizens of the United States to vote shall not be denied or abridged by the United States or any State on account of sex.

[2] Congress shall have power to enforce this article by appropriate legislation.

## Amendment XX (1933)

**Section 1.** The terms of the President and Vice President shall end at noon on the 20th day of January, and the terms of Senators and Representatives at noon on the 3d day of January, of the years in which such terms would have ended if this article had not been ratified; and the terms of their successors shall then begin.

**Section 2.** The Congress shall assemble at least once in every year, and such meeting shall begin at noon on the 3d day of January, unless they shall by law appoint a different day.

**Section 3.** If, at the time fixed for the beginning of the term of the President, the President elect shall have died, the Vice President elect shall become President. If the President shall not have been chosen before the time fixed for the beginning of this term, or if the President elect shall have failed to qualify, then the Vice President elect shall act as President until a President shall have qualified; and the Congress may by law provide for the case wherein neither a President elect nor a Vice President elect shall have qualified, declaring who shall then act as President, or the manner in which one who is to act shall be selected, and such person shall act accordingly until a President or Vice President shall have qualified.

**Section 4.** The Congress may by law provide for the case of the death of any of the persons from whom the House of Representatives may choose a President whenever the right of choice shall have devolved upon them, and for the case of the death of any of the persons from whom the Senate may choose a Vice President whenever the right of choice shall have devolved upon them.

**Section 5.** Sections 1 and 2 shall take effect on the 15th day of October following the ratification of this article.

**Section 6.** This article shall be inoperative unless it shall have been ratified as an amendment to the Constitution by the legislatures of three-fourths of the several States within seven years from the date of its submission.

## Amendment XXI (1933)

**Section 1.** The eighteenth article of amendment to the Constitution of the United States is hereby repealed.

**Section 2.** The transportation or importation into any State, Territory, or possession of the United States for delivery or use therein of intoxicating liquors, in violation of the laws thereof, is hereby prohibited.

**Section 3.** This article shall be inoperative unless it shall have been ratified as an amendment to the Constitution by conventions in the several States, as provided in the Constitution, within seven years from the date of the submission hereof to the States by the Congress.

## Amendment XXII (1951)

**Section 1.** No person shall be elected to the office of the President more than twice, and no person who has held the office of President, or acted as President, for more than two years of a term to which some other person was elected President shall be elected to the office of President more than once. But this Article shall not apply to any person holding the office of President when this Article was proposed by the Congress, and shall not prevent any person who may be holding the office of President, or acting as President, during the term within which this Article becomes operative from holding the office of President or acting as President during the remainder of such term.

**Section 2.** This article shall be inoperative unless it shall have been ratified as an amendment to the Constitution by the legislatures of three-fourths of the several States within seven years from the date of its submission to the States by the Congress.

## Amendment XXIII (1961)

**Section 1.** The District constituting the seat of Government of the United States shall appoint in such manner as the Congress may direct:

A number of electors of President and Vice President equal to the whole number of Senators and Representatives in Congress to which the District would be entitled if it were a State, but in no event more than the least populous state; they shall be in addition to those appointed by the states, but they shall be considered, for the purposes of the election of President and Vice President, to be electors appointed by a state; and they shall meet in the District and perform such duties as provided by the twelfth article of amendment.

**Section 2.** The Congress shall have power to enforce this article by appropriate legislation.

## Amendment XXIV (1964)

**Section 1.** The right of citizens of the United States to vote in any primary or other election for President or Vice President, for electors for President or Vice President, or for Senator or Representatives in Congress, shall not be denied or abridged by the United States, or any State by reason of failure to pay any poll tax or other tax.

**Section 2.** The Congress shall have power to enforce this article by appropriate legislation.

## Amendment XXV (1967)

**Section 1.** In case of the removal of the President from office or of his death or resignation, the Vice President shall become President.

**Section 2.** Whenever there is a vacancy in the office of the Vice President, the President shall nominate a Vice President who shall take office upon confirmation by a majority vote of both Houses of Congress.

**Section 3.** Whenever the President transmits to the President pro tempore of the Senate and the Speaker of the House of Representatives his written declaration that he is unable to discharge the power and duties of his office, and until he transmits to them a written declaration to the contrary, such powers and duties shall be discharged by the Vice President as Acting President.

**Section 4.** Whenever the Vice President and a majority of either the principal officers of the executive departments or of such other body as Congress may by law provide, transmit to the President pro tempore of the Senate and the House of Representatives their written declaration that the President is unable to discharge the powers and duties of his office, the Vice President shall immediately assume the powers and duties of the office as Acting President.

Thereafter, when the President transmits to the President pro tempore of the Senate and the Speaker of the House of Representatives his written declaration that no inability exists, he shall resume the power and duties of his office unless the Vice President and a majority of either the principal officers of the executive department or of such other body as Congress may by law provide, transmit within four days to the President pro tempore of the Senate and the Speaker of the House of Representatives their written declaration and the President is unable to discharge the powers and duties of his office. Thereupon Congress shall decide the issue, assembling within forty-eight hours for that purpose if not in session. If the Congress, within twenty-one days after receipt of the latter written declaration, or, if Congress is not in session, within twenty-one days after Congress is required to assemble, determines by two-thirds vote of both Houses that the President is unable to discharge the powers and duties of his office, the Vice President shall continue to discharge the same as Acting President; otherwise the President shall resume the powers and duties of his office.

## Amendment XXVI (1971)

**Section 1.** The right of citizens of the United States, who are eighteen years of age or older, to vote shall not be denied or abridged by the United States or by any State on account of age.

**Section 2.** The Congress shall have power to enforce this article by appropriate legislation.

# Appendix B
# Selected Statutes

*Note to Students:* The following important federal statutes have been excerpted and edited as an aid to study. Often important portions of these laws have been omitted because of lack of relevance to the matters studied in the text.

## FEDERAL JURISDICTION (28 U.S. CODE)

**Section 1331. Federal Question Jurisdiction.** The district courts shall have original jurisdiction of all civil actions arising under the Constitution, laws, or treaties of the United States.

**Section 1332. Diversity of Citizenship; Amount in Controversy; Costs.**

(a) The district courts shall have original jurisdiction of all civil actions where the matter in controversy exceeds the sum or value of $10,000, exclusive of interest and costs, and is between—

**(1)** citizens of different States;

**(2)** citizens of a State and citizens or subjects of a foreign state;

**(3)** citizens of different States and in which citizens or subjects of a foreign state are additional parties; and

**(4)** a foreign state . . . as plaintiff and citizens of a State or of different States.

(b) . . . where the plaintiff who files the case originally in the Federal courts is finally adjudged to be entitled to recover less than the sum or value of $10,000, . . . the district court may deny costs to the plaintiff and, in addition, may impose costs on the plaintiff.

. . . .

## THE FEDERAL ANTITRUST LAWS

### The Sherman Antitrust Act (July 2, 1890, as amended)

**Section 1.** Every contract, combination in the form of trust or otherwise, or conspiracy, in restraint of trade or commerce among the several States, or with foreign nations, is hereby declared to be illegal. Every person who shall make any such contract or engage in any such combination or conspiracy shall be deemed guilty of a felony, and, on conviction thereof, shall be punished by fine not exceeding one million dollars if a corporation, or, if any other person, one hundred thousand dollars or by imprisonment not exceeding three years, or by both said punishments in the discretion of the court.

**Section 2.** Every person who shall monopolize, or attempt to monopolize, or conspire with any other person or persons, to monopolize any part of the trade or commerce among the several States, or with foreign nations, shall be deemed guilty of a felony, and, on conviction thereof, shall be punished by fine not exceeding one million dollars if a corporation, or, if any other person, one hundred thousand dollars or by imprisonment not exceeding three years, or by both said punishments, in the discretion of the court.

## The Clayton Act as Amended by the Robinson-Patman Act (Oct. 15, 1914, amended June 19, 1936)

**Section 2.** This section is also known as the Robinson-Patman amendment to Section 2 of the Clayton Act. (a) That it shall be unlawful for any person engaged in commerce, in the course of such commerce, either directly or indirectly, to discriminate in price between different purchasers of commodities of like grade and quality, where such ... commodities are sold for use, consumption, or resale within the United States or any Territory thereof ... and where the effect of such discrimination may be substantially to lessen competition or tend to create a monopoly in any line of commerce, or to injure, destroy, or prevent competition with any person who either grants or knowingly receives the benefit of such discrimination, or with customers of either of them: Provided, That nothing herein contained shall prevent differentials which make only due allowance for differences in the cost of manufacture, sale, or delivery resulting from the differing methods or quantities in which such commodities are to such purchasers sold or delivered: Provided, however, That the Federal Trade Commission may, after due investigation and hearing ... fix and establish quantity limits, ... as to particular commodities or classes of commodities, where it finds that available purchasers in greater quantities are so few as to render differentials on account thereof unjustly discriminatory or promotive of monopoly in any line of commerce; and the foregoing shall then not be construed to permit differentials based on differences in quantities greater than those so fixed and established: And provided further, That nothing herein contained shall prevent persons engaged in selling goods, wares, or merchandise in commerce from selecting their own customers in *bona fide* transactions and not in restraint of trade: And provided further, That nothing herein contained shall prevent price changes from time to time where in response to changing conditions affecting the market for or the marketability of the goods concerned, such as but not limited to actual or imminent deterioration of perishable goods, obsolescence of seasonal goods, distress sales under court process, or sales in good faith in discontinuance of business in the goods concerned.

(b) Upon proof being made, at any hearing on a complaint under this section, that there has been discrimination in price or services or facilities furnished, the burden of rebutting the *prima facie* case thus made by showing justification shall be upon the person charged with a violation of this section, and unless justification shall be affirmatively shown, the Commission is authorized to issue an order terminating the discrimination: Provided, however, That nothing herein contained shall prevent a seller rebutting the *prima facie* case thus made by showing that his lower price or the furnishing of services or facilities to any purchaser or purchasers was made in good faith to meet an equally low price of a competitor, or the services or facilities furnished by a competitor.

(c) That it shall be unlawful for any person engaged in commerce, in the course of such commerce, to pay or grant, or to receive or accept, anything of value as a commission, brokerage, or other compensation, or any allowance or discount in lieu thereof, except for services rendered in connection with the sale of purchase of goods, wares, or merchandise, either to the other party to such transactions or to an agent, representative, or other intermediary therein where such intermediary is acting in fact for or in behalf, or is subject to the direct or indirect control, of any party to such transaction other than the person by whom such compensation is granted or paid.

(d) That it shall be unlawful for any person engaged in commerce to pay or contract for the payment of anything of value to or for the benefit of a customer of such person in the course of such commerce as compensation or in consideration for any services or facilities furnished by or through such customer in connection with the processing, handling, sale, or offering for sale of any products or commodities manufactured, sold, or offered for sale by such person, unless such payment or consideration is available on proportionally equal terms to all other customers competing in the distribution of such products or commodities.

(e) That it shall be unlawful for any person to discriminate in favor of one purchaser against another purchaser or purchasers of a commodity bought for resale, with or without processing, by contracting to furnish or furnishing, or by contributing to the furnishing of, any services or facilities connected with the processing, handling, sale, or offering for sale of such commodity so purchased upon terms not accorded to all purchasers on proportionally equal terms.

(f) That it shall be unlawful for any person engaged in commerce, in the course of such commerce, knowingly to induce or receive a discrimination in price which is prohibited by this section.

**Section 3.** That it shall be unlawful for any person engaged in commerce, in the course of such commerce, to lease or make a sale or contract for sale of goods, wares, merchandise, machinery, supplies, or other commodities, whether patented or unpatented, for use, consumption, or resale within the United States or ... other place under the jurisdiction of the United States, or fix a price charged therefor, or discount from, or rebate upon, such price, on the condition, agreement, or understanding that the lessee or purchaser thereof shall not use or deal in the goods, wares, merchandise, machinery, supplies, or other commodities of a competitor or competitors of the lessor or seller, where the effect of such lease, sale, or contract for sale or such condition, agreement, or understanding may be to substantially lessen competition to tend to create a monopoly in any line of commerce.

**Section 4.** That any person who shall be injured in his business or property by reason of anything forbidden in the antitrust laws may sue therefor ... without respect to the amount in controversy, and shall recover threefold the damages by him sustained, and the cost of suit, including a reasonable attorney's fee.

. . . .

**Section 4C.** (a) (1) Any attorney general of a State may bring a civil action in the name of such State, as *parens patriae* on behalf of natural persons residing in such State ... to secure monetary relief ... for injury sustained by such natural persons to their property by reason of any violation of [the Sherman Act.]

. . . .

**Section 6.** That the labor of a human being is not a commodity or article of commerce. Nothing contained in the antitrust laws shall be construed to forbid the existence and operation of labor, agricultural or horticultural organizations, instituted for the purposes of mutual help, and not having capital stock or conducted for profit, or to forbid or restrain individual members of such organizations from lawfully carrying out the legitimate objects thereof; nor shall such organizations or the members thereof, be held or construed to be illegal combinations or conspiracies in restraint of trade, under the antitrust laws.

**Section 7.** That no corporation engaged in commerce shall acquire, directly or indirectly, the whole or any part of the stock or other share capital and no corporation subject to the jurisdiction of the Federal Trade Commission shall acquire the whole or any part of the assets of another corporation engaged also in commerce, where in any line of commerce in any section of the country, the effect of such acquisition may be substantially to lessen competition, or to tend to create a monopoly.

No corporation shall acquire, directly or indirectly, the whole or any part of the stock or other share capital and no corporation subject to the jurisdiction of the Federal Trade Commission shall acquire the whole or any part of the assets of one or more corporations engaged in commerce, where in any line of commerce in any section of the country, the effect of such acquisition, of such stocks or assets, or of the use of such stock by the voting or granting of proxies or otherwise, may be substantially to lessen competition, or to tend to create a monopoly.

This section shall not apply to corporations purchasing such stock solely for investment and not using the same by voting or otherwise to bring about, or in attempting to bring about, the substantial lessening of competition. Nor shall anything contained in this section prevent a corpo-

ration engaged in commerce from causing the formation of subsidiary corporations for the actual carrying on of their immediate lawful business, or the natural and legitimate branches or extensions thereof, or from owning and holding all or a part of the stock of such subsidiary corporations, when the effect of such formation is not to substantially lessen competition.

. . . .

Nothing contained in this secton shall apply to transactions duly consummated pursuant to authority given by the Civil Aeronautics Board, Federal Communications Commission, Federal Power Commission, Interstate Commerce Commission, the Securities and Exchange Commission. . . .

**Section 8. . . .** No person at the same time shall be a director in any two or more corporations any one of which has capital, surplus, and undivided profits aggregating more than $1,000,000 engaged in whole or in part in commerce, ... if such corporations are or shall have been theretofore, by virtue of their business and location of operation, competitors, so that the elimination of competition by agreement between them would constitute a violation of any of the provisions of the antitrust laws. . . .

## The Federal Trade Commission Act (1914)

**Section 5.** (a) (1) Unfair methods of competition in or affecting commerce, and unfair or deceptive acts or practices in or affecting commerce, are hereby declared unlawful.

(2) The Commission is hereby empowered and directed to prevent persons, partnerships, or corporations ... from using unfair methods of competition in or affecting commerce and unfair or deceptive acts or practices in or affecting commerce.

## The Federal Labor Laws

## The National Labor Relations Act, As Amended

**Section 1. . . .** (b) Industrial strife which interferes with the normal flow of commerce and with the full production of articles and commodities for commerce, can be avoided or substantially minimized if employers, employees, and labor organizations each recognize under law one another's legitimate rights in their relations with each other, and above all recognize under law that neither party has any right in its relations with any other to engage in acts or practices which jeopardize the public health, safety, or interest.

It is the purpose and policy of this Act, in order to promote the full flow of commerce, to prescribe the legitimate rights of both employees and employers in their relations affecting commerce, to provide orderly and peaceful procedures for preventing the interference by either with the legitimate rights of the other, to protect the rights of individual employees in their relations with labor organizations whose activities affect commerce, to define and proscribe practices on the part of labor and management which affect commerce and are inimical to the general welfare, and to protect the rights of the public in connection with labor disputes affecting commerce.

### Section 2. Definitions.

When used in this Act—

(1) The term "person" includes one or more individuals, labor organizations, partnerships, associations, corporations, legal representatives, trustees, trustees in bankruptcy, or receivers.

. . . .

(5) The term "labor organization" means any organization of any kind, or any agency or employee representation committee or plan, in which employees participate and which exists for the purpose, in whole or in part, of dealing with employers concerning grievances, labor disputes, wages, rates of pay, hours of employment, or conditions of work.

. . . .

(11) The term "supervisor" means any individual having authority, in the interest of the employer, to hire, transfer, suspend, lay off, recall, promote, discharge, assign, reward, or discipline other employees, or responsibly to direct them, or to adjust their grievances, or effectively to recommend such action, if in connection with the foregoing the exercise of such authority is not of a merely routine or clerical nature, but requires the use of independent judgment.

(12) The term "professional employee" means—

(a) any employee engaged in work (i) predominately intellectual and varied in character as opposed to routine mental, manual, mechanical, or physical work; (ii) involving the consistent exercise of discretion and judgment in its performance; (iii) of such a character that the output produced or the result accomplished cannot be standardized in relation to a given period of time; (iv) requiring knowledge of an advanced type in a field of science or learning customarily acquired by a prolonged course of specialized intellectual instruction and study. . . .

(b) any employee, who (i) has completed the courses of specialized intellectual instruction and study described in clause (iv) of paragraph (a) and (ii) is performing related work under the supervision of a professional person to qualify himself to become a professional employee as defined in paragraph (a).

. . . .

### Section 3. National Labor Relations Board.

(a) The National Labor Relations Board (hereinafter called the "Board") . . . as an agency of the United States, shall consist of five . . . members, appointed by the President by and with the advice and consent of the Senate . . . for terms of five years each,. . . . The President shall designate one member to serve as Chairman of the Board. Any member of the Board may be removed by the President, upon notice and hearing, for neglect of duty or malfeasance in office, but for no other cause.

. . . .

### Section 6.

The Board shall have authority from time to time to make, amend, and rescind, in the manner prescribed by the Administrative Procedure Act, such rules and regulations as may be necessary to carry out the provisions of this Act.

### Section 7. Rights of Employees.

Employees shall have the right to self-organization, to form, join, or assist labor organizations, to bargain collectively through representatives of their own choosing, and to engage in other concerted activities for the purpose of collective bargaining or other mutual aid or protection, and shall also have the right to refrain from any or all of such activities except to the extent that such right may be affected by an agreement requiring membership in a labor organization as a condition of employment as authorized in section 8(a) (3).

### Section 8. Unfair Labor Practices.

(a) It shall be an unfair labor practice for an employer—

(1) to interfere with, restrain, or coerce employees in the exercise of the rights guaranteed in section 7;

(2) to dominate or interfere with the formation or administration of any labor organization or contribute financial or other support to it: Provide, that subject to rules and regulations made and published by the Board pursuant to section 6, an employer shall not be prohibited from permitting employees to confer with him during working hours without loss of time or pay;

(3) by discrimination in regard to hire or tenure of employment or any term or condition of employment to encourage or discourage membership in any labor organization: Provide, that nothing in this Act . . . shall preclude an employer from making an agreement with a labor organization . . . to require as a condition of employment membership therein. . . . Provided further, that no employer shall justify any discrimination against an employee for nonmembership in a labor organization (A) if he has reasonable grounds for believing that such membership was not available to the employee on the same terms and conditions generally applicable to other members, or (B) if he has reasonable grounds for believing that membership was denied or terminated for reasons other than the failure of the employee to tender periodic dues and initiation fees uniformly required as a condition of acquiring or retaining membership;

(4) to discharge or otherwise discriminate against an employee because he has filed charges or given testimony under this Act;

(5) to refuse to bargain collectively with the representatives of his employees, subject to the provisions of section 9(a).

(b) It shall be an unfair labor practice for a labor organization or its agents—

(1) to restrain or coerce (A) employees in the exercise of the rights guaranteed in section 7: Provided, that this

paragraph shall not impair the right of a labor organization to prescribe its own rules with respect to the acquisition or retention of membership therein; or (B) an employer in the selection of his representatives for the purposes of collective bargaining or the adjustment of grievances;

(2) to cause or attempt to cause an employer to discriminate against an employee in violation of subsection (a) (3) or to discriminate against an employee with respect to whom membership in such organization has been denied or terminated on some ground other than his failure to tender the periodic dues and the initiation fees uniformly required as a condition of acquiring or retaining membership;

(3) to refuse to bargain collectively with an employer, provided it is the representative of his employees subject to the provisions of section 9 (a).

(4) (i) to engage in, or to induce or encourage any individual employed by any person engaged in commerce or in an industry affecting commerce to engage in, a strike or a refusal in the course of his employment to use, manufacture, process, transport, or otherwise handle or work on any goods, articles, materials, or commodities or to perform any services; or, (ii) to threaten, coerce, or restrain any person engaged in commerce or in an industry affecting commerce, where in either case an object thereof is:

(A) forcing or requiring any employer or self-employed person to join any labor or employer organization or to enter into any agreement which is prohibited by section 8 (e);

(B) forcing or requiring any person to cease using, selling, handling, transporting, or otherwise dealing in the products of any other producer, processor, or manufacturer, or to cease doing business with any other person, or forcing or requiring any other employer to recognize or bargain with a labor organization as the representative of his employees unless such labor organization has been certified as the representative of such employees.... Provided, that nothing contained in this clause (B) shall be construed to make unlawful, where not otherwise unlawful, any primary strike or primary picketing;

(C) forcing or requiring any employer to recognize or bargain with a particular labor organization as the representative of his employees if another labor organization has been certified as the representative of such employees....

(D) forcing or requiring any employer to assign particular work to employees in a particular labor organization or in a particular trade, craft, or class....

Provided, that nothing contained in this subsection (b) shall be construed to make unlawful a refusal by any person to enter upon the premises of any employer (other than his own employer), if the employees of such employer are engaged in a strike ratified or approved by a representative of such employees whom such employer is required to recognize under this Act: Provided further, that for the purposes of this paragraph (4) only, nothing contained in such paragraph shall be construed to prohibit publicity, other than picketing, for the purpose of truthfully advising the public, including consumers and members of a labor orga-

nization, that a product or products are produced by an employer with whom the labor organization has a primary dispute and are distributed by another employer, as long as such publicity does not have an effect of inducing any individual employed by any person other than the primary employer in the course of his employment to pick up, deliver, or transport any goods, or not to perform any services, at the establishment of the employer engaged in such distribution;

(5) to require of employees covered by an agreement authorized under subsection (a) (3) the payment, as a condition precedent to becoming a member of such organization, of a fee in an amount which the Board finds excessive or discriminatory....

(6) to cause or attempt to cause an employer to pay or deliver or agree to pay or deliver any money or other thing of value, in the nature of an exaction, for services which are not performed or not to be performed; and

(7) to picket or cause to be picketed, or threaten to picket or cause to be picketed, any employer where an object thereof is forcing or requiring an employer to recognize or bargain with a labor organization as the representative of his employees, or forcing or requiring the employees of an employer to accept or select such labor organization as their collective bargaining representative, unless such labor organization is currently certified as the representative of such employees:

(A) where the employer has lawfully recognized in accordance with this Act any other labor organization and a question concerning representation may not appropriately be raised under section 9(c) of this Act.

(B) where within the preceding 12 months a valid election under section 9(c) of this Act has been conducted, or

(C) where such picketing has been conducted without a petition under section 9(c) being filed within a reasonable period of time not to exceed 30 days from the commencement of such picketing: Provided, that when such a petition has been filed the Board shall forthwith, without regard to the provisions of section 9(c) (1) or the absence of a showing of a substantial interest on the part of the labor organization, direct an election in such units as the Board finds to be appropriate and shall certify the results thereof: Provided further, that nothing in this subparagraph (C) shall be construed to prohibit any picketing or other publicity for the purpose of truthfully advising the public (including consumers) that an employer does not employ members of, or have a contract with, a labor organization, unless an effect of such picketing is to induce any individual employed by any other person in the course of his employment, not to pick up, deliver or transport any goods or not to perform any services.

Nothing in this paragraph (7) shall be construed to permit any act which would otherwise be an unfair labor practice under this section 8(b).

(c) The expressing of any views, argument, or opinion, or the dissemination thereof, whether in written, printed, graphic, or visual form, shall not constitute or be evidence of an unfair labor practice under any of the provisions of this Act, if such expression contains no threat of reprisal or force or promise of benefit.

(d) For the purposes of this section, to bargain collectively is the performance of the mutual obligation of the employer and the representative of the employees to meet at reasonable times and confer in good faith with respect to wages, hours, and other terms and conditions of employment, or the negotiation of an agreement, or any question arising thereunder, and the execution of a written contract incorporating any agreement reached if requested by either party, but such obligation does not compel either party to agree to a proposal or require the making of a concession: Provided, that where there is in effect a collective bargaining contract covering employees in an industry affecting commerce, the duty to bargain collectively shall also mean that no party to such contract shall terminate or modify such contract, unless the party desiring such termination or modification—

(1) serves a written notice upon the other party to the contract of the proposed termination or modification 60 days prior to the expiration date thereof, or in the event such contract contains no expiration date, 60 days prior to the time it is proposed to make such termination or modification;

(2) offers to meet and confer with the other party for the purpose of negotiating a new contract or a contract containing the proposed modifications;

(3) notifies the Federal Mediation and Conciliation Service within 30 days after such notice of the existence of a dispute. . . .

(4) continues in full force and effect, without resorting to strike or lockout, all the terms and conditions of the existing contract for a period of 60 days after such notice is given or until the expiration date of such contract, whichever occurs later.

. . . .

(e) it shall be an unfair labor practice for any labor organization and any employer to enter into any contract or agreement, express or implied, whereby such employer ceases or refrains or agrees to cease or refrain from handling, using, selling, transporting, or otherwise dealing in any of the products of any other employer, or to cease doing business with any other person, . . . Provided, that nothing in this subsection (e) shall apply to an agreement between a labor organization and an employer in the construction industry relating to the contracting or subcontracting of work to be done at the site. . . .

## Section 10. Prevention of Unfair Labor Practices. (a)
The Board is empowered, as hereinafter provided, to prevent any person from engaging in any unfair labor practice affecting commerce. This power shall not be affected by any other means of adjustment or prevention that has been or may be established by any other means of adjustment or prevention that has been or may be established by agreement, law, or otherwise. . . .

(b) Whenever it is charged that any person has engaged in or is engaging in any such unfair labor practice,

the Board . . . shall have power to issue and cause to be served upon such person a complaint stating the charges in that respect, and containing a notice of hearing before the Board or a member thereof, or before a designated agent or agency, at a place therein fixed, not less than five days after the serving of said complaint. . . . The person so complained of shall have the right to file an answer to the . . . complaint and to appear in person or otherwise and give testimony. . . .

(c) The testimony taken by such member, agent, or agency or the Board shall be reduced to writing and filed with the Board. Thereafter, in its discretion, the Board upon notice may take further testimony or hear argument. If upon the preponderance of the testimony taken the Board shall be of the opinion that any person named in the complaint has engaged in or is engaging in any such unfair labor practice, then the Board shall state its findings of fact and shall issue and cause to be served on such person an order requiring such person to cease and desist from such unfair labor practice, and to take such affirmative action including reinstatement of employees with or without back pay, as will effectuate the policies of this Act. . . . If upon the preponderance of the testimony taken the Board shall not be of the opinion that the person named in the complaint has engaged in or is engaging in any such unfair labor practice, then the Board shall state its findings of fact and shall issue an order dismissing the said complaint. No order of the Board shall require the reinstatement of any individual as an employee who has been suspended or discharged, or the payment to him of any back pay, if such individual was suspended or discharged for cause.

. . . .

(e) The Board shall have power to petition any court of appeals of the United States, . . . for the enforcement of such order and for appropriate temporary relief or restraining order, and shall file in the court the record in the proceedings. . . . Upon the filing of such petition, the court shall cause notice thereof to be served upon such person, and thereupon shall have jurisdiction of the proceeding and of the question determined therein, and shall have power to grant such temporary relief or restraining order as it deems just and proper, and to make and enter a decree enforcing, modifying, and enforcing as so modified, or setting aside in whole or in part the order of the Board.

. . . .

(j) The Board shall have power, upon issuance of a complaint as provided in subsection (b) charging that any person has engaged in or is engaging in an unfair labor practice, to petition any district court of the United States. . . . for appropriate temporary relief or restraining order. . . .

. . . .

## Section 13. Limitations. Nothing in this Act, except as specifically provided for herein, shall be construed so as to interfere with or impede or diminish in any way the right to strike, or to affect the limitations or qualifications on that right.

**Section 14.** (a) Nothing herein shall prohibit any individual employed as a supervisor from becoming or remaining a member of labor organization, but no employer subject to this Act shall be compelled to deem individuals defined herein as supervisors as employees for the purpose of any law, either national or local, relating to collective bargaining.

(b) Nothing in this Act shall be construed as authorizing the execution or application of agreements requiring membership in a labor organization as a condition of employment in any State or Territory in which such execution or application is prohibited by State or Territorial law.

. . . .

### Section 19. Individuals with Religious Convictions.
Any employee who is a member of and adheres to established and traditional tenets or teachings of a bona fide religion, body, or sect which has historically held conscientious objections to joining or financially supporting labor organizations shall not be required to join or financially support any labor organization as a condition of employment; except that such employee may be required in a contract between such employee's employer and a labor organization in lieu of periodic dues and initiation fees, to pay sums equal to such dues and initiation fees to a nonreligious, nonlabor organization chartiable fund exempt from taxation under section 501(c) (3) of title 26 of the Internal Revenue Code. . . .

. . . .

### Section 206. National Emergencies.
Whenever in the opinion of the President of the United States, a threatened or actual strike or lockout affecting an entire industry or a substantial part thereof engaged in trade, commerce, transportation, transmission, or communication among the several States or with foreign nations, or engaged in the production of goods for commerce, will, if permitted to occur or continue, imperil the national health or safety, he may appoint a board of inquiry into the issues involved in the dispute and to make a written report to him within such time as he shall prescribe. Such report shall include a statement of the facts with respect to the dispute and to make a written report to him within such time as he shall prescribe. Such report shall include a statement of the facts with respect to the dispute, including each party's statement of its position but shall not contain any recommendations. The President shall file a copy of such report with the [Federal Mediation and Conciliation] Service and shall make its contents available to the public.

. . . .

**Section 208.** (a) Upon receiving a report from a board of inquiry the President may direct the Attorney General to petition any district court of the United States having jurisdiction of the parties to enjoin such strike or lockout or the continuing thereof, and if the court finds that such threatened or actual strike or lockout—

(i) affects an entire industry or a substantial part

thereof engaged in trade, commerce, transportation, transmission, or communication among the several States or with foreign nations, or engaged in the production of goods for commerce; and

(ii) if permitted to occur or to continue, will imperil the national health or safety, it shall have jurisdiction to enjoin any such strike or lockout, or the continuing thereof, and to make such other orders as may be appropriate.

. . . .

**Section 209.** (a) Whenever a district court has issued an order under section 208 enjoining acts or practices which imperil or threaten to imperil the national health or safety, it shall be the duty of the parties to the labor dispute giving rise to such order to make every effort to adjust and settle their differences, with the assistance of the [Federal Mediation and Conciliation] Service created by this Act. Neither party shall be under any duty to accept, in whole or in part, any proposal of settlement made by the Service.

(b) Upon the issuance of such order, the President shall reconvene the board of inquiry which has previously reported with respect to the dispute. At the end of a 60 day period (unless the dispute has been settled by that time), the board of inquiry shall report to the President the current position of the parties. . . . The President shall make such report available to the public. The National Labor Relations Board, within the succeeding 15 days, shall take a secret ballot of the employees of each employer involved in the dispute on the question of whether they wish to accept the final offer of settlement made by their employer as stated by him and shall certify the results thereof to the Attorney General within 5 days thereafter.

**Section 210.** Upon certification of the results of such ballot or upon a settlement being reached, whichever happens sooner, the Attorney General shall move the court to discharge the injunction, which motion shall then be granted and the injunction discharged. . . .

# THE FEDERAL CIVIL RIGHTS LAWS

## 42 U.S. Code, Section 1982. (1866)

All persons within the jurisdiction of the United States shall have the same right in every State and Territory and the District of Columbia to make and enforce contracts, to sue, be parties, give evidence, and to the full and equal benefit of all laws and proceedings for the security of persons and property as is enjoyed by white citizens, and shall be subject to like punishment, pains, penalities, taxes, licenses and exactions of every kind, and no other.

## 42 U.S. Code, Section 1982. (1866)

All citizens of the United States shall have the same right, in every State and Territory, as is enjoyed by white citizens thereof to inherit, purchase, lease, sell, hold and convey real and personal property.

# 42 U.S. Code, Section 1983. (1871)

Every person who, under color of any statute, ordinance, regulation, custom, or usage, of any State or Territory, subjects, or causes to be subjected, any citizen of the United States or other person within the jurisdiction thereof to the deprivation of any rights, privileges, or immunities secured by the Constitution and laws, shall be liable to the party injured in an action at law, suit in equity, or other proper proceeding.

# Title II of the Civil Rights Act of 1964—The Public Accomodations Section

**Section 201.** (a) All persons shall be entitled to the full and equal enjoyment of the goods, services, facilities, privileges, advantages, and accomodations of any place of public accomodation, as defined in this section, without discrimination on the ground of race, color, religion, or national origin.

(b) Each of the following establishments which serves the public is a place of public accomodation within the meaning of this title if its operations affect commerce, or if discrimination or segregation by it is supported by State action:

(1) any inn, hotel, motel, or other establishment which provides lodging to transient guests, other than an establishment located within a building which contains not more than five rooms for rent or hire and which is actually occupied by the proprietor of such establishment as his residence;

(2) any restaurant, cafeteria, lunchroom, lunch counter, soda fountain. . . .

(3) any motion picture house, theater, concert hall, sports arena, stadium. . . .

(4) any establishment (A) (i) which is physically located within the premises of any establishment otherwise covered by this subsection, or (ii) within the premises of which is physically located any such covered establishment, and (B) which holds itself out as serving patrons of such covered establishment.

(c) The operations of an establishment affect commerce within the meaning of this title if (1) it is one of the establishments described in paragraph (1) of subsection (b); (2) in the case of an establishments described in paragraph (2) of subsection (b), it serves or offers to serve interstate travelers or a substantial portion of the food which it serves, or gasoline or other products which it sells, has moved in commerce; (3) in the case of an establishment described in paragraph (3) of subsection (b), it customarily presents films, performances, athletic teams, exhibitions, or other sources of entertainment which move in commerce; and (4) in the case of an establishment described in paragraph (4) of subsection (b), it is physically located within the premises of, or there is physically located within its premises, an establishment the operations of which affect commerce within the meaning of this subsection. For purposes of this section, "commerce" means travel, trade, traffic, commerce, transportation, or communication among the several States, or between the District of Columbia and any State, or between any foreign country or any territory or possession and any State or the District of Columbia, or between points in the same State but through any other State or the District of Columbia or a foreign country.

**Section 202.** All persons shall be entitled to be free, at any establishment or place, from discrimination or segregation of any kind on the ground of race, color, religion, or national origin, if such discrimination or segregation is or purports to be required by any law, statute, ordinance, regulation, rule, or order of a State or any agency or political subdivision thereof.

**Section 203.** No person shall (a) withhold, deny, or attempt to withhold or deny, or deprive or attempt to deprive, any person of any right or privilege secured by section 201 or 202, or (b) intimidate, threaten, or coerce, or attempt to intimidate, threaten, or coerce any person with the purpose of interfering with any right or privilege secured by section 201 or 202, or (c) punish or attempt to punish any person for exercising or attempting to exercise any right or privilege secured by section 201 or 202.

. . . .

# Title VII of the Civil Rights Act of 1964—The Employment Discrimination Section

**Section 703. Unlawful Employment Practices.** (a) It shall be an unlawful employment practice for an employer—

(1) to fail or refuse to hire or to discharge any individual, or otherwise to discriminate against any individual with respect to his compensation, terms, conditions, or privileges or employment, because of such individual's race, color, religion, sex, or national origin; or

(2) to limit, segregate, or classify his employees or applicants for employment in any way which would deprive or tend to deprive any individual of employment opportunities or otherwise adversely affect his status as an employee, because of such individual's race, color, religion, sex, or national origin.

(b) It shall be an unlawful employment practice for an employment agency to fail or refuse to refer for employment, or otherwise to discriminate against, any individual because of his race, color, religion, sex, or national origin, or to classify or refer for employment any individual on the basis or his race, color, religion, sex, or national origin.

(c) It shall be an unlawful employment practice for a labor organization—

(1) to exclude or to expel from its membership, or otherwise to discriminate against, any individual because of

his race, color, religion, sex, or national origin;

(2) to limit, segregate, or classify its membership or applicants for membership, or to classify or fail or refuse to refer for employment any individual, in any way which would deprive or tend to deprive any individual of employment opportunities, or would limit such employment opportunities or otherwise adversely affect his status as an employee or as an applicant for employment, because of such individual's race, color, religion, sex, or national origin; or

(3) to cause or attempt to cause an employer to discriminate against an individual in violation of this section.

(d) It shall be an unlawful employment practice for any employer, labor organization, or joint labor-management committee controlling apprenticeship or other training or retraining, including on-the-job training programs to discriminate against any individual because of his race, color, religion, sex, or national origin in admission to, or employment in, any program established to provide apprenticeship or other training.

(e) Nothwithstanding any other provision of this subchapter,

(1) it shall not be an unlawful employment practice for an employer to hire and employ employees, for an employment agency to classify, or refer for employment any individual, for a labor organization to classify its membership or to classify or refer for employment any individual, or for an employer, labor organization, or joint labor-management committee controlling apprenticeship or other training or retraining programs to admit or employ any individual in any such program, on the basis of his religion, sex, or national origin in those certain instances where religion, sex, or national origin is a bona fide occupational qualification reasonably necessary to the normal operation of that particular business or enterprise, and

(2) it shall not be an unlawful employment practice for a school, college, university, or other educational institution or institution of learning to hire and employ employees of a particular religion if such school, college, university, or other educational institution or institution of learning is, in whole or in substantial part, owned, supported, controlled, or managed by a particular religion or by a particular religious corporation, association, or society, or if the curriculum of such school, college, university, or other educational institution or institution of learning is directed toward the propagation of a particular religion.

(f) As used in this subchapter, the phrase "unlawful employment practice" shall not be deemed to include any action or measure taken by an employer, labor organization, joint labor-management committee, or employment agency with respect to an individual who is a member of the Communist Party of the United States or of any other organization required to register as a Communist-action or Communist-front organization. . . .

(g) Notwithstanding any other provision of this subchapter, it shall not be an unlawful employment practice for an employer to fail or refuse to hire and employ any individual for any position, for an employer to discharge any individual from any position, or for an employment

agency to fail or refuse to refer any individual for employment in any position, or for a labor organization to fail or refuse to refer any individual for employment in any position, if—

(1) the occupancy of such position, or access to the premises in or upon which any part of the duties of such position is performed or is to be performed, is subject to any requirement imposed in the interest of the national security of the United States . . . and

(2) such individual has not fulfilled or has ceased to fulfill that requirement.

(h) Notwithstanding any other provision of this subchapter, it shall not be an unlawful employment practice for an employer to apply different standards of compensation, or different terms, conditions, or privileges of employment pursuant to a bona fide seniority or merit system, or a system which measures earnings by quantity or quality of production or to employees who work in different locations, provided that such differences are not the result of an intention to discriminate because of race, color, religion, sex, or national origin, nor shall it be an unlawful employment practice for an employer to give and act upon the results of any professionally developed ability test provided that such test, its administration or action upon the results is not designed, intended or used to discriminate because of race, color, religion, sex, or national origin. . . .

(j) Nothing contained in this subchapter shall be interpreted to require any employer, employment agency, labor organization, or joint labor-management committee subject to this subchapter to grant preferential treatment to any individual or to any group because of the race, color, religion, sex, or national origin of such individual or group on account of an imbalance which may exist with respect to the total number of percentage of persons of any race, color, religion, sex, or national origin employed by any employer, referred or classified for employment by any employment agency or labor organization, or admitted to, or employed in, any apprenticeship or other training program, in comparison with the total number or percentage of persons of such race, color, religion, sex, or national origin in any community, State, section, or other area, or in the available work force in any community, State, section, or other area.

. . . .

**Section 704. Other Unlawful Employment Practices.** (a) It shall be an unlawful employment practice for an employer to discriminate against any of his employees or applicants for employment, for an employment agency, or joint labor-management committee controlling apprenticeship or other training or retraining, including on-the-job training programs, to discriminate against any individual, or for a labor organization to discriminate against any member thereof or applicant for membership, because he has opposed any practice made an unlawful employment practice by this subchapter, or because he has made a charge, testified, assisted, or participated in any manner in an investigation, proceeding, or hearing under this subchapter.

(b) It shall be an unlawful employment practice for an employer, labor organization, employment agency, or joint labor-management committee controlling apprenticeship or other training or retraining, including on-the-job training programs, to print or publish or cause to be printed or published any notice or advertisement relating to employment by such an employer or membership or any classification or referral for employment by such a labor organization, or relating to any classification or referral for employment by such an employment agency, or relating to admission to, or employment in, any program established to provide apprenticeship or other training by such a joint-labor-management committee, indicating any preference, limitation, specification, or discrimination, based on race, color, religion, sex, or national origin, except that such a notice or advertisement may indicate a preference, limitation, specification, or discrimination based on religion, sex or national origin when religion, sex, or national origin is a bona fide occupational qualification for employment.

## The Federal Civil Rights Act of 1968

**Section 803.** (a) Subject to the provisions of subsection (b) and section 807, the prohibitions against discrimination in the sale or rental of housing set forth in section 804 shall apply:

(1) . . . to (A) dwellings owned or operated by the Federal Government; (B) dwellings provided in whole or in part with the aid of loans, advances, grants, or contributions made by the Federal Government. . . . (C) dwellings provided in whole or in part by loans insured, guaranteed, or otherwise secured by the credit of the Federal Government. . . . (D) dwellings provided by the development of real property purchased, rented, or otherwise obtained from a State or local public agency receiving Federal financial assistance for slum clearance or urban renewal. . . .

(2) . . . to all dwellings covered by paragraph (1) and to all other dwellings except as exempted by subsection (b).

(b) Nothing in section 804 . . . shall apply to—

(1) any single-family house sold or rented by an owner: Provided, That such private individual owner does not own more than three such single-family houses at any one time: Provided further, That in the case of the sale of any such single-family house by a private individual owner not residing in such house at the time of such sale or who was not the most recent resident of such house prior to such sale, the exemption granted by this subsection shall apply only with respect to one such sale within any twenty-four month period: Provided further, That such bona fide private individual owner does not own any interest in, nor is there owned or reserved on his behalf, under any express or voluntary agreement, title to any right to all or a portion of the proceeds from the sale or rental of, more than three such single-family houses at any one time: Provided further, That . . . the sale or rental of any such single-family house shall be excepted from the application of this Title only if such house is sold or rented (A) without the use in

any manner of the sales or rental facilities or the sales or rental services of any real estate broker, agent, or salesman, or of such facilities or services of any person in the business of selling or renting dwellings, or of any employee or agent of any such broker, agent, or salesman, or person and (B) without the publication, posting, mailing, after notice, of any advertisement or written notice in violation of section 804(c) of this title; . . . or

(2) rooms or units in dwellings containing living quarters occupied or intended to be occupied by no more than four families living independently of each other, if the owner actually maintains and occupies one of such living quarters for his residence.

(c) for the purposes of subsection (b), a person shall be deemed to be in the business of selling or renting dwellings if—

(1) he has, within the preceding twelve months, participated as principal in three or more transactions involving the sale or rental of any dwelling. . . .

(2) he has, within the preceding twelve months, participated as agent . . . in two or more transactions involving the sale or rental of any dwelling. . . .

(3) he is the owner of any dwelling designed or intended for occupancy by, or occupied by, five or more families.

### Section 804. Discrimination in the Sale or Rental of Housing.
As made applicable by section 803 and except as exempted by sections 803(b) and 807, it shall be unlawful—

(a) to refuse to sell or rent after the making of a bona fide offer, or to refuse to negotiate for the sale or rental of, or otherwise make unavailable or deny, a dwelling to any person because of race, color, religion, sex, or national origin.

(b) To discriminate against any person in the terms, conditions, or privileges of sale or rental of a dwelling, or in the provision of services or facilities in connection therewith, because of race, color, religion, sex, or national origin.

(c) To make, print or publish, . . . any notice, statement, or advertisement, with respect to the sale or rental of a dwelling that indicates any preference, limitation, or discrimination based on race, color, religion, sex, or national origin, or an intention to make any such preference, limitation, or discrimination.

(d) To represent to any person because of race, color, religion, sex, or national origin that any dwelling is not available for inspection, sale, or rental when such dwelling is in fact so available.

(e) For profit, to induce or attempt to induce any person to sell or rent any dwelling by representations regarding the entry or prospective entry into the neighborhood of a person or persons of a particular race, color, religion, sex, or national origin.

**Section 807.** Nothing in this title shall prohibit a religious organization, association, or society, or any nonprofit institution or organization operated, supervised, or controlled by or in conjuction with a religious organization, association or society, from limiting the sale, rental or occupancy of dwellings which it owns or operates for other than a commercial purpose to persons of the same religion, or from giving preference to such persons, unless membership in such religion is restricted on account of race, color, sex, or national origin. Nor shall anything in this title prohibit a private club not in fact open to the public, which as an incident to its primary purpose or purposes provides lodging which it owns or operates for other than a commercial purpose, from limiting the rental or occupancy of such lodgings to its members or from giving preference to its members.

. . . .

# UNIFORM COMMERCIAL CODE (SELECTED PROVISIONS)

## Section 2-302. Unconscionable Contract or Clause.

(1) If the court as a matter of law finds the contract or any clause of the contract to have been unconscionable at the time it was made the court may refuse to enforce the contract, or it may so limit the application of any unconscionable clause as to avoid any unconscionable result.

(2) When it is claimed or appears to the court that the contract or any clause thereof may be unconscionable the parties shall be afforded a reasonable opportunity to present evidence as to its commercial setting, purpose and effect to aid the court in making the determination.

## Section 2-313. Express Warranties by Affirmation, Promise, Description, Sample.

(1) Express warranties by the seller are created as follows:

(a) Any affirmation of fact or promise made by the seller to the buyer which relates to the goods and becomes a part of the basis of the bargain creates an express warranty that the goods shall conform to the affirmation or promise.

(b) Any description of the goods which is made part of the basis of the bargain creates an express that the goods shall conform to the description.

(c) Any sample or model which is made part of the basis of the bargain creates an express warranty that the whole of the goods shall conform to the sample or model.

(2) It is not necessary to the creation of an express warranty that the seller use formal words such as "warrant" or "guarantee" or that he have a specific intention to make a warranty, but an affirmation merely of the value of the goods or a statement purporting to be merely the seller's opinion or commendation of the goods does not create a warranty.

## Section 2-314. Implied Warranty: Merchantability; Usage of Trade.

(1) Unless excluded or modified (Section 2-316), a warranty that the goods shall be merchantable is implied in a contract for their sale if the seller is a merchant with respect to goods of that kind. Under this section the serving for value of food or drink to be consumed either on the premises or elsewhere is a sale.

(2) Goods to be merchantable must be at least such as

(a) pass without objection in the trade under the contract description; and

(b) in the case of fungible goods, are of fair average quality within the description; and

(c) are fit for the ordinary purposes for which such goods are used; and

(d) run, within the variations permitted by the agreement, of even kind, quality and quantity within each unit and among all units involved; and

(e) are adequately contained, packaged, and labeled as the agreement may require; and

(f) conform to the promises or affirmations of fact made on the container or label if any.

(3) Unless excluded or modified (Section 2-316) other implied warranties may arise from course of dealing or usage of trade.

## Section 2-315. Implied Warranty: Fitness for Particular Purpose.

Where the seller at the time of contracting has reason to know any particular purpose for which the goods are required and that the buyer is relying on the seller's skill or judgment to select or furnish suitable goods, there is unless excluded or modified under the next section an implied warranty that the goods shall be fit for such purposes.

## Section 2-316. Exclusion or Modification of Warranties.

(1) Words or conduct relevant to the creation of an express warranty and words or conduct tending to negate or limit warranty shall be construed wherever reasonable as consistent with each other; but subject to the provisions of this Article . . . negation or limitation is inoperative to the extent that such construction is unreasonable.

(2) Subject to subsection (3), to exclude or modify the implied warranty of merchantability or any part of it in the language must mention merchantability and in case of a writing must be conspicuous, and to exclude or modify any implied warranty of fitness the exclusion must be by a writing and conspicuous. Language to exclude all implied warranties of fitness is sufficient if it states, for example, that "There are no warranties which extend beyond the description on the face hereof."

599

(3) Notwithstanding subsection (2)

(a) unless the circumstances indicate otherwise, all implied warranties are excluded by expressions like "as is," "with all faults," or other language which in common understanding calls the buyer's attention to the exclusion of warranties and makes plain that there is no implied warranty; and

(b) when the buyer before entering into the contract has examined the goods or the sample or model as fully as he desired or has refused to examine the goods there is no implied warranty with regard to defects which an examination ought in the circumstances to have revealed to him; and

(c) an implied warranty can also be excluded or modified by course of dealing or course of performance or usage of trade.

(4) Remedies for breach of warranty can be limited in accordance with the provisions of this Article on liquidation or limitation of damages and on contractual modification of remedy. . . .

## Section 2-318. Third-Party Beneficiaries of Warranties Express or Implied.

**Alternative A**  A seller's warranty whether express or implied extends to any natural person who is in the family or household of his buyer or who is a guest in his home if it is reasonable to expect that such person may use, consume or be affected by the goods and who is injured in person by breach of the warranty. A seller may not exclude or limit the operation of this section.

**Alternative B**  A seller's warranty whether express or implied extends to any natural person who may reasonably be expected to use, consume or be affected by the goods and who is injured in person by breach of the warranty. A seller may not exclude or limit the operation of this section.

**Alternative C**  A seller's warranty whether express or implied, extends to any person who may reasonably be expected to use, consume or be affected by the goods and who is injured by breach of the warranty. A seller may not exclude or limit the operation of this section with respect to injury to the person of an individual to whom the warranty extends.

## Section 2-714. Buyer's Damages for Breach in Regard to Accepted Goods.

(1). . . .

(2) The measure of damages for breach of warranty is the difference at the time and place of acceptance between the value of the goods accepted and the value they would have had if they had been as warranted, unless special circumstances show proximate damages of a different amount.

(3) In a proper case any incidental and consequential damages under the next section may also be recovered.

## Section 2-715. Buyer's Incidental and Consequential Damages.

(1) Incidental damages resulting from the seller's breach include expenses reasonably incurred in inspection, receipt, transportation and care and custody of goods rightfully rejected, any commerically reasonable charges, expenses or commissions in connection with effecting cover and any other reasonable expense incident to the delay or other breach.

(2) Consequential damages resulting from the seller's breach include

(a) any loss resulting from general or particular requirements and needs of which the seller at the time of contracting had reason to know and which could not reasonably be prevented by cover or otherwise; and

(b) injury to person or property proximately resulting from any breach of warranty.

## Section 2-719. Contractual Modification of Limitation of Remedy.

(1) Subject to the provisions of subsections (2) and (3) of this section and of the preceding section on liquidation and limitation of damages,

(a) the agreement may provide for remedies in addition to or in substitution for those provided in this Article and may limit or alter the measure of damages recoverable under this Article, as by limiting the buyer's remedies to return of the goods and repayment of the price or to repair and replacement of non-conforming goods or parts; and

(b) resort to a remedy as provided is optional unless the remedy is expressly agreed to be exclusive, in which case it is the sole remedy.

(2) Where circumstances cause an exclusive or limited remedy to fail of its essential purpose, remedy may be had as provided in this Act.

(3) Consequential damages may be limited or excluded unless the limitation or exclusion is unconscionable. Limitation of consequential damages for injury of the person in the case of consumer goods is prima facie unconscionable but limitation of damages where the loss is commercial is not.

# Glossary

The list of terms in this glossary is not meant as a substitute for a good law dictionary. Students should be aware that various terms have "shades" of meaning, which can only be derived from the context of a case or a particular discussion. The definitions provided are merely the most useful definition of the term for the purposes of this text. Words in italics are defined elsewhere in this glossary. It may be necessary to look those words up in order to be sure of a full definition.

**acceptance**  (contract law) agreement or acquiescence to the terms of an offer; compliance by an offeree with the terms and conditions of the terms of an offer.

**act of state doctrine**  the rule of international law that the courts of one nation will not sit in judgment on the acts of the government of another nation.

**activists**  judges who see the courts' role as advocate and protector of the interests of the weak and disadvantaged (see *restraintists*; *neutralists*).

**ad hoc**  for this purpose only; on a case-by-case basis.

**adjudicatory function**  (administrative law) the function of administrative agencies in deciding cases that arise under their authority.

**administrative agency**  (1) any *independent regulatory commission* or *line agency*; (2) for purposes of the *due process* clause, any governmentally related entity or person.

**Administrative Law Judge (ALJ)**  an officer who hears administrative cases before *administrative agencies*. Although these judges are attached to a particular agency, they are hired under the Civil Service system and have a measure of independence from the agency they serve.

**administrative regulations**  rules enacted by administrative agencies pursuant to a delegation of authority to make such rules by a legislative body. Although such regulations are not law, they have the force of law.

**adversary system**  the system of law in the United States, Great Britain, and the British Commonwealth. In the adversary system, lawyers for opposing sides present their cases, and the judge acts as a neutral decision maker. The assumption is that the truth will surface from the conflict of opposing forces (see *inquisitorial system*).

**adverse possession**  a method of acquisition of title to property. Possession must be actual, notorious, open, and hostile for a statutorily specified period of time. That period may often be shortened by payment of real estate taxes and "color of title," that is, some legal claim to the property.

**advisory opinions**  opinions issued by a court or other authority based upon a hypothetical question rather than a real case involving adversary interests.

**affecting commerce**  having an impact on goods or people moving between states.

**affirm**  to confirm a former judgment, usually of a lower court judgment by a higher appellate court.

**affirmative action**  policies attempting to remedy historic segregation through racial quotas or advantages to minorities, especially in employment and public education.

**affirmative defense**  a portion of an *answer* to a *complaint* that agrees that the plaintiff's complaint is accurate but asserts that there is more to the story. The defendant usually has the burden of proving affirmative defenses.

**agency**   (1) a legal relationship in which one person (the *agent*) acts for and on behalf of another person (the *principal*); (2) short for *administrative agency*.

**agency by estoppel**   an *agency* (definition 1) created by operation of law, and established by proof of such acts of the principal as reasonably lead others to conclude that the agency exists.

**agency coupled with an interest**   an irrevocable *agency*; an agency in which the agent has both the authority to act and an interest in the subject matter of the agency.

**agency shop**   (labor law) a form of *open shop agreement* in a labor contract in which employees are not required to join a union but are required to pay a portion of the union dues attributable to collective bargaining activities (see *union shop*).

**agent**   one who acts for and on behalf of another (see *agency*).

**amicus curiae**   literally "friend of the court"; a person or group not directly involved in a lawsuit but permitted to make an argument in the case.

**anarchy**   the complete absence of government.

**annual report**   (securities regulation) a yearly report filed with the Securities and Exchange Commission by all corporations subject to the 1934 Securities and Exchange Act.

**answer**   a responsive *pleading* in a lawsuit, filed by the *defendant* or other party in response to a *complaint* filed against that party, denying, admitting, or stating that the defendant is without information to answer the allegations of the complaint.

**antidumping laws**   laws controlling *dumping* of goods by foreign sellers.

**antifraud provisions**   (securities regulation) provisions of the securities laws outlawing specific practices in dealing with securities such as fraud, market manipulation, and corporate mismanagement.

**apparent authority**   a method of creation of agency relationships in which the *principal* places another in a position in which it reasonably appears to third persons that the *agent* has authority to deal on behalf of the principal.

**appellant**   the person filing an appeal; the appealing party.

**appellate jurisdiction**   the power to hear a case at the appellate level; the right to review a case decided by a lower court or an administrative agency.

**appellee**   the person against whom an appeal is filed; the party defending the judgment of the lower court.

**appropriate bargaining unit**   (labor law) the proper unit, whether shop, company, trade, or other, that is to elect a union representative, as determined by the National Labor Relations Board.

**arbitration**   submitting a dispute for final and binding settlement to a third person (the arbitrator), outside of the judicial process. If such submission is required by law, it is compulsory arbitration.

**Articles of Confederation**   the first attempt at a written constitution in America. The articles were proposed in 1777 and ratified in 1781 but were little more than a treaty or alliance between the states, with little power in the central government.

**articles of incorporation**   the grant of authority from the state to a *corporation* to act in the corporate form that defines the specific powers of the corporation.

**association**   any group of persons joined together for a particular purpose, but especially any *partnership* or other business form that is taxed as a corporation but has not organized as a corporation.

**assumed-name statutes**   state laws requiring that businesses that operate under some name other than the name(s) of the owner must register the business name with state or local government officials.

**assumption of risk**   a *tort* doctrine in which a person who assumes the consequences of injury occurring through the fault of another may not recover for such injuries; a voluntary exposure to a known risk.

**authorization cards**   cards signed by workers authorizing a union to request an election. Such cards are not membership cards.

**authorized shares**   the number of shares of stock a corporation is permitted to issue by virtue of its articles of incorporation, as amended.

**bait and switch**   a deceptive sales device wherein the seller offers a product at a low price and then convinces the consumer to switch to a higher-priced version of the product.

**bargaining order**   an order from the NLRB requiring the employer and the union to bargain over a particular issue.

**beneficiary**   a person who is to receive the benefits from something, especially of a *trust*, an insurance policy, or an estate.

**bfoq**   see *bona fide occupational qualification.*

**bilateral**   two-sided; containing two parts.

**bill of lading**   a negotiable receipt issued by the shipper of goods.

**Bill of Rights**   commonly understood to be the first ten amendments to the U.S. Constitution but often defined to include the thirteenth, fourteenth, and fifteenth amendments; those portions of the U.S. Constitution that protect individual liberties.

**blacklist**   a list of employees active in union affairs or the labor movement that is circulated to employers, who then refuse to hire such individuals.

**blackmail picketing**   an *unfair labor practice* by unions in which a union or employees picket in order to gain representation or obtain union members, if certain conditions are present: (1) when the employer has already recognized another union; (2) when an NLRB election has been held in the last twelve months; or (3) if a representation petition is not filed within thirty days of the onset of picketing.

**blockbusting**   inducing a person to sell or rent by making representations about the prospective entry of persons of a particular race or other prohibited category into a neighborhood; inducing panic selling.

**blue sky laws**   state statutes regulating the sale of securities or requiring registration of securities brokers or dealers, and usually containing *antifraud* provisions.

**bona fide occupational qualification**   an exception to the general prohibition of discrimination in employment, permitting classification on the basis of religion, sex, or national origin (but not race or color) if such classification is "reasonably necessary to the normal operation of that particular business or enterprise."

**bond**   (1) a debt security of a corporation secured by a pledge or mortgage on corporate property; (2) all debt securities (improper, but common usage).

**breach of duty**   one of the elements of any *tort*; violation or omission of some legally recognized duty.

**brief**   a written or printed document, prepared by counsel, which serves as the basis for argument before a court. Briefs are almost always filed in appellate cases and are sometimes used to present arguments in trial courts as well.

**broker**   (securities regulation) a person engaged in the business of making transactions in securities for the account of others (see *dealer; broker-dealer*).

**broker-dealer**   (securities regulation) a person who has both the status of *broker* and the status of *dealer* under the federal securities laws.

**bubble doctrine**   the theory that all parts of a single industrial plant should be treated as a single pollution source, and that offsetting increases and decreases in pollution from parts of the same plant should be permitted.

**bundle of rights theory**   the concept of ownership of *property* as a group of rights enabling the holder of those rights to deal with the property in certain ways.

**burden of proof**   the duty or necessity of affirmatively proving a fact or facts in dispute by a certain level of evidence. In most civil cases that level is by a "preponderance of the evidence," but in criminal cases it is "beyond a reasonable doubt." Some types of civil cases require a higher level, such as by "clear and convincing evidence."

**business judgment rule**   the rule that corporate officers and directors may manage the corporation within the bounds of the discretion granted to them by law, the *articles of incorporation*, and the corporate *by-laws*, all without interference by the courts.

**business trust**   a form of business organization in which investors give money or property to a board of trustees, which then uses that money or property for business purposes for the benefit of the investor-beneficiaries.

**by-laws**   rules adopted by a corporation, through its board of directors, for the operation of corporate affairs.

**capacity**   (contracts) the legal ability of a person to contract.

**case law**   judicial decisions in written form that act as precedent for future cases (see *stare decisis*).

**case or controversy requirement**   a Constitutional requirement that the federal courts cannot act and have no *jurisdiction* unless there is an actual, adverse case between parties.

**cause of action**   a legally recognized basis for a lawsuit.

**caveat emptor**   literally "let the buyer beware"; the general rule that a purchaser must examine a product before it is purchased, and in the event of defect, the buyer must bear the loss.

**cease and desist orders**   orders from an administrative agency to stop a certain act or practice; especially, an order of the NLRB to an employer or union.

**CEQ**   see *Council on Environmental Quality*.

**certiorari**   a petition to an appellate court, especially the U.S. Supreme Court, for leave to file an appeal to that court.

**C.F.R.**   see *Code of Federal Regulations*.

**challenge for cause**   an objection to a juror's serving on a case for some reason, such as potential bias or prejudice (see *peremptory challenge*).

**charging order**   an order by a court requiring a *partnership* to pay over a partner's income from a partnership to a personal creditor of the partner.

**chose in action**   a personal right to sue; a right of property not in possession.

**churning**   an unlawful practice by securities *brokers* involving making numerous unnecessary transactions in a customer's account in order to obtain the commission on those transactions.

**civil cases**   lawsuits between two or more private persons, including cases in which the government acts as a private party, usually asking for *damages* or *equitable relief*.

**class action**   suits filed on behalf of a group or class of individuals who are injured in the same way by the same or similar acts of the same defendant.

**classical deregulation**   the removal or alleviation of direct *economic regulation*.

**class voting**   a method of voting in a corporation in which each class of stock has different voting rights; also known as *series voting*.

**close corporation**   a small corporation; a corporation managed by its shareholders and often owned by a family.

**Code of Federal Regulations (C.F.R.)**   the comprehensive compilation of all federal administrative regulations.

**collective bargaining**   negotiations on behalf of a group of employees for a common employment contract, usually through a labor union.

**collective negotiation laws**   state statutes requiring negotiation between public employee unions and their employers. Such laws usually do not require agreement but do require the parties to negotiate.

**comfort letter**   a written statement by independent public accountants that reports filed with the SEC do not contain any false or misleading information, is written for the protection of the issuer and the underwriter of stock issues, and imposes liability on the accountants if false or misleading information is present unless the accountant used *due diligence*.

**Commerce Clause**   article 1, section 8, clause 3 of the U.S. Constitution, which provides much of the authority by which Congress regulates matters that are either *in commerce* or *affecting commerce*.

**commercial speech**   one of the exceptions to the first amendment rule that Congress may not make laws limiting freedom of speech. Commercial speech, such as advertising, may be limited by both federal and state governments in most cases.

**commingle**   to mix; to mix one's own property with the property of another.

**common law**   (1) the body of law that developed in England, as distinguished from civil law systems which developed on the European continent; (2) the body of law derived from the customs and usages of history or from the judgments of courts recognizing such customs and usages; (3) all of the positive law of any state or nation.

**common market**   an economic association of countries with no internal *tariffs* and a common external tariff.

**common situs**   a common employment site, such as a construction site, where several employers are at work at the same time.

**common stock**   one of the types of shares in a corporation, usually granting voting rights but receiving dividends after dividends are paid to preferred shares (see *preferred stock; participating preferred stock; equity financing*).

**community ethic**   the *societal ethic* that places primary emphasis on society and often justifies the sacrifice of individual rights for the greater good. At its extreme, this ethic corresponds to Marxism and totalitarianism, while in its more moderate aspects it reflects a simple concern for the good of the community.

**Community Relations Service**   a federal agency created by the Public Accommodations section of the Civil Rights Act of 1964 for the purpose of obtaining voluntary compliance with those sections of the act.

**compact theory**   see *natural rights theory*.

**company-dominated unions**   unions that are dependent on the employer for their existence or support; company unions.

**comparative negligence**   the doctrine accepted in many states that weighs the fault in *negligence* cases and permits a pro rata recovery based on the differences in guilt of the parties to the case, as opposed to *contributory negligence*.

**compensatory damages**   money awarded to the *plaintiff* in a civil action to make good or replace the loss caused by the injury and to put the plaintiff in the same position as before the injury.

**complaint**   the first *pleading* on the part of a *plaintiff* in a lawsuit, setting forth facts and allegations on which his or her claim for relief is based; sometimes called a petition in some types of cases or in some courts.

**Compliance Safety and Health Officers (COs)**   inspectors who conduct investigations and inspections regarding violations of OSHA.

**concentration**   (antitrust law) the degree to which an industry is gathered into one or a few hands, as in the case of *monopoly* or *oligopoly*.

**conclusive presumption**   a presumption that cannot be overcome by evidence, as opposed to a *rebuttable presumption*, which can be overcome by evidence.

**concurrent jurisdiction**   two or more courts with the power to hear the same subjects or cases.

**confession of judgment clause**   a clause in a contract or promissory note permitting the creditor to sue and obtain *judgment* against the debtor without notice, and that waives the right to notice, *summons*, and trial.

**confirming bank**  a bank located near the seller of goods that acts as a correspondent bank with the *issuing bank* in a documentary sale.

**conflicts of laws**  legal rules used to choose between the law of two or more states or nations that may apply to the same case.

**conglomerate merger**  (antitrust law) *corporate integration* between firms that are not related horizontally or vertically as competitors, buyers, or suppliers (see *product extension merger; market extension merger; pure conglomerate merger*).

**consent decree**  (antitrust law) negotiated settlements of government antitrust cases, which cannot be used as *prima facie proof* of violations in subsequent civil antitrust cases.

**consideration**  (contract law) the inducement to a contract; the cause, motive, price, or impelling influence that induces a party to enter into a contract; an act, forbearance, or promise of an act or forbearance, which is offered by one party to an agreement and accepted by another: the quid pro quo of the agreement.

**consolidation**  a method of *corporate integration* in which two firms join together to form a new third firm and both of the preexisting firms cease to exist.

**constitution**  a charter of government that expresses both the powers of government and limitations on those powers.

**contract**  an agreement between two or more persons that creates, modifies, or destroys a legal relationship.

**contracts clause**  a part of article 1, section 10 of the U.S. Constitution that prohibits the states from passing laws which impair the obligation of contracts. The clause is rarely used, because states may pass laws within their *police powers*, even though they affect private contracts.

**contributory negligence**  (tort law) the rule that if one party was in any way *negligent*, that party may not recover for injuries suffered as a result of another's negligence (see *comparative negligence*).

**copyright**  the grant of a limited *monopoly* to the author of a work.

**corporate charter**  see *articles of incorporation*.

**corporate integration**  any method by which two firms join together.

**corporate mismanagement**  (securities regulation) a requirement of Rule 10b-5 of the SEC that corporate officers may not make fraudulent or misleading statements in transactions in the shares of their own company.

**corporation**  a business form that is created by the state; is granted limited legal liability to the owners, or shareholders; and is treated as a separate legal entity for most purposes (see *not-for-profit corporations; articles of incorporation*).

**corrective advertising**  see *retroactive advertising*.

**cosigner**  a guarantor of a debt; a person who agrees to pay a debt on behalf of another and who is liable for the debt if the debtor defaults.

**cost–benefit analysis**  a balancing of the costs of an activity versus the benefits of that activity, usually measured in dollars.

**Council for Mutual Economic Aid (COMECON)**  a *common market* of communist nations.

**Council on Environmental Quality (CEQ)**  (environmental law) a three-member board appointed by the President to coordinate environmental programs and advise and assist the President on environmental matters.

**counterclaim**  a case filed by the *defendant* in a civil case against the *plaintiff* in the same case. Counterclaims may be mandatory ones, which arise from the same transaction and therefore must be filed, or permissive ones, which arise from other transactions or occurrences between the parties and which are not lost if not filed as a counterclaim.

**counteroffer**  (contracts) a response to an initial *offer* that materially or substantially changes the initial offer. Counteroffers are treated in the same way as a *rejection* of the initial offer and create a power of acceptance in the initial offeror.

**countervailing duties**   a *duty* imposed by the U.S. government on goods sold below market value (see *dumping*).

**country**   a *sovereign* political body; a *state* (definition 1).

**Court-Packing Plan**   a plan proposed to Congress by President Franklin Roosevelt in 1937 to increase the number of judges on the Supreme Court by one new judge for each existing judge over the age of seventy. The plan was proposed because of the Supreme Court's resistance to New Deal programs and was withdrawn after the Court's decision in *NLRB v. Jones & Laughlin Steel* and resistance to the plan by Congress.

**Courts of Chancery**   the equity courts originally set up in England to mitigate the harsh results sometimes obtained in the law courts. Judges in such courts were called chancellors (see *equity*, definition 2).

**covert conspiracy**   a concealed conspiracy.

**criminal conspiracy statutes**   (labor law) state laws that forbade organization of labor unions.

**criminal law**   law that punishes individuals for injuring the public at large.

**cross-claim**   an action filed by a *defendant* against a codefendant arising from the same transaction as the *plaintiff's* complaint.

**cross-elasticity of demand**   an economic concept that determines the interchangeability of goods; whether, given a price increase in one product, consumers will readily shift to another product; the principle of substitutability. The concept is used in antitrust law in determining the *relevant product market*.

**cross-examination**   the questioning of an opposing witness; the first examination of an adverse witness.

**cumulative dividends**   corporate stock dividends that accumulate if they are not paid from year to year.

**cumulative voting**   a method of voting in a corporation in which a shareholder receives a number of votes equal to the number of shares of stock owned times the number of directors to be elected, permitting the shareholder to apply those votes in any way he or she sees fit.

**current report**   a report filed with the SEC by any firm subject to the 1934 Securities and Exchange Act if certain events take place, and which is filed in addition to *annual* and *quarterly reports*.

**custodial interrogation**   one of the requirements of the *Miranda* decision. Warnings must be given when a suspect is "in custody" and being interrogated.

**customs duties**   a tax on imported items.


**damages**   money paid to a person who has suffered loss, detriment, or injury to person, property, or rights as a result of actions of another and under the *judgment* of a court (see *nominal damages; compensatory damages; punitive damages*).

**dealer**   for purposes of the federal securities laws, a person engaged in the business of buying and selling securities for his or her own account (see *broker; broker-dealer*).

**deauthorization elections**   (labor law) elections held by the NLRB to determine whether to withdraw the authority of a union representative to continue a union shop agreement (see *decertification elections*).

**debenture**   a form of corporate debt unsecured by corporate property or mortgages on corporate property.

**debt financing**   financing a corporation through borrowed money (see *equity financing; bond; debenture*).

**deceptive nondisclosure**   failure to tell consumers some important fact about a product, such as its foreign origin, product hazards, or important matters regarding its contents or construction.

**decertification elections**   (labor law) elections held by the NLRB to determine whether to retain the current bargaining representative (see *deauthorization elections*).

**declaratory judgment**   an action of a court that states the rights of parties to a case but does not result in *damages* or *equitable relief.*

**deed**   a written document, signed by the *grantor* of *real property*, in which *title* to or interests in real property are transferred from the grantor to the *grantee.*

**deep-pocket theory**   (1) (agency or tort law) the theory of *respondeat superior*, based on the idea that the employer is better able to bear the risk of loss because of greater financial resources; (2) (antitrust law) in *conglomerate mergers*, the theory that one part of an integrated firm may subsidize another part of the same firm to drive competitors from the market and thereby obtain a greater market share. The theory has not been accepted as an "anticompetitive effect" in dealing with conglomerate mergers.

**de facto segregation**   separation that exists in fact, as opposed to separation by mandate of law (see *de jure segregation*).

**defamation**   *libel* and *slander*; intentional falsehoods written or spoken about a living person, bringing injury to that person's reputation.

**default judgment**   a judgment entered against a defendant because he or she failed to answer a *summons.*

**defendant**   the person against whom a lawsuit, civil or criminal, is filed.

**de jure**   by law; by right; legitimate, whether or not true in actual fact (see *de facto*).

**de jure segregation**   separation required by law, as opposed to that resulting from custom or social forces (see *de facto segregation*).

**delectus personae**   literally "the choice of the person"; the doctrine in partnership law that changing the combination of partners in a *partnership* destroys the previous relationship and terminates the partnership.

**delegation**   (1) (administrative law) the grant, from the legislative branch to an administrative agency, of authority to make rules and regulations; (2) (contact law) the transfer of a contract duty to another; (3) (agency law) the transfer of authority from the principal to an agent.

**de minimus**   small; unimportant; trifling.

**de minimus violations**   unimportant violations of OSHA for which no penalty is imposed.

**de novo entry**   entry into a market by creation of new facilities, as opposed to entry through acquisition or merger.

**democratic government**   a government of all of the people, who govern themselves (see *republican government*).

**deposition**   a part of *discovery*; the written record of a witness's sworn testimony taken outside of court.

**derivative action**   a form of lawsuit brought by corporate stockholders on behalf of the corporation to enforce rights of the corporation.

**dicta**   statements in a judicial opinion that are not essential to the case and are unnecessary to reach the result in the case; statements in a judicial opinion that are not binding as *precedent* (see *stare decisis*).

**dilution of shares**   any change in the corporate stock relationships that changes the relative proportion of ownership of corporate assets that a share represents.

**diminishing returns**   the economic doctrine that teaches that after a business reaches a certain optimal size, *economies of scale* no longer take place and each unit of output becomes increasingly expensive to produce.

**direct action**   a form of lawsuit by a shareholder to enforce his or her individual rights as a shareholder (see *derivative action*).

**direct examination**   the first questioning of one's own witnesses in a trial or other hearing (see *cross-examination*).

**directors** persons elected by the shareholders of a corporation to manage the affairs of the corporation; also, the persons elected or appointed to manage the affairs of a not-for-profit corporation.

**disability benefits** benefits payable under social security to injured or disabled workers who are eligible under the Social Security Act.

**disclaimer of warranties** a statement or attempt to limit or foreclose *warranties* implied by law.

**discovery** the exchange of information between the sides in a lawsuit, generally through *interrogatories, depositions, requests to produce*, and special motions.

**discrimination against interstate commerce** treating the goods and other commerce of other states differently than the goods and commerce of the "home" state.

**disparagement** false statements regarding the goods or services of another; commercial *libel* or *slander*.

**disparate treatment** overtly different treatment of persons in employment because of race, color, religion, national origin, or sex, under the Civil Rights Act of 1964, as amended (see *disproportionate impact*).

**disproportionate impact** employment policies that are apparently neutral but that have a different effect on employees because of race, color, religion, national origin, or sex, under the Civil Rights Act of 1964 (see *disparate treatment*).

**disproportionate voting** voting in a corporation in which one class of shares receives greater voting rights than other shares (see *class voting*).

**disregarding the corporate fiction** (see *piercing the corporate veil*).

**dissenters' rights** the rights of shareholders of a corporation to sell their stock to the corporation if a *merger, consolidation,* or sale or exchange of all or a substantial part of the assets is proposed. Such rights must be exercised before the shareholders of the corporation vote on the move.

**distinguish** to point out differences between cases, usually based on distinctions between the facts of two cases.

**diversity jurisdiction** the authority of the federal courts to hear cases between citizens of more than one state, if the amount in controversy between them is more than $10,000.

**divestiture** (antitrust law) the remedy under section 7 of the Clayton Act that forces improperly merged firms to undo the *merger* and become separate firms once again.

**dividends** distribution of earnings of a corporation to shareholders. Dividends may take the form of money, property, or shares of stock.

**divine right of kings** the philosophy that kings rule by a grant from God and, therefore, that the king can do no wrong.

**domestic corporation** a corporation created under the laws of the state in question (see *foreign corporation*).

**double jeopardy** the requirement under the fifth amendment to the U.S. Constitution that no person may be tried twice for the same offense; not to be confused with *res judicata*.

**draft convention** a model treaty proposed by some international body for consideration and potential adoption by a group of nations.

**due diligence** (securities regulation) the requirement that accountants who certify reports filed with the SEC use proper care in reviewing those reports and in obtaining information about the material in those reports.

**due process** a part of a clause found in both the fifth and fourteenth amendments to the U.S. Constitution. The clause generally requires both fair procedures (*procedural due process*) and fair laws (*substantive due process*).

**dumping** selling goods in a foreign country at less than the comparable price in the exporting nation.

**duty** (1) a human action required by law. Duty is the correlative of right, in that if one person has a right, there must rest upon some other person a corresponding duty; that which is due from a person; (2) a *tariff* on imports.

**duty of fair representation** the duty of a union to exercise its right to represent workers fairly and without discrimination.

**duty to bargain** the requirement under the National Labor Relations Act that both the union and management bargain with each other on certain topics. There is no requirement that they agree, however.

**economic regulation** licensing, certification, and direct economic supervision of certain industries, such as government-granted monopolies, public utilities, and certain other industries; "close" regulation.

**economic school of law** the philosophy that the law is the expression of economic forces, in which each actor assesses the costs and gains of every action, including the legal costs and gains.

**economic strikers** persons who strike to gain some economic concession from the employer.

**economies of scale** the economic doctrine that as more is produced, each unit of output becomes less expensive to produce, up to a certain point (see *diminishing returns*).

**eminent domain** the power of the government to take private property for a public use or purpose, subject to the government's duty to pay just compensation for that property.

**enabling act** a legislative act that creates an *administrative agency* and grants it authority to make rules by the *delegation* of authority. Some enabling acts grant additional authority to existing agencies.

**entitlement legislation** laws creating rights to particular types of public welfare or other benefits, such as social security or veterans' benefits; social welfare legislation.

**entity theory** the doctrine that certain business firms, such as corporations, are separate legal "persons" under the law.

**enumerated powers** the *granted powers* of the federal government; those powers expressly set out in the Constitution.

**Environmental Impact Statement (EIS)** a report on the effects of any federal project that "significantly affects the quality of the human environment" filed by the federal agency involved in the project and filed with the *Council on Environmental Quality*, as required by the National Environmental Policy Act.

**Equal Protection Clause** a part of the fourteenth amendment that prohibits various forms of discriminatory *state action*. Under the amendment, any classification scheme must have a *reasonable basis*, unless it involves *fundamental rights* or a protected category such as race, in which case the courts will subject the classification to the *strict scrutiny test*.

**equitable maxim** a general statement of law universally admitted or applied in *equity* cases; an aphorism of law. Such maxims may take the place of decided cases in equity cases.

**equitable relief** relief granted by a court of *equity*; usually in the form of a court order, such as an *injunction* or *specific performance*, but not including *damages*.

**equity** (1) the spirit of fairness, justice, and fair dealing; (2) a system of jurisprudence administered by special courts, which was developed to mitigate the harsh results of the Law Courts through direct recourse to the King and which gives types of relief, such as *injunctions* and *specific performance*, that the law courts are incompetent to give (see *common law*, definition 2); (3) the difference between the value of property and the amount of the mortgages and liens on that property; the net value of property.

**equity financing** financing through investment and ownership in a corporation through stock or shares (see *stockholder*; *debt financing*; *common stock*; *preferred stock*).

**escheat** the reversion of property to the state or other unit of government in the event no person is competent to inherit the property upon the owner's death.

**establishment clause**   one of two parts of freedom of religion under the first amendment to the U.S. Constitution that generally forbids government from establishing, supporting, or favoring a particular religion or sect (see *free exercise clause*).

**estates in land**   any interest in land; any property interest in land, including both *freehold estates* and *leasehold estates*.

**ethical dilemma**   a clash between two or more ethical notions; a situation in which an individual cannot fulfill his or her personal ethics completely but must choose between two or more ethical notions.

**ethics**   (1) the set of rules, norms, and values by which each person judges the actions of others and of himself or herself; (2) the set of commonly held beliefs, rules, norms, and values of a particular group or society (see *societal ethics*); (3) a branch of philosophy that studies the actions of human beings and their relationships, as opposed to metaphysics, which studies the relationship of human beings to the universe, natural and supernatural.

**European Economic Community (EEC)**   a *common market* made up of twelve European nations.

**European Parliament**   the assembly of the *European Economic Community* which functions as a legislative body.

**exchange markets**   (securities law) the two national stock exchanges and the several regional stock exchanges.

**exclusionary rule**   a rule adopted by the courts to enforce the various criminal procedure requirements of the Constitution under the fourth, fifth, and sixth amendments. The rule generally states that evidence seized in violation of those amendments may not be introduced into evidence.

**exclusive dealing arrangements**   (antitrust law) business contracts in which a purchaser agrees to deal only with a certain supplier (see *requirements contracts*), or a supplier agrees to deal only with a certain purchaser. Such arrangements may be illegal under either the Sherman or Clayton act.

**executive privilege**   the doctrine that the executive branch need not turn over certain types of evidence to the legislative or judicial branches of government.

**exhaustion of remedies**   (administrative law) the rule that before one may appeal an administrative judgment to the courts, all of the existing administrative procedures for review of that judgment must be used. The doctrine has many exemptions.

**ex parte**   with only one side present; without participation by all of the parties.

**express liability**   (securities law) express statements in the securities laws providing for civil actions to redress grievances for violations of those laws (see *implied liability*).

**express warranty**   an explicit promise regarding a *contract* or the subject of the contract, made either orally or in writing.

**expropriation of property**   seizure of foreign-owned property by a government.

**fact finding**   (labor law) mediation of a labor dispute, particularly those in the public sector, followed by a public airing of the dispute and the positions of the parties by the mediator if an impasse is not resolved.

**Fair Trade laws**   state statutes that permitted *resale price maintenance* under the Miller-Tydings Act.

**fair use doctrine**   the rule that permits the use of copyrighted material without permission for purposes of criticism, comment, news reporting, teaching, scholarship, or research.

**featherbedding**   clauses in union-management contracts that require the employer to hire workers who are not needed.

**Federalist Papers**   a set of essays written by Alexander Hamilton, John Jay, and James Madison that argued for the ratification of the Constitution. Much of our knowledge of the "intent of the framers" comes from those essays.

**federal question jurisdiction**   the authority of the federal courts to hear cases arising under the federal Constitution or federal law.

**Federal Register**   an official publication of the U.S. government that contains, among other things, notice of proposed administrative rules, in order to fulfill the "notice" requirement of *notice and comment rule making.*

**Federal Trade Commission (FTC)**   an *independent regulatory commission* created in 1914 and given authority over all "unfair and deceptive trade practices," together with a wide variety of other federal regulations of commerce.

**fee simple**   (property law) an *estate in land* given to a person and his or her heirs absolutely, without condition or limitation; total ownership; the greatest interest in land that one may own (see *fee simple determinable; life estate*).

**fee simple determinable**   (property law) also known as a fee simple conditional, base fee, or qualified fee; a *fee simple* subject to termination upon the happening of a certain condition, e.g., "to A and his heirs forever, unless the property is used for the sale of alcoholic beverages."

**fellow-servant rule**   (tort law) the doctrine that one employee cannot recover *damages* from his or her employer for injuries caused by the *negligence* of another employee of the same employer; an exception to the doctrine of *respondeat superior.*

**felony**   a serious crime, usually punishable by imprisonment in a state facility rather than a county jail, or by death.

**fiduciary**   a person who stands in a relationship of trust and confidence to another.

**fiduciary duties**   the duties imposed on any *fiduciary* by the law, including the duties of care, obedience, to account, loyalty, and notice.

**final judgment**   the last action by a court from which appeals may be taken to a higher court.

**final prospectus**   (securities law) any written communication that offers a security for sale or confirms the sale of a security. The final prospectus must contain much of the information required to be in the *registration statement.*

**fiscal policy**   the theory that the economy can be controlled through taxing and spending policies.

**fixture**   a piece of personal property permanently affixed to real estate, thus becoming a part of the real estate.

**fool's standard**   the FTC and judicial standard that the FTC advertising rules protect all consumers, not just the "reasonable person," and include the "ignorant, the unthinking, and the credulous."

**foreign corporation**   a corporation formed under the law of some state other than the state in question (see *domestic corporation*).

**formal rule making**   a procedure for making rules in an *administrative agency* that involves a trial-type hearing prior to the adoption of a new rule; required only if the *enabling act* requires the rule-making procedure to be "on the record."

**forum non conveniens**   literally "the court is not convenient"; the doctrine that provides that if two or more courts have proper *venue,* the court may determine which of those courts should hear the case based on fairness and convenience to the parties.

**foundation**   a form of nonprofit organization, usually organized as a charitable *trust.*

**fourth-line competition (injury to)**   (antitrust law) injury to customers in competition with a customer of a customer of the supplier's favored customer, caused by price discrimination.

**four unities**   (property law) one of the basic requirements to create a *joint tenancy.* In order to create a joint tenancy with the right of survivorship, the property must be acquired by the owners (1) at the same time, (2) under the same title, (3) with the same proportionate interest, and (4) with equal rights of possession (see *joint tenancy; tenancy in common*).

**franchise** (1) a business arrangement in which an individual or firm buys the right to sell the products and services of a company and to use that company's name or trademark to do business; (2) a grant of a special privilege by a unit of government, such as the right to provide water or utility service to a community; (3) a grant of the privilege to incorporate by the government, usually by special act of the legislature; (4) any grant of a special privilege.

**franchise tax** a tax paid by corporations for the privilege of being incorporated, usually paid annually and varying with the net worth or some other financial variable of the company.

**fraud** a misrepresentation of a material fact that induces another to take some action to his or her detriment.

**free exercise clause** one of two parts of freedom of religion under the first amendment to the Constitution that generally forbids government from interfering with personal religious beliefs (see *establishment clause*).

**freehold estate** an ownership interest in land, as distinguished from a *leasehold estate*, which grants only temporary rights of possession by lease. The term also includes all *future interests*.

**free riders** nonunion employees in an *open shop* who receive the benefits of a union contract but who do not join the union or pay union dues.

**frolic and detour** (tort law) the exception to the doctrine of *respondeat superior* that a master is not responsible for the torts of his or her servants if the tort was committed while the servant was not acting within the scope of employment but for personal purposes.

**FTC** see *Federal Trade Commission*.

**FTC Guides** general guidelines of the Federal Trade Commission regarding certain problem areas, particularly deceptive trade practices and advertising, and providing information about what the law and FTC rules require.

**full warranty** under the Magnuson-Moss Act, any warranty in which the warrantor agrees to remedy or repair a defect within a reasonable time, which does not limit the duration of the *implied warranties*, in which the warrantor agrees to replace the product if the defect cannot be remedied in a reasonable number of attempts and in which the consumer need only notify the warrantor to remedy the defect. Any other warranty must be designated as a *limited warranty*.

**fundamental rights** those rights secured by the *Bill of Rights*; those rights which, if impaired, will cause the courts to apply the *strict scrutiny test* as opposed to the *reasonable basis test* in questions involving the *equal protection clause*.

**fungible** interchangeable goods; goods easily replaced by others that are identical. Fungible goods are usually sold by weight or volume, such as flour or wheat.

**future interest** interests in lands or other things in which the right of possession and enjoyment is delayed until the future. Such interests may be *vested*, in which case the holder of the future interest will take possession at some future time, or contingent, in which case the holder may take possession if certain events take place.

**General Agreement on Tariffs and Trade (GATT)** a series of treaty rules generally requiring a *most favored nation* clause in every trade agreement established by a member country.

**general duty clause** the clause under the Occupational Safety and Health Act that requires employers to provide their employees with a workplace free from recognized hazards of employment.

**general intent** the intent to perform a specific act, such as the intent to pull the trigger on a gun, as opposed to the *specific intent*, such as to shoot someone with intent to obtain a specific result, in this case, to kill or injure.

**general jurisdiction** the authority of a court to hear any type of case arising within the geographical area that the court serves.

**general partnership**   a partnership in which all of the partners have a right to manage the affairs of the partnership equally and in which all of the partners are personally liable for the debts of the partnership (see *partnership; limited partnership*).

**geographic market division**   see *market division*.

**Gissel remedy**   an order by the National Labor Relations Board that, because unfair labor practices by an employer have so tainted a union election, a fair election cannot be held and, therefore, no election is required. The union is automatically considered to be the bargaining representative, even though no election is held and even if the union lost the election.

**government in the sunshine statutes**   open meetings laws; laws that require meetings of government bodies to be open to the public.

**granted powers**   the doctrine that the federal government and its branches have only those powers expressly granted to them by the Constitution (see *implied powers*).

**grantee**   the person receiving property by *deed*.

**grantor**   the person conveying property by *deed*.

**grievance procedure**   the portions of a labor contract that spell out how differences between employees and the employer are to be resolved.

**group boycotts**   agreements between two or more persons that they will not purchase goods from another firm, or that they will not sell goods to another firm; a *per se* violation of the Sherman Act.

**hazardous air pollutant**   a pollutant for which no *National Ambient Air Quality Standard* has been established, but which may contribute to mortality or serious illness.

**hearsay**   repetition in court of a statement made by some person outside of court that is admitted to prove the truth of the out-of-court statement.

**Herfindahl-Hirschman Index (HHI)**   a numerical index of *concentration* of industries used in the Justice Department's *Merger Guidelines*. The percentage of market share of each firm is squared, and the squares of all of the firms are added together to find the HHI of the industry.

**HHI**   see *Herfindahl-Hirschman Index*.

**historical school of jurisprudence**   the philosophy of law that teaches that all law and legal institutions are the result of historical forces.

**Hobbesian philosophy**   the philosophy of Thomas Hobbes (1588–1679), which teaches that power gives right, based on the natural outcome of a "war of each against all," and that the stronger is the legitimate ruler, at least until someone still stronger appears.

**holding company**   a company whose sole purpose is holding stocks or securities in other companies.

**horizontal agreements**   agreements between competitors; agreements between firms or individuals at the same level of the distribution process of the same good or service (see *vertical agreements*).

**horizontal geographic market division**   see *market division*.

**horizontal mergers**   mergers or other corporate integration between competing firms.

**hot-cargo agreements**   a part of a labor contract providing that employees are not required to handle or work on goods or materials going to or coming from an employer the union designates as "unfair."

**impasse resolution techniques**   methods of resolving disputes in public sector labor conflicts, instead of striking; *mediation*, *fact finding*, voluntary *arbitration*, and compulsory *arbitration*.

**implied liability**   (securities regulation) liabilities imposed by the courts in the absence of an express statement in those laws permitting private civil actions to redress violation of the securities laws.

**implied partnership**   partnership found by the acts of the parties, rather than by express agreement of the partners; a failed attempt to form a corporation or a limited partnership may create an implied general partnership, for example.

**implied powers**   the powers of the federal government not expressly granted to the branches of government but "necessary and proper" to the execution of the *granted powers.*

**implied warranties**   warranties imposed by law, as opposed to *express warranties,* which are made by agreement of the parties.

**implied warranty of fitness for a particular purpose**   the *implied warranty* that a product will serve a consumer's special needs. The warranty is found if (1) the seller knows of the buyer's specific requirements for the product and (2) the buyer relies on the seller's skill and judgment in choosing the item. The warranty is given by both *merchants* and nonmerchant sellers.

**implied warranty of merchantability**   an *implied warranty* given by *merchants* that goods are fit to be sold, under six specific definitions of the term found in the Uniform Commercial Code.

**implied warranty of title**   a promise that the seller has the right to transfer goods, that the title to the goods is satisfactory, and that there are no outstanding *liens* or claims on the goods.

**in commerce**   goods or commerce actually moving between states, as opposed to *affecting commerce,* in which goods are not moving between states but have an impact on *interstate commerce.*

**independent contractor**   one who acts for another (an *agent*) on an independent basis without being subject to the control of the *principal* (see *master-servant relationship; respondeat superior*).

**independent regulatory commission (IRC)**   administrative agencies that are somewhat independent from the executive branch, in that the members of the commission are appointed for overlapping terms longer than that of the President and generally cannot be fired from their position without the consent of Congress (see *line agency*).

**indication of interest**   (securities regulation) a statement by a potential investor that he or she may purchase a stock or other security once it is available for sale after SEC review of the issue (see *waiting period; preliminary prospectus; tombstone ad*).

**indictment**   a formal accusation of a crime made by a grand jury (see *information*).

**individualist ethic**   the *societal ethic* that teaches that the individual is supreme and the interests of the community must submit to those of the individual. At its extreme, this ethic becomes anarchism and social Darwinism, while in its more moderate aspects it simply holds that the interests of the individual must be protected against undue limitation (see *community ethic*).

**informal rule making**   see *notice and comment rule making.*

**information**   a formal accusation of a crime made by a prosecutor or other public official, often on oath, but not presented to a grand jury (see *indictment*).

**informational picketing**   picketing to inform the public rather than force some action on the part of the employer.

**injunction**   an order issued by a court of *equity* directing a person not to do a certain act or stopping the continuance of that act (see *mandatory injunction.*)

**inquisitorial system**   the system of law in most of the world aside from the United States and Great Britain. In the inquisitorial system, all parties, including the judge, actively seek evidence to arrive at the truth. The judge usually represents the state's interest in the trial and searches for evidence independent of the parties (see *adversary system*).

**insider**   (securities regulation) a person who has access to nonpublic information about a corporation by way of a position within the corporation.

**insider trading**   (securities regulation) trading of securities of a corporation by *insiders* (see *tippee*).

**institutional decisions**   (administrative law) a method of administrative decision making in *adjudicatory* proceedings in which a hearing officer or *Administrative Law Judge* takes the evidence on the record and then forwards the record to the agency's board, which makes the final decision based on that record.

**insured status**   (social security law) the status of an employee necessary to be covered by the Social Security Act. There are three forms: (1) fully insured, (2) currently insured, and (3) insured for disability benefits. The insured status is determined by quarters of eligibility, i.e., the number of three-month segments a person has worked under the Social Security Act.

**interlocking directorates**   (antitrust law) when one or more persons serve on the boards of directors of two or more corporations; a violation of the Clayton Act if the corporations are competing, although some businesses are exempt from this provision.

**interlocutory appeal**   an appeal of something other than a *final judgment*, such as appeal of an order of discovery or a pretrial motion. Interlocutory appeals are permitted only in exceptional circumstances.

**International Bank for Reconstruction and Development**   an agency of the *United Nations* that makes loans for development; the *World Bank*.

**International Center for Settlement of Investment Disputes**   an international arbitration body available to decide investment disputes.

**International Court of Justice**   the principal judicial arm of the *United Nations*; the *World Court*.

**International Monetary Fund**   a specialized agency of the *United Nations* that acts as a consultant on world money problems and seeks to stabilize exchange rates.

**interrogatories**   a part of *discovery*; a list of written questions submitted to a party to a lawsuit by another party, which must be answered under oath and in writing (see *deposition*).

**interstate commerce**   commerce moving between two or more states (see *intrastate commerce*; *in commerce*; *affecting commerce*).

**intestate succession**   a succession to property owned by a person who had no will or whose will is void, as determined by state statutes that determine who shall inherit property (see *estate succession*; *law of descent and distribution*).

**intraenterprise conspiracy**   (antitrust law) an agreement or conspiracy between individuals or firms that are a part of the same firm, e.g., agreements between a parent company and its subsidiaries or between the officers of the same firm.

**intrastate commerce**   commerce totally within one state (see *interstate commerce*; *in commerce*; *affecting commerce*).

**investigative function**   the function of *agencies* to collect data to aid in their *rule-making* and *adjudicatory* functions.

**investment advisers**   (securities regulation) persons who advise others regarding *securities* for compensation.

**investment bankers**   bankers who specialize in marketing securities, often acting as *underwriters* for issues of stock or securities.

**investment company**   a corporation formed for the purpose of investing in the stock of another company.

**invidious discrimination**   objectionable discrimination; in a legislative act, discrimination or classification based on impermissible categories, such a race.

**issued shares**   *authorized shares* that have in fact been issued to shareholders.

**issuing bank**   a bank that issues a *letter of credit*.

**jingle rule**   a rule of priority between personal creditors of partners and partnership creditors. Individual creditors must proceed against individual assets of partners, partnership creditors must proceed against partnership assets, and each must stand behind the other if assets are insufficient.

**joint stock association**    an unincorporated business form in which investors pool their funds and receive stock certificates in return, and which is managed by a board of directors elected or appointed by the shareholders.

**joint tenancy**    (property law) ownership of *property* by two or more persons whereby at the death of one of the joint tenants, the surviving joint tenants automatically and as a matter of law take the deceased joint tenant's share (see *four unities*). State statutes usually prescribe strict rules for the formation of joint tenancies, including the use of certain specific language in a deed creating the joint tenancy (see *tenancy in common*).

**joint venture**    a *partnership*, usually temporary, between two or more business entities, for joint participation in an endeavor.

**judgment**    the official and final decision of a court on the rights and claims of the parties to a lawsuit; the law's last word on a controversy.

**judgment n.o.v.**    literally, "judgment notwithstanding the verdict"; a motion filed by a party after an adverse *verdict*, asking that the court enter *judgment* contrary to the verdict.

**judgment on the pleadings**    a motion made by a party asserting that there is no issue to resolve after the pleadings are filed and asking judgment without further proceedings.

**judicial review**    the doctrine that the courts, particularly the U.S. Supreme Court, have the right to hold acts of the executive and legislative branches unconstitutional and void.

**jurisdiction**    (1) the power and authority to hear a case; (2) the geographical area a court serves; (3) the persons and subject matter over which a court has authority to hear cases and make decisions (see *venue*).

**jurisprudence**    the study of philosophy of law; the study of law itself.

**jury instructions**    oral or written instructions to the jury from the judge regarding the law that the jury is to apply in a case.

**laissez faire**    literally "let the people do as they choose"; the doctrine of opposition to governmental interference, particularly in economic affairs.

**Law Merchant**    the system of rules, customs, and usages applied by traders in England and later incorporated into the common law to regulate contracts and transactions in goods.

**law of descent and distribution**    a statute in each state providing how property is to be distributed in the event a person dies without a will (see *interstate succession*).

**Law of Neutrality**    the international law that requires warring countries to respect neutral nations.

**Law of Peace**    the international law that establishes the rights and duties of nations at peace with one another.

**Law of War**    the international law that provides restrictions on nations at war with one another.

**leasehold estates**    (property law) an *estate in land* under a lease; an estate for a fixed term or a period of time, sometimes renewable or at will; an estate of temporary possession of land.

**legal fiction**    an assumption or statement of the law that is not true but is given effect by the law, e.g., that a corporation is a "person."

**legality**    (contract law) one of the elements of a *contract*, which requires that an agreement, in order to be considered a valid contract, must be legal both in its object and in the means by which it is to be accomplished.

**legal realism**    the school of legal philosophy that teaches that all we can be concerned about in any analysis of the law is a description of the law itself; also called legal *positivism*.

**legislative veto**    the retention in an *enabling act* of the right of the legislature to override the actions of the *administrative agency* to which power was delegated, usually by legislative actions involving less formality than formal lawmaking activity, e.g., by the vote of one house of Congress. Held unconstitutional in *Chadha v. INS*.

**lessee**    one who holds property under a lease; a tenant.

**lessor**    one who grants possession of land to another under a lease; a landlord.

**letter of credit**   a promise by an *issuing bank* to the seller of goods that the bank will pay the contract price to the seller, if the seller produces a *bill of lading*.

**libel**   a written *defamation* (see *slander*).

**lien**   a claim on *property* that is allowed by law, which usually receives priority over other claims based merely on contract or other grounds.

**life estate**   (property law) a *freehold estate* in which *property* is granted to another for his or her lifetime only, as in a grant "to A for life, then to B." A common variant is a life estate *pur autrie vie* (for the life of another) in which the measuring life is some other person than the holder of the life estate, as in "to A for the life of C, then to B."

**limited jurisdiction**   the power and authority of a court to hear a case that is somehow less than *general jurisdiction* (see *jurisdiction*).

**limited liability**   the concept that business investors may only be liable to the extent of their investment, and creditors of the business may not attack personal assets of investors to satisfy business debts (see *corporation*; *limited partnership*).

**limited partnership**   a form of partnership available under statute in which certain partners may invest in the partnership and be liable only to the extent of the funds invested for partnership debts; such limited partners may not take part in the management of the partnership, and there must be at least one general partner (see *partnership*; *general partnership*).

**limited warranty**   any warranty that does not fulfill the requirements of a *full warranty*, under the Magnuson-Moss Warranty Act.

**line agency**   (administrative law) an *administrative agency* directly responsible to the executive and usually headed by a single administrator, who serves at the pleasure of the executive (see *independent regulatory commission*).

**line of commerce**   part of the language of section 7 of the Clayton Act, which requires that an anticompetitive effect of a *merger* must take place in a particular *relevant product market*.

**lockouts**   (labor law) plant closings by employers to force employees to submit to employer demands.

**long-arm statutes**   state statutes that permit the courts of a state to exercise *jurisdiction* over persons or property outside of that state.

**malice**   ill will or bad motive; having no moral or legal justification.

**malicious competition**   a common law *tort* forbidding competition for a predatory purpose.

**malum in se**   literally, "evil of itself"; crimes that are also morally wrong in the eyes of most people, such as murder or robbery (see *malum prohibitum*).

**malum prohibitum**   literally, "evil because it is prohibited"; crimes that are crimes only because the law makes them so, rather than because the acts are morally wrong, such as traffic laws (see *malum in se*).

**management**   a general term indicating those who actually run a business; in the corporate form the term refers to the board of directors and the *officers*.

**mandamus**   a court order requiring a public official to perform his or her duties.

**mandatory bargaining topics**   (labor law) issues over which labor and management must bargain, such as wages, work rules, union status, and conditions of work.

**mandatory injunction**   a court order issued by an equity court ordering a person affirmatively to perform an act, as distinguished from an *injunction*, which orders a person not to perform an act.

**margin**   (securities regulation) purchasing stock on credit; the margin is the amount of credit extended (see *margin maintenance rules*; *margin requirements*).

**margin maintenance rules**   (securities regulation) rules imposed by many securities exchanges requiring the payment of additional margin if the value of stocks purchased on credit declines (see *margin*; *margin requirements*).

**margin requirements** (securities regulation) rules of the Federal Reserve Board specifying the maximum amount of credit that may be given by brokers on the sale of stock and further specifying how much of a "down payment" is required (see *margin; margin maintenance requirements*).

**market division** (antitrust law) also known as horizontal geographic market division, the concept involves agreements between competing firms to divide up a market geographically and create regional monopolies; a *per se* violation of the Sherman Act.

**market extension merger** (antitrust law) a merger between firms that produce identical products but sell them in different regions.

**market manipulation** (securities regulation) trading in shares that, of itself, affects the price of the shares for the benefit of the person trading (see *wash sales*).

**marketplace theory of speech** the idea that all ideas should be allowed to enter the "marketplace of ideas," because the public will only accept those ideas that are valid and good and will refuse to "buy" those that are invalid or untrue; one of the principal justifications for the first amendment to the Constitution.

**Massachusetts trust** see *business trust*.

**master** an employer (see *master-servant relationship; respondeat superior*).

**master-servant relationship** (agency law) a type of *agency* relationship, distinguished from that involving an *independent contractor*, whereby the master has the right to control the work of the *servant*. The distinction is factual and based on the degree to which the principal may control the activities of the agent (see *respondeat superior*).

**mediation** a dispute settlement technique in which an outside third party (a mediator) tries to settle a dispute through persuasion. The mediator has no power to force a settlement (see *arbitration*).

**Mediation and Conciliation Service** (labor law) an independent federal agency that offers a neutral third party to mediate labor disputes, either on its own motion or at the request of either party (see *mediation*).

**Medicare** (social security law) a 1965 amendment to the Social Security Act, which provides medical insurance to those otherwise eligible for any form of social security.

**meet and confer laws** (labor law) in public employee labor negotiations, statutes that require the union and the employer to meet and discuss issues prior to the adoption of policies by the employer-government (see *impasse resolution techniques*).

**meeting competition defense** (antitrust law) a defense to a charge of *price discrimination* under the Robinson-Patman Act, based on lowering one's price to a specific purchaser to meet (but not beat) a competitor's price to that customer.

**mental element** a part of the proof required in many criminal statutes of a particular mental state or intention on the part of the defendant, such as "knowingly," or "intentionally," or "recklessly."

**merchant** a special status accorded or imposed by the Uniform Commercial Code on persons who regularly deal in goods of the kind sold, or who hold themselves out as having knowledge or skill peculiar to the goods sold, or who deal through *agents* who hold themselves out as having such special knowledge or skill.

**merger** (1) a method of *corporate integration* in which one firm acquires and absorbs another, causing the acquired firm to cease to exist; (2) sometimes used to refer to all methods of corporate integration, somewhat improperly.

**Merger Guidelines** (antitrust law) a set of guides established by the U.S. Department of Justice, first in 1968, substantially amended in 1982, and reamended in 1984, which provides guidelines for business regarding which *mergers* or other *corporate integrations* will be prosecuted by the department. The guidelines are not binding on the department or on the courts.

**misappropriation** a common law *tort* forbidding asserting that another's product is one's own.

**misdemeanor**   a less serious criminal offense, usually punishable by imprisonment in a facility other than the state penitentiary, or by fine.

**Model Business Corporation Act**   a model act specifying most of the law relating to *corporations* and adopted in whole or in part in many states.

**monopolization**   (antitrust law) an offense under section 2 of the Sherman Act, consisting of (1) possession of *monopoly* power in the *relevant market*; and (2) willful acquisition or maintenance of that power.

**monopoly**   total *concentration* of an industry in the hands of one person or firm.

**most favored nation clause**   a treaty clause, required by the *General Agreement on Tariffs and Trade (GATT)*, that every nation will receive the same treatment in tariffs and trade that is received by the most favored nation.

**motion to dismiss**   a motion filed at the outset of a case, claiming that a *complaint* is deficient in some way and should be dismissed, either with or without prejudice to filing an amended complaint.

**motion to suppress**   the legal procedure used to obtain exclusion of evidence from trial under the *exclusionary rule*.

**multilateral**   many-sided; having many aspects.

**mutuality**   (contract law) sometimes considered an element of a *contract*, in that both parties are mutually bound to the agreement, and no party is bound unless all are bound.

**NAAQS**   see *National Ambient Air Quality Standards*.

**NASD**   see *National Association of Securities Dealers*.

**nation**   (1) a sovereign country; (2) some homogeneous group of people who look on themselves as a group, regardless of political independence.

**National Ambient Air Quality Standards (NAAQS)**   (environmental law) standards for air quality, established by the EPA (see *primary standards*; *secondary standards*).

**National Association of Securities Dealers (NASD)**   (securities regulation) a private association of securities *dealers* and *brokers* that has established rules regarding *securities*.

**National Institute for Occupational Safety and Health (NIOSH)**   a research body established by OSHA to aid in the formulation of health and safety standards for the Secretary of Labor.

**nationality principle**   the rule of international law that a state has jurisdiction over its own citizens, no matter where located.

**National Labor Relations Board (NLRB)**   a federal *independent regulatory commission* established by the Wagner Act with authority to make rules, to hold elections on labor matters, and to hold hearings on *unfair labor practice* charges.

**natural rights theory**   the doctrine that government arose out of a *contract* (compact) between human beings, in which each person gave up the right to rule him- or herself in return for the protection of government, and therefore government ruled by the consent of the governed; the basis of the American Declaration of Independence.

**negligence**   the failure to do that which an ordinary and prudent person would do under like circumstances.

**neutralists**   judges who find certain fixed principles of justice in the Constitution and apply the "plain meaning" of the words in the Constitution. Such judges think of themselves as "mere conduits" through which the Constitution speaks (see *activists*; *restraintists*).

**nexus**   a connection.

**NIOSH**   see *National Institute of Occupational Safety and Health*.

**NLRB**   see *National Labor Relations Board*.

**nominal damages**   damages in name only; money, usually one dollar plus costs of suit awarded to a plaintiff who has suffered some injury to a right, but no other loss compensable in money (see *damages*; *compensatory damages*; *punitive damages*).

**nonattainment areas** (environmental law) areas in which the National Ambient Air Quality Standards have not been met.

**noncumulative dividends** *dividends* that do not accumulate from year to year if they are not paid.

**nonparticipating preferred shares** *preferred stock* that receives its own *dividends* prior to *common stock* but that does not receive a dividend with the common stock, as in the case of *participating preferred shares*.

**nonsigner's clause** (antitrust law) clauses in a *resale price maintenance* agreement between a manufacturer and a retailer that bind all other sellers of that product to the agreement, regardless of whether they are parties to the agreement.

**no-strike clauses** (labor law) provisions of a labor contract prohibiting strikes during the contract period (see *wildcat strike*).

**not-for-profit corporation** a special form of organization permitting *limited liability* for participants and specifying organization and structure of nonprofit or charitable organizations.

**notice and comment rule making** (administrative law) a method of administrative *rule making* wherein the *agency* is required by the Administrative Procedure Act to give advance notice to the public of a proposed rule and provide an opportunity to the public to comment on that rule before the rule becomes effective.

**notice of appeal** the first paper filed in an appeal, usually setting out in general terms the fact that an appeal is intended and the general nature of the appeal, and required to be filed within a specific time of the final *judgment* of the lower court.

**Nuclear Regulatory Commission (NRC)** the federal agency (previously the Atomic Energy Commission) responsible for licensing of nuclear power plants, research in atomic energy, and inspection of nuclear facilities.

**nuisance** something or some activity that annoys or disturbs unreasonably (see *private nuisance; public nuisance*).

**Occupational Safety and Health Administration** a part of the Department of Labor established by the Occupational Safety and Health Act to enforce the provisions of the act and the rules established by the Secretary of Labor for workplace safety.

**offer** (contract law) an act on the part of one person giving to another the legal power to create a contract; a proposal to make a contract.

**offeree** (contract law) the person to whom an *offer* is made.

**offering circular** (securities regulation) a document, similar to a *prospectus*, that gives information about a stock issue and a corporation not subject to the prospectus requirement because the issue is under $5 million (see *Regulation A exception*).

**offeror** (contract law) the person making an *offer*.

**officers** the persons elected or appointed by the board of directors to manage the day-to-day affairs of a corporation; usually the president, vice-president, secretary, and treasurer.

**offset** (environmental law) in *nonattainment areas*, polluters may obtain permits to build new pollution sources only if they shut down existing ones, thus creating an offset.

**old-age benefits** (social security law) benefits payable in the form of a pension to workers who have reached a certain age and are otherwise eligible to receive social security benefits.

**oligopoly** concentration of an industry in a few hands.

**open meetings acts** see *government in the sunshine statutes*.

**open shop agreements** (labor law) union contracts that permit employees either to join or not join the labor union that is the bargaining representative of the employees (see *union shop; right-to-work laws*).

**option** (contract law) an irrevocable *offer*; an offer in which the *offeree* has given consideration for the offer to remain open for a period of time.

**original jurisdiction**   the power of a court to try a case, as opposed to *appellate jurisdiction*.

**OSHA**   *Occupational Safety and Health Administration*; also stands for Occupational Safety and Health Act.

**outstanding shares**   *issued shares* that remain in the hands of stockholders, as opposed to *treasury shares*, which are issued shares that have been reacquired by the corporation.

**overt conspiracy**   an open conspiracy; one made publicly or without attempt at concealment.

**over-the-counter market (OTC market)**   (securities regulation) the market in which securities not listed on any national or regional stock exchange are traded. This "market" has no physical location (see *exchange market*).

**parallel action**   similar action by two or more parties without express agreement or communication, as in *price leadership*.

**parens patriae action**   (antitrust) a remedy that permits state attorneys general to sue under the federal antitrust laws on behalf of the citizens of their states.

**participating preferred shares**   *preferred stock* that receives its own preferred *dividend* and also receives a dividend with the common shares (see *nonparticipating preferred shares*).

**partnership**   under the *Uniform Partnership Act*, an association of two or more persons to carry on as co-owners a business for profit (see *general partnership*; *limited partnership*).

**partnership property**   a form of *property* ownership created by the *Uniform Partnership Act*, which consists of "all property originally brought into a partnership or subsequently acquired by purchase or otherwise, on account of the partnership."

**passing off**   common law *tort* that forbids asserting that one's product was made by another (see *product simulation*).

**patent**   (1) the grant of a limited *monopoly* to the inventor of a product; (2) the original grant of title to land from the government to a private individual; the first grant of private ownership.

**perceived potential competition**   (antitrust law) a doctrine used to show the anticompetitive effect of *product extension* and *market extension mergers* by showing that persons in a market changed their competitive behavior based on their perception that a particular firm might enter the market; the "wings" effect (see *potential competition*; *actual potential competition*).

**per curiam**   literally "by the court"; a decision of the whole court; a unanimous decision, often without written opinion.

**peremptory challenge**   an objection, for no expressed reason, to a juror's serving on a case. Usually attorneys receive a set number of peremptory challenges in a case and may excuse jurors until that number runs out, unless there is a reason for excusing the juror sufficient to provide grounds for a *challenge for cause*.

**perfect competition**   an ideal economic state of small buyers and small sellers, none of which can affect price, and creating optimal economic benefits of low price and high output and efficiency.

**permissive bargaining topics**   (labor law) all topics over which labor and management may bargain; all bargaining topics except those designated as *mandatory bargaining topics* by the National Labor Relations Act.

**per se rules**   literally "of itself." In antitrust law, exceptions to the *Rule of Reason*, which provides that in-depth analysis of whether a particular restraint of trade is unreasonable or unnecessary; situations in which the courts hold that a restraint of trade always occurs.

**personal ethics**   individually held notions of right and wrong; an individual's moral code, by which he or she judges the actions of others and of himself or herself.

**personal jurisdiction**   *jurisdiction* over an individual, obtained through *service of process*.

**personal property**   all property not considered a *freehold estate* or an interest in land; movable property, including both tangible and intangible property.

**piercing the corporate veil**   imposing personal liability on shareholders for actions of the corporation in instances where the corporation is a "mere shell" and the shareholders have treated the corporation as an "alter ego" of themselves; disregarding the corporate fiction.

**plaintiff**   the party who files a lawsuit; the injured party seeking relief from the court.

**plea bargaining**   a process in criminal cases in which the defendant and prosecutor agree that the defendant will plead guilty to certain charges, and the prosecutor will either dismiss other charges or recommend a certain sentence or punishment (see *prosecutorial discretion*).

**pleadings**   the formal, written statements filed by the parties to a lawsuit, consisting of the *complaint, answer(s), cross-claims, counterclaims, third-party complaints*, and the *answers* to them, and sometimes including *motions to dismiss*.

**plenary power**   full, complete, or unqualified power.

**pluralism**   any form of government in which the government's authority is limited in some way.

**point source**   (environmental law) a single source of water pollution, such as a pipe or drainage tile.

**police power**   the inherent power of the states to regulate for purposes of health, welfare, safety, and morals.

**poll tax**   a tax on the right to vote, or on all persons within a specific jurisdiction of a particular class, such as on all males or all voters.

**pool**   a voluntary association of competing firms, operating together and physically dividing a market between them.

**positivism**   see *legal realism*.

**potential competition**   (antitrust law) the doctrine that firms in a market change their competitive behavior based on the threat of entry into the market by other firms; the "wings" effect (see *actual potential competition; perceived potential competition*).

**precedent**   see *stare decisis*.

**preclusion of review**   (administrative law) a statement in a statute which provides that courts may not review the actions of an *administrative agency*.

**predatory conduct**   (antitrust law) some conduct, legal or illegal, evidencing an intent to obtain a larger market share by anticompetitive means.

**preemption**   the doctrine that state laws in conflict with legitimate federal laws or administrative regulations are void under the supremacy clause (article VI. section 2) of the U.S. Constitution.

**preemptive rights**   the doctrine that shareholders should have the right of first refusal of stock that may dilute their ownership interests.

**preferred stock**   stock that gets special rights, usually to *dividends* or assets, over other shares; often the preferred stock must give up voting rights in order to receive rights to dividends or assets (see *common stock; participating* and *nonparticipating preferred shares*).

**preliminary prospectus**   (securities regulation) also known as a "red herring" prospectus; a document used to solicit *indications of interest* during the *waiting period* of SEC review of a stock issue (see *final prospectus*).

**premerger notification**   (antitrust law) the requirement under the Hart-Scott-Rodino Antitrust Improvements Act of 1976 that firms over certain thresholds must notify the Justice Department and the FTC before actually merging.

**presumption**   an inference as to the existence of some fact not yet proven, drawn from the existence of some other fact already proven.

**pretrial conference**   a meeting prior to trial between the attorneys for all sides and the judge, at which the *pleadings* are settled, *discovery* is finalized, and settlement is discussed.

**price discrimination**   (antitrust law) charging different prices to different customers for goods of the same type in two reasonably contemporaneous sales.

**price fixing**   (antitrust law) an agreement between two or more persons to set the price of a product or service. *Horizontal* price fixing involves agreements between competitors to set the price of a good or service, whereas *vertical* price fixing is an agreement between a supplier and a purchaser that the purchaser's resale price will be set at a certain level. Both forms are *per se* illegal.

**price leadership**   a form of *parallel action* in which competitors follow the lead of one firm in setting prices.

**prima facie proof**   evidence that suffices for the proof of a particular fact until overcome or contradicted by other evidence.

**primary-line competition (injury to)**   (antitrust law) injury caused by *price discrimination* to the seller's competitors.

**primary standards**   (environmental law) air-quality standards that are necessary to protect the public health (see *National Ambient Air Quality Standards*).

**principal**   one on whose behalf an *agent* acts (see *agency*, definition 1).

**Printer's Ink Model Statute**   a "uniform act" first proposed by the advertising trade journal *Printer's Ink* and adopted by many states, which outlaws deceptive advertising.

**prior restraint**   regulation of speech or press before the speech or printed word is disseminated; prior censorship, as opposed to punishment after dissemination.

**private law**   law that regulates the relationships between private individuals, including the law of *contracts, torts, agency, partnerships, corporations,* and *property* (see *public law*).

**private nuisance**   a *tort* involving special harm to the plaintiff arising from some unreasonable use of property (see *public nuisance*).

**private offering**   (securities regulation) an offering for sale of a security to a single individual or group of individuals, rather than to the public as a whole.

**privileges**   the right or duty of certain persons to withhold evidence under certain circumstances, e.g., spousal privilege, attorney-client privilege, doctor-patient privilege, or priest-penitent privilege. Others may exist by statute in some states.

**privity of contract**   the doctrine that only the parties to a *contract* may sue for breaches of the contract.

**probable cause**   one of the requirements for a valid search and seizure under the fourth amendment; it generally means "reasonable cause" or "reasonable ground for belief," which must exist before a warrant may issue or a search may be made.

**procedural due process**   fair procedures, both in the courtroom and in administrative hearings, requiring at least notice of the proceedings and a right to be heard.

**procedural law**   the legal machinery for carrying on a lawsuit, as distinguished from *substantive law* such as contracts, torts, etc.

**product extension merger**   (antitrust law) a *corporate integration* between firms involved in similar but noncompeting products.

**product simulation**   intentional duplication of the physical characteristics of a competitor's product (see *passing off*).

**products liability**   that field of *tort* and *contract* law which imposes liability on sellers or others for injuries or damages resulting from the sale of defective or unsafe products.

**promissory estoppel**   (contract law) a promise that the promisor should reasonably expect to induce action or forbearance of the promisee; a promise on which another relies, to his or her detriment.

**property**   an aggregate of rights protected by the government; a *bundle of rights* in some tangible or intangible thing.

**proprietorship**   see *sole proprietorship*.

**prosecutorial discretion**   the right of prosecutors to run cases in the way they see fit, including the right to dismiss or refuse to dismiss and the right to *plea bargain*.

**prospectus**   see *final prospectus; preliminary prospectus*.

**protectionism**   political pressure for high import duties or embargoes against the products of other nations.

**protective legislation**   laws that protect the public from some perceived danger.

**protective principle**   the rule of international law that a nation may deal with conduct that occurs outside of its territory but which threatens its security as a state or the operation of its government operations.

**proximate cause**   that which, in a natural and continuous sequence, and unbroken by any intervening cause, produces an injury; that without which the result would not have occurred; the immediate, direct cause.

**proxy**   voting by representation in a *corporation*; the statement by which a shareholder gives another the right to vote stock.

**proxy solicitation rules**   (securities regulation) restrictions on obtaining and soliciting *proxies*.

**proxy statement**   (securities regulation) a statement filed with the SEC when *proxies* are solicited, disclosing all of the material facts regarding the matters to be voted upon at the meeting for which the proxy is solicited; one of the *proxy solicitation rules*.

**publicity picketing**   see *informational picketing*.

**public law**   the law regulating the relationship between the government and individuals, including Constitutional law, criminal law, and administrative law (see *private law*).

**public nuisance**   a crime involving injury to the public arising from an unreasonable use of land (see *private nuisance*).

**public offering**   (securities regulation) a solicitation to sell securities made to the general public (see *private offering*).

**punitive damages**   money damages over and above *compensatory damages* awarded to the *plaintiff* to punish the *defendant* for a malicious or intentional (and in a few states, reckless) act; exemplary damages (see *damages; nominal damages*).

**purchase of assets**   a form of *corporate integration* in which one firm pays cash to another firm in return for all of the assets of that firm. The acquired firm usually must liquidate, because all of its assets are in the form of cash.

**purchase of stock**   a form of *corporate integration* in which one firm purchases all or a controlling portion of the stock of another corporation (see *tender offer*).

**pure conglomerate merger**   a merger between firms involved in the production, sale, or distribution of totally unrelated products or services (see *conglomerate merger; product extension merger; market extension merger*).

**quarterly report**   a report filed quarterly with the SEC by firms subject to the 1934 Securities and Exchange Act (see *annual report; current report*).

**ratification**   to approve after the fact, as when a *principal* approves an action taken on his or her behalf by an *agent* without authority.

**real property**   (property law) land and all things permanently affixed to the land, and including all interests in land.

**reasonable basis test**   the test to determine whether a classification system in a statute violates the *Equal Protection Clause* of the fourteenth amendment, if the classification scheme is not based on a *suspect classification* or does not involve *fundamental rights*. The issue in such cases is whether the legislature had a "reasonable basis" for making the classification (see *strict scrutiny test*).

**rebuttable presumption**   a *presumption* that may be overcome by evidence, as distinguished from a *conclusive presumption*, which cannot be overcome by evidence.

**reciprocity**   (antitrust law) an agreement or requirement that one firm will sell to or buy from another firm on condition that the second firm will sell to or buy from a subsidiary or parent of the first firm.

**recklessness**   carelessness, heedlessness, inattention or indifference to consequences; willful and wanton disregard of known circumstances.

**recognition clause**   (labor law) a clause in a labor contract in which the employer recognizes the union as the exclusive bargaining agent of the employees.

**recognition letter**   (labor law) a letter from a union to management requesting recognition of the union as the bargaining representative of the employees based on an *authorization-card* majority.

**record on appeal**   the formal, written account of a case, consisting of all of the papers filed with the court and either a transcript of the proceedings or a summary of the evidence as agreed to by the parties and the judge.

**record review**   (administrative law) a review of an administrative decision by a court based on the record before the agency; no new evidence may be presented before the court (see *review de novo*).

**redirect examination**   the second examination of one's own witnesses, following the opponent's *cross-examination* (see *direct examination*).

**reformation**   (contract law) a remedy granted by a court of *equity* to the parties to a written instrument, which reforms the instrument to conform to the real intent of the parties.

**registration statement**   (securities regulation) a form filed with the SEC by any issuer of new securities, with certain exceptions, disclosing a description of the issuing firm's business, a description of the security, information about the management of the firm, and financial statements prepared by independent accountants.

**Regulation A exception**   (securities regulation) an exemption from the registration requirements of the 1933 Securities Act covering small issues of securities; an *offering circular* is required, however.

**rejection**   refusal to accept the terms of an *offer* to make a *contract*, expressed to the *offeror*.

**relevant evidence**   evidence that bears upon and has a tendency to prove a fact in issue.

**relevant geographic market**   (antitrust law) the geographic area within which two or more firms effectively compete.

**relevant product market**   (antitrust law) the products that effectively compete with each other.

**remand**   to send a case back to a lower court for further proceedings, usually in conjunction with a reversal of that court's judgment, when there is something more to be done by the lower court, such as take additional evidence or retry the case (see *reverse; affirm*).

**removal**   the transfer of a case from one court to another, particularly the transfer of a case from the state courts to the federal courts.

**republican government**   a government by representatives chosen by the people (see *democratic government*).

**request to produce**   a letter or other document, from one side of a case to another, requesting that evidence be turned over for inspection and copying; a part of *discovery*.

**requirements contracts**   an agreement by a purchaser that it will purchase all of its requirements of a particular good or service from a particular supplier.

**resale price maintenance**   (antitrust law) a vertical *price-fixing* agreement; agreement between buyer and seller that the buyer will charge a certain price for the products purchased upon resale.

**rescission**   the canceling out of a *contract* and return of the parties to their original position.

**res ipsa loquitor**   literally "the thing speaks for itself"; the *tort* doctrine that shifts the burden to the defendant to prove that he or she was not responsible for an injury, if the plaintiff proves that the injury was caused by an instrumentality in the exclusive control of the defendant, and the incident is of a type not ordinarily caused except by *negligence*.

**res judicata**   literally "the thing has been adjudicated"; the rule that once a court has decided a case or an issue, that case or issue cannot be adjudged again, and the prior decision must be accepted unless it is overturned on appeal; not to be confused with the Constitutional doctrine of *double jeopardy*.

**respondeat superior**   literally "let the superior respond"; a *tort* and *agency* doctrine in which an employer *(master)* is liable for the torts of his or her employees *(servants)* if the tort is committed in the scope of the employee's employment; the master is not liable for the torts of *independent contractors*, however.

**restraintists**   judges who counsel restraint in dealing with Constitutional matters and who avoid Constitutional confrontations whenever possible. Such judges typically use a "balancing-of-interests" approach to such controversies (see *activists*; *neutralists*).

**restrictive covenants**   *contracts* that involve a condition that one party will not enter into competition with another party, usually found in contracts for the sale of a business or employment contracts. Such contracts may be valid if they are reasonable, both in their duration and in the geographic areas in which a party is restricted from competing.

**retroactive advertising**   a judicial remedy for deceptive or misleading advertising in which the court orders the guilty party to advertise, at its own expense, corrections of past deceptions; corrective advertising.

**reverse**   to vacate or set aside a prior judgment, usually of a lower court (see *remand*; *affirm*).

**review de novo**   (administrative law) a review of the actions of the *administrative agency* by the courts in which the court permits evidence to be presented, usually by retrying the entire case (see *record review*).

**revocation**   (contract law) the recall or withdrawal of an *offer* by an *offeror*.

**right of privacy**   a Constitutional right found by interpretation of several parts of the Constitution, generally prohibiting government interference with those aspects of a person's life the courts consider private.

**right of rescission**   the right given to consumers under some federal laws and regulations to terminate a *contract* within a certain period of time; the consumer must return whatever he or she received under the contract, and the seller must return the money paid and void the contract.

**right-to-work laws**   (labor law) state statutes that outlaw *union-shop* contracts.

**rule making**   (administrative law) the function of *administrative agencies* in making rules and regulations pursuant to a *delegation* of authority from the legislature (see *enabling act*).

**Rule of Reason**   (antitrust) the doctrine that, even though the Sherman Act prohibits "every contract, combination . . . or conspiracy . . . in restraint of trade," the legislators really intended that only unreasonable restraints be prohibited. The doctrine requires a full-scale economic analysis in each case, unless a *per se rule* applies.

**runaway shop**   (labor law) the shutting down or moving of a plant to avoid unionization or union pressure.

**scalping**   (securities regulation) an illegal practice of securities *brokers* who make recommendations to customers to purchase securities in which the broker has personally invested, in order to make the value of the broker's stock go up.

**scienter**   knowingly or with guilty knowledge; with intent to defraud or deceive.

**scope of employment doctrine**   the rule that a *master* is only liable for the torts of his or her servants that are committed while in the limits of the employment authority (see *respondeat superior*).

**SEC**   see *Securities and Exchange Commission*.

**secondary boycotts**   (labor law) union pressure on one employer not to deal with another employer or with the goods of another employer.

**secondary-line competition (injury to)**   (antitrust law) injury to competitors of the buyer caused by the seller's *price discrimination*.

**secondary standards**   (environmental law) air-quality standards necessary to protect nonhuman elements, such as buildings, animals, and crops (see *primary standards*; *National Ambient Air Quality Standards*).

**section of the country**   (antitrust) a part of the statutory language of section 7 of the Clayton Act, which has been interpreted to require proof in *merger* cases of an anticompetitive effect in some *relevant geographic market*.

**Securities and Exchange Commission (SEC)**   the federal independent regulatory commission created in 1934 to regulate the sale of securities and related matters.

**security**   (1) (securities regulation) any investment of money or property in a common enterprise for profit; (2) (contract law) any *lien*, mortgage, collateral, or other device used to assure a creditor of repayment.

**security interest**   a *lien* or claim on property given to secure payment of a debt; may be foreclosed, resulting in the sale of the property to pay the debt.

**selective incorporation doctrine**   the idea that the fourteenth amendment *due process* clause applies certain portions of the Bill of Rights to the states, notably those parts that are *fundamental rights* or are "essential to the concept of ordered liberty;" a part of the fourteenth amendment, *substantive due process*.

**self-executing subpoena**   a *subpoena* that is a court order, the violation of which is itself a contempt of court and punishable as such.

**semidisclosed agency**   an *agency* in which a third party knows that an *agent* is working for some *principal*, but the identity of the principal is not known (see *undisclosed agency*).

**separate but equal doctrine**   the historic doctrine that the *equal protection clause* was satisfied by providing equal but segregated facilities. The doctrine was repudiated in *Brown v. Board of Education* in 1954.

**series voting**   see *class voting*.

**servant**   (agency law) an *agent* over whom a *principal* has the right of control; an ordinary employee (see *master*; *master-servant relationship*; *independent contractor*; *respondeat superior*).

**service of process**   the delivery of a *summons* by an authorized person to the *defendant* or other party in a lawsuit, thereby conferring *personal jurisdiction* over the person served.

**set-off**   a claim by a *defendant* against a *plaintiff* that the defendant wishes to have credited against the claim by the plaintiff against the defendant, usually arising from some transaction other than that which formed the basis of the plaintiff's original complaint.

**settlor**   the person who creates a *trust* by transferring property to a *trustee* for the benefit of the *beneficiary*. The settlor may also be the trustee or beneficiary.

**shared monopoly**   (antitrust law) the theory that in certain markets a highly concentrated *oligopoly* will behave like a *monopoly*, and is therefore subject to a charge of "monopolization" under section 2 of the Sherman Act. The theory has not been accepted by the courts.

**shareholder democracy**   a concept of actual control of corporations by their shareholders, in which shareholders have real power as opposed to control by *management*.

**shingle theory**   the theory under the securities laws that holding one's self out as a security *investment adviser*, *broker*, or *dealer* ("hanging out a shingle") is equivalent to a representation that one has expertise in securities.

**short-swing profit**   (securities regulation) a profit on a *security* of a corporation made by an *officer*, director, or owner of more than 10% of the shares, made within a six-month period.

**SIPs**   see *State Implementation Plans*.

**slander** an oral *defamation*.

**small-issues exception** see *Regulation A exception*.

**social contract theory** see *natural rights theory*.

**social Darwinism** the social philosophy that holds that the "fittest" should survive and the less fit should not, even in a social and economic context.

**societal ethics** widely held beliefs of right and wrong, including all religions and political ideologies; systems of belief held by groups of people (see *personal ethics*).

**sociological school of jurisprudence** the philosophy that the law and legal institutions are the expression and tool of social forces.

**sole proprietorship** an unincorporated business owned by one person.

**sovereign immunity** the immunity of government from suit. In international law, the immunity of one government from suits in the courts of other nations.

**sovereignty** the supreme political power and authority over a geographic area.

**specific intent** the intent to obtain a specific result. Many criminal statutes require proof of a specific intent, such as assault with intent to kill, in which case the prosecution must prove the defendant committed the act while maintaining that specific type of intent (see *general intent*).

**specific performance** a remedy afforded by a court of *equity* ordering a party to a contract to comply with the terms of the contract and to perform the acts required by the agreement.

**standing** the doctrine that a person must have a legally protected private interest before he or she may bring an action in federal court; the right to sue; the interest upon which suit may be based (see *case or controversy requirement*).

**stare decisis** literally "look to the decided cases"; the doctrine of precedent; the rule that lower courts will follow the previously decided cases of the appellate courts having *jurisdiction* over those lower courts (see *case law*).

**state** (1) a sovereign country or nation; (2) one of the constituent political units within the United States.

**state action** the doctrine that the equal protection clause of the fourteenth amendment only prohibits discrimination that has as its source or is aided by the authority of state governments. Private discrimination is not prohibited by the equal protection clause unless it is aided by state action.

**State Implementation Plans (SIPs)** (environmental law) state plans to reach the goals set by the EPA administrator in the *National Ambient Air Quality Standards*.

**stationary sources** (environmental law) sources of air pollution that do not move, as opposed to automobiles, for example.

**Statute of Frauds** (contracts) a statute originally passed by Parliament and adopted in every English-speaking jurisdiction in the world. The statute makes unenforceable certain types of oral agreements and requires some additional proof of those agreements other than a mere oral statement by one of the parties that they exist.

**statutes** rules and laws enacted by legislatures, including the federal Congress, state legislatures, and local legislative bodies such as city councils.

**statutory prospectus** see *final prospectus*.

**steering** falsely representing that a dwelling is unavailable in order to encourage or maintain racially segregated housing.

**stipulation** an agreed piece of evidence.

**stockholder** a person who owns shares in a *corporation*; an investor, as opposed to a lender (see *equity financing*).

**stock options** rights to purchase stock at a previously agreed price, at some time in the future.

**stock subscriptions** the initial agreement to purchase stock in a *corporation* when it is formed, revocable at any time by the subscriber prior to acceptance by the corporation.

**straight bankruptcy**   a bankruptcy proceeding in which the debtor is relieved of payment of his or her debts (see *wage earner plans*).

**straight voting**   a method of voting in *corporations* in which each shareholder receives one vote per share for each director to be elected, and which requires those votes to be used for a specific director's seat (see *cumulative voting*).

**street name**   (securities regulation) a security *broker's* name; many securities are held for customers in the name of the broker for convenience and ease of sale.

**strict liability**   liability without fault; liability without proof of a mental element, such as negligence, recklessness, or intention.

**strict scrutiny test**   the test to determine whether a classification scheme in a statute violates the equal protection clause of the fourteenth amendment if the classification scheme involves *fundamental rights* or a *suspect classification* (see *reasonable basis test*).

**strike**   a work stoppage by employees.

**strikebreakers**   (labor law) thugs hired by employers to force employees through violence to go back to work during a strike.

**strike suit**   a legal action filed against a *corporation*, its officers, or its directors to force a settlement with the plaintiffs rather than to force payment to the stockholders of the corporation in a *derivative action*.

**subject-matter jurisdiction**   the authority of the courts to hear particular kinds of cases (see *jurisdiction*).

**subpoena**   a court order requiring a person to appear in court and give evidence, punishable by contempt of court proceedings for failure to appear (see *subpoena duces tecum*).

**subpoena duces tecum**   a court order requiring a person to appear in court and produce certain documents or articles specified in the *subpoena*. Like a simple subpoena, a *subpoena duces tecum* is punishable by contempt of court proceedings for failure to appear.

**subsidization**   see *deep-pocket theory*, definition 2.

**substantial evidence test**   (administrative law) the rule that a court will not overturn a decision by an *administrative agency* if there is substantial evidence on which that decision was based.

**substantive due process**   the requirement under the fifth and fourteenth amendments that laws not be unreasonable, arbitrary, or capricious and that the means bear a reasonable relationship to the ends of the law (see also *selective incorporation doctrine*).

**substantive law**   the part of the law that creates, defines, and regulates legal rights and duties.

**summary judgment**   the process by which cases may be decided without trial if there is no material fact in issue between the parties; summary judgment may be rendered on parts of cases as well; "trial by affidavit."

**summary procedures**   (administrative law) action by an administrative agency with no due process procedures prior to the action, generally taken only in emergency situations, and requiring a hearing after the action is taken.

**summons**   a paper delivered by the sheriff or other officer notifying a person of the existence of a lawsuit filed against that person and requiring the person to file an answer or appear in court or face a *default judgment*.

**sunset legislation**   automatic termination of administrative agencies or other laws, requiring an affirmative act on the part of the legislature to extend or continue the operation of the law beyond a specific date.

**superfund**   (environmental law) a fund financed by a tax on the production of toxic chemicals to be used to clean up toxic-waste sites and created by the Comprehensive Environmental Response, Compensation and Liability Act of 1980.

**survivor's insurance benefits**   (social security law) benefits payable under social security to minor dependent children and sometimes spouses of deceased workers who are eligible under the Social Security Act.

**suspect classification**    a classification by group, in which (1) membership in the group carries some "obvious badge" such as race or sex, (2) treatment of the members of the group has been historically pervasive and severe, and (3) members have been subjected to absolute deprivation of benefits available to nonmembers (see *strict scrutiny test*).

**switch after sale**    a variant of *bait and switch*, in which the bait is actually sold to the consumer but is somehow unsatisfactory, and upon the consumer's complaint, the seller agrees to "trade up" to a more expensive product.

**tariff**    (1) a tax on imports; (2) a rule regarding a closely regulated industry, particularly a public utility.

**taxpayer suits**    suits filed by taxpayers, alleging that a certain use of public **funds** is illegal and basing their *standing* to sue on their status as taxpayers.

**tenancy by the entireties**    (property law) a form of *joint tenancy*, with the right of survivorship, which cannot be broken by a single party acting alone and without the consent of the other party. This form exists only in marital situations and exists only in a few states.

**tenancy in common**    (property law) a form of concurrent ownership of property, to be distinguished from *joint tenancy* and *tenancy by the entireties*. No right of survivorship is involved, and if one tenant in common dies, his or her interest passes on to his or her heirs rather than to the surviving tenants. Proportionate interests are permitted, and the *four unities* are not required for its creation.

**tender offer**    a public offer by one corporation to purchase outstanding stock of another corporation in a sufficient amount to obtain control over the corporation.

**territorial principle**    the rule of international law that a state has jurisdiction over conduct that takes place within its territory.

**testate succession**    transfer of *property* by will (see *intestate succession*).

**third-line competition (injury to)**    (antitrust law) injury to customers in competition with customers of the supplier's favored buyer, caused by *price discrimination*.

**third-party complaints**    suits filed by existing parties in a lawsuit against new parties to the case.

**tie-in contracts**    (antitrust law) also called "tying contracts"; agreements or conditions wherein a seller of two goods or services will not provide one without the other. Such contracts are *per se* illegal if the seller has market power in the tying product.

**tippee**    (securities regulation) a person who receives information from a corporate *insider* (see *insider trading*).

**toehold acquisition**    entry into a market through *merger* with one of the smaller competitors already in the market.

**tombstone ad**    (securities regulation) an advertisement stating that a *security* will be available for sale; used to attract *indications of interest*.

**tort**    a private wrong or injury; a wrong not based on *contract*. The four elements of every tort are (1) a legal duty not depending on contract, (2) a breach of that duty, (3) an injury, and (4) proximate causal relationship between the breach of duty and the injury (see *proximate cause*).

**totalitarianism**    a form of government in which there is no limit on the government's authority.

**trademark**    a distinctive mark, symbol, word, phrase, or picture used to identify a particular firm or product.

**treasury shares**    *issued shares* that have been reacquired by the corporation, as opposed to *outstanding shares*, which remain in the hands of stockholders.

**treaty**    an agreement between *sovereign states*.

**Treaty of Rome**   the 1957 agreement that created the *European Economic Community (EEC)*.

**treble damage actions**   (antitrust law) a remedy in private antitrust actions whereby the injured party may collect three times its actual *damages*; a type of *punitive damages*.

**trespass**   (1) doing a wrongful act to the injury of another's person or property; (2) unlawful entry or presence upon the land of another.

**trust**   (1) a right of property held by one party (the *trustee*) for the benefit of another party (the *beneficiary*); (2) (antitrust) a form of agreement in which the voting rights of the stock in competing corporations is assigned to a board of trustees, who then operate all of the competing firms as one firm in an anticompetitive manner (see also *business trust*).

**trustee**   a person who holds property under a *trust* for the benefit of another.

**trust indenture**   an agreement between a *corporation* issuing *bonds* and an independent *trustee* to secure payment of those bonds, usually containing a mortgage or pledge of corporate property as *security* for repayment (definition 2).

**tying contract**   see *tie-in contract*.

**ultra vires**   actions of a corporation that are beyond the powers granted to it by law or in its *articles of incorporation*.

**unconscionability**   gross unfairness; particularly sales practices so unfair that a court will not permit them, as established by the Uniform Commercial Code.

**underwriter**   a person or firm specializing in giving financial advice, management, and marketing of issues of securities.

**undisclosed agency**   an *agency* in which a third party dealing with an *agent* does not know that the agent is representing someone else.

**undue burdens on interstate commerce**   an even-handed, nondiscriminatory but "too heavy" burden on *interstate commerce* imposed by a state.

**unemployment compensation**   state systems providing benefits to unemployed workers, financed in part by the federal government.

**unfair labor practices**   (labor law) practices by either unions or employers that are illegal under the National Labor Relations Act or its amendments.

**unfair labor practice strikers**   (labor law) employees striking because of some employer *unfair labor practice* (see *economic strikers*).

**Uniform Commercial Code (UCC)**   a model act consisting of ten articles dealing with various subjects of commercial law, e.g., sales, negotiable instruments, investment securities, and others, and adopted in whole or in part in every state.

**Uniform Consumer Credit Code (UCCC)**   a model act adopted in several states dealing with credit practices and generally requiring full disclosure in a manner similar to federal Truth in Lending.

**Uniform Partnership Act (UPA)**   a model act governing *general partnerships*, adopted in many states.

**Uniform Securities Act**   a model act regulating sales of securities at the state level.

**unilateral**   one-sided; having only one aspect.

**Union Members Bill of Rights**   (labor law) a statement of the rights of union members in relation to their own unions as found in the Landrum-Griffin Act of 1959.

**union shop**   (labor law) a labor contract which provides that all employees in the bargaining unit must become union members as a condition of employment (see *open shop*; *right-to-work laws*).

**unlawful employment practices**   discriminatory practices in employment as defined by the Civil Rights Act of 1964.

**unlawful housing practices**   discriminatory practices in the sale or rental of housing made illegal by the Civil Rights Act of 1968.

**usury statutes**   state laws limiting the amount of interest that may be charged on loans or credit purchases; sometimes called "loan shark acts."

**venue**   the courts of a particular county, city, or other geographical region that hear a case; not to be confused with *jurisdiction*; venue refers to the determination of which of the courts with jurisdiction should hear the case.

**verdict**   the decision of a jury; not to be confused with *judgment*; judges sitting without a jury may render a verdict as well, to be followed later by a judgment.

**vertical agreements**   (antitrust law) agreements between parties involved at different levels of the distribution process of the same good or service, e.g., an agreement between a supplier and a retailer of the same product (see *horizontal agreements*).

**vertical merger**   (antitrust law) a *corporate integration* between two firms which stand in the relationship of buyer and seller or could potentially stand in that relationship.

**vertical territory limitations**   (antitrust law) limitations imposed by a seller on a buyer on the area within which the buyer may operate.

**vested**   absolute; with a fixed right; having a right that cannot be taken away.

**vicarious liability**   liability for an act committed by another, e.g., the liability of the *master* under the doctrine of *respondeat superior*.

**wage and benefit provisions**   (labor law) parts of a labor contract spelling out the financial parts of the labor agreement.

**wage assignment**   a clause in a contract or promissory note that requires the debtor's employer to pay the debtor's salary directly to the creditor upon demand.

**wage earner plans**   (bankruptcy law) a procedure under the federal Bankruptcy Act in which a debtor pays off his or her debts but obtains a delay in payment in accordance with a "plan" filed with the court.

**waiting period**   (securities regulation) the time between the filing of the registration documents with the SEC of a new issue of stock and the approval by the SEC of that issue (see *indications of interest*; *preliminary prospectus*; *tombstone ads*).

**warrants**   options to buy stock.

**warranty**   a promise, either contained in a *contract* or implied by law (see various forms of *implied warranty*; *limited warranty*; *full warranty*).

**wash sales**   (securities regulation) also known as "matched orders"; a technique of inflating the price of stock by placing large orders to buy and sell the same stock, thus increasing volume and indicating to unsophisticated investors that there is activity in the stock, thereby raising the price of the stock (see *market manipulation*).

**watering of shares**   see *dilution of shares*.

**wildcat strikes**   (labor law) a strike in violation of a *no-strike clause* in a labor contract.

**winding up**   (partnership law) the process of terminating a *partnership*, including gathering of assets, payment of debts, and distribution of remaining assets to the partners.

**wings effect**   see *perceived potential competition*.

**workable competition**   (antitrust law) a compromise of classical competition (the theories of Adam Smith), which holds that although "perfect competition" cannot be attained, government policy should be aimed at achieving the best possible competitive conditions.

**worker's compensation statutes**   (labor law) state laws that provide benefits to employees whose injuries arose out of their employment and that assess those benefits directly against their employers.

**work-preservation clause**   an agreement by an employer in a *collective bargaining* agreement that it will not close the plant without prior opportunity to negotiate by the union or, alternatively, an agreement not to close the plant under any circumstances.

**World Bank**    the International Bank for Reconstruction and Development.

**World Court**    the *International Court of Justice.*

**yellow dog contracts**    (labor law) employment contracts that required employees never to join a labor union and provided that any employee who joined such a union would automatically lose his or her job.

**zoning**    state laws or local ordinances that regulate the uses to which land may be put.

# INDEX